207-

MATHEMATICAL BIOPHYSICS

PHYSICO-MATHEMATICAL FOUNDATIONS OF BIOLOGY

THIRD REVISED EDITION

By

N. RASHEVSKY
Professor and Chairman, Committee on Mathematical Biology
The University of Chicago

VOLUME TWO

DOVER PUBLICATIONS, INC.
NEW YORK NEW YORK

Published simultaneously in Canada by McClelland and Stewart, Ltd.

Published in the United Kingdom by Constable and Company Limited, 10 Orange Street, London, W.C. 2.

This new Dover edition, first published in 1960, is the third revised edition of the work first published by the University of Chicago Press. The work originally appeared in one volume but now appears in two volumes.

Manufactured in the United States of America

Dover Publications, Inc.
180 Varick Street
New York 14, New York

TO MY WIFE

PREFACE TO VOLUME II OF THE THIRD EDITION

The amount of new material added in this edition necessitated the publication of the whole work in two volumes.

The first part of this volume contains all of Part III of the Second Edition,[1*] with some additions. A general introduction (chapter i) has been added. In chapter xi a brief discussion of the Pitts-McCulloch theory of the Gestalt, and of J. Culbertson's theory has been added. Those theories differ appreciably from our theory which is presented in chapter xi in exactly the same form as it was presented in 1938 in the first edition of this work. Short additions have been made to chapters xiv and xix. Two new chapters, namely xii and xx, have been added.

The second part of this volume is a considerable extension of Part IV of the Second Edition. Whereas all the discussions in Volume I and in Part I of this volume are concerned with different physico-mathematical and formal mathematical *models* of various biological phenomena, in Part II we attempted to formulate some *general mathematical principles* of biology. The formulations are still tentative, and different possibilities of refining them are indicated. What we originally called the *Principle of Maximum Simplicity*, we prefer now to formulate as the *Principle of Optimal Design*. In this connection we devoted a new chapter (xxvii) to David Cohn's interesting work which leads to the newer and somewhat more precise formulation.

Another general principle, discussed in chapters xxviii to xxxv, which are all newly added in this edition, deals with the basic relational similarity of all organisms. Those chapters contain the presentation of the work of the author and his associates, the publication of which began in 1954. The material here is presented not in the chronological order as it was originally published. The studies which led to chapters xxx and xxxi preceded by a couple of years those which are presented in chapter xxix. We felt, however, that a systematic presentation in a book required a rearrangement of the material.

* In this book all numbered references are given at the end of each chapter.

The reader should not receive the impression that the mathematical approach to relational biology presented here is the first systematic approach that ever has been made. A detailed system of relational biology, based on mathematical logic and in particular on the theory of relations, was developed long ago by J. H. Woodger[2] in a series of writings of which we mention only one in the references. Woodger's approach and ours seem to have very little in common, except that both deal with relational aspects of biology. The type of conclusions which we reach seem to be outside of the scope of Woodger's approach and vice versa. Professor Alfred Tarski made a remark in a conversation a couple of years ago somewhat like the following: "The difference between Woodger's approach and yours is due to the fact that Woodger is interested in the logical foundations of biology, while you are interested in the biological foundations." This is probably very true. Yet the logical and biological aspects do overlap, as will be seen for example from chapter xxix. It is not impossible that the two approaches, in spite of their difference, eventually may be found to be merely two different but equivalent mathematical ways of treating the same problem, just as the matrix and the wave-mechanical approach in quantum theory are different but equivalent.

In its first publication the material of chapters xxx and xxxi preceded that of chapter xxix. Thus our later work is in a sense less geometrical.

After this volume had been written and delivered to the publisher, it was found[3] that the results of chapter xxix could be obtained without making the sets considered there into spaces by the introduction of a topology. All we need is the requirement that the mappings leave invariant certain relations between the elements of the sets. This is still very different from Woodger's ideas. Perhaps, however, by following this approach further, a connection eventually may be established between our work and Woodger's.

In the meantime, the work of Robert Rosen on the application of the theory of categories, very briefly described in chapter xxxiii, has also been developed further[4] and opens a still different mathematical approach to relational biology. We like to venture the opinion that all those different roads will eventually lead to the same goal.

I do not know of course whether in my own work the gradual transition from a geometrical approach to an approach *via* theory of relations was the result of an inherent logical development, as it seems to me, or whether I have been subconsciously influenced by Woodger's work. If so, I certainly owe Woodger a debt of gratitude.

I have been familiar with his writings ever since the time of their first publication, but for a long time I have underestimated their value; an error on my part, which I hasten to acknowledge and to correct. To Woodger goes the credit for having first introduced systematically relational mathematics into biology.

I wish again to express my indebtedness to my wife, who, as always, prepared the manuscript of this volume and helped with proofreading. Without her help neither this volume nor probably my other books would have ever been written. As a small tribute to her faithful help and encouragement this volume is dedicated to her.

I also wish to thank my friends and colleagues who helped me with their discussion of different chapters. Herbert D. Landahl read and discussed chapter xii; Anatol Rapoport made valuable comments on chapter xx; Robert Rosen carefully read in manuscript, and then again in proof, chapters xxviii to xxxv inclusive; Ernesto Trucco was very helpful with the preparation of chapter xxvii.

To Mrs. Elaine Smith I am indebted for the preparation of the Index.

Last but not least I wish to express my sincere gratitude to the Administration and Staff of Dover Publications, Inc., for their unfailing cooperation during the preparation of this volume.

CHICAGO, ILLINOIS
AUGUST 20, 1959.

N. RASHEVSKY

REFERENCES

1. N. Rashevsky, *Mathematical Biophysics*. Revised Edition. (Chicago: University of Chicago Press, 1948).

2. J. H. Woodger, *The Axiomatic Method in Biology*. (Cambridge: Cambridge University Press, 1937).

3. N. Rashevsky, *Bull. Math. Biophysics*, 21, 101-6, 1959.

4. Robert Rosen, *Bull. Math. Biophysics*, 21, 109-28, 1959.

TABLE OF CONTENTS

PREFACE TO VOLUME II OF THE THIRD EDITION vii

I. MATHEMATICAL BIOPHYSICS OF THE CENTRAL NERVOUS SYSTEM

I. A GENERAL SURVEY OF THE FIELD 1

II. GENERAL CONSIDERATIONS ON CENTRAL EXCITATION AND INHIBITION 5

III. GENERAL CONSIDERATION ON CENTRAL EXCITATION AND INHIBITION: CONTINUED 19

IV. MATHEMATICAL BIOPHYSICS OF SOME SIMPLE NEUROLOGICAL STRUCTURES: APPLICATIONS TO REACTION TIMES 37

V. DISCRIMINATION OF INTENSITIES 46

VI. MATHEMATICAL BIOPHYSICS OF PSYCHOPHYSICAL DISCRIMINATION 57

VII. HYSTERESIS PHENOMENA IN PHYSICOCHEMICAL SYSTEMS 69

VIII. A NEUROLOGICALLY INTERESTING CASE OF HYSTERESIS 74

IX. MATHEMATICAL BIOPHYSICS OF CONDITIONED REFLEXES 80

X. DISCRIMINATION OF RELATIONS 94

XI. MATHEMATICAL BIOPHYSICS OF THE GESTALT PROBLEM 98

XII. MATHEMATICAL BIOPHYSICS OF COLOR VISION AND OF FLICKER PHENOMENA 116

XIII. MATHEMATICAL BIOPHYSICS OF DELAYED REFLEXES AND ITS APPLICATION TO THE THEORY OF ERROR ELIMINATION 127

XIV. APPLICATIONS OF THE FOREGOING TO LEARNING 136

XV. MATHEMATICAL BIOPHYSICS OF RATIONAL LEARNING AND THINKING 144

XVI. PERCEPTION OF VISUAL PATTERNS AND VISUAL AESTHETICS.. 154

XVII. MATHEMATICAL BIOPHYSICS OF ABSTRACTION 175

XVIII. MATHEMATICAL BIOPHYSICS OF SOME MENTAL PHENOMENA.. 185

XIX. BOOLEAN ALGEBRA OF NEURAL NETS 207

XX. RANDOM NETS 230

II. GENERAL MATHEMATICAL PRINCIPLES IN BIOLOGY

XXI. OUTLINE OF A NEW MATHEMATICAL APPROACH TO GENERAL BIOLOGY 245

XXII. FORM OF PLANTS 251

XXIII. LOCOMOTION AND FORM OF SNAKES 256

XXIV. FORM AND LOCOMOTION OF SOME QUADRUPEDS 262

XXV. FLIGHT OF BIRDS AND INSECTS IN RELATION TO THEIR FORM 270

XXVI. THE INTERNAL STRUCTURE OF ANIMALS 280

XXVII. ANOTHER APPLICATION TO THE INTERNAL STRUCTURE OF ANIMALS 292

XXVIII. RELATIONS WITHIN AND BETWEEN ORGANISMS MAPPINGS IN BIOLOGY AND MATHEMATICS 306

XXIX. A GENERAL PRINCIPLE AND ITS APPLICATIONS 325

XXX. ORGANISMS AND GRAPHS 345

XXXI. SOME CONSEQUENCES OF THE FOREGOING 371

XXXII. COMPARISON OF THE SET—THEORETICAL AND COMBINATORIAL APPROACHES POSSIBLE OUTLOOKS 385

XXXIII. THE ORGANISM AS A SET OF MAPPINGS CATEGORIES AND EQUIVALENCES 390

XXXIV. AN INTERESTING CASE OF BIOTOPOLOGICAL TREATMENT OF THE ORGANISM 395

XXXV. THE GEOMETRIZATION OF BIOLOGY 404

XXXVI. THE ORGANIC WORLD AS A WHOLE 424

INDEX 439

PART I

MATHEMATICAL BIOPHYSICS OF THE CENTRAL NERVOUS SYSTEM

CHAPTER I

A GENERAL SURVEY OF THE FIELD

The mathematical biology of the central nervous system is possibly one of the most challenging problems offered to the mathematical biologist. Now, due to the ingenuity of the engineers and applied mathematicians, machines such as high speed electronic computers have been built and put to extensive use. Those machines imitate, true enough within a very narrow range, some properties of the human brain. But within this limited range the imitation is much more perfect than the object imitated. No human brain can attain either the speed or the accuracy of an electronic computer. Yet the versatility of the human brain as compared with that of the computer is so much larger, that any such designation for the computers as "electronic brains" or "giant brains" must be considered as highly hyperbolic figures of speech.

Nevertheless the development of computers and of other automata resulted in the circumstance that nowadays probably everybody will agree that the difference between a machine and a human brain is only a matter of degree of complexity. This difference in degree of complexity is tremendous. It has been variously put at from 10^8 to 10^{12} times. However, as long as scientists are convinced that we deal here only with different degrees of complexity, they have no reason to doubt that the basic principles which underlie the workings of the human brain are essentially the same physicochemical principles which underlie the working of an automaton. Such was not the situation some thirty years ago. Though the usefulness of the physicochemical and even physicomathematical approach was already well recognized then by biologists, many voices were heard which claimed that some of the most interesting properties of the brain, namely those connected with learning in its most general aspects and with the "acquiring of experience" were of a nature which made them forever refractory to a physicomathematical approach[1]. With this point of view in mind the author undertook in 1929 a theoretical investigation as to whether physicochemical systems are possible which exhibit those very characteristic properties of the brain. The answer to the question was very soon found to be a definite "yes." It was, however, not our purpose to develop a good theory of the actual human brain. Our purpose was a very different one: We wanted merely to show that physicochemical systems were conceivable which exhibited some of the most striking properties of the human brain. We therefore did not bother at first to investigate systems which in any way resembled the brain in their structure. In fact, the earliest systems which were shown to exhibit some properties of learning and recognition of patterns or Gestalts, were conceived as almost homogeneous on the larger scale level, their heterogeneity being manifested only on the molecular level[2]. We know that the brain of man and animals shows a highly heterogeneous structure even to the almost naked eye.

Further studies led us to systems which showed somewhat better resemblance to actual brains in that they consisted of a very large number of elements, connected into different more or less complex heterogeneous structures. We did not hesitate, for sake of conveniences, to call those elements "neurons," though in their assumed properties those neurons differed very much from the neurons of the neurophysiologist or neuroanatomist. Keeping in mind our primary purposes, we postulated some very simple laws of interaction between our hypothetical "neurons." Those laws dealt with continuous quantities and were expressed by simple ordinary linear differential equations which were patterned after those of the two-factor theory of excitation discussed in part II of Volume I of this work.

Once the laws of interaction were assumed, then, for any prescribed arrangement or configuration of our hypothetical neurons, we could derive the properties of the arrangement, barring purely mathematical difficulties. The study proceeded by way of investigating more and more complex configurations of the hypothetical neurons. Surprisingly enough we found that many of those configurations exhibited not only simple properties of the brain but even such properties as the recognition and invariance of Gestalt or even the recognition of abstract relations, such as "greater than" or "less than."

At this stage of development our studies were presented in the third part of the first edition (1938) of this book, which appeared in one volume of some 300 odd pages. But very soon afterwards the work of Herbert D. Landahl, Alston S. Householder, and others revealed even a much more astounding fact. Not only did our hypothetical models, which were not patterned according to known neurophysiological data, represent well qualitative properties of the brain, but many quantitative relations observed in experimental psychology and neuropsychology, were amazingly well represented by the equations which described our hypothetical structures. Even some quantitative relations in aesthetic perception of simple geometric patterns found a fair representation by the equations which governed our abstract models.

It seemed that in our basic postulates we did inadvertently hit upon something better than a mere abstract analogy. Yet with the development of experimental knowledge of the laws of interaction of actual neurons, the inadequacy of our postulates became more and more evident. The "mystery" deepened further when in 1943 Warren S. McCulloch and Walter Pitts[3] published their epoch making paper in which they showed that the proper mathematical tool for representing the observed *discontinuous* interaction between neurons was not the differential equation, but the Boolean Algebra or Logical Calculus.

Naturally it was immediately tried to reinterpret all our previous findings in terms of the new approach. But the result was a failure. Thus we faced a paradox: Using a theory based on definitely unrealistic postulates, we obtained a number of quantitatively correct results, while using a theory based on much more realistic postulates, we were unable to obtain those results. It took several years to solve the paradox and, as frequently in such cases, the solution was quite simple. In all experiments such as measurements of reaction times (chapter iv), psychophysical judgment (chapter vi), just noticeable differences (chapter v), we deal with phenomena which involve not a few, but hundreds if not thousands of actual neurons and axons. It turned out that in such a case the discontinuous laws of interaction of individual neurons lead to a sort of average continuous effect which is described by the differential equations postulated originally. The situation is not unlike that found in physics where the discontinuous molecular impacts against the wall of a gas container average out, for a very large number of molecules, into a continuous pressure which is described by the differential equations of aerodynamics. Thus dealing with "large scale" psychological phenomena, where very many neurons are involved, we can safely use our old approach. But when dealing with a few neurons as the neurophysiologist frequently does in his experiments, the McCulloch-Pitt's approach should be used. A possible connection between the two approaches is discussed in chapter ii. This is, however, not the only possible way of reconciling the two approaches. In chapter xx we shall discuss the work of Anatol Rapoport and his associates on "random nets." This work is still more in a mathematical than in an applicable stage, so far as the theory of brain is concerned. It offers, however, a much more general approach to the problem of the relation between "macroscopic" and "microscopic" properties than does the discussion of chapter ii.

A very interesting different approach to the "paradox" has recently been suggested by H. D. Landahl[4]. He points out that quasi-continuous types of interaction between neurons may be obtained even for very few neurons. The quasi-continuity results from the fact that the number of end-feet on the body of a neuron is usually very large and that the threshold for the response of a neuron is given in terms of the number of excited end-feet. A neuron fires namely only if a minimal number of end-feet on its body is excited. Landahl shows that under certain very plausible conditions the interaction of even two neurons may be described in terms of the old continuous differential equations, provided we consider the frequency of discharge of a neuron as the measure of its excitation.

REFERENCES

1. L. v. Bertalanffy, Literarische Berichte aus dem Gebiete der Philosophie. No. 17/18, p. 5, 1928.
2. N. Rashevsky, *J. Gen. Psychology*, 5, 207, 1931, *Ibid.*, 5, 368, 1931.
3. W.S. McCulloch and W. Pitts, *Bull. Math. Biophysics.*, 5, 115, 1943.
4. H. D. Landahl, unpublished.

CHAPTER II

GENERAL CONSIDERATIONS ON CENTRAL EXCITATION AND INHIBITION

In the first edition of this book we attempted to develop a systematic abstract mathematical theory of the functions of the central nervous system. The fundamental idea was to postulate a few mathematically definite laws of interaction between two adjacent neuroelements and then to consider to what consequences such laws of interaction lead when applied to different geometrical arrangements of the interacting elements. In other words, the attempt was made to reduce the tremendous complexity of functions of the central nervous system to the complexity of its structure, keeping the fundamental dynamic processes as simple as possible. A different line of approach is also possible, namely, to consider theoretically the structure of the central nervous system, with its tremendous number of neuroelements, as quasi-homogeneous and to try to account for the enormous complexity of its functions as postulating correspondingly complex dynamical laws of interaction between the individual elements.

It appears that the first point of view may be considered as indirectly better justified by actual observation. As far as experience goes, there does not seem to exist any too pronounced fundamental difference between the elementary physiological properties of the neuron of the frog and those of the neuron of man. One would therefore naturally tend to explain the enormous difference in the functions of the brain of the frog and that of man by the equally enormous difference in the complexity of the structure of their brains. Theoretically, also, the first approach seems to be the more promising one. In some earlier publications[1] we have attempted to develop the second point of view. While some rather interesting general conclusions were thus obtained, nothing of a quantitative nature seems to be gained without a large number of additional and rather disconnected assumptions. The interesting speculations of W. Köhler,[2] which implicitly assume the second point of view, also do not materially contribute to a quantitative mathematical theory of the brain. On the other hand, the first point of view not only has led to a rather natural systematic mathematical theory of the brain but has also shown its empirical usefulness by leading to quantitative relations that are found to be verified experimentally.

The abstract concept from which we start the development of the mathematical theory of the central nervous system is that of an aggregate of a very large number of irritable elements, which all can be divided into two groups: exciting and inhibiting. The presence of some sort of inhibitory elements in the nerve centers is directly suggested by various manifestations of central inhibition.[3] We begin by a systematic study of the simplest cases of interaction which may occur in such an aggregate. Those interactions will depend on the assumptions which we make both about the geometrical arrangement of the neuroelements and about the mechanism of interneuronic excitation and inhibition. Let us first discuss the latter assumptions.

When those fundamental postulates of the mathematical biophysics of the central nervous system were first developed *in abstracto* in the first edition of this book, they were suggested, on the one hand, by the earlier observations of E. D. Adrian[4] regarding the relation between frequency of discharge in a peripheral fiber and the intensity of the stimulus and, on the other hand, by a possible generalization of the two-factor theory of peripheral excitation. The earlier abstract developments of the theory were not too much concerned with the direct relation of the fundamental postulates to actual observations: the main interest centered around the proof that very complicated phenomena could be systematically described by a rather simple system of postulates. When, however, some of the consequences of the theory, elaborated principally by A. S. Householder and H. D. Landahl, turned out to be in good agreement with actual observations, it became evident that the postulated equations are something more than mere mathematical assumptions. Yet those postulates seemingly did not agree with the accumulated experimental evidence on the interaction of two neurons at the synapse, as well as with other observations.

Eventually, the usefulness of the postulates became firmly established.[5,6,7] At the same time W. S. McCulloch and W. Pitts,[8] using Boolean algebra, developed a theory of nervous activity which was based more directly on observations about synaptic transmission. All the successful applications of the older postulates of mathematical biophysics of the central nervous system remained outside the scope of this new theory, although some suggestions as to how the apparent gap between the two approaches may be bridged were made by H. D. Landahl, W. S. McCulloch, and W. Pitts.[9,5] In 1945 N. Rashevsky[10] suggested a simple interpretation of the original postulates in terms of the neurophysiological findings. All the results of the previous developments of the theory could thus be translated into terms familiar to the neurophysiologist.

In this chapter we shall outline the original postulates, as given in the first edition of this book, and then give the above-mentioned neurophysiological interpretation. In subsequent chapters we shall develop various aspects of the theory based on those postulates.

While a continuous excitation of a nerve fiber by means of a constant current usually results in a release of a single excitation impulse, the qualitative and quantitative nature of which is entirely independent of the stimulus, provided that the latter is strong enough to exceed the threshold, the situation for physiological stimuli, such as pressure, light, etc., is different. Studies by Adrian[4] and others show that a continuous stimulus sets off a volley of nerve impulses following one another at approximately equal intervals. The stronger the stimulus, the shorter the intervals or the higher the frequency of the sequence of the impulses. While each individual impulse may be entirely independent of the intensity of the stimulus, thus preserving the "all-or-none law," yet the phenomenon as a whole gives a graded response to a graded stimulus. For an intensity of the external stimulus which is not too strong, the frequency of the volleys is approximately proportional to the intensity of the stimulus. We introduce the concept of the intensity of excitation, E, of a fiber, defining E as a quantity proportional to the frequency ν of the impulses and to the intensity, I, of each individual impulse. Thus,

$$E = I\nu . \tag{1}$$

If the all-or-none law holds for all fibers, then I is independent of the intensity, S, of the external stimulus and is a constant, characteristic of the fiber. The frequency ν, however, is proportional to S; but, since S must, in general, exceed a threshold, h, in order that excitation may be released at all, ν is zero for $S = h$; hence,

$$\nu = \alpha(S - h), \tag{2}$$

where, however, the factor of proportionality α may vary from fiber to fiber. In fact, for peripheral sensory fibers α will be of different physical dimensionality for different fibers, because of the different physical nature of the stimulus S. Equations (1) and (2) give

$$E = \alpha I(S - h) = \beta(S - h). \tag{3}$$

From physiological considerations it follows that (2) can at best be only an approximation. The interval between two successive impulses cannot be smaller than the refractory time θ of the fiber. Hence, $\nu \leqslant 1/\theta$ no matter how strong S is. As S increases indefinitely, ν must tend asymptotically to the value $1/\theta$; while for small values of S, equation (2) holds approximately. There is, of course, an infinite number of functions which satisfy this requirement. Inasmuch as we have, as yet, no empirical data to guide our choice, we may choose the simplest one possible, namely,

$$\nu = \frac{1}{\theta}\left[1 - e^{-\alpha\theta(S-h)}\right]. \tag{4}$$

For small values of $(S - h)$ we have

$$e^{-\alpha\theta(S-h)} = 1 - \alpha\theta(S-h),$$

and therefore (4) reduces to (2).

Now, using (1) and (4), instead of (1) and (2), we obtain

$$E = \frac{I}{\theta}\left[1 - e^{-\alpha\theta(S-h)}\right]. \tag{5}$$

As an alternate possibility we may consider

$$E = I\alpha h \log \frac{\dfrac{S}{h}}{1 + \delta \dfrac{S}{h}}; \qquad \delta = e^{-1/\alpha h\theta}. \tag{6}$$

Let $\alpha h\theta << 1$, so that $\delta << 1$. For small values of S/h we have

$$E = I\alpha h \log \frac{S}{h} = I\alpha h \log\left(1 + \frac{S-h}{h}\right) = I\alpha(S-h),$$

while, for very large S,

$$E = I\alpha h \log \frac{1}{\delta} = \frac{I}{\theta}.$$

In most of the following we shall restrict our considerations, unless explicitly mentioned otherwise, to such small values of S that equations (2) and (3) may be used. Every formula derived in this fashion presents only a limiting case and offers a problem for its generalization.

When a nerve fiber conducting a volley of impulses branches off into two or more fibers, it is, in general, possible that in each branch I will be different from that of the original fiber, for I may well depend on the radius of the fiber. Though less likely, it may be that ν also will change at a branching-point. Thus, generally, a fiber excited to the intensity E may give rise to excitation in collaterals with different intensities: E_1, E_2, E_3, and E_4. However, we shall at present restrict ourselves to the simplest possible case, namely, that all branches of a fiber have the same I and ν, so that E does not vary within the branches of the same neuron. Very likely this assumption does not correspond to the real situation, but it will serve as a first approximation. In the further development of the theory the more general case will have to be studied also.

We shall now consider the mechanism of transmission of excitation and the mechanism of inhibition. We assume that at the end of every excitatory fiber an excitatory factor, ε, is produced, according to the equation

$$\frac{d\varepsilon}{dt} = AE - a\varepsilon , \tag{7}$$

where A and a are positive constants. We do not give any particular physical interpretation to this factor ε. It may be a special substance secreted in the immediate neighborhood of the end of the axon, or it may be some other physicochemical quantity which follows, approximately, equation (7). The development of the consequences of (7) is quite independent of such special assumptions. In the future, of course, a physical interpretation of all equations introduced here formally, such as (6) and (7), is to be attempted. But this will most likely bring us back to problems discussed in the first part of this book.

For an inhibitory fiber we assume, similarly, that its end produces an inhibitory factor, j, according to

$$\frac{dj}{dt} = BE - bj , \tag{8}$$

where B and b are positive constants.

From (7) and (8) it follows that, when for a long time the fibers are not excited at all, the values of ε and j are practically zero; for, when $E = 0$, we have

$$\frac{d\varepsilon}{dt} = -a\varepsilon \quad \text{and} \quad \frac{dj}{dt} = -bj ,$$

which give, upon integration,

$$\varepsilon = \varepsilon_0 e^{-at} \quad \text{and} \quad j = j_0 e^{-bt} ,$$

where the quantities ε_0 and j_0 are initial values. Both ε and j tend to zero in the absence of excitation of corresponding fibers. Since

A, B, and E are always positive, ε and j are also always positive.

Now we must specify the effect of ε and j on a neighboring, adjacent fiber which lies in the vicinity of the end of the axon that produces either ε or j. We shall postulate that, whenever $\varepsilon > j$, $\varepsilon - j$ acts as an excitatory stimulus on any such adjacent fiber. That is, if h_2 is the threshold of such an adjacent fiber, then, if $\varepsilon - j > h_2$, this fiber becomes excited, with an intensity given by (3) or, more generally, by (5) or (6), in which $\varepsilon - j$ is substituted for S. For such $\varepsilon - j$ we thus have for the intensity E_2 of the adjacent fiber

$$E_2 = \alpha_2 I_2 (\varepsilon - j - h_2) = \beta_2 (\varepsilon - j - h_2). \tag{9}$$

When $\varepsilon - j < h_2$, and, a fortiori, when $\varepsilon < j$, no excitation occurs.

Consider, now, an excitatory fiber which at its peripheral end is stimulated with a constant intensity S_1 beginning at $t = 0$. Let one of the branches of the neuron, to which fiber I belongs, form a connection with a fiber II of another neuron (Fig. 1). The intensity of excitation of I is

FIG. 1

$$E_1 = \alpha_1 I_1 (S_1 - h_1). \tag{10}$$

Owing to a finite velocity of propagation, the excitation reaches the connection at $t = t_p$. At the connection it produces ε, according to equation (7). When $E = E_1 =$ constant, the integral of (7) with initial conditions $\varepsilon = 0$ at $t = t_p$ is given by

$$\varepsilon = \frac{AE_1}{a} [1 - e^{-a(t-t_p)}] \tag{11}$$

(cf. eq. [3], chap. xxxi of Vol. I. The quantity ϵ increases from zero to the asymptotic value AE_1/a. If h_2 is the threshold of II, then II becomes excited as soon as $\epsilon \geqslant h_2$, since $j = 0$. By putting $\epsilon = h_2$ in (11) and solving it with respect to t, we find for the time at which II becomes excited

$$t_1 = t_p + \frac{1}{a} \log \frac{AE_1}{AE_1 - ah_2} = t_p + \frac{1}{a} \log \frac{A\alpha_1 I_1 (S_1 - h_1)}{A\alpha_1 I_1 (S_1 - h_1) - ah_2}. \tag{12}$$

The interval

$$t_s = t_1 - t_p = \frac{1}{a} \log \frac{A\alpha_1 I_1 (S_1 - h_1)}{A\alpha_1 I_1 (S_1 - h_1) - ah_2} \tag{13}$$

represents the delay at the connection. From (13) it follows that this delay, t_s, is not only a function of the constants characterizing the nervous system but also a function of the intensity of the peripheral stimulus, S_1.

For *II* to become at all excited, we must have

$$\frac{AE_1}{a} > h_2. \tag{14}$$

Once the excitation has taken place at $t = t_1$, the intensity E_2 of this excitation is given by

$$E_2 = \alpha_2 I_2 (\varepsilon - h_2). \tag{15}$$

As ε tends to AE_1/a, E_2 tends to

$$E'_2 = \alpha_2 I_2 \left(\frac{AE_1}{a} - h_2 \right) = \alpha_2 I_2 \frac{A\alpha_1 I_1 (S_1 - h_1) - ah_2}{a}. \tag{16}$$

If S_1 is kept constant for a sufficiently long time, the intensity of excitation of *II* will also be a constant and will be given by (16). Equations (1)-(9) are sufficient to describe quantitatively any situation arising from the interaction of any number of neurons arranged according to a definite geometrical pattern. Provided that we can master the purely mathematical complexity of any such problem, we can proceed to the consideration of various forms of neuronic circuits and their functions. They form the basis of the mathematical biophysics of the central nervous system, as developed originally in the first edition of this book and as used in the subsequent literature.

The relation between frequency of discharge and intensity of a continuous stimulus, postulated above, holds, however, only in a limited sense and in a limited number of cases. For slowly adapting fibers, such as those of the muscle end-organs,[11, 12, 13, 14] the postulated relations hold for a constant stimulus except for the short period of the initial volleys of higher frequency. They also may hold in some cases of visual stimuli.[15] For the fibers of the acoustic nerve, the relation between the intensity of the stimulus and frequency of response is very similar to that postulated above, but the process is complicated by the fact that the frequency of the sound enters as a parameter.[16] On the other hand, for rapidly adapting fibers, such as those conveying the sensation of touch,[17] the postulated relations do not hold even with remote approximation.

Thus, while for slowly adapting fibers the postulated relations (2) or (4) between frequency of discharge and intensity of stimulation may hold fairly well for constant S, they certainly do not hold for sufficiently rapidly varying values of S. Formally, however, this may be remedied by considering the rate of change $\dot{S} = dS/dt$ itself as a stimulus and considering a fiber as reacting both to the stimulus S and to dS/dt. Very rapidly adapting fibers like those of the tactile receptors, which do not discharge at all for continuous stimuli,[17] may be considered as responding to S only. It can be shown that these formal assumptions are made plausible biophysically by considerations of the two-factor theory of peripheral nerve excitation. Such considerations also throw light on the facts mentioned in the preceding paragraph.

An actual stimulus usually involves a very large number of fibers, this number increasing with the intensity due to the differences in thresholds. Therefore, even if we have a number of perfectly adapted fibers, each of which responds to a continuous stimulus with a frequency independent of the intensity S, still the total number, ν_T, of impulses per unit time for the whole set of fibers will increase with S, the relation between ν_T and S being given for physiological reasons by a curve convex upward, except perhaps in the neighborhood of the threshhold. Hence, if the actual units to which the above postulates (1)–(9) apply are not fibers but *large groups of fibers,* then for such groups the relations (2) or (4) will still hold with sufficient approximation, h now denoting the lowest threshold of the group.

The problem of synaptic transmission is more complicated. When a neuron, N_1, synapses with a higher-order neuron, N_2, then a number of branches of the axon of N_1 forms contact with the body of N_2, through so-called "terminal bulbs." Those are small (*ca.* 10^{-4} cm) bulblike structures at the end of each branch. In order for the neuron N_2 to become excited, or to "fire," it is necessary that a minimal number, m^*, of terminal bulbs be excited simultaneously or almost simultaneously, that is, within an interval of about 0.2 ms. This interval is called the period of "latent addition." In other words, a short nervous impulse must arrive nearly simultaneously to at least m^* terminal bulbs. If this happens, then after a synaptic delay of about 0.5 ms, which is independent of the intensity of stimulation and is rather constant for different types of neurons,[18, 19, 20, 21, 22, 23] neuron N_2 will become excited and send off *one* short impulse. The frequency of a presynaptic discharge is not modified at the synapse, at least in sympathetic ganglia.[24] To each presynaptic impulse there corresponds one postsynaptic, if a sufficient number of terminal bulbs is excited, or no postsynaptic impulse at all if the number of simultaneously excited terminal bulbs is below m^*. After a neuron has fired, it remains unexcitable for the period of this refractory phase, which lasts approximately 0.5 ms. There is evidence[25] for the existence of inhibitory fibers which do not transmit any excitation to neuron N_2 but, instead, raise the threshold m^* of N_2 so that an excitatory neuron N_1 may be prevented from exciting N_2. The transmission of excitation from a terminal bulb is apparently an all-or-none phenomenon.

All the above contradicts equations (1), (9), and (13). Moreover, as we shall see in chapter iii, the application of (13) to some experimental data, while leading to very good agreement, requires that the quantity t_s in (13) be of the order of seconds or even longer.

In the first edition of this book and in all the literature on the mathematical biophysics of the central nervous system until 1945, the word "synapse" was used to designate a connection between two neurons through which excitation can be transmitted according to equation (9). It was not used in the same sense as a neurophysiologist uses it. In the following we shall use the word "synapse" to designate the actual synapse of the neurophysiologist. The word "connection" will be used to describe the structure which has been designated hitherto as "synapse" in mathematical biophysics and for which the expression (9) is assumed. We shall also refer henceforth to a "nerve fiber" as meaning the actual fiber. When we refer to large groups of fibers, we shall speak of "pathways."

What is the relation between that abstract concept of connection and the real synapse, and what is the neurophysiological meaning of the factors ε and j?

Consider either a single very slowly adapting fiber or a group of parallel fibers, I (Fig. 2) stimulated with an intensity, S. The total average number of impulses per unit time in that fiber, or group of fibers, will then be a monotonically increasing function of S, described approximately by one of equations (2) or (4). Let each fiber of the group send off a large number of collaterals, each forming a chain of neurons I', as indicated in Figure 2. Each chain

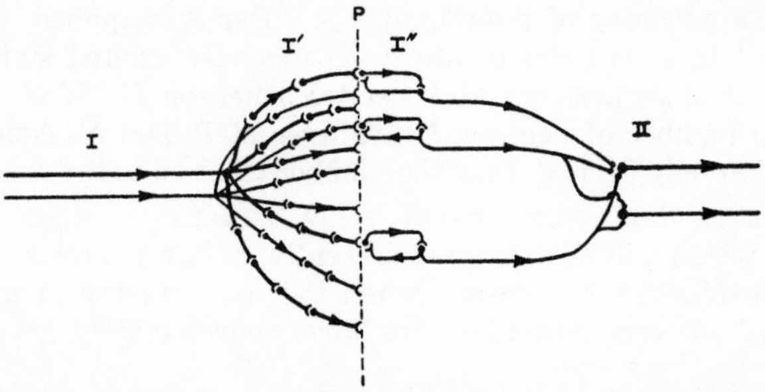

FIG. 2.—For simplicity, only two fibers of pathway I and their branches are shown in the drawing. For the same reason, only three circuits I'' are shown.

may, in general, contain a different number of neurons. Let the axons of the last neurons of each of those chains end on a surface P, and let the collaterals of all the fibers I be thoroughly "mixed" in the surface P so that each element of area ΔP receives collaterals from all the fibers I. Because of slight variations in the individual synaptic delays of the different neurons, even a regular sequence of impulses in a fiber, I, will not result in a set of synchronous impulses arriving at the surface, P. This will hold, a fortiori, for the impulses arriving at P from different fibers I if the frequencies of discharges of the latter are statistically independent. Hence the surface P will receive a large number of impulses per unit time, this number being constant only on the average. But this average number, $\bar{\nu}$, will be proportional to the total average frequency, ν_T, in the group of fibers I.

Let each axon of the system I' form in the surface P a synapse with a neuron I'', which forms a closed chain of two or more neurons.

If the number of terminal bulbs at all synapses of such a closed chain is higher than the necessary threshold value, then, if a neuron of the chain is once excited, the excitation will travel along the chain and will eventually excite the initial neuron again. Thus such a chain, once excited, remains excited permanently. Each neuron will fire periodically at intervals equal to the synaptic delay times the number of neurons in the chain.

Let each axon I' excite the corresponding neuron I'' just above the threshold so that relatively slight accidental fluctuations of the thresholds of I'' may make them occasionally unexcitable by I'. Let α denote the probability that an impulse arriving at P excites the corresponding I''.

Consider the case in which all the neurons I'' are unexcited before the application of the stimulus S. After S is applied, a circuit connected to I'' is thrown into a permanently excited state every time an impulse arriving at P excites a neuron I''. If N_0 denotes the total number of neurons I'' available at P, and N_i denotes the number already excited, then the number of circuits thrown into an excited state during the time dt is $dN_i = \alpha\bar{\nu}(N_0 - N_i)dt$. If, for reasons which will be explained presently, N_i always remains much less than N_0, in other words, when the total reserve of available neurons N_0 is very large, then we have, approximately,

$$\frac{dN_i}{dt} = \alpha\bar{\nu}N_0. \tag{17}$$

But $\bar{\nu}$ is proportional to ν_T, and the latter is taken to be a measure of the intensity E of excitation of the whole pathway I. Hence, let us denote by A a constant:

$$\frac{dN_i}{dt} = AE. \tag{18}$$

Each of the circuits, once excited, would remain so indefinitely if everything within it and its environment were constant. But such a constancy as a rule does not occur in biological systems. Thresholds fluctuate even in controlled experiments[26, 27] (cf. chap. xxxiv of Vol. I). It may be that the number of terminal bulbs exciting each neuron in the circuit is so much larger than the necessary minimum one[28] that every neuron receives a highly superthreshold excitation. A slight variation in the threshold in such a case will not affect the reverberation of the circuit. But if the number of the terminal bulbs is just sufficient to excite, then a slight variation in threshold or an accidental failure of only a few terminal bulbs to function will break the circuit and bring it back into the unexcited state. It may be worth calling attention to the fact that at ordinary values of the pH there are very few hydrogen ions per terminal bulb. The number of molecules of other substances may also be very small. The physicochemical conditions of a single terminal bulb must therefore fluctuate very strongly.

We thus see that, depending on the number of the terminal bulbs, the circuits will possess a greater or lesser degree of instability. Owing to accidental fluctuations, there will always be a probability that a number of excited circuits will be spontaneously broken during the interval of time dt. The probability of a given circuit's failing within the interval dt is constant and equal to $a\,dt$, a being a coefficient of proportionality. Hence, the natural "rate of decay" of the excited circuits will be proportional to their total number, N_i. Therefore, when, owing to impulses arriving from I', a certain number of circuits is thrown per unit time into the excited state, the rate of change of N_i is given by

$$\frac{dN_i}{dt} = AE - aN_i. \tag{19}$$

But this is formally identical with the differential equation for ε or j.

If the re-entrant part of each circuit sends off excitatory fibers, as shown in Figure 2, which converge upon a group of fibers II, then the total intensity of excitation of II will at any moment be a linear function of the number N_i of excited circuits. On the other hand, if the circuits send off *inhibitory* fibers to *II*, we have an inhibition proportional to N_i. In view of D. Lloyd's[25] work, we assume, with W. S. McCulloch and W. Pitts,[8] the existence of specific inhibitory fibers rather than explain inhibition by the action of special internuncials, as has been suggested by some authors.[29] This assumption is, however, irrelevant for the general argument.

Equation (19) holds only approximately when $N_i << N_0$ or, what is the same thing, when $AE/a << N_0$. For very high intensities, E, of excitation, equation (19) will have to be modified. The fact that equations of the form (19) can be used successfully for ε and j within a rather wide range of E indicates that N_0 is very large.

If no other limitations, except the obvious one, $N_i < N_0$, are imposed upon N_i, then we have, instead of (19), the following:

$$\frac{dN_i}{dt} = \alpha\bar{\nu}N_0 - (\alpha\bar{\nu} + a)N_i. \tag{20}$$

Since $\bar{\nu} \propto E$, so that $\alpha\bar{\nu} = cE$, we may write the solution of (20) for a constant E and for $N_i(0) = 0$ as follows:

$$N_i = \frac{cN_0E}{cE + a}[1 - e^{-(cE+a)}]. \tag{21}$$

The time constant now depends on E and hence on the intensity, S, of the stimulus. Equation (21) reduces to the usual form for ε (or j) when $cE << a$; $cN_0 = A$.

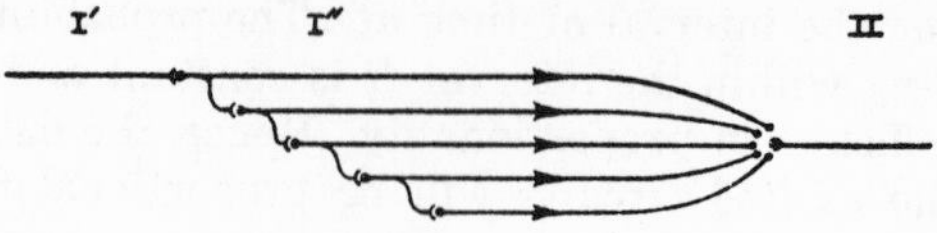

FIG. 3

Instead of assuming that neurons I'' form parts of closed circuits [interneurons C of R. Lorente de Nó[23, 28]], we may consider them as having a structure shown in Figure 3 [Type M of R. Lorente de Nó[23, 28]]. Such a group, if excited at a time t, will send a regular train of impulses to a neuron of II on which it converges, for a time equal to $r\sigma$, where r is the number of branches and σ the synaptic delay. Such a group always has a finite life-span equal to $r\sigma$. If, however, the probability of the spontaneous failure of any one synapse of the group is large enough, the "natural" life-span may practically never be reached. If the "average" life-span of such a group, determined by the probability of failure of a synapse, is much smaller than the "natural" life-span, then again the rate of decay of such excited groups will be proportional to their number.

Thus we are led to interpret a connection as a rather complex structure which includes all the internuncial neurons, by means of which the excitation of one pathway is transmitted to another. The factors ε and j are interpreted as a measure of the number of excited groups of interneurons of a certain type. Since the stability of such groups may vary within a very wide range, we obtain a very wide range of variations of the "connection delay."

To sum up, the units of which we here consider the central nervous system to be built up and the dynamics of which is described by equations (1)-(9) are not individual neurons or nerve fibers but groups of neurons and pathways. Wherever such groups of neurons are considered as units, we shall refer to them as "neuroelements." The relations (1)-(9) and the factors ε and j must be interpreted statistically as describing the behavior of very large numbers of actual neurons and fibers.

In chapter xix we shall discuss the theory of some phenomena in which individual neurons and fibers seem to be involved.

In conclusion, it may be added that H. D. Landahl[30] and N. Rashevsky[31] have also suggested interpretations of the ε- and j-factors which are different from the one given here.

REFERENCES

1. N. Rashevsky, *Jour. Gen. Psychol.*, 5, 368, 1931; 13, 82, 1935.
2. W. Köhler, *Gestalt Psychology* (New York: Liveright, 1929).
3. *Handb. d. norm. u. path. Physiol.*, 9, 645 (Berlin: J. Springer, 1929).
4. E. D. Adrian, *The Mechanism of Nervous Action* (Philadelphia: University of Pennsylvania Press, 1932).
5. A. S. Householder and H. D. Landahl, *Mathematical Biophysics of the Central Nervous System* (Bloomington, Ind.: Principia Press, 1945).
6. N. Rashevsky and V. Brown, *Bull. Math. Biophysics*, 6, 119, 1944.
7. N. Rashevsky and V. Brown, *ibid.*, p. 163.
8. W. S. McCullough and W. Pitts, *Bull. Math. Biophysics*, 5, 115, 1943.
9. H. D. Landahl, W. S. McCulloch, and W. Pitts, *Bull. Math. Biophysics*, 5, 135, 1943.
10. N. Rashevsky, *Bull. Math. Biophysics*, 7, 151, 1945.
11. J. F. Fulton, *Physiology of the Nervous System* (New York, London, and Toronto: Oxford University Press, 1943).
12. B. H. C. Matthews, *Jour. Physiol.*, 71, 64, 1931.
13. B. H. C. Matthews, *ibid.*, 72, 153, 1931.
14. B. H. C. Matthews, *ibid.*, 78, 1, 1933.
15. H. K. Hartline and C. H. Graham, *Jour. Cell. and Comp. Physiol.*, 1, 277, 1932.
16. R. Galambos and H. Davis, *Jour. Neurophysiol.*, 6, 39, 1943.
17. McKeen Cattel and H. Hoagland, *Jour. Physiol.*, 72, 392, 1931.

18. R. Lorente de Nó, *Amer. Jour. Physiol.*, 112, 595, 1935.
19. R. Lorente de Nó, *ibid.*, 113, 505, 1935.
20. R. Lorente de Nó, *ibid.*, p. 524.
21. R. Lorente de Nó, *Jour. Neurophysiol.*, 1, 187, 1938.
22. R. Lorente de Nó, *ibid.*, p. 194.
23. R. Lorente de Nó, *ibid.*, p. 207.
24. D. W. Bronk, *Jour. Neurophysiol.*, 2, 380, 1939.
25. D. P. C. Lloyd, *Jour. Neurophysiol.*, 4, 184, 1941.
26. C. Pecher, *Arch. internat. physiol.*, 49, 129, 1939.
27. H. D. Landahl, *Bull. Math. Biophysics*, 3, 141, 1941.
28. R. Lorente de Nó, *Jour. Neurophysiol.*, 2, 402, 1939.
29. H. S. Gasser, *Volume jubilaire publié en l'honneur du Prof. J. Demoor* (Liège, 1937), p. 218.
30. H. D. Landahl, *Bull. Math. Biophysics*, 7, 219, 1945.
31. N. Rashevsky, *Bull. Math. Biophysics*, 7, 223, 1945.

CHAPTER III

GENERAL CONSIDERATIONS ON CENTRAL EXCITATION AND INHIBITION: CONTINUED

We shall now proceed with a systematic discussion of some circuits of pathways. A more general theory of complex circuits has been developed by A. S. Householder[1] and by Walter Pitts.[2] An excellent presentation of this theory is given in the book by A. S. Householder and H. D. Landahl,[3] *Mathematical Biophysics of the Central Nervous System*, in which the reader will find much interesting material.

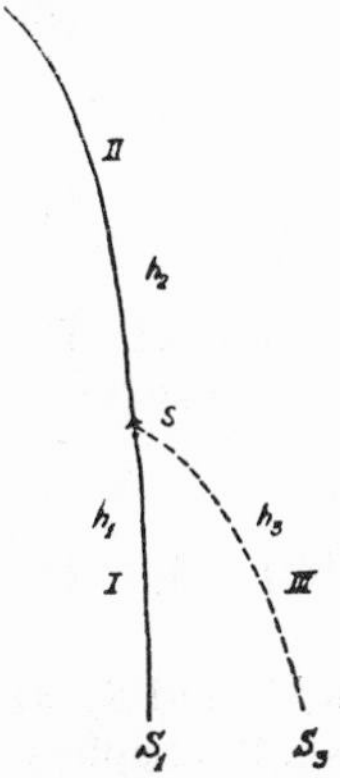

FIG. 1

Let an inhibitory pathway (Fig. 1, *III*) with a threshold h_3 also reach the connection s. Let it be stimulated with a constant intensity S_3, beginning at some moment $t_0 > 0$, so that the excitation reaches the connection at a moment t_0', at which ε, and therefore also E_2, have practically reached their asymptotic values.* Then an amount of j is produced at the connection, according to

$$j = \frac{BE_3}{b}[1 - e^{-b(t-t_0')}], \tag{1}$$

with

$$E_3 = a_3 I_3 (S_3 - h_3), \tag{2}$$

and j tends asymptotically to BE_3/b. At $t = t_0'$, $j = 0$, and therefore $\varepsilon - j = AE_1/a$. Now, as j increases according to (1), $\varepsilon - j$ decreases. If

$$\frac{BE_3}{b} < \frac{AE_1}{a} - h_2, \tag{3}$$

then $\varepsilon - j$ will reach, after a while, its minimum value

$$(\varepsilon - j)_{\min} = \frac{AE_1}{a} - \frac{BE_3}{b} > h_2. \tag{4}$$

The pathway *II* will still be excited, but the intensity of excitation,

* The assumption that the inhibitory pathway *III* is directly stimulated from the periphery is, of course, made here for simplicity. It may actually be stimulated by a peripheral excitatory pathway. This does not affect any of the following conclusions.

E_2, will drop from the value given by equation (16) of chapter ii to

$$\left.\begin{aligned} E_2'' &= \alpha_2 I_2 \left(\frac{AE_1}{a} - \frac{BE_3}{b} - h_2 \right) \\ &= \alpha_2 I_2 \frac{bA\alpha_1 I_1 (S_1 - h_1) - aB\alpha_3 I_3 (S_3 - h_3) - abh_2}{ab} \, . \end{aligned}\right\} \tag{5}$$

If, however $BE_3/b > [(AE_1/a) - h_2]$, then *II* will become completely inhibited. When both *I* and *III* are stimulated nearly simultaneously, then, if (3) holds, after a sufficient lapse of time an excitation of intensity (5) will occur. At the early stages of development of ε and j, things may be more complicated. Let S_1 be applied at $t = t_{01}$, and S_3 at $t = t_{03}$. Then ε varies according to

$$\varepsilon = \frac{AE_1}{a} [1 - e^{-a(t - t_{01} - t_p)}] \, , \tag{6}$$

and j according to

$$j = \frac{BE_3}{b} [1 - e^{-b(t - t_{03} - t_p')}] \, , \tag{7}$$

where t_p' is the time it takes the excitation to travel along *III*. The time t_1 at which, under those conditions, *II* will become excited is given by

$$\varepsilon - j = \frac{AE_1}{a} [1 - e^{-a(t_1 - t_{01} - t_p)}] - \frac{BE_3}{b} [1 - e^{-b(t_1 - t_{03} - t_p')}] = h_2 \tag{8}$$

and will depend, in general, on E_1 and E_3, that is, on S_1 and S_3, as well as on the value of $t_{01} - t_{03}$ of the interval between the application of S_1 and S_3, and on other constants. Under those conditions

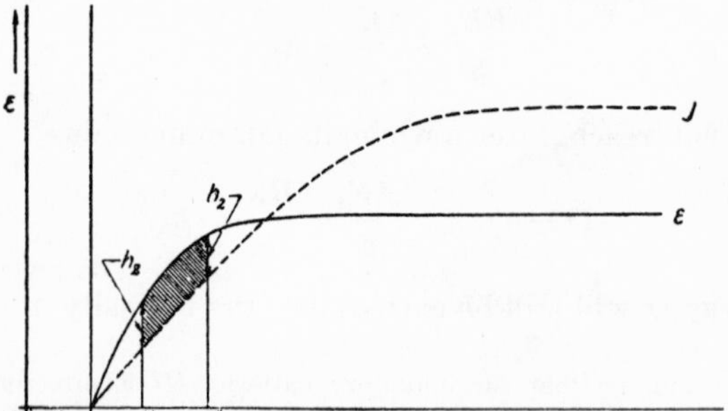

FIG. 2

we may have a short excitation of II even when (3) does not hold. Such a case is represented, for instance, by Figure 2, with $t_{01} = t_{03} = 0, t_p = t_p', AE_1 > BE_3,$ and $a >> b,$ so that $AE_1/a < BE_3/b.$ From (6) and (7) we see that in this case

$$\frac{d\varepsilon}{dt} = AE_1 e^{-a(t-t_p)}, \quad \frac{dj}{dt} = BE_3 e^{-b(t-t_p)}.$$

Hence, for $t = t_p$ the slope of the ε-curve is equal to AE_1; that of the j-curve, to BE_3. The quantity ε first rises more rapidly than j. Between $t = t'$ and $t = t''$, $\varepsilon - j > h_2$ and there is a temporary excitation of II.

Equation (8) gives us the effect of the stimulation of an inhibitory pathway on the connective delay of the excitatory, since this delay, $t_s = t_1 - t_{01} - t_p$, is a function of S_3 and of t_{03}. The study of the various relations following from (8) offers a simple, but interesting, mathematical problem, which may suggest some experimental studies.

Let us now consider a more complex case, namely, that of an excitatory and an inhibitory pathway, each producing both ε and j, only that an excitatory pathway is characterized by an excess of ε and an inhibitory by an excess of j. In terms of the neurophysiological interpretation given in chapter ii, this means that some of the interneurons I'' of Figure 2 of chapter ii send off excitatory fibers, and some send off inhibitory fibers. Let the excitation of a central end of an excitatory pathway result in a variation of ε according to

$$\frac{d\varepsilon}{dt} = A_e E - a_e \varepsilon, \tag{9}$$

and in a variation of j according to

$$\frac{dj}{dt} = B_e E - b_e j, \tag{10}$$

with

$$A_e > B_e, \quad a_e > b_e, \quad \text{and} \quad \frac{A_e}{a_e} > \frac{B_e}{b_e}. \tag{11}$$

Similarly, at the central end of an inhibitory neuroelement, let

$$\left.\begin{aligned} \frac{d\varepsilon}{dt} &= A_j E - a_j \varepsilon, \\ \frac{dj}{dt} &= B_j E - b_j j, \end{aligned}\right\} \tag{12}$$

with

$$B_j > A_j, \quad b_j > a_j, \quad \frac{B_j}{b_j} > \frac{A_j}{a_j}. \tag{13}$$

In a subsequent chapter we shall also consider intermediate cases, namely,

$$\left.\begin{aligned} A_e < B_e, \quad &\text{with} \quad a_e < b_e \quad \text{and} \quad \frac{A_e}{a_e} > \frac{B_e}{b_e}; \\ A_j > B_j, \quad &\text{with} \quad a_j > b_j, \quad \text{and} \quad \frac{A_j}{a_j} < \frac{B_j}{b_j}. \end{aligned}\right\} \tag{14}$$

The first case (14) gives, for a continuous constant stimulus, a brief inhibition followed by a continuous lasting excitation. The second case gives a brief excitation followed by a continuous inhibition (cf. Fig. 5, chap. ix).

If at $t = 0$ the excitatory pathway I (Fig. 1 of chap. ii) is stimulated, then, at $t = t_p$, $\varepsilon - j$ begins to vary at the connection according to

$$\varepsilon - j = \frac{A_e E_1}{a_e}[1 - e^{-a_e(t-t_p)}] - \frac{B_e E_1}{b_e}[1 - e^{-b_e(t-t_p)}].$$

Because of (11), $\varepsilon - j$ is always positive. For $t = \infty$, $\varepsilon - j$ becomes equal to

$$\left(\frac{A_e}{a_e} - \frac{B_e}{b_e}\right)E_1. \tag{15}$$

Hence, if the expression (15) is larger than h_2 or if

$$E_1 > \frac{h_2 a_e b_e}{A_e b_e - B_e a_e}, \tag{16}$$

then, at some moment $t_1 > t_p$, II will be excited. This moment t_1 is obtained from the equation

$$\frac{A_e E_1}{a_e}[1 - e^{-a_e(t_1-t_p)}] - \frac{B_e E_1}{b_e}[1 - e^{-b_e(t_1-t_p)}] = h_2. \tag{17}$$

This is transcendental in t_1 and cannot be solved exactly with respect to t_1 or to $t_s = t_1 - t_p$. Solving, however, with respect to E_1, we find

$$E_1 = \frac{h_2}{\dfrac{A_e}{a_e} - \dfrac{B_e}{b_e} + \dfrac{B_e}{b_e}e^{-b_e t_s} - \dfrac{A_e}{a_e}e^{-a_e t_s}}. \tag{18}$$

Substituting for E_1 its value given by equation (10) of chapter ii, we find

$$S_1 = \frac{h_2}{\alpha_1 I_1 \left(\frac{A_e}{a_e} - \frac{B_e}{b_e} + \frac{B_e}{b_e} e^{-b_e t_s} - \frac{A_e}{a_e} e^{-a_e t_s} \right)} + h_1, \tag{19}$$

which gives us a relation between the connection retardation t_s and intensity S_1 of the peripheral stimulus. For $t_s = \infty$,

$$S_1 = \frac{h_2}{\alpha_1 I_1 \left(\frac{A_e}{a_e} - \frac{B_e}{b_e} \right)} + h_1 > 0. \tag{20}$$

The expression

$$\frac{B_e}{b_e} e^{-b_e t_s} - \frac{A_e}{a_e} e^{-a_e t_s} \tag{21}$$

is negative for $t_s = 0$, being equal to $-[(A_e/a_e) - (B_e/b_e)]$. Hence, for $t_s = 0$, $S_1 = \infty$. The expression (21) is zero for $t_s = \infty$, and it also becomes zero for a value $t_s' > 0$ of t_s. This value is obtained by equating (21) to zero. This gives

$$\frac{B_e}{b_e} e^{-b_e t_s'} = \frac{A_e}{a_e} e^{-a_e t_s'},$$

or

$$e^{-b_e t_s'} = \frac{A_e b_e}{B_e a_e} e^{-a_e t_s'},$$

or, taking logarithms,

$$-b_e t_s' = \log \frac{A_e b_e}{B_e a_e} - a_e t_s'.$$

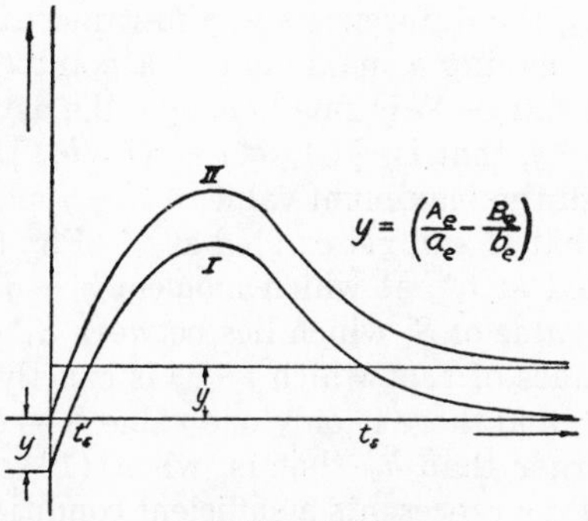

FIG. 3

Solving the foregoing for t_s', we find

$$t_s' = \frac{1}{a_e - b_e} \log \frac{A_e b_e}{B_e a_e}. \tag{22}$$

Because of (11), $t_s' > 0$. Hence, for $t_s > t_s'$, expression (21) is positive. The variation of (21) is represented by Figure 3, curve *I*. The expression in parentheses in the denominator of (19) is obtained by adding to (21) $(A_e/a_e) - (B_e/b_e)$. This expression is represented by Figure 3, *II*. Hence, we see that the denominator of (19) is zero for $t_s = 0$, is positive for $t_s = \infty$, and has a maximum for a finite t_s. Therefore, S_1 is positive for $t_s = \infty$, has a minimum for a finite t_s, which we shall call t_s^*, and is infinite for $t_s = 0$.

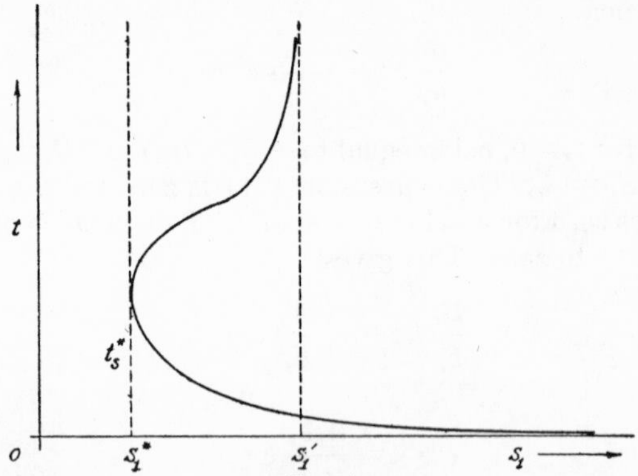

FIG. 4

This relation between S_1 and t_s is represented by Figure 4. At first, this graph looks somewhat puzzling, but its physical meaning becomes clear from the following consideration. For a given S_1, that is, for a given E_1, the difference $\varepsilon - j$ first increases and then decreases (Fig. 5), having a maximum at a point t^*. When E_1 or—what is the same thing—S_1 is small enough, the asymptotic value of the difference $\varepsilon - j$, that is, $[(A_e/a_e) - (B_e/b_e)]E_1$, will be smaller than h_2, though the maximum value of $\varepsilon - j$ may be larger than h_2. This means that *II* will get excited at t_s' (Fig. 5) but will again cease to be excited at t_s'', at which moment $\varepsilon - j$ again drops below h_2. For any value of S_1 which lies between S_1^* and S_1' there are therefore two values of t_s at which $\varepsilon - j$ is exactly equal to h_2. For $S_1 > S_1'$, $t_s'' = \infty$, and there is only one value $t_s = t_s'$. This happens when (15) is larger than h_2, that is, when (16) is satisfied. The inequality (16) thus represents a sufficient condition, but not a necessary condition for the excitation of *II*. It is necessary only for a constant continuous stimulus S_1 to cause a continuous excitation of *II*.

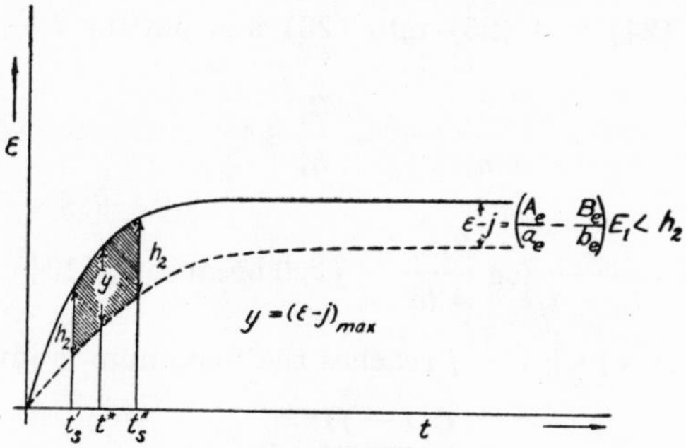

FIG. 5

Now, consider the case in which *III* (Fig. 1) is stimulated continuously alone for a long time. At the connection, then, $\varepsilon - j$ has the asymptotic value

$$(\varepsilon - j)_j = \left(\frac{A_j}{a_j} - \frac{B_j}{b_j} \right) E_3. \tag{23}$$

Because of (13), $\varepsilon - j$ (asymptotic) is less than zero. Hence no excitation occurs in *II*. But now, at some moment $t = t_1$, let the stimulation S_3 cease. Then ε will decrease according to

$$\varepsilon = \frac{A_j}{a_j} E_3 e^{-a_j(t-t_1)}, \tag{24}$$

while j will be given by

$$j = \frac{B_j}{b_j} E_3 e^{-b_j(t-t_1)}. \tag{25}$$

Since, because of (13), $b_j > a_j$, the j-curve will fall off more rapidly than will the ε-curve (Fig. 6) ; and, after a while, $\varepsilon - j$ will become positive, reach a maximum, and drop to zero. The moment t at

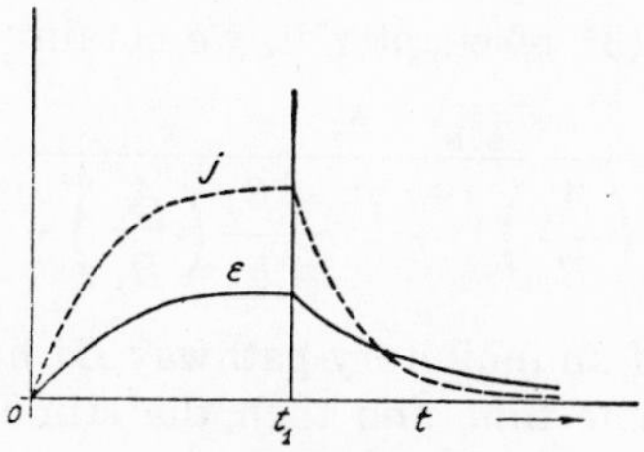

FIG. 6

which $\varepsilon - j$ becomes positive is given by the equation

$$\varepsilon - j = 0. \tag{26}$$

Introducing (24) and (25) into (26) and putting $t - t_1 = t'$, we find

$$\frac{A_j}{a_j} e^{-a_j t'} = \frac{B_j}{b_j} e^{-b_j t'},$$

or

$$t' = \frac{1}{b_j - a_j} \log \frac{B_j a_j}{A_j b_j} \qquad (> 0 \text{ because of } [13]). \tag{27}$$

The time t_m at which $\varepsilon - j$ reaches the maximum is given by

$$\frac{d(\varepsilon - j)}{dt} = 0. \tag{28}$$

Again introducing (24) and (25) into (28), we find

$$A_j e^{-a_j(t_m - t_1)} = B_j e^{-b_j(t_m - t_1)},$$

or

$$t_m = t_1 + \frac{1}{b_j - a_j} \log \frac{B_j}{A_j} > 0. \tag{29}$$

The actual value of $\varepsilon - j$ at its maximum is obtained by introducing (29) for t in (24) and (25) and taking the difference. This gives

$$(\varepsilon - j)_{\max} = E_3 \left\{ \frac{A_j}{a_j} \left(\frac{A_j}{B_j} \right)^{a_j/(b_j - a_j)} - \frac{B_j}{b_j} \left(\frac{A_j}{B_j} \right)^{b_j/(b_j - a_j)} \right\}.$$

If $(\varepsilon - j)_{\max}$ is greater than h_2, then *II* will be excited for a short time. The requirement $(\varepsilon - j)_{\max} > h_2$ gives

$$E_3 > \frac{h_2}{\frac{A_j}{a_j} \left(\frac{A_j}{B_j} \right)^{a_j/(b_j - a_j)} - \frac{B_j}{b_j} \left(\frac{A_j}{B_j} \right)^{b_j/(b_j - a_j)}}, \tag{30}$$

or, using equation (3) of chapter ii, we obtain

$$S_3 > \frac{h_2}{a_3 I_3 \left[\frac{A_j}{a_j} \left(\frac{A_j}{B_j} \right)^{a_j/(b_j - a_j)} - \frac{B_j}{b_j} \left(\frac{A_j}{B_j} \right)^{b_j/(b_j - a_j)} \right]} + h_3. \tag{31}$$

We thus find that, if an inhibitory pathway *III* has been stimulated continuously for some time and then the stimulation is suddenly stopped, a short excitatory process will occur in *II*, provided that the intensity of stimulation, S_3, of *III* is sufficiently large. This reminds one of the so-called "rebound phenomenon," studied by Sherrington and others.[4] The value

$$(\varepsilon - j) = E_3 \left(\frac{A_j}{a_j} e^{-a_j t'} - \frac{B_j}{b_j} e^{-b_j t'} \right) \tag{32}$$

is first negative, then reaches a positive maximum, and then, remaining positive, drops to zero at $t' = \infty$. Hence, if (31) is satisfied, the $\varepsilon - j$ curve will intercept the horizontal line $\varepsilon - j = h_2$ at two points (Fig. 7), which lie the farther apart, the larger the

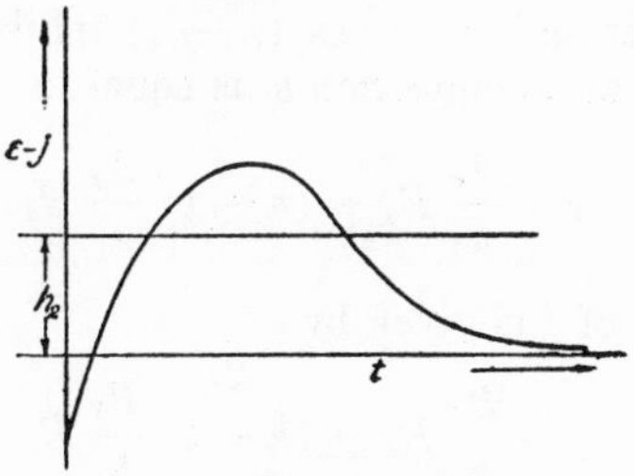

FIG. 7

E_3, since an increase of E_3 increases all ordinates of the $\varepsilon - j$ curve in the same proportion. The stronger the S_3, the longer the duration of the rebound phenomenon.

Consider, now, a number n of similar peripheral excitatory pathways N_i (where $i = 1, \cdots, n$), which we shall call "pathways of class *I*," each leading to a connection s_i with a neuroelement of higher order of N_i' of class *II*. Let each of those pathways N branch off, between its peripheral end and the connection, with a pathway, which will, in turn, form a connection s_i' with an inhibitory pathway $\bar{N}_i$, which sends pathways to every connection s_h for $h \neq i$ (Fig. 8). Thus, each connection s_i receives an excitatory pathway from the periphery and $(n - 1)$ inhibiting pathways from other neuroelements. Let us consider the case that all the n excitatory pathways are peripherally stimulated with equal intensity, S_1, of constant indefinite duration. At any of the

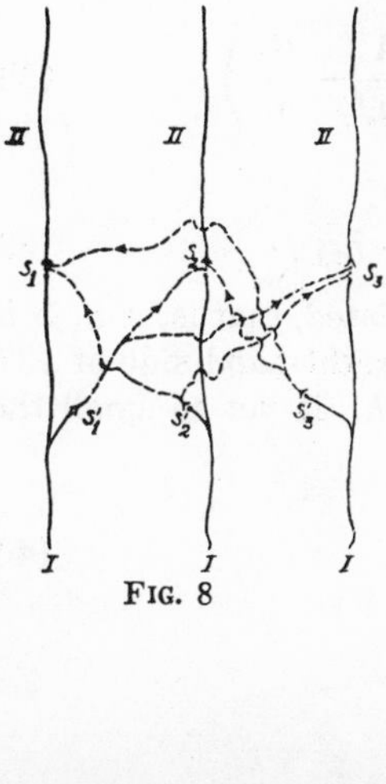

FIG. 8

connections s_i we then have the following situation:

Each of the excitatory pathways gives rise, when the stationary state is reached, to an amount A_eE_1/a_e of ε and B_eE_1/b_e of j, with

$$\frac{A_eE_1}{a_e} - \frac{B_eE_1}{b_e} > 0. \tag{33}$$

Each of the inhibitory pathways of class *III* give rise similarly to an amount A_jE_3/a_j of ε and B_jE_3/b_j of j, with

$$\frac{A_jE_3}{a_j} - \frac{B_jE_3}{b_j} < 0. \tag{34}$$

Since each connection s_i receives $(n-1)$ inhibitory pathways, the total amount of ε at a connection s_i is equal to

$$\varepsilon = \frac{A_e}{a_e} E_1 + (n-1) \frac{A_j}{a_j} E_3. \tag{35}$$

The total amount of j is given by

$$j = \frac{B_e}{b_e} E_1 + (n-1) \frac{B_j}{b_j} E_3. \tag{36}$$

The difference $\varepsilon - j$ is therefore equal to

$$\varepsilon - j = \left(\frac{A_e}{a_e} - \frac{B_e}{b_e}\right) E_1 + (n-1)\left(\frac{A_j}{a_j} - \frac{B_j}{b_j}\right) E_3. \tag{37}$$

But E_3 is the intensity produced by stimulating any of the pathways $\bar{N}_i$ by the amount of $\varepsilon - j$ at each connection s_i'. This amount is equal to $[(A_e/a_e) - (B_e/b_e)]E_1$. Hence,

$$E_3 = \alpha_3 I_3 (PE_1 - h_3)\,; \quad P = \left(\frac{A_e}{a_e} - \frac{B_e}{b_e}\right), \tag{38}$$

and, because of equation (10) of chapter ii,

$$E_3 = \alpha_3 I_3 [P\alpha_1 I_1 (S_1 - h_1) - h_3]\,. \tag{39}$$

If the pathways of class *I* are actually stimulated, that is, if $S_1 > h_1$, then, because of (33), the first term of the right-hand side of (37) is positive. If S_1, while being larger than h_1, is yet so small that $P\alpha_1 I_1 (S_1 - h_1) - h_3 < 0$, which means that

$$h_1 < S_1 < h_1 + \frac{h_3}{P\alpha_1 I_1}, \tag{40}$$

then, as seen from (39), $E_3 = 0$ (since negative values of E are excluded), and therefore in (37) $\varepsilon - j > 0$. If $\varepsilon - j > h_2$, then all pathways of class *II* will be excited. This requires that

$$PE_1 = P\alpha_1 I_1 (S_1 - h_1) > h_2 ,$$

or

$$S_1 > h_1 + \frac{h_2}{P\alpha_1 I_1}. \tag{41}$$

Equations (40) and (41) are compatible only if

$$h_2 < h_3 . \tag{42}$$

If, however,

$$S_1 > h_1 + \frac{h_3}{P\alpha_1 I_1}, \tag{43}$$

so that $E_3 > 0$, then, because of (34), the second term of the right-hand side of (37) is negative. By introducing equation (10) of chapter ii and (39) into (37), the latter may be written

$$\left.\begin{aligned} \varepsilon - j = & P\alpha_1 I_1 (S_1 - h_1) \\ & - (n-1) Q\alpha_3 I_3 [P\alpha_1 I_1 (S_1 - h_1) - h_3] , \end{aligned}\right\} \tag{44}$$

with

$$P = \frac{A_e}{a_e} - \frac{B_e}{b_e} > 0; \quad Q = -\left(\frac{A_j}{a_j} - \frac{B_j}{b_j}\right) > 0. \tag{45}$$

The quantity $(\varepsilon - j)$ is then represented as a difference of two positive terms. If S_1 is given, then $\varepsilon - j$ will be negative when n is sufficiently large, namely, when

$$n > 1 + \frac{P}{Q} \frac{\alpha_1 I_1}{\alpha_3 I_3} \frac{S_1 - h_1}{P\alpha_1 I_1 (S_1 - h_1) - h_3}. \tag{46}$$

The right-hand side of (46) is positive because of (43). In this case a stimulation of n neuroelements at the periphery with equal intensity results in a complete inhibition at the connection, and neuroelements of class *II* remain unexcited, although the peripheral stimuli may be superliminal.

The right-hand side of (46) decreases with increasing S_1, whenever S_1 is large enough to make the denominator positive, that is, when (43) is satisfied. This is seen by writing the right-hand side of (46) in the form

$$\frac{P}{Q}\frac{\alpha_1 I_1}{\alpha_3 I_3}\frac{1}{P\alpha_1 I_1 - \dfrac{h_3}{S_1 - h_1}}. \tag{47}$$

Hence, if n is given, we can choose a sufficiently small S_1, such as to make the denominator of (46) as small as we wish and, therefore, the right side as large as we wish, so that (46) will not hold; and therefore $\varepsilon - j$ will be positive. This still does not insure that the pathways of class *II* will become excited, because for this to happen we must have $\varepsilon - j > h_2$, which gives, because of (44),

$$n < 1 + \frac{P\alpha_1 I_1 (S_1 - h_1) - h_2}{Q\alpha_3 I_3 [P\alpha_1 I_1 (S_1 - h_1) - h_3]}.$$

However, out of n pathways, let $m < n$ be stimulated with an intensity $S_1' > S_1$, while the remaining $n - m$ pathways are stimulated as before. Then, at each of the m connections s_i^m corresponding to the m pathways, we have, for continuous stimulation, the production of ε by the corresponding pathway of class *I* itself, the production of ε by $m - 1$ inhibitory pathways, stimulated by the remaining $m - 1$ pathways of class *I*, and the production of ε by $n - m$ inhibitory nerves, stimulated by the $n - m$ pathways of class *I*. Altogether,

$$\varepsilon = \frac{A_e}{a_e} E_1' + (m-1)\frac{A_j}{a_j} E_3' + (n-m)\frac{A_j}{a_j} E_3, \tag{48}$$

with

$$\left.\begin{aligned} E_1' &= \alpha_1 I_1 (S_1' - h_1), \\ E_3' &= \alpha_3 I_3 (PE_1' - h_3) = \alpha_3 I_3 [P\alpha_1 I_1 (S_1' - h_1) - h_3], \end{aligned}\right\} \tag{49}$$

and E_3 given by (39).

Similarly, we have for j at each connection s_i^m

$$j = \frac{B_e}{b_e} E_1' + (m-1)\frac{B_j}{b_j} E_3' + (n-m)\frac{B_j}{b_j} E_3. \tag{50}$$

The value $(\varepsilon - j)_1$ of $\varepsilon - j$ at a connection s_i^m is then given by

$$(\varepsilon - j)_1 = PE_1' - (m-1)QE_3' - (n-m)QE_3. \tag{51}$$

For a connection s_i^{n-m} corresponding to the $n - m$ pathways, we obtain, in a similar manner,

$$(\varepsilon - j)_2 = PE_1 - (n-m-1)QE_3 - mQE_3'. \tag{52}$$

Introducing equations (10) of chapter ii, (39), and (49) into (51) and (52), we find

$$\left.\begin{aligned}(\varepsilon - j)_1 = &P\alpha_1 I_1 (S_1' - h_1)\\ &- (m-1) Q\alpha_3 I_3 [P\alpha_1 I_1 (S_1' - h_1) - h_3]\\ &- (n-m) Q\alpha_3 I_3 [P\alpha_1 I_1 (S_1 - h_1) - h_3] ,\\ (\varepsilon - j)_2 = &P\alpha_1 I_1 (S_1 - h_1)\\ &- (n-m-1) Q\alpha_3 I_3 [P\alpha_1 I_1 (S_1 - h_1) - h_3]\\ &- mQ\alpha_3 I_3 [P\alpha_1 I_1 (S_1' - h_1) - h_3] .\end{aligned}\right\} \tag{53}$$

Since $S_1' > S_1$, we have

$$\left.\begin{aligned}(\varepsilon - j)_2 < &P\alpha_1 I_1 (S_1 - h_1)\\ &- (n-1) Q\alpha_3 I_3 [P\alpha_1 I_1 (S_1 - h_1) - h_3] .\end{aligned}\right\} \tag{54}$$

The right-hand side of expression (54) is identical with that of (44). If, therefore, conditions (43) and (46) are satisfied, we shall have $(\varepsilon - j)_2 < 0$. All connections s_i^{n-m} will be inhibited. At the same time, we have, similarly, $(\varepsilon - j)_1 > (\varepsilon - j)_2$. Therefore, $(\varepsilon - j)_1$ is not necessarily negative under the same conditions. With such values of S_1 and n as to satisfy (46), we still can dispose of S_1' so as to make $(\varepsilon - j)_1 > h_2$, which requires

$$\left.\begin{aligned}S_1' > &h_1\\ &+ \frac{h_2 + Q\alpha_3 I_3 [(n-m) P\alpha_1 I_1 (S_1 - h_1) - (n-1) h_3]}{P\alpha_1 I_1 [1 - (m-1) Q\alpha_3 I_3]} .\end{aligned}\right\} \tag{55}$$

Thus, when out of n peripheral pathways a smaller group $m < n$ is stimulated with an intensity S_1', which is sufficiently larger than the intensity of stimulation of the remaining pathways, the excitation of this group will pass through the connection and result in further excitation of some centers. Among simple psychological experiences this has its analogies in our inability to react definitely to a situation in which too many stimulı of equal intensity are present. Only if a smaller group of stimuli has a much stronger intensity, do we turn our attention to it without perceiving the details of the background. There is also direct experimental evidence[5] that, for instance, two pain stimuli mutually inhibit each other. The foregoing scheme, while rather simplied, perhaps represents roughly a rather general structure of the brain.

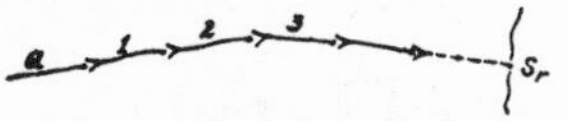

FIG. 9

An afferent excitatory pathway a (Fig. 9) may send an inhibitory stimulus to a connection s_r not through one inhibitory pathway but through a chain of excitatory pathways (Fig. 9, solid lines) which ends in an inhibitory pathway (Fig. 9, dotted line). The excitation of the first pathway is given by

$$E_1 = \alpha_1 I_1 (PE_0 - h_1), \tag{56}$$

where the subscript refers to the first pathway and E_0 is the intensity of excitation of the afferent pathway. The intensity of excitation E_2 of the second pathway is given by

$$E_2 = \alpha_2 I_2 (PE_1 - h_2) = \alpha_2 I_2 [P\alpha_1 I_1 (PE_0 - h_1) - h_2] ,$$

while that of the ith branch is generally

$$E_i = \alpha_i I_i (PE_{i-1} - h_i). \tag{57}$$

This is an equation in finite differences which determines E_i as a function of i. Since the last rth pathway is an inhibitory one, the inhibitory effect at s_r will be given by $QE_r = f(r)$.

If the individual pathways 1, 2, 3, $\cdots$, r (Fig. 9) are very short and are densely arranged, the intensity of excitation E_i may be considered not as a function $f(i)$ of the ordinal-number i but as a function $u(x)$ of the distance x taken from the origin of the neuronic chain (Fig. 9) and measured along the chain to the point at which the ith neuroelement is located. Thus, the inhibitory effect of the whole chain is a function of its length. The shape of this function is determined by the values $\alpha_1, \alpha_2, \cdots, \alpha_i$; $I_1, I_2, \cdots, I_i$; and $h_1, h_2, \cdots, h_i$. If the variation of α, I, and h from a preceding neuroelement to a following is prescribed analytically, $u(x)$ is hereby determined. Neuronic chains which have the same morphological structures may have different distributions of α, I, and h along them, and thus give rise to quite different $u(x)$. The chain in Figure 9 may also not contain an inhibitory last link but may consist exclusively of excitatory neuroelements. Then the excitatory action of the chain will be a function of its length.

Quite generally, if one nerve center excites or inhibits another center through a chain of neuroelements, the excitatory and inhibitory effects depend on the distance between those two centers, the dependence being determined by the distribution of α, I, and h along the chain.

It must, however, be noted that, in general, E_i is not equal to E_0 times a function of i but is of the form $E_i = f(E_0, i)$. If all h_i are very small and can be neglected as compared to PE_{i-1}, then the solution of (57) is of the form

$$E_i = P^i \alpha_1 \alpha_2 \cdots \alpha_i I_1 I_2 \cdots I_i E_0 = E_0 P^i \prod_1^i \alpha_i I_i .$$

The product $\Pi \alpha_i I_i$ is a given function of (i) which is determined by the choice of α_i and I_i. In the limiting continuous case we then have $E(x) = E_0 f(x)$. We shall use, in the future, this simplified particular case.

Some interesting special cases have been studied by A. S. Householder[6] and H. D. Landahl.[7]

We may have, now, any arbitrary distribution of S as $S_1^{(1)}$, $S_1^{(2)}$, $S_1^{(3)}$, $\cdots$, $S_1^{(n)}$. At any connection s_i we have

$$(\varepsilon - j)_i = PE_1^{(i)} - Q \sum_{k=1}^{k=n}{}' f_{ki}(PE_1^{(k)} - h_3), \tag{58}$$

where Σ' denotes that the summation is to be taken over all elements except the ith one and where f_{ki} is the intensity of excitation of the inhibitory pathway coming from the kth excitatory pathway to the ith connection. We may consider a somewhat different arrangement, namely, that at each connection s_i, pathway I excites

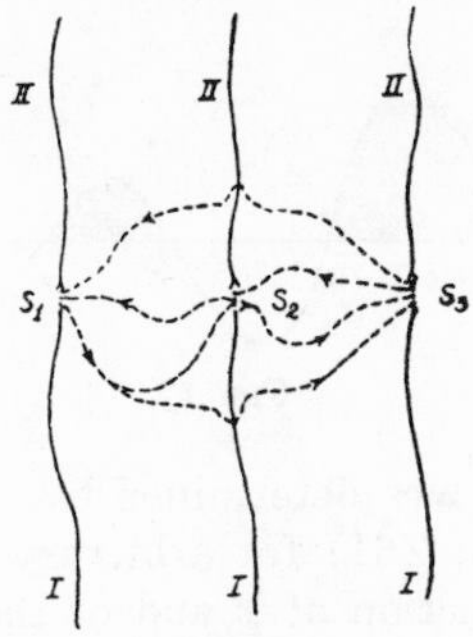

FIG. 10

an inhibitory pathway, which goes to other connections. In other words, s_i' is also located at s_i (Fig. 10). Then we have at each connection

$$(\varepsilon - j)_i = PE_1^i - Q \sum_k{}' f_{ki}[(\varepsilon - j)_k - h_{ki}], \tag{59}$$

where h_{ki} is the threshold of the inhibitory neuroelement, transmitting from the kth to the ith connection. If the neuroelements are distributed linearly and very densely, we may, for a large number of neuroelements, substitute integrals for sums. Then f_{ki} becomes a function of the distance $x - \xi$ of the neuroelements located at x and at ξ. Setting $(\varepsilon - j)_x = \phi(x)$, we then have, instead of (58), for the case of a linear (one-dimensional) arrangement of connections,

$$\phi(x) = PE_1(x) - Q \int_a^b K(x-\xi)[PE_1(\xi) - h_3]d\xi\,, \quad (60)$$

and, instead of (59),

$$\phi(x) = PE_1(x) - Q \int_a^b K(x-\xi)[\phi(\xi) - h(x,\xi)]d\xi\,. \quad (61)$$

Similar equations are obtained for a more general three-dimensional arrangement. Equation (61) is an integral equation, with one peculiarity, however. Since only those connections $s(\xi)$ contribute to the inhibition at $s(x)$ in which $\phi(\xi) - h(x, \xi) > 0$, therefore the integration must be extended over only the positive parts of the integrand. If $\phi(x) = 0$ has several roots, then (Fig. 11) we actually have to integrate only from ξ_1 to ξ_2, ξ_3 to ξ_4, etc. But

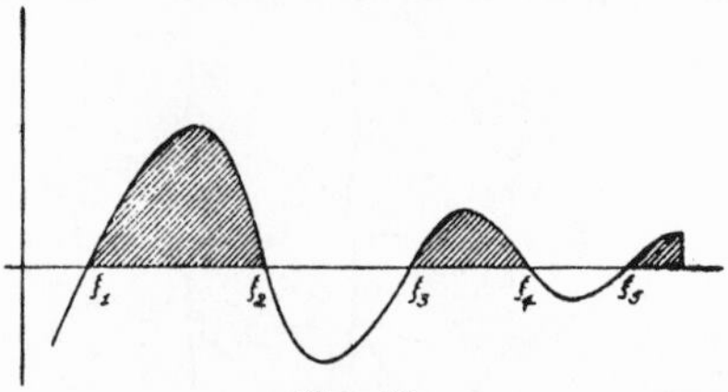

FIG. 11

these roots are themselves determined by $\phi(x)$. The procedure to follow is this: We solve (61) for arbitrary $a = a'$ and $b = b'$, and thus obtain ϕ as a function of x and of the parameters a' and b', $\phi(a', b', x)$. Then we determine the roots $x_1, x_2, \cdots$, etc., of

$$\phi(a', b', x) = 0\,. \quad (62)$$

Let $\phi > 0$ between x_1 and x_2, x_3 and x_4, $\cdots$, etc. Then we must have $a' = x_1$, $b' = x_2$, $a' = x_3$, $b' = x_4$, $\cdots$, etc. Hence the values a' and b' are obtained from

$$\phi(a', b', a') = 0; \quad \phi(a', b', b') = 0\,. \quad (63)$$

Since $h(x, \xi)$ is known, (61) may be written

$$\phi(x) = PE_1(x) - Q \int_{a'}^{b'} K(x-\xi)\phi(\xi)d\xi + QF(x), \quad (64)$$

where

$$F(x) = \int_{a'}^{b'} K(x-\xi)h(x,\xi)d\xi \quad (65)$$

is a known function. Equation (61) thus reduces to the usual form

$$\phi(x) = a(x) - Q \int_{a'}^{b'} K(x - \xi) \phi(\xi) d\xi \, , \tag{66}$$

where

$$a(x) = PE_1(x) - QF(x) \tag{67}$$

is a known function. We may ask the following question: For what $E_1(x)$ or—what amounts to the same thing—for what $S_1(x)$ will $\int_a^b \phi(x) dx$ have a maximum? In other words, what particular distribution of peripheral stimulation gives the largest total excitation at the center? This total central excitation may measure, for instance, the emotional value of a peripheral stimulus pattern. This problem has an obvious bearing on the theory of aesthetic values of various stimulus patterns.

A peculiar difficulty arising here must, however, be kept in mind. All the foregoing integral equations are based on the approximate equation (3) of chapter ii, which gives an infinite E_1 for infinite S_1. In that case it is clear that any central excitation, as large as we wish, may be obtained by stimulating a single afferent neuroelement with a sufficiently strong stimulus S_1. The problem of an optimum stimulus pattern $S_1(x)$ which would give a maximum central excitation then becomes meaningless.

This, however, does not hold when we use, instead of equation (3) of chapter ii, the exact equations (5) or (6) of the same chapter. The argument remains the same as that used in establishing equations (60), (61), and (66); but the integral equations now obtained are nonlinear, and their solution presents great difficulties. Here is a challenging problem for the mathematician, a problem which will throw most interesting light on numerous problems of Gestalt psychology. It is interesting that, starting with rather simple fundamental postulates, we arrive so soon at such mathematical complexities. This should not surprise us, since we are dealing with a biological system of a tremendous intrinsic complexity. But this gives us hope that even the behavior of such complex systems is reducible to rather simple general laws.

In the integral equation (66) the solution $\phi(x)$ depends both on the prescribed stimulus pattern $E_1(x)$ and on $K(x, - \xi)$. The latter, however, depends, as we have seen, on the physical constants of the neuronic chain between the connections $s(x)$ and $s(\xi)$. In other words, $K(x - \xi)$ depends on the characteristic of the brain of the individual. If we consider a case in which the excitation pattern $\phi(x)$ determines, for instance, the excitation of a center which is responsible for the sensation of pleasure, then we may say that the same external pattern $E_1(x)$ will produce a different degree of pleasure in different individuals, depending on their $K(x - \xi)$ function. The function $K(x - \xi)$ may be said to characterize the taste of the individual. The reaction of any individual to a stimulus pattern depends thus, as is actually the case, both on the nature of the pattern and on the psychophysical constitution of the individual.

If, instead of continuous stimulation, we consider stimuli varying with respect to time, we obtain more complex functional equations. At each connection the variation of ε and j is given by (9), (10), and (12), in which for E we have to substitute $\int K(x - \xi)[\phi(\xi) - h(x,\xi)]d\xi$, taken at a previous moment $t - \tau(x, \xi)$, where τ is the time it takes the excitation to travel from ξ to x. We then find

$$\left.\begin{aligned}\frac{\partial \varepsilon(x,t)}{\partial t} &= A_e E_1(x,t) + A_j \int K(x-\xi)[\phi\{\xi, t-\tau(x,\xi)\} \\ &\qquad - h(x,\xi)]d\xi - (a_e + a_j)\varepsilon(x,t) \\ \text{and}& \\ \frac{\partial j(x,t)}{\partial t} &= B_e E_1(x,t) + B_j \int K(x-\xi)[\phi\{\xi, t-\tau(x,\xi)\} \\ &\qquad - h(x,\xi)]d\xi - (b_e + b_j)j(x,t).\end{aligned}\right\} \quad (68)$$

These are integrodifferential equations. For a prescribed variation of $E(x, t)$ with respect to time, $\varepsilon(x)$ and $j(x)$ vary in a definite way, as determined by the solution of (68). We may ask what form of $E(x, t)$ makes $\int_{t_1}^{t_2}\int_a^b [\varepsilon(x,t) - j(x,t)]dxdt$ a maximum. This will determine a sequence of stimuli which gives a maximum central excitation.

REFERENCES

1. A. S. Householder, *Bull. Math. Biophysics*, 3, 63, 105, 137, 1941; 4, 7, 1942.
2. Walter Pitts, *Bull. Math. Biophysics*, 4, 121, 169, 1942; 5, 23, 1943.
3. A. S. Householder and H. D. Landahl, *Mathematical Biophysics of the Central Nervous System* (Bloomington, Ind.: Principia Press, 1945).
4. *Handb. d. norm. u. path. Physiol.*, 9, 657.
5. K. Dunker, *Psych. Forsch.*, 21, 311, 1937.
6. A. S. Householder, *Psychometrika*, 3, 69, 1938.
7. H. D. Landahl, *Psychometrika*, 3, 291, 1938.

CHAPTER IV

MATHEMATICAL BIOPHYSICS OF SOME SIMPLE NEUROLOGICAL STRUCTURES: APPLICATIONS TO REACTION TIMES

Having established in the previous chapter the fundamental equations which govern the interaction between neuroelements, we shall now follow the procedure clearly indicated. We must systematically study different, more or less complex, geometrical arrangements of neuroelements and mathematically derive their properties. We shall start with the simplest possible cases and then gradually complicate the picture.

The simplest possible structure is that of a neuroelement with a peripheral pathway connecting with a neuroelement of higher order. As we have seen in the previous chapters, we do not need to enter into the considerations of the detailed structure of the connection in order to apply our fundamental equations. We shall therefore represent two connecting neuroelements schematically, as shown in Figure 1 of chapter ii simply by adjacent lines. In the first edition of this book we indicated by arrows, placed at the connection, the direction of transmission. Inasmuch as a forklike scheme is used in neurological diagrams to represent schematically the branchings of the pathway at the connection and a point is used to represent schematically the body of the higher-order neuroelement, our former notation appeared somewhat confusing to the neurologists,[1] for in the classical neurological notations the nervous impulse travels from the fork of one neuroelement to the point of the other, that is, in the direction opposite to that assumed in our notations, since a fork can be looked upon as an inverted arrow. Therefore in some diagrams, the cuts for which were taken from subsequent publications, the arrows are placed in the middle of the lines which represent the neuroelements. It must be noted, however, that some neurologists use the same convention as we used.[2]

We may now consider various stimuli, S, which are different with regard to their variation with respect to time, as being applied to the afferent end of the neuroelement I. We shall confine ourselves here to the consideration of a stimulus of constant intensity S_1, applied suddenly and kept indefinitely.

In this case neuroelement I will be subject to a suddenly established intensity of excitation E_1, connected to S_1 by one of the equations discussed in chapter ii. From the moment that the excitation arrives at the connection, the two factors ε and j will vary according to

$$\varepsilon = \frac{A_e E_1}{a_e}(1 - e^{-a_e t}); \quad j = \frac{B_e E_1}{b_e}(1 - e^{-b_e t}). \tag{1}$$

As soon as $\varepsilon - j$ reaches or exceeds the threshold h_2 of the neuroelement II, the latter becomes excited, and the excitation is transmitted farther along it. The time that elapses between the moment of arrival of the excitation along the pathway I at the connection and the moment when the neuroelement II becomes excited —in other words, the connective delay—is obtained by solving, with respect to t, the equation $\varepsilon - j = h_2$, after introducing into the latter the values for ε and j from equations (1). The details of the calculations are given in chapter iii. The relations become particularly simple when B_e is very small—in other words, when neuroelement I produces very little of the inhibitory factor j, so that the latter may be neglected, as compared with ε. In this case the connection delay is given by (p. 10, eqs. [12] ff.)

$$t_s = \frac{1}{a_e} \log \frac{A_e E_1}{A_e E_1 - a_e h_2}. \tag{2}$$

The relation for the general case is more complicated, though similar in general, to the foregoing (chap. iii).

Equation (2) shows that the stronger the intensity of excitation E_1, the shorter the connection delay t_s. Since E_1 increases with increasing intensity S_1 of the peripheral stimulus, the stronger the stimulus S_1, the shorter should be the connection delay t_s. To obtain a relation between t_s and S_1, we must use one of the equations of the previous chapter. Assuming relation (6) of chapter ii to hold, we find, approximately, for not too large values of S_1,

$$t_s = \frac{1}{a_e} \log \frac{A_e I_1 \alpha_1 h_1 \log S_1 - A_e I_1 \alpha_1 h_1 \log h_1}{A_e I_1 \alpha_1 h_1 \log S_1 - A_e I_1 \alpha_1 h_1 \log h_1 - a_e h_2}, \tag{3}$$

in which the subscript 1 indicates that the constants refer to the neuroelement I.

Putting

$$H_1 = \log h_1; \quad H_2 = \frac{a_e h_2}{A_e I_1 \alpha_1 h_1},$$

we obtain equation (3) in the form

$$t_s = \frac{1}{a_e} \log \frac{\log S_1 - H_1}{\log S_1 - H_1 - H_2}. \tag{4}$$

Using the approximate expression (2) of chapter ii, we find for t_s an expression of the form (chap. ii, eq. [13])

$$t_s = \frac{1}{a_e} \log \frac{A_e \alpha_1 I_1 (S_1 - h_1)}{A_e \alpha_1 I_1 (S_1 - h_1) - a_e h_2}. \qquad (5)$$

Consider a chain of neuroelements transmitting the excitation successively to one another, and let the velocity of propagation along each individual link of the chain be independent of the intensity

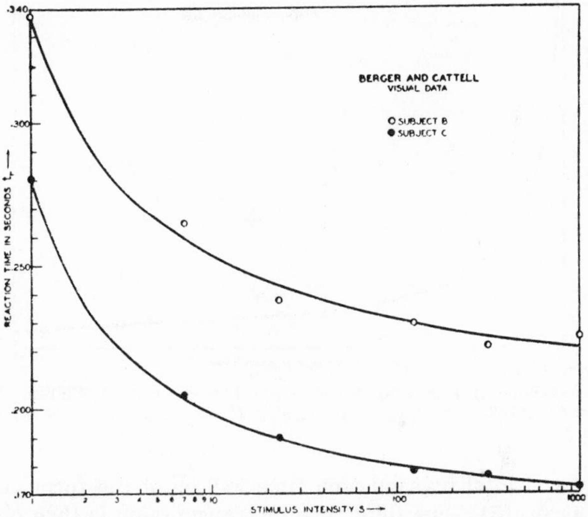

FIG. 1.—Reaction time for visual stimuli, plotted against stimulus intensity. The curves represent equation (4). The circles represent experimental values by G. O. Berger and J. McK. Cattell for two different subjects. The following values for the constants in equation (4) were used. Subject B: $1/a_e = 0.413$ sec; $H_1 = -1.96$; $H_2 = 0.57$. Subject C: $1/a_e = 0.279$ sec; $H_1 = -1.57$; $H_2 = 0.57$. From H. D. Landahl.[3]

of excitation. In that case a *qualitatively* similar relation between the intensity of the peripheral stimulus and the total time of transmission along the chain must hold—that is, the stronger the peripheral stimulus, the shorter the total time of transmission along the chain. We cannot expect equations (4) and (5), which were derived for a single connection, to hold *quantitatively* in that case. However, in one particular case, (4) or (5) may hold even for such a chain of neuroelements—while not exactly, yet with good approximation. This will occur when all connections but one in the chain have, for given conditions, approximately equal and very short delays, t_s, while the one exceptional connection (or perhaps a very few connections) has a much larger connection delay. Then the total time of transmission along the chain will be controlled mainly by the one "long" connection, and the relation between stimulus

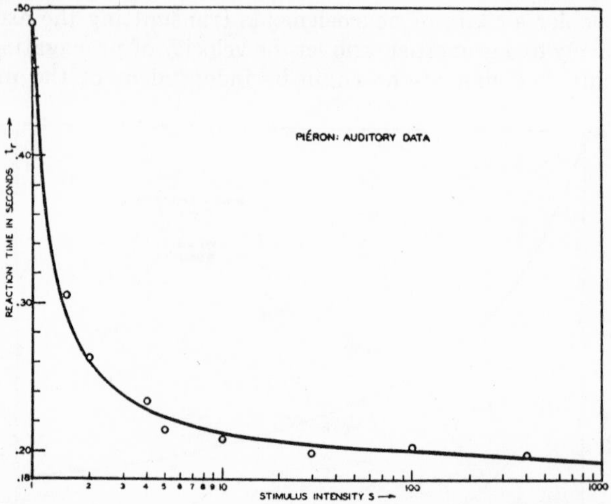

FIG. 2.—Same as Fig. 1 for a set of auditory data by H. Piéron. The values of the constants are: $1/a_e = 0.304$ sec; $H_1 = -0.37$; $H_2 = 0.23$. From H. D. Landahl.[3]

intensity and total transmission time will be of the form given by either (4) or (5). The total time of transmission is then obtained by adding to t_s a constant time, t_0, which represents the duration of the transmission along each pathway, delays at end-organs, etc.

On the other hand, since a connection actually contains a very large number of internuncials, there would be nothing surprising if the simple relations, derived for two connected pathways, actually applied to reflex arcs containing a large number of synapses.

In view of these facts, it may be of interest to compare equations (4) or (5), with a constant term added, to experimental data for reaction times. Such a comparison has been made by H. D. Landahl,[3] and the results are shown in Figures 1, 2, and 3. Visual and auditory data (Figs. 1 and 2) are well represented by an equation of the form of (4), while the simpler equation (5) is sufficient to represent the gustatory data. For discussion of details we must refer to the original paper by H. D. Landahl.[3]

A more complex neuronic structure is represented in Figure 4.

Here a neuroelement *II* of second order is excited by two neuroelements, *I* and *III*, of the first order. We may consider cases in which the stimuli S_1 and S_3 are applied at different times. Of particular interest is the case in which S_3 is too weak to produce a response in neuroelement *II* and is always applied before S_1. Follow-

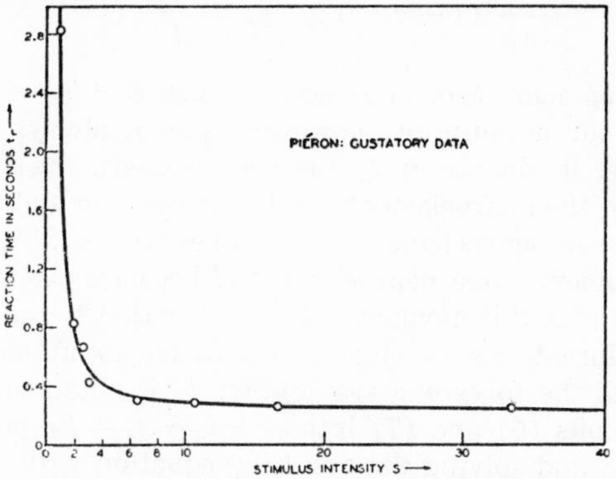

FIG. 3.—Reaction times for gustatory data, plotted against intensity of stimulus. The curve represents the theoretical equation (5). The circles are experimental values by H. Piéron. The values of the parameters in equation (5) are, in this case: $1/a_e = 3.8$ sec; $h_1 = 0.6$; $a_e h_2 / A_e a_1 I_1 = 0.2$. From H. D. Landahl.[3]

ing H. D. Landahl, we shall consider a special case, namely, where neuroelement *I* produces only the factor ε, while neuroelement *III* produces both ϵ and j but is of the excitatory type (chap. iii, expressions [11]). Later on we shall discuss a more general assumption regarding neuroelement *I*. The constants A, a, B, and b are considered as different for the three neuroelements and are denoted by corresponding subscripts. It is assumed that $A_3/a_3 = B_3/b_3$, although $A_3 > B_3$ and $a_3 > b_3$.

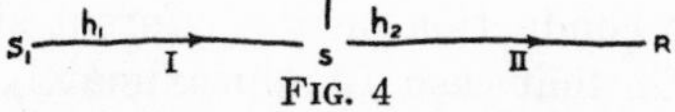

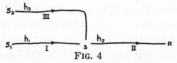

FIG. 4

If a constant stimulus S_1 of indefinite duration is applied suddenly to the neuroelement *I*, then at the connection the amount ε_1 of ε produced by that neuroelement is given by

$$\varepsilon_1 = \frac{A_1 E_1}{a_1} (1 - e^{-a_1 t_1}) , \tag{6}$$

the time t_1 being counted from the moment of arrival of the excitation of *I* at the connection. Denoting by t_3 the time from the moment of arrival of the excitation of neuroelement *III* at the connection, we have, similarly, for the variation of the amounts ε_3 and j_3 of the factors ε and j produced by neuroelement *III*:

$$\varepsilon_3 = \frac{A_3 E_3}{a_3}(1 - e^{-a_3 t_3}); \qquad j_3 = \frac{B_3 E_3}{b_3}(1 - e^{-b_3 t_3}). \tag{7}$$

Excitation of neuroelement *II* occurs when $\varepsilon_1 + \varepsilon_3 - j_3 = h_2$. According to our assumption, however, $\varepsilon_3 - j_3$ always remains less than h_2. Let us denote by t_1' the time between the arrival of the excitation of the neuroelement *I* at the connection and the initiation of excitation in neuroelement *II*. In other words, t_1' is the value of t_1 at the moment when neuroelement *II* becomes excited. Let t_3' be the value of t_3 at this moment. (Remember that t_1 and t_3 are counted from different origins, since S_1 and S_3 are not applied simultaneously.) With the foregoing assumption, t_1' is obtained by introducing expressions (6) and (7) into $\varepsilon_1 + \varepsilon_3 - j_3 = h_2$, putting $t_1 - t_1'$ and $t_3 = t_3'$, and solving the resulting equation with respect to t_1'. This gives

$$t_1' = -\frac{1}{a_1}\log\left\{1 - \frac{a_1}{A_1 E_1}\left[h_2 - \frac{A_3 E_3}{a_3}(1 - e^{-a_3 t_3'}) + \frac{B_3 E_3}{b_3}(1 - e^{-b_3 t_3'})\right]\right\}. \tag{8}$$

The total time t_r between the application of stimulus S_1 and the final reaction of the end-organ is obtained under similar assumptions, as before, by adding to t_1' a constant t_0.

Of particular interest is the study of the relation between the reaction time t_r and the time t_3' for the case in which the intensities of both stimuli are kept constant and the conduction time along neuroelements *I* and *III* is very short, as compared with either t_3' or t_1'. In other words, we consider that most of the constant time t_0 is due to conduction on the efferent side and to delays at the end-organs. In that case, t_3' approximately represents the time between the presentation of the stimulus S_3 and the beginning of the reaction less the time t_0.

These considerations can be applied to some experiments on the effect of a warning or preparatory stimulus upon the length of the reaction time. In such experiments the subject is to react to a given stimulus; but some time before that stimulus is applied, a different preparatory or warning stimulus is given. We may tentatively identify our stimulus S_1 with the stimulus to which the reaction takes place, while S_3 may be considered as the warning stimulus. In practice the interval t_w between S_3 and S_1 is always much larger than the reaction time t_r. In other words,

$$t_w = t_3' - t_1' >> t_r = t_1' + t_0 .$$

In that case we have approximately

$$t_w = t_3' .$$

Putting

$$t_3' = t_w; \quad M = 1 - \frac{a_1 h_2}{A_1 E_1}; \quad J = \frac{A_3 E_3 a_1}{A_1 E_1 a_3} = \frac{B_3 E_3 a_1}{A_1 E_1 b_3}, \tag{9}$$

we obtain from expression (8)

$$t_r = t_1' + t_0 = t_0 - \frac{1}{a_1} \log \left[M + J \left(e^{-b_3 t_w} - e^{-a_3 t_w} \right) \right], \tag{10}$$

which is the relation between the preparatory interval t_w and the

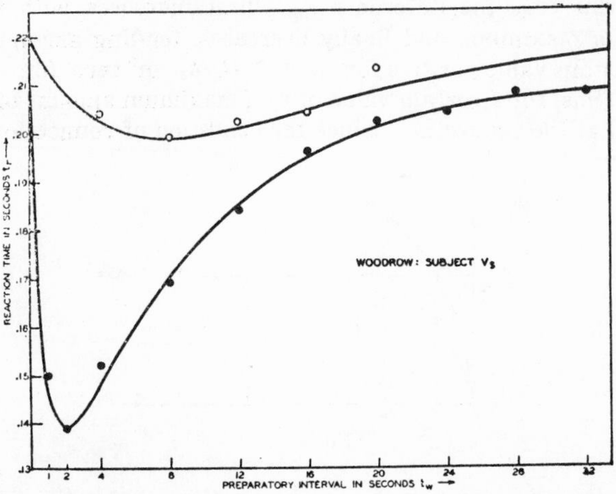

FIG. 5.—Reaction time plotted against the interval between warning and final stimulus. The curves represent equation (10). The points and circles represent observations by H. Woodrow. The two sets of data were obtained on the same subject but under different conditions. For the case represented by circles the subject did not know the lengths of the warning period, whereas in the other cases the subject was given practice with a particular warning period, after which his responses with that warning period were recorded. The values of the parameters are as follows: Upper curve: $t_0 = 0.13$ sec; $1/a_1 = 0.2$ sec; $M = 0.638$; $J = 2$; $a_3 = 0.132$ sec^{-1}; $b_3 = 0.12$ sec^{-1}. Lower curve: $t_0 = 0.13$ sec; $1/a_1 = 0.2$ sec; $M = 0.67$; $J = 0.41$; $a_3 = 1.28$ sec^{-1}; $b_3 = 0.128$ sec^{-1}. From H. D. Landahl.[3]

reaction time t_r. In Figure 5 are shown two sets of actual data,[3] compared with curves represented by equation (10).

It is of interest to note that the value of $1/a_e$ is of the same order of magnitude for the following curves (Fig. 5) as for the visual data (Fig. 1) and the auditory data (Fig. 2), although there is no apparent connection between the curves. However, it should be noted here that the intensity-time curves are largely determined by the quantity $H_1 + H_2$, the value t_0, and the product of H_2 and $1/a_e$. As long as H_2/a_e remains constant, changes in H_2 or in $1/a_e$ do not appreciably affect the shape of the curve. Then, making the value $1/a_e$ the same for two different situations imposes a condition upon H_2. If, then, any one is determined independently, the others are fixed. Thus we see that the curve of equation (4) is, apart from the constant term added, practically a two-parametric curve.

The peculiar minimum of the t_r, t_w-curves is due, in the present theory, to the fact that the constants of neuroelement *III* satisfy relations (11) of chapter iii. As has been shown on page 25, in this case the difference $\epsilon_3 - j_3$ first increases with t_3', then reaches a maximum, and finally decreases, tending asymptotically to a constant value positive for $A_e/a_e > B_e/b_e$, or zero for $A_e/a_e = B_e/b_e$. Thus, for a certain value of t_3' a maximum amount of $\varepsilon_3 - j_3$ is added at the connection. Since the condition of connection trans-

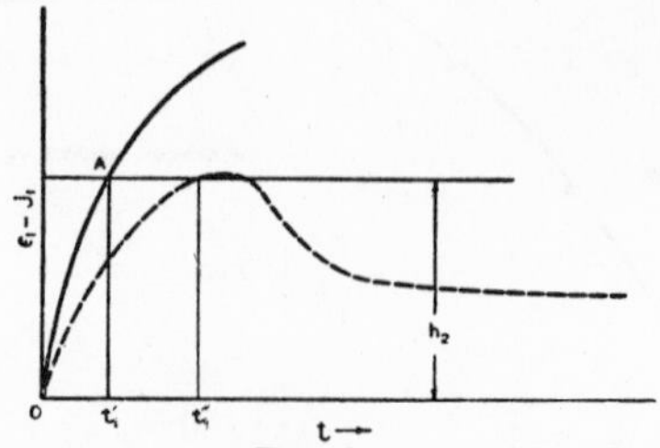

FIG. 6

mission is $\varepsilon_1 + \varepsilon_3 - j_3 = h_2$, the larger the $\varepsilon_3 - j_3$, the smaller is the necessary amount of ε_1 and the sooner will this necessary amount be reached according to equation (6).

If we consider the more general case in which neuroelement *I* also produces both ε and j, things become more complicated. However, approximately the same relation will hold for the case in which S_1 is sufficiently larger than the threshold necessary to produce any reaction at all. In this general case the difference $\varepsilon_1 - j_1$ of ε and j produced by neuroelement *I* will vary with respect to

t_1', as shown in Figure 6. When S_1 and, therefore, E_1 are near threshold, then the excitation of neuroelement *II* begins at the time t_1'' (Fig. 6, dotted line). When S_1 and E_1 are large, then neuroelement *II* is excited at the time t_1' (Fig. 6, full line). But in this case the segment *OA* of the curve may be represented, with sufficient accuracy, by equation (6).

As we have seen in chapter ii (eq. [21]), in general the time factors of ε and j may depend on the intensity of the stimulus. It would be of interest to look for possible indications of an increase of the time constant for very strong stimuli. This would show, for instance, on reaction times, which should decrease more rapidly for very strong values of S than is predicted by the theory discussed in this chapter.

REFERENCES

1. G. von Bonin, *Psychometrika*, 4, 69, 1939.
2. G. E. Coghill, *Anatomy and the Problem of Behaviour* (Cambridge: At the University Press, 1929).
3. H. D. Landahl, *Bull. Math. Biophysics*, 1, 95, 1939.
4. A. S. Householder, *Psychometrika*, 3, 273, 1938.
5. N. Rashevsky, *Psychometrika*, 2, 199, 1937.
6. A. S. Householder and H. D. Landahl, *Psychometrika*, 4, 255, 1939.
7. Cf. a number of papers on this subject in *Cold Spring Harbor Symp. Quant. Biol.*, 4, 1936.
8. H. D. Landahl, *Psychometrika*, 3, 291, 1938.
9. A. S. Householder, *Psychometrika*, 3, 69, 1938.

CHAPTER V

DISCRIMINATION OF INTENSITIES

Let a stimulus of intensity S_1 be applied to a sense organ. Under actual physiological conditions, perceptible stimuli, no matter how weak and how sharply localized, excite not one but a large number of peripheral pathways. A nerve innervating a given sense organ usually consists of a large number of pathways with different thresholds. A stimulus of a given intensity, S_1, excites only a fraction of those pathways, namely, those whose thresholds are less than S_1. If we apply to the same sense organ a stronger stimulus of intensity, $S_2 > S_1$, then that second stimulus will excite all the pathways which were excited by the first one, plus an additional number of pathways, namely, those whose thresholds lie between S_1 and S_2. An excessively strong stimulus, such that its intensity exceeds the highest threshold of the bundle of nerve pathways in the nerve trunk, will excite all the pathways.

Whether each peripheral pathway is connected by a chain of neuroelements with a corresponding single pathway of an effector end-organ or whether through branches and collaterals this peripheral pathway becomes connected to several pathways of the effector end-organ, thus producing a sort of "multiple response," the foregoing considerations lead to the conclusion that a response due to a weaker stimulus is, so to speak, always "contained" in the response for any stronger stimulus of the same type. In this simple scheme, whenever a stimulus, S_1, produces a reaction, R_1, then a stronger stimulus, $S_2 > S_1$, necessarily produces such a reaction, R_2, that it includes the reaction R_1. However, the fact that we can ac-

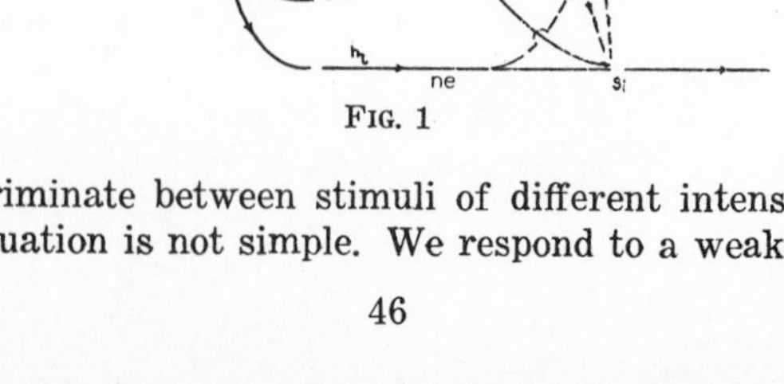

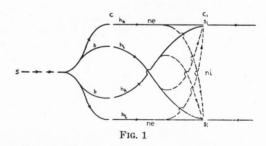

FIG. 1

tually discriminate between stimuli of different intensities shows that the situation is not simple. We respond to a weaker stimulus by calling it "weaker" and to a stronger stimulus by calling it "stronger." The words "weaker" and "stronger" themselves constitute certain motor reactions of the lungs, pharynx, and tongue to the corresponding stimuli; and neither of these reactions "includes" the other in the above-mentioned sense. A still better illustration is obtained by considering cases in which we are taught to respond to a weaker stimulus in a way qualitatively different from our response to a stronger one. Thus a weak sound of a given pitch may be used as a signal for beginning to read a book, while a stronger sound of the same pitch may be used as a signal for an entirely different action.

Hence some neurological mechanism must exist which provides for the possibility of a *qualitatively* different response to *quantitatively* different stimuli. Such mechanism can be provided by the existence of inhibitory pathways, intercalated in a proper way between excitatory ones.

Let us consider the structure shown in Figure 1, and let us confine ourselves to stationary states—that is, we shall consider constant stimuli of sufficiently long duration so that at all connections the factors ε and j have practically reached their constant limiting values. In that case ε is proportional to E (cf. eq. [1] of chap. iv). A sensory peripheral pathway or a chain of pathways eventually divides into several branches. Each of these branches connects with a neuroelement *ne*, of higher order. The thresholds, h, of the neuroelements, *ne*, are, in general, different and are distributed according to some distribution function, $N(h)$. That is, if we take h as abscissa and plot the number $N(h)$ of neuroelements *ne* having a threshold between h and $h + dh$, where dh is a very small fixed quantity, we shall obtain a curve of some sort, which represents $N(h)$ as a function of h. If, as in chapter iii, we consider the simpler case in which, whenever a pathway divides into several branches, the intensity E of excitation in each branch is the same as in the original pathway, then we have the following situation.

For a given intensity S of the peripheral stimulus, there corresponds a definite value E_1 of intensity of excitation in each branch (chap. iii). If the chain consists of only one pathway, then E_1 is a linear function of S. In general, however, E_1 is a more complicated function of S, depending on the constants of the individual members of the chain

$$E_1 = F(S). \tag{1}$$

The intensity of excitation, E_{ne}, of each neuroelement *ne* is given by (chap. iii)

$$E_{ne} = \beta(PE_1 - h). \tag{2}$$

The total intensity of excitation of all neuroelements (ne) which have a threshold $h < PE_1$ is then given by

$$E(h) = \beta(PE_1 - h)N(h). \tag{3}$$

If $N(0) = 0$, as would be expected from general considerations, then $E(h)$ is zero for $h = 0$ and for $h = PE_1$ and is positive within this interval. Hence, in that interval $E(h)$ has at least one maximum. Let us first consider the case in which it has only one maximum, $h = h_m$, h_m being a function of E_1.

Let all neuroelements ne send pathways to a region of the brain, C_1, in which all neuroelements ne with the same threshold h form a connection with the same neuroelement of third order ne_3; and, moreover, let each neuroelement ne of threshold h_k send off a collateral which excites inhibitory pathways ni, leading to all the connections s_i corresponding to neuroelements of a different threshold h_l. Consider, for simplicity, that all thresholds h_i of ni are the same. Each connection s_i is excited by an amount of $(\varepsilon - j)_1$ due to neuroelements ne and proportional to the quantity $E(h)$ in equation (3). Morover, each of these connections receives from neuroelements ni a certain amount of $(j - \varepsilon)_2 > 0$. Since each neuroelement ni is excited by a neuroelement ne, its intensity of excitation is stronger, the stronger the intensity of excitation of the corresponding neuroelement ne. The few connections, s_i, corresponding to such a value of h that $E(h)$ is very high, will receive a large amount of $(\varepsilon - j)_1$ from the ne neuroelements and relatively lesser amounts $(j - \varepsilon)_2$ from the inhibitory pathways, coming from other less excited neuroelements ne. The total amount of $\varepsilon - j$ will therefore be positive and large enough, and the corresponding neuroelements ne_3 will be excited. But the large number of connections, corresponding to such values of h for which $E(h)$ is much smaller will receive little $(\varepsilon - j)_1$ from their ne neuroelements and a large amount of $(j - \varepsilon)_2$ from the strongly excited neuroelements ne. As a result of this, only those connections which correspond to sufficiently large values of $E(h)$ will transmit excitation to neuro-

FIG. 2

elements ne_3. But such $E(h)$ has a maximum for a value h_m of h_1, and therefore only those connections s_i will transmit excitation that correspond to values of h, that lie in the neighborhood of h_m, and that are therefore included between two fixed values, h_1 and h_2 (Fig. 2). Since, according to equation (3), h_m is a function of E_1 and hence also a function of S, the h_1 and h_2 are also functions of S. If, by varying the intensity S of the peripheral stimulus, we vary E_1, this will result in a variation of h_m; and if, for a new value E_1' of E_1, the corresponding h_m' will be sufficiently different from the h_m, then entirely different groups of connections s_i will be excited by the stimulus S' than by S. Thus to any intensity S of the peripheral stimulus there is a corresponding excitation of a definite group of connections s_i. A stimulus of intensity S will produce a reaction R through a group s_i of connections, while a stimulus of a different intensity, S', will not produce R because it involves a totally different group, s_i' of connections. Each intensity S of the same stimulus has thus a representative individual group of connections in the nerve centers, and therefore *each intensity may, in a way, be considered as a different stimulus pattern.*

However, things will happen in this fashion only if the difference between the intensities S and S' is sufficiently large. If this is not the case, then h_m and h_m' differ very little, and the corresponding intervals (h_1, h_2) and (h_1', h_2') will partially overlap (Fig. 2). If, now, S produces reaction R, then S' also produces R through all the connections which correspond to the interval (h_1', h_2) (Fig. 2). Since, because of equation (3), h_1 and h_2, as well as h_m, are functions of E_1, or, what amounts to the same thing, functions of S, the minimum difference $\Delta S = S - S'$ for which the intervals (h_1, h_2) and (h_1', h_2') do not overlap at all is itself a function of S. The determination of this function $\Delta S = U(S)$ is, in principle, a simple problem, which may, however, involve some complicated algebra. The function $U(S)$ is determined by $F(S)$ in equation (1) and by $N(h)$. Several problems suggest themselves at this stage. For instance, we may ask the following question. How should $F(S)$ and $N(h)$ be chosen in order that $\Delta S = U(S)$ may have a prescribed form—say, that of Fechner's Law?

When (h_1, h_2) and (h_1', h_2') partially overlap, we may investigate the relative intensity of R, as produced by S', compared to that produced by S. In the simplest case this relative intensity will be given by the ratio η of all neuroelements lying in the interval (h_1', h_2') (Fig. 2) to those lying in the interval (h_1, h_2). That is,

$$\frac{R'}{R} = \eta = \frac{\int_{h_1'}^{h_2} N(h)\,dh}{\int_{h_1}^{h_2} N(h)\,dh}. \tag{4}$$

If we make more complicated assumptions about the possible interaction of the neuroelements which lie on the efferent side of the connections s_i, we shall obtain expressions different from (4). This leads to another interesting group of problems.

The case in which $E(h)$ has several maxima in the interval $(0, PE_1)$ is more complicated but is treated in a similar way.

A similar, but slightly different, situation is obtained by considering the case in which the inhibitory pathways are not collaterals of the *ne* neuroelements but are themselves excited at the connections s_i (Fig. 3). This case has been discussed in more de-

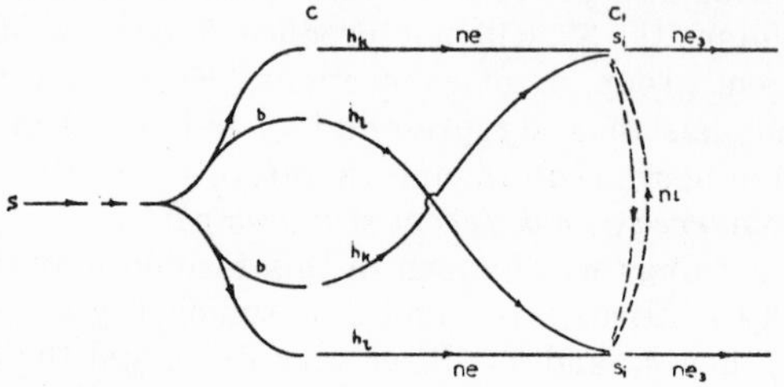

FIG. 3

tail in chapter iii and has been used by A. S. Householder to develop a quantitative theory of discrimination along the lines outlined above. We shall now follow Householder's presentation.[1]

The quantity $E(h)$ in equation (3) is a function of h and of the parameter S. Let us denote it by $\Phi(S, h)$. Assuming that the relation (1) is a linear one, we can bring (3), by a suitable choice of units, into the form

$$\Phi(S, h) = (S - h) f(h). \tag{5}$$

Since ε is proportional to E, we may, by a proper choice of units, make $\varepsilon = \Phi$. Let each connection s_h' be connected with each other connection s_h by an inhibitory pathway. Then the *net amount* $\varepsilon - j$ at s_h, to be denoted by $\sigma(S, h)$, will be obtained by subtracting from $\Phi(S, h)$ the amount of j produced by all inhibitory pathways leading from other connections to s_h. Moreover, $\sigma(S, h)$ is the effective stimulus acting upon all inhibitory pathways leading from s_h. To set up the equation giving σ, we make the following *assumptions concerning the inhibitory pathways*: (*a*) they are all similar; (*b*) for each pathway the amount of j produced is a linear function of σ; and (*c*) the threshold of each pathway is negligible.

Then the total amount of j *produced by these pathways at any connection* s_h *is*

$$I(S) = \lambda \int \sigma(S, h)\, dh\,,$$

where λ is a constant of proportionality measuring the activity of the inhibitory pathways. The integration is to be extended over all values of h for which $\sigma > 0$. Hence,

$$\sigma(S, h) = \Phi(S, h) - \lambda \int \sigma(S, h)\, dh\,.$$

We may suppose $f(h)$ to be at least continuous and to vanish at $h = 0$. Then $\Phi(S, h)$ vanishes at $h = 0$ and at $h = S$, for any given S. Hence, $\Phi(S, h)$ has at least one maximum in the interval. If we suppose it to have only one maximum, then for any S the graph of Φ will have just two points of ordinate I—say, at h_1 and at h_2—and for values of h between these two values σ will be positive. Call this interval over which $\sigma > 0$ the "excited interval."

Putting

$$I(S) = \lambda \int_{h_1}^{h_2} \sigma(S, h)\, dh\,, \tag{6}$$

we find

$$\sigma(S, h) = \Phi(S, h) - I(S)\,;$$

and hence,[2]

$$I(S) = \frac{\lambda \int_{h_1}^{h_2} \Phi(S, h)\, dh}{1 + \lambda(h_2 - h_1)}\,. \tag{7}$$

For determining $h_1(S)$ and $h_2(S)$ we have

$$\Phi(S, h_1) = \Phi(S, h_2) = \frac{\lambda \int_{h_1}^{h_2} \Phi(S, h)\, dh}{1 + \lambda(h_2 - h_1)}\,, \tag{8}$$

since at these points σ vanishes.

We now define the Weber ratio $\delta(S)$ by the equation

$$h_2(S) = h_1(S + S\delta)\,. \tag{9}$$

This is equivalent to saying that discrimination between the intensities S and $S(1 + \delta)$ is possible (in a suitable percentage of trials) when the excited intervals are just distinct.

By simple considerations A. S. Householder proves[1] that, for very large values of S, equation (9) is inconsistent with the foregoing assumption. In other words, the above-described mechanism does not work when S is excessively large. The limits of possible variations of S are approximately defined by the value h^* corresponding to the maximum of $f(h)$. Neurophysiologically, there is nothing unlikely in that result, inasmuch as any observed regularities hold with sufficient exactness only within more or less limited ranges of stimulus intensities.

Under those conditions we need consider only the ascending branch of $f(h)$. Since nothing is known about that function, we may make the simplest assumption, namely, that over a wide range of values of S, the function $f(h)$ is, with sufficient approximation, linear, so that

$$\Phi(S, h) = h(S - h). \tag{10}$$

In that case the graph $\Phi(S, h)$ is an inverted parabola with a maximum at $S/2$. Hence, h_1 and h_2 are equidistant from $S/2$. Define the "relative interval," x, by

$$Sx = S - 2h_1 = 2h_2 - S\,. \tag{11}$$

Thus,

$$\Phi(S, h_1) = \Phi(S, h_2) = \frac{S^2(1 - x^2)}{4}, \tag{12}$$

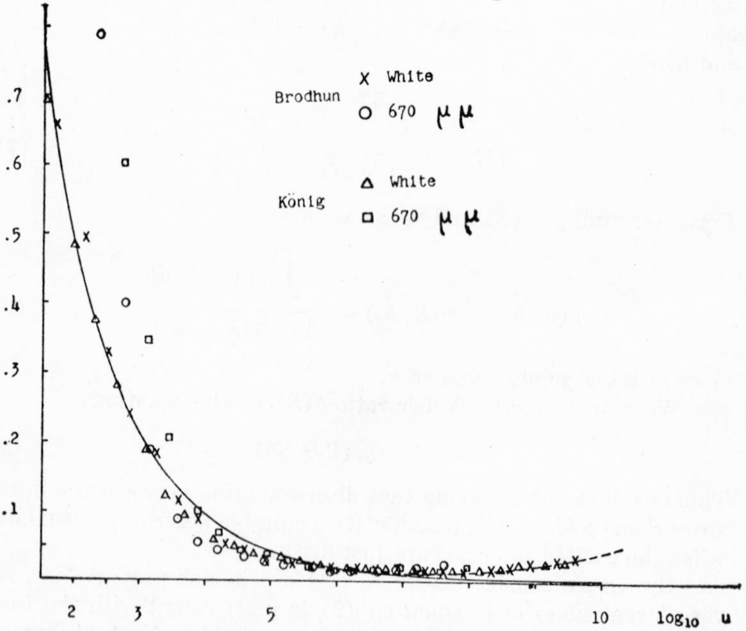

FIG. 4.—The curve represents the theoretical relation between the Weber ratio δ, as defined by equation (9), and the quantity u, as defined by equation (15). The points are values determined experimentally by E. Brodhoon and by A. König for the case of comparison of intensities of light of different wave lengths. From A. S. Householder.[1]

$$\int_{h_1}^{h_2} \Phi(S,h)\,dh = \frac{S^3 x(3-x^2)}{12}. \tag{13}$$

Then equation (8) becomes

$$2\lambda S x^3 + 3x^2 - 3 = 0. \tag{14}$$

If we set

$$u = \frac{2\lambda S}{3}, \tag{15}$$

we obtain

$$ux^3 + x^2 - 1 = 0. \tag{16}$$

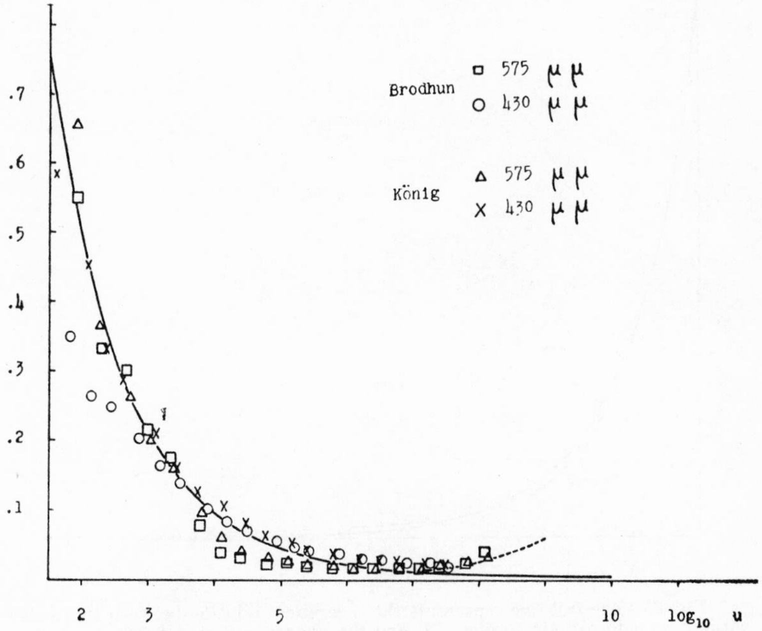

FIG. 5.—Same as Fig. 4 but for another set of data.

To calculate δ we use equation (9). Let $\bar{x}$ and $\bar{u}$ be the values of x and u corresponding to the values $S(1+\delta)$ of the stimulus. Then we have

$$\bar{u} = u(1+\delta). \tag{17}$$

From equations (9) and (11) and the definition of $\bar{x}$ we obtain, after simple transformations,

$$\bar{x} = \frac{\delta - x}{\delta + 1}. \tag{18}$$

Then by defining a new variable z by the equation

$$\delta = x + z\,, \tag{19}$$

we obtain

$$uz^3 - 2(x+1)z - (x+1)^2 = 0\,. \tag{20}$$

Eliminating z from (19) and (20), we shall find an equation connecting u, δ, and x. Then, eliminating x from that equation and from (16), we obtain a relation between δ and u. Since u is con-

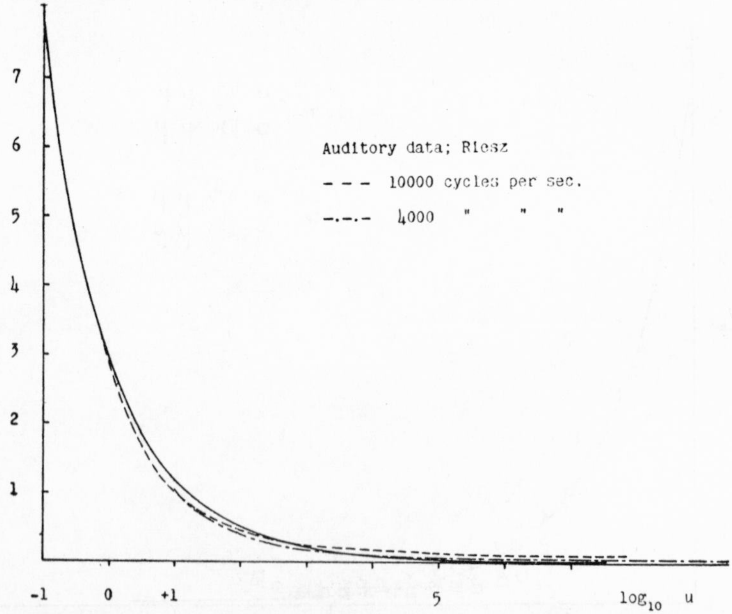

FIG. 6.—The full line represents the theoretical relation between the Weber ratio δ, as defined by equation (9), and the quantity u, as defined by equation (15). The broken and alternate lines represent relations found experimentally by R. Riesz for auditory stimuli. From A. S. Householder.[1]

nected to the intensity S of the stimulus by means of (15), being actually proportional to S, we thus arrive at a relation between the Weber ratio δ and the stimulus intensity S.

For further details and discussion of the foregoing equations we must refer the reader to the original paper by A. S. Householder.[1] Figures 4–8, taken from Householder's paper, show a comparison of the calculated and observed relations between δ and S (or, what amounts to the same thing, between δ and u). For convenience δ is plotted not against u but against $\log_{10} u$. From equations (15), (16), and (20) it follows that only one parameter, namely, the quantity λ, is involved in the final relation between δ and S.

If the relation (1) between E_1 and S is not a linear one, then (5) is not strictly equivalent to (3). If $F(S)$ in (1) is of the type

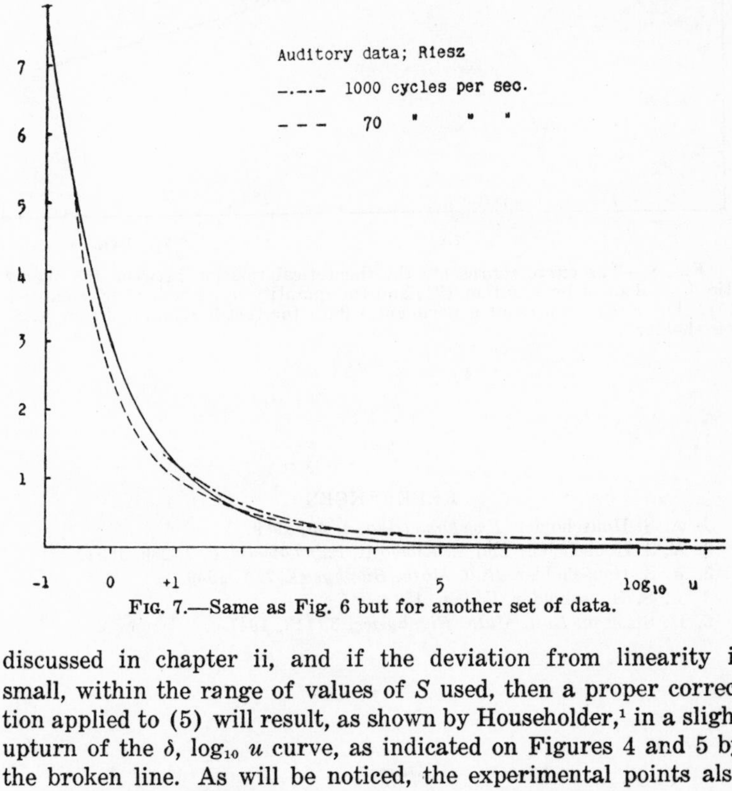

FIG. 7.—Same as Fig. 6 but for another set of data.

discussed in chapter ii, and if the deviation from linearity is small, within the range of values of S used, then a proper correction applied to (5) will result, as shown by Householder,[1] in a slight upturn of the δ, $\log_{10} u$ curve, as indicated on Figures 4 and 5 by the broken line. As will be noticed, the experimental points also indicate such an upturn.

A. S. Householder[3] has also developed a similar theory for discriminations of weights[3] and visual lengths and distances.[4] Agreement between theory and experiment is good. Henry Stanton discussed the above mechanism of discrimination in connection with monocular depth perception.[5]

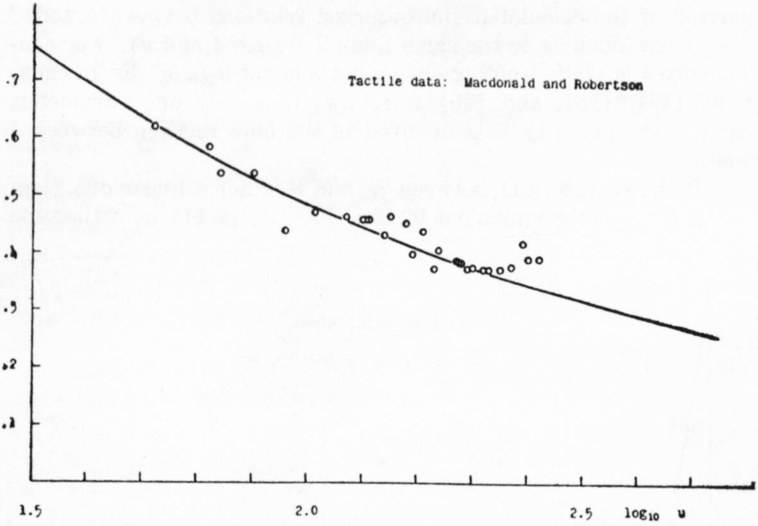

FIG. 8.—The curve represents the theoretical relation between the Weber ratio δ, as defined by equation (9), and the quantity u, as defined by equation (15). The circles represent experimental data for tactile stimuli. From A. S. Householder.[1]

REFERENCES

1. A. S. Householder, *Psychometrika*, 4, 45, 1939.
2. A. S. Householder and E. Amelotti, *Psychometrika*, 2, 255, 1937.
3. A. S. Householder, *Bull. Math. Biophysics*, 2, 1, 1940.
4. A. S. Householder, *ibid*, p. 157.
5. H. Stanton, *Bull. Math. Biophysics*, 3, 113, 1941.

CHAPTER VI

MATHEMATICAL BIOPHYSICS OF PSYCHOPHYSICAL DISCRIMINATION

Hitherto we have discussed the problem that arises when we ask whether two intensities which are only slightly different from each other are definitely perceived as different or not. This problem, however, has another aspect. The two intensities or, more generally, the two stimuli may be so close to each other that a definite discrimination is impossible. Yet, even then, there may be a certain probability for a correct statement with regard to whether the two stimuli are equal or not. The problem acquires a still slightly different aspect when we ask not merely for a statement as to whether the stimuli are equal or different but also for a statement as to which of the two stimuli is the greater (or the stronger) one. The closer the two stimuli are to each other with respect to their intensities, the less will be the probability for a correct judgment. We may ask for the functional relation between the difference of the two stimuli and the probability of a correct judgment.

An interesting approach to this problem has been made by H. D. Landahl[1] by considering the neurological structure shown in

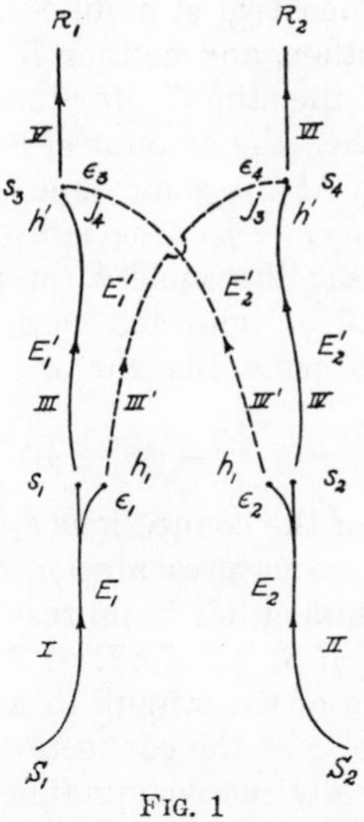

FIG. 1

Figure 1. This structure is a particular instance of the structure considered in chapter iii.

Let the stimulus S_1 (Fig. 1) elicit a reaction R_1 through a chain of excitatory pathways connected by connections s_1 and s_3, while the stimulus S_2 elicits the reaction R_2 through connections s_2 and s_4. However, let the connections s_1 and s_2 also excite inhibitory pathways which are arranged as shown on Figure 1. We have essentially the well-known scheme of reciprocal innervation.

For simplicity, let us consider the case in which the excitatory pathways are of purely excitatory type (chap. iii, p. 21), while the inhibitory ones are of a purely inhibitory type. That is, the former produce only the ε-factor; the latter, only the j-factor. This restriction is not an essential one.

The stimuli S_1 and S_2 result in the production, at the connection s_3, of an amount ε_3 of ε by pathway *III* and an amount j_4 of j by pathway *IV'*. Similarly, at the connection s_4 we have the amounts ε_4 and j_3 when the stimuli S_1 and S_2 are applied. If the constants of all the pathways are the same and, in particular, when $A = B$ and $a = b$, then we always have $\varepsilon_3 = j_3$ and $\varepsilon_4 = j_4$. When $S_1 = S_2$, then at the connections s_3 and s_4 we have, correspondingly,

$$\varepsilon_3 = \varepsilon_4 \,; \qquad j_3 = j_4 \,;$$

and hence

$$\varepsilon_3 - j_4 = \varepsilon_4 - j_3 = 0\,. \tag{1}$$

In other words, when two stimuli, S_1 and S_2, are equal, they mutually inhibit each other, and neither R_1 nor R_2 is produced.

If, however, one of the stimuli—for instance, S_1—is much larger than the other, S_2, then the amount ε_3 is increased, resulting in an increase of $\varepsilon_3 - j_4$. At the same time, j_3 is also increased, resulting in a decrease of $\varepsilon_4 - j_3$. Therefore, when $\varepsilon_3 - j_4$ becomes so large as to exceed the threshold h' of pathway V, R_1 will be elicited, but R_2 will still be inhibited because $\varepsilon_4 - j_3 < 0$. For a perfectly symmetrical scheme, like the one shown in Figure 1, we have, quite generally,

$$\varepsilon_4 - j_3 = -(\varepsilon_3 - j_4)\,. \tag{2}$$

Therefore, at only one of the connections s_3 or s_4 can $\varepsilon - j$ be positive. Hence the simultaneous presentation of S_1 and S_2, regardless of their intensities, results either in no reaction at all ($S_1 = S_2$) or in only one reaction (R_1 if $S_1 >> S_2$; R_2 if $S_1 << S_2$).

Instead of speaking of the stimuli S_1 and S_2, we may speak of the amounts ε_1 and ε_2 of ε at the connections s_1 and s_2, since these amounts are monotonically increasing functions of S_1 and S_2, respectively. In order to produce the response R_1, the quantity $\varepsilon_3 - j_4$ at the connection s_3 must exceed the threshold h. But in order that this may happen, we must have a sufficient excess of ε_1 over ε_2; in other words, $\varepsilon_1 - \varepsilon_2$ must exceed a threshold value h, so that

$$\varepsilon_1 - \varepsilon_2 > h\,. \tag{3}$$

The quantity h is not to be confused with the threshold h' of the pathways *III, IV, V,* and *VI* or with the threshold h_0 of the pathways *I* and *II*. The quantity h is a function of h', but it involves other parameters also.

This situation holds only as long as all neurophysiological processes are perfectly regular and constant, not being subject to any external or internal disturbances. However, in general, we must expect spontaneous fluctuation of excitation to occur in the central nervous system. Such fluctuations may be due to fluctuations of metabolic activity or to excitation carried to a given region from a number of other regions of the brain, which are randomly excited by the stream of oncoming exteroceptive, as well as proprioceptive and enteroceptive, stimuli.

Let us consider such fluctuations at the connections s_1 and s_2. They result in an addition of a varying amount of $\varepsilon - j$ to either ε_1 or ε_2. In the absence of fluctuations, whenever we have $\varepsilon_1 - \varepsilon_2 > h$, the reaction R_1 is produced. Since an increase of ε_1 is equivalent to a reduction of ε_2, as far as the release of R_1 is concerned, we may consider fluctuations of ε_1 at the connection s_1 only.

In the presence of such fluctuations the following will generally occur. Suppose $S_1 >> S_2$; then $\varepsilon_1 >> \varepsilon_2$. In the absence of fluctuations this will result in the reaction R_1. But if, owing to the fluctuations, an amount $(\varepsilon - j)' < 0$ is added to ε_1 at the connection s_1, then if the absolute value of this amount $(\varepsilon - j)$ is sufficiently large, the net $\varepsilon - j$ at the connection s_1 will become less than h; and, therefore, either no reaction at all will be produced or a reaction R_2 will occur because of a decrease of j_3 at the connection s_4, in spite of the fact that $S_1 > S_2$. Let us use the designation "correct response" for the response R_1 when $S_1 > S_2$, or for R_2 when $S_1 < S_2$; and the term "wrong response" for the reaction R_1 when $S_1 < S_2$ or for R_2 when $S_1 > S_2$. With this terminology we see that the spontaneous fluctuations of excitation may result in wrong responses. The probability of a large fluctuation $(\varepsilon - j)'$ is smaller than the probability of a small fluctuation. Since, when $S_1 > S_2$, the larger the $S_1 - S_2$, the larger must be the absolute value of the additional $(\varepsilon - j)' < 0$ in order to produce the wrong response; therefore, the probability of a wrong response increases when the difference $S_1 - S_2$ decreases.

Quantitatively, we can determine the relation between the probability of a given response and the difference of the stimuli in the following way.[1, 2] From the preceding discussion it follows that, in order to produce a reaction R_1, we must have (cf. eq. [3])

$$[\varepsilon_1 + (\varepsilon - j)'] - \varepsilon_2 > h\,. \tag{4}$$

The wrong reaction is produced when the left-hand side of (4) is less than $-h$. When the left-hand side of (4) lies between $-h$ and $+h$, no response is produced.

Hence,

I. If $(\varepsilon - j)' > -(\varepsilon_1 - \varepsilon_2 - h)$, the correct response is made;

II. If $(\varepsilon - j)' < -(\varepsilon_1 - \varepsilon_2 + h)$, the wrong response is made; and

III. If $-(\varepsilon_1 - \varepsilon_2 - h) \geqq (\varepsilon - j)' \geqq -(\varepsilon_1 - \varepsilon_2 + h)$, no response is made at all. In other words, things occur as if $S_1 = S_2$. We shall call this last case "equality response."

Let

$$p(\varepsilon - j)'\, d(\varepsilon - j)'$$

denote the probability of having the fluctuation lie between $(\varepsilon - j)'$ and $(\varepsilon - j)' + d(\varepsilon - j)'$. We have

$$\int_{-\infty}^{+\infty} p(\varepsilon - j)' d(\varepsilon - j)' = 1\,. \tag{5}$$

Since the correct response is made whenever case I is satisfied, the probability P_c of the correct response is equal to the probability of having $(\varepsilon - j)'$ lie in the interval $[-(\varepsilon_1 - \varepsilon_2 - h), +\infty]$, a probability given by

$$P_c = \int_{-(\varepsilon_1-\varepsilon_2-h)}^{\infty} p(x)\,dx\,; \quad x = (\varepsilon - j)'. \tag{6}$$

Similarly, we have for the probability P_w of the wrong response and for the probability P_e of the equality response from cases II and III, respectively,

$$P_w = \int_{-\infty}^{-(\varepsilon_1-\varepsilon_2+h)} p(x)\,dx \tag{7}$$

and

$$P_e = \int_{-(\varepsilon_1-\varepsilon_2+h)}^{-(\varepsilon_1-\varepsilon_2-h)} p(x)\,dx\,. \tag{8}$$

If the function $p(x)$ is given, then equations (6), (7), and (8) give us P_c, P_w, and P_e in terms of ε_1, ε_2, h, and of any parameters of the function $p(x)$. On the other hand, the quantities ε_1 and ε_2 can be expressed in terms of intensities of constant stimuli S_1 and S_2 and the duration, t, of their application. In fact, denoting the intensities of excitation of pathways I and II (Fig. 1) by E_1 and E_2, respectively, we have (chap. ii)

$$\left.\begin{aligned} \varepsilon_1 &= \frac{AE_1}{a}(1-e^{-at}); \\ \varepsilon_2 &= \frac{AE_2}{a}(1-e^{-at}). \end{aligned}\right\} \tag{9}$$

Using now, together with (9), relation (6) of chapter ii, which gives, approximately,

$$\left.\begin{aligned} E_1 &= K \log \frac{S_1}{h_0}, \\ & \qquad\qquad K = Iah_0, \\ E_2 &= K \log \frac{S_2}{h_0}, \end{aligned}\right\} \tag{10}$$

where h_0 is the threshold of pathways I and II, we find relations between ε_1 and S_1 and ε_2 and S_2. Thus, equations (6), (7), and (8) express the probabilities P_c, P_w, and P_e, in terms of S_1, S_2, the time t, and the different parameters entering into the function $p(x)$. In the experiment to be described later, to which some of the present considerations are applied, the time t is kept constant.

If we assume for $p(x)$ the normal distribution function[3]

$$p(x) = \frac{1}{\sqrt{2\pi}\sigma} e^{-x^2/2\sigma^2}, \tag{11}$$

then (6), (7), and (8) express P_c, P_w, and P_e in terms of S_1, S_2, and the two parameters h and σ. In this case, if we take two observed values of either P_c, P_w, or P_e for any two pairs of S_1 and S_2, we can calculate h and σ and then calculate the values of P_c, P_w, and P_e for any other pair S_1, S_2. Since in the case of a normal distribution (11) the integrations in (6), (7), and (8) cannot be made in closed form, numerical tables of the probability integral have to be used.

Other distribution functions, such as, for instance,

$$p(x) = \frac{\sigma_1}{2} e^{-\sigma_1|x|}, \tag{12}$$

may also be considered. In equation (12) σ_1 is a constant and $|x|$ denotes the absolute value of x. In this case the integrals in (6), (7), and (8) can be calculated in closed form. A comparison of the functions (11) and (12) is shown in Figure 2.

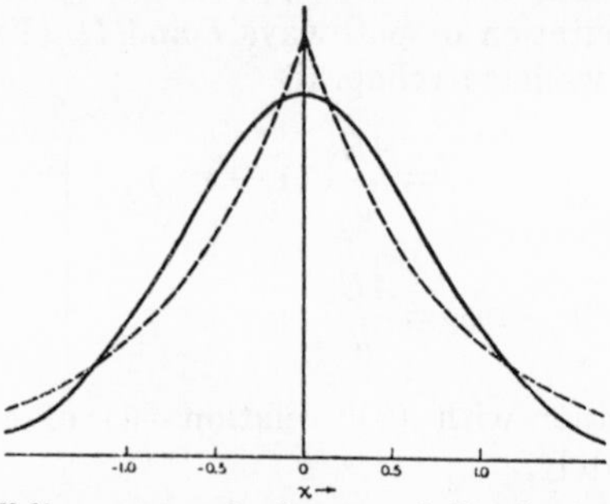

FIG. 2.—The full line represents the normal distribution function, equation (11). The broken line represents the function given by equation (12). The areas of the two curves on this figure are equal.

These theoretical results have been applied by H. D. Landahl[1] to the cases of discrimination of weights. Table 1 shows the experimental data. This table means, for instance, that when a standard weight of 200 gm (S_1) is compared with another one of 195 gm (S_2), in 15 per cent of the judgments by a subject the actually greater weight was estimated as being smaller, in 25 per cent both weights were estimated as equal, and in 60 per cent the correct estimate was made. The second lines, corresponding to the weights in the first column, are obtained by modifying the experiment somewhat, namely, by allowing only "greater-than" or "less-than" judgments, excluding the equality judgments. In this case, for instance, when a comparison of the 195-gm weight with the standard 200-gm weight is made, it is found that there are 20 per cent wrong judgments and 80 per cent correct ones.

The theoretical argument leading to this second mode of experimenting needs a little more discussion. Whenever condition III is satisfied, neither R_1 nor R_2 is produced—in other words, the subject does not state either stimulus to be greater than the other. If, however, the subject is instructed not to make any equality judgments but always to decide on a "greater-than" or "less-than" judgment, this will result in an effort to sharpen his own acuity for the case, when he otherwise would pronounce an equality judgment. Such an effort may be interpreted biophysically as a general increase in excitability, resulting in a lowering of the threshold h.

TABLE 1
EXPERIMENTAL DATA

S (Gm)	P_w	P_e	P_c
185	0.05 .05	0.04	0.91 (.95)
190	.12 .15	.18	.70 .85
195	.15 .20	.25	.60 .80
200	.30 .52	(.42)	.28 .48
205	.10 .15	.35	.55 .85
210	.12 .15	.18	.70 .85
215	.06 0.07	0.09	.85 0.93

TABLE 2
THEORETICAL VALUES

S (Gm)	P_w	P_e	P_c
185	0.03 .05	0.06	0.91 .95
190	.07 .11	.13	.80 .89
195	.14 .24	.27	.59 .76
200	.29 .50	.42	.29 .50
205	.14 .24	.28	.58 .76
210	.07 .12	.14	.79 .88
215	.04 0.06	0.07	.89 0.94

When $h = 0$, then from (8) we have $P_e = 0$. For $h \gtrless 0$, we find from (5), (6), (7), and (8)

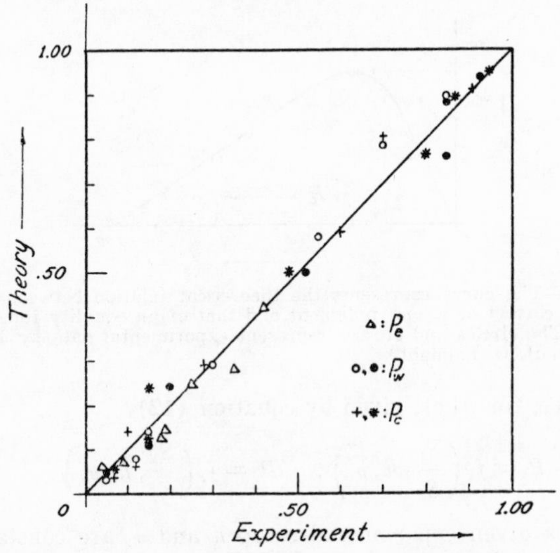

FIG. 3.—Graphs showing the comparison between the experimental data in Table 1 and the theoretical data in Table 2, for probabilities of correct, wrong, and equality judgments. A perfect agreement would bring all points onto the straight line. From H. D. Landahl.[1]

$$P_c + P_w + P_e = \int_{-\infty}^{+\infty} p(x)\,dx = 1\,. \tag{13}$$

For $h = 0$, we have

$$P_c + P_w = 1\,, \tag{14}$$

as we should expect from physical considerations.

In using data for "two-category" judgments only, we put $h = 0$ in our equations. In this way we can calculate σ from any one pair, S_1, S_2.

The values in parentheses in Table 1 have thus been used for computing h and σ_1, assuming for $p(x)$ the distribution function (12). With the values thus found, all the remaining probabilities for other values S_1, S_2 were calculated; Table 2 shows these calculated values. A comparison of the two tables is best made graphically and is shown in Figure 2, in which the theoretically calculated values are plotted against the experimental values.

From equations (6), (7), and (8) it is seen that P_c, P_w, and P_e are functions of the difference $\varepsilon_1 - \varepsilon_2$. For a constant value t of the duration of stimuli, such as is used experimentally, we see from (9) and (10) that therefore P_c, P_w, and P_e are functions of the ratio S_1/S_2.

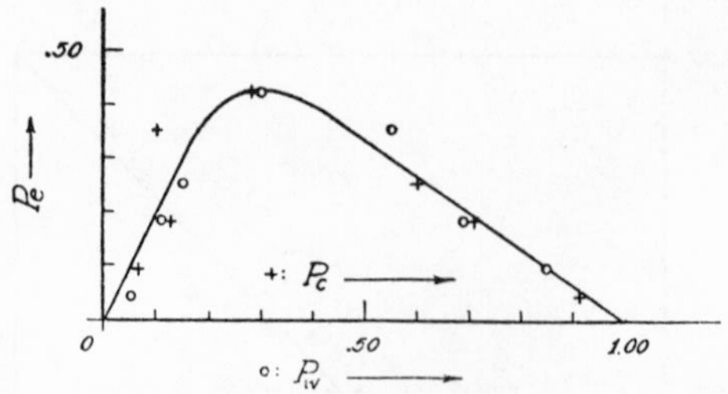

FIG. 4.—The curve represents the theoretical relation between the probability of a correct or wrong judgment and that of an equality judgment (cf. eq. [14]). The circles and crosses represent experimental data by J. P. Guilford.[4] From H. D. Landahl.[1]

Hence, for $p(x)$, given by equation (12),

$$P_c = f_1\left(\frac{S_1}{S_2}, h, \sigma_1\right); \quad P_e = f_2\left(\frac{S_1}{S_2}, h, \sigma_1\right). \tag{15}$$

Since for a given experimental setup h and σ_1 are constants, the elimination of S_1/S_2 from the two equations (14) gives us a relation between P_c and P_e. Similarly, a relation is obtained between P_w and P_e. The theoretical relation obtained by numerical evaluation of the integrals involved is compared with experimental data in Figure 4.

For a different set of data on weight discrimination, similar comparison was made by using a normal distribution function, represented by (11). The results of the comparison of the theory with experimental data are shown in Tables 3 and 4 and in Figures 5 and 6.

One complicating circumstance must, however, be discussed in this case. The functions (11) and (12) are symmetric with re-

TABLE 3
EXPERIMENTAL DATA

S (Gm)	P_w	P_e	P_c
84	0.012	0.027	0.961
	.020		.980
88	.021	.082	.897
	(.053)		.947
92	.096	(.181)	.723
	.185		.815
96	.275	.266	.459
	.420		.580
100	.502	.267	.231
	(.683)		.317
104	.055	.103	.842
	.080		.920
108	.020	0.065	.915
	0.037		0.963

TABLE 4
THEORETICAL VALUES

S (Gm)	P_w	P_e	P_c
84	0.0039	0.0207	0.9754
	.0103		.9897
88	.0248	.0774	.8978
	(.0530)		.9470
92	.1027	(.1811)	.7162
	.1791		.8209
96	.2845	.2646	.4509
	.4092		.5908
100	.5512	.2502	.1986
	(.6830)		.3170
104	.0642	.1401	.7957
	.1203		.8797
108	.0135	0.0545	.9320
	0.0337		0.9663

spect to $x = 0$. This means that a positive fluctuation is as likely to occur as a negative one. This occurs physically when there is no bias of any sort in favor of one of the stimuli. Frequently, however, a bias is introduced by the experimental setup. In the experiments of J. P. Guilford,[4] represented in Table 1, the two weights to be compared were presented in different orders several times. In the experiments of F. M. Urban,[5] represented in Table 3, the standard weight was always presented first. This results, in the case of Urban, in a bias of the subject in favor of the second weight, which appears to be larger. Such a bias has the same effect as shifting the distribution function to the right or to the left along the axis of the abscissae. This gives, instead of (11),

$$p(x) = \frac{1}{\sqrt{2\pi}\sigma} e^{-(x-x_0)^2/2\sigma^2}, \qquad (16)$$

where x_0 is another parameter. A corresponding modification is introduced into function (12). Since, now, the distribution function is a two-parametric one, we have, altogether, three parameters: h, σ, and x_0. Therefore, three values from the experimental Table 3 are now used in order to calculate the remaining ones.

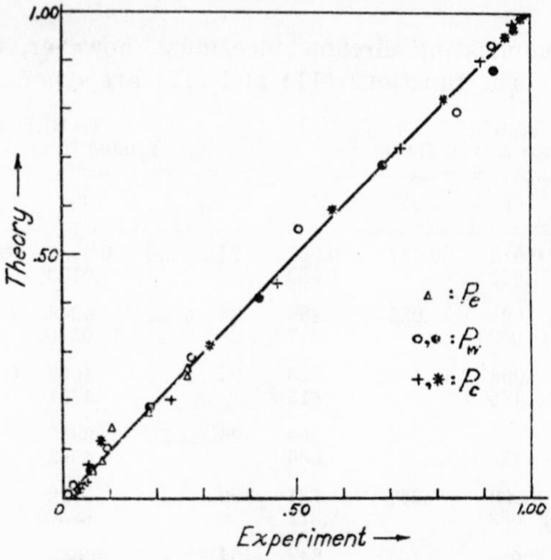

FIG. 5.—Same as Fig. 3 but for a different set of data, as given in Tables 3 and 4. Computed by H. D. Landahl.

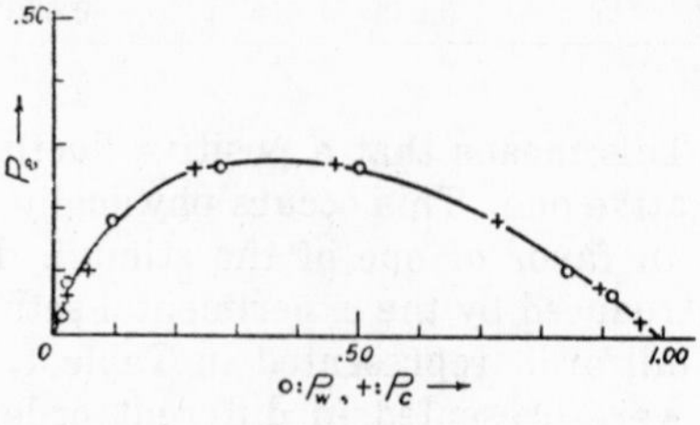

FIG. 6.—Same as Fig. 4 but for a different set of data. Computed by H. D. Landahl.

Another difference to be noted between the data of J. P. Guilford and those of F. M. Urban is that, in the former, all observations were made on one subject, while, in the latter, seven subjects were used, so that Table 3 is obtained by averaging for all subjects.

One interesting point may be noted. If ε and j measure the number of excited groups of interneurons (chap. ii), then the statistical fluctuations of ε and j in the stationary state, such as introduced by H. D. Landahl, follow immediately. Both the building-up of ε or j and their decrease follow equation (19) of chapter ii only statistically. The decay, for instance, does not proceed *exactly* according to an exponential. If $\bar{m}$ in the average number of groups decays during the time t, that is,

$$\bar{m} = aN_i t \,, \tag{17}$$

then[6] the probability that, in the interval t, actually m groups will decay is given by

$$p_m = \frac{\bar{m}^m}{m!} e^{-\bar{m}} \,, \tag{18}$$

or, for large values of $\bar{m}$,

$$p_m = \frac{1}{\sqrt{2\pi\bar{m}}} e^{-\frac{(m-\bar{m})^2}{2m}} \tag{19}$$

Denoting by Δ_m the average absolute deviation $m - \bar{m}$, we have for the relative variation,

$$\Delta_m / \bar{m} = 1/\sqrt{\bar{m}} \,. \tag{20}$$

Owing to the fluctuation of the decay, the stationary values of ε and j will also fluctuate, even if the building-up rate is constant. The fluctuation of the latter will complicate the picture further. But, in general, we shall find that the fluctuations will decrease with increasing ε and j. Such relations may be, in principle, verified experimentally by comparing theoretical and experimental data for psychophysical discriminations,[1, 2] but using a very wide range of intensities of stimuli.

Analysis of visual and auditory data have also been made by H. D. Landahl.[2] He has also discussed more complex cases of more than two stimuli, as well as a relation between the probability of a correct response, the difference between the stimuli, and the time allowed for comparison of the stimuli.[1] This leads us into the interesting problem of the relation between the performance, the difficulty of a task, and the time allowed. For details we must refer the reader to the original papers.

REFERENCES

1. H. D. Landahl, *Psychometrika*, 3, 107, 1938.

2. H. D. Landahl, *Bull. Math. Biophysics*, 1, 159, 1939; 2, 73, 1940; A. S. Householder and H. D. Landahl, *Mathematical Biophysics of the Central Nervous System* (Bloomington, Ind.: Principia Press, 1945).

3. R. A. Fisher, *Statistical Methods for Research Workers* (Edinburgh and London: Oliver & Boyd, 1938).

4. J. P. Guilford, *Psychometric Methods* (New York and London: McGraw-Hill Book Co., 1936), pp. 187 and 195, Tables 28 and 30.

5. F. M. Urban, *The Application of Statistical Methods to Problems of Psychophysics* (Philadelphia: Psychological Clinic Press, 1908).

6. W. Bothe, *Handb. d. Physik*, ed. H. Geiger and Scheel (Berlin: J. Springer, 1926), 22, 179.

CHAPTER VII

HYSTERESIS PHENOMENA IN PHYSICOCHEMICAL SYSTEMS

In chapter xxiii of Vol. I we met an interesting case of hysteresis, in which the state of a cell is determined not only by the instantaneous state of the surrounding conditions but also by the conditions previous to those for which the cell is observed. By saying that a physicochemical system shows hysteresis we understand, in general, that the properties and reactions of a system are determined not merely by its present surroundings but also by the conditions of those surroundings at previous times, or, in other words, that those properties are determined by the past history of the system. From this point of view various phenomena in the central nervous system, such as are connected with learning, adaptation, etc., are merely complex forms of hysteresis. Inasmuch as we shall attempt to develop special mechanisms to explain some of these phenomena, it is appropriate to discuss here some general properties of all systems which exhibit hysteresis phenomena, regardless of the particular mechanism which is responsible for the hysteresis in different, special cases.

We may say, quite generally, that any system which is capable of several configurations of equilibria for given constant external conditions exhibits hysteresis.[1] The kind of a system we consider is quite immaterial. It may be a mechanical system, possessing several configurations of equilibria, like a ball on a curved surface which has several "hills" and "valleys."[2] Or it may be a complex physicochemical system, in which the entropy has not one but several maxima, or in which the free energy has several minima.[3]

The circumstance that a system possesses several configurations of equilibria shows already that its actual configuration is not determined uniquely by the specification of the external constants. If under given external conditions the system is in one of the several possible configurations of equilibrium, and if a small disturbance displaces the system from this configuration, then the system will again return to it after the disturbance is removed. But a sufficiently strong disturbance may bring the system into a different configuration of equilibrium, in which it remains even after the disturbance is removed. It will now require a disturbance in the opposite direction to bring the system back into its original configuration. A disturbance that brings the system from an equilibrium configuration A into another equilibrium configuration B either may bring the same system from a configuration C into a configuration D or may be inadequate to displace the system sufficiently from C, depending on the relative stability of the configurations A, B, C, and D. Mathematically, the foregoing may be expressed as follows:

Let $\lambda_1, \lambda_2, \cdots, \lambda_n$ be the quantities that describe the configuration of the system, and let $\eta_1, \eta_2, \cdots, \eta_m$ be those quantities that describe the external conditions. For instance, λ may be the concentration ratio of two reversibly interacting substances which constitute the system, while η may represent the external temperature. The equilibrium configuration is characterized by a minimum of some function, which we shall denote by G (for instance, the potential energy in mechanical systems, the negative of the entropy, or the free energy in thermodynamics, etc.). This function G is a function of the λ_i and η_k, and the equilibrium is determined by n equations

$$\frac{\partial G}{\partial \lambda_i} = 0, \tag{1}$$

which determine the values of λ_i for prescribed η_k. For stability of equilibrium it is sufficient that the matrix

$$\left(\frac{\partial^2 G}{\partial \lambda_i \partial \lambda_j} \right) \tag{2}$$

be positive definite. If equations (1) have s solutions,

$$\left. \begin{array}{l} \lambda_1^1, \lambda_2^1, \cdots, \lambda_n^1, \\ \lambda_1^2, \lambda_2^2, \cdots, \lambda_n^2, \\ \cdots\cdots\cdots\cdots, \\ \lambda_1^s, \lambda_2^s, \cdots, \lambda_n^s, \end{array} \right\} \tag{3}$$

satisfying conditions (2), then in the $n+1$ dimensional space the hypersurface

$$\lambda_0 = G(\lambda_1, \lambda_2, \cdots, \lambda_n, \eta_1, \eta_2, \cdots, \eta_m), \tag{4}$$

which depends on the m parameters η_k, has relative minima for such values of λ_i as given by (3).

If the parameters η_k vary continuously, the hypersurface (4) is deformed. In general, not only does such a deformation result in the change of the coordinates (3) of the minima, but those minima themselves may change by becoming more or less pronounced, owing to a change of λ_0. The situation is illustrated for the two-dimensional case by Figure 1 ($n = m = 1$).

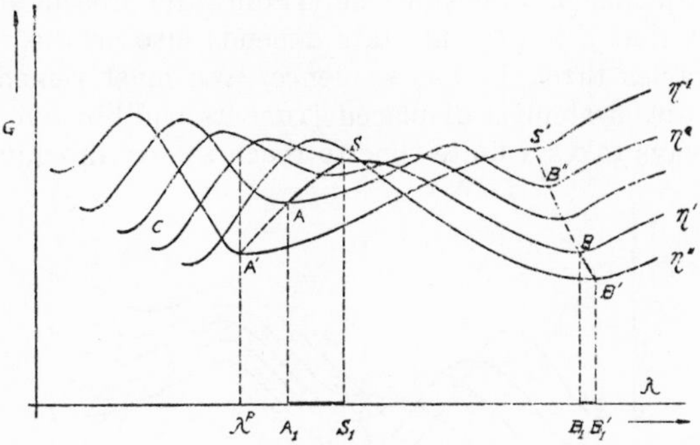

FIG. 1

Let the system be in the configuration A for the value η^0 of the parameter. If η varies from η^0 to η', the equilibrium value of λ which corresponds to the minimum A moves along A_1S_1.

As long as (2) is satisfied, all such variations of the system are reversible, because they form a succession of stable equilibria. However, a variation of the minima involves, in general, a variation of $\partial^2G/\partial\lambda_i\partial\lambda_j$ as well as of higher derivatives of G; and it may happen that for some values of η_k the minima of the hypersurface (4) degenerate into saddle-points. If for the value $\eta_k{}^0$ the system has a configuration of equilibrium, corresponding to a minimum A of λ_0, and if the η_k's vary in such a way that they take values $\eta_k{}'$ for which this particular minimum A degenerates into a saddle-point (inflection-point in a two-dimensional case), then the system "jumps over" into a next equilibrium configuration, B, as soon as the values $\eta_k{}'$ are reached (Fig. 1). Of course, the "jump" may occur both "forward" (Fig. 1) or "backward" (Fig. 2).

A further variation of η_k in the same direction (that is, from η' to η'' in Figs. 1 and 2) causes the equilibrium value of λ to move along $B_1B_1{}'$.

In all cases, however, the "jumping" is an irreversible process. If after such a "jump" the η_k's vary in the reverse direction, the configuration-point of the system moves along $B'B''$. When the original value $\eta_k{}^0$ is re-established, the system has an equilibrium configuration different from the original. It now requires a change of η_k in the opposite direction (η^{-1}, Fig. 1) in order to bring the system back into the original configuration, A. It may happen, however, that no variation of η_k is possible to bring the system back to A, once it has been displaced into another minimum of G.

An important property of such systems is not only that the previous sequence of values of η determines the present state of the system but that this present state depends also on the speed with which η varies through that sequence. We must remember that, whenever any system is displaced from its equilibrium configuration, it always takes a finite time to reach the equilibrium again.

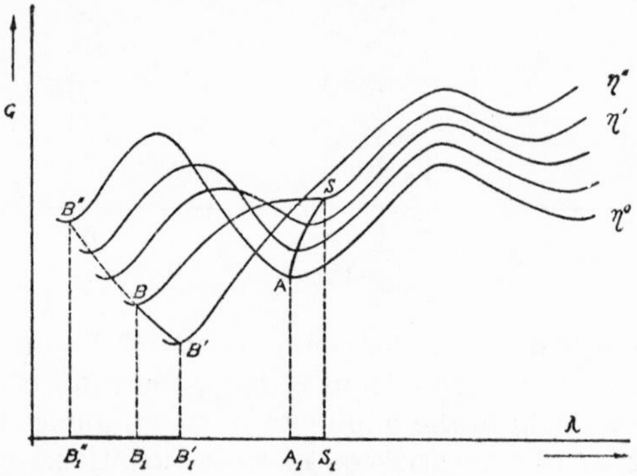

FIG. 2

If the variation of η_k is very slow as compared with the speed of "adjustment" of the system to its equilibrium, then everything happens as discussed above. At each moment the system has a configuration, corresponding to the values of η_k at this moment and to the initial configuration of the system. If, however, η_k varies very rapidly, the following may happen (Fig. 1).

Let the system have originally the configuration A' so that for a slow variation of the parameter η the configuration-point would have moved along $A'S$. The η_k's have reached such values η_k' for which the system would already have "jumped over" to B. However, if the variation of η is very rapid, λ will have, at that moment, a value still close to the original λ^p. However, to this value, λ^p of λ corresponds, for the value η_k', such a part of the curve which lies much nearer to a minimum C than to B. Therefore, while for a slow variation of η the system will jump over into B, for a very rapid variation of η it will jump over into C.

Such very complex physicochemical systems as are exemplified by living organisms are likely to possess many equilibria configurations and to exhibit hysteresis. The above-discussed dependence of the final state of a system on the rate of variation of the external parameters suggests an interesting possibility for the interpretation of the failure to produce any organism artificially. The evolution of the organic world took millions of years. Starting with some particular configuration of organic molecules, the slow changes in the environment resulted finally in the formation of a simplest living cell. It may be quite possible for us to obtain in the laboratory the same original configuration of organic molecules and subject them to exactly the same variations of the environment. Yet the end-result may be quite different unless those changes are so slow as to require millions of years. The slowness of the geological changes may be the thing responsible for the origin of life on our planet.

In some cases, as in chapter xxiii of Vol. I. the equilibrium configuration is defined not in terms of an extremum of a function but in more kinetic terms, such as the configuration, for which the reaction velocities or velocities of change of the variables λ_i are zero. Formally, this case can sometimes be reduced to the foregoing one by the following consideration:

The velocity of change of a λ_i is, in general, a function of all the λ_i's; thus

$$\frac{d\lambda_i}{dt} = v_i(\lambda_1, \lambda_2, \cdots, \lambda_n).$$

In equilibrium we have

$$v_i(\lambda_1, \lambda_2, \cdots, \lambda_n) = \frac{d\lambda_i}{dt} = 0. \tag{5}$$

If $\partial v_i/\partial\lambda_j = \partial v_j/\partial\lambda_i$, then, introducing

$$G = -\int \sum_{i=1}^{i=n} v_i d\lambda_i, \tag{6}$$

we find that (5) becomes identical with (1). Because

$$\frac{\partial^2 G}{\partial\lambda_i \partial\lambda_j} = -\frac{\partial v_i}{\partial\lambda_j} = -\frac{\partial v_j}{\partial\lambda_i},$$

the requirement (2) is replaced by the requirement that the matrix

$$\left(-\frac{\partial v_i}{\partial\lambda_j}\right) \tag{7}$$

should be positive definite.

REFERENCES

1. N. Rashevsky, *Zeitschr. f. Phys.*, 53, 102, 1929.
2. N. Rashevsky, *Jour. Gen. Psychol.*, 5, 207, 1931.
3. N. Rashevsky, *Zeitschr. f. Phys.*, 59, 562, 1930; 61, 511, 1930.

CHAPTER VIII

A NEUROLOGICALLY INTERESTING CASE OF HYSTERESIS

Hysteresis of various types, as described in the foregoing chapter, may be found in physicochemical systems of different degrees of complexity. Thermodynamic systems which possess some peculiar hysteresis properties have been studied by N. Rashevsky.[1] In relatively simple cases of interaction of van der Waalsian gases or of concentrated solutions, such phenomena do occur.

Let us now consider the following structure, which is suggested by some neurological observations: An arrangement of neuroelements forming a "closed circuit," as represented by Figure 1, has frequently been observed and described. In this arrangement one neuroelement is stimulated by another; and the latter, in turn, stimulates the first neuroelement. Various possible significances of such an arrangement have been discussed. Let us consider it from the point of view which interests us.

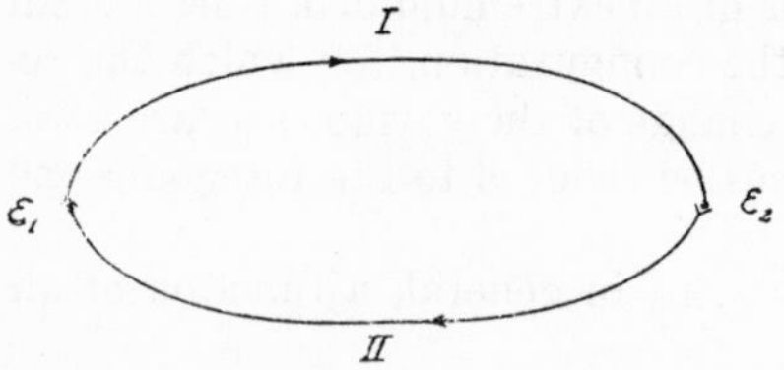

FIG. 1

Let the threshold of I be h_1, and that of II be h_2. In the absence of any external stimulation, neither of the two neuroelements will be excited. However, at the left end let an amount of $(\varepsilon - j)_1$ be present such that $(\varepsilon - j)_1 > h_1$. This will produce a finite intensity of excitation E_1 in I, which, in its turn, will result in a production of $(\varepsilon - j)_2$ at the right end. If $(\varepsilon - j)_1 - h_1$ is sufficiently small, E_1 also will be sufficiently small, and therefore $(\varepsilon - j)_2$ will be less than h_2. Hence, II will not be excited. When under those conditions $(\varepsilon - j)_1$ again acquires the value zero, E_1 becomes zero. Everything returns to its original state of nonexcitation. However, let $(\varepsilon - j)_1$ exceed h_1 by such a large amount that E_1 and, therefore, also $(\varepsilon - j)_2$ become so large that $(\varepsilon - j)_2 > h_2$. Then II will also become excited with an intensity E_2, which will result in the production of additional $(\varepsilon - j)_1$ at the left end. This, in its turn, will result in an increase of E_1 and therefore in an increase of $(\varepsilon - j)_2$. The latter again increases E_2, and the process will then tend automatically to infinity if the linear relation between intensity of stimulation and intensity of excitation holds exactly. As we have seen in chapter ii, actually E_1 and E_2 tend to upper limits, I_1/θ_1 and I_2/θ_2. Therefore, the above-described "self-energizing" process will also actually stop when E_1 and E_2 cannot increase any further, in spite of an increase of $(\varepsilon - j)$. But, if we now bring the initial $(\varepsilon - j)_1$ back to zero, it is possible that the additional $(\varepsilon - j)_1$ produced by E_2 will be large enough to maintain E_1 excited and that the system will remain in a continuous state of excitation even in the absence of an external stimulus.

These rather crude general considerations are borne out by mathematical analysis. To simplify the problem, we shall here discuss in detail only the limiting case in which both I and II produce only the excitatory factor ε. We shall denote the value of ε at the left end (Fig. 1) by ε_1 and that at the right by ε_2. Furthermore, we shall introduce a simplification which considerably reduces the mathematical complexity of the problem. We shall assume that both I and II are very short and that the velocity of propagation of the excitation in both the pathways is very large, so that the time t which it takes for any variation of intensity of excitation at one end to reach the other is very small. In fact, we consider it to be so small that during this time neither ε_1 nor ε_2 can change appreciably. We have

$$\left.\begin{aligned} \frac{d\varepsilon_1}{dt} &= AE_2 - a\varepsilon_1, \\ \frac{d\varepsilon_2}{dt} &= AE_1 - a\varepsilon_2. \end{aligned}\right\} \tag{1}$$

Substituting for E_1 and E_2 their expressions from equation (5) of chapter ii, we obtain

$$\left.\begin{aligned} \frac{d\varepsilon_1}{dt} &= \frac{AI_2}{\theta_2}\left[1 - e^{-a\theta_2(\varepsilon_2 - h_2)}\right] - a\varepsilon_1, \\ \frac{d\varepsilon_2}{dt} &= \frac{AI_1}{\theta_1}\left[1 - e^{-a\theta_1(\varepsilon_2 - h_1)}\right] - a\varepsilon_2. \end{aligned}\right\} \tag{2}$$

The analytic solution of the nonlinear system (2) is not known. We shall, therefore, investigate its property by a graphical method. The derivative $d\varepsilon_1/dt \geqslant 0$ when

$$\frac{AI_2}{\theta_2}\left[1 - e^{-a\theta_2(\varepsilon_2 - h_2)}\right] - a\varepsilon_1 \geqslant 0,$$

or when

$$\varepsilon_1 \leqslant \frac{AI_2}{a\theta_2}\left[1 - e^{-a\theta_2(\varepsilon_2 - h_2)}\right]. \tag{3}$$

Consider ε_1 and ε_2 as Cartesian coordinates in a plane. The equality sign in (3) gives the equation of a line which is zero for $\varepsilon_2 = h_2$ and tends asymptotically to $AI_2/a\theta_2$ with increasing ε_2. It is represented by the solid line in Figure 2. For all points below that line, $d\varepsilon_1/dt > 0$; for all points above it, $d\varepsilon_1/dt < 0$. Similarly, $d\varepsilon_2/dt \geqslant 0$ when

$$\frac{AI_1}{\theta_1}\left[1 - e^{-a\theta_1(\varepsilon_1 - h_1)}\right] - a\varepsilon_2 \geqslant 0,$$

which may be written

$$e^{-a\theta_1(\varepsilon_1 - h_1)} \leqslant 1 - \frac{a\theta_1\varepsilon_2}{AI_1} = \frac{AI_1 - a\theta_1\varepsilon_2}{AI_1} < 1.$$

Taking logarithms, we obtain

$$-\alpha\theta_1(\varepsilon_1 - h_1) \leqslant \log\frac{AI_1 - a\theta_1\varepsilon_2}{AI_1} < 0.$$

Hence

$$\varepsilon_1 \geqslant h_1 + \frac{1}{\alpha\theta_1}\log\frac{AI_1}{AI_1 - a\theta_1\varepsilon_2}. \tag{4}$$

The sign of equality in (4) gives the equation of a line shown by the broken line in Figure 2. For $\varepsilon_2 = 0$, $\varepsilon_1 = h_1 > 0$. As ε_2 increases,

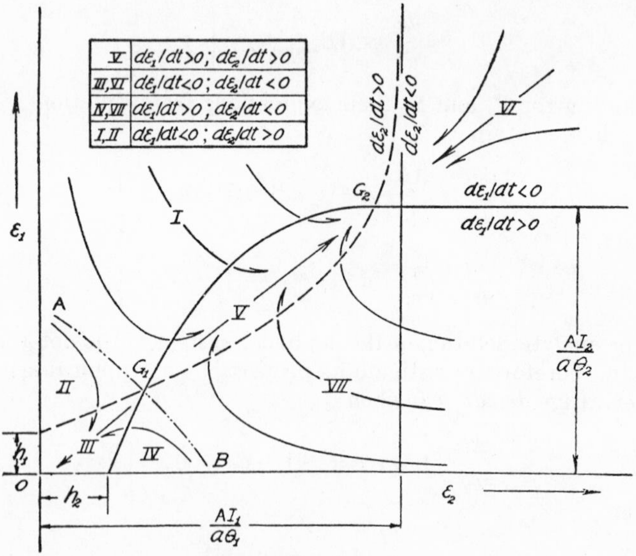

FIG. 2

ε_1 also increases. When $\varepsilon_2 = AI/a\theta_1$, the denominator of the log becomes zero and $\varepsilon_1 = \infty$. For still larger values of ε_2, ε_1 has no real values.

For all points to the right of the curve, $d\varepsilon_2/dt < 0$; for all points to the left, $d\varepsilon_2/dt > 0$.

If, as represented by Figure 2, the two curves intersect at all for $\varepsilon_1 > 0$ and $\varepsilon_2 > 0$, then they intersect at two points, G_1 and G_2. For values of ε_1 and ε_2 corresponding to these two points $d\varepsilon_1/dt = 0$ and $d\varepsilon_2/dt = 0$. Hence the system does not change and is in equilibrium. It is, however, seen from inspection of Figure 2 that, while the configuration G_2 is stable, G_1 is unstable. Let the configurational point $(\varepsilon_1, \varepsilon_2)$ of the system be displaced from G_2 into region *VI*. Here, as we see, $d\varepsilon_1/dt < 0$ and $d\varepsilon_2/dt < 0$; therefore both ε_1 and ε_2 will decrease until they reach G_2, as shown by the arrows. If the point $(\varepsilon_1, \varepsilon_2)$ is in region *V*, then $d\varepsilon_1/dt > 0$ and $d\varepsilon_2/dt > 0$, and the system moves again to G_2. In region *I*, $d\varepsilon_1/dt < 0$ but $d\varepsilon_2/dt > 0$; the configurational point moves, as indicated by the arrows, until it comes into region *V*, where it moves, as we have seen, to G_2. In region *VII*, $d\varepsilon_1/dt > 0$ and $d\varepsilon_2/dt < 0$, and we have a similar situation. Figure 2 indicates clearly that, while for any small displacement from G_2 the system returns to G_2, for any small displacement from G_1 it will move either to $\varepsilon_1 = \varepsilon_2 = 0$ or to G_2. The only exception is for displacements along the line *AB*, for which the system does return to G_1.

The foregoing results can be demonstrated analytically by expanding the right-hand side of (2) around G_1 and G_2 and keeping only the lower terms. We then obtain in the immediate vicinity of G_1 and G_2 for ε_1 and ε_2 a system of ordinary linear equations, the stability of whose solutions is determined and studied in the usual way. In this way it is also proved that the slope of the line *AB* at the point G_1 is equal to $-\sqrt{\alpha_1 I_1/\alpha_2 I_2}$.

Thus the system considered has, in this case, in the absence of any external stimulation, the two stable states of equilibrium. One corresponds to $\varepsilon_1 = \varepsilon_2 = 0$; the other, to $\varepsilon_1 = \varepsilon_{01}$; $\varepsilon_2 = \varepsilon_{02}$. Then there is a line *AB* of unstable equilibrium, dividing the two states. As soon as, by any external disturbance, the system which was originally in a state $\varepsilon_1 = \varepsilon_2 = 0$ is brought into a state represented by a point to the right of *AB*, it "tips over" into $G_2(\varepsilon_{01}, \varepsilon_{02})$ and remains there after the removal of the external disturbance.

If, as represented by Figure 3, the full and broken lines do not intersect at all, then, in the absence of any external stimulation, the only stable state is $\varepsilon_1 = \varepsilon_2 = 0$. Whether we shall have the case

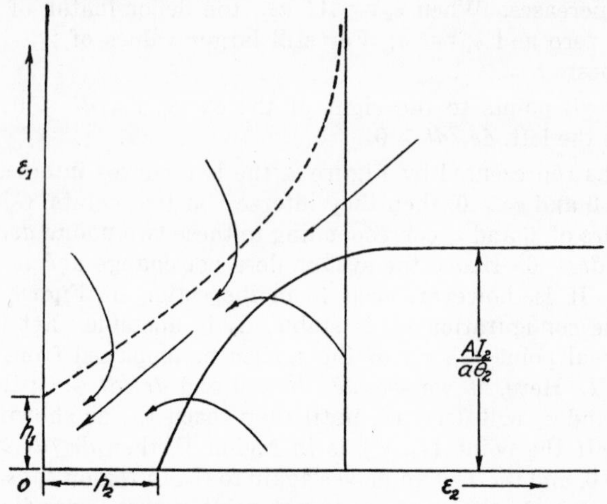

FIG. 3

of Figure 2 or that of Figure 3 depends merely on the numerical values of the constants involved in our equations. The physical meaning of the case represented by Figure 3 is that the limiting value I_1/θ_1 of E_1 is so small that, even when it is reached, $\varepsilon_2 = (A/a)E_1 = AI_1/a\theta_1$ is still less than h_2, and therefore *II* does not get excited; or that the limiting value I_2/θ_2 of E_2 is too small to excite *I*.

In the more general case, when *I* and *II* each produce both ε and j, we shall have fundamentally a similar situation, though the problem becomes much more complex because we are dealing now with four variables. A detailed study of it will probably reveal some interesting mathematical and biological peculiarities.

From all the foregoing it is clear that the particular relation between *E* and *S*, as given by equation (5) of chapter ii, is not at all essential for the results obtained. Any relation between *E* and *S*, such that *E* eventually increases more slowly than *S*, will give the same result. It is not even necessary, so far as those results are concerned, that *E* have an upper limit for infinite *S*.

The above-considered system, when it is in the state G_2, represents a source of spontaneous nerve activity in the absence of any external stimulation. This may have a bearing on spontaneous activities of the brain centers, as observed in the autonomous system and as revealed in the cortex by electric measurements.[2]

A more detailed analytical study of the circuit discussed here has been made by A. S. Householder.[3] H. D. Landahl and A. S.

Householder[4] and G. Sacher[5] have studied more complex circuits which contain both excitatory and inhibitory neuroelements.

REFERENCES

1. N. Rashevsky, *Zeitschr. f. Phys.*, 59, 562, 1930; **61**, 511, 1930.

2. Cf. H. Davis, *Cold Spring Harbor Symp. Quant. Biol.*, 4, 285, 1936, as well as other articles on that subject in the same volume.

3. A. S. Householder, *Psychometrika,* 3, 273, 1938.

4. H. D. Landahl and A. S. Householder, *Psychometrika,* 4, 255, 1939; also *Mathematical Biophysics of the Central Nervous System* (Bloomington, Ind.: Principia Press, 1945).

5. G. Sacher, *Bull. Math. Biophysics,* 4, 77, 1942.

CHAPTER IX

MATHEMATICAL BIOPHYSICS OF CONDITIONED REFLEXES

Let us now consider a structure represented by Figure 1. Let the stimulus, S_u, produce an excitation in the pathway I^u with the threshold h_u. This excitation, carried over a number of connections s, finally results in some reflex or reaction, R. Let another series

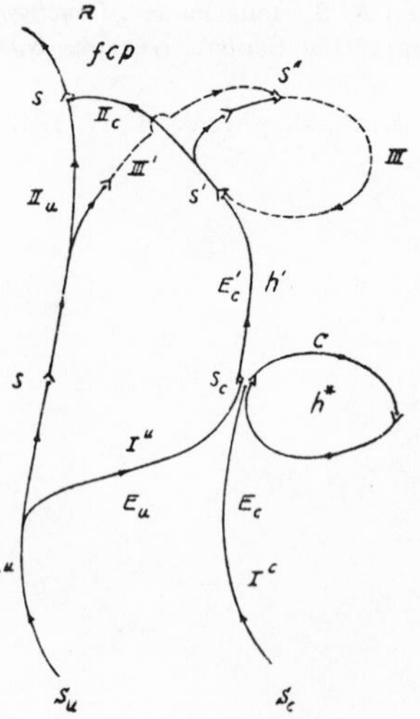

FIG. 1.—The pathway leading from connection s_c to connection s^1 is referred to in the text as II_c'. The role of connections s' and s'', as well as that of pathways III and III', is explained on page 441.

of pathways, stimulated by a different stimulus S_c, acting on the pathway I^c with the threshold h_c, lead the excitation to a connection s_c at which it connects with a pathway II_c' which, when excited, also produces R through a final common path (fcp). Let this connection s_c be excited also by a collateral of I^u, and let it also connect to one end of a circuit such as that studied in the preceding chapter. Let that circuit be in an unexcited state; and let the external excitation that is necessary to bring it into the excited state be h^*. Thus, h^* represents the hysteresis threshold of this circuit. Let h' be the threshold of II_c', and let ε_0 be the value of ε at the left end of the circuit when it is in the stable excited state. Using for E_u and E_c equation (5) of chapter ii, and using subscripts u and c to refer to the constants of the pathways I^u and I^c, let the limiting value I_u/θ_u of E_u and I_c/θ_c of E_c be such that

$$P\frac{I_c}{\theta_c} < h'; \quad P = \frac{A_e}{a_e} - \frac{B_e}{b_e} \tag{1}$$

and

$$P\frac{I_c}{\theta_c} < h^*; \quad P\frac{I_u}{\theta_u} < h^*, \tag{2}$$

but that

$$P\left(\frac{I_u}{\theta_u} + \frac{I_c}{\theta_c}\right) > h^* \tag{3}$$

and

$$P\frac{I_c}{\theta_c} + \varepsilon_0 > h'. \tag{4}$$

If a sufficiently strong stimulus, $S_u > h_u$, is applied, the reflex R is produced. However, a stimulus S_c, no matter how strong, does not, under these conditions, produce R because of (1), since PE_c is the maximum value that $\varepsilon - j$ ever reaches for a continuous constant excitation E_c and since I_c/θ_c is the maximum possible value of E_c. If, however, both S_u and S_c are applied simultaneously and kept continuous for a sufficient time, then the amount $\varepsilon - j$ at s_c will be

$$PE_u + PE_c = P(E_u + E_c).$$

Because of (3), this will become larger than h^* if S_u and S_c are sufficiently strong, so that E_u and E_c are close enough to their limiting values I_u/θ_u and I_c/θ_c.

This will bring the circuit C into an excited state in which, in the absence of any external stimuli, there will be an amount ε_0 of ε produced at the connection s_c. Now, when S_c is again applied alone, the total amount of ε at the connection s_c will be, for a continuous stimulation, $PE_c + \varepsilon_0$; and this is, because of (4), enough to excite II_c' and therefore produce a reflex R, provided that S_c is again sufficiently strong so that E_c is close to its limiting value, I_c/θ_c. Because of (2), application of S_u alone will not bring C into an excited state. The simultaneous application of S_u and S_c is essential.

We have here some of the principal features of Pavlov's conditioned reflex.[1] In this simple scheme many fundamental details are, however, still missing. Let us now discuss the modifications of the scheme necessary in order to account for other features of the conditioned reflex.

When S_u and S_c are applied simultaneously, the variation of ε and j at the connection s_c is given by

$$\left.\begin{aligned} \frac{d\varepsilon}{dt} &= A_e(E_u + E_c) - a_e\varepsilon\,, \\ \frac{dj}{dt} &= B_e(E_u + E_c) - b_e j\,, \end{aligned}\right\} \tag{5}$$

considering, as we have done before, the special case that A_e, B_e, a_e, and b_e are the same for all nerve pathways.

For the case of continuous stimulation and a simultaneous application of S_u and S_c, we have, as in chapter iii, neglecting the small possible difference in times of arrival of excitation from S_u and S_c to the connection s_c,

$$\left.\begin{aligned} \varepsilon &= \frac{A_e}{a_e}(E_u + E_c)(1 - e^{-a_e t})\,, \\ j &= \frac{B_e}{b_e}(E_u + E_c)(1 - e^{-b_e t})\,; \end{aligned}\right\} \tag{6}$$

and the time t_c at which $\varepsilon - j = h^*$ is given by

$$(E_u + E_c)\left[\frac{A_e}{a_e}(1 - e^{-a_e t_c}) - \frac{B_e}{b_e}(1 - e^{-b_e t_c})\right] = h^*. \tag{7}$$

This is formally the same equation as (17) of chapter iii, which gave us the connection delay. Therefore, we obtain, quite similarly, a relation between $E_u + E_c$ and t_c:

$$E_u + E_c = \frac{h^*}{\dfrac{A_e}{a_e} - \dfrac{B_e}{b_e} + \dfrac{B_e}{b_e}e^{-b_e t_c} - \dfrac{A_e}{a_e}e^{-a_e t_c}}. \tag{8}$$

Since (eq. [3], chap. ii)

$$E_u = \beta_u(S_u - h_u)\,; \quad E_c = \beta_c(S_c - h_c)\,, \tag{9}$$

we find

$$\beta_u S_u + \beta_c S_c = \frac{h^*}{\dfrac{A_e}{a_e} - \dfrac{B_e}{b_e} + \dfrac{B_e}{b_e}e^{-b_e t_c} - \dfrac{A_e}{a_e}e^{-a_e t_c}} + \beta_u h_u + \beta_c h_c. \tag{10}$$

Exactly in the same way as in chapter iii, we obtain the curve *1* of Figure 2, as representing the relation between the linear combination $(\beta_u S_u + \beta_c S_c)$ of the intensities of stimuli and the time

t_c necessary to bring C into the excited state or—which is the same thing—the time necessary for conditioning. The actual time of conditioning is now given by the lower branch AB of the curve (Fig. 2).

When $S = \beta_u S_u + \beta_c S_c$ exceeds the threshold H (Fig. 2), then the stronger the S or the stronger the S_u and the S_c, the shorter the

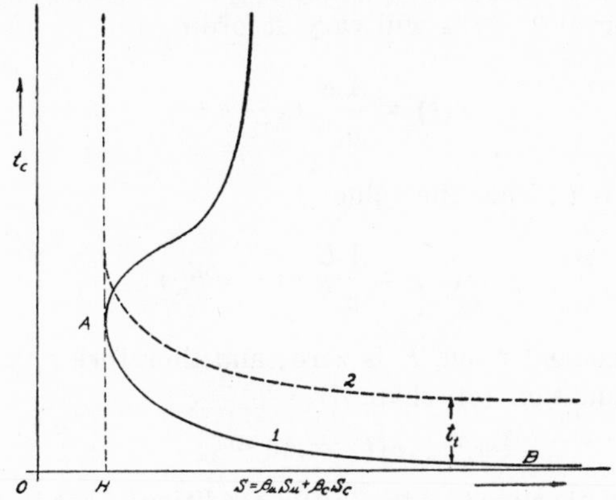

FIG. 2

time of their simultaneous application necessary to produce conditioning. The upper branch of the curve has no interest now; for, once C has passed into the excited state, it remains there even if $\varepsilon - j$ decreases below h^*. We must, however, keep in mind that, from the moment that $\varepsilon - j$ at s_c reaches the value h^* and to the moment that the system C reaches the state G_2, a finite time t_t

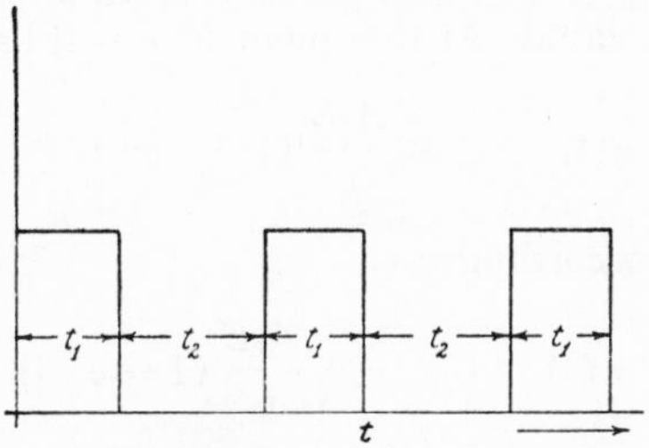

FIG. 3.—Abscissae, time. Ordinates, the value of $E = E_u + E_c$.

elapses. The total conditioning time is therefore obtained by adding t_c and t_t, which gives curve 2 of Figure 2.

Since in actual practice the conditioned and unconditioned stimuli are not kept together continuously but are usually repeated together at regular intervals, we shall investigate the variation of ε and j when $E = E_u + E_c$ is not constant but has a constant value for a time t_1, then drops to zero suddenly and remains zero for an interval of time t_2, then again suddenly rises to E, remaining constant for a time t_1, etc., as represented by Figure 3.

Let such a variation of E begin at $t = 0$ (Fig. 3). Then, during the interval $0 - t$, ε will vary according to

$$\varepsilon(t) = \frac{A_e E}{a_e}(1 - e^{-a_e t}). \tag{11}$$

Hence, at $t = t_1$, ε has the value

$$\varepsilon(t_1) = \frac{A_e E}{a_e}(1 - e^{-a_e t_1}). \tag{12}$$

From the moment t_1 on, E is zero; and therefore ε varies according to the equation (cf. chap. ii)

$$\varepsilon(t) = A e^{-a_e t}, \tag{13}$$

where A is determined by the initial conditions, that is, by the value of ε at $t = t_1$. This value is equal to $\varepsilon(t_1)$ as given by (12). Hence,

$$A e^{-a_e t_1} = \varepsilon(t_1) \quad \text{or} \quad A = \varepsilon(t_1) e^{a_e t_1}.$$

Hence, using (12), we obtain

$$\varepsilon(t) = \frac{A_e E}{a_e}(1 - e^{-a_e t_1}) e^{-a_e(t - t_1)}. \tag{14}$$

After an interval t_2, that is, for $t = t_1 + t_2$, E again acquires suddenly a constant value. At this moment ε will have the value

$$\varepsilon(t_1 + t_2) = \frac{A_e E}{a_e}(1 - e^{-a_e t_1}) e^{-a_e t_2}. \tag{15}$$

Now, ε changes according to

$$\varepsilon(t) = C_0 e^{-a_e t} + \frac{A_e E}{a_e}(1 - e^{-a_e t}), \tag{16}$$

in which C_0 has the value $\varepsilon(t_1 + t_2)$ given by (15) and t is counted from the moment $t_1 + t_2$ of the establishment of E. Introducing the foregoing value for C_0, we find

$$\varepsilon(t) = \frac{A_e E}{a_e}(1 - e^{-a_e t_1}) e^{-a_e t_2} e^{-a_e t} + \frac{A_e E}{a_e}(1 - e^{-a_e t}). \tag{17}$$

The excitation E now lasts again for an interval t_1. Hence, at the end of the interval we have

$$\varepsilon(2) = \frac{A_e E}{a_e}(1 - e^{-a_e t_1})\,e^{-a_e(t_1+t_2)} + \frac{A_e E}{a_e}(1 - e^{-a_e t_1}),$$

or

$$\varepsilon(2) = \frac{A_e E}{a_e}(1 - e^{-a_e t_1})\,[1 + e^{-a_e(t_1+t_2)}]. \tag{18}$$

Denoting by $\varepsilon(n)$ the value of ε at the end of the nth interval t_1, and by $\varepsilon(n')$ its value at the end of nth interval t_2, we shall now show that if

$$\varepsilon(n) = \frac{A_e E}{a_e}(1 - e^{-a_e t_1})\,[1 + e^{-a_e(t_1+t_2)} + \dots + e^{-(n-1)a_e(t_1+t_2)}], \tag{19}$$

then

$$\left.\begin{aligned}\varepsilon(n+1) = \frac{A_e E}{a_e}(1 - e^{-a_e t_1})\,[1 &+ e^{-a_e(t_1+t_2)} \\ &+ \dots + e^{-(n-1)a_e(t_1+t_2)} + e^{-na_e(t_1+t_2)}].\end{aligned}\right\} \tag{20}$$

Since we established that (19) holds for $n = 2$, this will prove that it holds for any n.

From (19) and (13) it follows that

$$\varepsilon(n') = \frac{A_e E}{a_e}(1 - e^{a_e t_1})\,[1 + e^{-a_e(t_1+t_2)} + \dots + e^{-(n-1)a_e(t_1+t_2)}]\,e^{-a_e t_2}. \tag{21}$$

From the end of the nth interval t_2, ε varies according to (16), with $C_0 = \varepsilon(n')$. Hence, since this variation lasts during an interval t_1,

$$\begin{aligned}\varepsilon(n+1) &= \frac{A_e E}{a_e}(1 - e^{-a_e t_1})\,[1 + e^{-a_e(t_1+t_2)} \\ &\qquad + \dots + e^{-(n-1)a_e(t_1+t_2)}]\,e^{-a_e(t_1+t_2)} + \frac{A_e E}{a_e}(1 - e^{-a_e t_1}) \\ &= \frac{A_e E}{a_e}(1 - e^{-a_e t_1})\,[1 + e^{-a_e(t_1+t_2)} + \dots + e^{-na_e(t_1+t_2)}],\end{aligned}$$

which is the same as (20).

The expression in brackets of equation (19) is the sum of n terms of a geometric progression

$$1 + q + q^2 + \dots + q^{n-1}$$

with a common ratio $q = e^{-a_e(t_1+t_2)}$, and is therefore equal to

$$\frac{1-q^n}{1-q} = \frac{1-e^{-na_e(t_1+t_2)}}{1-e^{-a_e(t_1+t_2)}}.$$

Hence, putting $E = E_u + E_c$, equation (19) reduces to

$$\varepsilon(n) = \frac{A_e(E_u + E_c)}{a_e} \frac{(1-e^{-a_e t_1})}{(1-e^{-a_e(t_1+t_2)})} [1 - e^{-a_e(t_1+t_2)n}]. \qquad (22)$$

For $n = 0$, this reduces to zero; and for $n = \infty$, $\varepsilon(n)$ tends asymptotically to

$$\frac{A_e(E_u + E_c)}{a_e} \frac{1-e^{-a_e t_1}}{1-e^{-a_e(t_1+t_2)}} < \frac{A_e}{a_e}(E_u + E_c), \qquad (23)$$

because

$$1 - e^{-a_e t_1} < 1 - e^{-a_e(t_1+t_2)}.$$

Equation (22) gives formally the same relation between ε and n as equation (6) gives between ε and t, except for the different expression of the coefficients. Similarly, we obtain

$$j(n) = \frac{B_e(E_u + E_c)}{b_e} \frac{(1-e^{-b_e t_1})}{(1-e^{-b_e(t_1+t_2)})} [1 - e^{-b_e(t_1+t_2)n}]. \qquad (24)$$

Hence the curve that gives us the number of repetitions necessary to make $\varepsilon - j \geqslant h^*$ will also be of the same kind as that of Figure 2. The asymptotic values of ε and j are decreased by increasing t_2, the interval between the stimulations. For $t_2 = \infty$, the maximum value $\varepsilon(n)$ will reach is

$$\frac{A_e(E_u + E_c)}{a_e}(1 - e^{-a_e t_1}).$$

Increasing t_1 for a constant t_2 increases the asymptotic value. In any case, if $\varepsilon(n) - j(n)$ exceeds h^*, it does so after a finite number of repetitions, this number being the smaller, the stronger the $E_u + E_c$ or the $\beta_u S_u + \beta_c S_c$.

The peculiar result of the foregoing considerations is that conditioning, while requiring a finite number of repetitions, occurs suddenly after the necessary number of repetitions has been made, for the circuit C of Figure 1 is not affected so long as $\varepsilon - j$ at s_c is less than h^*.

However, this situation obtains only when we consider that each peripheral stimulus involves only a single neuroelement, to be conditioned to another. Actually, even the simplest stimuli do involve a large number of neuroelements, both on the afferent and on the efferent side. Let the total number of neuroelements involved in the stimulation of the afferent side be N_a, and the number involved in the production of the reflex R be N_e. The conditioning will be considered as completed when any stimulus S_c stimulates all N_e of the efferent neuroelements. Therefore, actually, in order to complete the conditioning, at least N_e new connections must be made. The conditioning connections s_c of different neuroelements will vary, in general, as regards the thresholds h^*. Hence, they will vary as regards the number of repetitions that it is necessary to make during conditioning with given intensities S_u and S_c. In general, of course, β_u and β_c will also vary from neuroelement to neuroelement. At present let us confine ourselves to the simplest case that all β are the same and that only the h^* vary. Let, out of N_e connections involved, $N(h^*)dh^*$ be the number having the threshold between h^* and $h^* + dh^*$. For $N(h^*)$ we may take any plausible distribution function, since there are no actual indications as to its shape. We shall consider here two cases: first,

$$N(h^*) = cN_e e^{-ch^*}, \quad c > 0, \tag{25}$$

and next

$$N(h^*) = c^2 N_e h^* e^{-ch^*}, \quad c > 0, \tag{26}$$

so that

$$N_e = \int_0^\infty N(h^*)\,dh^*.$$

These cases are represented by Figure 4.

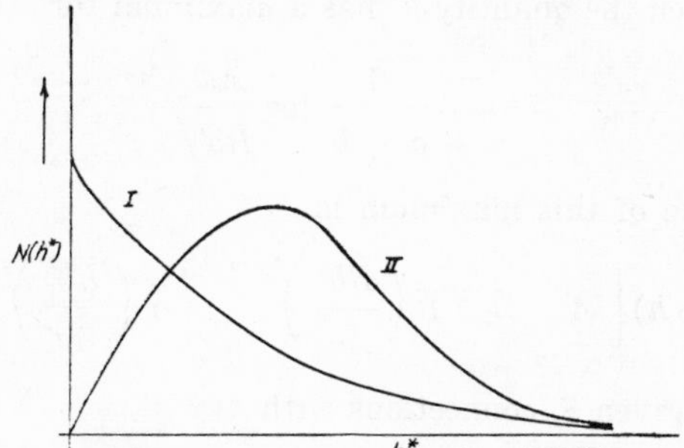

FIG. 4

Since, as we have seen in chapter ii, a neuroelement and a pathway are already statistical concepts involving a large number of actual neurons, what we are doing here in effect is to postulate a statistical structure of higher order.

As we have seen, in the case of a single connection s_c, the relation between $\beta_u S_u + \beta_c S_c$ and n is the same as the relation (10) between $\beta_u S_u + \beta_c S_c$ and t, except that now we must substitute for A_e/a_e, B_e/b_e, a_e, and b_e the quantities

$$\left.\begin{aligned} \bar{A} &= \frac{A_e}{a_e}\,\frac{1-e^{-a_e t_1}}{1-e^{-a_e(t_1+t_2)}}; \quad & \bar{B} &= \frac{B_e}{b_e}\,\frac{1-e^{-b_e t_1}}{1-e^{-b_e(t_1+t_2)}}; \\ a' &= a_e(t_1+t_2); & b' &= b_e(t_1+t_2). \end{aligned}\right\} \tag{27}$$

Denoting also, for abbreviation,

$$\beta_u h_u + \beta_c h_c = h; \quad \beta_u S_u + \beta_c S_c = S, \tag{28}$$

we now have

$$S = \frac{h^*}{\bar{A} - \bar{B} + \bar{B}e^{-b'n} - \bar{A}e^{-a'n}} + h. \tag{29}$$

An analysis similar to that on page 23 shows that the $n - s$ graph is represented by a curve similar to the curve in Figure 2.

Consider, first, the case of the distribution function (25). Equation (29) gives

$$h^* = (S-h)(\bar{A} - \bar{B} + \bar{B}e^{-b'n} - \bar{A}e^{-a'n}). \tag{30}$$

When the stimulus combination S is kept constant,

$$dh^* = (S-h)(\bar{A}a'e^{-a'n} - \bar{B}b'e^{-b'n})\,dn. \tag{31}$$

If $a' > b'$, then the quantity h^* has a maximum for

$$n = \frac{1}{a'-b'}\log\frac{\bar{A}a'}{\bar{B}b'},$$

and the value of this maximum is

$$h^*_{\max} = (S-h)\left[\bar{A} - \bar{B} + \bar{B}\left(\frac{\bar{B}b'}{\bar{A}a'}\right)^{b'/(a'-b')} - \bar{A}\left(\frac{\bar{B}b'}{\bar{A}a'}\right)^{a'/(a'-b')}\right]. \tag{32}$$

Hence for a given S, connections with

$$h^* > h^*_{\max} \tag{33}$$

will never become conditioned. Therefore, the maximum number of connections that may be conditioned by a sufficient number of repetitions is given by

$$N_m = \int_0^{h^*_{max}} N(h^*)\,dh^*. \tag{34}$$

By introducing (30) into either (25) or (26), N becomes a function of n and of the parameter S, $\bar{N}(S, n)$, giving the number of connections that, for a given stimulus S and a given t_1 and t_2, require n repetitions to become conditioned.

If n repetitions have been made, then the total number of connections that have become conditioned is given by

$$\int_0^n \bar{N}(S, n)\,dn = F(S, n). \tag{35}$$

As we increase n to infinity, we gradually condition all the connections which can be conditioned at all for a given S, that is, we condition the number N_m given by (34). Thus,

$$F(S, \infty) = N_m(S). \tag{36}$$

The function $F(S, n)$ is obtained by introducing into $\int_0^{h^*} N(h^*)\,dh^*$ the expression (30). Thus, for the distribution (25)

$$F(S, n) = N_e[1 - e^{-c(S-h)(\bar{A}-\bar{B}-\bar{A}e^{-a'n}+\bar{B}e^{-b'n})}]. \tag{37}$$

For $n = \infty$, this reduces to

$$F(S, \infty) = N_e[1 - e^{-c(S-h)(\bar{A}-\bar{B})}]. \tag{38}$$

Introducing (25) into (34), we find the same expression for N_m, as should, of course, be the case. Using (26), we find a different expression:

$$\left.\begin{aligned} F(S, n) &= N_e\{1 - [c(S-h)(\bar{A} - \bar{B} - \bar{A}e^{-a'n} \\ &\qquad + \bar{B}e^{-b'n}) + 1]e^{-c(S-h)(\bar{A}-\bar{B}+\bar{B}e^{-b'n}-\bar{A}e^{-a'n})}\}; \\ F(S, \infty) &= N_e\{1 - [c(S-h)(\bar{A} - \bar{B}) + 1]e^{-c(S-h)(\bar{A}-\bar{B})}\}. \end{aligned}\right\} \tag{39}$$

As S is kept constant but n increases, the number $F(S, n)$ of efferent neuroelements that produce R increases continuously from zero to its maximum value, according to both (37) and (39). The intensity of excitation E_c' of each fiber II_c' (Fig. 1) after conditioning, and when S_c is applied alone, is given by

$$E_c' = \beta_c'(PE_c + \varepsilon_0 - h') \tag{40}$$

or by

$$E_c' = \beta_c'[P\beta_c(S_c - h_c) + \varepsilon_0 - h']. \tag{41}$$

If we restrict ourselves to the very special case in which all β_c, ε_0, h', and h_c are the same, then E_c' will also be the same for all pathways II_c'. The intensity of R is proportional to the intensity E_c' of excitation of each pathway and to the number of pathways. In this case, therefore, using (37) and (41), we have

$$R = \beta_c'[P\beta_c(S_c - h_c) + \varepsilon_0 - h']N_e[1 - e^{-c(S-h)(\bar{A}-\bar{B}-\bar{A}e^{-a'n}+\bar{B}e^{-b'n})}]. \quad (42)$$

Equation (42) gives the intensity of the conditioned reflex produced by S_c alone after n simultaneous repetitions of S_u and S_c.

For n's that are not too large, the exponentials $e^{-a'n}$ and $e^{-b'n}$ in the exponent of (42) may be written

$$e^{-a'n} = 1 - a'n; \qquad e^{-b'n} = 1 - b'n. \quad (43)$$

Introducing this into (42) and denoting by K the factor before the brackets, we obtain, as a very rough approximation,

$$R = K[1 - e^{-c(S-h)(\bar{A}a'-\bar{B}b')n}]. \quad (44)$$

The intensity R of the reflex increases with n more rapidly, the greater the S.

Much more complex expressions would be obtained if we should consider the more general case in which not only h^* but also other constants differ for different neuroelements.

While no sufficiently exact data are available to compare with (42) or with a corresponding different expression derived from (39), the foregoing study has the value of suggesting definite experimental questions. In order to obtain any experimental results that could be checked against the expressions here derived, one must pay particular attention to the requirement that, during the process of conditioning, both conditioned and unconditioned stimuli should be kept constant and repeated at constant intervals. The influence of the interval could then be studied and compared with the influence required by (42), in which $\bar{A}$, $\bar{B}$, a', and b' are connected with the time interval according to (27). While in reality there are undoubtedly a number of other factors that affect the conditioning curve, the simpler factors considered here should be given proper attention before we may hope to unravel the more complex relations.

An important feature of the conditioned reflex is that when, after conditioning, the conditioned stimulus S_c is repeated several times alone, without "reinforcement" by S_u, it gradually loses its effectiveness.[1] Pavlov himself attributes this to an inhibitory mechanism. The following scheme may account for the phenomenon.

If, for instance, on the efferent side of the circuit C the pathway II_c gives off a collateral which through a connection s'' excites an inhibitory pathway III, which ends at the connection s', then, after s_c has become conducting, a continuous stimulation of I^c produces a gradual increase of j at s' and thus inhibits the conditioned response. We have here the elements of internal inhibition of a conditioned reflex. If the pathway II_u sends off through a collateral an inhibitory pathway III' to the connection s'', so that III' inhibits the excitation of the inhibitory pathway III, then a simultaneous stimulation of I^u and I^c does not result in an inhibition of s'.

The mathematical theory of the phenomenon can be developed along similar lines as before and offers a number of interesting problems concerning the effects of interaction of excitation and inhibition in a circuit represented by Figure 1. The phenomenon described by Pavlov[2] as external inhibition due to neutral stimuli, or the phenomenon of disinhibition, can be readily described on the same basis; and a quantitative theory of these phenomena can be developed. Again, after developing the theory for a single circuit of the type represented by Figure 1, we shall have to consider statistically the effect of a large number of such circuits with a given distribution of various parameters.

In a more complex scheme, which probably is somewhat closer to the actual situation, we should consider a large number of connections between the peripheral afferent nerve and the conditioning system C. A complex stimulus pattern S_1, consisting of a large number of individual stimuli and involving a large number of peripheral pathways, causes the excitation of N_1 neuroelements in the centers. These may be imagined to be connected each with a corresponding s_c connection, just as the neuroelement I^c of Figure 1 is connected to s_c. Thus, each of the N_1 neuroelements may become conditioned to some response R. By combining the pattern S_1 with an appropriate unconditioned stimulus, we may condition S_1 to the response R.

If, now, a different pattern, S_2, is presented, which has some similarity to S_1, then it causes, in the centers, the excitation of N_2 neuroelements, of which N^* may be common to the group of N_1 neuroelements excited by the stimulus pattern S_1. While the remaining $N_2 - N^*$ neuroelements, not being previously conditioned to R, will not produce any response, R will be produced via the N^* neuroelements common to N_1 and N_2. Since $N^* < N_1$, the response R to S_2 will be weaker than to S_1. If S_2 is repeated several times without reinforcement by the appropriate unconditioned stimulus, then the N^* neuroelements previously conditioned to R become inactive, owing to internal inhibition, and S_2 itself becomes ineffective. When, however, S_1 is presented again, it will produce R via the $N_1 - N^*$ originally conditioned and not inhibited neuroelements. We thus have a mechanism that produces a discrimination of similar but not identical stimulus patterns by differential inhibition.[3] Two stimuli of different intensities also involve different numbers of central neuroelements. A similar mechanism then provides for a discrimination of absolute intensities.

In the above-discussed scheme the stimuli S_c and S_u must be applied simultaneously in order to produce conditioning. In actual cases it appears[4] to be essential that S_c should be applied always slightly before S_u. While such a requirement may possibly be deduced from the present theory merely by complicating the circuit still further, thus increasing the complexity of interactions of various elements, the following suggestion seems of interest. Again consider the scheme represented in Figure 1. However, now let I^u be an inhibitory neuroelement of the intermediate type (eq. [14], chap. iii), so that

$$A_j > B_j\,, \quad \text{with } a_j > b_j \quad \text{and} \quad \frac{A_j}{a_j} < \frac{B_j}{b_j}. \tag{45}$$

In that case the variation of ε and j at s_c, for a suddenly established constant E_u, is represented by Figure 5. Owing to a larger A_j, the ε-curve exceeds for a while the j-curve, though in the long run j

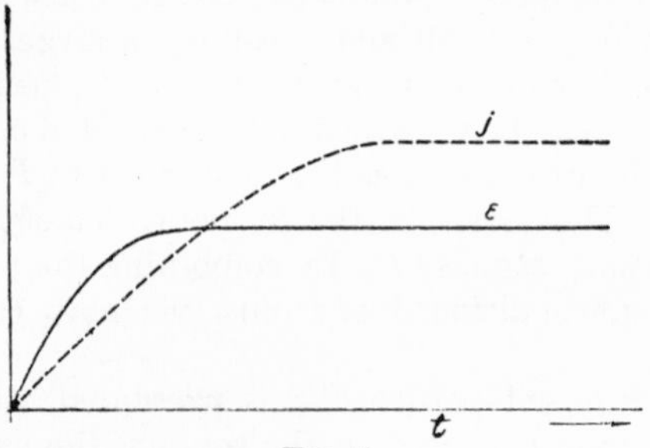

FIG. 5

exceeds ε. This means that, if S_c is applied after S_u, $\varepsilon - j$ at s_c may never exceed h^*, no matter how strong S_c, for the already insufficient excitation E_c is counteracted at s_c by an inhibition produced by E_u. If, however, S_c is applied first, and then S_u is applied, when the corresponding stationary state of $\varepsilon - j$, due to E_c, is almost established, then the transient excess of ε over j, due to E_u, will be added to the already existing $\varepsilon - j$ at s_c, and h^* may be exceeded.

REFERENCES

1. I. P. Pavlov, *Conditioned Reflexes* (New York: Oxford University Press, 1927).

2. *Ibid.*, pp. 33, 48.

3. *Ibid.*, p. 110.

4. *Ibid.*, p. 27.

CHAPTER X

DISCRIMINATION OF RELATIONS

Consider a stimulus S being conditioned to some response R. To each intensity S_i of the stimulus there corresponds a definite number N_i of neuroelements in the nerve centers, which are conditioned to R, so that $N_i > N_k$ if $S_i > S_k$ (chap. ix). In this way, as we have seen in the previous chapter, we may condition R to a specific absolute intensity S_r of the stimulus, by differential inhibition against stimuli S_i, S_k, etc.

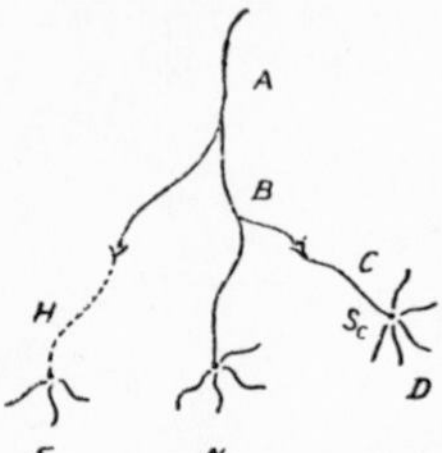

FIG. 1

Let the afferent pathway A (Fig. 1), carrying the excitation due to the stimulus S, excite through a collateral pathway B a fiber C, which is of the intermediate type mentioned on page 22 (chap. iii, eq. [14]), with

$$B_j < A_j; \quad b_j < a_j; \quad \frac{A_j}{a_j} < \frac{B_j}{b_j}. \tag{1}$$

Let C excite, through the connection S_c, a center D, consisting of a group of neuroelements. If a constant stimulus S_k is suddenly established at $t = 0$, then at the connection s_c the variation of ε and j will be represented by Figure 2. Because of (1), ε will first

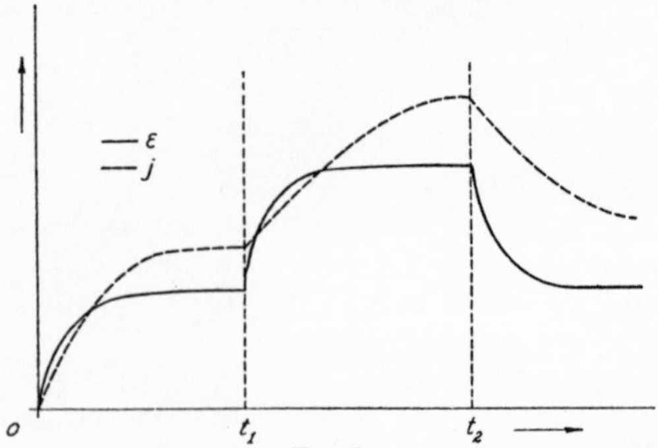

FIG. 2

exceed j; but when the asymptotic state is reached, we shall again have $\varepsilon < j$. If, after the asymptotic state is reached, we suddenly increase S_k to $S_i > S_k$ and keep S_i constant, ε and j will vary, as can readily be seen by an argument similar to that used in chapter xxxii of Vol. I (eq. [36]), as represented by Figure 2, in the interval from t_1 to t_2. That is, again for a short time there will be $\epsilon - j > 0$, followed by a state of inhibition, provided that $S_i - S_k$ is sufficiently large. If, on the contrary, we decrease S from S_i to $S_m < S_i$, ϵ and j will vary, as shown in Figure 2, to the right of the point t_2, and no excitation will occur. If $S_i - S_k$ exceeds a certain value Δ, which depends on the absolute value of S_k and on the thresholds of the center D, then a sudden transition from S_k to $S_i > S_k$ will be accompanied by a short excitation of D. But a transition from S_i to $S_k < S_i$ will not be accompanied by such an excitation.

Let us now present to the subject a pair of stimuli S_i and $S_k < S_i$, alternately, and combine the stimulus S_i with an unconditioned stimulus, producing the response R. Then, as we have seen in chapter ix, R will become conditioned to the absolute value of S_i.

However, if we present each time, during the process of conditioning, a different pair, S_m and $S_r > S_m$, and always combine the stronger stimulus with the unconditioned stimulus for R, then, since every time different neuroelements, N_m, N_r, etc., are involved, the absolute value of the stimulus S does not become conditioned to R. But every time a stronger stimulus is presented after a weaker one, D is excited, provided that the difference between the stimuli is large enough. Hence, D becomes conditioned to R.

If we now present alternately a pair of stimuli, S_p and $S_q > S_p$, which were never used during the process of conditioning, then presentation of S_q after S_p will produce R via D. But the presentation of S_p after S_q will not do that, since D then remains unexcited. We have here a response to the abstract relation "larger than."

This simple scheme leads to the following consequences. The presentation of a single stimulus of sufficient intensity is accompanied by an excitation of D. Therefore, an animal or subject, trained to respond to a single stimulus S_i, will, when presented alternately with two other stimuli, S_p and $S_q > S_p$, always choose the bigger one, S_q. In some cases this may perhaps actually be so. In cases when this does not hold, we must complicate our scheme somewhat. We may, for instance, assume that a spontaneously and constantly excited center, of the type considered in chapter vi, excites an inhibitory pathway which normally inhibits D. A stimulus S, through a proper connection, may inhibit the inhibitory pathway (chap. viii) and thus disinhibit D. If, however, the time τ which it takes to disinhibit D by S is longer than the interval during which $\varepsilon - j > 0$, then a continuous presentation of S_i does not excite D, unless S_i is repeated at intervals shorter than τ.

Several other complications and generalizations of this scheme are apparent and suggest a number of mathematical investigations to derive relations between the thresholds Δ of discrimination, the interval between presentation of the two stimuli, etc.

Connecting the pathway A (Fig. 1) to a center F, through a pathway H of the ordinary inhibitory type (chap. iii, eq. [13]), results in an excitation of F only when a weaker stimulus is presented after a stronger one. The mechanism is quite similar to that of the rebound phenomenon studied in chapter iii, page 27. Compare, also, Figure 6 of chapter iii. In this way we obtain a mechanism corresponding to the relation "smaller than."

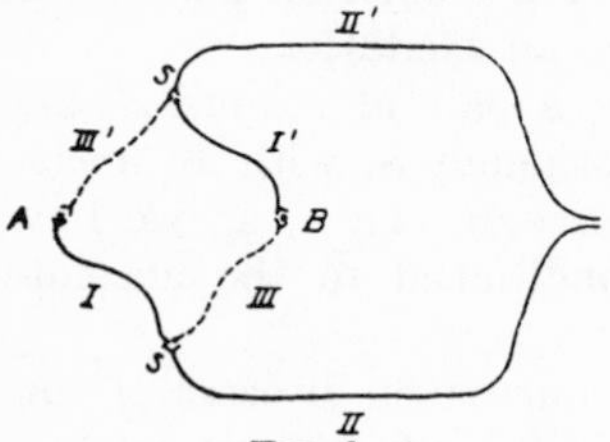

FIG. 3

Now, consider two centers, A and B (Fig. 3), in a state of constant excitation with intensities E_A and E_B. Those excitations act as stimuli on the two pathways I and III, of which the first is an excitatory, the other an inhibitory, pathway and both of which lead to the connection s with an excitatory pathway II. Let the intensities of excitation E_1 and E_3 of these pathways be given not by the approximate linear equation (3) of chapter ii but by equation (6), of which (3) is a limiting case. In a rather wide range of values of S we may then have, with good approximation,

$$E = I\alpha h \log \frac{S}{h}. \tag{2}$$

Referring again to Figure 3 and remembering that the role of S is now played by E_A and E_B, we have

$$E_1 = I_1 \alpha_1 h_1 \log \frac{E_A}{h_1}; \qquad E_3 = I_3 \alpha_3 h_3 \log \frac{E_B}{h_3}. \tag{3}$$

Let

$$\alpha_1 = \alpha_3 = \alpha; \qquad I_1 = I_3 = I; \qquad h_1 = h_3 = h. \tag{4}$$

At s pathway I gives

$$(\varepsilon - j)_1 = PI\alpha h \log \frac{E_A}{h} > 0, \tag{5}$$

and pathway III gives

$$(\varepsilon - j)_3 = -QI\alpha h \log \frac{E_B}{h} < 0\,, \tag{6}$$

with P and Q being defined by equation (45) of chapter iii. The total amount of $\varepsilon - j$ at s is equal to

$$\varepsilon - j = I\alpha h\left(P \log \frac{E_A}{h} - Q \log \frac{E_B}{h}\right). \tag{7}$$

If, now, besides (4) we also have, in this particular case, $P = Q$, then

$$\varepsilon - j = PI\alpha h \log \frac{E_A}{E_B}. \tag{8}$$

The intensity of excitation E_2 of pathway II being a function of $\varepsilon - j$ only is, as we see, a function of the ratio E_A/E_B of the excitation of the two centers A and B and is independent of the absolute values of E_A and E_B. If $E_A < E_B$, pathway II is, however, unexcited, $\varepsilon - j$ being negative. However, by considering a perfectly symmetric arrangement of another set of pathways, I', III', and II' (Fig. 3), corresponding identically with pathways I, III, and II, we shall find, by a similar argument, that the pair of pathways II and II' is always excited in the same way for a constant ratio E_A/E_B, regardless of the absolute values of E_A and E_B.

CHAPTER XI

MATHEMATICAL BIOPHYSICS OF THE GESTALT PROBLEM

In this chapter we shall discuss, from the point of view of the postulates developed in the preceding chapters, one of the most important and difficult problems of brain physiology, which so far has been emphasized more from the psychological side. We mean that group of phenomena usually known under the name of "Gestalt transposition."

When a square is presented to us in various positions, we still recognize it as a square—in other words, we respond to it always in the same way although the retinal elements involved are quite different each time. Again, the square may be of any color, or of the same color but of different brightness. It may be drawn in black lines on a white background or in white lines on a black background. It is still recognized as a square.

In the following discussion we do not attempt to give any extensive theory of those complex phenomena and shall endeavor merely to outline some possible mechanisms that may explain some of the gross characteristics of those phenomena.[1]

It is naturally admitted that neural elements of different kinds are involved in color discrimination and brightness discrimination. The last-mentioned circumstance, however, suggests very strongly that there are special neural elements for "contour perception" or, rather, for sharp contrast. If the same line in exactly the same position is presented first as black on white and then as white on black, and yet should produce the same excitation pattern in the brain or at least in some region of the brain, the conclusion is unavoidable that it is not the white that causes excitation, or the black, but the sharp contrast of black and white at the edge of the line. Such a conclusion is not at variance with known neurophysiological facts. We do not need to assume the existence of the special kind of neural elements in the retina. There is nothing that would support such an assumption. But the existence of this special kind of neural elements in the brain centers can be readily understood. Admitting, as most neurologists do, that there is a "point-to-point correspondence" between the retina and the occipital lobes and considering the latter as a kind of central retina, we may take as starting-point of our considerations the distribution of excitation on that "central retina." Through myelinated brain tracts the excitation of one neuroelement can be conducted to another definite neuroelement, thus giving a point-to-point correspondence between two regions of the brain. In nonmyelinated regions there may be greater probability of a spreading of excitation from any neuroelement to all adjacent ones. Therefore, owing to the existence of other brain tracts connecting the occipital lobes with other regions, there may be point-to-point correspondence between the central retina and a few other regions.

Consider the following structural arrangements of the neuroelements. Let all pathways of class *I* coming from the central retina (*C.R.*) form connections s_i, all lying in a surface *C* (Fig. 1).

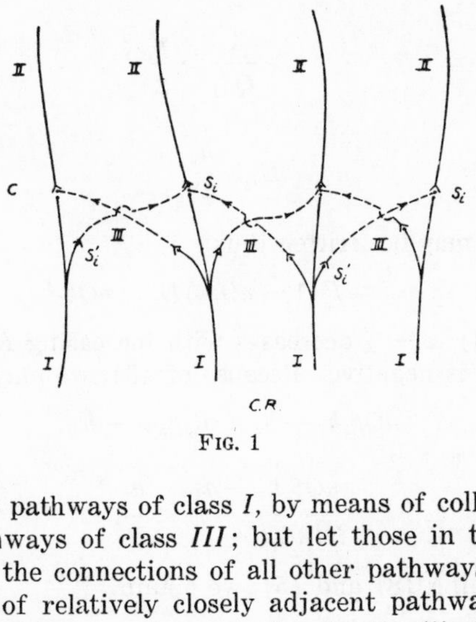

FIG. 1

Let each of the pathways of class *I*, by means of collaterals, excite inhibitory pathways of class *III*; but let those in this particular case not reach the connections of all other pathways but only the connections s_i of relatively closely adjacent pathways of class *I*. At each connection s_i we have, as in chapter iii, for a continuous stimulation at the central retina

$$\varepsilon = PE_1; \quad j = nQE_3, \tag{1}$$

where n denotes the number of excited pathways of class *I* adjacent to any pathway of this class. If we have a regular arrangement, n can be specified from it. In general, n varies slightly from pathway to pathway, and we consider some average value of n for an aggregate of randomly distributed pathways.

Using equation (38) of chapter iii, we have, from (1),

$$(\varepsilon - j) = PE_1 - nQ\beta_3(PE_1 - h_3); \quad (\beta_i = \alpha_i I_i). \tag{2}$$

This equation holds only for $PE_1 > h_3$. If $PE_1 < h_3$, we have simply $\varepsilon - j = PE_1$. Let

$$h_2 > h_3 . \tag{3}$$

Then, if

$$PE_1 < h_3 ,$$

we shall also have

$$PE_1 < h_2 ;$$

and therefore, if E_1 is too small to excite the inhibitory pathways, then, even in the absence of any effect of those pathways at the connections s_i, the pathways of class *II* will not be excited, because

$$\varepsilon - j = PE_1 < h_2 .$$

Now let

$$n > \frac{1}{Q\beta_3} > \frac{n}{2} \tag{4}$$

and

$$E_1 > \frac{h_3}{P}. \tag{5}$$

Equation (2) may be written thus:

$$\varepsilon - j = P(1 - nQ\beta_3)E_1 + nQ\beta_3 h_3 . \tag{6}$$

Because of (4), $\varepsilon - j$ decreases with increasing E_1, since the coefficient of E_1 is negative. Because of (3), we may write

$$nQ\beta_3 h_3 - h_2 < nQ\beta_3 h_3 - h_3 , \tag{7}$$

which gives

$$\frac{nQ\beta_3 h_3 - h_2}{P(nQ\beta_3 - 1)} < \frac{h_3}{P}. \tag{8}$$

Hence, combining (8) and (5), we obtain

$$E_1 > \frac{nQ\beta_3 h_3 - h_2}{P(nQ\beta_3 - 1)},$$

or

$$nQ\beta_3 h_3 - P(nQ\beta_3 - 1)E_1 < h_2 . \tag{9}$$

Comparison of (9) with (6) shows that, if (3) holds, then for the case $PE_1 > h_3$ we still have, at s_i, $\varepsilon - j < h_2$, so that the elements *II* are not excited.

Consider, now, that at the central retina all the neuroelements lying within an area limited by a closed contour Γ are excited with the same intensity E_1. To this contour Γ let there correspond a contour Γ' on C (Fig. 1). Then at each connection s_n lying within Γ',

$\varepsilon - j$ will be negative, and none of the pathways of class *II* will be excited. Outside Γ'' there will also be no excitation at any connection, since there $\varepsilon - j = 0$. But for each pathway and its corresponding connection, lying on the contour line Γ'', we have a number of adjacent excited pathways n' equal to only half of n,

$$n' = \frac{n}{2}. \tag{10}$$

Each connection s_i on the contour line receives only n' inhibitory pathways. Hence at such a connection we have, instead of (6),

$$\varepsilon - j = P(1 - n'Q\beta_3)E_1 + n'Q\beta_3 h_3 . \tag{11}$$

Because of (4) the coefficient of E_1 in (11) is positive, and therefore $\varepsilon - j$ is positive for any $E_1 > 0$. If we also have

$$E_1 > \frac{h_2 - n'Q\beta_3 h_3}{P(1 - n'Q\beta_3)}, \tag{12}$$

then at each such "contour connection" $\varepsilon - j > h_2$, and the corresponding pathways of class *II* will be excited. Under the same conditions, if we consider that on the central retina all neuroelements lying outside Γ are excited with an intensity E_1, and none are excited inside, we shall still obtain the same effect at C. That is, only connections which lie on the contour line Γ'' will be excited.

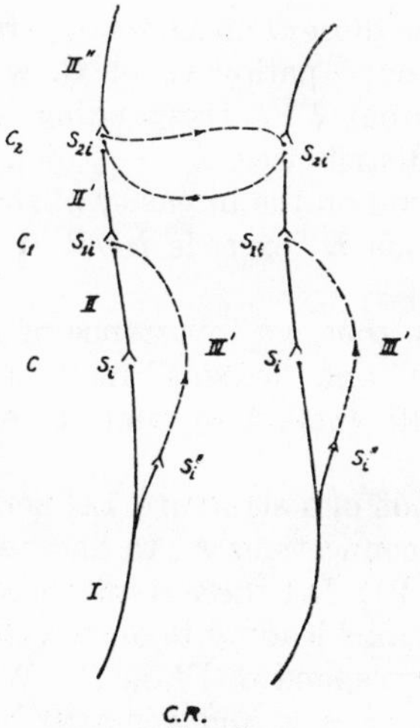

FIG. 2

To sum up, we now have the following situation: If the constants characterizing the neuroelements of our system satisfy relations (3) and (4), then, when E_1 is very small, neither the elements of class *II* nor those of class *III* are excited. If E_1 increases so as to excite the pathways of class *III*, still none of the pathways of class *II* are excited. Only when E_1 satisfies (12) do the elements of class *II*, which correspond to the contour, get excited. All others remain unexcited.

Now let each of pathways *II* end in a connection s_{1i} in a higher center C_1 (Fig. 2). Let each ith pathway of class *I* send a collateral pathway which, through a connection s_i'', excites an inhibitory pathway III' to s_{1i}. We then have at s_{1i}

$$\varepsilon - j = PE_2 - QE_3' . \tag{13}$$

From equation (9) of chapter ii and from (11) we have

$$E_2 = \beta_2[P(1 - n'Q\beta_3)E_1 + n'Q\beta_3 h_3 - h_2]. \tag{14}$$

Also,

$$E_3' = \beta_3'(PE_1 - h_3'). \tag{15}$$

Hence, at s_{1i}

$$\varepsilon - j = P\beta_2[P(1 - n'Q\beta_3)E_1 + n'Q\beta_3 h_3 - h_2] - Q\beta_3'(PE_1 - h_3'),$$

or

$$\varepsilon - j = [P^2\beta_2(1 - n'Q\beta_3) - PQ\beta_3']E_1 + PQn'\beta_2\beta_3 h_3 - P\beta_2 h_2 + Q\beta_3' h_3' .$$

If

$$P\beta_2(1 - n'Q\beta_3) - Q\beta_3' = 0$$

and

$$Q\beta_3' h_3' - P\beta_2(h_2 - Qn'\beta_3 h_3) = L > 0 , \tag{16}$$

where L is a constant, then

$$\varepsilon - j = L > 0$$

is constant at all connections s_{1i}. But, since those connections s_{1i} are receiving impulses only from the "contour" pathways of C, we therefore have now on C_1 an excited contour Γ'' corresponding to the contour Γ on the central retina. The distribution of $\varepsilon - j$ along this contour is constant and does not depend on the intensity of the excitation on the central retina so long as E_1 exceeds h_3'/P (cf. eq. [5]).

The structure here considered offers, thus, an invariance of a geometrical figure with respect to "inside" and "outside" illumination, as well as, within certain limits, with respect to intensity of illumination.

We now consider a further complication of a structure. Let neuroelements of third order II' lead from connections s_{1i} to another set of connections s_{2i} in a center C_2 (Fig. 2). Let these connections excite a number of inhibitory neuronic chains leading to other connections s_{2i} . Let a contour Γ''' on C_2 correspond to Γ'' on C_1. We thus have, as in chapter iii, putting $\epsilon - j = \phi$ and denoting by S the distance measured along the contour Γ''' from any fixed point on it,

$$\phi(S) = L - Q \int_S K(S, S')[\phi(S') - h_2]dS' , \tag{17}$$

the integration being taken along the whole contour. We shall confine ourselves here to the case in which the structure at C_2 is isotropic, so that $K(S, S') = f(S - S') = f(r)$ is a function of the distance r only of the points S and S'. If all h_2 are the same in C_2, then, introducing $\psi(S) = \phi(S) - h_2$, (17) may be written

$$\psi(S) = L' - Q \int_S K(S, S')\, \psi(S')\, dS'; \qquad L' = L - h_2. \tag{18}$$

Let the contour Γ''' be given by the equation in polar coordinates

$$\bar{r} = u(\theta), \tag{19}$$

where $\bar{r}$ denotes the radius vector from the origin. Then the distance r between any two points of the contour is equal to

$$r = \sqrt{u^2(\theta) + u^2(\theta') - 2u(\theta)u(\theta') \cos(\theta - \theta')}; \tag{20}$$

and therefore, if $K(S, S') = f(r)$, where f is a known function,

$$\left.\begin{aligned} \psi(\theta) &= L' \\ &- Q \int_{\theta'=0}^{\theta'=2\pi} u(\theta') f[\sqrt{u^2(\theta) + u^2(\theta') - 2u(\theta)u(\theta') \cos(\theta - \theta')}] \\ &\qquad \psi(\theta')\, d\theta'. \end{aligned}\right\} \tag{21}$$

For a given $f(r)$, $\psi(\theta)$ will depend on the choice of $u(\theta)$, that is, on the shape of the contour. Any variation in any part of the contour results, in general, in a variation of $\psi(\theta)$ at all other points of it.

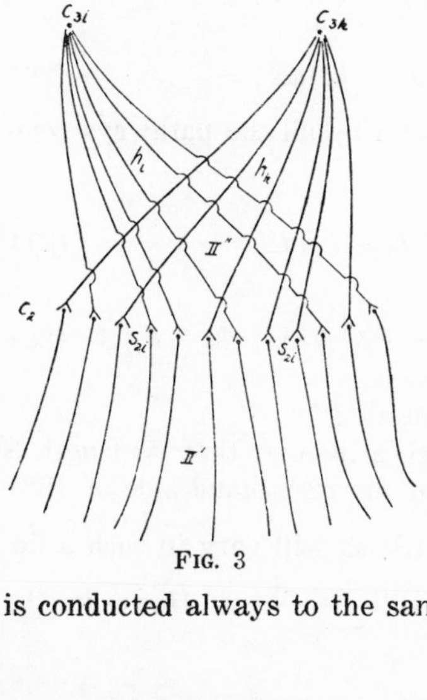

FIG. 3

Let us further consider the following arrangement of neuroelements. Let the connections s_{2i} transmit to neuroelements of the fourth order, II'', which have different thresholds h_i. Let the pathways with the same threshold be distributed entirely at random or "macroscopically uniformly" in C_2. But let, in their further course, all pathways with a threshold h_i be segregated in a separate tract, converging to a center C_{3i}, so that, whenever a neuroelement of threshold h_i is excited in any region of C_2, the excitation is conducted always to the same region C_{3i} of C_3 (Fig. 3). Under those conditions and with $K(S, S') = K(r)$, no matter how the contour Γ''' is situated on C_2, as long as it preserves its size and shape it will produce the same excitation in any center C_{3i}, and hence the distribution of the excitations between various C_{3i} is invariant with respect to a displacement of Γ''' on C_2 and hence of Γ on $C.R.$

If N is the number of connections s_{2i} per unit length and if $N(h_i)$ denotes the number of pathways per unit length with a threshold h_i, then

$$\sum_i N(h_i) = N . \tag{22}$$

At the point S of Γ''',

$$\varepsilon - j = \phi(S) = \psi(S) + h_2 . \tag{23}$$

At this point, therefore, each pathway II'' with a threshold h_i is excited with the intensity

$$E_2'' = \beta_2''(\varepsilon - j - h_i) = \beta_2''[\psi(S) + h_2 - h_i] . \tag{24}$$

The total number of such pathways in the element dS is $N(h_i)dS$. Therefore, the total number of pathways II'' with threshold h_i which converge to C_{3i} from the element dS is equal to $N(h_i)dS$. Each pathway produces at C_{3i} an amount $\varepsilon - j$ equal to

$$PE_2'' = P\beta_2''[\psi(S) + h_2 - h_i] . \tag{25}$$

Hence the total amount of $\varepsilon - j$ produced at C_{3i} by pathways coming from the element dS is

$$PN(h_i)\beta_2''[\psi(S) + h_2 - h_i]dS , \tag{26}$$

and the total amount of $\varepsilon - j$ produced by all the pathways coming to C_{3i} from the whole contour is

$$(\varepsilon - j)_i = P\beta_2''N(h_i)\int_S [\psi(S) + h_2 - h_i]dS \tag{27}$$

$$= P\beta_2''N(h_i)\int_S \psi(S)dS + P\beta_2''N(h_i)(h_2 - h_i)S , \tag{28}$$

where S denotes the length of the contour Γ'''.

If we deform the contour in such a manner that its length S remains the same, the second term of the right-hand side of (28) does not vary; but, in general, $\int_S \psi(S)dS$ will vary in such a deformation, and therefore $(\varepsilon - j)_i$ will also vary. However, the distribution of $(\varepsilon - j)_i$ is, in general, not in a one-to-one correspondence to the shape of the contour. We may have, as a rule, contours of different shapes, such that $\int_S \psi(S)\,dS$ remains the same. Whether a particular distribution of $(\varepsilon - j)_i$ can be obtained by only one or by more than one shape, that is, whether S and $\int_S \psi(S)\,dS$ specify only a limited or a wide class of geometrical shapes, depends on the function $f(r)$. It is an interesting mathematical problem to investigate the different types of contours possessing, for a given $f(r)$ and S, the same $\int_S \psi(S)\,dS$ and thus producing the same $(\varepsilon - j)_i$.

A more unique correspondence of a geometrical shape to a given $(\varepsilon - j)_i$ distribution is obtained by slightly modifying our hypothesis.

Let us consider that the pathways II'' are characterized by such constants that for them the approximate equation (3) of chapter ii cannot be used and, instead, equation (5) of that chapter must be employed. Then, instead of (24), we shall have

$$\left.\begin{aligned} E_2'' &= \frac{I_2''}{\theta_2''}\left[1 - e^{-\alpha_2''\theta_2''(\varepsilon - j - h_i)}\right] \\ &= \frac{I_2''}{\theta_2''}\left[1 - e^{-\alpha_2''\theta_2''[\psi(S) + h_2 - h_i]}\right] \\ &= F[I_2'', \theta_2'', \alpha_2'', h_i; \quad \psi(S)], \end{aligned}\right\} \tag{29}$$

where I_2'', θ_2'', α_2'', and h_i are parameters and $\psi(S)$ is the argument of the function F. Now, let the pathways characterized by a given set of $\alpha_i = \alpha_2''$, $\theta_i = \theta_2''$, $I_i = I_2''$, and h_i be segregated into a center C_{3i}, and let them have on C_2 a distribution function $N_i = N(\alpha_i, \theta_i, I_i, h_i)$. More generally we may consider the case in which all indices are different, so that we have

$$N_{iklm} = N(\alpha_i, \theta_k, I_l, h_m).$$

We shall, however, consider as an illustration only the more limited case. We have

$$\sum_i N(\alpha_i, \theta_i, I_i, h_i) = N. \tag{30}$$

Then each center $C_{3i}(\alpha_i, \theta_i, I_i, h_i)$ has an amount of $\varepsilon - j$ given by

$$(\varepsilon - j)_i = PN(\alpha_i, \theta_i, I_i, h_i) \int_S F[I_i, \alpha_i, \theta_i, h_i, \psi(S)]dS. \quad (31)$$

If Γ''' varies, it may happen that, for a particular i,

$$\int F[\alpha_i, \theta_i, I_i, h_i; \psi(S)]dS = \int F_i[\psi(S)]dS$$

will remain the same. But, in general, for another i',

$$\int F_{i'}[\psi(S)]dS \quad (32)$$

will not remain the same. Only such shapes give identical distributions of $(\varepsilon - j)_i$ for which (32) is invariant for any i'.

Now let the contour Γ or, what is the same thing, Γ''' increase in size, remaining similar to itself. This, in general, will result in a change of $\psi(S)$. However, while $\psi(S)$ changes, the expression (32) may remain invariant. Whether it will do so or not depends on $f(r)$. We now have the following problem: to determine what conditions the function $f(r)$ in equation (21) must satisfy in order that a transformation

$$x_1 = \lambda x; \quad y_1 = \lambda y; \quad z_1 = \lambda z \quad (33)$$

may leave invariant the k expressions,

$$\int F_1[\psi(S)]dS, \int F_2[\psi(S)]dS_1, \cdots, \int F_k[\psi(S)]dS, \quad (34)$$

in which $F_1, F_2, F_3, \cdots, F_k$, are k-given functions. If this problem has a solution, this solution resolves, at the same time, our problem of Gestalt transposition; for, if $f(r)$ on C_2 is so chosen as to satisfy the foregoing conditions, then, because of (31), the distribution $(\varepsilon - j)_i$ will be invariant not only with respect to displacements of Γ''' on C_2 but also with respect to a change of size of Γ'''.

Pending such a solution, we shall discuss here a different mechanism. Let $K(S, S') = f(r) = A/r$. The transformation (33) transforms dS' into

$$dS_1' = \lambda dS', \quad (35)$$

while $K(S, S')$ will become

$$K(S_1, S_1') = \frac{A}{\lambda r} = \frac{K(S, S')}{\lambda}. \quad (36)$$

Hence, $K(S, S')\,dS'$ remains invariant; and, since L is a constant, $\psi(S_1) = \psi(S)$ in (18). Therefore

$$F_i[\psi(S_1)] = F_i[\psi(S)]\,. \tag{37}$$

The new value of $(\varepsilon - j)_i$, after Γ''' has undergone the transformation (33) is

$$(\varepsilon - j)_i' = PN_i \int F_i[\psi(S_1)]\,dS_1\,,$$

which, because of (35) and (37), may be written

$$(\varepsilon - j)_i' = \lambda PN_i \int F_i[\psi(S)]\,dS = \lambda(\varepsilon - j)_i\,. \tag{38}$$

If Γ''' increases in size λ times, the relative distribution of $(\varepsilon - j)_i$ remains the same; but each $(\varepsilon - j)$ is multiplied by λ. Strictly speaking, owing to the finite size of neuroelements, we cannot have $f(r) = A/r$, which would become infinite for $r = 0$. We should take $f(r) = A/(r_0 + r)$, where r_0 is of the order of magnitude of the size of a cell (10^{-3} cm). Then, for contours which involve a sufficiently large number of neuroelements, the foregoing considerations will hold approximately.

Thus, by varying the position of Γ we do not vary anything at C_{3i}, while by varying the size of Γ we change only the absolute

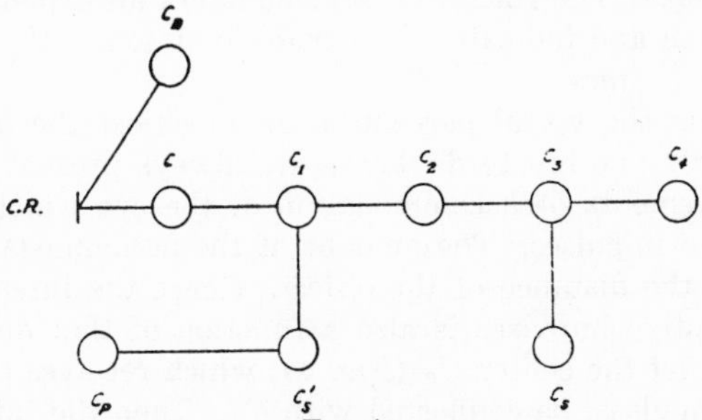

FIG. 4

values of excitation intensities of the different C_{3i}, leaving their ratios invariant. But in chapter x we have studied a mechanism that gives an invariant response to a constant ratio of excitation of two or more centers. Such a mechanism, C_4, connected to C_{3i} farther centrally, will thus insure a complete invariance of response to Γ, regardless of the latter's position or size.

We thus arrive at the following scheme. Any given geometrical pattern on the retina produces the same response via C_1, C_2, C_3, and C_4, regardless of its position, size, or intensity. Variations of size will involve, as we have seen, a change of intensity of excitation of the centers C_{3i}. The peculiar property of the neuroelements C_4 of higher order, discussed in chapter x, "levels out" these changes. But, if each center C_{3i} (Fig. 4) is connected directly to another region, C_S, in which it is directly conditioned to various efferent paths, then those paths which are conditioned at C_S will produce different responses for patterns of the same shape but of different size. C_S is the center for discrimination of sizes. Therefore, since the change in size involves also a change of number of excited neuroelements at C_1, sizes may be discriminated also through a center C_S', directly connected to C_1 (Fig. 4). Another conditioning center, C_B, connected directly with the central retina, will discriminate brightness, regardless of shape or size.

Lesion of C_S produces loss of ability to discriminate sizes, with preserved ability to discriminate shapes and intensities. Lesion of C_B produces loss of ability to discriminate intensities. Lesion of C_4, C_3, or C_2 produces loss of ability to discriminate and recognize geometrical forms but not size.[2]

Experiments by W. Köhler and by others on monkeys show another remarkable property of the central nervous system,[3] namely, the recognition of the constancy of the size of an object at various distances when the retinal images of the object are quite different in size. The foregoing scheme offers an explanation of this phenomenon and indicates the existence of some other connections of various centers.

During the visual perception of an object the optic nerve is not the only one involved. There are always present certain muscular movements of accommodation of the eye which set up proprioceptive impulses. The amount of the accommodation is determined by the distance of the object. Hence the intensity of those proprioceptive impulses is also a function of that distance.

Now, let the center C_P (Fig. 4), which receives those proprioceptive impulses, be connected with C_S'. Then the intensity of excitation of C_P will depend, on the one hand, on the retinal size (l) of the object and, on the other hand, on the amount of accommodation, and hence on the distance d of the object. So that at C_P we have

$$E = E_1(l) + E_2(d).$$

Changing the distance alters l, and hence E_1; but simultaneously it alters d, and hence E_2. In order to account for the experimental fact of constancy of size we must postulate

$$E_1(l) + E_2(d) = \text{const.} \tag{39}$$

Since $l = A/d$ and $E_1(l) = \lambda l$, λ being a constant, we have

$$E_2(d) = \text{const} - \frac{A}{d} \tag{40}$$

as the law of variation of E_2 with d, which secures a constancy of E at C_P.

A. S. Householder[4] has discussed numerical solutions of equation (17) in relation to some experimental data.

The mechanism of Gestalt perception developed here was first outlined in 1934 by N. Rashevsky and subsequently developed in its present form in the first edition (1938) of this book. There are no neurological justifications for this mechanism. It was invented and developed in order to demonstrate that mechanisms which exhibit the complex properties of Gestalt invariance and Gestalt transposition, are possible. A not too successful attempt at extending similar ideas to acoustic Gestalts was made in 1942 by N. Rashevsky[5].

In 1947 Walter Pitts and Warren McCulloch suggested a very different approach to the problem of Gestalt[6]. Whereas we limited ourselves above to optical Gestalts, Pitts and McCulloch approach the problem much more generally. They begin by considering any kind of perceptual Gestalts, caused by any conceivable combination of stimulus patterns. Those patterns may even be composed of stimuli of different modalities. The authors then outline a general theory of Gestalt invariance with respect to any kind of transformation. This very generality makes the treatment of the problem of necessity much less definite. Pitts and McCulloch's paper may perhaps best be described as an outline of a formal theory of general properties of some neural mechanisms which may produce Gestalt invariance.

Space does not permit here to give a detailed presentation of the theory of Pitts and McCulloch. We shall therefore merely outline the basic ideas of their paper, referring the reader to the original for details. We shall follow here very closely the presentation given by N. Rashevsky elsewhere[7].

Optical Gestalts on the retina or on the central retina are two-dimensional patterns. They can therefore be characterized by two variable coordinates x and y. If we consider any stimulus patterns, consisting even of stimuli of different modalities, then the number of coordinates necessary to describe them may be quite high. Let there be in general n such coordinates, $x_1, x_2, \ldots, x_n$. For brevity we shall denote the whole set of n coordinates by a single symbol x.

In the case of optical two-dimensional Gestalts we considered the distribution of excitation on a surface. This distribution is in general a function $\phi(x, y, t)$ of the coordinates x and y and of the time t. Similarly we shall now consider with Pitts and McCulloch a distribution function $\phi(x_1, \ldots, x_n, t) = \phi(x, t)$ in an n-dimensional space.

Consider now a transformation of the stimulus-pattern. For example, in a simple case it may be a displacement of the image on the retina. In the case of a simple translation, the new pattern is obtained from the old one by merely substituting for x and y the values

$$x' = x + \xi ; y' = y + \eta, \tag{41}$$

where ξ and η are the components of the translation in the direction of the x and y axes respectively. The transformation (41) changes the function ϕ (x, y, t) into another, ϕ' (x', y', t).

Transformations of the type (41) form what is known as a *group*. That means that if a pattern is transformed into another by a transformation (41) with particular values of ξ and η, say ξ_1 and η_1, and if that other pattern is transformed into a third one by means of (41) in general with a different set of ξ and η, say ξ_2 and η_2, then the first pattern transforms into the third by means of a transformation of the same form, in which ξ and η have the values $\xi_1 + \xi_2$, $\eta_1 + \eta_2$ correspondingly. Or to put it in a simple language, if one pattern is changed into another by means of a translation, and the other changed into a third by means of a translation, then the first changes into the third by means of a translation also.

Geometrically speaking a transformation which represents a translation may be as small as we wish. For a given geometrical pattern in a limited area of a plane there are therefore an infinite number of translations possible and therefore an infinite number of different positions. Biologically, however, the situation is different. A pattern on the retina, if shifted by an amount much less than the size of a neuron, does not change the distribution of the intensities of excitation among the neurons. Such a small shift is ineffectual. Therefore for a pattern on the retina there is a finite, though very large number of physiologically different positions. In other words, the number of possible transformations of type (41) is finite, though very large.

Pitts and McCulloch point out that this situation holds for any transformation of any stimulus pattern, because they all involve a finite number of neurons. Therefore, in their approach they consider a finite group of transformations of very general type. Let the number of transformations in a group be N. Symbolically a transformation is denoted by T. A distribution $\phi(x, t)$ is transformed into a different one, denoted by $T\phi(x, t)$, or more briefly, by $T\phi$, which is called the transform of ϕ.

Now consider what is known as a *functional* of the function $T\phi$. A functional is a variable quantity, the value of which depends not on any number of independent variables, but on the form of a function. For example if we take some function $\psi(x)$, then the definite integral of $\psi(x)$ between two fixed limits is a functional of $\psi(x)$. By taking different forms of $\psi(x)$, for example x^2, e^x, $\sin x$, etc. we obtain different values of the integral. But, whereas there is usually a unique value of the functional for a given function, the inverse is not true. Different functions may yield the same value of a definite integral.

Consider now an arbitrary functional $f[T\phi]$ of the function $T\phi$ and form the average value of that functional over all the N transformations T of the group. Denote that average by a. Thus

$$a = \frac{1}{N} \sum_T f[T\phi] \tag{42}$$

Since the sum includes *all* possible transformed functions $T\phi$ and there is a finite number of them, no matter with what particular $\phi(x, t)$ we begin, a remains the same. Beginning with a different $T\phi$ merely changes the order of the components of the sum.

Thus a is an invariant for any transformation of a stimulus pattern $\phi(x, t)$.

As we have seen, different functions may yield the same value of a functional. Therefore, in general, the same value of a will be obtained for a number of different initial patterns $\phi(x, t)$. In other words, while a pattern will be recognized as the same under any transformation, some different patterns will be considered as identical and confusion will result. To obviate this difficulty, Pitts and McCulloch introduce a number of different functionals $f_1, f_2, \ldots f_m$. Each of them leads to a corresponding invariant, so that we now have m invariants, $a_1, a_2, \ldots, a_m$. Though each invariant a_i does not specify $\phi(x, t)$ uniquely, yet, if m is large enough, all of them give a desired degree of accuracy in specifying $\phi(x, t)$.

Thus far we remained on a very general and abstract mathematical level. The next step is to apply the above considerations to actual neural nets. Pitts and McCulloch suggest the following general structure. Let the original pattern $\phi(x, t)$ be projected on some region of the brain. Let there be $N - 1$ other regions which are connected with the first region by means of a suitable mechanism which in each of the $N - 1$ regions produces one of the transforms $T\phi$ of $\phi(x, t)$. Let there be, furthermore, a mechanism in each of the $N - 1$ regions, which constructs a functional f of the corresponding $T\phi$, and let the corresponding results be added in some separate place of the brain, to which appropriate neurons from all the $N - 1$ regions converge.

Without specifying the actual neural mechanism for the formation of the functionals f_i, Pitts and McCulloch remark that the above scheme would require too large a number of neurons to be plausible. They do not give, however, any figures in support of this statement. Economy of neurons is obtained by the following device.

Let the threshold of all the $N - 1$ regions be so high, that they are not excited by the fibers coming from the region on which the original ϕ is projected. Let each of the $N - 1$ regions, however, receive fibers from an outside source, and let the thresholds be such that a region is excited if and only if it receives excitation both from the initial region and from another sources. Let that other source provide a mechanism, by means of which the additional excitation is received not simultaneously but successively by each of the $N - 1$ regions. Then the different transforms $T\phi$ will appear successively in the different regions. By appropriate fibers these transforms $T\phi$ may now be relayed to a single region Q, where they will appear *in succession.* A single "computer" which forms the functional f can now be used in the region Q for all the transforms $T\phi$, instead of having $N - 1$ such "computers."

We now come to the problem, as to what the neural mechanisms which construct the necessary transforms $T\phi$ and the functionals f look like.

Concerning the first, Pitts and McCulloch suggest specific mechanisms for two cases. First, when T represents a displacement in one dimension, and second, when T represents a uniform constriction or expansion. The first mechanism is quite simple. The $N - 1$ regions consist of $N - 1$ parallel rows of neurons. Each row is connected with the subsequent in such a way, that a neuron with a coordinate x of one row excites a neuron with a coordinate $x + \Delta$ in the other, where Δ is the distance between the neurons. Thus any excitation pattern in the initial row is merely displaced by $p\,\Delta$ in the pth row. Pitts and McCulloch apply this scheme to the theory of transposition of musical patterns along the pitch scale, assuming, as there is good evidence to believe, that different pitches are projected on a linear structure in the temporal lobe.

For invariance with respect to displacements on the retina, Pitts and McCulloch suggest a different principle. They believe that this invariance is due to the circumstance, that through a proper mechanism the eye always adjusts itself in such a way, that the center of gravity of the brightness of a pattern comes to lie in the optical axis. "If a square should appear anywhere in the field, the eyes turn until it is centered, and what they see is the same, whatever the initial position of the square" (p. 137). It may be somewhat doubted whether this mechanism is sufficient to explain known situations. Recognition by peripheral vision seems to occur also.

The contour effect is not discussed at all.

When we come to possible neural mechanisms for computing the functionals we are still left to guess what they might look like. The only suggestion we find is that of a ". . . deeper layer, a mass capable of reverberations and summation over time, that may well constitute the set of $f(T\phi, \xi)$ computers . . ." (p. 133). It must be said, however, that the construction of specific neural mechanisms which compute the functionals does not present any great difficulties.

As regards the neuron-saving scanning mechanism, the authors suggest its connection with the alpha-rhythm.

Though the authors do not give any specific suggestion for what is perhaps the most important part of the total mechanism, they consider extensive neurological evidence which might indicate in what particular parts of the brain the mechanisms which possess the necessary properties may be located. They go into a rather detailed analysis of that problem both for acoustic and optic perceptions.

Both the mechanism developed by N. Rashevsky and the one suggested by Pitts and McCulloch, in spite of their great difference, have this important feature in common: The destruction of a fairly large number of individual elements of which the mechanism is composed does not necessarily impair the functioning of the mechanism.

A still different approach to the problem of Gestalt was made in 1948 by James T. Culbertson[8].

In some respects Culbertson's approach is reminiscent of Pitts and McCulloch, though it is different in many essentials.

In chapter v of his book Culbertson discusses very specifically different neural mechanisms which produce invariance of optical Gestalts with respect to displacement and size. Like Pitts and McCulloch he assumes that all the transforms of the original

Gestalt are consecutively present in the brain. However, he does not place these transforms in separate regions, but assumes that they may all be present in the same region. He describes in great detail the neural nets which produce the transforms. For a simple translation in one direction the following scheme is, for example, used. Let *each* neuron on the central retina be connected to another neuron, which is located at a distance d to the right along the x-axis. The distance d corresponds to the smallest displacement still perceptible. If an optical pattern is projected on a group of neurons, then after a short time it is transmitted to the right and shifted by a distance d. From there it is again shifted by a distance d, and so forth, until it eventually reaches a limiting position on the right.

In this simple mechanism a pattern presented in any position along the x-axis moves to the right without change, and results in the same final response, no matter where it has been presented initially along the x-axis.

The above is, of course, only a very crude and simplified description of Culbertson's idea. He describes in great detail mechanisms for rotation of the pattern and for dilation. They are based on the same fundamental idea.

In Culbertson's theory it is not necessary either to construct additional functionals or to average over all the transforms. It may be said that in this theory any initial patterns is eventually transformed into a "canonic" form, which is one of the possible transforms of the pattern. It seems that Culbertson's mechanism produces the same effect as Pitts' and McCulloch's but in a simpler manner.

Culbertson also discusses the "contour effect". The mechanism which he proposes (p. 123) looks like a more complicated version of the mechanism proposed by Rashevsky and described above in detail. Inasmuch as Culbertson's mechanism gives the same performance, it is difficult to see why the complications are necessary or even desirable.

Two important problems, which neither Rashevsky nor Pitts and McCulloch discuss at all, are studied in great detail by Culbertson.

The first is the calculation of the number of neurons necessary to construct the mechanism suggested. Culbertson not only speaks of economy of neurons, but actually evaluates the necessary number of neurons as well as of dendrites to each neuron. He shows that the figures are biologically plausible.

The other, perhaps even more important, problem is the following. How much can a pattern be distorted and still be recognized as such? Culbertson discusses this problem and allied problems in detail. Space does not permit the presentation of Culbertson's ideas, and the reader is referred to his book[8].

REFERENCES

1. N. Rashevsky, *Jour. Gen. Psychol.*, **13**, 82, 1935; *Philosophy of Science*, **1**, 409, 1934.

2. K. Goldstein and A. Gelb, *Zeitschr. f. d. ges. Neurol. u. Psychiat.*, **41**, 1, 1918.

3. W. Köhler, *Gestalt Psychology* (Liveright, 1929), pp. 74, 81, 86, 93, 105, 133.

4. A. S. Householder, *Bull. Math. Biophysics*, **1**, 63, 1939.

5. N. Rashevsky, *Bull. Math. Biophysics*, **4**, 27, 1942; **4**, 89, 1942.

6. W. Pitts and W. S. McCulloch, *Bull. Math. Biophysics*, **9**, 127, 1947.

7. N. Rashevsky, *Thales*, **7**, 53, 1951.

8. J. T. Culbertson, *Bull. Math. Biophysics*, **10**, 37, 97, 1948; *Consciousness and Behavior. A Neural Analysis of Behavior and Consciousness.* (Dubuque, Iowa: Wm. C. Brown Co., Publishers, 1957.)

CHAPTER XII

MATHEMATICAL BIOPHYSICS OF COLOR VISION AND OF FLICKER PHENOMENA

It is found empirically that any color may be obtained by mixing in appropriate proportions, or in appropriate relative intensities, three so called "primary colors." For example green, yellow and red may be chosen as primary colors. But the primaries are not uniquely determined, and we may for example choose red, green and blue. This fact permits a simple graphical representation of colors by means of what is known as the color triangle[1]. Denote the three primary colors by C_1, C_2, C_3. Let each vertex of a triangle represent one of the three primaries. If we imagine each vertex of the triangle to be loaded with a mass which is proportional to the amount or intensity of the corresponding primary, then the center of gravity A of the three masses is the point which represents graphically a color, obtained by mixing C_1, C_2, and C_3 in given proportions. This point A is never on the outside of the triangle, though it may be located on one of the sides. If, for example, in any given mixture of primaries, C_1 is absent, then the point A lies somewhere on the side C_2C_3, its position depending on the relative intensities of C_2 and C_3. If C_2 and C_3 are absent, we have the pure primary color C_1.

If we connect the center of gravity O of the triangle, which represents the white color, to one of the vertices, say C_1, then all the points on the line OC_1 represent the primary color which corresponds to C_1, but in different degrees of saturation, in other words diluted to different extent with white. The closer to O, the less the saturation. The point C_1 represents the pure primary color, the point O — pure white.

There has been some argument as to whether three colors are completely sufficient to represent *any color and saturation,* and a color square instead of a color triangle has been discussed.

As far back as 1807 Thomas Young suggested that the mechanism of color vision is based on the presence of three different kinds of photosensitive cells in the retina, each kind being sensitive to one primary color. This concept was elaborated further by H. Helmholtz. Different explanations have also been suggested. Relatively recently C. H. Graham and H. K. Hartline[2], and R. Granit[3] have definitely established the actual existence of different types of photoreceptors, which are sensitive to different wave lengths. However, it turned out that there are at least four different kinds of photoreceptors. In vertebrates they are sensitive to red, yellow, green, and blue. Yet, empirically it seems that three primary colors are *necessary and sufficient* to obtain *any* color. Two are not enough. Four are not necessary. If true this implies that the four primary colors are not independent of each other, in the sense that the sensation of one of them may either be produced by stimulation of the corresponding photoreceptors, or by a combined stimulation of two or three of the other kinds of photoreceptors.

An interesting application to the theory of color vision of the ideas developed in chapter ii and iii has been suggested by A. S. Householder and H. D. Landahl[4], and developed further by H. D. Landahl[5]. Though the theory involves the existence of only three different types of photoreceptors, yet it is readily generalized to any number, and therefore is consistent with the experimental findings mentioned above. We shall present it first in its simplest form which involves only three types of photoreceptors, and then show how it can be generalized.

We assume that there are in the retina three different kinds of neurons, each kind forming corresponding neuroelements and pathways. We shall denote the three kinds by subscripts 1, 2, 3. In line with the experimental findings of R. Granit and others, we do not consider that each kind of neuroelements is sensitive to only one definite wave length of light. Each kind is sensitive to all wave lengths, but for each kind the sensitivity has a maximum for a particular wave length.

Consider equation (3) of chapter ii. Here S stands for the intensity of the optical stimulus. A light of a given wave length λ will produce a different effect on each of the three types of neuroelements. This means that for certain values of λ, the quantity S will be great, for other values of λ it will be very small. But for each of the three kinds of neuroelements the variation of S with λ will be different. Therefore for the ith kind of neuroelement ($i = 1, 2, 3$), S will be a function $p_i(\lambda)$ of λ.

Now let the retina be illuminated by light composed of different wave lengths, and let the intensity of that light which corresponds to a region of the spectrum between λ and $\lambda + d\lambda$ be $I(\lambda)\,d\lambda$. Then the total value S_i of S for the ith neuroelement will be

$$S_i = \int_0^\infty I(\lambda)\,p_i(\lambda)\,d\lambda. \tag{1}$$

Now, somewhat like in the preceding chapter, let us consider a two-dimensional region in the "central retina". To simplify the argument we shall consider this region as lying in a plane C and having otherwise some very simple geometric properties. Subsequently we shall show that those simplifications do not represent a loss in generality, and that the same argument can be extended to more realistic structures. In the plane C consider 3 points, C_1, C_2, and C_3, which form the vertices of an equilateral triangle. This geometric requirement also simplifies the argument considerably, and will be shown subsequently in a very simple manner not to be essential. We introduce a system of rectangular coordinates in the plane C, with its origin O in the center of the triangle $C_1C_2C_3$ and

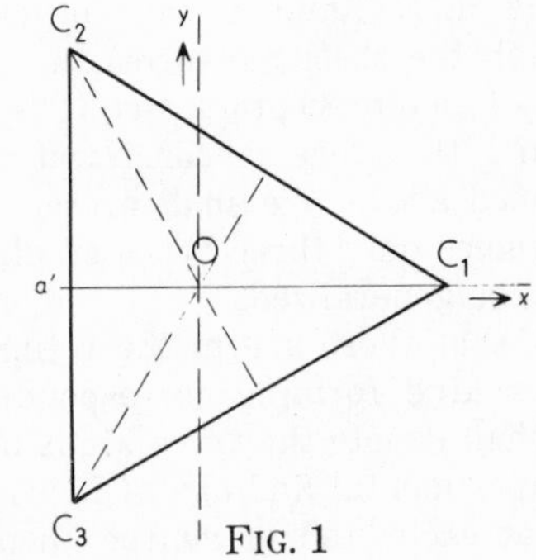

FIG. 1

the x-axis along the line OC_1 (Fig. 1). As unit of length we choose the distance OC_1. Since the triangle is equilateral, therefore $\angle OC_2a' = 30°$; $Oa' = \frac{1}{2}OC_2 = \frac{1}{2}OC_1 = \frac{1}{2}$. Hence the abscissae of either C_2 or C_3 is equal to $x = -\frac{1}{2}$. The ordinate of C_2 is $+\cos 30° = \frac{\sqrt{3}}{2}$, while that of C_3 is $-\frac{\sqrt{3}}{2}$. Thus the coordinates of C_1, C_2, and C_3 are:

$$\begin{aligned} C_1:&\quad x = 1, y = 0; \\ C_2:&\quad x = -\tfrac{1}{2}, y = \frac{\sqrt{3}}{2}; \\ C_3:&\quad x = -\tfrac{1}{2}, y = -\frac{\sqrt{3}}{2}. \end{aligned} \tag{2}$$

Let each peripheral neuroelement of type i ($i = 1, 2, 3$) send neural pathways to the plane C, and let the density of these pathways be non-uniform on C. Regions of C which receive per unit area more pathways from the ith kind of neuroelements will have a stronger intensity of excitation coming from neuroelements of type i, than regions which receive less pathways. Let the density of the pathways coming from the ith kind of neuroelements be greatest at the point C_i $(i = 1, 2, 3)$, and decrease with the distance d_i from C_i. This decrease may be due to a random scattering of the neuroelements around the point C_i. In that case the density σ_i of the pathways from neuroelements of the ith type will decrease with d_i according to a normal error distribution function which is of the form $\exp(-\gamma_i d_i^2)$. If we denote by σ_{oi} and γ_i two constants, then for not too large values of d_i the density σ_i will be represented by

$$\sigma_i(d_i) = \sigma_{oi}(1 - \gamma_i d_i^2). \tag{3}$$

The assumption of a random scattering of neuroelements around the point C_i leads to (3) as a first approximation, by expanding the error function and preserving only the lowest term in d_i. Equation (3) may just as well be introduced as an explicit assumption.

Applying to each of the three types of neuroelements equation (3) of chapter ii, we find for the intensity of excitation at the end of each pathway which terminates in the plane C the expressions:

$$E_i = \beta_i(S_i - h_i). \quad (i = 1, 2, 3) \tag{4}$$

In this expression the quantity S_i is given by equation (1) of the present chapter.

If we consider for the time being stationary states only, introduce the constants A_e, a_e, B_e, and b_e, used in equation (15) of chapter iii, and put

$$\frac{A_e}{a_e} - \frac{B_e}{b_e} = \eta, \tag{5}$$

then the net excitation at the end of each pathway of the ith type is equal to $\eta_i E_i$. The intensity of excitation per unit area in the plane C is given for each type of pathways by $\eta_i E_i \sigma_i(d_i)$. If we denote this density of excitation by ϕ_i, then from (3) and (4) we obtain:

$$\eta_i \beta_i \sigma_{oi}(S_i - h_i)(1 - \gamma_i d_i^2). \tag{6}$$

Introducing the notation

$$S_i' = \eta_i \beta_i \sigma_{oi}(S_i - h_i), \tag{7}$$

we find for the total density of excitation at the point x, y, *due to all three types of neuroelements:*

$$\phi(x, y) = \phi_1 + \phi_2 + \phi_3 = S_1' + S_2' + S_3' - \gamma_1 S_1' d_1^2 - \gamma_2 S_2' d_2^2 - \gamma_3 S_3' d_3^2. \tag{8}$$

We now shall show that $\phi(x, y)$ has a maximum which is always either inside the triangle $C_1C_2C_3$, or is located on one of its sides.

Since the coordinates of C_1 are, according to (2) : $x = 1$, $y = 0$, and d_1 is the distance from the point (x, y) to C_1, therefore

$$d_1^2 = (1 - x^2) + y^2. \tag{9}$$

Similarly, using the values (2) we find, putting

$$\frac{\sqrt{3}}{2} = c, \tag{10}$$

$$d_2^2 = (x + \tfrac{1}{2})^2 + (c - y)^2; \tag{11}$$

$$d_3^2 = (x + \tfrac{1}{2})^2 + (c + y)^2. \tag{12}$$

We now introduce (9), (11), and (12) into (8), and calculate the partial derivatives of ϕ (x, y) with respect to x and to y. Since the first three terms on the right side of (8) are constants, we need consider only the last three terms.

Introducing (9), (11), and (12) into (8) and differentiating with respect to x and to y, we find, after rearrangements:

$$\frac{\partial\phi}{\partial x} = -2(\gamma_1 S_1' + \gamma_2 S_2' + \gamma_3 S_3')x - (2\gamma_1 S_1' - \gamma_2 S_2' - \gamma_3 S_3'); \tag{13}$$

$$\frac{\partial\phi}{\partial y} = -2(\gamma_1 S_1' + \gamma_2 S_2' + \gamma_3 S_3')y - 2(\gamma_2 S_2' - \gamma_3 S_3')c. \tag{14}$$

Putting $\partial\phi/\partial x = 0$; $\partial\phi/\partial y = 0$, we find the coordinates of the extremum:

$$x = \frac{2\gamma_1 S_1' - \gamma_2 S_2' - \gamma_3 S_3'}{2(\gamma_1 S_1' + \gamma_2 S_2' + \gamma_3 S_3')};$$

$$y = \frac{(\gamma_2 S_2' - \gamma_3 S_3')c}{\gamma_1 S_1' + \gamma_2 S_2' + \gamma_3 S_3'}. \tag{15}$$

That the extremum is a maximum, can be seen by taking the second derivatives. We find from (13) and (14):

$$\frac{\partial^2\phi}{\partial x^2} = \frac{\partial^2\phi}{\partial y^2} = -2(\gamma_1 S_1' + \gamma_2 S_2' + \gamma_3 S_3') < 0; \quad \frac{\partial^2\phi}{\partial x \partial y} = 0. \tag{16}$$

We shall now show that the maximum never lies outside of the triangle $C_1C_2C_3$.

The equation of the line C_2C_1 (Fig. 1) is

$$y = \frac{\sqrt{3}}{3}(1 - x). \tag{17}$$

At C_1, where $x = 1$, $y = 0$. At C_2, where $x = -\frac{1}{2}$, $y = \frac{\sqrt{3}}{2}$, in agreement with (2).

Similarly the equation of the line C_3C_1 is

$$y = -\frac{\sqrt{3}}{3}(1 - x). \tag{18}$$

while the equation of the line C_2C_3 is

$$x = -\tfrac{1}{2}. \tag{19}$$

From expression (15) for the x — coordinate of the maximum, we find

$$\frac{\sqrt{3}}{3}(1 - x) = \frac{\sqrt{3}}{2} \quad \frac{\gamma_2 S_2' + \gamma_3 S_3'}{\gamma_1 S_1' + \gamma_2 S_2' + \gamma_3 S_3'}; \tag{20}$$

The y-coordinate of the maximum is given by the second expression (15). If the maximum is not to lie outside of the triangle $C_1C_2C_3$, one of the necessary conditions is that it should lie either *below* the line C_2C_1 or *on* that line. But according to (17) this means that

$$y \leqslant \frac{\sqrt{3}}{3}(1 - x). \tag{21}$$

Introducing expression (20) and the second expression (15) into (21), we obtain, after rearrangements:

$$\gamma_2 S_2' - \gamma_3 S'_3 \leqslant \gamma_2 S_2' + \gamma_3 S_3' \tag{22}$$

or

$$\gamma_3 S_3' \geqslant 0 \,, \tag{23}$$

a condition which is always satisfied. The equality sign holds, according to (7) when $S_i \leqslant h_i$ (c.f. chapter ii).

The requirement that the maximum would *not* lie outside of the triangle $C_1C_2C_3$ also requires that it lies either *on* or *above* the line C_3C_1, or that, because of (18), the inequality

$$y \geqslant \frac{\sqrt{3}}{3}(1 - x) \tag{24}$$

holds for its coordinates. In a similar manner as before we find that this requirement leads to

$$\gamma_2 S_2' \geqslant 0 \,, \tag{25}$$

which is also satisfied.

Finally the maximum must lie either on the line C_2C_3 or to the right of it. According to (19) this means that x-coordinate of the maximum, given by (15), must satisfy the inequality:

$$x \geqslant - \tfrac{1}{2} \,. \tag{26}$$

Introducing the first expression (15) into (26) we find:

$$\gamma_1 S_1' \geqslant 0 \,. \tag{27}$$

which is also always satisfied. Thus the maximum lies always either within or on the sides of the triangle $C_1C_2C_3$.

We notice that the equality sign in (23) is the condition for the maximum to be somewhere *on* the line C_2C_1. In other words, the absence of the primary 3 causes the maximum to be on the line C_2C_1. Similarly from (25) we see that the absence of the primary 2 makes the maximum to be located on the line C_1C_3; while from (27) we see that the absence of primary 1 causes the maximum to be located somewhere on the line C_2C_3. When $\gamma_1 S_1' = \gamma_2 S_2' = \gamma_3 S_3'$, then we find from (15) for the coordinates x and y of the maximum $x = y = 0$. In this case the maximum is in the center of the triangle $C_1C_2C_3$. Finally if $S_1' = S_2' = 0$, which according to (7) and (1), and according to chapter ii, means that the neuroelements which correspond to primaries 1 and 2 are not stimulated, and only the 3rd type of neuroelements is excited, then the maximum is located at C_3. Similarly, if only the 1st or only the 2nd type of neuroelements is excited, the maximum is located at C_1, respectively at C_2.

We notice that the point of maximum of $\phi(x, y)$ behaves within the triangle $C_1C_2C_3$ exactly as does the representative point for a color in the color triangle.

Consider now another plane C' somewhere in the central nervous system, to which higher order neuropathways go from the plane C. This time, however, we assume that the density distribution of those higher order neuroelements is the same on C and C'. Thus any excitation pattern on C is mapped exactly on C'. Let, however, those higher order neural pathways be mutually cross-inhibited, in a manner described in chapter iii, on pages 27 to 33. Then as we have seen in chapter iii [Equations (55) and the following discussion], and as we also discussed in chapter v, only those pathways arriving on C' will be excited, which come from the immediate neighborhood of the maximum of $\phi\ (x, y)$ on C. There will be no excitation anywhere else. To the points C_1, C_2, C_3 in the plane C there correspond the points C_1', C_2', and C_3' in the plane C', and the small excited region within the triangle $C_1'C_2'C_3'$ will represent the set of neuroelements in C' which are excited by a given color. As the composition of the color is varied by varying the relative intensities of the three primaries, the excited region will move within the triangle $C_1'C_2'C_3'$ just exactly as the representative points move within the color triangle when the relative intensities of the primaries are varied. The size of the excited region will depend on the parameters of the pathways. If two excited regions which correspond to two different colors are quite separate, the two colors can be discriminated. If the excited regions overlap, the corresponding colors cannot be discriminated[7]. The situation is quite analogous to that described in chapter v.

The assumption of planes C and C' and of equilateral triangles $C_1C_2C_3$ and $C_1'C_2'C_3'$ was made for simplicity only. It is of course quite unrealistic. The actual regions in the brain need not be in a plane (though they have to be on a thin surface-like a layer). Nor does the triangle have to be equilateral. We can always *continuously* map the triangles $C_1C_2C_3$ and $C_1'C_2'C_3'$ on any curved surface C in a one-to-one mapping. The mapping may be otherwise quite arbitrary. To the points within the triangles $C_1C_2C_3$ or $C_1'C_2'C_3'$ there will correspond points in C, though straight lines in C will not be straight in C. There will, however, be a maximum in C at the point which corresponds to the maximum in C. The situation is quite analogous to the fact that regular geometric figures projected on the retina are mapped in a distorted form somewhere in the occipital lobe. The density of excitation in C will depend on the distance in a very different manner from that given by equation (3). The relation of the excitation maximum to the excitation of the points C_1, C_2, and C_3 which correspond to C_1, C_2, and C_3 will, however, be the same. Dealing with almost arbitrary decreasing functions of distance would have complicated the argument. We can, however, continue to visualize the situation in the simple manner described above, and speak of an equilateral triangle in a plane.

If there are, as is actually the case, more than three types of photoreceptors, the argument still can be applied. Using the same model for m different kinds of receptors, we may consider in the plane C a polygon with m vertices. What is, however, the meaning of the fact that actually only three primary colors are needed to obtain any color? We have already remarked on p. 116 that $m - 3$ primary colors should then be obtained as mixtures of three chosen ones, though each of those $m - 3$ primary colors can also be obtained by direct excitation of the corresponding kind of neuroelements. In terms of the model which we discussed above, this could mean that 3 of the m points of the polygon on C should form a triangle, while the remaining $m - 3$ ones must be located either inside or on the sides of the triangle. This is illustrated in Figure 2, where $m = 8$, and where the sides of the 8 sided polygon are drawn in heavy lines. In terms of Landahl's model, the above means

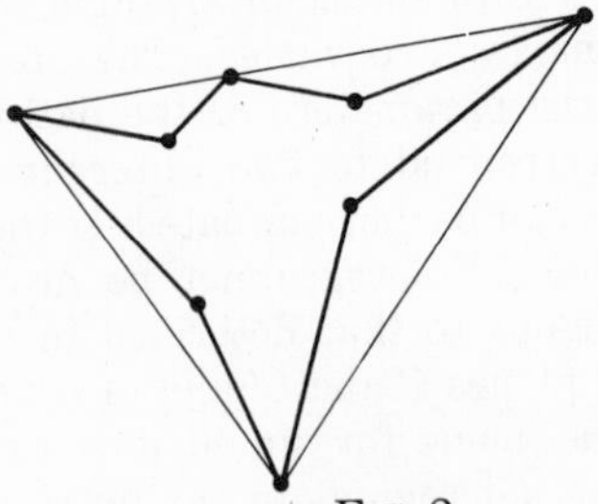

FIG. 2

that while three of the photoreceptors have the greatest density of their pathways at the three vertices of a triangle on C, any additional special photoreceptors will have the greatest density of their pathways either inside of the triangle $C_1C_2C_3$ or on one of its sides. If there are, let us say, four photoreceptors, which have their maximal sensitivity for four different wave lengths, λ_1, λ_2, λ_3 and λ_4 and if C_1, C_2, C_3 and C_4 are the points of greatest density of their pathways in the plane C, then either C_4 must not lie outside of the triangle $C_1C_2C_3$, or C_3 must not lie outside $C_1C_2C_4$, etc. In the first instance the sensation of the color C_4 is produced either by direct stimulation of the 4-th type of receptors, or by a stimulation of the 1st, 2nd, and 3rd photoreceptors with appropriate relative intensities, or both.

Thus we can apply all the above considerations to the more general case of more than three primary colors, and continue to use the triangular model. We shall therefore use the concept of three primary colors in the following discussion.

Suppose that we mix the three different primary colors in a given proportion. This results in a particular location of the excited region within the triangle $C_1'C_2'C_3'$. Let us keep the relative intensities of the primary colors the same, but present each of them intermittently. In chapter ix we have seen, that when a stimulus is applied intermittently, eventually stationary states for both excitatory and inhibitory factors ϵ and j are reached, but ϵ and j have now different values from those which they have in the stationary state for continuous stimulation. The values for intermittent stimulation are smaller than those for continuous one, as shown by expression (23) of chapter ix. The values of ϵ and j now depend on the length of t_1 of the period of stimulation, and on the length t_2 of the period of intermission. Moreover they depend, as seen from (23) and (24) of chapter ix, on the constants a_e and b_e. The afferent neuroelements of the three different type will in general have different values of a_e and b_e. That is why we provided the quantity η_i in expression (6) with an index i.

But this means that the stationary values of ϵ_i and j_i ($i = 1, 2, 3$) will be reduced by different amounts for the different kinds of neuroelements. This has the same effect as a change in the relative intensities of the primary colors. Therefore the excited region in C' will be displaced and a different color will be perceived. This consequence of the theory has been developed by H. D. Landahl[6], who also verified it experimentally. In particular, if the relative intensities of the primary colors are so chosen as to give white on continuous presentation, then on intermittent presentation it should produce a color effect. This has been first observed by T. Fechner, when disks with appropriate white and black patterns are rotated not too rapidly, but rapidly enough, so that the patterns cannot be clearly discerned. The colors obtained depend, as should be expected, both on the speed of rotation and on the relative widths of the white and black pattern, which determine t_1 and t_2 in expressions (23) and (24) of chapter ix.

The Fechner effect is, however, much less pronounced than the Landahl effect which can be demonstrated very easily with simplest equipment. To obtain a more pronounced Fechner effect it is necessary to make the pattern of white and black in such a manner, that the frequencies and durations of the off-and-on periods would be different for black and white. In other words, while, say, white is still on, black must already be off. For the Landahl effect this overlap is not necessary, and simple intermittence is sufficient. Landahl has discussed the theoretical basis of this difference[7].

By making use of the theory of intermittent stimulation developed in chapter ix, A. S. Householder and H. D. Landahl[4] have also developed a simple theory of flicker fusion. Later on H. D. Landahl[8] elaborated the theory in order to explain the effect of the illuminated area on the flicker fusion frequency.

REFERENCES

1. A. Linksz, *Physiology of the Eye*, II. *Vision.* (New York: Greene and Stratton, 1952).
2. C. H. Graham and H. K. Hartline, Jl. Gen. Physiol., 18, 917, 1935.
3. R. Granit, *Sensory Mechanisms of the Retina*, Oxford, Oxford University Press, 1947.
4. A. S. Householder and H. D. Landahl, *Mathematical Biophysics of the Central Nervous System.* Bloomington, Indiana, : Principia Press, 1945.
5. H. D. Landahl, *Bull. Math. Biophysics*, 14, 317, 1952.
6. H. D. Landahl, *Bull. Math. Biophysics*, 18, 137, 1956.
7. H. D. Landahl, (Unpublished).
8. H. D. Landahl, *Bull. Math. Biophysics*, 19, 157, 1957.

CHAPTER XIII

MATHEMATICAL BIOPHYSICS OF DELAYED REFLEXES AND ITS APPLICATION TO THE THEORY OF ERROR ELIMINATION

Let a neutral peripheral stimulus S_c result in an excitation of a pathway, or group of pathways, of the type discussed in chapter x, that is, for which

$$B_j < A_j; \quad b_j < a_j; \quad \frac{A_j}{a_j} < \frac{B_j}{b_j}. \tag{1}$$

Let each of these pathways lead to a multiple connection s with a number of other pathways N_c, whose thresholds are distributed according to some distribution function $N(h)$. For pathways characterized by (1) a suddenly established constant stimulus S_c results, as we have seen, in a transient increase of $\varepsilon - j$ up to a certain maximum positive value, followed by a continuous inhibitory state, with $\varepsilon - j < 0$. As $\varepsilon - j$ increases from 0 to its maximum value, the number of pathways excited through the connections s increases also, being given at each moment by

$$N(\varepsilon - j) = \int_0^{\varepsilon - j} N(h)\,dh. \tag{2}$$

If the intensity E of excitation of these pathways is given by

$$E = f(S - h) = f(\varepsilon - j - h), \tag{3}$$

where $f(S - h)$ is of the form discussed in chapter ii, then the total intensity of excitation of the pathways N_c is given by

$$E_T = \int_0^{\varepsilon - j} N(h) f(\varepsilon - j - h)\,dh \tag{4}$$

and is a monotonically increasing function of $(\varepsilon - j)$. As $\varepsilon - j$ reaches its maximum value and begins to decrease, E_T also decreases.

Consider the case in which the constants of the pathways N_c are such that for each pathway the asymptotic value E_a of E is practically reached for a rather small value Δ of $S - h$, and that E_a is the same for all neuroelements N_c. Then, for all pathways for which $S - h > \Delta$, the intensity of excitation will be E_a, independent of h. Hence,

$$E_T = E_a \int_0^{\varepsilon - j - \Delta} N(h)\, dh + \int_{\varepsilon - j - \Delta}^{\varepsilon - j} N(h) f(\varepsilon - j - h)\, dh\,. \tag{5}$$

When $\varepsilon - j$ is much larger than Δ, the second integral in (5) may be neglected. Thus, except for small values of $\varepsilon - j$, we have approximately

$$E_T = E_a \int_0^{\varepsilon - j} N(h)\, dh\,. \tag{6}$$

The intensity E_T is still a monotonically increasing function of $\varepsilon - j$.

Let each of the pathways N_c lead to a conditioning circuit of the type discussed in chapters vii and ix, so that the excitation of each pathway N_c may be made a conditioned stimulus to a reaction R, produced unconditionally by a stimulus S_u. Consider a time interval τ which is shorter than the time it takes for $\varepsilon - j$ to reach its maximum. In this interval E_T is a monotonically increasing function of the time t. Suppose we present at $t = 0$ the stimulus S_c and follow it exactly after τ seconds by S_u. At the time when S_u is applied, a number $N(\tau)$ of pathways N_c is excited by S_c, $N(\tau)$ being given by (2), in which $\varepsilon - j$ is taken for the time τ. The total intensity of their excitation is given by (6). If the procedure of the presentation of S_c, followed τ seconds by S_u, is repeated a sufficient number of times, then the $N(\tau)$ pathways become conditioned to R. If after this we present S_c alone, without following it by S_u, then at each time $t_1 < \tau$ the number of excited pathways $N(t_1)$ will be less than $N(\tau)$; also $E_T(t_1) < E_T(\tau)$. Both $N(t_1)$ and $E(t_1)$ will increase in the interval 0–τ. Hence, the intensity of R will also increase from zero to its maximum value at $t = \tau$. For $t > \tau$, the intensity of R will not increase, because, although the number of pathways excited by $\varepsilon - j$ does increase above $N(\tau)$, those additional pathways N_c with thresholds $h > (\varepsilon - j)_\tau$ have not been excited previously and therefore have not been conditioned to R, while the pathways of threshold $h < (\varepsilon - j)_\tau$ are all, except a small number, corresponding to Δ, excited with the same intensity E_a. Hence, the conditioned response R will reach its maximum for $t = \tau$. We have here one of the characteristics of a delayed reflex.[1]

In this case, however, the delayed reflex, while developing its maximum value at $t = \tau$, will have a finite value also for any $t_1 < \tau$. We may now complicate the picture by considering the case in which each pathway N_c with a threshold h_i sends inhibiting pathways to connections of all pathways of thresholds $h_k (k \neq i)$. If

$N(h)$ has a maximum for $h_m > 0$ and if the maximum value of $\varepsilon - j$ is less then h_m, so that we are confined to the ascending part of the $N(h)$-curve, then at $t = \tau$ the excited pathways with thresholds $h_\tau = (\varepsilon - j)_\tau - \Delta \sim (\varepsilon - j)_\tau$ are much more numerous than the pathways with thresholds $h_{t_1} = (\varepsilon - j)_{t_1}$, which were excited first at the moment $t_1 < \tau$. The inhibitory effect of the pathways with thresholds h_τ on those with thresholds h_{t_1} will therefore be greater than the inhibitory effect of pathways with threshold h_{t_1} on those with thresholds h_τ. As a result, those with thresholds h_{t_1} will be inhibited completely.

If the inhibition acts on the conditioning circuits so as to bring them back into the nonexcited state, then, as pathways of higher thresholds h_τ become conditioned, those of lower thresholds become permanently inhibited. Thus as $\varepsilon - j$ increases, upon presentation of S_c there will be no response until $\varepsilon - j$ exceeds a threshold h_r, which is pretty close to h_τ. Since those are excited only for a t which is close enough to τ, the delayed conditioned reflex will become "concentrated" around the moment τ.

Using the fundamental equations developed in chapters ii, viii, and ix and varying in different ways the foregoing scheme, we can develop an exact mathematical theory of the phenomenon. Here is a problem that offers interesting possibilities.

Previous to the development of the fundamental postulates discussed in chapter ii and of the theory of conditioning discussed in chapters viii and ix, N. Rashevsky[2] developed a somewhat different theory of delayed reflexes, a theory which has the disadvantage that, besides those adopted here, certain additional mechanisms are postulated. That theory also does not agree, except very roughly, with the equations for conditioning developed in chapter ix. Since, however, the mathematical setup used suggests a definite mathematical setup for the development of the above-outlined theory of delayed reflexes and since the results obtained are of some interest, we shall discuss it here.

The intensity of the conditioned response is taken to be proportional to

$$I(1 - e^{-an}), \tag{7}$$

where I is the intensity of the *central* excitation at the time of conditioning, n the number of repetitions of the conditioned and unconditioned stimuli taken simultaneously, and a a constant, depending, among other things, on the intervals between successive repetitions. We consider here the latter as being kept constant. Thus we have

$$R = FI(1 - e^{-an}), \tag{8}$$

where F is a factor of proportionality, itself depending on various other constants. Let us now consider that a conditioned peripheral stimulus S_c elicits a central excitation process which is propagated, wavelike, over a number of centers. Again we may make a number of different assumptions both as to the arrangement of the centers over which the excitation wave travels and as to the shape of the "wave." And again, for the sake of simplicity and definiteness, we shall pick out two simple hypotheses. Their choice is arbitrary but does not exclude any other more complex possibilities.

We consider a linear arrangement of the centers and consider that the "wave" has a very steep front, falling off to the rear (Fig. 1, solid line). With sufficient approximation, such a curve may be represented by

$$I(x) = I_0 e^{-\beta x}, \tag{9}$$

as shown by the dotted line. We also restrict ourselves in this paper to the case in which the "tail" of the wave falls off very rapidly—in other words, where $\beta > 1$. This does not introduce any limitations in principle but simplifies considerably our formulae.

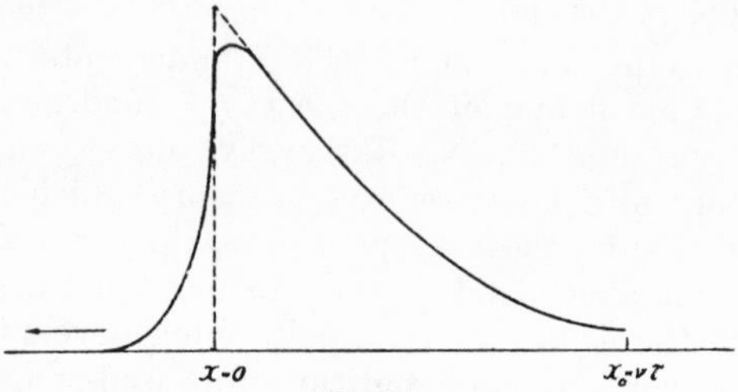

FIG. 1

Let the wave travel from right to left, with a constant velocity v. We shall choose for the point occupied by the "front" τ seconds after the stimulation, $x = 0$. Then at the moment of stimulation $t = 0$, the "front" of the wave is created and begins to travel from the point $x_0 = v\tau$. Any center, occupying the position x, is reached by the "front" of the wave at a time

$$t = \tau - \frac{x}{v} \quad (\text{where } 0 < x < x_0). \tag{10}$$

At the moment τ, that is, τ seconds after the conditioned stimulus, let an unconditioned stimulus S_u be produced, resulting in an unconditioned reflex R_u, and let the duration of S_u be so short that during this duration the wave produced by S_c does not move appreciably. Then, since any center between $x = 0$ and $x = x_0 = v\tau$ is being stimulated simultaneously with S_u, all those centers will begin to be conditioned to the reflex R_u; and if the whole procedure is repeated a sufficient number of times, the stimulation of any center x will result in a reflex $R_c(x)$, according to (8). But the quantity I in (8) is given by (9). Therefore, the intensity of the reflex $R_c(x)$ from any center x will be the weaker, the larger the x. If, after a sufficient number of repetitions, S_c is applied, then the excitation front reaches a center x at the time t given by (10). At this moment t the center x will elicit a response $R_c(x)$, the intensity of which will be proportional to

$$I(t) = I(x) = I_0 e^{-\beta x} = I_0 e^{-\beta v(\tau - t)}. \tag{11}$$

In other words, the conditioned response will be the stronger, the closer t is to τ. If, during the process of conditioning, the unconditioned stimulus is always applied τ seconds after the conditioned stimulus, then the maximum conditioned response will also be elicited through the center, which is reached by the wave-front exactly τ seconds after the conditioned stimulation.

At the moment t the wave-front reaches the center x. None of the centers which lie at $x' < x$ are stimulated yet. But all centers between x and x_0 are stimulated, the intensity of stimulation being given by (11). Therefore, the total response at the moment t, after conditioning is completed, is given by

$$\begin{aligned} R_c(t) &= F \int_x^{x_0} I(x)\,dx = \frac{FI_0}{\beta}\,(e^{-\beta x} - e^{-\beta x_0}) \\ &= \frac{FI_0}{\beta}\,(e^{-\beta v(\tau - t)} - e^{-\beta v\tau}). \end{aligned}$$

The response $R_c(t)$ is also strongest for $t = \tau$.

More complex and interesting results are obtained if we consider that the efferent conditioned pathways send inhibitory pathways to centers located along x. In this case, as we have seen, as a stronger reflex $R(x)$ from a center near $x = 0$ develops, it will inhibit the other centers lying farther from $x = 0$, so that eventually only centers in the immediate neighborhood of $x = 0$ will elicit a reflex; all others will be completely inhibited. Mathematically, the situation is described by stating that the intensity I in (8) is decreasing gradually as more neuroelements become conditioned in other centers. If a center x_1 elicits a response $R(x_1)$, then a center at x is inhibited to an extent proportional to $R(x_1)$, so that the intensity of excitation $I(x)$, which originally was $I_0e^{-\beta x}$, now becomes $I_0e^{-\beta x} - bR(x_1)$, b being a constant of proportionality. The total intensity at x is now given by

$$I(x) = I_0e^{-\beta x} - b \sum R(x_i), \tag{12}$$

the summation being taken over all those centers x_i which are not completely inhibited, owing to the activity of other centers. When the number of centers is very large, we can replace the sum by an integral and thus find for the determination of $I(x)$ the functional equation

$$I(x) = I_0e^{-\beta x} - b \int_0^k R(x)\,dx\,, \tag{13}$$

or, introducing for $R(x)$ its expression (8),

$$I(x) = I_0e^{-\beta x} - bF \int_0^k I(x)\,(1 - e^{-an})\,dx\,. \tag{14}$$

The upper limit k of integration is itself a function of n; for, as the conditioning of a center proceeds, $R(x)$ increases, the inhibition of the other centers increases also, and some of them, namely, those that had a small initial $I(x) = I_0e^{-\beta x}$, will become completely inhibited. Therefore, they will not contribute anything to the inhibition of other centers. We can determine k in the following way: We first solve (14) for any k, and thus obtain I as a function of the variable x and the parameters k and n:

$$I = I(x, k, n). \tag{15}$$

Then, since the integration in (14) is to be carried out only up to such a value of x for which the centers are not completely inhibited —in other words, for which $I > 0$—we find k as the root of the equation

$$I(k, k, n) = 0\,, \tag{16}$$

obtained from (15) by substituting k for x. Equation (16) then gives us k as a function of n.

The functional equation (14) was solved approximately by Rashevsky. Subsequently, A. S. Householder and E. Amelotti published an exact solution.[3] We now follow their presentation.

We notice that the last term in (14) is a constant independent of x. Let us denote it by μ. Then

$$\mu = \lambda \int_0^k I(x)\,dx\,, \tag{17}$$

where

$$\lambda = bF(1 - e^{-an}). \tag{18}$$

Hence, (14) may be written

$$I(x) = I_0 e^{-\beta x} - \mu\,. \tag{19}$$

Introducing (19) into (17) and solving, we find

$$\mu = \frac{I_0 \lambda (1 - e^{-\beta k})}{\beta (1 + \lambda k)}. \tag{20}$$

Hence,

$$I(x) = I_0 \left[e^{-\beta x} - \frac{\lambda (1 - e^{-\beta k})}{\beta (1 + \lambda k)} \right]. \tag{21}$$

To find k, we replace x by k in (21) and set the result equal to zero, according to (16). After rearrangements, we find

$$e^{\beta k} - \beta k - 1 = \frac{\beta}{\lambda}. \tag{22}$$

The left member of this equation in k vanishes with k and increases monotonically. It is, moreover, independent of λ. The right member is always positive and decreases as λ increases. Hence, for every λ, and therefore for every n, equation (22) is satisfied by a unique value of k; and this value decreases monotonically as λ, and hence as n, increases. For any such value of k, equation (21) may be written

$$I(x) = I_0 (e^{-\beta x} - e^{-\beta k}). \tag{23}$$

Thus we find that, as n increases, k decreases and $I(x)$ decreases at each center x. The conditioned response, which initially is spread over all the centers between 0 and $x_0 = v\tau$, gradually "concentrates" around $x = 0$ only. In other words, while in the early stages of conditioning a conditioned response will be elicited at any time t (where $0 < t < \tau$), after a sufficient number of repetitions a response will be produced only between t_1 and τ, where

$$0 < t_1 = \tau - \frac{k_0}{v}, \tag{24}$$

and where k_0 is the asymptotic value which k approaches with increasing λ, and which is obtained from (22) by replacing λ by bF.

Householder and Amelotti have also investigated the case in

which the inhibiting effect of one neuroelement upon another is an increasing or decreasing function of the distance between the two neuroelements.[3] The results, in general, are pretty much the same, though some quite new possibilities do appear in some special cases.

Consider, now, the following situation.[2] Let, at the moment $t = 0$, a stimulus S_0 produce an unconditioned response R_1, which, in turn, results in the production, after a time τ, of a stimulus S_1, resulting in an unconditioned response $\overline{R}_1$, the opposite of R_1. For instance, the sight of an alley in a maze may be considered as S_0; R_1 is the response to that, consisting in running into the alley. If the latter has a blind end, then this produces the reaction $\overline{R}_1$, the retracing of steps. If we consider, for simplicity, that the speed of the locomotion of the animal in the alley is constant and equal to q, then

$$\tau = \frac{l}{q}, \tag{25}$$

where l is the length of the alley.

If the procedure is repeated a sufficient number of times, then S_0 becomes conditioned to $\overline{R}_1$. The response $\overline{R}_1$ becomes a delayed conditioned reflex to S_0, the unconditioned stimulus being S_1. Since, during conditioning, the interval between S_0 and S_1 is equal to τ_1, therefore the maximum intensity of $\overline{R}_1$ as a conditioned reflex to S_0 will occur τ seconds after S_0, that is, at the same moment as $\overline{R}_1$ will be produced by S_1 unconditionally. But at the beginning of the conditioning process, when the inhibition is not yet complete, a certain amount of the response $\overline{R}_1$ will be elicited also at the time $t = 0$. This response will be elicited through the center $x = x_0$. Its intensity is therefore obtained by putting in (21) $x = x_0$ and introducing (21) into (8), in which we also put $R = \overline{R}_1$. Moreover, since we consider such early stages of conditioning, for which the response at $x = x_0$ is still positive, we must take $k = x_0$. This gives, because of (18)

$$\overline{R}_1(x_0, \lambda) = \frac{\lambda I_0}{b}\left\{e^{-\beta x_0} - \frac{\lambda(1 - e^{-\beta x_0})}{\beta(1 + \lambda x_0)}\right\}. \tag{26}$$

Remembering that $x_0 = v\tau$ and using (25), we obtain from (26)

$$\overline{R}_1(l, \lambda) = \frac{\lambda I_0}{b}\left\{e^{-\beta v l/q} - \frac{\lambda q(1 - e^{-\beta v l/q})}{\beta(q + \lambda v l)}\right\}. \tag{27}$$

For small values of λ or, because of (18), for small values of n, $\overline{R}_1$

at $t = 0$ increases with λ, and therefore also with n. Then, as the "concentration" effect, discussed above, becomes more and more pronounced, $\bar{R}_1$ at $t = 0$ will begin to decrease, until it may even become negative, which will happen when k becomes less than x_0. If in its initial increase $\bar{R}_1$ at $t = 0$ exceeds R_1, then S_0 will not produce R_1 at all, for, as R_1 is produced, it is immediately compensated by the opposite $\bar{R}_1$. Thus, after several entries into the alley, which result in returns, owing to a blind end, the sight S_0 of the alley will not produce R_1. The "wrong" alley is eliminated.

The number n of repetitions necessary to produce such an elimination, or the corresponding λ, is obtained as a root of the equation

$$\frac{\lambda I_0}{b}\left\{ e^{-\beta vl/q} - \frac{\lambda q(1 - e^{-\beta vl/q})}{\beta(q + \lambda vl)} \right\} = R_1. \tag{28}$$

This is quadratic in λ and does not always have real roots. In order that an elimination may be possible at all, some relations between the parameters, characterizing the brain of the animal, such as I_0, b, β, as well as between the length l of the alley and the speed q of the animal, must be satisfied. When the necessary relations are satisfied, then (28), together with (18), gives us the number of repetitions necessary to eliminate the alley, in terms of the constants characteristic of the animal and in terms of the length of the alley.

The foregoing scheme for the mechanism of the elimination of a wrong alley is decidedly too crude. Actually, the intensity of $\bar{R}_1$ as a conditioned reflex to S_0 increases more rapidly near the end of the alley, that is, for t approaching τ. When, after a sufficient number of repetitions, at some point $l' < l$, $\bar{R}_1$ becomes equal to and then exceeds R_1, the animal will turn back at that point. With each repetition l' becomes smaller, and this has an effect similar to a gradual reduction of the interval τ between the conditioned and the unconditioned stimulus during conditioning. We thus obtain a more complex picture of a gradual elimination of an alley. It leads to much more complex expressions, which have recently been derived and discussed by H. Landahl.[4]

REFERENCES

1. I. P. Pavlov, *Conditioned Reflexes* (London: Oxford University Press, 1927), p. 88.
2. N. Rashevsky, *Psychometrika*, 1, 265, 1936.
3. A. S. Householder and E. Amelotti, *Psychometrika*, 2, 255, 1937.
4. H. Landahl, *Psychometrika*, 3, 169, 1938.

CHAPTER XIV

APPLICATIONS OF THE FOREGOING TO LEARNING

An interesting application of the developments of chapters ix and xiii has been given by H. D. Landahl[1].

Consider the net shown in Figure 1. Let a stimulus S_c, presented alone, produce a response R_c. Let R_c produce a change either in the environment or in the organism, and let that change R_1 act as a stimulus itself, which, through the pathway V, excites a circuit C, which sends an excitatory pathway to the connection s_c. Similarly, the stimulus S_w, presented alone, produces a response R_w, which, through R_1, excites the circuit C', which *inhibits* the

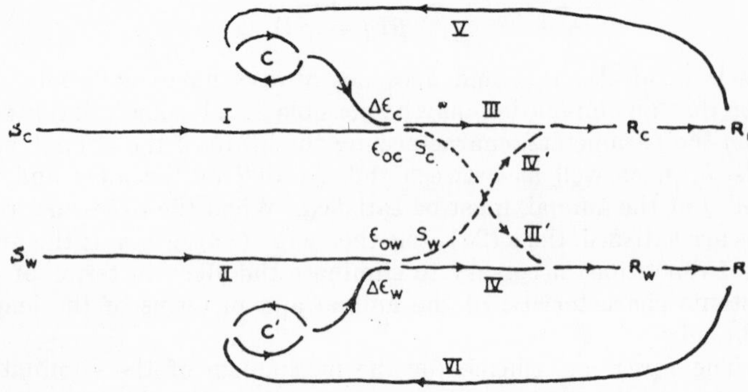

FIG. 1

connection s_w. Let the circuits C and C' each represent a large group of circuits of different thresholds. Let the part of the structure composed of neuroelements *III*, *III'*, *IV*, and *IV'* be equivalent to the corresponding part of Figure 1 of chapter vi. Now suppose that S_c and S_w are presented several times simultaneously and kept each time sufficiently long so that we can consider stationary states. At the first presentation, neither C nor C' was excited, and therefore the amounts ε_c and ε_w of ε which are developed at s_c and s_w respectively will be those produced by the pathways *I* and *II*. We shall denote them by ε_{0c} and ε_{0w} correspondingly. Let the stimuli S_c and S_w be of approximately the same intensity, and let the constants of pathways *I* and *II* be identical (chap. vi). Whether response R_c or R_w will be made on the first presentation will be determined by accidental fluctuations, such as were discussed in chapter vi. The probability P_w of R_w is determined by equation (7) of chapter vi, in which, instead of $\epsilon_1 - \epsilon_2$, we now substitute $\varepsilon_{0c} - \varepsilon_{0w}$. If the response R_c, which we shall call the "correct" response, is produced at the first presentation, then circuit C will be activated, and this results in a permanent increase of ϵ_c. According to what we have seen in chapter vi, this will increase the probability P_c of R_c at a subsequent presentation, because P_c increases with $\varepsilon_c - \varepsilon_w$. Each new repetition of R_c increases ε_c, because, according to the mechanism discussed in chapter ix (p. 87), each repetition of R_c throws more and more of the individual circuits C into an excited state. Hence, with each correct response R_c, the probability P_c of a further correct response increases. Similarly, we see that each "wrong" response R_w decreases the probability P_w of a subsequent wrong response by decreasing ε_w *at* s_w.

Suppose that, after S_c and S_w have been presented together n times, the response R_c has been made, say, c times and the response R_w, w times. We shall refer to n as the number of trials, c as the number of correct responses, and w as the number of wrong responses. Then P_c, the probability of a correct response, may be identified with the proportion of correct responses, so that, approximately,

$$P_c = \frac{dc}{dn}; \tag{1}$$

and, similarly,

$$P_w = \frac{dw}{dn}. \tag{2}$$

Thus

$$P_c + P_w = 1; \quad c + w = n. \tag{3}$$

As an approximation we may assume that the amount of ε_c increases linearly with the number c of correct responses, while the amount ε_w decreases linearly with the number w of wrong responses. Thus, denoting by b and β two positive constants, we have

$$\varepsilon_c = \varepsilon_{0c} + bc, \tag{4}$$

and

$$\varepsilon_w = \varepsilon_{0w} - \beta w. \tag{5}$$

Introducing equation (12) of chapter vi into equations (7) of chapter vi, evaluating the integral by elementary methods, and substituting $\varepsilon_c - \varepsilon_w$ for $\varepsilon_1 - \varepsilon_2$, we find,[2] for $\varepsilon_c > \varepsilon_w$:

$$P_w = \tfrac{1}{2} e^{-k(\varepsilon_c - \varepsilon_w)}. \tag{6}$$

The essential property of the mechanism shown in Figure 1 is that the correct stimulus in a sense "reinforces" itself; the wrong one inhibits itself. In actual situations we note that we tend to repeat any pleasant stimulus and avoid any unpleasant one. This suggests that the sensation of pleasure is connected with some sort of central excitation, while the sensation of pain is concerned with some central inhibition. Leaving the elaboration of this idea to a later chapter (xvi), we shall here tentatively identify such reactions as R_c with pleasant reactions, for example, with those leading to rewards, while such a reaction as R_w we shall identify with those leading to punishments.

Let up apply these results to the particular experimental situation which arises when Lashley's jumping apparatus is used. Here an animal is forced to jump toward either of two stimuli. Choice of one leads to reward, choice of the other may lead to punishment. If we then introduce equations (4) and (5) into (6) and eliminate P_w and c by means of (2) and (3), we obtain a differential equation in w and n. From this, with the initial condition $w = 0$ for $n = 0$, we obtain, by elementary integrations,

$$w = \frac{1}{k(b-\beta)} \log \frac{2be^{k(\varepsilon_{0c}-\varepsilon_{0w})}}{2be^{k(\varepsilon_{0c}-\varepsilon_{0w})} - (b-\beta)(1-e^{-kbn})} \tag{7}$$

for $b \neq \beta$. Equation (7) represents a curve which rises asymptotically to a limiting value. For $b = \beta$, the result represents also a rising curve which approaches a limit exponentially. In terms of the mechanism, we may consider the experiment as requiring a discrimination between two stimuli whose values, in effect,

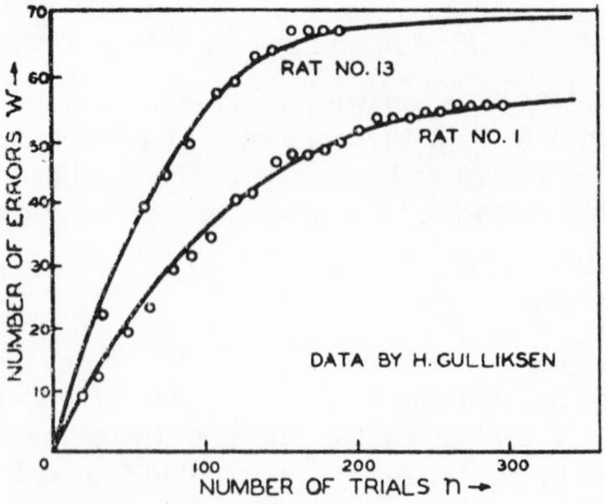

FIG. 2

change in successive trials. The correct stimulus becomes effectively larger owing to the conditioning, while the wrong decreases. Thus the probability of a wrong response diminishes.

In Figure 2 is shown a comparison between the theory and the experimental data by H. Gulliksen.[3] The lower and upper curves were obtained, respectively, by taking $\varepsilon_{0c} - \varepsilon_{0w} = 0$, $kb = 0.0121$, $\beta = 0$, and $k(\varepsilon_{0c} - \varepsilon_{0w}) = -0.46$, $kb = 0.0229$, $\beta = 0$. H. Gulliksen originally interpreted his data on the basis of a different theory.

In general, R_w does not necessarily need to inhibit the connection s_w. It may merely result in a lesser increase of ε_w than the increase in ε_c produced by R_c. The constants b and β are also, in general, functions of the times t_c and t_w between the presentation of any stimulus S_c or S_w and the responses R_c and R_w, respectively. Those more general cases have been discussed by H. D. Landahl,[1] and A. S. Householder and H. D. Landahl.[4]

It is possible to generalize the mechanism discussed above so as to include a choice from among any number N of stimuli, by constructing a net similar to that of Figure 1, but with N afferents and $\frac{1}{2}N(N-1)$ inhibitory pathways (cf. chap. iii). Suppose that out of the N stimuli there is but one correct stimulus, S_c. Instead of considering the individual wrong responses, we may consider their average effect. An expression somewhat different from (6) has been introduced by H. D. Landahl[1] for this case. Equation (6) shows that for two stimuli the probability P_w of a wrong response equals $\frac{1}{2}$ when the stimuli are equal. This is because in that case the correct and wrong responses are determined by pure chance. With increasing $\varepsilon_c - \varepsilon_w$, that is, with increasing bias toward a correct response, P_w tends exponentially to zero. If there are N *equal* stimuli, the probability of the correct response by pure chance is $1/N$, and therefore the probability P_w is

$$P_w = \frac{N-1}{N} \quad \text{for} \quad \varepsilon_c - \bar{\varepsilon}_w = 0. \tag{8}$$

The exact expression for the variation of P_w with $\varepsilon_c - \bar{\varepsilon}_w$ for the case of N stimuli has not been derived. H. D. Landahl assumes that it decreases approximately to zero exponentially with $\varepsilon_c - \bar{\varepsilon}_w$. He thus puts instead of (6):

$$P_w = \frac{N-1}{N} e^{-k(\varepsilon_c - \bar{\varepsilon}_w)}. \tag{9}$$

In the experimental situation, let a stimulus S_i' ($i = 1, 2, \cdots, M$) accompany a group of stimuli S_j ($j = 1, 2, \cdots, N$) of equal intensity, one and only one of which will elicit its response. Among the stimuli S_j is a stimulus S_{ic}, the "correct" stimulus corresponding to S_i', which, when chosen, results in a reward. Response to any other stimulus S_j when accompanied by S_i' results in punishment, or at least in no reward. The number N may be referred to as the number of possible choices, while the number M is the number of associations to be learned in the experiment. After a wrong response is made, the experimenter may choose to assist (prompt) the subject in making the correct response, or he may not. He may do so each time, not at all, or, in general, some fraction, $1-f$, of the times. Thus f is a variable under the control of the experimenter, just as M and N are. We shall assume that, throughout any particular experiment, M, N, and f are not changed. Then

$$\varepsilon_c = \varepsilon_{0c} + bc + b(1-f)w\,, \tag{10}$$

because conditioning improves with each correct response as well as with a fraction $(1-f)$ of the wrong responses. The prompted correct responses are not counted in c, so that we do not change the relation $n = c + w$. At each wrong choice, a quantity β is subtracted from ε_{0w}. This contributes only $\beta/(N-1)$ to the average. Thus

$$\bar{\varepsilon}_w = \varepsilon_{0w} - \frac{\beta w}{N-1}\,. \tag{11}$$

The parameter b gives a measure of the amount of learning per trial. If a response to one stimulus has no effect on the centers corresponding to other stimuli, the n is independent of M. But, if the response to one stimulus results in the stimulation of inhibitory neuroelements terminating at the various other conditioning centers, then b will be less when there are more items M to be learned. We may account for this by introducing, as a rough approximation, the relation

$$b = \frac{\eta}{k}\, e^{-\zeta M}\,, \tag{12}$$

where η and ζ are two parameters replacing bk.

Assuming $\varepsilon_{0w} = \varepsilon_{0c}$, substituting everywhere P and P_w' for P_c and P_w correspondingly, substituting (1), (10), and (11) in (13), and eliminating c by means of (3), we obtain a differential equation in w and n. With the initial condition $w = 0$ for $n = 0$ and with b eliminated by means of relation (12), the solution of the differential equation obtained by elementary integrations is, putting $Nf - f - \beta/b = A$,

$$w = \frac{(N-1)e^{\zeta M}}{\eta A} \log \frac{N}{e^{-\eta n e^{-\zeta M}} + N - A}. \tag{13}$$

In the experimental set-up, used by H. D. Landahl,[1] the subject did not pay attention to wrong answers. In such a case we may put $\beta = 0$ in equation (13).

This equation gives the number w of errors as a function of the number n of trials for any number M of items, for any number of N possible choices, and for any fraction $(1 - f)$ of prompting by the experimenter. All this involves only two parameters, ζ and η. As we have considered a highly oversimplified mechanism and introduced a number of approximations, it is not to be expected that the predictions of equation (13) will hold over too wide a range of values of M and N.

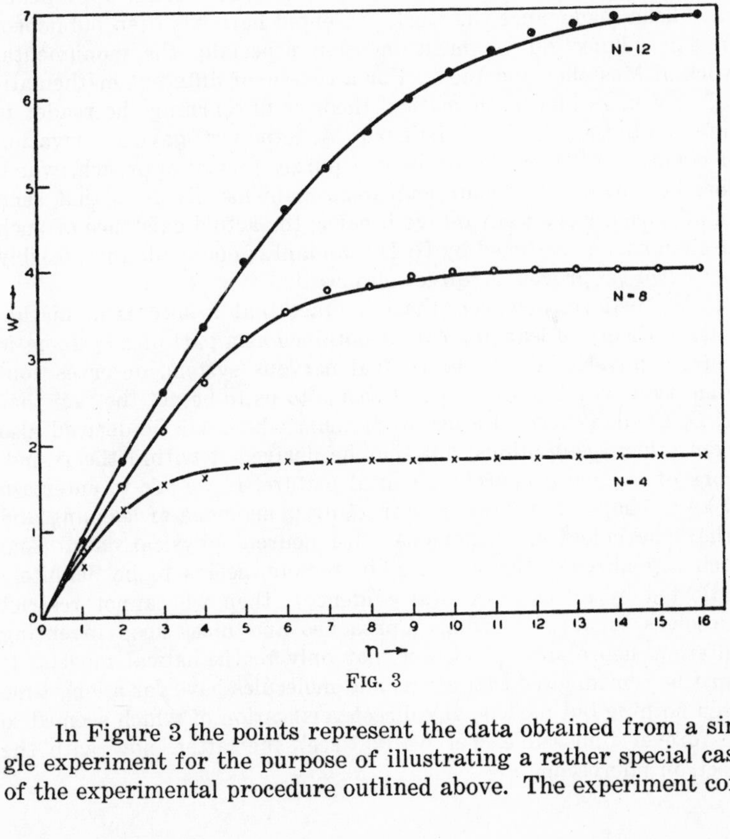

FIG. 3

In Figure 3 the points represent the data obtained from a single experiment for the purpose of illustrating a rather special case of the experimental procedure outlined above. The experiment corresponds to the case in which $M = N$ and $f = 1$. Taking $\eta = 1.15$ and $\zeta = 0.098$, we obtain the three theoretical curves for which $N = 4$, $N = 8$, and $N = 12$, respectively. These values of η and ζ are determined from one point of each of any two curves. The third curve is then completely determined. But another family of such curves is also determined by equation (13), without any additional parameters, for the case in which prompting follows each wrong response, i.e., $f = 0$. In fact, f can be given any value in the range of $0 \leqq f \leqq 1$, and M and N need not be equal.

It must be strongly emphasized here that the theory of learning developed by H. D. Landahl and presented in this chapter is not the only mathematically developed theory of learning. Prior to Landahl's work some formal theories of learning have been proposed. One of them, proposed by G. H. Gulliksen, has already been mentioned. A number of other different mathematical approaches have been made since the work presented here has been published. In this connection we must mention especially the monumental work of Mosteller and Bush[5]. For a review of different mathematical as well as non mathematical theories of learning the reader is referred to the book by E. Hilgard[6]. A. Rapoport[7] gave a derivation of equation (13) on the basis of a purely formal approach, which does not involve any neurological mechanisms. He feels that such an approach has an advantage because the actual existence of such mechanisms as assumed by H. D. Landahl is doubtful, and possibly can never be proven by direct observation.

We believe, however, that the fact that a successful mathematical theory of learning can be obtained as a part of a *systematic* neurobiophysical theory of central nervous system, deserves consideration. The important point seems to us to be not the fact that H. D. Landahl derived a useful formula which can be derived also from other assumptions, but that he derived it within the framework of a general neurobiophysical picture. If we are to entertain at all the hope of eventually connecting phenomena of learning and other psychological phenomena with neurobiophysical data, (and such a goal, even though possibly remote, seems to be definitely indicated by all experimental evidence), then we cannot restrict ourselves to purely formal approaches and must keep inventing different neurobiophysical, and not only mathematical models. It must be remembered that atoms and molecules have for a long time been nothing but models, any direct verification of which seemed to be forever impossible. Yet we do "see" the latter, now with the electron microscope.

Amongst other neurobiophysical models of learning, different from the one proposed by H. D. Landahl, we should mention the model of A. Shimbel[8].

REFERENCES

1. H. D. Landahl, *Bull. Math. Biophysics*, 3, 13, 71, 1941.
2. H. D. Landahl, *Psychometrika*, 3, 107, 1938.
3. H. Gulliksen, *Jour. Gen. Psychol.*, 11, 395, 1934.
4. A. S. Householder and H. D. Landahl, *Mathematical Biophysics of the Central Nervous System* (Bloomington, Ind.: Principia Press, 1945).
5. Robert R. Bush and Frederick Mosteller, *Stochastic Models or Learning*, (New York: John Wiley and Sons, 1955).
6. E. R. Hilgard, *Theories of Learning*, (New York: Appleton-Century-Crofts, Inc., 1956).
7. A. Rapoport, *Bull. Math. Biophysics*, 18, 317, 1956.
8. A. Shimbel, *Bull. Math. Biophysics*, 12, 241, 1956.

CHAPTER XV

MATHEMATICAL BIOPHYSICS OF RATIONAL LEARNING AND THINKING

Whenever an animal or individual, after having eliminated a given situation by trial, afterward eliminates some new wrong situations without trying them at all, we speak of the presence of "rational elements" in his learning. The case of pure rational learning is obtained when an elimination by trial of one wrong situation results in an elimination of all other wrong situations without trials, by "pure inference."

In order that the elimination of one possibility should result in a partial or total elimination of another, there must be some similarity between the corresponding two stimuli, or, in logical terms, there must be some criteria common to the two situations. If all situations to be tried out have no such common criterion, then, no matter how ingenious the person may be, he can never eliminate a case by reasoning based on previous experience. Thus, if a number of playing cards are scattered face down at random on a table and it is required to pick up, say, all the spades, keeping the right card and returning the wrong one to the table, then, no matter how ingenious a person may be, the elimination of one card does not increase his knowledge of the others. If, however, the spades are arranged all in the same direction, then, with a sufficient amount of intelligence, the person may pick up all correct cards after only one or two trials. Biophysically speaking, all this means that, in order to make any reasoning or insight possible, several different situations characterized by different stimulus patterns must have some elements of those patterns in common.

The case of a rational solution of a problem may be schematically represented in the following way. Let the past history of the individual be such that, whenever he reacted by the reaction R to a stimulus pattern $T_1 = (S_i, S_k, S_s)$, whether presented alone or in combination with other stimuli, R resulted in the delayed production of the opposite reaction $\bar{R}$. Let the individual meet several stimulus situations: T_2, T_3, etc. Let one of them, say,

$$T_i = (S_i, S_r, S_k, S_s, S_p, S_q),$$

contain among its elements the elements S_i, S_k, S_s, which constitute T_1, and let the others contain none of these elements. We say that

T_i "contains" T_1. Since T_1 and T_i have common elements, they excite some common neuroelements in the brain centers. If, in spite of the fact that in T_i the elements S_i, S_k, and S_s are, so to speak, "masked" by the presence of others, they still produce the reaction $\bar{R}$, to which T_1 has been conditioned, then $\bar{R}$ is produced by T_i also, although T_i may be presented for the first time. In other words, any pattern which contains the pattern T_1 is eliminated without any trial if T_1 has been previously eliminated by several trials. Similarly, we may consider the case in which the pattern T_i is eliminated not because it "contains" T_1 but because it has some elements in common with T_1.

Let us first consider the case in which the elements of the patterns are all similar quantitatively and qualitatively. Let the pattern T_1 consist of n such elements. Again considering the structure represented by Figure 8 of chapter iii, we may write equation (44) of that chapter, omitting the subscripts in the S's, thus:

$$\varepsilon - j = K_1 S - K_2(n-1)S + K_3(n-1) - K_4\,, \tag{1}$$

with

$$\left.\begin{aligned} &K_1 = P\alpha_1 I_1 > 0; \quad K_2 = PQ\alpha_1\alpha_3 I_1 I_3 > 0;\\ &K_3 = Q\alpha_3 I_3(P\alpha_1 I_1 h_1 + h_3) > 0; \quad K_4 = P\alpha_1 I_1 h_1 > 0;\\ &K_2 S > K_3\,, \end{aligned}\right\} \tag{2}$$

where P and Q are defined by equation (45) of chapter iii. As we have seen, when n exceeds a critical value, which now may be written

$$n > n_1 = 1 + \frac{K_1 S - K_4 - h_2}{K_2 S - K_3}\,, \tag{3}$$

the excitation is not transmitted through the connections. Hence a pattern with too many elements can neither produce a response nor be conditioned to one.

Consider, now, a stimulus combination T_i, consisting of $n + m$ elements, stimulated with equal intensity S; and let the n elements constitute the combination T_1, which has been previously conditioned to a response R. Owing to the inhibitory effect of the additional m elements, the amount of $\varepsilon - j$ at each of the connections s_i will now be less than that given by (1). It is now given by

$$\left.\begin{aligned} (\varepsilon - j)' = K_1 S - K_2(n+m-1)S&\\ + K_3(n+m-1) - K_4\,.& \end{aligned}\right\} \tag{4}$$

In order that $(\varepsilon - j)' < h_2$, so that no excitation will pass the connections s_i, we now must have

$$n > n_2 = 1 + \frac{K_1 S - K_4 - h_2}{K_2 S - K_3} - m. \tag{5}$$

Since $n_2 < n_1$, it may happen that

$$n_2 < n < n_1 . \tag{6}$$

In such a case the pattern T_1 will produce a response when presented alone; but the pattern T_i, which contains T_1, will not produce any response. A previously conditioned pattern becomes ineffective when a sufficient number m of new elements is added to it. If we consider n and $n + m$ as measuring the complexity of the combinations T_1 and T_i, then we may say that, if the complexity of T_1 is so great that T_1 can still just be conditioned to a response R, a relatively small addition makes T_1 unrecognizable, while less complex patterns are not so easily "masked." Moreover, if (6) holds, T_i cannot be conditioned at all to any response R, for T_i results in a complete central inhibition. We see that a pattern T_1 may be too complex to be rationally recognized as a part of another situation, yet can be learned alone by trial. But the other situation in this case is too complex to be learned even by trial.

Inequalities (3) and (5) imply also that $K_1 S - K_4 - h_2 > 0$, which means, physically, that S must be strong enough to stimulate at all.

We may consider a somewhat more general case, namely, that the additional m elements are stimulated with an intensity S' different from S. We then have, following the same argument that leads to equations (53) of chapter iii,

$$\left. \begin{aligned} (\varepsilon - j)' = K_1 S - (n-1)(K_2 S - K_3) \\ - K_4 - m(K_2 S' - K_3). \end{aligned} \right\} \tag{7}$$

Now $(\varepsilon - j)'$ becomes less than h_2 when

$$n > 1 + \frac{K_1 S - K_4 - h_2}{K_2 S - K_3} - \frac{K_2 S' - K_3}{K_2 S - K_3} m. \tag{8}$$

Comparison of (7) with (5) shows that, when $S' > S$, the inhibitory effect of the m additional elements is enhanced.

However, while (4) represents the value of $\varepsilon - j$ at any connection, corresponding either to one of the original n elements or to one of the additional m elements, (7) represents $\varepsilon - j$ only at connections corresponding to the n elements of T_1. At connections corresponding to the m additional elements we have

$$\left.\begin{aligned}(\varepsilon - j)'' = K_1 S' - K_4 - n(K_2 S - K_3) \\ - (m-1)(K_2 S' - K_3).\end{aligned}\right\} \qquad (9)$$

While, when (8) is satisfied, $(\varepsilon - j)' < 0$, $(\varepsilon - j)''$ still may be positive and even larger than h_2, provided that S' is sufficiently strong. We have the same situation as was discussed in chapter iii, page 31. If, then, $S' >> S$, the combination T_i can produce a response R through m connections. It can therefore also be conditioned to any response. In other words, we now have a situation T_i which is too complex to be learned rationally, owing to a previous experience of its part T_1, but which is simple enough to be learned by trial.

In chapter ii we developed equations for connective delays as functions of the intensities of external stimulations. Inasmuch as $\varepsilon - j$ acts on the pathways of class II as an external stimulus, similar considerations show that the larger the $\varepsilon - j$, the shorter the connection delay, both at s_i and at other connections lying more centrally. The exact expression for the total delay will, of course, depend on the special assumptions which we make about the arrangement of connections and the temporal character of the stimuli. This is an interesting problem, to be worked out along lines indicated in chapter iii. The total reaction time τ, which is a function of the connection delay, will be some function $f(\varepsilon - j - h_2)$ of $\varepsilon - j - h_2$:

$$\tau = f(\varepsilon - j - h_2), \qquad (10)$$

such that $f(x)$ decreases with increasing x. Since $(\varepsilon - j)$ decreases with increasing complexity $n + m$ of the situation, we see that τ will increase with increasing complexity. Formulae derived for τ should give us interesting relations for possible experimental verification.

In chapter iii we have seen that, while a total inhibition results when a sufficient number of afferent elements are excited equally, an excitation of a few centers will result if the corresponding few elements are excited much more strongly than the rest. We may describe this in psychological terms by saying that we perceive a few elements among a large group of others when they more strongly attract our attention, owing to stronger intensity, whereas a large number of simultaneous equal stimuli results in an absence of a definite perception.

Let us now consider a mechanism which consists of a spontaneous concentration of attention to a limited number p of elements for a period of time θ. In other words, when a number

$$m + n = N \tag{11}$$

of equal stimuli is presented, let a spontaneous physicochemical process in the brain increase the central excitation of p elements for a time θ, although the actual intensities of external stimuli of the p elements is the same as of the remaining $N - p$. Let this spontaneous process go on in a random fashion. That is, for an interval θ some p elements are spontaneously stimulated more strongly than the others. For another interval of duration θ, another group of p elements is spontaneously stimulated more strongly than the rest, and so on. Now let the situation T_i be presented, too complex to admit a recognition of T_1 as its part. Consider one particular set of p elements during a given interval. Let n' of those p elements belong to the n elements of the situation T_1, and m' to the additional m elements. Denote the uniform normal intensity of excitation of each element by S, while the excessive intensity of excitation of the p elements is

$$S' > \gamma S; \quad \gamma > 1 . \tag{12}$$

Let us first consider, for simplicity, the case in which both S and S' are constant. Remembering that

$$p = m' + n' , \tag{13}$$

we find for the value of $\varepsilon - j$ at the n' connections, corresponding to the elements of T_1, previously conditioned to R,

$$\left.\begin{aligned}(\varepsilon - j)_{n'} = K_1S' - K_4 - (p-1)(K_2S' - K_3)\\ - (K_2S - K_3)(N - p).\end{aligned}\right\} \tag{14}$$

In order to produce the response R, it is necessary that $(\varepsilon - j)_{n'} - h_2 > 0$. But even then it will take a time $\tau = f[(\varepsilon - j)_{n'} - h_2]$ to produce R. If $\theta < \tau$, then, before R is produced, the group of p selected elements will have changed; and for the new group the values n' and m', and therefore the value $(\varepsilon - j)_{n'}$ will, in general, be different. Hence, to insure a response always, it is necessary that

$$\theta \geqslant \tau , \tag{15}$$

or, on account of (10),

$$(\varepsilon - j)_{n'} - h_2 \geqslant \bar{f}(\theta), \tag{16}$$

where $\bar{f}(\theta)$ is the inverse function of $f(\theta)$, decreasing with increasing θ. Therefore, from (16) and (14) we get

$$\begin{aligned}K_1S' - K_4 - (p-1)(K_2S' - K_3)\\ - (N-p)(K_2S - K_3) - h_2 \geqslant \bar{f}(\theta),\end{aligned}$$

or, remembering (12),

$$p \leqslant 1 + \frac{K_1\gamma S - K_4 - (K_2 S - K_3)(N-1) - h_2 - f(\theta)}{K_2 S(\gamma - 1)}. \tag{17}$$

Because of (2), the right-hand side of (17) decreases with increasing N, having the largest value for $N = 1$. Hence, if

$$p > 1 + \frac{K_1\gamma S - K_4 - h_2 - f(\theta)}{K_2 S(\gamma - 1)}, \tag{18}$$

then (17) will never hold for any N, and no response to T_i will ever be produced. Again the right-hand side of (18) increases with S, tending, for very large S, to $1 + K_1\gamma/K_2(\gamma - 1)$. Therefore, if

$$p > 1 + \frac{K_1\gamma}{K_2(\gamma - 1)}, \tag{19}$$

then (18) is satisfied for any S, and (17) is never satisfied. But (19) expresses a relation between constants, characteristic of the individual. If those constants are such as to satisfy (19), a pattern T_1 will never be recognized by the individual as a part of the pattern T_i by a concentration of his attention to a fewer elements, if it is not recognized by direct inspection. No matter how many possible combinations $n' + m' = p$ the individual tries in this case, R will never be produced. If, however, (19) and (18) are not satisfied, then, for N which is not too large, (17) may be satisfied, in which case such a choice of n' and m' is possible, that R will be produced. If the random choice keeps up, R will finally be produced. We may say that for a sufficiently long contemplation of the problem, consisting in a recognition of T_1 as part of T_i, the problem will be solved rationally, provided N, the complexity, is not too large. However, individuals which are characterized by (19) cannot solve any problem of that type rationally.

In order, however, that a response R be obtained, it is not sufficient that p should satisfy (17). We must also require that, of the p chosen elements, at least one must belong to the n elements constituting T_1. In other words, we must also have $n' \geqslant 1$. Let us inquire for the probability of such a selection. The number of ways in which p elements can be selected from $(m + n)$ elements is equal to

$$\frac{(m+n)!}{p!(m+n-p)!}. \tag{20}$$

Let us find in how many ways these p elements can be selected so that n' of them will belong to the group T_1 of n elements.

Out of n elements, n' may be selected in

$$\frac{n!}{n'!(n-n')!} \tag{21}$$

ways. For each of these selections of n' elements we must add $p-n'=m'$ elements selected from the m additional elements. These can be selected in

$$\frac{m!}{m'!(m-m')!} \tag{22}$$

different ways. Hence, the number of ways in which we can select p elements so that n' of them will belong to T_1 is equal to

$$\frac{n!m!}{n'!m'!(n-n')!(m-m')!}. \tag{23}$$

The probability of selecting p elements so that n' of them will belong to T_1 is therefore equal to the ratio of (23) to (20), or

$$\left.\begin{aligned} &\frac{n!m!p!(m+n-p)!}{n'!m'!(n-n')!(m-m')!(m+n)!} \\ &\qquad =\frac{n!m!p!(m+n-p)!}{n'!(p-n')!(n-n')!(m-p+n')!(m+n)!}. \end{aligned}\right\} \tag{24}$$

Since, in order to produce R, n' must be either equal to or larger than unity, we obtain the probability that this will happen by taking the sum of (24) over all values of n' from 1 to p, if $p<n$:

$$\left.\begin{aligned} W(n'\geqslant 1) &= \frac{n!m!p!(m+n-p)!}{(m+n)!} \\ &\quad \times \sum_{n'=1}^{n'=p} \frac{1}{n'!(p-n')!(n-n')!(m-p+n')!}. \end{aligned}\right\} \tag{25}$$

If $p>n$, the summation is extended from 1 to n. Equation (25) expresses $W(n'\geqslant 1)$ in terms of m, n, and p.

Since each concentration act takes θ seconds, and the "correct" act is likely to happen once in $1/W$ times, it is likely to take a time

$$t=\frac{\theta}{W} \tag{26}$$

to produce the response R. The dependence of W, and hence of on m and n is a very complex one; but the larger the $N = m + n$, the smaller will be the W and the larger the t. It must also be noticed that W is always positive and finite as long as p satisfies the relations (17). Since this inequality contains constants which characterize the individual, they therefore express the conditions under which a given individual can rationally learn a situation or, if we state it in a slightly different way, can rationally solve a problem of a given complexity. A theoretical solution of an actual scientific problem does frequently amount to perceiving, in that problem, another one, which is already solved and which is therefore familiar to us. Thus, celestial mechanics has been developed by perceiving that the rather complex situation presented by the motion of planets contains in it a more familiar situation of the motion of material points. The development of theoretical optics consisted in establishing that phenomena of wave-dynamics form an essential constituent of optical phenomena; etc.

Formally a theoretical scientist, when faced with a new situation, always looks for a group of known elements contained in this situation. If he perceives in the new unknown situation a familiar constellation, to which he is somehow or other conditioned (or, putting it differently, of which he already knows something), he makes a correct reaction to the new, still unknown situation; or, in other words, he applies his knowledge to the unknown new situation, and *theoretically* he rationally predicts the outcome of the new situation. And, while in a relatively simple situation he may grasp the familiar aspects at a glance, in a more complex case he does mentally try out various combinations of a smaller number of elements, on which he concentrates his attention until the right combination is found. In a sense it is also a trial-and-error learning, only it occurs totally on the covert, cerebral plane. This trial-and-error character of mathematical thinking has been particularly emphasized by H. Poincaré.[1] From the point of view of the mechanism considered here, it takes a long time to solve a complex problem, simply because the probability of hitting on the right solution is small. This probability, as we have seen, depends partly on the nature of the problem and partly on the individual constants of the person. If the constants have such values that W is small even for a relatively simple problem, then the individual is not likely to solve a complex problem—at any rate, it will *probably* take a long time to solve it. But, inasmuch as we are dealing here only with probabilities, it is not excluded that an event with even a very small probability will occur upon the first few trials. It may thus happen that an individual who is not particularly smart at problem-solving and scientific creation may, once in his lifetime, solve a really complex problem and make one important scientific contribution. Such cases are not altogether unknown in the history of science, though they are rare, as they should be. On the other hand, some individuals may have constants which, for a given complexity N, do not satisfy (17). Such individuals are *physically unable* to solve a given problem theoretically, no matter how long they try.

The recognition of a known situation T_1 as a part of an unknown T_i may be considered as representing an elementary act of "abstraction." We recognize T_1 in T_i by abstracting the n elements relevant to T_1 and by "neglecting" the m irrelevant ones. By a fundamentally similar process we recognize, for instance, simple regularities in the great complexity of observable planetary motions.

It must be emphasized that the expression for the probability, derived here, is only one of many other possible ones. We may, for instance, consider a somewhat more special case, where the p elements, upon which the concentration is focused at a given moment, lie close together. In that case the calculation of W proceeds in a different way, and a simpler expression is obtained. On the other hand, we may consider a much more general case, namely, that S' is not constant but that, while being larger than S, it varies from element to element in a random fashion. The number p of elements, for which $S' > S$, may also vary, as well as the time θ. This problem is much more complex and presents some very interesting mathematical points.

Hitherto we have assumed that all elements of a situation were qualitatively equivalent, though we did not assume anything about their nature. They may be visual, auditory, thermal, tactile, etc. Such a simple case, while in itself presenting considerable theoretical interest, is undoubtedly very rare in reality. Even limiting ourselves to the visual field, the situation must be considered as much more complex. If n neuroelements are excited on the retina peripherally, then a much larger number of neuroelements is excited centrally. Furthermore, there are no point-to-point relations between periphery and some centers. Thus, the same geometrical figure may be projected on different parts of the retina, so that in neither case are there any common peripheral neuroelements. Yet in the center for shape-discrimination, in all cases exactly the same group will be excited (chap. xi). In order to generalize the preceding considerations to this more complicated case, we must consider the complexity of a situation as being characterized not by the number of external elements but by the number of neuroelements involved in the central nervous system. But inasmuch as the latter depends not only on the former but also on individual constants, we come to the conclusion that complexity, thus defined, is partly objective, partly subjective. What appears relatively complex to one may appear simple to another, although in certain cases an agreement may be reached. It is also interesting to note that complexity, essentially in the same sense as we use it, has been introduced by G. Birkhoff[2] in his remarkable pioneering studies on quantitative aesthetics. But Birkhoff considers only the objective complexity as defined by the number of external elements. This complexity enters as an essential constituent of Birkhoff's "aesthetic measure"; and therefore his aesthetic measure does not allow for the variation of "individual tastes." The generalized concept of complexity outlined above leads naturally to the possibility of including the individual taste as a mathematical parameter.

REFERENCES

1. H. Poincaré, *Science et méthode* (Paris: Ernest Flammarion, 1909), p. 43.
2. G. Birkhoff, *Aesthetic Measure* (Cambridge: Harvard University Press, 1933).

CHAPTER XVI

PERCEPTION OF VISUAL PATTERNS AND VISUAL AESTHETICS

As we have mentioned in chapter iii, when a constant stimulus is suddenly applied to a pathway characterized by

$$B < A; \quad b < a; \quad \frac{A}{a} < \frac{B}{b}, \tag{1}$$

then at first, for a short time, ε exceeds j; finally, however, j again exceeds ε and remains larger than ε as long as the stimulus lasts. This is due to the fact that, because $A/a < B/b$, the asymptotic value AE/a of ε is less than the asymptotic value BE/b of j. Yet, because $B < A$ and $b < a$, the quantity ε increases more rapidly at first and also approaches its asymptotic value more rapidly than the quantity j does. If, while the first stimulus S_0 lasts and j is therefore still larger than ε, we again apply, *suddenly,* an additional stimulus S_1, so that the total stimulus now becomes $S_0 + S_1$, then, as can be readily seen from Figure 2 of chapter x, again for a short time there will be excitation, followed again by a lasting inhibition. It is, however, necessary that the additional stimulus be applied sufficiently suddenly and that it exceed a certain threshold.

When such a pathway forms a connection with another pathway, then the latter becomes excited for a short time only when the intensity of excitation of the first pathway *suddenly increases.* If the first pathway is excited *continuously* with a constant intensity E, the second pathway is not excited. As we have seen, the intensity of excitation of the second pathway increases with increasing ΔE, where ΔE is the amount of sudden increment of E. As can be readily seen from the discussion in chapter x, the liminal ΔE which still produces an excitation of the second pathway is a linearly increasing function of E. Since E is, in general, a function $E = f(S)$ of the intensity of the peripheral stimulus, which involves the first pathway, this liminal ΔE will, in general, be a more or less complicated function of S, depending on the shape of $f(S)$.

If the second pathway leads to a region C_1, discussed in chapter v, then to each intensity of excitation of the second pathway there will correspond a definite group of excited neuroelements

ne_3. And, since a definite intensity E^* of excitation of the second pathway corresponds to a definite relative sudden increment $\Delta E/E$ of the intensity of excitation of the first pathway, while this relative increment itself corresponds to a definite relative increment $\Delta S/S$ of the peripheral stimulus, to every value of $\Delta S/S$ there will correspond a definite individual group of neuroelements ne_3. As has been shown in chapter x, a similar mechanism is obtained for a *sudden* decrease of E or of S—that is, for a negative $\Delta S/S$.

We thus have a situation in which a *sudden change* of intensity of a constant external stimulus results in a short excitation of a definite group of central neuroelements, different groups corresponding to different amounts of change.

Combining this result with that of chapter v, we may say that to each absolute value of intensity of a peripheral stimulus there is a corresponding excitation of a definite center consisting of a definite group of individual neuroelements ne_3; and to each value of relative change of the intensity of peripheral excitation there is also a corresponding excitation of a similar definite center. The finite, though very large, number of neuroelements in the brain causes an overlapping of some of these centers and thus causes the perception of continuity of the possible values of intensity of peripheral excitation.

We shall now introduce some neurophysiological assumptions which may appear rather questionable. We are introducing them here, not because we consider them to be any more likely than other possible assumptions, but in a tentative way, as a sort of working hypothesis, in order to show how, by means of such or similar assumptions, we may develop a physicomathematical theory of some phenomena of visual perception, the discussion of which has hitherto frequently remained on a purely qualitative level. Later on we shall discuss some possible modifications of these hypotheses—modifications which, however, may leave the fundamental formal results unaltered.

When we look at a segment of a straight line, we successively fix our attention on different points of this line. This results in movement of our eyes along that segment, back and forth. Experiments on eye movements[1] show that there is no simple relation between the shape of a figure contemplated and the path of the eye movement. Actual following of a rectangle gives a rather irregular path for the eye movement.[2] However, inasmuch as the eye muscles are innervated by several centers in a rather complicated fashion, the following hypothesis will not necessarily be at variance with observations. Suppose that there is a group of brain centers which innervate the eye muscles in such a way as to make the eye follow *exactly* a contour which is projected on the retina. Each eye muscle is, however, innervated by a number of other centers, which produce different movements, superimposed on the above-mentioned movements. Thus the actual movement of the eye

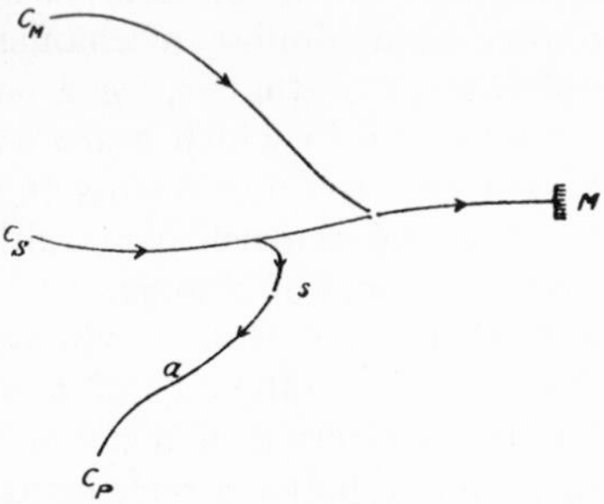

FIG. 1

may have no apparent relation to the shape of the contour contemplated; yet it contains *as a part* those movements which trace an exact replica of the geometrical pattern looked at.

In Figure 1, C_S represents schematically the center which would produce such exact movements of the eye, through the muscle M, while C_M stands for all other centers which may impart to M movements that have nothing to do with the shape of the contour. The character of the movement which would be produced by M under the influence of C_S alone depends on the character of excitation of C_S (intensity, duration). If through a connection s a pathway a is excited which leads to a sensory center C_P (Fig. 1), then to each definite type of excitation of C_S or, in other words, to each definite type of movement produced by M under the influence of C_S alone, there corresponds a definite intensity and duration of excitation of C_P. If M were to be innervated by C_S only, then the same type of excitation in C_P could be obtained through proprioceptive pathways, which would lead from M to C_P and which would be excited by the contraction of M. In such a case the proprioceptive impulses would have a definite relation to the shape of the contemplated pattern. Actually, because of the other centers C_M, the proprioceptive impulses coming from M have no relation to the shape of the pattern. But the impulses coming through s over a (Fig. 1) do have such a relation. In other words, according to the scheme represented by Figure 1, things will occur at C_P *as if* the movements produced by M exactly corresponded to the shape of the contour contemplated and *as if* these movements sent off proprioceptive impulses directly to C_P.

The considerations above therefore enable us to speak, for simplicity, of the eye as actually following the contemplated contour and of proprioceptive impulses *corresponding to such movements* being sent to some sensory centers. Although, actually, things are much more complex, by means of this scheme we may interpret our schematized statements in terms of a more exact neurophysiological picture. Thus, when in the following we say: "The contraction of the eye muscle sets up proprioceptive impulses which behave so and so," we do not mean it literally, but actually imagine a scheme like the one represented by Figure 1.

Neurological mechanisms that would produce such a movement can be readily suggested. For the time being, let us make, for simplicity and as a special, purely theoretical case, the assumption that this movement of the eyes goes on with constant velocity v. Let a line segment AB be placed in a vertical plane, and let its angle with the vertical be θ (Fig. 2). Neglecting the possible role of the oblique eye muscles, the movement of the eyes in the direction AB involves a contraction of the rectus superior of both eyes—the right rectus lateralis externus and the left rectus lateralis internus—and a relaxation of both recti inferiors—the right lateralis internus and left lateralis externus.[1]

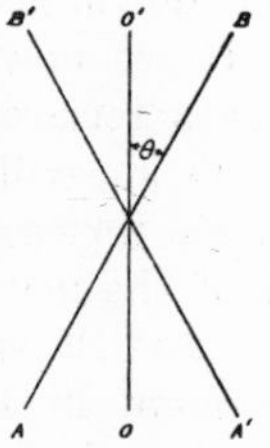

Fig. 2

Again assuming for simplicity that the coordinated movements of the left lateralis internus and the right lateralis externus are controlled from one common center and that the same holds for the right lateralis internus and the left lateralis externus, we may greatly simplify our considerations by considering only the movements of *one eye*—for instance, the right one. Then the movement in the direction AB (Fig. 2) involves a contraction of rectus superior and of lateralis externus and a relaxation of rectus inferior and lateralis internus, which may be written in an abbreviated form, thus:

$$AB\!:\! rs+;\quad le+;\quad ri-;\quad li-. \tag{2}$$

The movement in the direction BA involves

$$BA\!:\! rs-;\quad le-;\quad ri+;\quad li+. \tag{3}$$

The changes of muscular contraction of the four muscles produce proprioceptive impulses of different intensities; and if the proprioceptive pathways lead to a region C_1, discussed in chapter v, then any given intensity of contraction will produce excitation in a definite individual group of neuroelements ne_3. Again, for simplicity, we shall consider that only positive contractions produce proprioceptive impulses, a relaxation being characterized by a lack of such impulses. Let the intensity of these impulses be proportional to the *velocity* of the contraction of the muscles. Then, if v is the velocity of the eye movement, the velocities of contraction of rs and le in (2) are, respectively,

$$v \cos \theta \quad \text{and} \quad v \sin \theta ;$$

and the corresponding intensities of the proprioceptive impulses are

$$E_{rs} = av \cos \theta ; \quad E_{le} = av \sin \theta , \tag{4}$$

where a is a coefficient of proportionality.

The excitation E_{rs} excites a definite individual group of neuroelements ne_3 in a center which we shall call V (for vertical); while E_{le} excites a group of neuroelements in a center H (horizontal).

The movement of the eye in the direction BA produces the following excitation:

$$E_{ri} = av \cos \theta ; \quad E_{li} = av \sin \theta , \tag{5}$$

and causes the excitation of two other groups of neuroelements ne_3, one in V and one in H. If the eye moves up and down indefinitely, four groups of neuroelements are excited. If we now consider another segment of a straight line, which is characterized by a different $\theta = \theta'$, again four groups of neuroelements ne_3 will be excited; but these four groups will be different from the former four, because E_{rs}, E_{le}, E_{li}, and E_{ri} are different. Some of the new groups may partly overlap the old ones only when $\theta - \theta' = \Delta\theta$ is very small. Thus every position of a straight-line segment in a vertical plane corresponds to the excitation of four distinct individual centers, two in H and two in V.

Considering, now, the segment $A'B'$ (Fig. 2), symmetrical to AB with respect to the vertical OO', we shall find, by a similar argument, that the scanning of that segment with the eye in the direction $A'B'$ gives

$$E_{rs}' = av \cos \theta = E_{rs} ; \quad E_{li}' = av \sin \theta = E_{li} , \tag{6}$$

and in the direction $B'A'$ gives

$$E_{ri}' = av \cos \theta = E_{ri} ; \quad E_{le}' = av \sin \theta = E_{le} . \tag{7}$$

That is, AB and $A'B'$, scanned in both directions, *will excite identical groups of neuroelements* ne_3 *in* H *and* V. This difficulty can be avoided in several ways, only one of which we shall consider here.

As suggested by Gale Young, let the neuroelements of higher order, corresponding to *li*, *le*, and *ri*, have such high thresholds that they remain unexcited no matter how strong the excitation of the peripheral pathways. However, let those higher-order neuroelements also be excited by collaterals from *rs*, so that while, for instance, excitation of *li* alone does not result in any central excitation, yet simultaneous excitation of *rs* and *li* results in such a central excitation.

In that case a contraction of the muscle *rs*, that is, a movement of the eye upward, if accompanied by a lateral movement, produces an excitation both in V and in H. But a downward movement of the eye, produced by a contraction of *ri* and a relaxation of *rs*, does not result in any excitation in either V or H. Of course, other brain centers may be excited by such movement by means of other pathway connections. But at present we are interested only in V and H. We now have, for the movement along AB (Fig. 2),

$$AB : rs+\,; \quad le+\,; \quad ri-\,; \quad li-\,; \tag{8}$$

and for BA:

$$BA : rs-\,; \quad le-\,; \quad ri-\,; \quad li-\,. \tag{9}$$

For $A'B'$ we have

$$A'B' : rs+\,; \quad li+\,; \quad ri-\,; \quad le- \tag{10}$$

and

$$B'A' : rs-\,; \quad li-\,; \quad ri-\,; \quad le-\,. \tag{11}$$

From (8) and (9) it follows that scanning of AB in both directions results in

$$E_{rs} = av \cos\theta\,; \qquad E_{le} = av \sin\theta\,, \tag{12}$$

while scanning $A'B'$ in both directions results in

$$E_{rs}' = av \cos\theta\,; \qquad E_{li}' = av \sin\theta\,. \tag{13}$$

Both AB and $A'B'$ involve *rs* in the same amount and therefore excite the same group of neuroelements in V. But, while AB involves *le*, $A'B'$ involves *li*. Hence the two groups of neuroelements in the H-center, which correspond to the scanning of the two lines in both directions, will be different. Every segment of the straight line excites one group of neuroelements in H and one in V, the groups differing for different θ's. Lines symmetrical with respect to either a vertical or a horizontal line have a common group in V. Parallel segments produce identical excitation.

In order to obtain excitation in the H-center when a horizontal line is scanned, not involving any upward movement of the eye, we must introduce an additional assumption, namely, that only an actual downward movement of the eye results in a relaxation of rs, while holding the eye on the same level still requires a tonic contraction of rs.

The proprioceptive excitations, owing to the contemplation of any segment of a straight line, may thus, through V and H, be conditioned to a response R. A different segment will, in general, not produce R, because it involves different groups of neuroelements in V and H. A segment symmetrical to the original one with respect to a vertical line may, however, produce a weaker R through the group of neuroelements in V, which it has in common with the original segment.

Now consider two segments, AB and BC (Fig. 3), forming an angle at B. Following this figure with the eye results in the excitation of two groups of neuroelements in V and two in H. If, however, the proprioceptive pathways, leading from rs, li, and le to V and H, send off collaterals, which are characterized by relations (1) and each of which leads to a center A^*, A^* will become excited every time the eye passes the angle B, because of a sudden change in the intensity of excitation E_{rs} and E_{le} (or of E_{rs} and E_{li} for a differently oriented angle).

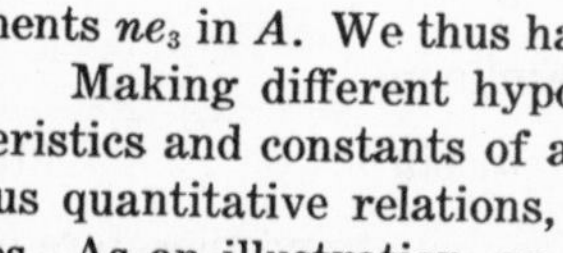

FIG. 3

To each value of the angle B there is a corresponding different intensity of excitation in A^*; and if A^* is connected to a center A, of the kind discussed in chapter v, then to each value of the angle B there corresponds a definite group of neuroelements ne_3 in A. We thus have a center for the perception of angles.

Making different hypotheses concerning the physical characteristics and constants of all centers involved, we may derive various quantitative relations, which may suggest experimental studies. As an illustration, an expression has been derived for the relation between the minimum perceptible angle formed by the two straight lines AB and BO and the angle which one of them—say, AB—forms with the vertical.[3]

Finally, we may consider not only that the speeds of the contraction of rs, li, and le control the excitation of some centers but that special pathways are provided in which the intensity of excitation is proportional to the amplitude of the muscular movements. In this fashion, by considerations similar to those above, we shall arrive at a picture in which a particular group of neuroelements ne_3 is excited in a center L, the group being characteristic for the length of the segment of straight line considered.

If a polygonal contour, consisting of n sides and n angles, is presented to the subject, then it follows from the foregoing that, as this contour is followed by the eye, in general, n groups of neuroelements will be excited in V, n groups in H, n groups in A, and n groups in L. The intensities of excitation of the different groups, even belonging to the same center, such as H or V, will generally be different. Two groups of neuroelements ne_3, corresponding to two different distinct intensities E, not only will be distinct but will, in general, contain different numbers of neuroelements. If the polygon possesses some symmetry properties, which result, for instance, in some of the angles being equal, this reduces the number of distinct groups in A. If there are m equal sides, then they all excite the same group of neuroelements ne_3 in L, etc. As the contour is followed by the eye, the excitation of each group comes and goes, discontinuously, occurring only when the attention is concentrated on the particular element (segment, angle, or length).

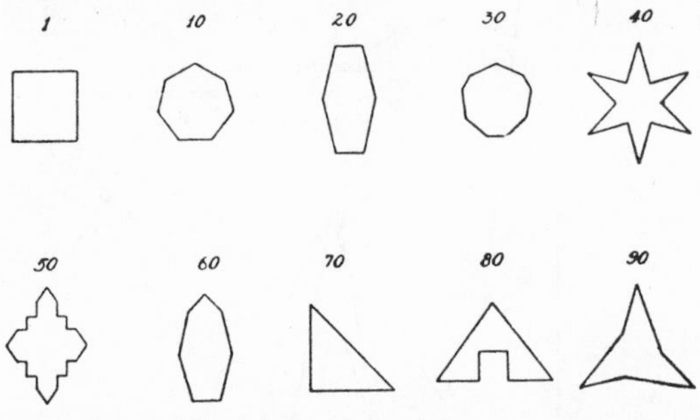

FIG. 4.—These ten polygons, selected from one hundred given in G. Birkhoff's book,[4] were used in the experiments of R. C. Davis[5] to determine the relative aesthetic values of different geometric patterns.

If, out of n elements, m are identical, the group ne_3 corresponding to the m identical elements k, will be excited, on the average per unit time, m times more often than those groups ne_3 which correspond to elements that have no other identical ones. Hence, *the average intensity of excitation* of the group corresponding to m identical elements k will be m times the excitation due to a single element k.

We may now consider a scheme, discussed in chapter v, in which an excitatory pathway leads from neuroelements of each center H, V, A, and L to neuroelements of higher corresponding centers, H', V', A', and L'. This excitatory pathway branches off into inhibitory pathways, leading to the neuroelements of all other centers. We may ask for the total excitation corresponding to a given polygonal contour. If this total excitation is transmitted to a center whose excitation results in a sensation of pleasure, then its intensity may be considered as a measure of the pleasantness or of the aesthetic value of a given contour. The problem is perfectly definite and can be treated, provided that the intensities of excitation of all the groups ne_3 in H, V, A, and L are given—in other words, provided that the distribution function $N(h)$, discussed in chapter v, for different centers, as well as the function given by equation (1) of chapter v, is specified. For different choices of these functions the problem will be of a different degree of mathematical difficulty. A particularly simple case is obtained when we consider a very special case in which the intervals (h_1, h_2) (cf. chap. v, Fig. 2) always contain the same number of neuroelements and in which the intensity of excitation of any such group, falling in any interval (h_1, h_2), is approximately con-

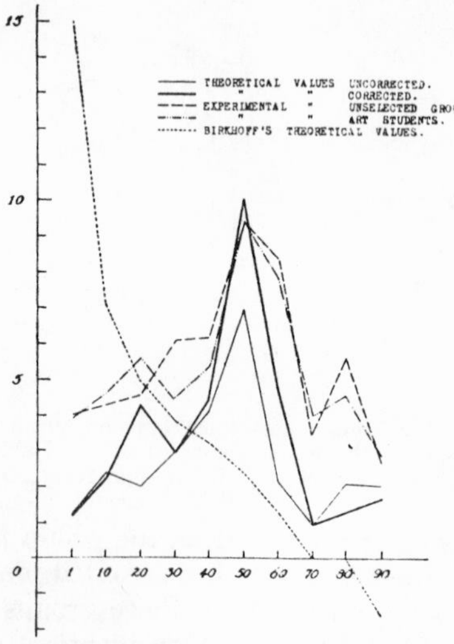

FIG. 5.—The two full lines represent the theoretical values of the intensity of aesthetic sensation in arbitrary units for the ten polygons represented in Fig. 4. The broken and the alternate lines represent the experimental data by R. C. Davis.[5] The dotted line represents theoretical values calculated by G. Birkhoff.[4]

stant. Such a case is rather unlikely to occur exactly, but it has been considered by N. Rashevsky[3] as a possible approximation. In that case two different elements—for instance, angles—are characterized by two distinct groups ne_3, having, however, the same total intensity of excitation E_0 when the element is perceived. To m identical elements there corresponds one group with an average intensity mE_0, since the group is stimulated m times more frequently.

Such considerations were applied to a group of polygons shown in Figure 4, for which G. Birkhoff[4] has calculated quantitative aesthetic values on the basis of some general considerations on complexity and order and for which those values have been measured by R. C. Davis[5] by the rank-order method. As seen in Figure 5, Rashevsky's results are in rather good agreement with the experiment, while Birkhoff's theory does not agree at all.[6]

In subsequent papers[7] N. Rashevsky generalized the theory by dropping the rather implausible assumption that all intervals (h_1, h_2) always contain the same number of neuroelements. Actually to calculate the number of neuroelements in that interval, we may proceed as follows: Consider the quantity $I(S)$ introduced in chapter v. This quantity $I(S)$, which is the total inhibition produced by cross-inhibitory pathways at any connection, is proportional to the total *net* excitation,

$$E(S) = \int \sigma(s, h)\, dh \, ,$$

at all the connections, so that

$$E(s) = \frac{1}{\lambda} I(S) \, ,$$

where λ has the same meaning as in chapter v. The function $E(S)$ determines the total intensity E of the whole discriminatory center as a function of the intensity S of the peripheral stimulus. Using again the same notations as in chapter v, we have the following expression for the function $E(S)$:

$$E(S) = \frac{\int_{h_1}^{h_2} \Phi(S, h)\, dh}{1 + \lambda(h_2 - h_1)} . \tag{14}$$

If, as in chapter v, we consider the simple case,

$$\Phi(S, h) = h(S - h) , \tag{15}$$

and define a quantity x by

$$Sx = S - 2h_1 = 2h_2 - S \, , \tag{16}$$

we have (chap. v, eq. [13])

$$\int_{h_1}^{h_2} \Phi(S, h)\,dh = \frac{S^3 x(3-x^2)}{12} \tag{17}$$

and

$$h_2 - h_1 = Sx\,. \tag{18}$$

Hence

$$E(S) = \frac{S^3 x(3-x^2)}{12(1+\lambda Sx)}\,. \tag{19}$$

The quantity x satisfies the equation

$$ux^3 + x^2 - 1 = 0; \quad u = \frac{2\lambda}{3} S. \tag{20}$$

Equations (19) and (20) give

$$E(u) = \frac{1}{\lambda^3} \frac{9u^3 x(3-x^2)}{32\left(1+\frac{3}{2}ux\right)}. \tag{21}$$

For large values of u, when $u >> 1$, $E(u)$ varies as u^2, since, for such values of u, x is practically constant, decreasing slowly with u. This can be seen if we plot x as a function of u, obtained by solving equation (20) graphically, for different values of u. Hence, defining a as the average value of $(3 - x^2)/12\lambda$ over the actually occurring range, we obtain

$$a = \overline{\frac{3-x^2}{12\lambda}}, \tag{22}$$

and we have, introducing S instead of u into expression (21),

$$E(S) = aS^2\,. \tag{23}$$

An actual graph shows that a relation of practically the same form as (23) holds also for small values of u, so that (23) may be used as a good approximation over a rather wide range of values of S.

Relation (23) may be applied to different problems in perception. We shall apply it to the problem of aesthetic judgments of geometrically similar patterns of different sizes.

Consider a series of similar polygons which are similarly oriented with respect to the observer, and each of which consists of p equal sides.[7] As far as the excitation of L-centers is concerned, contemplation of each polygon results in a p-fold excitation of one L-center, the total excitation being p times the quantity $E(S)$. As for the intensity, S, of the corresponding peripheral stimulus, we may assume it to be proportional to the length l of the side of the polygon[8] for not too large visual angles.

The total excitation of the L-center will thus be proportional to l^2. Since, in a series of similar and similarly oriented polygons, the excitation of the V, H, A, and possible symmetry centers remains the same, the total central excitation for each similar polygon should vary as

$$E_p = A + Bl^2. \tag{24}$$

It must, however, be remarked that the above relation cannot hold for extremely small values of l. For $l = 0$ the polygon shrinks to a point, and the excitations of the V-, H-, and A-centers vanish. Relation (24), has been verified experimentally by N. Rashevsky and Virginia Brown.[8, 9]

The next step in generalizing the theory is to find an expression for the excitation of the angle center, A^*, as a function of the size and position of the angle.

If the pathways leading to the V- or H-centers send off collaterals to other centers, A^*, these collaterals being mixed pathways, characterized either by

$$A > B; \quad a > b; \quad \frac{A}{a} < \frac{B}{b}, \tag{25}$$

or by

$$A < B; \quad a < b; \quad \frac{A}{a} > \frac{B}{b}, \tag{26}$$

then any sufficiently strong *sudden* increase of the vertical stimulus or of the horizontal stimulus will result in a brief excitation of A^*, through the collaterals satisfying relations (25). Similarly, any sufficiently strong sudden decrease of those stimuli will result in an excitation of A^* through pathways satisfying relations (26). For the sake of definiteness, let us consider the case of a sudden increase of the vertical component. The other cases are treated in a similar way.

The stimulus now consists in the sudden increase of the vertical component and is equal (Fig. 6) to

$$\left.\begin{aligned} S_{v+} &= a_1 av[\cos(\theta + \phi - \pi) - \cos\theta] \\ &= -a_1 av[\cos(\theta + \phi) + \cos\theta], \end{aligned}\right\} \tag{27}$$

where a_1 is again a coefficient of proportionality, different from a. Thus S_{v+} is a function both of the magnitude of the angle ϕ and of its position, as determined by θ.

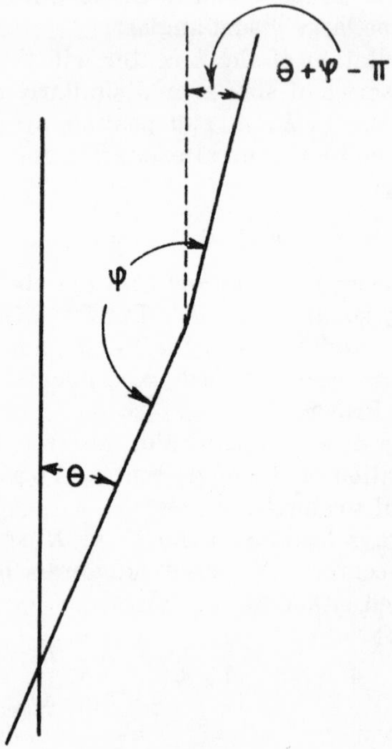

FIG. 6

Consider the simpler case in which the stimulation is the same every time that the vertical (or horizontal) component increases or decreases by the same amount and the coefficient of proportionality, a', is the same for the vertical and the horizontal component. Then we find

$$S(\phi) = a'(|\sin\theta_2 - \sin\theta_1| + |\cos\theta_2 - \cos\theta_1|). \tag{28}$$

But, as we have seen, the central excitation increases as the square of the peripheral intensity S. Hence, with a as another coefficient, we find for the intensity of excitation of the center corresponding to the perception of an angle ϕ the expression

$$e_{A\phi} = a(|\sin\theta_2 - \sin\theta_1| + |\cos\theta_2 - \cos\theta_1|)^2. \tag{29}$$

Relations such as (29) may be checked experimentally by

measuring aesthetic values of polygons in which lengths and positions of straight lines in the plane do not vary but angles do. This is obtained by permuting the sides of a polygon, leaving, however, the direction and length of each side invariant. Thus, starting with the sixteen-sided polygon shown in Figure 7, *a*, we may obtain by

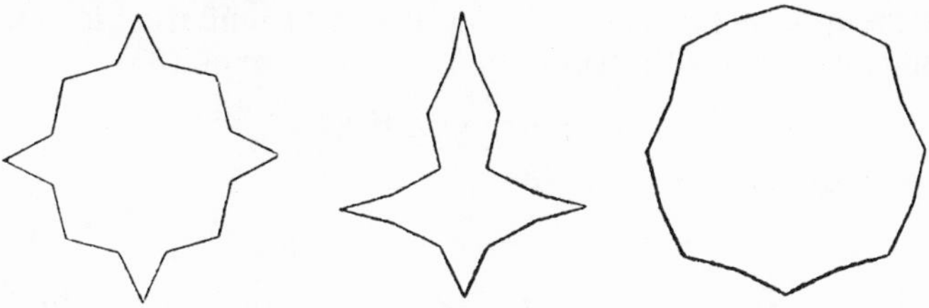

a b c

FIG. 7

permutation of the sides such polygons as those shown in Figure 7, *b* and *c*, and a large number of other widely different shapes. For all such polygons the number and the intensities of excitation of all *L*-, *V*-, and *H*-centers[7] are the same. However, the symmetry relations may change from case to case. Some of the polygons have a central symmetry, as in Figure 7, *a*. Some have a vertical and horizontal axis of symmetry, but no central symmetry. Some have only a vertical axis of symmetry. Some may have no symmetries whatsoever. A total of seventy-seven polygons obtained by permuting the sides of Figure 7, *a*, was used in an experimental study of their aesthetic values by the rank-order method. All seventy-seven polygons had a vertical axis of symmetry, but not all had a horizontal.

Consider n centers, of which n_1 are excited with an intensity e_1, n_2 with an intensity e_2 etc. We have

$$\sum_i n_i = n. \tag{30}$$

Let each center inhibit every other one with an intensity j_i proportional to its e_i, thus:

$$j_i = b_i e_i .$$

This will be the case when we neglect the threshold of the inhibitory fibers (chap. iii). The more general case of finite thresholds is treated in a similar way.

Each center in the group 1 receives an amount of inhibition:

$$b_1(n_1 - 1)e_1 + b_2 n_2 e_2 + \cdots = \sum_i n_i b_i e_i - b_1 e_1,$$

and, more generally, each center of the group k receives an amount of inhibition equal to

$$\sum_i n_i b_i e_i - b_k e_k .$$

Since there are n_k centers in the kth group, the total inhibition in that group is $n_k(\sum n_i b_i e_i - b_k e_k)$. The total inhibition is obtained by summing this with respect to k and, because of (30), is equal to

$$J = (n-1) \sum n_i b_i e_i .$$

The *net* excitation is equal to

$$E = \sum n_i e_i - (n-1) \sum n_i b_i e_i . \tag{31}$$

The n elements constituting a pattern are divided into different groups such as the A-centers, the L-centers, the V-centers, etc. It is plausible to assume that, although the inhibitory coefficients b_i may be different for different groups, they will be the same for the centers of the same group. We shall therefore denote by n_{ki}, b_{ki}, e_{ki}, the quantity referring to the ith neuroelement center of the kth group. (Thus $k = 1$ may stand for the group of A-centers, $k = 2$ for the group of L-centers, etc.) Then, assuming that $b_{ki} = b_k$ is constant for a constant k, we have from equation (31)

$$E = \sum_k [1 - (n-1) b_k] \sum_i n_{ki} e_{ki} , \tag{32}$$

$$n = \sum_k \sum_i n_{ki} . \tag{33}$$

If we consider a set of polygons in which all symmetries are the same and only the angles vary, then n is constant throughout the set. The sums $\sum_i n_{ki} e_{ki}$ are also constant; all except the one referring to the angles. Denoting, now, by b_A the value of b_k for the groups of A-centers, and correspondingly putting for that group $n_{ki} e_{ki} = n_A e_{Ai}$, we find, with C as a constant,

$$E = C + [1 - (n-1) b_A] \sum_i n_A e_{Ai} . \tag{34}$$

But n_A is known, being the total number of angles, and e_{Ai} is given by equation (29), where ϕ is the value of the ith angle. For every polygon the quantity $\sum_i n_A e_{Ai}$ can thus be calculated, and the observed aesthetic value should be a linear function of that quantity within a set of polygons with the same symmetry relations. For sets with different symmetry relations, the values of n will be different, because of different numbers of symmetry centers. Therefore, for different sets the slope of the straight line should be different, and the value of C, which is also a function of n, should vary also from set to set. From the slopes and intercepts of the straight lines for sets with different values of n it is possible to determine the values of the different b_k's.

The linear relation (34) has been confirmed experimentally.[10] Within the accuracy of the experiment it was found that the slopes and the intercepts of the straight lines were the same for all groups, except the ones with central symmetry. In the latter the slope is the same, but the value of C is greater. This has been interpreted as indicating the existence of a special center for perception of central symmetry,[10] for which the value of b_A is very small, while e_i is large. In order to obtain the values of b_A from such experiments, it will be necessary to use polygons with many more sides so as to increase n.

Owing to the above simplification caused by the smallness of b_A, we may use the expression

$$E = C_1 + C_2 + C_3 \sum_i n_A e_{Ai}, \tag{35}$$

where $C_1 = 0$ except for polygons with central symmetry. The quantity $\sum n_A e_{Ai}$ is calculated from equation (29) and still contains the factor a.

In Figure 8 the full line connects the experimentally observed aesthetic values; the broken line, those calculated from equation (35), with $C_1 = 1.9$, $C_2 = 2$, $aC_3 = 0.11$. The average difference between the observed and the calculated values is 10.5 per cent. The most frequently occurring difference is below 5 per cent.

A remark must be made about polygons *III-4* and *VII-4*. None of them has a central symmetry, but *III-4* has a full horizontal symmetry, while *VII-4* even has no horizontal symmetry. The theoretical values of E computed for those polygons with $C_1 = 0$ are, however, much too small, as shown by the crosses in Figure 8. If, however, we compute the value of E with $C_1 = 1.9$, as if they had central symmetry, the agreement becomes very good. The reason for this is that both polygons, while not *exactly* centrally symmetric, are approximately so. The deviations from central symmetry fall apparently for many individuals within the limits of discriminal error.

The theoretical values for polygons *XII-2*, *XII-3*, and *XII-4*, as shown in Figure 8, have been corrected for the end-effects of the rank-order scale.

Now consider the polygon of Figure 7, *a*, and derive from it a set of polygons in which the eight sides of the sharpest four angles have the same length l, while the remaining eight sides all have a different length l. All angles and symmetry relations are the same for all polygons of each set. By the same argument as before, we should now expect the aesthetic value E to be a linear function of $\sum_i n_L l_L$, where the subscript refers to the L-center. But $\sum_i n_L e_L$ is now proportional to $8l_0^2 + 8l_1^2$. Hence, denoting by A_1 and A_2 two constants,

$$E = A_1 + A_2(l_0^2 + l_1^2). \tag{36}$$

Figure 9 shows to what extent relation (36) is satisfied. The negative slope of the line indicates a large b_L, since A_2 is proportional to $1 - (n - 1)b_L$.

The influence of various symmetries, that is, the appearance of several identical elements, may be easily analyzed by considerations similar to those given in chapter iii. If we have, for instance, n equally externally excited, but different, elements, then each of the corresponding groups ne_3 receives an inhibition from $n - 1$ other groups. If m of these elements are identical, then we have only $n - m + 1$ groups. The total applied excitation remains the same. In the first case it was nE; now it is $(n - m)E + mE$. But the group corresponding to the m identical elements receives inhibitory pathways from $n - m$ other groups. Thus the total inhibition is decreased, and the net excitation increased. If we take, as a measure of complexity, the total number of elements in the pattern, then various types of symmetry have the effect of reducing the "effective" complexity; but this reduction occurs by a process of subtraction rather than by a process of division, as in Birkhoff's theory. It must also be remarked that, even when all elements are different, the total excitation in our case does not monotonically decrease with the complexity n. Equation (1) of chapter xv gives us the intensity of excitatory process at one of the n connections, corresponding to n different elements with equal intensity of excitation. The total intensity of excitation is obtained by multiplying that equation by n, which gives

$$E_{\text{tot}} = (K_1S - K_4)n - (K_2S - K_3)n(n-1).$$

This expression is zero for $n = 0$ and has a maximum for

$$n^* = \frac{(K_1 + K_2)S - (K_3 + K_4)}{2(K_2S - K_3)},$$

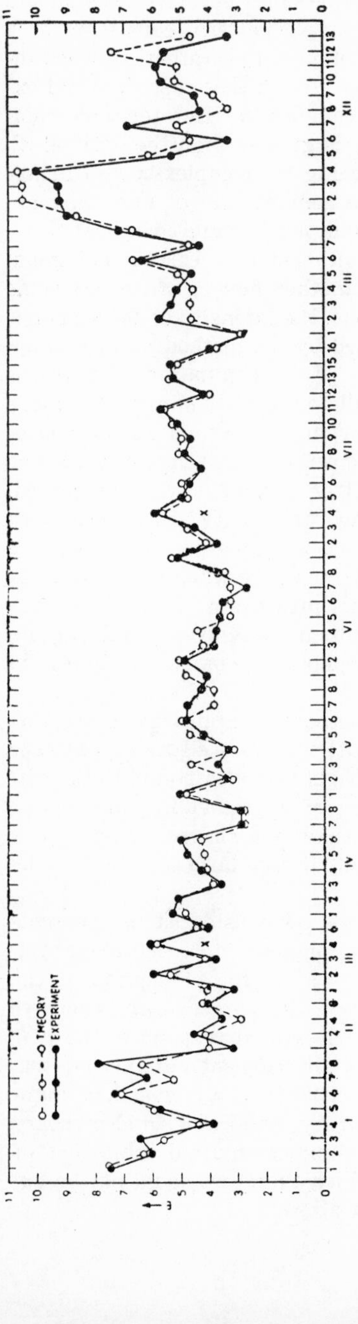

FIG. 8

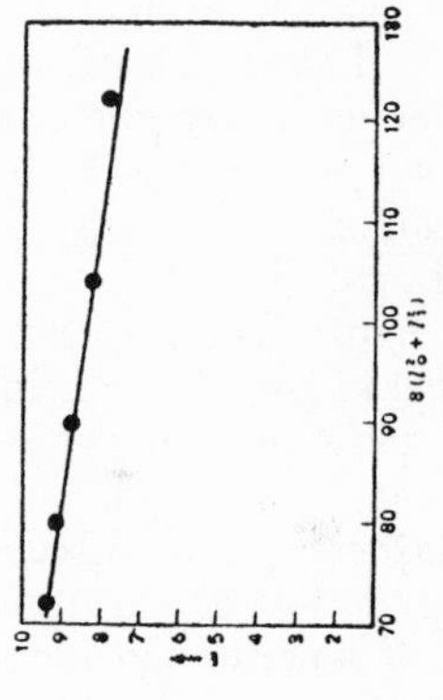

FIG. 9

after which it decreases to zero and becomes negative. We should therefore expect that in a rather simple pattern, consisting of a very few elements, too much symmetry will be rather a disadvantage from the aesthetic point of view, for in that case the total excitation increases with increasing complexity. But for very complex patterns, where the complexity is greater than the optimal n^*, some symmetry is pleasant, as reducing the complexity and bringing it closer to the optimal. In the general case of unequally excited elements, these relations become much more complicated.

If a subject or animal is conditioned to a certain polygonal figure and then is presented with another figure, which has some elements in common with the first one, the intensity of the response to the second figure can be calculated by the method used in chapter xv. Thus a quantitative theory of discrimination of patterns may be developed. Two patterns will be the more similar, the more they have common groups ne_3 in various centers. If all the neuroelements in A send off pathways to a center A_0, so that A_0 is always excited whenever any angle, no matter of what size, is presented, then A_0 is a center that responds to "angularity" in general. An animal trained to choose a square, when a square and a circle are presented, will choose the more angular figure when two other, but different, figures are presented. This provides a basis for the understanding of some interesting results of H. Klüver[11] on the equivalence or nonequivalence of certain pairs of geometrical figures in the behavior of monkeys.

N. Rashevsky[7] has discussed methods of approach to the theory of perception of curvilinear patterns, as well as of patterns composed of separate unconnected parts. He also points to the difference in the aesthetic appreciation of a geometric pattern and, for instance, a landscape, which is usually not characterized by any simple geometrical shape but contains a very large number of elements.

For simple geometrical patterns we considered as elements such things as straight lines, angles, lengths, etc. Neurobiophysical structures were outlined, with result in the perception of the above-mentioned things, as "elements." Similarly, we can conceive of neurobiophysical mechanisms which will correspond to the perception of a given color or shade as an "element" of the pattern. But a scenery or landscape painting consists of a tremendous number of such elements. The simple theory, applicable to elementary geometrical figures, would predict complete mutual inhibition of such a large number of elements, which therefore could not be expected to have any aesthetic value at all.

The situation is different, however, if we consider the finite thresholds of the inhibitory pathways, leaving the rest of the neurobiophysical scheme unchanged. Equations for that case have been developed in chapter iii.

Considering, as before, a set of n parallel excitatory neuronic chains corresponding to n peripheral stimuli or elements cross-connected by inhibiting chains and using the same notations, we find that, if

$$h_1 < S_1 < h_1 + \frac{h_3}{P\alpha_1 I_1} \tag{37}$$

(eq. [56] of chap. iii), then the inhibiting pathways remain unexcited, and a central excitation results, no matter how large the number n of elements of intensity S_1. As a matter of fact, the total central excitation increases under these conditions with increasing n.

If, however,

$$S_1 > h_1 + \frac{h_3}{P\alpha_1 I_1} \tag{38}$$

(eq. [59] of chap. iii), then the inhibiting pathways come into play, and this results in a complete central inhibition, when

$$n > 1 + \frac{P}{Q}\frac{\alpha_1 I_1}{\alpha_3 I_3}\frac{S_1 - h_1}{P\alpha_1 I_1 (S_1 - h_1) - h_3}. \tag{39}$$

We may thus perceive a pattern consisting of a very large number of elements and derive an aesthetic satisfaction from it as long as the intensity of excitation of the different elements is not too great. The equations derived in chapter iii hold for the case when all n elements are excited with equal intensity. But this can be readily generalized for different intensities of excitation, S_i, provided that the S_i's satisfy inequalities (37). Under those conditions a reduction of n results in a reduction of E and hence of the aesthetic value. On the other hand, keeping n constant but increasing some of the S_i sufficiently strongly so as to satisfy inequality (39) may produce two effects. If the number of the strong S_i's is small and the strength of these S_i's is not too large, then, although they will to some extent inhibit the remaining weaker elements, yet, because of their own increased intensity of excitation, the total intensity E may even increase. If, however, many S_i's are strongly excited, a complete inhibition results.

We may inquire what neurobiophysical parameters determine whether an individual prefers, in general, visual patterns consisting of a relatively small number of relatively strongly excited elements or patterns which consist of a very large number of weakly excited elements. This question has also been studied by N. Rashevsky.[12]

REFERENCES

1. A. Tachermak, *Handb. d. norm. u. path. Physiol.*, 12, Part II, 1001 (Berlin: J. Springer, 1931).

2. *Ibid.*, p. 1059.

3. N. Rashevsky, *Psychometrika*, 3, 253, 1938.

4. G. Birkhoff, *Aesthetic Measure* (Cambridge: Harvard University Press, 1933).

5. R. C. Davis, *Jour. Gen. Psychol.*, 15, 231, 1936.

6. N. Rashevsky, *Advances and Applications of Mathematical Biology* (Chicago: University of Chicago Press, 1940).

7. N. Rashevsky, *Bull. Math. Biophysics*, 4, 177, 1942.

8. A. S. Householder, *Bull. Math. Biophysics*, 2, 117, 157, 1940.

9. N. Rashevsky and Virginia Brown, *Bull. Math. Biophysics*, 6, 119, 1944.

10. N. Rashevsky and Virginia Brown, *ibid.*, p. 153.

11. H. Klüver, *Behavior Mechanisms in Monkeys* (Chicago: University of Chicago Press, 1933).

12. N. Rashevsky, *Bull. Math. Biophysics*, 7, 41, 1945.

CHAPTER XVII

MATHEMATICAL BIOPHYSICS OF ABSTRACTION

Consider a pair of stimulus patterns, S_a and S_b, each containing, as its components, stimuli of different modalities which we shall designate by the subscript i. Thus we may write

$$S_a = S_a(S_{a1}, S_{a2}, \cdots S_{ai}, \cdots),$$

$$S_b = S_b(S_{b1}, S_{b2}, \cdots S_{bi}, \cdots).$$

Two stimuli, S_{ai} and S_{bi}, of the same modality i, in general, involve two different afferent pathways. Thus we may have sensations of touch from different parts of the skin or, in principle, visual sensations from different parts of the retina. Two stimuli of the same modality may, however, differ only in intensity. For this case a mechanism has been discussed in chapter v, which provides that stimuli of different intensities excite different groups of neurons somewhere in the brain. Hence, either already at the afferent level or at a higher level, we may consider two stimuli of the same modality as involving two distinct pathways.

Let us consider, therefore, a pair of stimuli, S_{ai} and S_{bi}, of the same modality, each affecting a separate pathway, as shown in Figure 1, in which, as usual, the full lines denote excitatory pathways and the broken lines inhibitory pathways. If the constants of all

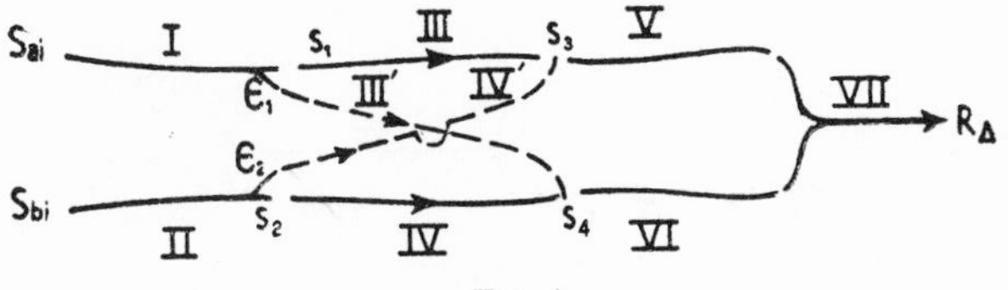

FIG. 1

pathways are the same, in particular if $A = B$ and $a = b$, then, as has been shown previously,[1, 2] the net excitation at the connections s_3 and s_4 is zero when $S_{ai} = S_{bi}$ or when $|S_{ai} - S_{bi}| = 0$. Let pathways V and VI connect to a common path. Then if $\Delta_i = |S_{ai} - S_{bi}| = 0$, the pathway VII remains unexcited. If, however, Δ_i is sufficiently larger than zero, a reaction R_Δ is produced via pathway VII. We may say that the organism perceives the difference Δ_i between S_{ai} and S_{bi} if it produces the reaction R_Δ. In other words, R_Δ indicates the perception of the difference Δ_i. From the above scheme it follows that the larger the Δ_i is, the stronger R_Δ will be.

We may now introduce as before[1] the fluctuations of the quantities ε_1 and ε_2. Again, because of the symmetry of the structure, we do not restrict the generality of our results by considering the fluctuations of ε_1 only.

In order to produce the response R_Δ, either pathway V or pathway VI must be excited. This requires that[1] $\varepsilon_1 - \varepsilon_2 > h$, or $\Delta_i > h_i$, where h is the threshold value determined by the different constants of all pathways and h_i is another constant proportional to h. The natural fluctuations of excitation at the connection s_2 result in temporary increases of ε_1 by an amount $(\varepsilon - j)'$. Let $p(\varepsilon - j)'d(\varepsilon - j)'$ be the probability of having the fluctuation lie between $(\varepsilon - j)'$ and $(\varepsilon - j)' + d(\varepsilon - j)'$.

If the standard deviation σ of the distribution function $p(\xi)$ is small as compared with h_i so that large fluctuations occur very rarely, then the probability that the reaction R_Δ will occur for very small values of Δ_i is very small. In order to produce the response R_Δ or to recognize the difference Δ_i with a high degree of certainty, Δ_i must be sufficiently larger than 3σ and h_i must be smaller than σ. If $\Delta_i < h_i$, then in the absence of fluctuations there would be no response R_Δ; in other words, the difference between S_{ai} and S_{bi} is not perceived.

For each modality i we have a mechanism as described above. Let the pathways VII of all modalities converge to a final common path, which produces a reaction $R_{\Delta T}$. This latter reaction, then, may be considered as corresponding to the total difference between the stimuli S_a and S_b.

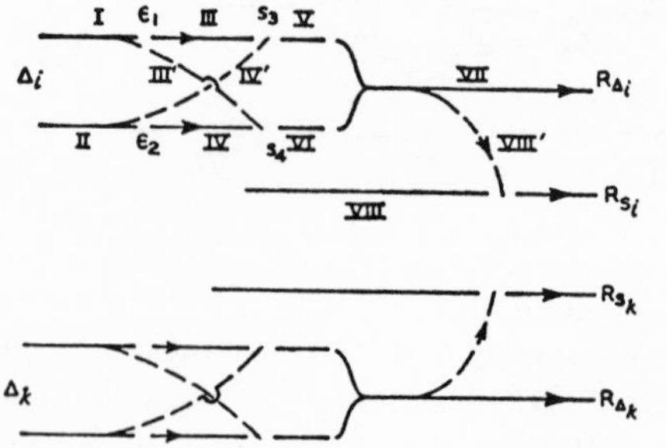

FIG. 2

The above mechanism has been suggested by H. D. Landahl,[3] who also suggests a different mechanism for perception of similarity. N. Rashevsky[4] modified somewhat the above mechanism.

We shall first somewhat simplify H. D. Landahl's mechanism for perception of similarity. Let a mechanism (Fig. 2) for perception of differences in one modality, such as suggested by H. D. Landahl, inhibit through the pathway *VIII′* a connection of a chain of pathways *VIII*, which produce a reaction R_s, the similarity or identity reaction. The chain *VIII* may be excited either by a permanent self-exciting center or, what is more natural, by either of the two stimuli acting on the "difference mechanism." In this case, if the difference $\Delta_i = 0$, then no "difference reaction," R_Δ, is produced, but the similarity reaction, R_s, is produced. If $\Delta_i > 0$, then R_Δ is produced, but R_s is absent.

According to this mechanism, similarity is a purely negative concept, meaning absence of difference. A situation, mentioned by H. D. Landahl, that two things may be neither similar nor different, may occur with the present mechanism also, if the chain of pathways *VIII* is broken or inhibited somewhere between the connection s_5 and the final path. Such a situation would, however, be pathological, whereas with Landahl's mechanism it may occur normally.

We shall now compute the probability p of a judgment of similarity in terms of Δ_i. The probability q of a judgment of difference is simply

$$q = 1 - p\,. \tag{1}$$

The probability p is the same as the probability P_e of a "doubtful judgment" in the mechanism for psychophysical discrimination discussed in chapter vi. We may take over directly some of the equations developed there. The quantity Δ_i is essentially the same as $\epsilon_1 - \epsilon_2$ of chapter vi. Assuming a distribution function, $p(\xi)$, for the fluctuation of excitation of the form

$$p(\xi) = \frac{k}{2}\, e^{-k|\xi|} \tag{2}$$

and evaluating the integral in equation (8) of chapter vi, we find[1] after somewhat elaborate calculations:

For $\Delta < h$:

$$p = 1 - e^{-kh} \cosh k\Delta\,, \tag{3}$$

$$q = e^{-kh} \cosh k\Delta\,. \tag{4}$$

For $\Delta = h$:

$$p = \tfrac{1}{2}(1 - e^{-2kh}), \qquad q = \tfrac{1}{2}(1 + e^{-2kh})\,. \tag{5}$$

For $\Delta > h$:

$$p = e^{-k\Delta} \sinh kh \,, \tag{6}$$

$$q = 1 - e^{-k\Delta} \sinh kh \,. \tag{7}$$

Equations (3) and (4) as well as (6) and (7) reduce to (5) for $\Delta = h$.

Instead of expression (2), N. Rashevsky[4] suggests the use of a fourth-degree curve with properly chosen coefficients, and he derives corresponding expressions for that case.

We shall now proceed to compute the probability of a similarity or dissimilarity judgment for two multimodal stimulus patterns. We may consider two different cases.

Case A.—For each modality there is a separate neuroelement chain for a reaction R_s. The whole mechanism consists of a number of such mechanisms, as represented in Figure 2. Let the subscript i refer to the ith modality. Then, if all R_{Δ_i}'s are zero, all R_{si}'s are produced. If only some R_{Δ_i}'s are zero, then only some of the R_{si}'s are produced. With this mechanism, an R_s reaction is produced whenever at least one R_{Δ_i} is zero. In other words, an individual will always notice a similarity whenever there is one in any respect.

The probability that a given Δ_i will give a no-difference response is $p(\Delta_i)$. The probability that a given Δ_i will give a no-difference response, but that all other Δ_i's will give one, is

$$p(\Delta_i) \prod_k q(\Delta_k) \,; \qquad (k \gtrless i) \,. \tag{8}$$

Hence the probability that any one Δ_i will give no difference response, while all others will, is

$$\sum_{i=1}^{i=n} p(\Delta_i) \prod_k q(\Delta_k) \,; \qquad (k \gtrless i) \,. \tag{9}$$

The probability that a given pair Δ_i and Δ_l will both fail to give a difference response, regardless of what the remaining Δ_k's do, is

$$p(\Delta_i) p(\Delta_l) \,. \tag{10}$$

The probability that the above-mentioned pair will give a no-difference response while all other Δ_k's give a difference response is

$$p(\Delta_i) p(\Delta_l) \prod_k q(\Delta_k) \,; \qquad (k \gtrless i; k \gtrless l) \,. \tag{11}$$

Hence the probability that any one pair will give a no-difference response, while all other Δ_k's give a difference response, is

$$\sum_i \sum_l p(\Delta_i) p(\Delta_l) \prod_k q(\Delta_k)\,; \qquad (k \gtrless i;\quad k \gtrless l;\quad i \gtrless l)\,. \tag{12}$$

Similar expressions are obtained for the probability that any three Δ's will give a no-difference response, all others giving a difference response, etc. Summing all those probabilities, we finally obtain for the total probability of a similarity response

$$\left.\begin{aligned} P = &\sum_i p(\Delta_i) \prod_k q(\Delta_k) + \sum_i \sum_l p(\Delta_i) p(\Delta_l) \prod_k q(\Delta_k) \\ &+ \cdots \sum_i \cdots \sum_r p(\Delta_i) \cdots p(\Delta_r) \prod_k q(\Delta_k)\,. \end{aligned}\right\} \tag{13}$$

Case B.—There is one common response path for R_s for all modalities (Fig. 3). Now R_s is produced only when all R_{Δ_i}'s are

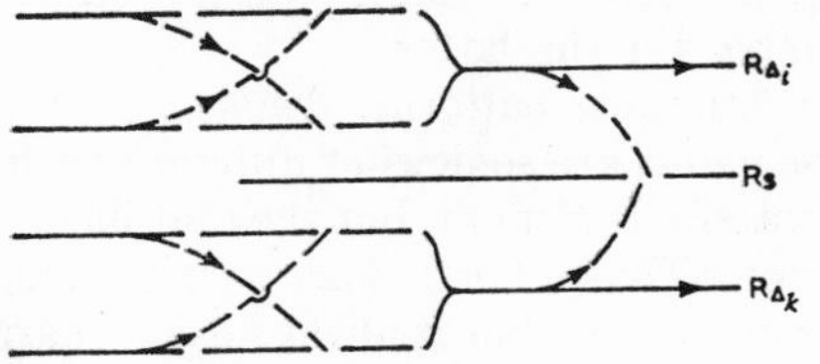

FIG. 3

zero. Hence the total probability P of R_s is equal to the probability of all Δ_i's failing simultaneously to give a reaction R_Δ. This is equal to

$$P = \prod_{i=1}^{i=n} p(\Delta_i)\,. \tag{14}$$

Using expressions (3), (5), and (6) for $p(\Delta_i)$, we can compute P as a function of all Δ_i's.

In order to compare (13) and (14) with experimental data, it is necessary to have a series of stimulus patterns with known values of Δ_i for each pair. For some modalities the differences Δ_i may be measured directly by the difference of some physical quantities. Thus we may have a set of objects of different size, weight, temperature, and perhaps saturation value of a given color or, still better, intensity of illumination. In some cases, however, the modalities may not be of a simple physical nature. Thus we may compare two objects in regard to the degree of their difference in being used to perform a certain function. For instance, a bell and a horn would be generally considered as more similar in regard to their use as sounding devices than a bell and a dishpan, although the latter may be used for sound-producing purposes. In such cases a scale of Δ_i-values may be established by standard psychological methods, for instance, the rank-order method or the method of paired comparisons. We may, for example, ask a large number of subjects to arrange a number of objects first in order of their use for a certain function, then in order of values of some other modality, etc. From such rankings, scale values for different modalities may be computed. Then pairs of those objects may be presented to *one* test subject many times, with the request to pass a judgment of similarity or dissimilarity *in general*, and from the observed probabilities of different responses equations (13) or (14) may be compared with the experiment.

Consider a stimulus pattern which becomes conditioned to a definite motor reaction, in particular to a verbal reaction. The verbal reaction is then the "name" of the stimulus pattern and stands as a symbol for the latter.

In general, stimulus patterns, denoted by the same word or having the same name, are somewhat different with respect to some of the component single stimuli, but they all have *some* component stimuli in common. Thus a "ball" may be large, small, white, black, made of leather or of steel, but it always has a characteristic shape.

Some attributes of an object, denoted by a given name, occur always in 100 per cent of the cases. Some others occur less frequently. Considering each of those attributes as a component stimulus of the pattern, we may say that those component stimuli occur with different frequencies. We may arrange them in order of the decreasing frequency of occurrence and represent them as equidistant points on a straight line, which we choose as abscissa. If we plot as ordinate the corresponding probability of occurence we shall obtain a line representing a monotonically decreasing function. The variable along the abscissa may be measured in terms of the arbitrarily chosen distance between the points. Denote the abscissa of each point by x_i. If a is the distance between any two points, then

$$x_i = ai\,. \tag{15}$$

Since each x_i represents a component stimulus of the pattern, we may speak of "the stimulus x_i."

The conditioning of the stimulus pattern $S(x_1, x_2, \cdots x_n)$ to a given verbal reaction R takes place gradually, as the pattern $S(x_1, x_2, \cdots x_n)$ is experienced a sufficient number of times. Each of the component stimuli x_i of the pattern S is thus conditioned to R. It is natural to assume that the intensity $R(x_i)$ of the reaction

R to the stimulus x_i will be the weaker, the smaller the frequency of occurrence of x_i in the total stimulus pattern $S(x_1, x_2, \cdots x_n)$.

Let us now consider[5, 6] a mechanism discussed in chapter xl. Let all efferent conditioned pathways send inhibitory pathways to the afferent centers of each stimulus x_i. Then a weaker stimulus x_k may be completely inhibited by the strong reactions $R(x_l)$. Let $N(x_i)$ represent the frequency of occurrence of x_i. Then the average intensity $I(x_i)$ of the stimulus x_i is proportional to $N(x_i)$ and equal to $b_1 N(x_i)$. The intensity $R(x_i)$ of the reaction R in the absence of inhibiting pathways is proportional to $I(x_i)$ and is equal to

$$R(x_i) = bI(x_i). \tag{16}$$

But, since each x_i center receives inhibitory pathways from all conditioned pathways $x_i - R$, the actual excitation $I(x_i)$ is given by

$$I(x_i) = b_1 N(x_i) - \lambda \sum_i R(x_i), \tag{17}$$

λ being a constant.

When the number of component stimuli is very large, we can replace the sum by an integral and thus obtain

$$I(x) = b_1 N(x) - \int_0^\kappa R(x)\, dx. \tag{18}$$

Introducing expression (16) into (18), we obtain

$$I(x) = b_1 N(x) - \lambda b \int_0^\kappa I(x)\, dx. \tag{19}$$

The upper limit is determined by considerations that those x's which are completely inhibited do not produce any $R(x)$ and do not therefore contribute anything to the inhibition of others.

As an illustration we shall discuss here the case in which

$$N(x) = e^{-\beta x}. \tag{20}$$

A component stimulus corresponding to $x = 0$ then occurs every time, the probability of its occurrence being 1. This assumption simplifies the following equations considerably but does not introduce any limitation in principle. We then have

$$I(x) = b_1 (e^{-\beta x} - e^{-\beta \kappa}), \tag{21}$$

where κ is the root of the equation

$$e^{\beta \kappa} - \beta \kappa - 1 = \frac{\beta}{b\lambda}. \tag{22}$$

As we have seen (p. 133), the quantity κ decreases with increasing λ.

We can find two approximate solutions of equation (22), one for the case that β is very large, $\beta/b\lambda > 0$, and another for very small values of β.

In the first case we may neglect in equation (22) $\beta\kappa$ and 1 compared with $e^{-\beta\kappa}$. We then have

$$e^{\beta\kappa} = \frac{\beta}{b\lambda}, \tag{23}$$

or

$$\kappa = \frac{1}{\beta} \log \frac{\beta}{b\lambda} > 0. \tag{24}$$

In the second case we expand $e^{\beta\kappa}$, omitting terms of third and higher powers. This gives

$$\kappa = \sqrt{\frac{2}{b\beta\lambda}}. \tag{25}$$

In any case, for very large values of λ, that is, for very strong inhibition, κ will be very small, and only those component stimuli will remain uninhibited which have a very small x, that is, which occur either always or almost always.

With the above mechanism, only such components of S will be associated with the reaction R as occur either always or almost always. Such components may be termed "essential," the remaining ones "accidental." We have here a rudimentary mechanism of abstraction. The verbal reaction R is now associated not with the whole accidental complex of component stimuli, entering into S, but only with the essential ones. Thus a mathematical biophysicist considers as the only essential feature of the cell its metabolism, this being the only feature which invariably occurs in all cells. An individual with a large λ and hence a small κ will abstract only such features which occur always. Individuals with smaller λ may, at least off-hand, include among "essential" features of an object those which occur very frequently, but not always. Individuals with very small λ and large κ will show inability to abstract and will consider as essential components even those which occur rather infrequently.

If λ is constant, then κ is constant, too. Any component whose frequency of occurrence $y(<1)$ is greater than $e^{-\beta\kappa}$ would be considered as essential and all others as accidental. But λ, which is a measure of the inhibitory effect, may itself fluctuate because of statistical physiochemical fluctuations in the organism. Then κ will fluctuate also. Under those conditions a component stimulus with a frequency y of occurrence may sometimes be considered as essential, sometimes as not. We may now compute the probability P_e that a stimulus of a given y will be considered essential, or the probability $P_u = 1 - P_e$ that it will be considered unessential.

Let the probability of λ's having a value between λ and $\lambda + d\lambda$ be $p(\lambda)\,d\lambda$, with $p(0) = p(\infty) = 0$, and consider the most likely case that $p(\lambda)$ has one and only one maximum at $\lambda = \lambda_0$. The probability $p_1(\kappa)\,d\kappa$ of κ's having a value between κ and $\kappa + d\kappa$ is obtained by substituting into $p(\lambda)\,d\lambda$ the expression of λ and $d\lambda$ in terms of κ and $d\kappa$, obtained from either (24) or (25). We shall use here as an illustration equation (25). It gives

$$\lambda = \frac{2}{b\beta\kappa^2}; \qquad d\lambda = -\frac{4d\kappa}{b\beta\kappa^3}. \tag{26}$$

Hence

$$p_1(\kappa)\,d\kappa = -\frac{4}{b\beta}\,p\left(\frac{2}{b\beta\kappa^2}\right)\frac{d\kappa}{\kappa^3}. \tag{27}$$

The abscissa x of a component of frequency y is

$$x_y = -\frac{1}{\beta}\log y > 0. \tag{28}$$

The component is considered as essential every time that $\kappa > x_y$. Hence the probability P_e is given by

$$P_e = \int_{-x_y}^{\infty} p_1(\kappa)\,d\kappa = -\frac{4}{b\beta}\int_{-(1/\beta)\,\log y}^{\infty} p\left(\frac{2}{b\beta\kappa^2}\right)\frac{d\kappa}{\kappa^3}. \tag{29}$$

Expression (29) gives us P_e in terms of β, which characterizes the external stimulus S, and in terms of the parameters of $p(\lambda)$, which contain the individual constants, in particular, λ_0.

Equation (29) can be compared with experiments. The quantity β can be controlled in principle. Thus we may show to a subject a large number of times the same object with different accidental characteristics. In a selected number of cases, for instance, the object will be green; in another selected number of cases it will be red; in some cases it will be made of wood; in some of metal; etc. We thus can artificially "construct" the function $e^{-\beta x}$ or, for that matter, any function $N(x)$. Expressions for P_u and P_e

may be derived in principle for any $N(x)$. After having presented the object a large number of times; we may ask the individual whether a given property— say, green—is an essential characteristic of the object or not. By recording the frequency of different replies, we may compare equations (29) or any other corresponding equation with experiment. We thus have a method of measuring quantitatively the ability to abstract. From such measurements some individual parameters of the subject may be calculated.

In connection with the above mechanism for abstraction, N. Rashevsky[4] has also suggested a mechanism for logical thinking. A different approach to that problem will be discussed in chapter xix.

REFERENCES

1. H. D. Landahl, *Psychometrika*, 3, 107, 1938.
2. H. D. Landahl, *Bull. Math. Biophysics*, 1, 159, 1939.
3. H. D. Landahl, *ibid.*, 7, 83, 1945.
4. N. Rashevsky, *Bull. Math. Biophysics*, 7, 133, 1945.
5. N. Rashevsky, *Psychometrika*, 1, 265, 1936.
6. A. S. Householder and E. Amelotti, *Psychometrika*, 2, 255, 1937.

CHAPTER XVIII

MATHEMATICAL BIOPHYSICS OF SOME MENTAL PHENOMENA

In this chapter we shall consider neurobiophysical mechanisms which may throw some light on the nature of consciousness and memory.

Let a number of afferent pathways *I* (Fig. 1) lead to the cortex and connect each with a pathway *II*, as well as with the usual cross-inhibitory pathways *III*. For simplicity, not all pathways *III* are shown in the figure. The scheme thus far is similar to the one studied before (chap. iii). If the stimulus pattern affecting the peripheral ends of pathways *I* is pleasant, then the same pattern will be duplicated in pathways *II*. For unpleasant stimuli some or all of the pathways *II* will not be excited because an unpleasant

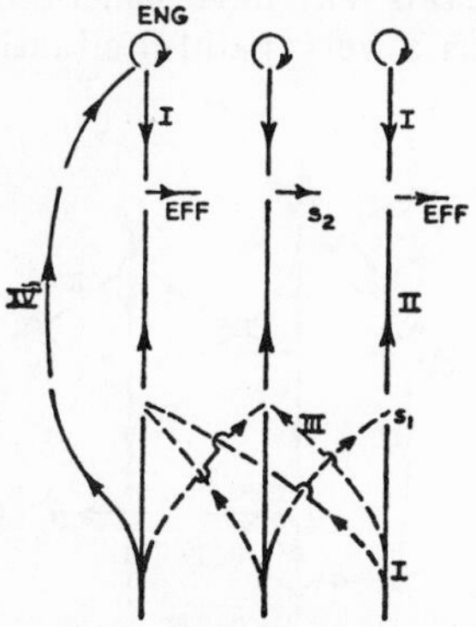

FIG. 1

stimulus results in a net inhibition of the set of connections s_1. However, let each pathway *I* send an excitatory pathway *IV* to a different cortical level, in which it excites a self-circuiting neuroelement[1] (chap. viii), *Eng*, which has a low permanent excitation threshold, so that a moderate or even a weak intensity of excitation E_{IV} of pathway *IV* throws it into a permanently excited state. Let each *Eng* send pathways *I′* downward, so as to produce an excitation of the efferent neuroelements *Eff*, connecting with *II* at s_2. With this arrangement, even an unpleasant stimulus pattern results in an excitation of the efferent and of *II*, as should be the case. Without this or a similar arrangement, we should be led to the absurd conclusion that an unpleasant stimulus pattern cannot produce any reaction at all. With the present mechanism, there is, however, an essential difference between pleasant and unpleasant stimuli. In the case of the former ones, the efferent nuroelements *Eff* are activated both through *II* and through *Eng*, while in the latter case the *Eff* neuroelements are activated through *Eng* only. The biophysical correlate of unpleasantness is inhibition of neuroelements *II*.

Each *Eng* neuroelement provides a memory trace or engram of the corresponding stimulus, since *Eng* remains excited after the stimulus subsides. At first glance, one might be inclined to assume that we perceive a stimulus pattern directly when the efferents *Eff* are excited through *II*, while we remember a stimulus pattern only if the afferent region is excited only through *Eng*. With this simple picture, however, a very unpleasant stimulus pattern which does not excite any neuroelements *II* would not be perceived as real at all, but only as a memory. This hardly corresponds to facts in general. However, this may have something to do with the feeling of unreality which a very painful situation produces in some individuals.

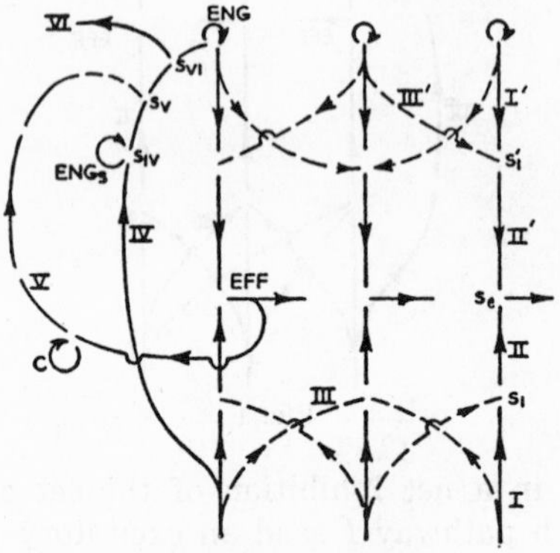

FIG. 2

We now complicate the picture by having excitatory pathways, perhaps rather weak ones, connect each neuroelement *I* with the corresponding efferent neuroelement *Eff*, by-passing the corresponding neuroelement *II*. The total excitation or inhibition of the neuroelements *II* still remains the measure of pleasantness or unpleasantness, but even the most painful situation will now give a feeling of reality because it will have excited the neuroelements *Eff* not through *Eng* only.

With this mechanism the memory of an unpleasant event is in no way different from that of a pleasant event. Neither memory involves neuroelements *II*. This in itself does not necessarily contradict any observations. We frequently think without particular pain of past events which at the time of their occurrence were extremely unpleasant. However, sometimes memories themselves are very painful. To account for this we must complicate somewhat our neural mechanism.

Let each *Eng* (Fig. 2) send "down" a pathway *I'*, connecting at s_1' with a pathway *II'*, which, in its turn, connects at s_e with the same efferent neuroelement as the corresponding neuroelement *II*. Let each *I'* send cross-inhibitory pathways *III'* to each s_1', so as to form a sort of mirror image of the system of neuroelements *I* and *II*. Moreover, let each neuroelement *I* and each neuroelement *I'* send excitatory pathways to the corresponding efferents, by-passing neuroelements *II* and *II'* correspondingly.

A directly perceived stimulus pattern is pleasant if it results in the excitation of neuroelements *II* and *II'*. A directly perceived stimulus pattern is unpleasant if it results in an inhibition of both neuroelements *II* and *II'*. A memory of a pleasant stimulus pattern exists when neuroelements *II'*, but not *II*, are excited while a memory of an unpleasant pattern exists when neuroelements *II* and *III* are not excited at all, but neuroelements *II'* and *III'* are excited in such a way that the net result is an inhibition at the connection s_1'.

In general, the memory of a pleasant event will be less pleasant than the event itself, since only neuroelements *II'*, instead of both *II'* and *II*, are excited and excite neuroelements *Eff*. The memory of an unpleasant event is less unpleasant than the event itself. This seems to agree with observations.

Events of which we are conscious we do usually remember to a greater or less degree. We speak of an unconscious act, if we do not ordinarily remember it. This suggests that the excitation of the *Eng* neuroelements corresponds to consciousness of an event.

If the connection delay along pathways *IV*, each of which may actually be a chain of pathways, is long, then some stimulus patterns may produce a reaction through the neuroelements *Eff*, *before* the neuroelements *Eng* are stimulated. Such a reaction is subconscious and is not consciously remembered. If each of the efferent neuroelements *Eff* sends an inhibitory pathway *V* to one of the connections of the corresponding chain of pathways *IV*, then, once such a subconscious reaction is produced, before the corresponding neuroelement *Eng* is excited, a subsequent excitement of that neuroelement *Eng* will be prevented. The act remains subconscious. In the absence of such an additional mechanism or when the reaction is short and therefore the inhibition of the chains *IV* is short, the neuroelements *Eng* may be stimulated after the corresponding efferent neuroelements. Thus we may or may not remember afterward an act of which we were not conscious at the time of its performance.

It is, however, known that subconscious acts may in a way be remembered also, though the memory itself is on the subconscious level. Under the action of some drugs, such as amytal sodium, such "subconscious" memories may be evoked. The above picture does not account for that, and we must complicate it further.

Let each of the pathways *V* be a chain of pathways, and let that chain at some given spot, s_{IV}, connect with a self-circulated neuroelement Eng_s. Let each of the chains of pathways *V*, mentioned above, inhibit through a last inhibitory link a connection of the chain *IV* somewhere between Eng_s and *Eng*. Moreover, let the chain of pathways *V* have at one of its connections a self-circuited *C*, whose permanent excitation threshold is such that when *V* is excited weakly the excitation is reversible but when *V* is excited strongly the circuit is excited permanently and the part of the chain *V* between the circuit and s_V (Fig. 2) remains permanently excited.

With this mechanism, once a sufficiently strong subconscious reaction is produced, the corresponding Eng_s are excited but not the corresponding neuroelements *Eng*. This may be interpreted as meaning that the individual will not consciously remember the event but that it will be stored in the subconscious memory. If through the action of some factor, for example, amytal sodium, the chain *V* between *C* and s_V is inhibited, the excitation of Eng_s causes an excitation of *Eng*, and the event is remembered.

The individual's reaction to such a "disinhibited" previously subconscious memory will be through *Eng*, *I'* s_1', and *II'*. In this case, once a subconscious memory is evoked into consciousness, it remains conscious. The chain *IV* may, however, branch off at s_{VI} an excitation chain *VI* which connects directly to *Eff*. In that case, disinhibition of s_V may produce a reaction through *VI* and *Eff*, without necessarily exciting the neuroelements *Eng*. The reaction may be interpreted as the individual's statement about a past event remembered only subconsciously. But when the disinhibition is over and the neuroelements *Eng* have not become excited, the individual will again not remember the event. All will depend on the intensity of excitation of Eng_s or of the intensity of excitation E_{IV} of the neuroelement chain between Eng_s and Eng. If E_{IV} is greater than the threshold h^* of the permanent excitation of Eng, the inhibition of V will result in a conscious memory of the event, even after the disinhibition is over. Otherwise, the individual will again forget consciously the event.

It is empirically known that memory of an event becomes weaker as time goes on. One might attempt to interpret that in terms of a gradual extinction of the excitation of the engramic neuroelement. Since memories may last for years, we must assume that the *Eng* neuroelements are rather stable, which is quite possible according to the discussion of chapter ii (p. 15). Inasmuch, however, as sometimes entirely forgotten events are again remembered, the assumption of an extinction of excitation of the *Eng* neuroelements presents some difficulties. The following scheme may therefore be suggested as an alternative:

Let each engramic neuroelement *Eng* send to every other one inhibitory pathways. In the stream of experience more and more engrams become excited. Hence each of the already excited engrams becomes more and more inhibited by the others. The memory for any event will gradually weaken because of inhibition by memories of new events. Thus a general weakening of memory will occur, as time goes on. But this weakening, contrary to facts, would affect equally the recent and the long-past memories. Only the strongest memories will eventually remain, the weaker ones being completely inhibited.

The network shown in Figure 2 provides for such a mechanism, though in a too restricted sense. According to Figure 2, we should not remember too complex situations nor remember several things at one time, for all involved engrams will become inhibited when their number exceeds a critical value n^*. With such a scheme we should find that if, on the average, a constant number of engrams are formed per unit time in the stream of experience, then after a finite time all engrams will become inhibited, and no memory will be possible.

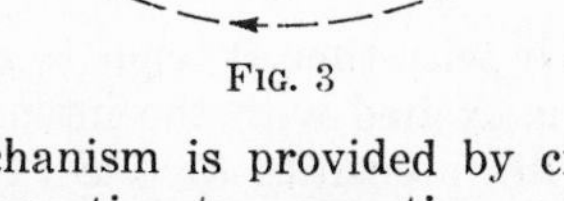

FIG. 3

A different mechanism is provided by cross-inhibitory pathways going from connection to connection, as shown in Figure 3.

Let E be the excitation of each engram. For simplicity we

now assume E to be the same for all of them. In the stationary state the value of ϵ produced at the connection is (chap. ii)

$$\varepsilon = \frac{A}{a} E = \gamma E . \tag{1}$$

Denoting by h the threshold of the cross-inhibitory pathways, we find that the excitation E_i of each of the inhibitory pathways is

$$E_i = \beta (\varepsilon - j - h) , \tag{2}$$

where j is the total amount of inhibitory factor at the connection, while the amount of inhibitory factor produced by each inhibitory pathway is

$$j^* = \frac{B}{b} E_i = \gamma_1 E_i . \tag{3}$$

Equations (2) and (3) give

$$j^* = \beta \gamma_1 (\varepsilon - j - h) . \tag{4}$$

If the total number of excited engrams is n, then at each connection

$$j = (n-1) j^* = \beta \gamma_1 (n-1) (\varepsilon - j - h) . \tag{5}$$

Putting

$$\varepsilon - j = \phi , \tag{6}$$

we have from (1) and (5)

$$\phi = \gamma E - \beta \gamma_1 (n-1) (\phi - h) , \tag{7}$$

which gives

$$\phi = \frac{\gamma E}{1 + \beta \gamma_1 (n-1)} + \frac{\beta \gamma_1 (n-1)}{1 + \beta \gamma_1 (n-1)} h . \tag{8}$$

For any finite n the excitation ϕ is positive and tends to h as n becomes infinite. If the threshold h is very small, we may neglect the second term of the right-hand side of (8) and obtain

$$\phi = \frac{\gamma E}{1 + \beta \gamma_1 (n-1)} . \tag{9}$$

Since n varies linearly with time, ϕ tends to zero as $1/t$.

If one engram is excited with the intensity E_1 and the other $(n-1)$ engrams with intensities $E_2 < E_1$, then we have, neglecting h,

$$\varepsilon_1 = \gamma E_1\,, \qquad \varepsilon_2 = \gamma E_2\,;$$
$$j_1 = \beta\gamma_1(n-1)\phi_2\,; \qquad j_2 = \beta\gamma_1(n-2)\phi_2 + \beta\gamma_1\phi_1\,. \tag{10}$$

Hence with

$$\beta\gamma_1 = \eta\,, \tag{11}$$

we have

$$\left.\begin{aligned} \phi_1 &= \gamma E_1 - \eta(n-1)\phi_2\,; \\ \phi_2 &= \gamma E_2 - \eta(n-2)\phi_2 - \eta\phi_1\,. \end{aligned}\right\} \tag{12}$$

This gives

$$\phi_1 = \frac{\gamma E_1 + \gamma\eta(n-2)E_1 - \gamma\eta(n-1)E_2}{(1-\eta)^2 + \eta(1-\eta)n}\,; \tag{13}$$

$$\phi_2 = \frac{\gamma E_2 - \gamma\eta E_1}{(1-\eta)^2 + \eta(1-\eta)n}\,. \tag{14}$$

For $E_1 = E_2$ those equations reduce to expression (9).

If E_1 and E_2 are of the same order of magnitude, then for ϕ_1 and ϕ_2 to be positive we must have $\eta << 1$. If $\eta << 1$ and $E_1/E_2 > 1/\eta$, then $\phi_2 < 0$. Physically, this means that none of the inhibitory pathways converging on the engram with excitation E_2 are excited. Hence in that case $\phi_1 = \alpha E_1$. Again only the strongest engram is excited at all, the others being inhibited.

The above mechanism results in a weakening of memories with time, the weakening being the same for recent and for long-past events. However, actually, recent events are remembered better than old ones, other conditions being equal. This suggests that, while newly formed engrams inhibit those formed previously, they themselves are not inhibited, at least appreciably, by those previous ones.

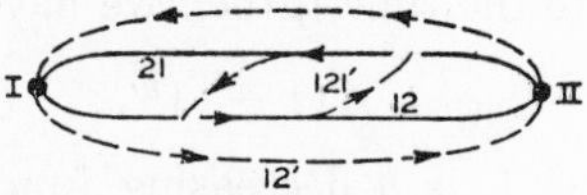

FIG. 4

The following mechanism provides for such a situation. Let any two engrams be connected as represented in Figure 4. Let the inhibitory pathways *12′* and *21′* be of the same strength as the excitatory pathways *12* and *21*. If *I* is excited first, then *12* and *12′* will cancel each other, and *II* will not be inhibited. But if, after that, *II* is excited, then *I* will be inhibited via *21′* because *21* is inhibited by the previous excitation of *121′*. The constants of *121* must be such that *121* is excited strongly even by weak stimuli, so that, when the excitation of *I* is reduced through inhibition by *II*, *121* would still inhibit *21*. Owing to the symmetry of the arrangement, if *II* is excited before *I*, *II* will be affected by *I*, but not *I* by *II*.

Consider, now, n engrams, all excited at different times. Denote by 1 the engram which is the last to be excited; by 2 the one before last, and so on. Let their intrinsic intensities of excitation be all the same and equal to E. Then for the first engram we have

$$\phi_1 = \alpha E \,, \tag{15}$$

since it is not inhibited by any others. For the second we have, neglecting the threshold of the inhibitory pathways,

$$\phi_2 = \alpha E - \eta\phi_1 = \alpha E(1-\eta)\,. \tag{16}$$

For the third we have

$$\left.\begin{aligned}\phi_3 &= \alpha E - \eta(\phi_1 + \phi_2)\\ &= \alpha E(1-2\eta+\eta^2) = \alpha E(1-\eta)^2.\end{aligned}\right\} \tag{17}$$

If

$$\phi_n = \alpha E(1-\eta)^{n-1}, \tag{18}$$

then

$$\left.\begin{aligned}\phi_{n+1} &= \alpha E - \eta(\phi_1 + \phi_2 \cdots \phi_n)\\ &= \alpha E\{1-\eta[1+(1-\eta)+(1-\eta)^2\\ &\quad +\cdots+(1-\eta)^{n-1}]\}\\ &= \alpha E\left\{1+\eta\frac{(1-\eta)^n-1}{\eta}\right\} = \alpha E(1-\eta)^n.\end{aligned}\right\} \tag{19}$$

Since equation (18) holds for $n = 1$ and 2, it holds for any n. If n is proportional to the time t, then we have

$$\phi_t = A(1-\eta)^{Bt}, \tag{20}$$

which, since $0 < \eta < 1$, is a decreasing function of t. Thus the longer ago the engram was formed, the weaker it is. If at some time an engram is formed with an intensity $E^* > E$ and is followed by $n-1$ engrams of intensity E, then

$$\left.\begin{aligned}\phi_n &= \alpha E^* - \eta(\phi_1 + \phi_2 + \cdots + \phi_{n-1})\\ &= \alpha E^* - \alpha E\eta[1+(1-\eta)+\cdots+(1-\eta)^{n-2}]\\ &= \alpha E^* - \alpha E[1-(1-\eta)^{n-1}].\end{aligned}\right\} \tag{21}$$

As n increases and as time goes on, ϕ_n decreases but tends to a constant value $\alpha(E^* - E)$. Thus a few strong memories outstanding in the stream of experience will slightly decrease but will then remain constant. Of course, all engrams are of different intensities, but we may consider them as of an average same intensity E, except for a few outstanding memories. If, on the average, outstanding memories occur every so often, then their intensity will also decrease with time to zero, since, as time goes on, their number mounts to infinity.

From the discrete case we may pass to the continuous and write, counting t backward,

$$\phi(t) = \alpha E(t) - \eta \int_0^t \phi(\xi)\,d\xi\,. \tag{22}$$

Differentiating and denoting

$$\frac{dE}{dt} = E'\,, \tag{23}$$

we find

$$\frac{d\phi}{dt} = \alpha E'(t) - \eta\phi. \tag{24}$$

The general solution of (24) is

$$\phi = e^{-\eta t}\,\{\phi_0 + \eta \int_0^t E'(t)\,e^{\eta t}dt\}\,. \tag{25}$$

If $E(t) = \text{const}$, then $E'(t) = 0$, and (25) gives

$$\phi = \phi_0 e^{-\eta t}\,, \tag{26}$$

where ϕ_0 is the intensity of memory just formed.

We shall assume here that the above-discussed mechanism of memory extinction holds only for the "conscious" memory. We shall consider that the neuroelements Eng_s do not cross-inhibit each other and that, therefore, subconsciously even the remotest events may be remembered. The number of events stored in the subconscious is limited only by the total number of neuroelements Eng_s available.

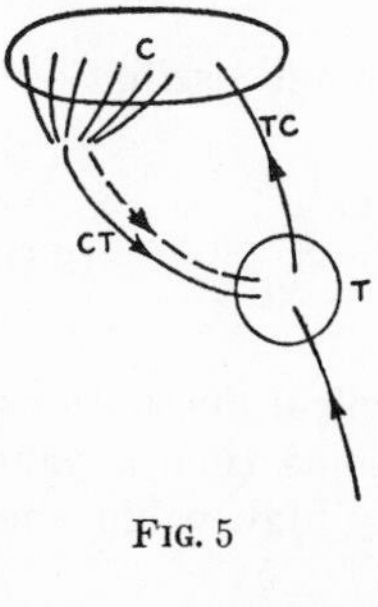

FIG. 5

In the stream of experience there is a constant increase of excitation on the level of neuroelements Eng_s. There is thus an accumulation of the level of the total net excitation $\phi = \varepsilon - j$ in the cortex. It is natural to assume some homeostatic mechanism which will tend to maintain a constant level ϕ_0. One of the simplest mechanisms of that kind would be that shown in Figure 5. The impulses coming from the external world are relayed to the cortex, C, through the thalamus, T. While we may consider that in an ordinary stream of experience not upset by any too unusual events, the *average* flow of impulses to the thalamus will be constant, yet, even then, the intensity S of the individual impulses will be scattered around the average according to some distribution function $E(S)$. Let all the Eng_s neuroelements of C send pathways to the pathways CT (Fig. 5), which are a pair of pathways, one excitatory, the other inhibitory. Since, ordinarily, the changes in the flow of outside stimuli are slow compared with the time constants of the neuroelements, we may consider the pathways CT as always in a quasistationary state of excitation.

The constants of the two pathways may be so chosen that for weak stimuli at C the excitatory pathway has almost reached its saturation value, while the inhibitory one is only weakly excited. For strong stimuli the excitation of the inhibitory pathway catches up with that of the excitatory and eventually exceeds it.

But then for high values of the total amount of $\phi_1 = \phi - \phi_0$ accumulated over a long period of time, the pair CT will act as an inhibitory pathway, raising the thresholds of the pathways TC, running from the thalamus to the cortex and thus cutting off from the cortex some of the weaker stimuli of the stream of experience. This will result in a decrease of the rate of accumulation, $d\phi_1/dt$. If the average rate of accumulation of ϕ_1, that is, the flow of stimuli, is constant and equal to S_0, then we have, denoting by a and λ two constants of proportionality,

$$\frac{d\phi_1}{dt} = aS_0 - \lambda \int_{-\infty}^{t} \phi_1 dt. \tag{27}$$

By differentiation we obtain from equation (27)

$$\frac{d^2\phi_1}{dt^2} = -\lambda\phi_1, \tag{28}$$

the solution of which represents undamped harmonic oscillations within a period

$$T = \frac{2\pi}{\sqrt{\lambda}} \tag{29}$$

In this simple case we should thus have periodical fluctuations of cortical excitation and inhibition. Unless at some time a particularly high value of S_0 has brought ϕ_1 to a very high value, the amplitude of the oscillations of ϕ_1 will be usually small. But if an external very strong experience has made ϕ_1 very large, the amplitude may become very large, and abnormally strong fluctuations of the state of excitation of the cortex will result, such as are observed in manic-depressive psychoses.

Let us consider the somewhat more general case in which S_0 is not constant but is itself a function, $S_0(t)$, of time. Then, instead of equation (28), we shall have, putting $dS_0/dt = S_0'(t)$,

$$\frac{d^2\phi_1}{dt^2} + \lambda\phi_1 = aS_0'(t). \tag{30}$$

Consider the following form of $S_0(t)$: Let, in general, S_0 be constant, except for a short time when it rapidly rises to some value S_{01}, then after an interval of time T_0 again drops to the original constant value. The quantity S_0' then will rise from zero to a maximum value, drop again to zero, become negative, and again return to zero. It will be represented by a curve like that shown in Figure 6. But then for that interval of time, equation (30) represents a forced harmonic oscillation. If T_0 is very close to $2\pi/\sqrt{\lambda}$, then even one "wave" of the external force, $S_0'(t)$, may increase the

FIGURE 6

amplitude of ϕ_1 very appreciably. An equal temporary increase of S_0 to the value S_{01} but for a period T_i, which is much different from $2\pi/\sqrt{\lambda}$ will not result in such abnormally high amplitudes. It must be noted that bringing, by some external means, ϕ_1 and even S_0 to zero at some moment does not necessarily result in the cessation of the fluctuations, because $d\phi_1/dt$ may remain at that moment either strongly positive or negative, depending on the value of the integral $\int_{-\infty}^{t} \phi_1 dt$.

Equation (27) should, of course, be considered only as a first approximation. The relation between $d\phi_1/dt$ and the cumulative value of ϕ_1 will, in general, be nonlinear. The addition of nonlinear terms will introduce harmonics into the oscillations and the possibility of very sudden periodical changes in ϕ_1 will be present.

If we consider another more general case, namely, that the Eng_s neuroelements inhibit each other, or that the Eng neuroelements also connect with *CT*, then in the cumulative effect the amount of ϕ_1 which corresponds to a more remote time contributes less than a recent ϕ_1. If we assume an exponential decay, as in (26), then, instead of (27), we obtain, for a constant S_0,

$$\frac{d\phi_1}{dt} = aS_0 - \lambda \int_{-\infty}^{t} \phi_1(\tau) e^{-\eta(t-\tau)} d\tau. \tag{31}$$

Bringing $e^{-\eta t}$ outside the sign of the integral, multiplying by $e^{\eta t}$, differentiating with respect to t, and then canceling $e^{-\eta t}$, we obtain

$$\frac{d^2\phi_1}{dt^2} + \eta \frac{d\phi_1}{dt} + \lambda\phi_1 = a\eta S_0, \tag{32}$$

which represents damped harmonic oscillations, the amplitude decreasing as $e^{-\eta t}$. The greater the η, in other words, the weaker the memory, the more rapidly the oscillations will die down. The value of ϕ_1 oscillates now not around $\phi_1 = 0$ ($\phi = \phi_0$) but around $\phi_1' = a\eta S_0/\lambda$.

The neurobiophysical mechanisms discussed above provide for aftereffects of past experiences through memory. We shall now briefly discuss mechanisms which will have to be studied for the interpretation of the effects of anticipation of future events upon the individual. Fundamentally, any idea of a future event presupposes that the different elements of that event have been experienced in the past. The *combinations* of those elements may be entirely new and never have been experienced before. But the elements themselves must have been given by previous experience.

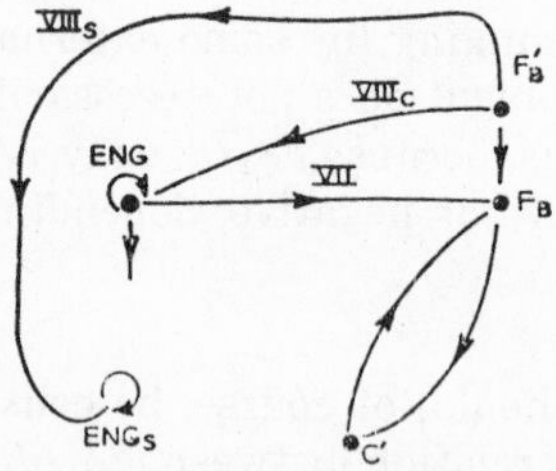

FIG. 7

It is natural to consider a generalization of the scheme of Figure 2, in which case each neuroelement *Eng* excites a pathway (Fig. 7, *VII*) leading to a neuroelement *F* in some different region of the brain. While the excitation of an *Eng* neuroelement corresponds to a memory of a past event, a similar excitation of a neuroelement F corresponds to the idea of the event's happening in the future. Since, according to that scheme, a present event also excites the corresponding F neuroelement, we may use the following interpretation:

An event is perceived directly when the corresponding peripheral afferents, the *Eng* and F, are excited. If only *Eng* and F are excited, we have the memory of the event. If only F is excited, we think of the event in the future.

If in the past an experience A has been followed several times by the experience B, then the temporal pattern $A \rightarrow B$ will be "remembered" through the corresponding neuroelements *Eng*. During the experiencing of the temporal pattern $A \rightarrow B$, the corresponding neuroelements F_A and F_B will also be excited. If the different neuroelements F are connected through "conditioning" pathways, discussed in chapter ix, then a simultaneous or closely successive excitation of F_A and F_B will have the result that excitation of F_A alone will, through the conditioning pathway, elicit the excitation of F_B.

Now let experience A happen alone. Through the corresponding neuroelement *Eng* it will produce the excitation of F_A. Through previous conditioning, F_B will become excited. But there will be no excitation of the peripheral afferents, nor will there necessarily be a very strong excitation of the *Eng* corresponding to the event B. Hence the occurrence of A will make us *anticipate* B *in the future*. We have here an elementary mechanism of foresight.

Such phenomena as rational problem-solving or planning are probably closely connected with the functioning of neuroelements F, involving mechanisms outlined in chapter xvi.

When an external event evokes our concern or thought of a future event, it is frequently in the biological interest of the individual to concentrate on that future event for a sufficient time. A mechanism for such a concentration may be provided by the scheme shown in Figure 7. A neuroelement F excites some other center C', which, in its turn, excites F. This enhances the excitation of F. With properly chosen constants of the neuroelements involved, the circuit $F_B C'$ will not remain excited if the original excitation of F is removed. But if in a pathological individual the constants of the circuit are different, then even the removal of the original stimulus A, which resulted in the excitation of F_B will leave the circuit $F_B C'$, and hence F_B, excited. The individual will not be able to bring to a stop his concern about the future event F_B. If, as is natural to assume in accordance with the general mathematical biophysics of the central nervous system, each F sends inhibitory pathways to other parts of the brain, such a strong excitation of one group F of neuroelements will result in an inhibition of other functions of the central nervous system. Such a general inhibition may be removed by cutting the circuit $F_B C'$.

It is plausible to assume that the F neuroelements are located in the frontal lobes. It may be suggested that what is achieved in prefrontal lobotomy is just the severing of the circuits $F_B C'$. Once those circuits are destroyed, not only does the permanent preoccupation with one idea cease, but it becomes impossible for an individual to *concentrate* properly on future events. Complaints of lobotomized patients about a certain "haziness" of the future have been occasionally recorded in the literature.

Let a pattern $A + B$ be several times followed by a stimulus C_1, which produces the reaction R_1. However, let A alone not be followed by C_1. As a part of the pattern $A + B$, A will continually produce reaction R_1. Let A, presented alone, be followed by a stimulus C_2, which unconditionally produces the reaction R_2. While A is experienced alone several times, it not only becomes conditioned to R_2, but (chap. ix) through it inhibits its own connection with R_1. With properly chosen constants of the pathways, the process of extinction of the conditioned reflex $A \rightarrow R_1$ is slow. Moreover, after a period of rest when A was not experienced at all, an experiencing of A will again result in the reaction R_1 until A has been repeated alone a sufficient number of times. Hence, in general, an experience of A will produce both R_1 and R_2. If the efferent paths of R_1 and R_2 cross-inhibit each other, only one of the reactions will be produced, namely, the stronger one.

If B has always been followed by C_1, while A alone has always been followed by C_2, then we may say that reaction R_1 is the "correct" reaction to B, while the reaction R_2 is the "correct" reaction to A alone. The experience A may have occurred accidentally several times in conjunction with B and thus have become conditioned to R_1. If $A \rightarrow R_1$ has been very strong, $A \rightarrow R_2$ will not overcome it, and A will always result in the wrong reaction. If, in the pattern $A + B$, the central neuroelements, which form the beginnings of the conditioned circuits, cross-inhibit each other, then the conditioning of A to R_1 when in conjunction with B is weaker than if A were alone; for that reason the reaction $A \rightarrow R_1$ will be weaker than $A \rightarrow R_2$. Hence, when A is presented alone, it will elicit the the correct reaction R_2.

But if the cross-inhibition between A and B is weak, the reflex $A \rightarrow R_1$ may become so strong as always to prevail over $A \rightarrow R_2$.

Let A stand for the experience by a person of seeing another individual, and let B stand for this individual's performance of some hostile act. R_1 may then be a fright reaction or the feeling that the other individual hates the person. On the contrary, R_2 may be a reaction of friendliness. If we always have $A \rightarrow R_1$, then the person has the feeling that every other individual is hostile to him or her. As follows from the above, this type of paranoia may be caused by too weak cross-inhibitory pathways between the afferent neuroelements.

The same situation may, however, be caused by an entirely different mechanism. Let R_1 be a very unpleasant reaction, which results in a general cortical inhibition. Then if we first have $A + B \rightarrow R_1$ with a resulting $A \rightarrow R_1$, the process of conditioning of A alone to R_2 is inhibited because, before the conditioned reaction $A \rightarrow R_2$ is established, the already existing reaction $A \rightarrow R_1$ produces inhibitions of all centers.

If, in particular, we assume that any unpleasant situation results in an excitation of a definite "pain" center, which sends off inhibitory pathways to other parts of the brain, then the above-discussed situation may be remedied by cutting the pathways leading from the rest of the cortex to the pain center. A surgical treatment of some paranoid conditions thus appears as a possibility.

As we have seen, qualitatively the same type of paranoid symptoms may be due to entirely different mechanisms. The next problem is to develop the different *quantitative* aspects of the two mechanisms by means already used in mathematical biophysics. In this way through *quantitative tests* it may be possible to establish which of the possible mechanisms is operating in a given case. This would have diagnostic value as well as give clues to possible therapeutic procedure.

Let it be possible to condition Eng_s to any reaction, and let the Eng's send inhibitory pathways to *all* conditioned pathways going from the corresponding Eng_s's. Then the mere bringing into consciousness of any subconsciously remembered event may abolish some subsconsciously formed undesirable reaction.

Now let F_B be excited by a center F_B', which also is connected with both the corresponding Eng and Eng_s by tracts VIII_c and VIII_s. The excitation of F_B' may be interpreted as corresponding to the desire of B. Owing to the type of connections shown in Figure 7, when we desire B, we also, *ipso facto,* think of B in the future. But we may think of B in the future (excitation of F_B) without desiring it.

Suppose at some time the desire for B was followed by an

event A, which produces reaction R. Since F_B' through VIII_c and VIII_s excites both Eng and Eng_s, either of which can be conditioned to produce R, R will be produced later on whenever the desire for B is experienced. If the excitation E_{VIII_c} of VIII_c is always stronger than E_{VIII_s} of VIII_s, then the "subconscious" part of the conditioning, that is, the conditioning of Eng_s to B, will be inhibited by the excitation of the corresponding Eng. Thus the reaction R will be produced quite consciously, and, if it is an undesirable reaction, it may be consciously suppressed. But if in an individual the connection VIII_c is always much weaker than VIII_s, then the reaction R will be produced subconsciously. Reaction R may be undesirable, even antisocial or even painful to the individual. Thus B may represent attention by others, while A may be some physiological disturbance or mild illness producing the reaction R—say, a headache or other symptom. If desire for attention (B) has been accidentally followed immediately by A and thus produced R, R may be produced again every time B is desired, although A (the actual physiological disturbance) may be absent. We have here a mechanism that produces some simple forms of hysteria. A hysterical individual, according to that picture, is characterized by $E_{VIII_c} < E_{VIII_s}$.

From this point of view, severing of VIII_s may abolish some types of psychoneurotic behavior. In this connection it may be interesting to speculate concerning the mechanism of the beneficial effects of prefrontal lobotomy. If all connections to and from the frontal lobes are severed, this would mean severing VIII, as well as the circuit $F_B - C'$ (Fig. 7). The severance of the latter would, as mentioned above, abolish some types of depressions connected with constant concern over the future. Severance of VIII_s would abolish certain types of hysterical behavior and subconscious habits. It may be worth noticing that improvements in psychoneurotics have been reported after lobotomy. Perhaps, with further experimental study and improvement of surgical technique, it may be possible to sever at will either VIII_s or circuit $F_B - C'$. Different kinds of "partial" lobotomies may perhaps be used in the future for different types of mental disorders. That a complete severance of *all* connections may not be necessary seems to be indicated by some recent work.[2]

Any given situation which confronts an individual has, as a rule, a large number of possible consequences, of different degrees of probability, as well as of different degrees of pleasantness. Thus, taking a walk may result in the mere sensation of walking, usually pleasant and very probable. Or it may result in getting wet in a rain, which may be less probable and more unpleasant; or it may result in being injured by an automobile, which is rather improbable but highly unpleasant; or it may result in finding a thousand-dollar bill, which is also highly improbable but exceedingly pleasant. Any given situation may be viewed as a complex stimulus pattern. Let us denote it by S.

If the same situation, or a set of similar situations, recurs frequently during the lifetime of an individual, then, since every time that it occurs it is followed by one of the possible consequences, it becomes eventually associated through conditioning with *all* those consequences. The strength of the association to a given consequence, x_i, will be the greater, the more frequently the sequence S, x_i has occurred in the past (chap. ix). But that frequency is proportional to the probability $P(x_i)$ of x_i's above, occurring when S is present.

Through the mechanism discussed when x_i becomes conditioned to or associated with S, then the experiencing of S makes us anticipate x_i in the future. The intensity of anticipation will be approximately proportional to the strength of association. Thus any situation S would make us anticipate all, or almost all, possible consequences, if our experience with S has been long enough.

However, let all the centers for anticipation of different x_i's be cross-inhibiting one another. Then only those that are most strongly excited, that is, the most probable ones, will remain excited, the remaining ones being inhibited. The intensity of excitation e_i of any x_i is given by

$$e_i = e_{0i} - b \sum_{k \neq i} e_{0k} \,, \tag{33}$$

where e_{0i} is the intensity as determined by the strength of association. For very large numbers of x_i, we may substitute an integral for the sum, considering x as a continuous variable:

$$e(x) = e_0(x) - b \int_0^\infty e_0(x)\,dx \,. \tag{34}$$

But with α as a coefficient,

$$e_0(x) = \alpha P(x) \,, \tag{35}$$

where $P(x)$ is the probability of x. Therefore,

$$e(x) = \alpha P(x) - \alpha b \int_0^\infty P(x)\,dx \,, \tag{36}$$

or, since

$$\int_0^\infty P(x)\,dx = 1\,, \tag{37}$$

$$e(x) = \alpha[P(x) - b]\,. \tag{38}$$

If the inhibitory constant b is larger than the probability P_m of the most probable consequence x of S, then no consequences will be anticipated at all. This is a particular case of the general phenomenon of mutual inhibition of too many centers (chap. iii).

According to the theory of pleasantness and unpleasantness suggested in chapter xvi, the pleasantness of an experience is measured essentially by the intensity of excitation E of certain cortical regions, or perhaps even of the cortex as a whole. Since each x, or the anticipation of it, itself acts as a stimulus, the experiencing of a given x or the anticipation of it will result in a definite intensity of excitation $E(x)$ in the cortex.

In discussing problems of discrimination of intensities of peripheral stimuli, we pointed out (chap. v) that, since different reactions may be produced by different intensities of the same stimulus, those different intensities must involve different neuroelements, even though the peripheral stimulus is always applied to the same afferent pathways. There is no sufficient reason to limit such considerations to intensities of peripheral excitation only. In fact, the generalization to central excitation is almost mandatory. We react quite differently when we exhibit different degrees of pleasure or displeasure. Hence we must postulate a similar mechanism, which results in the excitation of different groups of neuroelements $N_{E(x)}$ for different values $E(x)$ of the central excitation.

If we now make the rather plausible assumption that all conditioned and associative connections are two-way connections so that, if a stimulus s_1 is associated with a stimulus s_2, then s_2 is also associated with s_1, then we come to the conclusion that not only does the experiencing of x produce a central excitation $E(x)$ but, vice versa, if the central excitation has a given value $E(x)$, then, through the group of neuroelements $N_{E(x)}$, it will excite the center, whose functioning corresponds to the anticipation of x.

Now let the individual be confronted with the situation S and, at the same time, let the level of the central excitation be maintained at a given level $E(x')$ through some endogenous or exogenous influences. Then (35) will hold only for such values of x as are different from x'. For the latter we shall have

$$e_0(x') = \alpha P(x') + I\,, \tag{39}$$

where I denotes the additional excitation received by x' from the group of neuroelements $N_{E(x')}$. Instead of (34), we now have, for $x \neq x'$,

$$e(x) = e_0(x) - b\left[I + \int_0^\infty e_0(x)\,dx\right], \tag{40}$$

or, instead of (38),

$$e(x) = \alpha[P(x) - b] - bI\,. \tag{41}$$

For $x = x'$ we have

$$e(x') = \alpha[P(x') - b] + I\,. \tag{42}$$

Whereas, in the absence of the additional excitation I, only the most probable x's are excited, now, even if $b < P_m$, the most probable $x = x_m$ may remain unexcited, while the one which is additionally excited by $N_{E(x')}$ will be excited. Or it may happen that, although in the neighborhood of $x = x_m$ the x's still remain excited, an $x = x'$, having the additional excitation I, will also be excited, even more strongly than x_m.

Let us arrange all x's in decreasing order of their pleasantness, so that $x = 0$ is the most pleasant. In the average life of an average individual most situations are of such a nature that their most probable consequences are neither too pleasant nor too unpleasant. The extremely pleasant or extremely unpleasant consequences of S are, as a rule, improbable, as in the example given on page 200. Hence $P(x)$ will have its maximum value P_n for some value of $x = x_m$, which is of average pleasantness. For instance, let $P(x)$ be a normal distribution

$$P(x) = \frac{1}{\sqrt{2\pi}\,\sigma}\, e^{-(x_m - x)^2/2\sigma^2}. \tag{43}$$

If the individual is confronted with S at a time when his central excitation level is in the neighborhood of $E(x_m)$, then all highly pleasant and highly unpleasant x's will be inhibited, and only the x's in the range between the two roots of the equation

$$\alpha[P(x) - b] - bI = 0 \tag{44}$$

will be excited. The individual anticipates average, most probable events of average pleasantness. But if the situation S is confronted when the value $E(x)$ corresponds to $x' >> x_m$, then in the neighborhood of $x = x_m$ we shall have (41), but for x' we shall have expression (42). If $P(x)$ is given by (43), then

$$e(x') = \alpha \left[\frac{1}{\sqrt{2\pi}\,\sigma} e^{(x_m - x')^2/2\sigma^2} - b \right] + I, \tag{45}$$

$$e(x_m) = \alpha \left[\frac{1}{\sqrt{2\pi}\,\sigma} - b \right] - bI. \tag{46}$$

If

$$b < \frac{1}{\sqrt{2\pi}\,\sigma} < b\,\frac{I + \alpha}{\alpha}, \tag{47}$$

$$e(x') > 0, \tag{48}$$

then only x' will be excited. The individual anticipates such consequences of S as are unpleasant and unlikely. Because of equation (45), inequality (48) imposes a condition upon x'. Thus for given α, b, I, σ, and x_m, the probability of x' may have to be above a certain value in order that x' may be anticipated. If, however,

$$I > \alpha b, \tag{49}$$

then inequality (48) is always satisfied, but inequalities (47) may or may not be satisfied. If they are not, then, besides x', x's in the neighborhood of x_m will also be anticipated.

Thus the lowering of the excitatory level $E(x)$ results in a shift of associations and anticipations of the consequences of a given situation toward consequences which are unpleasant, and as a rule, highly improbable. We have an elementary mechanism of some anxiety neuroses when everything appears gloomy in the future and when an individual may worry over utterly unlikely possibilities. If at that moment a highly pleasant experience increases $E(x)$ and if this increase is not upset by some other influences (pathological conditions), the whole mood of the individual will change, and the future will appear "rosy."

Conversely, if an individual has an abnormally high level of $E(x)$, then, even in average circumstances, he will anticipate most pleasant, but unlikely, events ($x << x_m$). The choice of the constants α, b, and I, together with the individual's normal level $E(x)$ determine for a given situation whether the individual is an optimist or a pessimist.

There may be a very great number of factors which can determine the average level of $E(x)$. In an individual who reacts rather emotionally to eating and is very fond of good food, mere hunger or an upset stomach may lower $E(x)$ and temporarily produce a pessimistic attitude. On the other hand, a number of yet unknown or uncontrolled factors, like metabolism, endocrine activities, etc., may play an important role.

We have discussed above possible mechanisms of some forms of paranoia. It may be pointed out that the mechanism discussed here can very well also give rise to paranoid conditions. In the present instance the paranoia may be due not to any defect of the mechanism of logical thinking but to the *faulty choice of the premises*. A very large number of consequences *may* follow from a situation S. If, owing to the above-discussed mechanism, the individual chooses a very unlikely one, then, with impeccable logic, he will arrive at deductions that will be in conflict with reality and may lead the individual to social conflict. Thus, *purely logically*, there is the *possibility* that every other individual with whom an individual A comes in contact hates A and conspires against him. If A *accepts* this as the major premise, then, if he sees that B is actually very kind to him, the very impeccability of A's logic will force him to argue that B is kind to him in order to deceive him by his kindness. The roots of some paranoias may be not in the defect of logic but in the defect of choosing the major premises. In real life this choice has to be made in most cases on probability bases. The mechanism discussed here provides for the possibility of a forced choice of very improbable things.

Another interesting consequence of this theory is that an individual with low $E(x)$ will anticipate, as a rule, most unlikely things and is liable to overlook the more likely ones. This may result in a number of unpleasant situations, which might have been avoided had the individual thought of more likely things. The unpleasant situation will lower $E(x)$ further, and thus the situation gets worse, until it may end in a psychosis.

In general, $P(x)$ is a function of time, $P(x, t)$. Instead of equation (35) we have

$$e_0(x, t) = \alpha \int_0^t P(x, t)\, dt = \alpha F(x, t). \tag{50}$$

The effect of the past experience of the individual is thus made explicit.

In connection with the problem of psychoses and psychoneuroses we should mention here the interesting paper by J. Lettvin and W. Pitts.[4] L. Danziger and H. D. Landahl developed a mathematical theory of the mechanism of shock therapy,[5] which agrees fairly with some quantitative observations. N. Rashevsky discussed the nature of psychoses and psychoneuroses from the point of view of learning a "wrong" behavior.[6]

REFERENCES

1. A. S. Householder and H. D. Landahl, *Mathematical Biophysics of the Central Nervous System* (Bloomington, Ind.: Principia Press, 1945).

2. L. Hofstatter, A. Smolik, and A. K. Busch, *Arch. Neurol. and Psychiat.*, 53, 125, 1945.

3. N. Rashevsky, *Psychometrika*, 3, 253, 1938.

4. J. Lettvin and W. Pitts, *Bull. Math. Biophysics*, 5, 139, 1943.

5. L. Danziger and H. D. Landahl, *Bull. Math. Biophysics*, 7, 213, 1945.

6. N. Rashevsky, *Bull. Math. Biophysics*, 9, 1, 1947.

CHAPTER XIX

BOOLEAN ALGEBRA OF NEURAL NETS

If we consider neural structures which contain a relatively small number of neurons, then the equations developed in chapter ii cannot be applied. In studying the dynamics of such networks, we must take into account the actual discontinuous and all-or-none character of the synaptic transmission. W. S. McCulloch and W. Pitts[1] have suggested a convenient method of studying the properties of such networks through the use of Boolean algebra or symbolic logic.

For simplicity let us assume, with W. S. McCulloch and W. Pitts, that all synaptic delays are strictly constant, and let us use the synaptic delay as the unit of time. In Figure 1, *a*, let the neuron with the number *2*, which we shall designate by N_2, have a threshold of two terminal bulbs (chap. ii). Designate the neuron with the number *1* as N_1. Let no other neurons synapse with N_2. Then, neglecting the conduction time along the fibers, which for short fibers is much less than 0.5 ms, we may say: "N_2 fires at the moment t if, and only if, N_1 fires at the moment $t - 1$." If we denote the statement, "The neuron N_i fires at the time $t - x$", symbolically by $N_i(t - x)$ and if we denote by "$\equiv$" the phrase "if and only if," then the above statement about N_1 and N_2 may be written

$$N_2(t) \equiv N_1(t-1). \tag{1}$$

For the structure represented in Figure 1, *b*, the following statement holds: "The neuron N_3 fires at the time t if, and only if, either N_1 fires at the time t—1, or N_2 fires at the time t—1, or both N_1 and N_2 fire at the time t—1." Denoting by v the sign of logical disjunction,[2] that is, the statement "either ···· or ···· , or both," we may describe the properties of the structures shown in Figure 1, *b*, by the formula:

$$N_3(t) \equiv N_1(t-1) \mathbf{v} N_2(t-1). \tag{2}$$

In Figure 1, *c*, the neuron N_3 fires at the time t if, and only if, N_1 and N_2 both fire at the time t—1. Denoting by a dot $(\cdot)$ the sign of logical conjunction, that is, the relation "and," we describe the property of the structures shown in Figure 1, *c* by

$$N_3(t) \equiv N_1(t-1) \cdot N_2(t-1). \tag{3}$$

In Figure 1, *d*, let neuron N_2 be an inhibitory neuron, which we shall indicate graphically, following W. S. McCulloch and W. Pitts, by a loop at the apex of the higher-order neuron. Moreover, let the inhibition be absolute, that is, let an impulse arriving at the inhibiting synapse make the neuron N_3 entirely unexcitable at *that moment*. Then we may say: "N_3 fires at the time t if, and only if, N_1 fires at the time t—1 and N_2 does *not* fire at the time t—1." Denoting by a bar the negation of a statement, we have

$$N_3(t) \equiv N_1(t-1) \cdot \overline{N_2(t-1)}. \tag{4}$$

Given a neural net of any complexity, its property will always be described by a sentence of the form: "Neurons $N_i \cdots\cdots N_k \cdots\cdots N_e$ fire correspondingly at times $t_i \cdots\cdots t_k \cdots\cdots t_e$ if, and only if, other neurons $N_p \cdots\cdots N_r \cdots\cdots N_s$ fire correspondingly at times $t_p \cdots\cdots t_r \cdots\cdots t_s$, and certain other neurons $N_v \cdots\cdots N_w \cdots\cdots N_q$ do not fire correspondingly at times $t_v \cdots\cdots t_w \cdots\cdots t_q$."

Any sentence of that form may be decomposed into a series of simple statements, connected by conjunctions, disjunctions, and negations. Similarly, any complex network may be decomposed into, or built up from, the combination of the elementary networks shown in Figure 1*a* to *d*.

W. S. McCulloch and W. Pitts[1] give a formal method for constructing any complex net which has prescribed properties. The method, though powerful, has one serious limitation: It requires that all neurons fire at intervals which are integral multiples of the synaptic delay. In our notation it requires that they all fire at times which are represented by natural numbers.

We shall illustrate the method of W. S. McCulloch and W. Pitts in an example taken from actual observation. If a cold object is held to the skin for a moment and removed, a sensation of heat will be felt; if it is applied for a longer time, the sensation will be only of cold, with no preliminary warmth at all. It is known that we have special cutaneous receptors for heat and others for cold. Let N_1 and N_2 be the receptor neurons, respectively, for heat and for cold, and let N_3 and N_4 be the neurons whose activity implies a sensation of heat or cold respectively. Let us assume, for definiteness, that, if the cold stimulus is applied for only one unit of time but no longer, a sensation of heat results. We may describe the situation by

$$\left.\begin{aligned} N_3(t) &\equiv N_1(t-1) \vee [N_2(t-3) \cdot \overline{N_2(t-2)}], \\ N_4(t) &\equiv N_2(t-2) \cdot N_2(t-1). \end{aligned}\right\} \tag{5}$$

Now we shall construct a neural net which has the properties described by (5). To this end we introduce a "functor," S, defined by

$$SN_i(t) \equiv N_i(t-1). \tag{6}$$

We also define

$$S^2N_i(t) \equiv S[SN_i(t)] \equiv N_i(t-2)\,;\ \text{etc.} \tag{7}$$

It can readily be verified that in any equation of the type discussed here S can be "factored out." Thus, for instance, we may write

$$S^2N_i(t) \cdot SN_k(t) = S[SN_i(t) \cdot N_k(t)]. \tag{8}$$

Expressions (1)-(4) may now be written, correspondingly, as

$$\left.\begin{array}{ll} N_2(t) \equiv SN_1(t)\,; & N_3(t) \equiv SN_1(t) \vee SN_2(t)\,; \\ N_3(t) \equiv S[N_1(t) \cdot N_2(t)]\,; & N_3(t) \equiv S[N_1(t) \cdot \overline{N_2(t)}]. \end{array}\right\} \tag{9}$$

Expressions (5) for which we wish to construct a corresponding network, may now be written

$$N_3(t) \equiv S\{N_1(t) \vee S[(SN_2(t)) \cdot \overline{N_2(t)}]\}\,; \tag{10}$$

$$N_4(t) \equiv S\{[SN_2(t)] \cdot N_2(t)\}\,. \tag{11}$$

First, we construct a net for the function inclosed in the greatest number of brackets and proceed outward, that is, we construct a net which corresponds to the expression $SN_2(t)$. To this end we connect neuron N_2 to a neuron N_a in such a way as is shown in Figure 1, *a*. Thus

$$N_a(t) \equiv SN_2(t). \tag{12}$$

Next we construct a net corresponding to $[(SN_2(t) \cdot \overline{N_2(t)}]$ in (10) or, because of (12), to $N_a(t) \cdot \overline{N_2(t)}$. To do this we connect neuron N_a with a neuron N_b in a way indicated in Figure 1,*d*. Next we construct a net corresponding to $SN_2(t) \cdot N_2(t)$ in (11). To do this we connect N_a and N_e to N_4 in the way shown in Figure 1,*c*. Thus we now have

$$N_4(t) \equiv S[N_a(t) \cdot N_2(t)] \equiv S[(SN_2(t)) \cdot N_2(t)]\,, \tag{13}$$

which is nothing else but equation (11). We also have

$$N_b(t) \equiv S[N_a(t) \cdot \overline{N_2(t)}] \equiv S[(SN_2(t)) \cdot \overline{N_2(t)}]\,. \tag{14}$$

Finally, we use a structure of the form shown in Figure 1,*b*, to connect N_1 and N_b with N_3. We then have

$$\left.\begin{aligned} N_3(t) &\equiv S[N_1(t) \mathrm{v} N_b(t)] \\ &\equiv S\{N_1(t) \mathrm{v} S[(SN_2(t)) \cdot \overline{N_2(t)}]\}. \end{aligned}\right\} \quad (15)$$

Equations (15) and (13) are identical with (10) and (11) correspondingly, and our problem is thus solved. The final net is shown *in toto* in Figure 1,*e*.

A slight fallacy in the above picture has been pointed out by H. Epstein and A. Rapoport[13]. The first condition (5) requires that N_3 would fire at t if N_2 fires at $t - 3$, but does not fire at $t - 2$. The circuit of Figure 1e, constructed according to the method of W. S. McCulloch and W. Pitts, satisfies this requirement. But requirement (5) does not say anything about N_2 firing at $t - 4$, $t - 5$, or previous times. Therefore regardless of whether N_2 fired at, say $t - 4$ and $t - 5$, or not, as long as it fires at $t - 3$ and does not fire at $t - 2$, N_3 will fire at t. But if N_2 has fired also at $t - 4$ and $t - 5$, then we have a sensation of heat even though N_2 has been firing for a long time, that is even though the cold stimulus has been applied continuously. That this is so can be seen by a detailed analysis of the firing of circuit of Figure 1e.

Let N_2 fire at $t - 5$, $t - 4$, and $t - 3$, but not fire at $t - 2$. Then N_a fires at $t - 4$, but N_b is inhibited at that moment, and N_b does not fire at $t - 3$. Next N_2 fires at $t - 3$, but again N_a is inhibited at that moment and N_3 does not fire. Now N_a fires at $t - 2$ and since *at that time* N_2 does not fire, therefore N_b is not inhibited at $t - 2$, it fires and causes N_3 to fire at t. Hence N_3 fires at t, in spite of the fact that N_2 *did* fire at $t - 5$, $t - 4$, $t - 3$, and *did not fire* only at $t - 2$. We describe such a situation in physiological terms by saying that a short sensation of heat follows a cessation of continuous cold stimulus. But this is not what McCulloch and Pitts set out to do. Instead of the first expression (5) we should require

$$N_3(t) \equiv N_1(t-1) \mathrm{v} \\ [N_2(t-3) \cdot \overline{N_2(t-2)} \cdot \overline{N_2(t-m)} \cdot m > 3].$$

A circuit which satisfies this condition has been described by H. Epstein and A. Rapoport[13]. The above criticism does not of course alter the general validity of the approach by W. S. McCulloch and W. Pitts.

We shall now discuss some possible applications of the foregoing.[3]

The problem of a point-to-point correspondence between the retina and some region of the occipital lobes has been treated from the "macroscopic" point of view by H. D. Landahl.[4] It does not seem to be possible on this basis to account for the fact that, in certain parts, the number of optical fibers is about one hundred

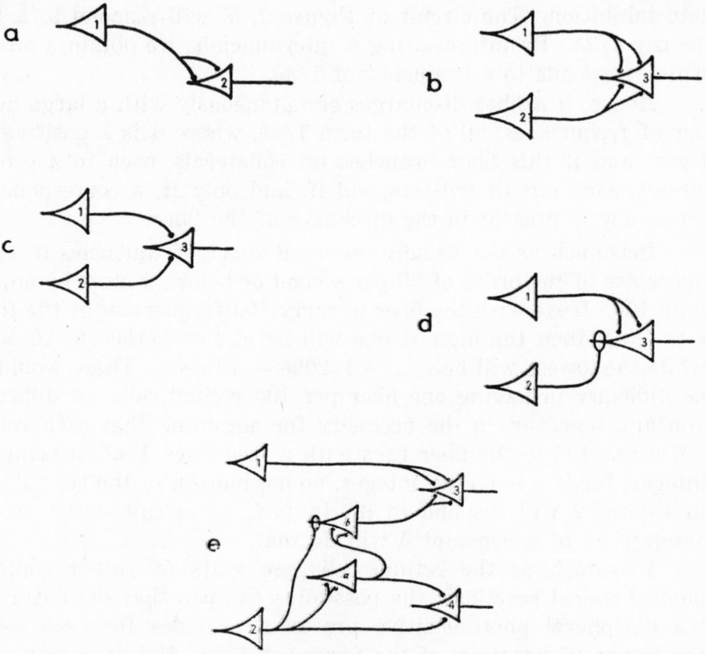

FIG. 1

times less than the number of cells which they connect. W. S. McCulloch (unpublished) has shown that, by considering rather general temporal patterns of discharge in a fiber, it is possible to construct a "microscopic" mechanism which will give the desired effect. It is interesting to consider as temporal patterns simple periodic discharges with different periods.

Assuming with W. S. McCulloch and W. Pitts[1] that all synaptic delays are approximately constant, being equal to about 0.5 ms, and denoting this constant by δ, it is readily seen that a circuit as shown in Figure 2,*a*, will respond only when the left fiber

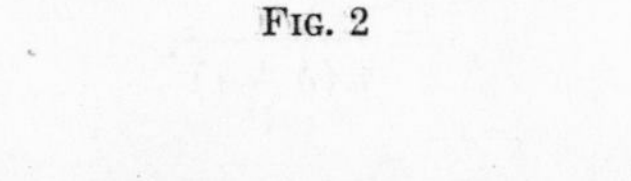

FIG. 2

fires regularly with a frequency $1/\delta$. Except where otherwise indicated, we symbolically assume[1] that a simultaneous excitation of two terminal bulbs is necessary to make a neuron fire. Inhibitory synapses are symbolized by loops, and we consider here only absolute inhibition. The circuit of Figure 2, *b*, will respond to a frequency $1/2\delta$. By intercalating n internuncials, we obtain a circuit which responds to a frequency of $1/n\delta$.

Hence, if a fiber discharges simultaneously with a large number of frequencies, all of the form $1/n\delta$, where n is a positive integer, and if this fiber branches off collaterals, each to a proper circuit, each circuit will respond if, and only if, a corresponding frequency is present in the discharge of the fiber.

Inasmuch as the usually observed steady frequencies in optic fibers are of the order of 20 per second or below, n must be no less than 100. If we wish the fiber to carry 100 frequencies of the form $\nu = 1/n\delta$, then the highest one will be $\nu_{\max} = 1/100\delta = 20 \text{ sec}^{-1}$, while the lowest will be $\nu_{\min} = 1/200\delta = 10 \text{ sec}^{-1}$. There would be no difficulty in having one fiber per 100 retinal cells. A difficulty appears, however, in the necessity for assuming that each retina cell connected to the fiber fires with a frequency $1/n\delta$, n being an integer, for if n is not an integer, no mechanism of the type shown in Figure 2 will respond to it. In fact, *no* circuit based on the assumption of a constant δ will do that.

Inasmuch as the retinal cells are seats of rather complex photochemical reactions, the possibility is open that the nature of the peripheral photosensitive processes provides for each cell a frequency of discharge of the form $\nu = 1/n\delta$. But at present this must be an explicit additional assumption.

The mechanism for discrimination of intensities discussed in chapter v is based on the macroscopic concept. However, using at the afferent end of a slowly adapting fiber such circuits as those shown in Figure 2, we see that a stimulus of a given intensity, S, which results in a steady frequency, $\nu(S)$, may be relayed to different parts of the brain, depending on its intensity. Empirically it is known that approximately

$$\nu = \log S \, . \tag{16}$$

But only frequencies of the form $1/n\delta$ will produce a response at all. In order to have a mechanism that will account for perception of a continuous range of frequencies, we must consider the period of latent addition τ (p. 12), and thus obtain

$$\nu = \frac{1}{n(\delta \pm \tau)} , \tag{17}$$

with $\tau < \delta$. The smallest discriminable difference, $\Delta\nu$, of frequencies is

$$\Delta\nu = \frac{1}{\delta \pm \tau}\left(\frac{1}{n} - \frac{1}{n+1}\right) = \frac{1}{\delta \pm \tau}\,\frac{1}{n(n+1)}. \tag{18}$$

For frequencies of the order of 200 sec^{-1} or less, $n > 10$, and, instead of (18), we have approximately

$$\Delta\nu = \frac{1}{\delta \pm \tau}\,\frac{1}{n^2}. \tag{19}$$

From equations (16), (17), and (18) it follows that

$$\frac{\Delta S}{S} = (\delta \pm \tau)\log^2 S, \tag{20}$$

which is contrary to experience. The "macroscopic" theory[9] is better in this case, although further modifications of the "microscopic" model may lead to different results.

We may consider a group of rapidly adapting fibers so that the frequency in each fiber is independent of the intensity S of the stimulus. Owing to differences in thresholds, however, let the number of excited fibers increase with S. The circuit shown in Figure 3 provides for an excitation of a different second-order neuron for sufficiently different values of S. But the relation between S and ΔS is now determined solely by the distribution function of the thresholds h_i, which must be chosen so as to give a correct relation between ΔS and S.

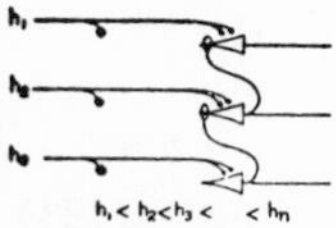

FIG. 3

A distribution function of thresholds enters also into the "macroscopic" theory of discrimination. All the work of A. S. Householder[5, 6, 7, 8] discussed in chapter v indicates, however, that the gross results of the theory do not depend on the exact form of that distribution function as they would in the present case.

We shall now discuss a mechanism for the discrimination of several temporally separated stimuli affecting the same end-organ. On a "macroscopic" scale a somewhat similar problem has been discussed by H. D. Landahl.[9]

We shall introduce two new structures corresponding to the unlimited existential operator, $(Ex)\ N(x)$, meaning "there is an x for which $N(x)$ holds" and the limited existential operator, (Ex) k$N(x)$, meaning "there is an x among the integers from 0 to k for which $N(x)$ holds."

Using δ as the unit of time, we find the following:

To the analytical expression

$$N_2(t) \equiv (Ex) N_1(t-x-1), \tag{21}$$

where x is an integer including zero, corresponds the circuit shown in Figure 4,*a*. To the expression

$$N_2(t) \equiv (Ex) \mathrm{k} N_1(t-x-1), \tag{22}$$

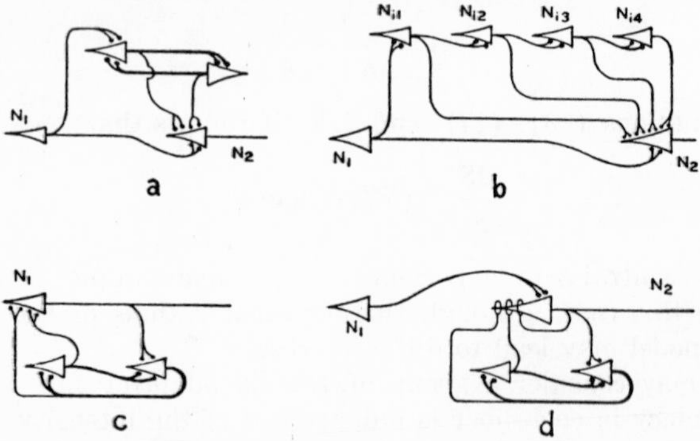

FIG. 4

corresponds a circuit of the kind shown in Figure 4,*b*, with k neurons N_{ij}.

A circuit, shown in Figure 4,*c*, corresponds to

$$N_1(t) \equiv (Ex) N_1(t-x-2); \tag{23}$$

and to the expression

$$N_2(t) \equiv N_1(t-1) \cdot (\overline{Ex}) N_2(t-x-1) \tag{24}$$

corresponds the circuit of Figure 4,*d*.

W. McCulloch and W. Pitts have remarked in their paper that the existential operator corresponds to a closed circuit. They made, however, the error of drawing a circuit in which the axon synapses with the body of its own neuron, in other words, a circuit consisting of only one neuron. Such a circuit cannot exist, because the impulse at the synapse will fall within the refractory phase created by a previous impulse. At least two neurons, as shown in Figure 4 are therefore necessary in a closed circuit. Self-circuited *neuroelements* may exist indefinitely in an excited state, but no self-circuited single neurons.

We now proceed to construct a network consisting of a single afferent N_0, and of m efferents $N_1, N_2, \cdots, N_m$, and having the following properties: Let N_0 fire at any irregular intervals, *provided that all those intervals are integer multiples of* δ; then, when N_0 fires for the first time, N_1, and only N_1, responds; when it fires for the second time, N_2, and only N_2, responds; when it fires for the jth time, N_j, and only N_j responds. Analytically, this is expressed by

$$N_j(t) \equiv N_0(t-1) \cdot (Ex)N_1(t-x-1) \cdot (Ex)N_2(t-x-1) \cdots (Ex)N_{j-1}(t-x-1)\,(\overline{Ex})N_j(t-x-1).$$

But this is equivalent to the requirement

$$N_j(t) \equiv N_0(t-1) \cdot (Ex)N_{j-1}(t-x-1). \tag{25}$$

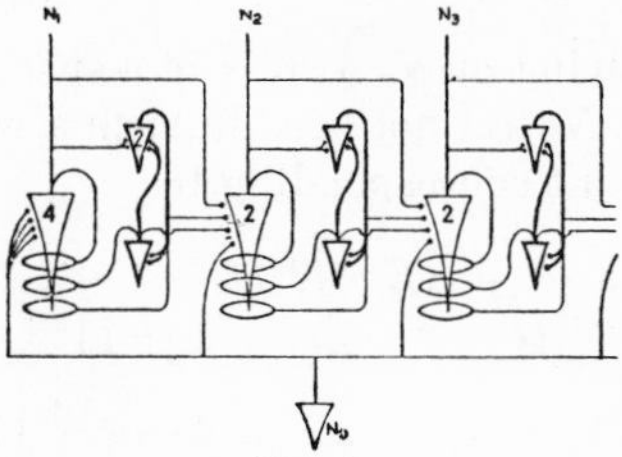

FIG. 5

The corresponding circuits are shown in Figure 5. The neuron N_1 is assumed to have a threshold of 4, while the neurons of the reverberating circuits and all other neurons N_j have thresholds 2.

Thus, if the same stimulus is applied to N_0 several times in succession, each application elicits the response of a different N_j. The activity of a given N_j may release a set of motor reactions, verbal or otherwise, which will be different for each repetition of the same stimulus. We have here an elementary process of counting.

If, instead of the unlimited existential operator, we use in expression (25) the limited existential operator, a circuit is obtained similar to that of Figure 5, but in which, instead of circles, structures shown in Figure 4,*b*, are used. Such a circuit will have the property that repetitions of the same stimulus will be "counted" only when the intervals between the individual repetitions do not exceed a certain value determined by the value of k in $(Ex)\boldsymbol{k}$. Speaking anthropopsychically, we may say that in this case we "forget" the preceding repetitions if the intervals become too large. This, perhaps, may correspond to actual situations.

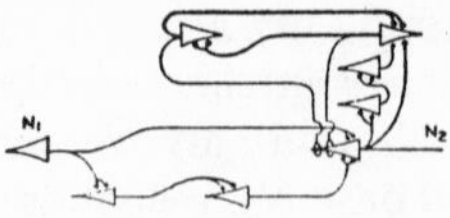

FIG. 6

Consider, now, the circuit shown in Figure 6. Denoting by $N(t, t+2)$ the statement that neuron N fires at the moments t and $t+2$, the analytical expression for the circuit of Figure 6 is

$$\left.\begin{array}{l} N_2(t, t+2) \equiv N_1(t-1). \\ (\overline{Ex})\,[N_2(t-x-2)\cdot N_2(t-x)]. \end{array}\right\} \tag{26}$$

In words: a single firing of N_1 results in a succession of two firings of N_2, provided that N_2 has not fired in such a way before. We may now construct a circuit corresponding to

$$\left.\begin{array}{l} N_j(t, t+2) \equiv N_0(t-1)\cdot(Ex)N_1(t-x-3, t-x-1) \\ \quad\cdot(Ex)N_2(t-x-3, t-x-1) \\ \quad\cdots(Ex)N_{j-1}(t-x-3, t-x-1) \\ \quad\cdot(\overline{Ex})N_j(t-x-2, t-x-1). \end{array}\right\} \tag{27}$$

Returning, again, to one afferent N_0 and n efferents N_j, we may conceive that N_0 is connected with each N_j both by means of a circuit 4,*d*, which is the fundamental unit used in constructing the circuit of Figure 5, and by means of circuits of Figure 6. In other words, we now construct a circuit which corresponds to both expressions (25) and (27). The circuit corresponding to expression (27) may, however, be inhibited by a permanently excited closed circuit C_1, which itself is inhibited by the single excitation of the nth efferent N_n. At the same time, let the excitation of N_n excite another closed circuit C_2, which inhibits all circuits of the type of Figure 4,*a*, at all the N_j's. Then up to n repetitions we shall have the situation described for Figure 3. But for the $(n+1)$st repetition of the stimulus, N_1 will fire twice; for the $(n+2)$d repetition, —N_2 will fire twice; and so forth. Putting

$$\left.\begin{array}{l} (E_1x)N_i(t-x) = [(Ex)N_i(t-x)] \\ \cdot[(\overline{Ey})N_i(t-y)]\cdot[x\neq y], \end{array}\right\} \tag{28}$$

we have, analytically,

$$\left.\begin{aligned} N_j(t) &\equiv N_0(t-1)\left[\sum_{i=1}^{i=j-1}(Ex)N_i(t-x-1)\right] \\ &\quad\cdot[(\overline{Ex})N_j(t-x-1)]\cdot[j<n]; \\ N_j(t,t+2) &\equiv N_0(t-1) \\ &\quad\cdot\left[\sum_{i=1}^{i=j-1}(Ex)N_i(t-x-3,t-x-1)\right] \\ &\quad\cdot[(\overline{Ex})N_j(t-x-3,t-x-1)] \\ &\quad\cdot[(E_1x)N_n(t-x-3)(j-1)]. \end{aligned}\right\} \quad (29)$$

The circuit becomes too complicated to permit a practically useful drawing.

The great disadvantage of the above mechanism is the requirement that all stimuli at N_0 be repeated at intervals which are integer multiples of δ, at least with an error not exceeding the period of latent addition. If this requirement is not fulfilled the mechanism breaks down.

The situation may be remedied in two ways. First, we may introduce some mechanism between N_0 and the rest of the system which will provide for such a regulation of the intervals, even for stimuli spaced differently in time. Second, we may construct a circuit similar to the one represented in Figure 5, in which, however, pathways are substituted for fibers. In other words, we may consider a similar mechanism on a "macroscopic" scale. The circuit then is considerably simplified, since, owing to the continuous excitation of the pathways, each neuron group N_i needs to connect with only one pathway from each preceding N_{i-1} (Fig. 7). The group of neurons N_0 must be of a mixed excitatory type (chap. iii) characterized by

$$A > B; \quad a > b; \quad \frac{A}{a} < \frac{B}{b}. \quad (30)$$

Otherwise, a continuous stimulus to N_0 will produce a successive series of responses N_1, N_2, N_3, etc. Moreover, the duration of excitation of N_0 for a continuous stimulus must be less than the delays at the connections s_j and s_j' (Fig. 7). Also the saturation value E_0 of N_0 must be reached for very small values of the intensity S of the stimulus applied to N_0 so that the intensities E_i' of excitation of all the N_i' are independent of the intensity of the stimulus at N_0. If, for simplicity, we assume that the constants of all the pathways converging on any connection, s_i, are the same, and if we denote by E_i'' the intensity of excitation of each of those pathways, while E_i denotes the intensity of excitation of the inhibiting pathways, then we must have

$$\frac{AE_i'}{a} - \frac{BE_i}{b} < h_i < \frac{AE_i'}{a} + \frac{AE_i''}{a} - \frac{BE_i}{b}. \qquad (31)$$

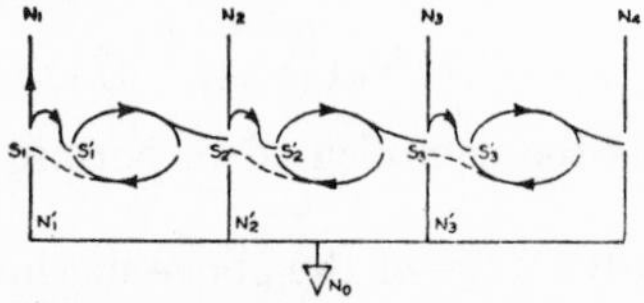

FIG. 7

With all the above requirements satisfied, the "macroscopic" network shown in Figure 7 will possess the necessary property. Various quantitative aspects may be studied by applying the fundamental equations of the mathematical biophysics of the central nervous system.

It seems somewhat awkward to have to construct by means of Boolean algebra, first, a "microscopic circuit" and then obtain a simpler one by a transition to the "macroscopic" picture. We should expect that a generalization of the application of Boolean algebra would be possible so as to permit its use for the construction of networks in which time relations are of a continuous, rather than of a quantized, nature.

An attempt to apply the Boolean algebra method to the problem of logical thinking has been made by N. Rashevsky[11]. To do this we must first interpret neurophysiologically the perception of such abstract relations as, for instance, "all A's are B's."

One of the simplest assumptions is to consider a statement like "all A's are B's" as a stimulus pattern consisting of the sequence of the stimulus A, a stimulus corresponding to the notion "all . . . . are," and of the stimulus B. In ordinary language the stimulus "A" is actually preceded by "All" and followed by "are." This complicates the situation somewhat but does not change it in principle. If we use symbolical notations, we may write "AaB," in which case we do have a sequence of three stimuli.

Therefore, without any loss of generality, we may consider that the statements "All A's are B's," "Some A's are B's," "No

A's are B's," and "Some A's are not B's" are temporal sequences of stimuli "AaB," "AiB," "AeB," and "AoB." Then we may say that a logical inference of the mode "barbara" is made if the presentation of the sequence "$AaBCaA$" is automatically followed by "CaB." Similarly, an inference of the mode "darii" is made when the sequence "$AaBCiA$" is followed by "CiB."

Let the perception of "A" correspond to the excitation of the neuron N_A, the notation "a" ("all-are"), to the excitation of neuron N_a, etc. Then a network which is described by

$$\left.\begin{aligned} N_C(t) &\equiv N_A(t-6)\cdot N_a(t-5)\cdot N_B(t-4) \\ &\quad \cdot N_C(t-3)\cdot N_i(t-2)\cdot N_A(t-1)\,; \\ N_i(t+1) &\equiv N_A(t-6)\cdot N_a(t-5)\cdot N_B(t-4) \\ &\quad \cdot N_C(t-3)\cdot N_i(t-2)\cdot N_A(t-1)\cdot N_C(t)\,; \\ N_B(t+2) &\equiv N_A(t-6)\cdot N_a(t-5)\cdot N_B(t-4) \\ &\quad \cdot N_C(t-3)\cdot N_i(t-2)\cdot N_A(t-1)\cdot N_C(t) \\ &\quad \cdot N_i(t+1), \end{aligned}\right\} \tag{32}$$

may be said to be able to "reason" in the mode of "darii." There is no difficulty in constructing networks for different modes of the Aristotelian logic, by using the method of W. S. McCulloch and W. Pitts.

Such a procedure, however, has several weak points, of which we first discuss one. The circuit, represented by (32), is timed in such a way that the stimuli A, a, B, C, i, A, etc., follow one another at intervals of one synaptic delay, that is, about 0.5 ms. By the intercalation of a proper number of internuncials, it is easy, however, to make this interval as long as desired. It is also possible to make the intervals between different stimuli of the sequence not equal. But in all cases *those intervals are fixed* in their magnitude. This is neurophysiologically and psychologically, to say the least, very implausible. What is needed, for instance, in the case of the mode "darii" is that the sequence "CiB" shall follow the sequence "$AaBCiA$," regardless of the intervals between the individual items of the sequence.

To construct such a circuit we must first study a simpler circuit, namely, one described by

$$\begin{aligned} N_3(t) \equiv [(Ex)N_1(t-x)]\cdot[(Ey)N_2(t-y)] \\ \cdot\,[x > y + m]\cdot[\,y \geqslant n]\,, \end{aligned} \tag{33}$$

where m and n are positive integers.

Such a circuit requires the introduction of closed circles of neurons. The circuit which realizes expression (33) for $m = 0$, $n = 3$, is represented in Figure 8. The thresholds of all the neu-

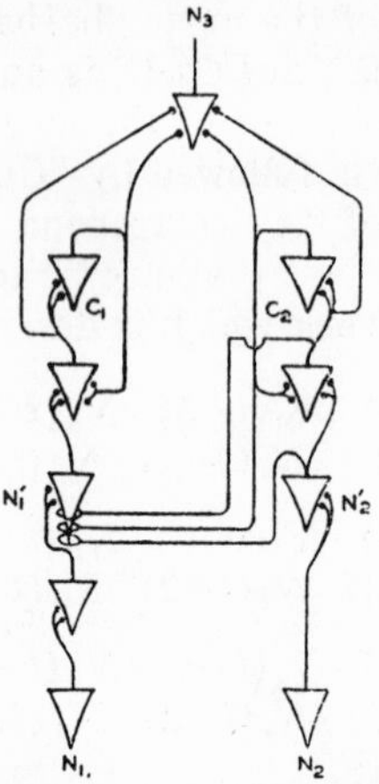

FIG. 8.—Because of the inhibitory fibers going from C_2 to N_1', C_1 cannot become excited if N_2 fires before N_1. If N_1 fires before N_2, then both C_1 and C_2 become permanently excited, and N_3 receives at regular intervals, σ, two impulses simultaneously.

rons, measured in terms of the minimum number of terminal bulbs which must be excited within the period of latent addition, are assumed to be equal to 2.

In any actual situation, the intervals between any stimuli involved in logical thinking are of the order of at least several hundred σ's and usually even much larger. This means a very large m. To simplify notations, we shall in the following write simply $x >> y$.

We introduce the following abbreviation, denoting by x, y, z, and u positive integers:

$$\left.\begin{aligned} N_i:N_k:N_p:\cdots N_r \equiv [(Ex)N_i(t-x)]\cdot[(Ey)N_k(t-y)] \\ \cdot[(Ez)N_p(t-z)]\cdot\ldots.[(Eu)N_r(t-u)] \\ \cdot[x >> y >> z >> \cdots >> u > n]. \end{aligned}\right\} \quad (34)$$

From such circuits as those shown in Figure 8 we may now construct a circuit which realizes the following expressions, in which p and q again denote positive integers,

$$\left.\begin{aligned} N_C(t) &\equiv N_A:N_a:N_B:N_C:N_i:N_A; \\ N_i(t+p) &\equiv (N_A:N_a:N_B:N_C:N_i:N_A)\cdot N_C(t); \\ N_B(t+p+q) &\equiv (N_A:N_a:N_B:N_C:N_i:N_A)\cdot N_C(t)\cdot N_i(t+p). \end{aligned}\right\} \quad (35)$$

The circuit, which realizes expressions (35) is shown in Figure 9, for $p = q = 1$, the time unit being the synaptic delay, σ.

The circuit has the property of "reasoning" in the mode of "darii," but only the time intervals of the "conclusion" "CiB" are

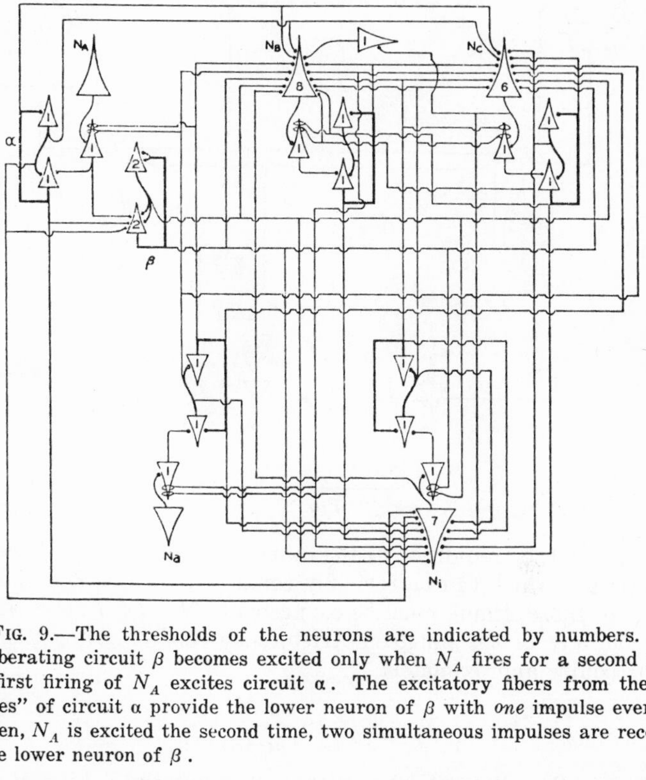

FIG. 9.—The thresholds of the neurons are indicated by numbers. The reverberating circuit β becomes excited only when N_A fires for a second time. The first firing of N_A excites circuit α. The excitatory fibers from the two "halves" of circuit α provide the lower neuron of β with *one* impulse every σ. If, then, N_A is excited the second time, two simultaneous impulses are received by the lower neuron of β.

fixed, those of the major and minor premises being arbitrary within the limitation imposed on all such circuits, namely, that they are all integer multiples of σ.

From the standpoint of *formal* logic, we should have a circuit which gives not only $AaBCiA \rightarrow CiB$ but also $BaCAiB \rightarrow AiC$, as well as any other of the six permutations of ABC. To this end we should connect in Figure 9 neuron N_B with N_A, N_a, N_i, N_B, and N_C in the same manner as N_A is connected with N_B, N_a, N_i, N_B, and N_C, etc. For the three stimuli alone we shall obtain a circuit of some sixty-nine neurons. (Some neurons may perhaps be used in common for all three circuits). Approximately the same number of

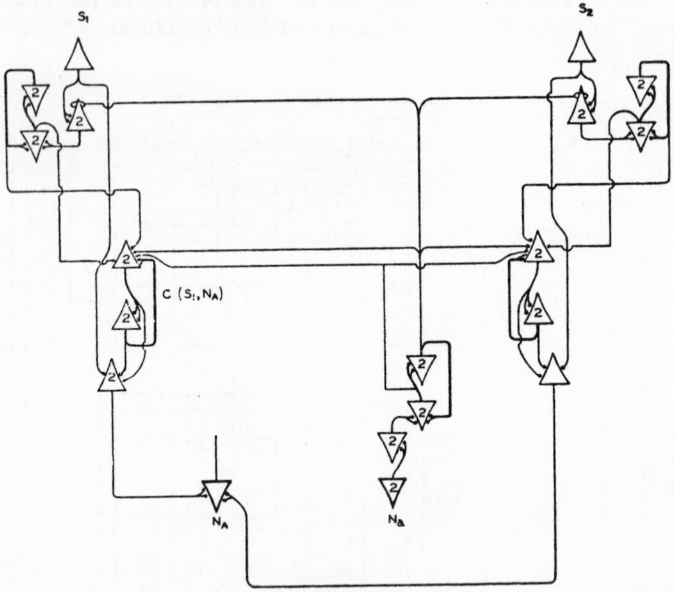

FIG. 10

neurons will be required for the other eighteen modes. If we have M stimuli, which can be formally connected by *a, e, i, o,* then *any three* of those stimuli must be connected to N_a, N_e, N_i, and N_0 so as to give any of the nineteen Aristotelian modes. Altogether, this will require approximately

$$N = 69 \times 19 \frac{M!}{(M-3)!3!} \tag{36}$$

neurons. For all practical purposes, M is infinite. Taking $M = 10^3$, which is too low an estimate, gives $N \sim 10^{11}$ neurons, which is biologically absurd, since the total number of neurons in the human brain is of the order of 10^{10}.

The solution of the difficulty may be sought in the following: When in formal logic we think (or say) "All A's are B's," the "A" stands actually for "the thing about which it is said 'All . . . . are.'" Similarly, "B" is merely the thing that follows "All A's are." Hence in the circuit shown in Figure 9, for the mode "darii," N_A must be excited every time when *any other* stimulus precedes

N_a; while N_B must be excited every time when *any other* stimulus follows N_a. Similar situations should hold for other circuits which correspond to other modes of logic. Hence we must construct a circuit such that if *any* neuron S_i fires before N_a, making a sequence S_iN_a, then S_i must become connected to N_A, so that henceforth *every* firing of S_i will be followed by a firing of N_A. The principle on which such a circuit is based is to have between each S_i and N_A a circle $C(S_i, N_A)$ (Fig. 10), the excitation of which is necessary for a permanent connection between S_i and N_A. If in expression (33) we substitute $C(S_iN_A)$ for N_3, S_i for N_1, and N_A for N_2, we obtain the expression describing the circuit. Such a circuit is shown in Figure 10 with only two S_i's. Any number of S_i's, however, can be used. The number of internuncials involved per S_i is only six, so that if the total number of S_i's is M, 6 M neurons are needed.

If in the circuit shown in Figure 10 the sequence $S_1S_2N_a$ is presented, then both S_1 and S_2 become connected to N_A. In this case, $S_1 + S_2$ is actually the stimulus preceding N_a.

Since similar connections must be made between any S_i and N_B and N_C, respectively, the total number of necessary neurons increases to 18 M. Next, connection between S_i's and N_A, N_B, and N_C must be made for sequences S_iN_i, S_iN_e, and S_iN_0, which would raise N to 72 M.

All those circuits, however, will still not fulfill all the requirements. The main difficulty arises when we have, for instance, a sequence $S_raS_pS_paS_q$, giving as a conclusion S_qiS_r (mode "bamalip"). Here S_p first follows "*a*" and then precedes it. Hence, after becoming connected to N_B, it will then become connected to N_A, and confusion will result. Moreover, while in the above sequence S_r will be excited before N_a, owing to time lags in the circuit of Figure 10, N_A may actually become excited *after* N_a, whereas for the working of the mechanism discussed on page 220 and exemplified in Figure 9 the excitation of N_A must precede that of N_a.

A way out of the difficulty may be found by taking a slightly different viewpoint. We may require that in any sequence, say $S_kaS_lS_miS_k$, constituting the premises of a syllogism, the *first* of the stimuli S connect with N_A; the *second*, different from the first, with N_B; and the *third* with N_C. Thus we shall have the connection S_k—N_A, S_l—N_B, S_m—N_C.

In a sequence $S_raS_pS_paS_q$, and S_r will become connected with N_a, S_p with N_B, and S_q with N_C. Since, when a sequence, say $S_raS_pS_paS_q$ occurs, the sequence S_qiS_r must follow automatically, the connection between the S's and the corresponding N_A, N_B, or N_C must be two-way connections, so that excitation of N_A results in an excitation of S_r, etc. However, this two-way connection must not be a closed self-reverberating circuit, which will keep both S_r and N_A, or other corresponding pairs, excited indefinitely.

First, we shall consider the problem of the connections *from* the S's to N_A, N_B, and N_C. Consider the structure represented in Figure 11. Let application of stimulus S_k result in the excitation

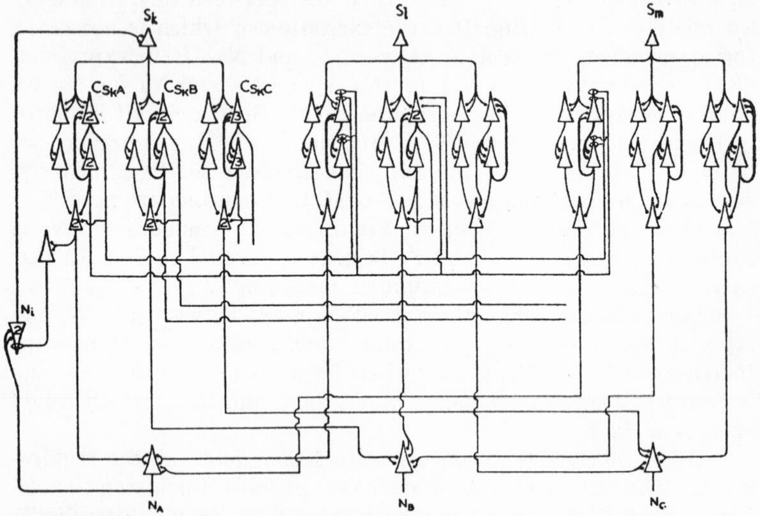

FIG. 11.—In order not to make the drawing too complicated, only a few connections are shown. Thresholds are indicated by numbers. The neurons of the circuit C_{S_kC} have a threshold 3, because they are excited only if, besides S_k, two other circuits, C_{S_jA} and C_{S_lB}, have already been excited. Those two circuits send each excitatory fiber to C_{S_kC}.

of neuron N_{S_k}, application of S_l in the excitation of N_{S_l}, and so forth. A simple firing of any S_k results in the permanent excitation of the circuits $C_{S_k}A$. Whenever a circuit of that kind is excited, a connection between S_k and N_A is established; and, if we have $S_k(t)$, then, with the structure shown in Figure 11, we shall have $N_A(t+4)$.

If we denote by the symbol $S_{kA}(t)$ the statement that there exists at the time t a connection between S_k and N_A such that an excitation of S_k results in an excitation of N_A; if we denote by $C_{S_kA}(t)$ the statement that at the time t the circuit C_{S_kA} is excited, and by $S_j(t)$ the statement that S_j is excited at the moment t, then we have

$$S_{kA}(t) \equiv C_{S_kA}(t)\,; \qquad S_{kB}(t) \equiv C_{S_kB}(t)\,; \qquad S_{kC}(t) \equiv C_{S_kC}(t)\,. \tag{37}$$

The requirements for our mechanism, mentioned on page 555, may now be written

$$S_{kA}(t) \equiv (Ex)S_k(t-x)\cdot(\overline{Ej})S_{jA}(t)\cdot(j \neq k)\,; \tag{38}$$

$$\left.\begin{aligned} S_{lB}(t) \equiv (Ex)S_l(t-x)\cdot(Ei)S_{iA}(t) \\ \cdot(\overline{Ej})S_{jB}(t)\cdot(i\neq l)\cdot(j\neq l)\,; \end{aligned}\right\} \tag{39}$$

$$\left.\begin{aligned} S_{mC}(t) \equiv (Ex)S_m(t-x)\cdot(Ei)S_{iA}(t)\cdot(Ej)S_{jB}(t) \\ \cdot(\overline{Er})S_{rC}(t)\cdot(i\neq m)\cdot(j\neq m)\cdot(r\neq m)\,. \end{aligned}\right\} \tag{40}$$

Introducing expressions (37) into (38), (39), and (40), we find

$$C_{S_kA}(t) \equiv (Ex)S_k(t-x)\cdot(\overline{Ej})C_{S_jA}(t)\cdot(j\neq k)\,; \tag{41}$$

$$\left.\begin{aligned} C_{S_lB}(t) \equiv (Ex)S_l(t-x)\cdot(Ei)C_{S_iA}(t) \\ \cdot(\overline{Er})C_{S_jB}(t)\cdot(i\neq l)\cdot(j\neq l)\,; \end{aligned}\right\} \tag{42}$$

$$\left.\begin{aligned} C_{S_mC}(t) \equiv (Ex)S_m(t-x)\cdot(Ei)C_{S_iA}(t)\cdot(Ej)C_{S_jB}(t) \\ \cdot(\overline{Er})C_{S_rC}(t)\cdot(i\neq m)\cdot(j\neq m)\,; \qquad (r\neq m)\,. \end{aligned}\right\} \tag{43}$$

In realizing expressions (41), (42), and (43) by a network, we see that the second term in the conjunction of the right side of expression (41) requires that each circuit C_{S_jA} send inhibitory fibers to all other circuits C_{S_pA}, where $p \neq j$. The second term of the conjunction on the right side of expression (42) indicates that every circuit C_{S_lB} will be thrown into excitation only if it is excited simultaneously by S_l and by the already excited circuit, C_{S_kA}. According to expression (10), there can be only one such circuit at a time. Hence every circuit C_{S_kA} must send excitatory fibers to all circuits C_{S_iB} with $j \gtrless k$. The third term of the right-hand side of expression (42) requires that each circuit C_{S_jB} send inhibitory fibers to all other circuits C_{S_lB}, with $l \neq j$. A similar analysis of expression (43) shows that each circuit C_{S_iA} and C_{S_jB} sends excitatory fibers to each circuit C_{S_mC}, while each C_{S_rC} sends inhibitory fibers to all others C_{S_mC}, where $m \neq r$.

With this arrangement, which for the sake of clarity is only partly shown in Figure 11, any of the neurons S_i, which is excited first, will become connected to N_A; any S_i, which is excited second, will become connected to N_B; and any S_i, excited third, will become connected to N_C.

It may be worth mentioning that such a mechanism provides us in principle with the theory of the concept of ordinal numbers. Instead of three neurons, N_A, N_B, N_C, we may have a large number N_1, N_2, N_3, $\cdots$, and every first-stimulated S_i will connect to N_1, the second to N_2, etc. Thus, regardless of their nature, the stimuli S become labeled: the first, the second, etc. Together with the mechanism for "counting" the number of repetitions of the same stimulus discussed before (p. 215), we may have here a basis for a general theory of the conception of ordinal numbers.

There remains now to connect N_A (or N_B or N_C) with the corresponding S_i in such a way as to fulfil the requirements given on page 223. The way to do it is shown in Figure 11 for the connection between S_k and N_A. When S_k fires for the first time at the moment t, N_A will fire at $t+4$; but this firing will not make S_k fire again, because at $t+4$ the internuncial, N_i, also receives an inhibitory impulse. But, if at any time after the connection S_{kA} is established, N_A fires, then S_k will fire two σ's later.

Hence when, for instance, a sequence $S_k a S_l S_m i S_k$ produces the sequence $N_A a N_B N_C i N_A$, which, by means of the mechanism shown in Figure 9, produces $N_C i N_B$, the sequence $S_m i S_l$ will result, provided that the time lag between the firing of N_C and of N_i is greater than that between N_C and S_k. This can always be achieved by making p and q sufficiently large in expressions (35). In fact, it is sufficient to have $p > 2$. This can be obtained by adding an appropriate amount of internuncials in the circuit of Figure 9.

Finally, a mechanism must be added which disconnects the S_i's from N_A, N_B, and N_C as soon as the syllogism is completed. This can be done by having a neuron N_F respond to, and only to, the whole sequence, say, $N_A a N_B N_C i N_A N_C i N_B$, which can be obtained by realizing expressions similar to expression (35). Then make N_F send inhibitory fibers to *all* circuits $C_{S_i A}$, $C_{S_i B}$, $C_{S_i C}$.

With the mechanism discussed in this section and represented in Figure 11, there are 17 interneurons corresponding to each S_i. Hence the total number of neurons necessary is 17 M. Even with M 10^5, which is the order of magnitude of the sensory fibers reaching the sensory projection areas of the cortex, we find the total number to be about 2×10^6, which is a very small portion of all neurons available. The total number of neurons involved in mechanisms like that shown in Figure 9 will, including all additional internuncials discussed above, not exceed the same figure, so that, all told, $N \sim 2 \times 10^6$ neurons.

All the foregoing discussions are of interest as providing a mechanism for logical thinking. The theory is, however, not directly amenable to quantitative predictions and experimental tests. To obtain that, we must consider possible failures of the mechanism and attempt to evaluate the probabilities of correct and wrong conclusions or of the inability of making a conclusion at all.[11] One of the ways of developing a theory of errors in the present case is to consider that the neurons N_a, N_i, N_e, and N_o are excited by a previous excitation of four corresponding pathways, *I, II, III,* and *IV*, which are activated by stimuli S_a, S_i, S_e, and S_o, which are cross-inhibiting one another, as discussed previously. We have here a generalization to four stimuli of H. D. Landahl's[12] circuit discussed in chapter vi. Now N_a will fire only if S_a is much stronger than the other stimuli, and so on. But, owing to fluctuations of excitation in a certain percentage of cases, N_i may, for example, become excited, although S_a is applied. General expressions for the probabilities of such occurrences have been given by H. D. Landahl.[12] They may be elaborated and applied to our problem. An error in logical thinking is ascribed according to this picture of the fact that, although, for instance, actually $S_k S_a S_l$ is presented, the central mechanism will give $S_k N_i N_e$. A confusion thus results.

The difficulty of having all intervals between the stimuli $S_k S_l S_m$, etc., equal to integer multiples of σ still remains. This difficulty may be overcome, as suggested above, by constructing corresponding "macro-circuits." In the present instance, however, we may run into the difficulty of requiring more neurons than are actually available.

A different solution of the difficulty leads to interesting consequences and suggestions. If the intervals between the stimulation of N_A, N_a, N_B, N_i, and N_C are all integer multiples of σ, then, for instance, all eight terminal bulbs synapsing with neuron N_B in Figure 9 will be receiving simultaneous impulses at regular intervals σ. If, however, the above-mentioned intervals between the excitation of the neurons N_A, N_a, etc. are not integer multiples of σ, then, although each bulb will receive impulses at regular intervals σ, they will not act synchronously, and neuron N_B will not fire at all, if the impulses do not fall within the period of latent addition. This, however, would be the case only if all synaptic delays were perfectly constant and all equal to σ. Such a situation appears to be biologically rather implausible. It is more likely that, although the synaptic delay of a given neuron is, *on the average*, equal to σ, it actually fluctuates around that value according to some distribution function. Let τ be the actual synaptic delay; then the probability of a given value of τ, $\tau + d\tau$ will be given by

$$F(\tau)\,d\tau\,, \tag{44}$$

with

$$\int_0^\infty F(\tau)\,d\tau = 1; \quad \int_0^\infty \tau F(\tau)\,d\tau = \sigma\,. \tag{45}$$

Instead of being concentrated all at the ends of the interval σ, the eight impulses arriving at N_B now are distributed at random within the interval σ. If τ were constant, then the distribution of the individual impulses within the interval σ would be the same for all consecutive intervals. But, because of the fluctuations of τ, this distribution will vary from interval to interval σ. We may ask for the probability that, because of fluctuations, all eight impulses fall within the period σ_l of latent addition. The greater the dispersion of $F(\tau)$, the greater will be this probability, and therefore the shorter the probable time which it will take for this event to occur. But this probable time measures the probable speed of response to the premises of the syllogism, or speed of reasoning. For zero dispersion of $F(\tau)$, that is, for a constant τ $(=\sigma)$, the probability will be zero, and the speed of reasoning will be zero.

The actual calculation of the probability would have to proceed as follows: For a given average distribution of impulses in the interval σ we can calculate the probability that each impulse will fall within a given fixed interval σ_l, and take the product of all those probabilities. Then we shall have to sum over all possible positions of σ_l within σ. Finally, we shall have to sum over all possible average distributions of the impulses, which are determined by the exact intervals (N_A, N_a), (N_a, N_B), (N_C, N_i), (N_i, N_A). Here we should have to consider the finite duration, τ^*, of an impulse and consider the probability of a given position of any impulse in the interval σ as equal to τ^*/σ. The probability of a given distribution then is $(\tau^*/\sigma)^n$, where n is the number of impulses considered. (In the present instance, $n = 8$.) The total number of possible distributions would be equal to the number of possible ways of selecting n numbers out of $(\sigma/\tau^*) > n$. This is

$$\frac{(\sigma/\tau^*)\,!}{[(\sigma/\tau^*) - n]\,!n\,!}\,. \tag{46}$$

We shall end by making the following important remark: The same considerations apply to the mechanism for counting, discussed on page 215; they will lead to an expression for the maximum speed with which a stimulus may be repeated and still be able to be counted. Assuming that the function $F(\tau)$ is the same for the whole cortex, we shall find a relation between speed of logical reasoning and this limiting speed in counting. Both will vary from individual to individual.

An interesting theory of neural networks which perform logical thinking has been developed along the lines of the McCulloch-Pitts theory by F. H. George[14]. See also "Automata Studies"[15].

REFERENCES

1. W. S. McCulloch and W. Pitts, *Bull. Math. Biophysics*, 5, 115, 1943.
2. D. Hilbert and W. Ackerman, *Grundzüge der theoretischen Logik* (Berlin: J. Springer, 1928).
3. N. Rashevsky, *Bull. Math. Biophysics*, 7, 203, 1945.
4. H. D. Landahl, *Bull. Math. Biophysics*, 1, 95, 118, 1939.
5. A. S. Householder, *Psychometrika*, 4, 45, 1939.
6. A. S. Householder, *Bull. Math. Biophysics*, 2, 1, 1940.
7. A. S. Householder, *ibid.*, p. 157.
8. A. S. Householder and H. D. Landahl, *Mathematical Biophysics of the Central Nervous System* (Bloomington, Ind.: Principia Press, 1945).
9. H. D. Landahl, *Bull. Math. Biophysics*, 2, 37, 1940.
10. N. Rashevsky, *Bull. Math. Biophysics*, 8, 29, 1946.
11. N. Rashevsky, *ibid.*, 7, 133, 1945.
12. H. D. Landahl, *Psychometrika*, 3, 107, 1938.
13. H. Epstein and A. Rapoport, *Bull. Math. Biophysics*, 13, 21, 1951.
14. F. H. George, *Bull. Math. Biophysics*, 18, 337, 1956; 19, 187, 1957.
15. C. Shannon and J. McCarthy (ed.), *Automata Studies* (Princeton: Princeton University Press, 1956).

CHAPTER XX

RANDOM NETS

The development in all the preceding chapters are based on a study of different type of structures, or configurations of either neuroelements and pathways, or of neurons and axons. Those configurations or circuits were constructed rather *ad hoc,* in order to explain some neurophysiological or neuropsychological phenomena. Whether anything resembling such structures actually occurs in the brains of men and animals, in any case such structures constitute useful working hypotheses to the extent that they permit to explain some occasionally rather complicated phenomena or even lead to quantitative conclusions which are verified by experiment.

The use of such structures has, however, one serious theoretical disadvantage. The vast majority of the structures discussed in this book are highly specific, in the sense that a slight variation of the structure or a possible break-down of a part of it renders the whole mechanism inoperative. True enough in the discussion of the Gestalt problem, of discrimination of intensities, of color vision, and of some other phenomena, we did use the concept of a certain *randomness* of distribution of neuroelements and pathways. In fact we first came across such a randomness in chapter ii, when we discussed the possible structures of a connection (p. 13). Basically, however, our approach rests on the assumption of very definite and specific neural structures. This holds even more for discussion which involves actual neurons (chapter xix) rather than neuroelements.

Actually some rather complicated and rather definite structures are found in the brain. Those structures, however, usually involve neither individual neurons nor even neuroelements, but rather large groups of neuroelements. Those larger groups are arranged in very definite patterns. Nothing so definite is found on the microscopic level, as anyone can see by examining a microphotograph of some region of the brain in a textbook of neurology. But those patterns do not seem to be as specific, as those discussed previously, especially not so specific as the structures discussed in the preceding chapter. As we already remarked, in any of the structures discussed in chapter xix, the failure of a single neuron will render the whole net inoperative. It is, however, well known that sometimes even rather extensive lesions of the brain do not necessarily cause a complete loss of the corresponding functions, especially in lower animals. Very minute lesions which involve only few neurons are unlikely to cause any changes in behavior.

Moreover while even rather complicated anatomical patterns may be formed due to the action of various factors in the course of embryonic development, the probability of formation in the brain of *exactly* such neuronic circuits as have been discussed in the preceding chapter is extremely small. Yet, according to the discussion of the preceding chapter, those circuits *must* possess *exactly* a given structure, in order to perform given functions.

Such considerations led Anatol Rapoport and Alfonso Shimbel to an entirely different approach to the whole problem of mathematical biology of the central nervous system. Considering the tremendous number of neurons in the brain (10^{13} in man), we may expect that even if *all* connections or synapses between them occur entirely at random, some definite types of pattern will occasionally be formed by pure chance. Thus there always is a finite probability for two neurons to form a closed circuit, neuron A synapsing on B, and neuron B — on A. We may ask ourselves quite legitimately the question, as to what is the probability of such circuits being formed by chance, and how does this probability depend on such parameters as total number of neurons, number of axons per neuron, average distance between neurons, etc. We may inquire into the probabilities of formation by chance of more complicated structures. Then, given the probabilities of such structures, we may investigate the probabilities of definite patterns of spread of excitation in such a random net under specified conditions. It may well be expected that such studies may become very revealing for the understanding of some important neurophysiological phenomena.

Actually the neural nets found in the brain are not entirely random. Certain orderly patterns are superimposed on a random distribution. Such not entirely random nets A. Rapoport calls "nets with bias." The bias may be of different nature. Thus the probability of a neuron A to synapse with neuron B may depend on the distance between A and B, or it may depend on the direction of the lines AB. Rapoport's aim is to provide in the theory of random nets a point of departure for the neurologically more important biased nets.

Since 1948 A. Rapoport, A. Shimbel and their co-workers have published a very large number of papers on this subject[1]. A complete presentation of the whole available material would require a book of fair size. We shall therefore limit ourselves to giving only two examples which illustrate the basic idea of their approach. Because of the nature of the problem, a great deal of preliminary purely theoretical work has to be done in this field before any concrete practical applications can be expected. Curiously enough, as we shall see at the end of this chapter, some very interesting applications of Rapoport's work were obtained in a field in which to begin with they were least of all expected.

We first shall discuss the following problem[2]. Given $N + 1$ neurons, each having *one* axon, and each axon forming a synapse on *some* other neuron, what is the probability that certain pairs of neurons will form closed circuits, or that in general closed circuits consisting of k neurons will be formed?

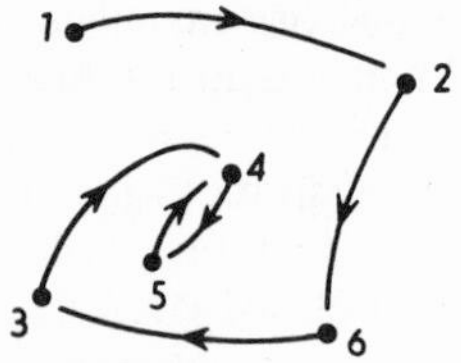

FIG. 1

First of all we notice that the conditions of our problem require that each neuron sends out one and only one axon, which synapses on *another* neuron; but they do not require that each neuron receives an axon from another neuron. Figure 1 illustrates the situation for $N = 5$. Neurons are denoted for simplicity by points, and axons by lines, with arrows indicating the direction *away* from the neuron to which they belong. This is of course also the direction of conduction. In Figure 1 neuron 1 does not receive any axon. Neurons 4 and 5 form a closed circuit.

The problem as stated above is not yet definite, because the answer to it will in general depend on how the probability of a neuron A synapsing on neuron B depends on the distance between A and B. We shall study here, for illustration only, the simplest possible case, namely that in which this probability does not depend on the distance between A and B. Thus we consider the case where it is equally probable for a neuron to synapse with any other neuron.

In that case the probability of a given neuron A to synapse with any one of the remaining N neurons is equal to one, because we assume that the axon of every neuron synapses with some other neuron. In order that neuron A would belong to a cycle consisting of *two* neurons, it is necessary that the neuron with which A synapses, sends its axon back to neuron A. Since it can send its axon with equal probability to anyone of the N neurons, therefore the probability that it sends it to A is $1/N$. This then is the probability C_2 that a given neuron A will belong to a two neuron closed circuit.

Now let us consider the probability of A belonging to a circuit which consists of three neurons, A, B, and C, such that A synapses on B, B on C, and C on A, where B and C are *any* two neurons different from A.

Again A will synapse with certainty on *some* neuron B. The probability that B synapses on any neuron C which is different from A is $(N-1)/N$, because B can synapse with N neurons, of which $N-1$ are different from B. The probability that C synapses exactly on A is $1/N$, because it can synapse on any of the N neurons different from C. Hence the probability C_3 that a given neuron belongs to a closed circuit which consists of three neurons is $(N-1)/N$ times $1/N$, or $(N-1)/N^2$.

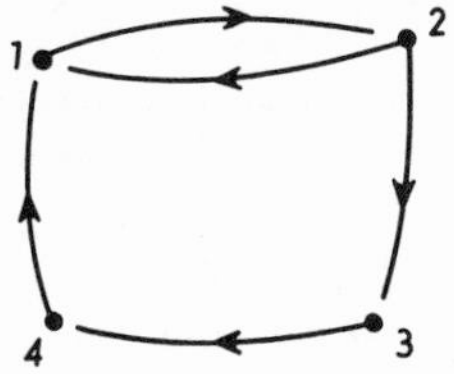

FIG. 2

By a similar argument we find that the probability that a given neuron belongs to a closed circuit which consists of k neurons is

$$C_k = \frac{(N-1)(N-2)\ldots(N-k+2)}{N^{k-1}}, \tag{1}$$

Because each neuron has only one axon, therefore it cannot belong at once to more than one closed circuit. If it could, then it should have at least two axons, as seen in Figure 2, where neuron (2) belongs simultaneously to a two-neuron circuit (1, 2) and to a four-neuron circuit (1, 2, 3, 4). Hence the probability that a given neuron belongs to *any kind* of closed circuit, regardless of the number of neurons in that circuit, is equal to the sum of all C_k's taken for all values of k from 2 to $N+1$. We shall denote this probability by C and call it with Rapoport the *cycle saturation*. The greater C, the more cycles of *any* kind are present in a given aggregate of neurons.

We thus have:

$$C = \sum_{k=2}^{N+1} C_k = \frac{1}{N} + \frac{N-1}{N^2} + \ldots \frac{(N-1)!}{N^N}. \tag{2}$$

For small values of k the probability C can be directly computed. For $N = 2$ we have $C = 1$, which means that in an aggregate consisting of only two neurons both neurons are members of the same cycle. For $N = 3$, we have $C = 1/2 + 1/4 = 3/4$ that is the probability of a neuron being a member of a cycle in an aggregate of 3 neurons is 3/4. For $N = 4$, $C = 17/27$, etc.

For very large values of N we proceed as follows: from (2) we have:

$$NC = 1 + \frac{N-1}{N} + \ldots \frac{(N-1)!}{N^{N-1}} = \frac{N-1}{N^{N-1}}\left[1 + N + \frac{N^2}{2!} + \ldots \frac{N^{N-1}}{(N-1)!}\right]. \tag{3}$$

For very large N we have with great approximation $(N-1)!/N^{N-1} = N!/N^N$ and we can use Stirlings formula

$$N!\,N^{-N} = \sqrt{2\pi N}\, e^{-N}. \tag{4}$$

Introducing this into (3) we find:

$$NC = \sqrt{2\pi N}\, e^{-N}\left(1 + N + \frac{N^2}{2!} + \ldots \frac{N^{N-1}}{(N-1)!}\right) = \sqrt{2\pi N}\, e^{-N} \sum_{m=0}^{N-1} \frac{N^m}{m!}. \tag{5}$$

We now make use of the formula[3]

$$\lim_{N \to \infty} e^{-N} \sum_{m=0}^{N-1} \frac{N^m}{m!} = \frac{1}{\sqrt{2\pi}} \int_0^\infty e^{-t^2/2}\, dt = \tfrac{1}{2}. \tag{6}$$

For very large values of N the expression on the left side of (6) will be sufficiently close to its limit 1/2. Therefore, for very large values of N we find from (5) and (6):

$$C = \sqrt{\frac{\pi}{2N}}. \tag{7}$$

The expected number of neurons which are members of a cycle is equal to the total number $N + 1$ of neurons times the probability C of a given neuron to be a member of a cycle. Hence, replacing $N + 1$ by N, we have for that number N_c:

$$N_c = (N+1)\sqrt{\frac{\pi}{2N}} = \sqrt{\frac{\pi N}{2}}. \tag{8}$$

For large values of N the number of neurons which are members of cycles increases as the square root of N.

We now shall discuss a different example[4]. Consider an aggregate of N neurons each of which may have more than one axon. The number of axons may vary from neuron to neuron. For each neuron this number is of course an integer. However, the *average* number a of axons per neuron will in general be a fractional number. Thus if two out of three neurons have two axons each, and one has one axon, the average number of axons per neuron in the aggregate of 3 neurons is 5/3. We again assume that every axon does synapse on some neuron, not excluding now the possibility of it synapsing on its own neuron, thus forming a one-neuron closed circuit. Again we assume that the probability of a neuron A to synapse with neuron B does not depend on the distance between A and B and is a constant.

If a neuron A synapses on B, B on C, and C on D, so that an impulse from A can travel to D, we shall say that there exists a path from A to D. A path does not necessarily exist between *any* two neurons of an aggregate such as those which we are now considering. Thus in Figure 3 there exists a path from neuron A to neuron 8; but there exists *no* path from either A to B, or from B to A, although geometrically A and B are connected by a line of axons. The direction of those axons is, however, not everywhere the same between A and B.

Our problem is to find the fraction γ of neurons in the aggregate to which there exist paths from a given neuron.

We shall say that neuron B is one axon removed from A, if A synapses directly on B. We shall say that C is two axons removed from A, if A synapses on a neuron B, and B — on C; etc. Thus in Figure 3 neurons 2, 3, and 5 are each one axon removed from A; neurons 1, 4, 6, and 7 are each two axons removed from A.

Denote by $x(t)$ the number of neurons which are removed from a given neuron A by *not more than* t axons. In this number are included all neurons removed by 1, 2, . . . , $(t - 1)$, and t axons. Thus in Figure 3 $x(2)$ equals to the number of all neurons marked by crosses. In other words here $x(2) = 7$. The number of all neurons marked by either crosses or circles in Figure 3 is $x(3)$. Thus in Figure 3 $x(3) = 15$. We see from Figure 3 that $x(3) - x(2) = 8$ is the number of neurons which are *exactly* 3 axons removed from A. It is readily seen that quite generally $x(t+1) - x(t)$ is the number of neurons which are exactly $t + 1$ axons removed from a given neuron A.

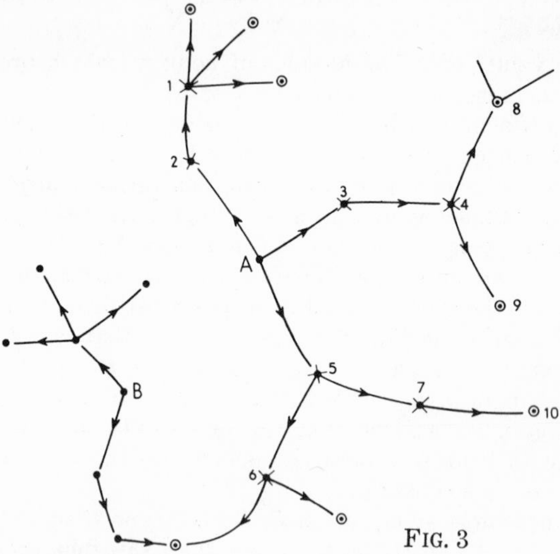

FIG. 3

There are thus $x(t) - x(t-1)$ neurons, which are exactly t axons removed from A. Since the average number of axons per neuron is a, therefore those $x(t) - x(t-1)$ neurons send out altogether

$$s = a\,[x(t) - x(t-1)]\,. \tag{9}$$

axons which eventually synapse with the $x(t+1) - x(t)$ neurons which are exactly $t + 1$ axons removed from A. How many of those $x(t+1) - x(t)$ neurons are there? Axons from different neurons of those exactly t axons removed from A may synapse on the same neuron which is $t + 1$ axons removed from A. The synapsing occurs at random, by pure chance. The probability that one of the s axons will synapse on a particular neuron is $1/N$. Therefore the probability that it will *not* synapse on that particular neuron is $1 - \dfrac{1}{N}$.

The probability that *none* of the s axons will synapse on that particular neuron is thus:

$$\left(1 - \frac{1}{N}\right)^{s}. \tag{10}$$

Hence the probability that one or more of the axons s will synapse on a given neuron is:

$$1 - \left(1 - \frac{1}{N}\right)^{s}. \tag{11}$$

Therefore the expected number of neurons on which one or more of the s axons will synapse is equal to the total number N of neurons times the probability (11), or to

$$N\left[1 - \left(1 - \frac{1}{N}\right)^{a[x(t) - x(t-1)]}\right].$$

But of these neurons the fraction $x(t)/N$ has already been contacted. Hence the expected number of newly contacted neurons will be given by

$$x(t+1) - x(t) = [N - x(t)]\left[1 - (1 - 1/N)^{a[x(t) - x(t-1)]}\right]. \tag{12}$$

Equation (12) enables us to determine $x(t + 1)$ if $x(t)$ and $x(t - 1)$ are known.

Put

$$N - x(t) = y(t). \tag{13}$$

Introducing this into (12) we find, after rearrangements:

$$y(t+1) = y(t)\left(1 - \frac{1}{N}\right)^{a[y(t-1) - y(t)]} \tag{14}$$

or, multiplying both sides by $(1 - 1/N)^{ay(t)}$:

$$y(t+1)\left(1 - \frac{1}{N}\right)^{ay(t)} = y(t)\left(1 - \frac{1}{N}\right)^{ay(t-1)}. \tag{15}$$

From (15) we see that for all values of t:

$$y(t+1)\left(1 - \frac{1}{N}\right)^{ay(t)} = \text{Const.} = K. \tag{16}$$

From (16) we have:

$$y(t+1) = K\left(1 - \frac{1}{N}\right)^{-ay(t)}. \tag{17}$$

From the definition (13) of $y(t)$, the latter represents the expected number of all neurons which are *not* at most t axons removed from A. In other words $y(t)$ is the number of neurons which are not contacted on the t-th step from A if we consider the conservative synapsings as steps from A. Neuron A is the only one which is zero axons removed from A. The remaining $N-1$ neurons are not included in the set of neurons which are zero axons removed from A, hence

$$y(0)=N-1. \tag{18}$$

The given neuron A sends out on the average a axons, which can contact any of the N neurons (including A itself). By an argument similar to the one which led to expression (12), we find that the probability of a given neuron *not* to receive any of the a axons is given by $(1-1/N)^a$. There are altogether $N-1$ neurons which may or may not receive axons from A. Hence the expected total number $y(1)$ of neurons which are not at most 1 axon removed from A is equal to

$$y(1)=(N-1)\left(1-\frac{1}{N}\right)^a=(N-1)^{a+1}N^{-a}. \tag{19}$$

Putting in expression (17) $t=0$, using (18) and (19), and solving for K we find:

$$K=N^{-aN}(N-1)^{aN+1}. \tag{20}$$

As t increases by one unit and $y(t)$ changes to $y(t+1)$ the number of uncontacted new neurons either decreases or remains the same. The latter will take place in the relatively unlikely situation in which all axons sent by neurons at most t axons removed from A will synapse on some of those $x(t)$ neurons, and on no new ones. Thus $y(t+1)\leqslant y(t)$. On the other hand $y(t)\geqslant 0$ for all values of t. It follows that as t increases without bound, $y(t)$ must approach a limit Y. Thus

$$\lim_{t\to\infty} y(t)=Y. \tag{21}$$

Introducing (21) into (17), we find:

$$y(t+1)=N^{-aN}(N-1)^{aN+1}\left(1-\frac{1}{N}\right)^{-ay(t)}=$$

$$(N-1)\left(1-\frac{1}{N}\right)^{aN(1-y(t)/N)}. \tag{22}$$

As t increases, both $y(t+1)$ and $y(t)$ approach the limit Y. Hence from (22) we find:

$$Y=(N-1)\left(1-\frac{1}{N}\right)^{Na(1-Y/N)}. \tag{23}$$

Since with increasing N the expression $(1 - 1/N)^N$ tends to e^{-1}, where e is the base of natural logarithms, therefore for very large values of N we have with very good approximation:

$$Y = Ne^{a(Y/N - 1)}, \tag{24}$$

or

$$\frac{Y}{N} = e^{a(Y/N - 1)}. \tag{25}$$

At the outset we were interested in the fraction γ of neurons to which there exist paths from any given neuron A. This fraction is nothing but the ratio $x(t)/N$ for $t = \infty$, in other words $\gamma = x(\infty)/N$. But, by definition (13) of y this is also equal to $1 - Y/N$. Hence, from (25) we find:

$$\gamma = 1 - e^{-a\gamma} \tag{26}$$

a transcendental equation which determines γ.

Equation (26) is satisfied for any value of a by $\gamma = 0$. If $\gamma \neq 0$ we can solve equation (26) for a and obtain:

$$a = \frac{-\log(1 - \gamma)}{\gamma}. \tag{27}$$

The graph of a versus γ obtained from (27) is shown in Figure 4. It is turned by 90°, so as to give γ as a function of a, represented by the line cc'. As γ tends to zero, we may expand $\log(1 - \gamma)$ preserving only the linear term: $\log(1 - \gamma) = -\gamma$. We thus see that $a = 1$ for $\gamma = 0$. Thus the curve which represents γ as a function of a has two branches: one represented by cc', the other by the axis of abscissae. Since γ is essentially a positive quantity, therefore the branch of the curve cc' which is shown by the broken line has no physical meaning. We now shall show that for $a > 1$ the branch shown by the axis of abscissae also cannot physically exist. To this end we go back to equation (23). From the latter we obtain:

$$Y/(N - 1) = (1 - 1/N)^{a(N - Y)}, \tag{28}$$

or

$$\log Y - \log(N - 1) = a(N - Y)\log(1 - 1/N). \tag{29}$$

From (28) we find

$$a = \frac{\log Y - \log(N - 1)}{(N - Y)\,[\log(N - 1) - \log N]}. \tag{30}$$

Put $Y = N - \phi(N) = N\,[1 - \phi(N)/N]$. Then equation

(30) may be written thus:

$$\log N - \log(N-1) + \log[1 - \phi(N)/N] = a\phi(N)[\log(N-1) - \log N]. \quad (31)$$

Since $\phi(N) < N$ for all N, we may expand the last term of the left side of (31) and obtain

$$\log N - \log(N-1) - \phi(N)/N - \tfrac{1}{2}[\phi(N)/N]^2 - \tfrac{1}{3}[\phi(N)/N]^3 \ldots = a\phi(N)[\log(N-1) - \log N]. \quad (32)$$

We now expand $\log(N-1) - \log N$, which appears in the righ side of (32) and obtain after rearrangements:

$$\log N - \log(N-1) = \frac{\phi(N)}{N}\left[1 - a + \frac{\phi(N) - a}{2N} + \frac{[\phi(N)]^2 - a}{3N^2} + \cdots\right.$$
$$< \frac{\phi(N)}{N}\left[1 - a + (1 - \phi(N)/N)^{-1}\right]. \quad (33)$$

Now if a is fixed and greater than unity, the limit of $\phi(N)/N$ can not be zero as N increases without bound, because otherwise for N sufficiently large the right side of the inequality in (33) become negative, while the left side remains always positive. This woul contradict the inequality. Therefore, the limit of Y/N, as N in creases without bound, cannot be unity for $a > 1$. But this mean that $\gamma \neq 0$ if $a > 1$. Hence, for $a > 1$, the non-zero branch of ou curve is the only meaningful one.

The problem just discussed has had two interesting applica tions in two very different fields. The first application was made b A. Rapoport and by H. G. Landau and A. Rapoport[5] to the sprea of epidemics. Rapoport observed that formally the process of on neuron synapsing with another is analogous to one person contact ing another. If an epidemic is spread through contacts of differen persons, person A infecting B, and B infecting C, etc.; if the proba bilities of contacts between any two persons in a given populatio is the same; and if the average number of contacts which a perso makes is given; then if we substitute for our a the average numbe of contacts, the quantity γ gives us the fraction of all individual in a population, which may be infected directly or indirectly by a given individual. In actual situations the probabilities of contac are not the same for any pair of individuals. To such cases expres sions must be applied, which have been derived by Rapoport for neuronic nets in which probabilities of synapses between two neurons depend on the distance[6].

Even more striking applications have been made by Rapoport and his co-workers to the process of rumor spreads[7]. Here again we have a formal mathematical analogy with the problem discussed above. Just as a neuron may be one, two or more axons removed from a given neuron, so can an individual hear of a rumor either directly from the person who starts it, or through one, two, or more intermediate persons. The theoretical work of Rapoport has found a wide use in the experimental researches on rumor spread, conducted by the Washington Public Opinion Laboratory under the direction of Stuart C. Dodd[8].

All of which shows that by applying mathematical methods to the study of fundamental mechanisms of different natural phenomena, we are likely to uncover quite unsuspected similarities between such widely different fields as neurophysiology, epidemiology, and sociology.

REFERENCES

1. A. Shimbel and A. Rapoport, *Bull. Math. Biophysics,* **10**, 41, 1948; A. Rapoport and A. Shimbel, *ibid.*, **10**, 211, 1948; A. Rapoport, *ibid.*, **10**, 145, 1948; **10**, 221, 1948; **12**, 109, 1950; **12**, 187, 1950; **12**, 317, 1950; **12**, 327, 1950; N. Anderson and A. Rapoport, *ibid.*, **13**, 47, 1951; A. Rapoport, *ibid.*, **13**, 85, 1951; **13**, 85, 1951; R. Solomonoff and A. Rapoport, *ibid.*, **13**, 107, 1951; A. Rapoport, ibid., **13**, 179, 1951; **14**, 35, 1952; **14**, 73, 1952; **14**, 159, 1952; **14**, 351, 1952; **19**, 257, 1957; H. G. Landau, *ibid.*, **14**, 203, 1952; E. Trucco, *ibid.*, **14**, 365, 1952.

2. A. Rapoport, *Bull. Math. Biophysics.*, **10**, 145, 1948.

3. J. V. Uspensky, *Introduction to Mathematical Probability*, pp. 135-136; New York: McGraw-Hill, 1937.

4. R. Solomonoff and A. Rapoport, *Bull. Math. Biophysics*, **13**, 107, 1951.

5. H. G. Landau and A. Rapoport, *Bull. Math. Biophysics*, **15**, 173, 1953.

6. A. Rapoport, *Bull. Math. Biophysics*, **13**, 85, 1951.

7. A. Rapoport, and L. Rebhun, *Bull. Math. Biophysics*, **14**, 375, 1952; A. Rapoport, *ibid.*, **15**, 523, 1953; **15**, 535, 1953; **16**, 75, 1954.

8. Stuart C. Dodd and Staff, "Testing Message Diffusion in C-Ville". *Research Studies in the State College of Washington*, **20**, 83, 1952; Washington Public Opinion Laboratory, *Project Revere*, Vol. III, 1952. (Mimeographed Report).

PART II

GENERAL MATHEMATICAL PRINCIPLES IN BIOLOGY

CHAPTER XXI

OUTLINE OF A NEW MATHEMATICAL APPROACH TO GENERAL BIOLOGY

The development of mathematical biophysics has made considerable strides. Not only is the theoretical edifice wall erected and systematically developed, but a very large number of experimental facts, ranging from cell respiration to experimental aesthetics, have been quantitatively represented in an adequate manner and in some cases even predicted by the theory.

Naturally, as in every science, the more a theory is developed, the more new problems appear in it. Also the more experimental facts have been explained, the more new experimental facts call for an explanation. The progress of any science may almost be measured by the width of the new horizon it uncovers to us.

Whether there is such a thing as a possible exhaustion of a science—a stage in which everything is discovered and nothing remains to be done—is more a metaphysical question, and we shall not discuss it here. Premature worries in regard to the possibilities of explaining some of the yet unexplained phenomena and anxieties lest such an explanation should turn out to be impossible should not take place with scientists. Whenever such worries and anxieties have occurred, they usually were rather ridiculed by further developments by investigators who went ahead heedless of such worries.

Nevertheless, at every stage of development of a science, when we have before us a vista of unsolved problems, it is useful, and perhaps even necessary, to consider, so to speak, the general plan of campaign in attacking those problems. We may not be expected to tell actually how to solve those problems, for that would practically amount to a solution. But we should be able to see, at least in principle, how those problems may be solved practically.

If we survey from this point of view the field of mathematical biophysics, we find that, while in some directions the method of further conquest is already indicated by merely following and extending present techniques, in some other directions the adoption in the future of new methods and techniques is strongly indicated.

The first case is exemplified mainly by the mathematical biophysics of the central nervous system. We may have to modify somewhat the fundamental equations. But, in principle, the rather formal method used hitherto, namely, the study of geometrically more and more complex circuits, to which the formal, phenomenological equations are applied, still offers almost unlimited possibilities.

The second case is exemplified by the mathematical biophysics of cell aggregates and of the organism as a whole. While, by the introduction of drastic simplifications, remarkable progress has been made in the dynamics of cell division, as well as in the theory of cell aggregates, yet an impartial survey of the situation shows that it is pretty difficult even to conceive in principle how the present methods are going to be applied *practically* to some more complex cases. We have outlined a couple of possible approaches to the problem of the form of animals. In principle, the development of those suggested approaches should well lead us to the solution of the problem. *Practically,* however, as it is easy to see even now, we shall soon run into almost insuperable difficulties if we try to extend even the present approximate treatment of the metabolic forces to such complex shapes as are offered by various organisms. Any oversimplification of the problem must have a limit, beyond which the problem becomes completely distorted and unreal and a further simplification of the present "approximate method" would likely exceed that limit. Something else must be done.

Difficulties of a similar nature, but perhaps even more severe in extent, are met when we remember that, hitherto, mathematical biophysics has studied only a very small section of the organic world. The interaction between the organisms and the surrounding environment has been taken into account from the very beginning. This interaction forms often an essential feature of the theory, as, for instance, in the case of cell division. Yet the properties of the environment considered have been oversimplified almost to the limit. Only a very small fraction of the environment of an organism is inorganic. The largest part of that environment is formed by other organisms. Almost every organism depends for its existence on the presence of other organisms, with the exception, perhaps, of some of the simplest unicellular organisms. With this exception the concept of an organism or even of a number of organisms of the same kind, in the absence of other kinds of organisms, is a fiction.

Again we may say, or at least we may hope, that in the final analysis all these complex interactions are reducible to physico-chemical metabolic forces of tremendous complexities. But that very complexity makes it again rather doubtful whether *practically* we may achieve anything by such a reduction. Again something else must be done.

Situations of that nature are not unfamiliar to the physicist. The latter does not doubt that even the most complex mechanical or electromechanical phenomena are ultimately reducible to activities of individual atoms. Nevertheless, in studying, for instance, a complex electric circuit, a physicist does not fall back on the equations of the electron theory but uses some general *formal* principles in his computations. It is quite true that at present almost all such formal principles can be shown directly to be deducible from atomic theory. But there was a time when this was not known, and yet those formal principles were used just as safely. We may be reminded, by way of example, of Fourier's theory of heat conduction, Ohm's law, etc.

We therefore propose to introduce in mathematical biology a few such formal principles, which may be used to advantage in the development of a theory of more complex biological phenomena, regardless *at present* of their reducibility to the principles used hitherto. It must be kept in mind that the adoption of such formal principles in no way competes with the use of the former ones, which are more *physical* and less formal in nature. The two sets are quite compatible. The introduction of the formal principles opens, however, new horizons, hitherto unseen.

It may be worth noticing that the mathematical biophysics of the central nervous system, which offers, as we remarked, almost unlimited possibilities for further developments with the present method, is essentially based on a few formal phenomenological principles.

Whether a single cell or a complex metazoan plant, every organism is a metabolizing system. But, whereas in a single cell metabolism is perhaps the most outstanding thing, complex metazoan organisms are usually characterized by other essential physico-chemical attributes. One of the most important of those, which occurs in single cells even, is motility. Another important attribute is the nervous coordination and integration. The velocity of locomotion of any organism varies largely under different circumstances. We may, however, consider every mobile metazoan as endowed with an *average* velocity of locomotion, v, characteristic of the species. Similarly, the amount of nervous coordination and integration varies largely from case to case. But again, we may consider average values, characteristic of the species. This average amount of coordination will be some increasing function of the amount n of nerve tissue per unit mass of the organism.

With the exception of some protozoa, the locomotion of all organisms is produced by a system of levers. In such cases as snakes or fishes the body as a whole is used as a lever. In other cases the extremities are such systems of levers.

Although quite a considerable amount of research has been done on the kinematics of movements of the vertebrates and of some other organisms,[1] a systematic theory of what may be called *lever-propelled metabolizing systems* is yet completely lacking. The principal reason for this lies probably in the fact that the equations of motion of chains of linked levers present almost insuperable mathematical difficulties.[2] An elaboration of such a systematic abstract theory, as a preliminary to actual biological applications, is strongly indicated.

Given a metabolizing system of mass M, average metabolism q ergs gm^{-1} per unit mass, average amount of nervous tissue nM gm, the average velocity of locomotion v will be determined by the particular structure of the systems of levers which constitute the locomotory system. If we have a systematic classification of such systems of levers and of their properties, we can calculate, for a given lever system, the value of v in terms of M, q, and n. In general, we may expect that for given M, q, and n the same value of v may be obtained by means of several lever structures.

In developing a systematic theory of lever-propelled metabolizing systems, we may, among other things, classify those systems by their degree of complexity. Provisionally, we may consider the complexity as measured by the number of single rigid levers of the system. A more detailed theory should, however, take into consideration also the different types of joints between the levers. A joint with two degrees of freedom will be considered as more complex than a joint with one degree of freedom. In such a case the complexity may be measured by the number of kinematic degrees of freedom of the whole system.

We shall now introduce the following formal principle:

A lever-propelled metabolizing system, characterized by given values of M, q, n, *and* v *has the simplest lever structure which for the given values of* M, q, *and* n *gives the required value of* v.

Since the lever structure of an organism determines to a large extent its shape, we thus may describe the shape of an organism in terms of M, q, n, and v.

More generally we may postulate that *the shape of any or-*

ganism is determined by the requirements of performing certain mechanical and physiological functions. Such a more general view is better applicable to the problems of the form of plants, which are not lever-propelled systems. Formally, however, we may consider a plant as a system for which $v = n = 0$.

The simplest method of propulsion of a lever-propelled system is by a process of consecutive foldings and unfoldings. Locomotion of some caterpillars is of a similar nature. The locomotion of snakes is more complicated, as shall be seen in chapter xxiii. During the folding, the "front" end (Fig. 1,*a*) remains in fixed

FIG. 1

contact with the ground, during the unfolding the "rear" end does it (Fig. 1,*b*).

This type of movement requires relatively little coordination, and therefore a relatively small n will be sufficient. We may set as a requirement, $n > n_1$, where n_1 is the minimum n required for such types of movements.

All these cases of locomotion may be generally described as "crawling." For all of them a considerable frictional resistance of ground must be present. This resistance may set an upper limit for the velocity of locomotion for a given M and q. In more complex types of locomotion, which involve the use of extremities, this may not be the case. Thus the requirement of a certain velocity v may require the presence of extremities. The definite proof that this is the case is still lacking. The discussion in the subsequent chapters tends, however, to support this contention.

It appears that the speed of locomotion is not essentially increased by addition of more extremities above two. Hence it would at first appear as if our fundamental formal principle would allow only organisms with only one pair of extremities. This, however, is not so, if we consider the role of the quantity n. With only one pair of extremities both locomotion and quiet standing are unstable processes. The maintenance of standing posture with only two extremities requires a very complex mechanism of nervous coordination and hence a sufficiently large n. Let us denote by n_2 the smallest value of n which will provide for the necessary coordination.

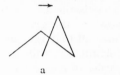

As a measure of n_2 we may perhaps take the total number of muscular movements, which is involved, on the average, per unit of time in order to maintain an erect posture on two extremities.

A standing posture on four extremities requires much less coordination, although mechanically it is not quite stable, considering that the extremities are not rigidly joined to the body. A certain minimum amount of muscular coordination is still necessary to maintain a standing position. Let a value n_4 correspond to that minimum. Then we find four extremities only within the range $n_2 > n > n_4$. For $n_4 > n > n_6$ we find six extremities, etc.

There is another factor which plays a role in the determination of the number of extremities. That is the size of the organism relative to the average "roughness" of the ground on which it is moving around. Even a human uses all four extremities when climbing over a rough mountainous terrain, when the average size of the "bumps" becomes of the same order of magnitude as that of our bodies. For very rough terrain we have to use our fingers, which are additional levers, to take hold of the unevennesses. Hence a system of even four rigid extremities will not be sufficient in such a case, and it is necessary to introduce additional levers, either by adding more joints at the ends of the extremities or by adding more extremities.

From kinematic considerations it may be readily seen that, in the first instance at least, two "fingers" have to be added to each extremity to provide for sufficient hold. Hence the second case introduces less additional joints. The smaller the number of joints, the smaller may be n. Hence for small values of n the stabilization will take place by addition of new extremities. And, since the relative roughness of the ground in general increases as the size of the organism decreases, we shall find six or eight extremities for small values of both M and n. Such is the case with insects. When M and n are large, only four extremities may be sufficient, but they will be provided with "second-order" extremities.

REFERENCES

1. A. Bethe, *Handb. d. norm. u. path. Physiol.*, Vol. 15, Part I (Leipzig: J. Springer, 1930).

2. O. Fischer. *Theoretische Grundlagen für eine Mechanik der lebenden Körper* (Leipzig: Teubner, 1906). C.f. also a series of papers by W. Braune, and O. Fischer, in *Abh. d. Sächs. Gesellsch. d. Wiss.*, **20**, 5–84, 1893; **21**, 153–322, 1895; **22**, 55–197, 1895; **25**, 1–130, 1899; **26**, 87–170, 1900; **26**, 471–556, 1901; **27**, 485–588, 1902; **28**, 321–418, 533–617, 1904. M. Winkelmann and R. Grammel, "Kinetik der starren Korper," *Handb. d. Physik, herausgegeben von H. Geiger und K. Scheel*, 5, 373–483 (Berlin: J. Springer, 1927).

CHAPTER XXII

FORM OF PLANTS

The absence of locomotion and therefore the impossibility of running after food require a much larger specific surface of the organism through which food can be absorbed from the surrounding medium. Hence the general "branched" character of plants.

Let l_0 be the length of the main trunk, r_0 its radius. Let l and r be the average length and radii of the branches. Let the total number of branches be n, and the average density of the plant δ. Then

$$M = \pi\delta(l_0 r_0^2 + nlr^2). \tag{1}$$

Since qM is proportional to the total number of leaves, it is approximately proportional to the area of the branches. Hence

$$qM = knlr, \tag{2}$$

k being a coefficient.

From mechanical considerations, the length of a branch cannot exceed a certain value, determined by its radius, lest the branch break. Therefore.

$$l = f(r, \delta). \tag{3}$$

Since the smaller the r and the greater the l, the greater for a given M the specific surface of the tree, if the latter has a maximum, the relation (3) must hold.

Similarly,

$$l_0 = f_0(r_0, \delta, M). \tag{4}$$

Moreover, the total flow of metabolites through the trunk is limited by r_0 and by the diffusion properties of the material. Considering that r_0 is always just such as to allow the necessary flow, we have for the trunk

$$r_0 = f_1(qM, \delta), \tag{5}$$

and for each branch

$$r = f_1\left(\frac{qM}{n}, \delta\right). \tag{6}$$

Altogether, we have six equations, to determine the six quantities l_0, r_0, n, l, r, and δ in terms of M and q. But the first five quantities already largely determine the gross shape of the plant. Small l_0 and r_0 and large n give us a bush. Small l_0, large r_0, small n, and large l give us the form of Figure 1,*a*. Large l_0, r_0, n, l, and r give

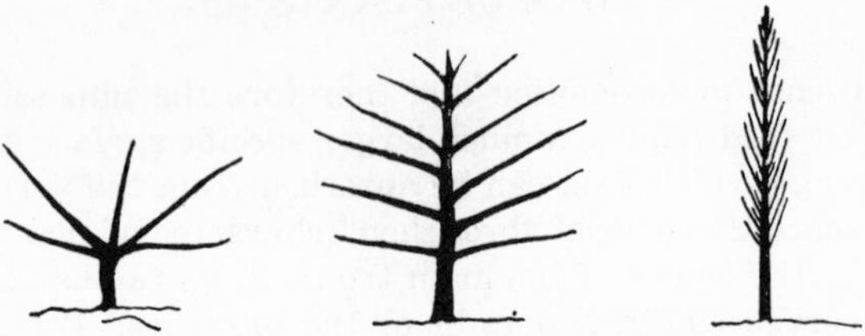

a b c

FIG. 1

the shape of Figure 1,*b*, while large l_0, r_0, and n but small l and r give something like Figure 1,*c*. By using plausible expressions for $f(r, \delta)$, f_0, and f_1, those different forms are actually obtained as functions of M and q.

The following is intended only as an illustration of the method and does not necessarily bear any relation to real cases.

A very rough idea about f may be obtained in the following manner. A horizontal rigid rod of length l, fixed at one end and loaded at the other end with a load P, will sag at the free end by the amount[1]

$$x_0 = \frac{P}{3EJ} l^3, \tag{7}$$

where E is the modulus of elasticity and J is defined by

$$J = \int x^2 d\sigma . \tag{8}$$

Here x denotes the coordinate in the direction of the force P, and $d\sigma$ is the element of surface of the cross-section. Hence the dimensionality of J is [cm^4]. From equation (7) we find the bending per unit length to be

$$\Delta x_0 = \frac{x_0}{l} = \frac{P}{3EJ} l^2, \tag{9}$$

and, from the above dimensional considerations, this quantity will be, in general, of the form

$$\Delta x_0 \propto \frac{Pl^2}{3Er^4}. \tag{10}$$

On the other hand, considering that the rod bends under the influence of its own weight, we have

$$P \propto \delta l r_0^2 . \tag{11}$$

Hence

$$\Delta x_0 \propto \frac{l^3 \delta}{3Er^2}.$$

E is likely to increase with δ, and therefore, as a first approximation, we may put, assuming $E \propto \delta$,

$$\Delta x_0 \propto \frac{l^3}{r^2}. \tag{12}$$

When Δx_0 exceeds a certain constant determined by the strength of the wood, the branch breaks. That constant, in general, increases with δ. Let us put it proportional to δ^p. Then we have

$$l = a\delta^{p/3} r^{2/3} , \tag{13}$$

a being a coefficient. This determines f.

As regards f_0, we may consider that the trunk is compressed by a force $M/\pi r_0^2$ per square centimeter of cross-section and that, if that quantity exceeds a limit, which we again set approximately proportional to δ^p, the wood breaks under compression. Hence, b being another coefficient,

$$M = b\delta^p r_0^2 . \tag{14}$$

The function f_1 may be determined roughly by considering that the total metabolic flow in the trunk, which is proportional to qM, is proportional to the cross-section and approximately inversely proportional to δ. Hence, with c as a coefficient,

$$qM = \frac{cr_0^2}{\delta}; \qquad \frac{qM}{n} = \frac{cr^2}{\delta}. \tag{15}$$

Together with (1) and (2), equations (13), (14), and (15) determine δ, l_0, r_0, l, r, and n in terms of q and M.

Solving those equations, we obtain rather unwieldy expressions. They simplify considerably, however, if we consider the case in which $p << 1$. Since we are interested here only in illustrating the method and not in any actual relations, we can limit ourselves to that case. Denoting by C a coefficient, we then find that the six quantities, δ_1, l_0, r_0, l, r, and n vary approximately in the following way:

$$\delta \propto \frac{1}{q}; \quad l_0 \propto \left(q - \frac{C}{q^2} \right); \quad r_0 \propto M^{\frac{1}{2}} q^{p/2};$$
$$l \propto \frac{1}{q^2}; \quad r \propto \frac{1}{q^3}; \quad n \propto M q^6. \tag{16}$$

The value of l_0 is negative for $q < q_1 = \sqrt[3]{C}$. A negative l_0, physically, would probably mean $l_0 = 0$, that is, a form of a bush. If the actual range of variation of q is in the neighborhood of q_1, then l_0 increases with q rather rapidly. For $p << 1$, l_0 is first negative, then increases to $+ \infty$. Here again l_0 increases very rapidly with q in the neighborhood of q_1, though for large q, approximately $l_0 \propto q$. Assuming that the actual range of variation of q is in the neighborhood of q_1, we find that the ratio l_0/r_0 increases very rapidly with q. If $u(q)$ denotes this rapidly increasing function of q, then,

$$\frac{l_0}{r_0} \propto \frac{u(q)}{\sqrt{M}\, q^{p/2}}, \tag{17}$$

$$\frac{l}{l_0} \propto \frac{1}{q^2 u(q)}, \tag{18}$$

$$n \propto M q^6, \tag{19}$$

$$\frac{r}{r_0} \propto \frac{1}{q^3 \sqrt{M}}. \tag{20}$$

For a constant M, small q gives us a small l_0/r_0, large l/l_0, large r/r_0, and small n—hence a shape like Figure 1, *a*. An increasing q increases l_0/r_0, and n but decreases l/l_0 and r/r_0, and we have the shape of Figure 1, *b*. An increase of M increases n, and to a lesser extent decreases l_0/r_0 and r/r_0. Hence a large M and sufficiently large q give us the shape of Figure 1, *c*. The density, δ, decreases with increasing q.

Instead of equal branches, we may introduce a distribution function $n(l)$, such that $\int_0^\infty n(l)\,dl = n$ and determine $n(l)$ from some extremum requirement.

N. Rashevsky[2] outlined a further generalization of the theory to take into account branches of higher order, as well as the size and shape of leaves. Other studies on the relation of mechanical properties of trees to their form have been made by I. Opatowski[3] and M. H. M. Esser.[4]

REFERENCES

1. J. W. Geckeler, *Handb. d. Physik*, **6**, 165. 1928.
2. N. Rashevsky, *Bull. Math. Biophysics*, **5**, 33, 1943; **6**, 1, 1944.
3. I. Opatowski, *Bull. Math. Biophysics*, **6**, 113, 153, 1944; **7**, 1, 1945; **8**, 41, 1946.
4. M. H. M. Esser, *Bull. Math. Biophysics*, **8**, 65, 95, 1946.

CHAPTER XXIII

LOCOMOTION AND FORM OF SNAKES

There are, apparently, at least three different types of locomotions of snakes.[1,2] Of those we shall consider the one which is regarded as the most common one. According to W. Mosauer, the snake assumes an approximately sinusoidal shape and moves forward in such a way that each point along the body follows the same sinusoidal path. The physical mechanism of such a locomotion seems at first somewhat puzzling. As we shall presently see, however, this type of locomotion may be obtained by assuming that the coefficients of static friction of the snake against the ground are different in the direction of the body axis and in the direction normal to it. The reasons for such a possibility will be discussed presently.

Inasmuch as the exact shape of the curve formed by the body of the snake has never been ascertained and may, in a strict mathematical sense, be not a sinusoid at all, we shall in the following discussion make some very crude approximations, by assuming instead of a smooth, wavy line a zigzag line (Fig. 1), of total length L. The expressions derived are more of the nature of dimensional relations

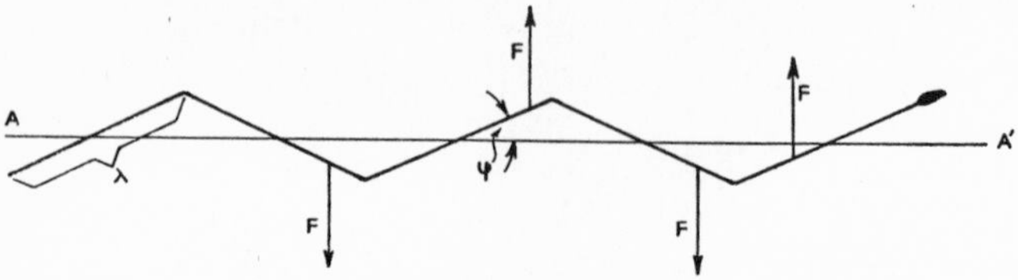

FIG. 1

and establish orders of magnitudes rather than exact equations. However, even those rough approximations throw interesting light on the problem. Let the length of each straight segment be λ. Let at every point a muscular force f per unit length tend to displace the different parts of the body at a right angle to AA', as shown by the arrows (Fig. 1). The component of this force along the snake's axis is

$$f_l = f \sin \phi; \tag{1}$$

the component normal to the direction of the body axis is

$$f_n = f \cos \phi \,. \tag{2}$$

Let the static friction r_l for displacement along the axis be less than the static friction r_n for displacement perpendicular to that axis:

$$r_l < r_n \,. \tag{3}$$

This may be due either to a peculiarity of the surface of the skin of the snake or to the fact that the snake, because of its weight, makes an impression in the ground. Such an impression tends to prevent lateral displacements. Longitudinal displacements may be easier, because of the wedgelike action of the snake's head. The total force acting along the snake's axis is

$$F_l = f_l L = fL \sin \phi \,. \tag{4}$$

The total force acting normally to the axis is

$$F_n = f_n L = fL \cos \phi \,. \tag{5}$$

If

$$F_n < r_n ; \quad F_l > r_l \,, \tag{6}$$

then the body of the snake will glide along its own axis. Let the velocity of this gliding be v cm sec^{-1}.

A zigzag, or a wave-line, shape of the body of the snake is produced by contraction of muscles on the "concave" sides of each "peak" and by relaxation of the muscles on the "convex" side of it. Hence, if the body of the snake glides along its axis with the velocity v, a wave of contraction must move along the body of the snake with the same velocity v. If the zigzag line is periodical, as we shall consider to be the case, then, denoting by 2λ the wave length, this contraction wave will have a period

$$T = \frac{2\lambda}{v} \,, \tag{7}$$

or a frequency

$$\nu = \frac{v}{2\lambda} \,. \tag{8}$$

Since the dry friction of the moving snake against the ground is independent of the velocity, any force acting along the axis that is strong enough to set the body in motion will keep this motion accelerated indefinitely, if other limiting factors do not enter into play. In the present case such a limiting factor is found in the condition that, as the snake moves along its axis with the velocity v, a contraction wave must move along its muscles with the same velocity. A snake cannot move with respect to the ground with a velocity greater than the velocity of the contraction wave with respect to its body. Thus the factors limiting the velocity of the snake must be sought in the properties of the snake's muscular apparatus.

From (8) we have

$$v = 2\lambda\nu\,. \tag{9}$$

Since $2\lambda < L$, the velocity v of the contraction wave is limited fundamentally by ν. This latter is probably limited by the viscosity of the muscle.[3] The greater the ν, the faster must be the velocity u of contraction of the muscle, and that velocity is limited by the viscosity.

As an illustration we may consider the following line of thought. For a viscous rod of length l, cross-section s^2, viscosity η, we have

$$\frac{1}{l}\frac{dl}{dt} = \frac{1}{3\eta}\frac{F}{s^2}, \tag{10}$$

where F is the total force. Hence, if a denotes a constant and

$$F = as^2\,, \tag{11}$$

as happens to be approximately the case with muscles, then

$$u = \frac{dl}{dt} = \frac{al}{3\eta}. \tag{12}$$

The greater the amplitude A of the wave, the larger must be the relative shortening Δl of the muscles. It is also larger, the greater the thickness s of the body of the snake. Moreover, the smaller the wave length, the larger the curvature of the body and therefore the larger the Δl. Hence

$$\Delta l \propto \frac{As}{\lambda}, \tag{13}$$

and

$$u \sim \frac{\Delta l}{T} = \nu\Delta l \propto \frac{As}{\lambda}\nu. \tag{14}$$

Since the length l of the contracting mass of muscles is of the order of λ,

$$l \sim \lambda; \tag{15}$$

hence, from (12),

$$u \propto \frac{a\lambda}{3\eta}. \tag{16}$$

Equations (14) and (16) give

$$As\nu \propto \frac{a\lambda^2}{3\eta}, \tag{17}$$

or

$$\nu \propto \frac{a\lambda^2}{3A\eta s}. \tag{18}$$

Introducing this into (9) and making the plausible assumption that

$$\lambda \propto L, \tag{19}$$

we have

$$v \propto \frac{2aL^3}{3A\eta s}. \tag{20}$$

The force f per unit length may be assumed to be proportional to s^2, because of its approximate proportionality to the cross-section of the muscles. If we increase s, we increase both the circumference and the thickness of the muscles. Hence their cross-section varies approximately as s^2. Hence, denoting by a_1 a constant,

$$f = a_1 s^2 . \tag{21}$$

Therefore, (4) and (6) give

$$a_1 s^2 L \sin \phi > r_l , \tag{22}$$

or

$$\sin \phi > \frac{r_l}{a_1 s^2 L} = \frac{r_l}{a_1 V} , \tag{23}$$

where V is the volume of the snake.

But, from Figure 1,

$$A \sim \lambda \sin \phi ; \tag{24}$$

hence

$$A \sim \frac{\lambda r_l}{a_1 V}. \tag{25}$$

Introducing expression (25) into (20) we find, remembering (15) and (19),

$$v \sim \frac{L^2 V}{\eta s r_l}. \tag{26}$$

The quantity v is the velocity of the snake along its axis. Along AA' the velocity is

$$\bar{v} = v \cos \phi . \tag{27}$$

Since the density of the snake is close enough to unity, we have, from (23),

$$\sin \phi = \frac{r_l}{a_1 M}; \tag{28}$$

hence

$$\cos \phi = \sqrt{1 - \frac{r_l^2}{a_1^2 M^2}}. \tag{29}$$

Therefore (26) and (27) give

$$\bar{v} \propto \frac{L^2 M}{\eta s r_l} \sqrt{1 - \frac{r_l^2}{a_1^2 M^2}}. \tag{30}$$

Since

$$L s^2 = M , \tag{31}$$

s may be eliminated from (30), and this determines L in terms of M and v; s is then determined from (31). *Hence* v *and* M *determine the shape of the snake.*

It seems paradoxical that $\bar{v}$ should increase with M. If r_l increases with M, the latter may drop out of the equation.

The weakest points in the reasoning are relations (13) and (15). In (13) we may perhaps consider, instead of λ, the length of the individual muscles. This will introduce a parameter characterizing the inner anatomical structure. Instead of (15), a more exact relation should be established.

A more rigorous procedure would be to establish from more exact considerations of the viscous losses a maximum value of ν in terms of λ, a relation to replace (18). Let the relation be

$$\nu = \nu(\lambda) ;$$

then the exact equation (9) gives

$$\nu = 2\lambda\nu(\lambda). \tag{32}$$

It may happen, that $\lambda\nu(\lambda)$ has a maximum for $\lambda_m << L$. In this case the equation

$$\frac{d[\lambda\nu(\lambda)]}{d\lambda}=0 \qquad (33)$$

may be considered as determining the actual value of λ.

The physical reason why $\bar{v}$ increases with M is due to the fact that, with the assumption made, the total force is proportional to M (eqs. [4] and [21]), while the viscous resistance increases with L and decreases with s.

It must also be kept in mind that the above considerations hold only for uniform motion. The acceleration at the beginning will be expressed in a more complicated way, and it seems likely that, at least approximately, the acceleration will not depend on M.

If we wish to connect the velocity of locomotion to the available metabolic energy Mq, we must compute for a given ν and λ, and hence v, the energy losses, E, per unit time and also remember that the energy loss due to friction against ground is $r_l v$ ergs sec^{-1}. Hence

$$E + r_l v = Mq\,. \qquad (34)$$

If E is known as a function of v, equation (34) determines the latter in terms of M and q.

Since the actual values of r_l and r_n, as well as of other constants, are not known, it is impossible at present to compute the limiting speed of locomotion for a given q. It appears plausible, however, that, owing to the very large frictional area, those speeds would be low. According to Mosauer,[1] the largest observed speeds of snakes are of the order of 1 meter per second. To obtain higher speeds, different bodily structures must be used, which would involve extremities.

A further improvement of the theory outlined above would consist in considering, instead of a zigzag line, a continuous line. One might then investigate what kind of continuous periodical line gives a maximum velocity, other parameters being kept constant. In any case the possible relation between the size and shape of snakes and their speed should be made the object of careful quantitative studies.

REFERENCES

1. W. Mosauer, "*The Locomotion of Snakes and Its Anatomical Basis.*" (Thesis, University of Michigan, 1931).

2. W. Mosauer, *Zool. Jahrb., Abt. f. allg. Zool. u. Physiol. d. Tiere*, 52, 191, 1932.

3. A. V. Hill, *Muscular Movements in Man* (New York: McGraw-Hill Book Co., 1927).

CHAPTER XXIV

FORM AND LOCOMOTION OF SOME QUADRUPEDS

In a very rough way, a quadruped, such as a horse or an elephant, may be considered from a mechanical point of view as a bar supported at its ends. This sets definite limits to the length of the trunk for a given width. The actual supporting structure is the vertebral column. However, not only the ribs but even the soft muscular and other tissues contribute to some extent to the mechanical strength of the trunk. The study of different factors and conditions affecting the mechanical strength of the trunk of quadrupeds is a most interesting, but extremely complex, problem. Its development will result in many relations which will offer clues for biometric studies.

We shall not tackle that general problem at present. Inasmuch as we are as yet confining our study to extremely oversimplified pictures, we shall, *for the sake of illustration only*, investigate the situation that would prevail if the trunk of a quadruped could be considered as a uniform bar of length L and width W, supported at its ends.

If such a bar is uniformly loaded with a load p per unit length, then the sagging f in the middle is[1]

$$f \propto \frac{pL^4}{W^4}; \tag{1}$$

hence the relative sagging is

$$f/L \propto \frac{pL^3}{W^4}. \tag{2}$$

By definition

$$p = \frac{M}{L}, \tag{3}$$

where M is the mass of the trunk, which may be set approximately equal to the total mass of the animal. Hence

$$f/L \propto \frac{ML^2}{W^4}. \tag{4}$$

The relative sagging should not exceed a certain threshold value, lest the bar break. Assuming this value to be a constant and that f/L is always a given fraction of that constant, we have

$$\frac{ML^2}{W^4} = \text{const} \quad \text{or} \quad \frac{L^2}{W^4} \propto M^{-1}. \tag{5}$$

Moreover, we have, approximately,

$$LW^2 = M. \tag{6}$$

Expressions (5) and (6) give

$$L \propto M^{1/4}; \quad W \propto M^{3/8}; \quad \frac{L}{W} \propto M^{-1/8}; \quad W \propto L^{3/2}. \tag{7}$$

The heavier the animal, the shorter its trunk relative to its width.

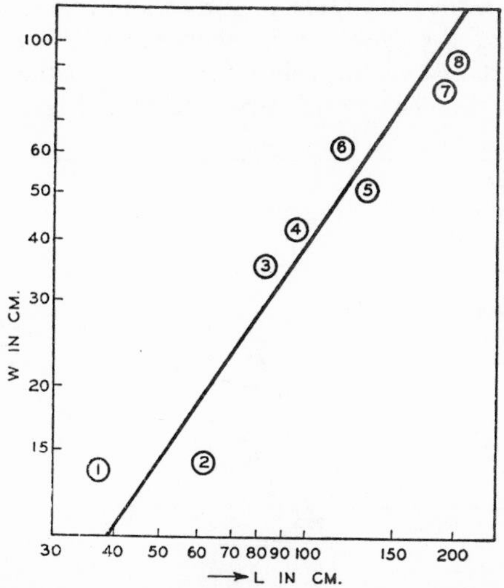

FIG. 1.—Width W of trunk plotted against length L of trunk on logarithmic scale. The straight line has the theoretically predicted slope 3/2. 1, cat; 2, dog; 3, dog; 4, goat; 5, ass; 6, saw; 7, elk; 8, ox. Data from Muybridge (1887).

Of course, we cannot expect such simple relations to hold exactly in reality. It is interesting, however, that, to some degree of approximation, the relation $W \propto L^{3/2}$ does actually hold, as is seen from Figure 1, where W is plotted against L on logarithmic scale.

Similar crude considerations lead us to expect that the cross-section of the legs will be roughly proportional to the mass M of the quadrupeds, since they have to be mechanically strong enough to support the body. Such an approximation is even cruder than the one made above about the trunk. The strength of the legs is determined not only by their role as "pillars" supporting the body but by numerous other functions. The trend toward thicker legs in heavier animals is, however, unmistakable. Actual data are very scarce. To make even a rough comparison, the following procedure was used. Denoting the thickness of the extremities by d, its cross-section is roughly d^2. We expect approximately $d^2 \propto M$, or, because of relations (7), $d^2 \propto L^4$ or $d \propto L^2$. Hence $d/L \propto L$ or

$$\frac{d}{L} \propto M^{1/4}. \tag{8}$$

The values of d/L were taken from pictures in Volume 2 of the *Anatomy of Vertebrates* by R. Owen[2]; the values of M from tables compiled by G. Crile[3] and from C. Oppenheimer and L. Pincussen.[4] The thickness of the femur was taken for d, the length between the shoulder blades and the pelvis for L. The values of d are extremely inaccurate. The results are plotted in Figure 2.

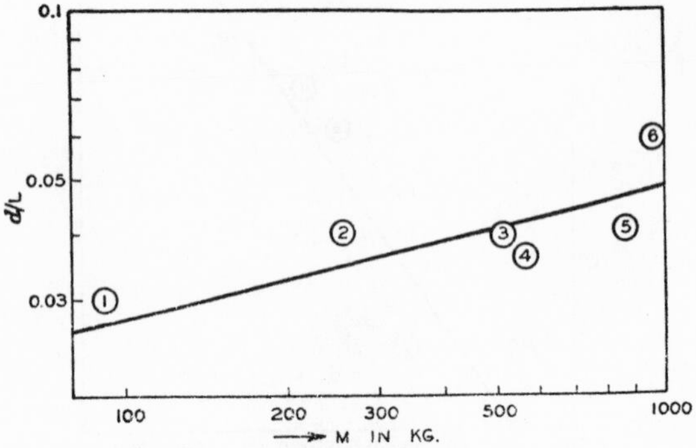

FIG. 2.—Ratio of thickness d of extremities to length L of trunk, plotted on logarithmic scale against mass M. The straight line has the theoretically predicted slope 1/4. 1, lion; 2, polar bear; 3, horse; 4, ox; 5, giraffe; 6, hippopotamus. For sources of data see text.

Thus, from a purely theoretical point of view, we see that the mass M *of a quadruped in principle may determine the size and shape of its trunk and the thickness of the extremities. This already specifies to a large extent its general form.*

It must be remarked that relations (7) determine L and W and hence the surface of the animal in terms of M. Since Rubner's law requires that the total metabolism vary approximately as the surface of the body, this raises the question as to whether M and q may be considered independent. However, the surface of the extremities is not negligible as compared with that of the trunk, and therefore no definite conclusion can be drawn at this stage. Here is a problem to be kept in mind.

A relation between the mass of an animal, the thickness of its extremities, and their *length* is provided by considerations of the mechanism of locomotion, especially of running. An exact theory of such a locomotion presents almost insuperable difficulties because, as mentioned in chapter xxi, the equations of motions of chains of linked levers are extremely complex. By using very rough approximations, N. Rashevsky[5] establishes a few general theorems. He shows that speeds such as are actually observed would be unattainable if the extremities of animals were rigid rods, merely swinging to and fro. At least one joint in the middle of the extremity must be provided, so that it can fold. In that case, when running is a result of *repulsion* of the body from the ground by the unfolding extremity, actually observed speeds may be obtained.

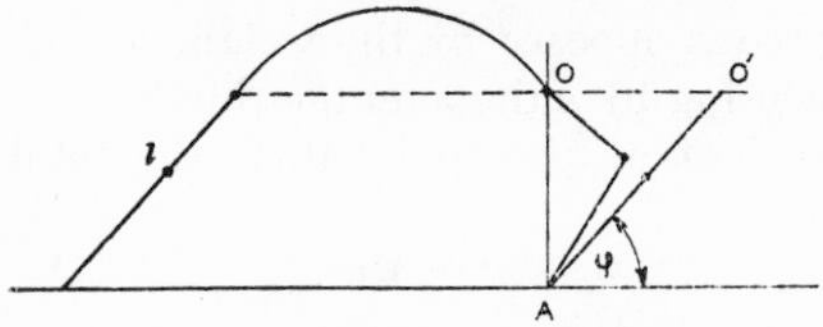

FIG. 3

Let the repelling action of an extremity impart to the center of gravity of the body a velocity v, forming an angle ϕ with the horizontal, and cause the system to be detached from the ground. The center of gravity then describes a parabola, and the horizontal distance traveled by the center of gravity until it reaches the same horizontal level is

$$x_h = 2\frac{v^2}{g}\sin\phi\cos\phi. \tag{9}$$

The time it takes to cover that distance is

$$t_0 = \frac{x_h}{v\cos\phi} = \frac{2v\sin\phi}{g}. \tag{10}$$

If we neglect, for the time being, the length of the extremity, then t_0 is essentially the duration of the step, while

$$\bar{v} = v\cos\phi \tag{11}$$

is the speed of running.

Let the forward-swinging extremity hit the ground in such a position that the line OA (Fig. 3) is vertical, so that, approximately, only the vertical component $v \sin \phi$ of the velocity is lost. Then the horizontal velocity $\bar{v}$ remains the same, and, as the extremity now unfolds, it communicates to the body the lost vertical momentum, which is regained when the extremity is in the "unfolded" position AO'. During this period the body moved the distance $OO' = l \cos \phi$, and this takes a time

$$t_1 = \frac{l \cos \phi}{v \cos \phi} = \frac{l}{v}. \tag{12}$$

Since, to a first approximation, only the vertical component of v is affected in that case, we see that during the time l/v the velocity changes from 0 to $v \sin \phi$. Hence the average acceleration is $(v^2 \sin \phi)/l$, and the average force is $(Mv^2 \sin \phi)/l$. This force is supplied by the muscles of the extremity and is approximately proportional to their cross-section, other conditions being equal.[5] The muscular force is opposed by the weight of the body, which is equal to Mg. Denoting by s the average thickness of the extremity and by f a coefficient of proportionality, the total force is very roughly equal to

$$fs^2 - Mg\,.$$

Putting this expression equal to $(Mv^2 \sin \phi)/l$, we find, because of equation (11),

$$\bar{v} = \sqrt{\frac{(fs^2 - Mg)l}{M \sin \phi}} \cos \phi\,. \tag{13}$$

Equation (13) may be written

$$\bar{v} = \sqrt{\frac{fs^2 l}{M \sin \phi} - \frac{gl}{\sin \phi}} \cos \phi\,. \tag{14}$$

The quantity $s^2 l$ is the volume of the extremity, which is roughly proportional to its mass. Hence, for similarly built animals, $s^2 l/M = \gamma =$ const. If the second term is small as compared with the first, then

$$\bar{v} = \sqrt{\frac{f\gamma}{\sin \phi}} \cos \phi\,. \tag{15}$$

Hence, *for similarly built animals the maximum velocity is independent of the size of the animal, other physicochemical conditions (which enter in* f) *being the same.* This result has been previously obtained in a different way by A. V. Hill.[6]

On the other hand, if we assume that s^2 is proportional to M, so that, denoting by k a constant, $s^2 = kM$, then, again neglecting the term in g,

$$\bar{v} = \sqrt{\frac{fkl}{\sin\phi}}\cos\phi. \tag{16}$$

A comparison of such a relation with observations presents great difficulties, in view of the scarcity of data. Hitherto, almost the only available data on the speed of animals are given by the series of instantaneous photographic pictures published by E. Muybridge.[7] They give interesting insight into different modes of locomotion, such as walking, trotting, galloping. In no case do we have the certainty that the *maximum* speed has been observed in any of the locomotions. For comparison with equation (16) we must choose the speediest form of locomotion—galloping. A few data could thus be found in Muybridge's publication, and they are represented in Figure 4. For a greyhound the observed velocity is, however, much too high.

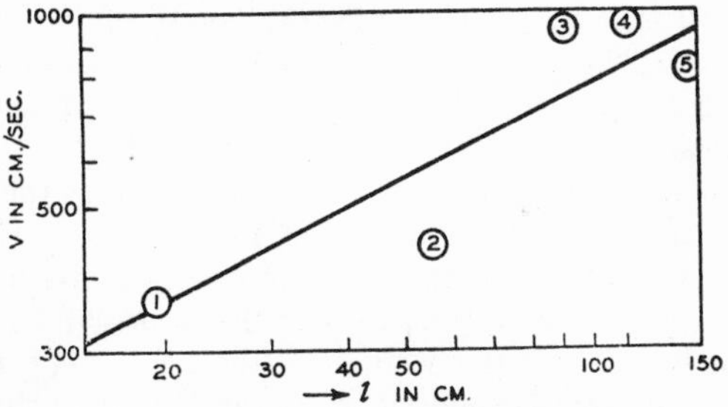

FIG. 4.—Velocity v of galloping plotted against length l of extremities on logarithmic scale. The straight line has the theoretically required slope 1/2. 1, cat; 2, goat; 3, elk; 4, horse; 5, camel. Data from Muybridge (1887).

It would certainly be of interest to obtain more detailed data on various animals by means of a cinema film. The quantity f could, in principle, be measured for each animal, and the cross-section s^2 can also be directly determined. Thus it would be possible to compare equation (13) directly with observations.

Before any worth-while discussion of the available data can be made, the theory will have to be considerably improved. Instead of using average velocities and accelerations, it will be necessary to establish more exact, although still approximate, equations of motion for the folding and unfolding of an extremity. The relative dimensions of each part of the extremity, in other words, *the location of the joints,* may then be determined by the requirement of a maximum possible velocity, considered as a function of those dimensions. The next extension would be to determine from similar considerations *the optimum number of joints.* Besides considerations of locomotion, other considerations will enter into that problem. An extremity ending in a thin stump would be of little use on a soft ground. This alone, regardless of other reasons, may require an extra joint, forming the foot.

The requirements of maximum *short-time velocity* or of maximum acceleration are different from those of sustained running. The study of this aspect of locomotion will lead into a theory of jumping and require considerations of *extremities of unequal length.* Even the role of an additional extremity in jumping—the tail—may be brought quantitatively into those studies. All such studies will determine more closely the external shape of the animal. But, even with the present crude approximation, we have the following result:

For a given mass of the animal, the size and shape of its trunk are determined by relations (7), while the thickness of the extremities is determined by relation (8), the length of the extremities is given by (16). The general outside shape of the animal is thus determined quantitatively to quite a large extent even by those simple considerations.

In addition to that, it may readily be seen that the total length of the neck must be of the order of magnitude of the length of the extremities, in order that the animal may be able to reach food on the ground. The thickness of the neck will be determined, for a given length, by the weight of the head. The latter, in its turn, is approximately proportional to the weight of the brain. The latter may be assumed to be proportional to the quantity n discussed in chapter xxi. G. W. Crile finds, however, empirically[3] that the brain weight of animals is approximately proportional to the total metabolism,* qM. *If this is so, then* q *and* M *determine, together with the shape of the trunk and the thickness and length of extremities, the size of the head and the length and width of the neck.* If Crile's selection does not hold, then q, M, and n determine the shape of the animal.

With the exception of the tail, we thus have a fairly complete description of the general shape of a quadruped in quantitative terms.

The approximate proportionality of the weight of the brain

* Crile does not give the source of his data for q, and we feel, therefore, that the above relation must be taken with due reservation.

and of qM awaits a theoretical explanation. Perhaps it may be found through the consideration that the more complex a brain, the larger the number of innervated muscle fibers and other end-organ units, the tonic activity of which consumes energy.

If the above-mentioned linear relation between qM and the weight of the brain is corroborated, this would require a revision of the assumption, suggested in chapter xxi, that the weight of the brain is an independent parameter. The reasons why most animals use four extremities for locomotion, when two seem to be sufficient, may have to be sought elsewhere and may well lie in some details, as yet not studied, of the dynamics of locomotion.

As regards arthropods, the larger number of extremities in those animals will likely be explained by the "relative roughness" of the ground (chap. xxi) and other similar considerations. The locomotion of jumping insects, like fleas or grasshoppers, is more aptly described as "biped."

All the foregoing holds, on the assumption of the constancy of other parameters, in particular of f. The latter is largely determined by the physicochemical constituents of the animal. It may well happen that f may itself be considered as an independent determining parameter of the organism. This does not alter anything in the general situation. We determine the shape of the organism in terms of continuously varying biological parameters, which describe the physicochemical constitution and the physiological functions of the organisms.

In another paper[8] N. Rashevsky makes a more detailed study of the mechanism of locomotion discussed above. He attempts to determine the optimal number of joints, as well as the angle ϕ. He also considers the role of muscular viscosity.

REFERENCES

1. J. W. Geckeler. "Elastostatik," *Handb. d. Physik, herausgegeben von H. Geiger und K. Scheel*, 6, (Berlin: J. Springer, 1928) 141–308.

2. R. Owen, *On the Anatomy of Vetebrates* (London: Longmans, Green & Co., 1866), Vol. 2.

3. G. W. Crile, *Intelligence, Power, and Personality* (New York: McGraw-Hill Book Co., 1941), p. 234.

4. C. Oppenheimer and L. Pincussen, *Tabulae biologicae*, Vol. 6 (Berlin: W. Junk, 1930).

5. N. Rashevsky, *Bull. Math. Biophysics*, 6, 17–32, 1944.

6. A. V. Hill, *Muscular Movements in Man* (New York: McGraw-Hill Book Co., 1927).

7. E. Muybridge, *Animal Locomotion* (Philadelphia: J. B. Lippincott Co., 1887).

8. N. Rashevsky, *Bull. Math. Biophysics*, 10, 11–23, 1948.

CHAPTER XXV

FLIGHT OF BIRDS AND INSECTS IN RELATION TO THEIR FORM

Even a remotely exact theory of the flight of birds and insects meets with almost insuperable difficulties at present. In fact, the relatively simpler problems of aircraft design are still based on semi-empirical foundations, since a complete synthetic theory of aerodynamics is still wanting. The relative simplification of the problems of aircraft engineering is due partly to the circumstance that the two principal types of aerodynamical structures involved are the ordinary wing and the propeller. The action of both involves, to a large extent, stationary aerodynamical states, when continuous operation is considered. The situation with birds is different. While the wing represents an aerodynamical profile, yet its movement through air is anything but stationary. Inertial forces due to acceleration, which do not enter into the theory of the airplane wing, probably play here a very important role.

From studies by E. J. Marey[1] and from pictures by E. Muybridge,[2] one gets the following general impression of the mechanism of the flight of a bird.

During the downstroke (Fig. 1,*a*) the wing moves down and forward, with the velocity v. The lift A has thus a component directed forward, A_x. The resistance W was a horizontal component W_x directed backward. Apparently $A_x - W_x > 0$ and causes the bird to move forward. The vertical components $A_y + W_y$ compen-

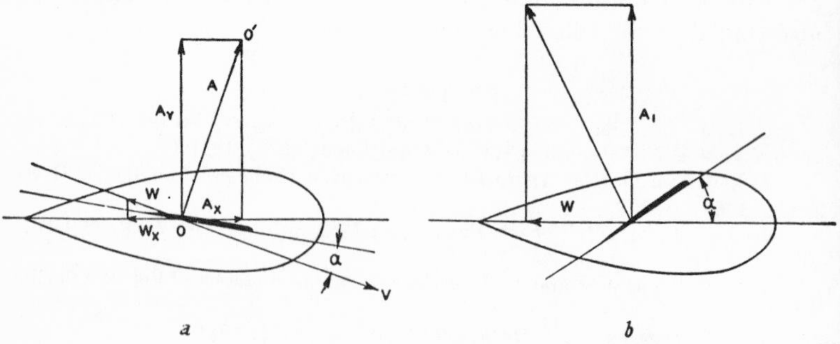

FIG. 1

sate at least partly for the force of gravity Mg, M being the mass of the bird and g the acceleration of gravity. Actually, $A_y + W_y$ is less than Mg, because, according to Marey, during the downstroke the bird loses slightly in altitude.

During the upstroke, the wings move backward and upward much more slowly than during the downstroke. The bird moves forward, owing to the momentum imparted previously by $A_x - W_x$, with a velocity v_1 (Fig. 1,*b*), which gradually decreases owing to resistance. Because of a larger angle of attack α, the lift A_1, which is now directed vertically, is greater than A_y before, so that $A_1 > Mg > A_y$, and the bird again gains altitude.

While, in a sense, the wing acts as an aerodynamic profile both during the downstroke and during the upward stroke, yet in no case can the ordinary theory of an airplane wing be applied with any accuracy; for neither the velocity v in Figure 1,*a*, nor v_1 in Figure 1,*b*, is uniform. Nor is the direction of the velocity with respect to the wing constant. In fact, in both cases the tip of the wing has a much higher velocity than the point of attachment, which remains stationary with respect to the body of the bird. This suggests that the wing may be acting as a propeller blade,[3] rotating approximately around the axis OO' (Fig. 1,*a*) and propelling itself in that direction. The vertical component then provides for the maintenance of altitude; the horizontal, for the forward movement. But again the fundamental difference between a theory of such an action and that of a propeller is that the former does not correspond to a stationary state of rotation. Moreover, the two wings must be considered as two propeller blades moving in opposite directions, and their mutual disturbance will be very complex. Thus we have in a bird a new type of aerodynamic lifting surface, which is neither a stationary moving wing nor a propeller, but a system *sui generis*, the theory of which must still be developed.

From Marey's studies it appears that the flight of insects is based on a somewhat similar mechanism.

At the end we shall suggest a rough, but somewhat detailed, analysis of the process of flight discussed above. Now we shall confine ourselves to very rough and general approximations, based largely on dimensional considerations.

Whatever the details of the actual mechanism may be, we may consider that the total velocity of locomotion $\bar{v}$ of the animal through air is less than, but of the same order of magnitude as, the velocity v of the wing through air. Thus

$$\bar{v} \sim v \,. \tag{1}$$

Denoting by L the length of a wing and by S its width, by ρ the density of air ($\rho = 1.2 \times 10^{-3}$ gm cm^{-3}) and by c_a and c_w the lift and resistance coefficients of the wing, we find from aerodynamical considerations[3] for the force of resistance, F_r, approximately

$$F_r = \tfrac{1}{2} c_w \rho L S v^2 . \tag{2}$$

If the frequency of wing movements is ν, then the average velocity v is

$$v \sim L\nu . \tag{3}$$

Since this velocity v is acquired approximately during a time $1/\nu$, the average acceleration is

$$\dot{v} \sim L\nu^2 . \tag{4}$$

If we put the density of the wing equal to ρ' and its average thickness to Δ, we have for its mass, M_w,

$$M_w \sim LS\rho'\Delta . \tag{5}$$

Hence the average inertial force is

$$F_i = M_w \dot{v} \sim L^2 S \nu^2 \Delta \rho' . \tag{6}$$

The total force $F_i + F_r$ must be exercised by the body in order to move the wing with the desired velocity. This muscular force may be put as roughly proportional to $M^{2/3}$, since it is proportional to the cross-section of the muscles, and for *similarly* built birds that cross-section is proportional to the total surface, which is proportional to $M^{2/3}$. Hence we have from (2) and (6), denoting by a_1' and f two coefficients,

$$a_1' L^2 S \Delta \nu^2 \rho' + \tfrac{1}{2} c_w \rho L S v^2 \propto f M^{2/3} , \tag{7}$$

or, because of (3), with a_1 as a new coefficient and remembering that there are two wings, so that F_r must be doubled:

$$a_1 S \Delta \rho' v^2 + c_w \rho L S v^2 \propto f M^{2/3} . \tag{8}$$

The lifting force of the two wings is equal to $c_a \rho L S v^2$, and this must be equal to Mg. Hence

$$LS \propto \frac{Mg}{c_a \rho v^2} . \tag{9}$$

Solving expressions (8) and (9) for L and S, we find, with $\varepsilon = c_w / c_a$,

$$L \propto \frac{a_1 M \Delta g \rho'}{c_a \rho (f M^{2/3} - \varepsilon M g)} = \frac{A\Delta}{\dfrac{f}{\sqrt[3]{M}} - \varepsilon g} , \tag{10}$$

and

$$S \propto \frac{fM^{2/3} - \varepsilon Mg}{a_1 \Delta \rho' v^2}. \tag{11}$$

A relation, determined by questions of mechanical strength, exists between L, S, Δ, and M. The thickness Δ must be greater, the greater the L and M. The situation is similar to the problem of the thickness of a branch of a tree or the length of the trunk of an animal. Thus,

$$F(L, S, M, \Delta) = 0. \tag{12}$$

Equations (10), (11), and (12) give us the size of the wing in terms of M and $\bar{v}$, since $\bar{v} \propto v$.

Equation (10) shows that there is a limit of the mass of a bird; for, when $M > f^3/\varepsilon^3 g^3$, L becomes infinite. The actual limit is, of course, much below $(f/\varepsilon g)^3$, since for structural reasons the length of the wing cannot exceed a certain size, which is of the order of magnitude of the size of the body. With $f \sim 10^5$, a value which we obtain by considering that the cross-section of the muscles in question is about 1 per cent of the cross-section of the body, $(f/\varepsilon g)^3 \sim 10^9$ gm $= 10^6$ kg.

If $\Delta \propto L$, then L and S cannot be determined from equations (8) and (9), since only the product LS enters into them. In that case equation (9) gives us LS, while equation (10) establishes a relation between the different parameters, which must hold, in order for flying to be possible at all. In particular, putting $\Delta = \beta L$, we have

$$c_a = \frac{a_1 g \beta \rho'}{\rho \left(\frac{f}{\sqrt[3]{M}} - \varepsilon g \right)}, \tag{13}$$

which shows that the larger the M, the greater must be c_a. Hence for larger animals, like birds, the profile of the wing must be much more perfect an aerodynamic profile than it needs to be for insects. Actually, this is the case, the wing of a bird being much more perfect aerodynamically than the wing of an insect.

Actually, in equation (10) we may have, more generally, a "less than" sign instead of an equality sign. This, with $\Delta = \beta L$, will result in a "greater than" sign in expression (13). Thus the conditions imply inequalities rather than rigid equalities.

To give one illustration of the above: The load per square centimeter in birds is of the order of 0.4–1.5 gm cm^{-2} or 4×10^2–15×10^2 dynes cm^{-2}. With velocities of the order of 10^3 cm sec^{-1}, this gives values of c_a between 0.6 and 2. For insects, the load per square centimeter is 1/10–1/100 of the above. With velocities of the same order of magnitude, this gives a correspondingly smaller c_a.

For approximately similar animals the mass varies as the cube of the linear dimensions l, while the area of the wings varies as l^2. Hence the load per unit area varies as l. The velocity v varies as $l\nu$, hence the resistance as $l^2v^2 = l^4\nu^2$. The acceleration varies as $l\nu^2$, and the mass of the wing as l^3, hence the inertial force varies as $l^4\nu^2$ also. The sum of the resistance and inertial force must be proportional to the muscular force, which, being proportional to the cross-section of the muscles, varies as l^2. Hence

$$\nu^2 l^4 \propto l^2 ,$$

or, remembering that l is proportional to the load m per square centimeter of the wing,

$$\nu \propto \frac{1}{l}; \qquad \nu \propto \frac{1}{m}. \tag{14}$$

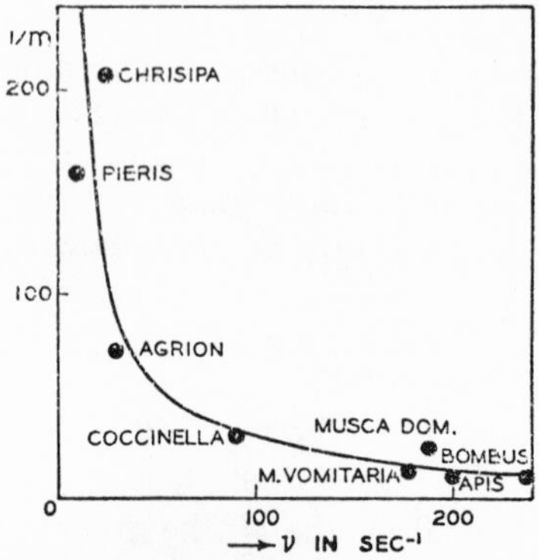

FIG. 2.—Frequency ν of wing beats of some insects plotted against the inverse of load per square centimeter of wing. Experimental points compared with the theoretical curve. Adapted from Buddenbrock.[4]

These relations hold, however, only for similarly built animals. In approximately similarly built insects it is actually observed that the larger the animal, the smaller the ν, so that, at least qualitatively, relation (14) is verified.[4]

If, however, we consider animals which have approximately the same mass but wings of different sizes, we obtain a different relation. The inertial and resistance forces are again proportional to $l^4\nu^2$. But the muscular force is now roughly constant. Hence $\nu^2 l^4 = \text{const}$ and $\nu \propto 1/l^2$. But for constant mass, l^2 is inversely proportional to the load m per square centimeter of the wing. Hence, instead of the second relation in (14), we have

$$\nu \propto m \,. \tag{15}$$

Relation (15) is very well verified by observation for some insects (Fig. 2), although they differ appreciably from one another with respect to their mass.

It is known, however, that larger insects fly more rapidly than smaller ones do. This, at first, seems to contradict the above considerations, since $v \propto l\nu = \text{const}$. But we must remember that v differs from $\bar{v}$. The coefficient of proportionality between v and $\bar{v}$ apparently varies with size. This is still a problem to be studied.

If we compare the empirical values of c_a and c_w for aerodynamical profiles and for plane plates, we find[5] that a value of $c_a \sim 1$ may be obtained with either. However, in order to obtain such a high value of c_a for a plate, α must be taken rather large. Then c_a turns out to be about ten times as large for a plate as for a profile. For larger animals, like birds, a wing in form of a flat plate would require very high energy expenditure and great force, owing to a high c_w. For insects c_a may be about ten times lower. Therefore, a flat plate can be used with a much smaller α, in which case c_w will also be reduced correspondingly. Thus insects may have smaller c_a than birds, but approximately the same c_w. The resistance, as we have seen, varies as $l^4\nu^2$, the coefficient of proportionality being determined by c_w. Muscular force varies as l^2. The relation $\nu = 1/m$ (eq. [15]) should hold over the whole range of birds and insects, if c_w is about the same.

If $\Delta \propto L$ and only LS is determined, then the determination of L and S separately is made in the following way. For a given LS the induced resistance will be the smaller, the greater the L. Hence c_w is itself a function of L and S separately. Thus we still have two equations for the two variables, L and S, although they will be rather unmanageable. In general, L should be taken as large as is compatible with structural requirements, such as lead to equation (12).

If the velocity v is to be sustained, then we have an equation which relates that velocity to q. The work done by the force F_r per unit time is for the two wings,

$$2\bar{v}F_r = c_w \rho L S v^3 \,. \tag{16}$$

The work done by F_i per downstroke is approximately

$$L^3 S \nu^2 \Delta\rho' . \qquad (17)$$

Hence per unit time, because of (3),

$$L^3 \nu^3 S \Delta\rho' = \Delta\rho' S v^3 . \qquad (18)$$

The sum of expressions (16) and (18) must be equal to Mq, if Mq is the excess metabolism over the resting one. Hence

$$(\Delta\rho' + c_w \rho L) S v^3 = Mq . \qquad (19)$$

Since L, S, and Δ are determined from (10), (11), and (12), equation (19) gives a relation between q, M, and v. Hence q and M alone determine the motion and form of the animal.

Now we shall briefly outline a more detailed, but very rough, approach to the problem of the flight of birds.

In glancing over the graphs representing the empirical relations between c_a and α (angle of attack) and c_w and α^3, we find that with some approximation, within a fairly wide range of α's, we have

$$c_a = A + B\alpha ; \qquad c_w = C + D\alpha^2 . \qquad (20)$$

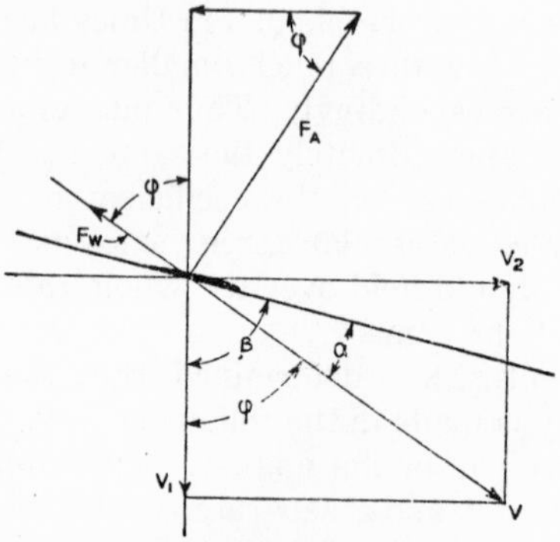

FIG. 3

Let (Fig. 3) the bird hold the wing at an angle β to the vertical and swing it downward. The resulting forces will move the wing forward, so that its resulting velocity will be v, making an angle ϕ with the vertical. The vertical force due to the lift F_A and resistance F_w is equal to

$$F = F_A \sin\phi + F_w \cos\phi \qquad (21)$$

and is directed upward. In order to move the wing down, it is necessary to apply a downward force, F_v. If M_w is the mass of the wing and v_v its instantaneous vertical velocity, then

$$M_w \frac{dv_v}{dt} = F_v - F. \tag{22}$$

Let v_1 (Fig. 3) be the *average* vertical velocity, then the duration, t_1, of a downward stroke is approximately

$$t_1 = \frac{L}{v_1}. \tag{23}$$

Hence the average acceleration is

$$\bar{\dot{v}}_1 = \frac{v_1^2}{L}. \tag{24}$$

Averaging equation (22), we have

$$\frac{M_w v_1^2}{L} = F_v - F. \tag{25}$$

But, as before, we may put

$$F_v = fM^{2/3}. \tag{26}$$

On the other hand, for each wing,

$$F_A = \tfrac{1}{2} c_a \rho L S v^2; \qquad F_v = \tfrac{1}{2} c_w \rho L S v^2. \tag{27}$$

Hence, introducing (20) into (27), the latter into (21), and the latter with (26) into (25), we have

$$\left.\begin{aligned} \frac{M_w v_1^2}{L} = fM^{2/3} - \tfrac{1}{2}\rho LS\{[A + B(\beta - \phi)] \sin \phi \\ + [C + D(\beta - \phi)^2] \cos \phi\} v^2. \end{aligned}\right\} \tag{28}$$

Furthermore, we have

$$v_1 = v \cos \phi. \tag{29}$$

The sum of the horizontal components of F_A and F_w is

$$F' = F_A \cos \phi - F_w \sin \phi \tag{30}$$

and must be positive.

If M is the mass of the bird and R the coefficient of resistance of the body to the horizontal movement, we have, denoting by v_{h1} the velocity of the body in the horizontal direction,

$$M\frac{d\dot{v}_{h1}}{dt}=F'-Rv_{h1}^{2}. \tag{31}$$

Since the duration of the downstroke period is given by (23), the average acceleration is

$$\bar{\dot{v}}_{h1}=\frac{\bar{v}_{h1}}{t_1}=\frac{v_1 v_{h1}}{L}. \tag{32}$$

Equation (31) now gives

$$\frac{Mv_1\bar{v}_{h1}}{L}=F'-R\bar{v}_{h1}. \tag{33}$$

We also have the requirement that, at least approximately,

$$F=Mg. \tag{34}$$

Expressing in (33) and (34) F' and F in terms of v, LS, β, and ϕ, we thus have four equations—(28), (29), (33), and (34)—which determine v, LS, ϕ, and $\bar{v}_{h1}\,(< v_1)$ for a given β. The distance traveled during the downstroke period is

$$\bar{v}_{h1}t_1=\frac{L\bar{v}_{h1}}{v_1}. \tag{35}$$

For the upstroke we can consider the movement of the wings relative to the body as slow and compute the loss of velocity and gain of altitude by putting

$$M\frac{dv_{h2}}{dt}=-(c_w\rho LS+R)v^2_{h2}. \tag{36}$$

Easily integrated, (36) gives v_{h2} as a function of time, with the initial conditions $v_{h2}(0)=\bar{v}_{h1}$. The value of c_w is now to be taken for a different α. The duration of the upstroke period is given by the requirement that

$$c_a\rho LSv^2_{h2}\geqq Mg. \tag{37}$$

The moment that inequality (37) ceases to hold, the new downstroke must begin.

The duration t_1 and t_2 of the two periods as well as the average velocities during those periods thus known, the total average velocity $\bar{v}$ is obtained in terms of M, L, S, α_1, α_2, etc.

The angle α may be chosen so as to maximize $\bar{v}$.

REFERENCES

1. E. J. Marey, *Animal Mechanism* (New York: D. Appleton & Company, 1893).

2. E. Muybridge, *Animal Locomotion* (Philadelphia: J. B. Lippincott Co., 1887).

3. M. H. Fischer, *Handb. d. norm. u. path. Physiol., herausgegeben von A. Bethe et al.*, Vol. 15, Part I (Berlin: J. Springer, 1930).

4. W. von Buddenbrock, *Handb. d. norm. u. path. Physiol., herausgegeben von A. Bethe et al.*, 15, Part I (Berlin: J. Springer, 1930).

5. A. Betz, *Handb. d. Physik, herausgegeben von H. Geiger und K. Scheel*, Vol. 7 (Berlin: J. Springer, 1927).

CHAPTER XXVI

THE INTERNAL STRUCTURE OF ANIMALS

The size and shape of different internal organs may also be considered as determined by the requirements put on them by the performance of their functions. Hence a general physicomathematical theory of organic form should include the internal structure of animals as well as their external shape. A step in that direction is to be made in this section, which, however, must be left even sketchier than the preceding ones.

Let M denote the mass of an animal and q^* the metabolic rate necessary to supply the energy for sustained locomotion. A continuous supply of the energy, $Q = Mq^*$ per unit time, requires a definite continuous supply of oxygen. If V_L denotes the amplitude of the volume of the lungs, and ν_L the frequency of respiration, then the supply of oxygen is proportional to $\nu_L V_L$. But the oxygen supplied goes not only for the energy supply of the running mechanism but also to supply the energy, Q_L, necessary to maintain the movements of the lungs; the energy, Q_c, necessary to maintain the circulation of the blood; the energy, Q_i, necessary to maintain the peristaltic movements of the intestinal tract; and the energy, $Q_0 = Mq_0$, necessary to maintain the nonmobile cells of the organism. Denoting, therefore, by a_1 and a_2 two coefficients which are determined by the efficiency of the lung (a_1) and by the energy equivalent of the oxygen, we have

$$a_1 \nu_L V_L = a_2 (Mq^* + Q_L + Q_c + Q_i + Q_0). \tag{1}$$

But the maximum frequency, ν_L, is determined by V_L. The latter determines the size of the musculature that contracts and expands the lungs. This size determines, first of all, the possible force acting on the lungs, as well as the viscous resistance of the muscles. By appropriate mechanical considerations, also involving possibly the inertial terms, we shall arrive at an equation,

$$\nu_L = f_L(V_L). \tag{2}$$

Furthermore, if ν_L and V_L are given, the rate Q_L of energy supply necessary to maintain the periodic contractions and expansions of the lungs is also given:

$$Q_L = F_2(\nu_L, V_L). \tag{3}$$

The adequate supply of oxygen is provided also by the circulatory system. Denoting by V_c the effective volume of the heart per beat and by ν_c the frequency of heart-beats, we see that $\nu_c V_c$ is proportional to the sum of all the Q's. Hence, with a_3 as a constant,

$$\nu_c V_c = a_3 (Mq^* + Q_L + Q_c + Q_i + Q_0). \qquad (4)$$

And again we have

$$\nu_c = f_c (V_c), \qquad (5)$$

where f_c is different from f_L.

For Q_c we must remember that it depends not only on ν_c and V_c but also on the size and structure of the blood vessels. For the same values of ν_c and V_c, the quantity Q_c will be greater, the longer the total lengths, l_c, of the circulatory circuit and the less its effective cross-section, s_c. Thus

$$Q_c = F_c (\nu_c, V_c, l_c, s_c). \qquad (6)$$

But l_c is determined by the over-all length of the body L, and of the extremities l. Thus

$$l_c = f_1 (L, l). \qquad (7)$$

Similarly, the value of s_c is determined by the total size of the animal. For an adequate supply of all tissues with oxygen and adequate removal of waste products, there must be so many capillaries per unit volume, and they must be of a given size, to have the necessary surface. Hence

$$s_c = f_2 (M). \qquad (8)$$

Denoting by l_i and s_i the length and average radius of the intestinal tract, we find that the total area $2\pi l_i s_i$ must be proportional to $(Q_0 + Q_L' + Q_c' + Q_i')$, where Q_L', Q_c', and Q_i' denote the necessary energy supply to the lungs, heart, and intestines in a resting organism, that is, when $q^* = 0$. The reason for the proportionality is the necessity of a given rate of resorption, which we assume to be proportional to the surface. Hence

$$2\pi l_i s_i = a_4 (Q_0 + Q_L' + Q_c' + Q_i'). \qquad (9)$$

Similarly, the volume of the intestinal tract is determined by the same quantity, since the latter determines the amount of food that must daily be held in the intestinal tract:

$$l_i s_i^2 = f_i (Q_0 + Q_L' + Q_c' + Q_i'). \qquad (10)$$

Also we have

$$Q_i' = F_i (l_i, s_i). \qquad (11)$$

The length of the body may be determined by mechanical considerations from its mass M, as was done in chapter xxiv. We have, in general,

$$L = F_2(M). \tag{12}$$

For the thickness s_e of the legs we have, as in chapter xxiv,

$$s_e^2 = a_5 M; \tag{13}$$

and, finally, we have expression (16) of chapter xxiv, giving l in terms of the maximum velocity $\bar{v}$:

$$l = a_6 \bar{v}^2. \tag{14}$$

For an animal at rest, $q^* = 0$, and $Q_L = Q_L'$, $Q_c = Q_c'$, $Q_i = Q_i'$. The latter remains true also for $q^* > 0$, when the animal runs.

Putting $q^* = 0$ into equation (1) and (4), we have fourteen equations for the determination of the fourteen quantities:

$$\nu_L', V_L', Q_L', Q_c', Q_i, \nu_c', V_c', l_c, s_c, l_i, s_i, L, s_e, l, \tag{15}$$

in terms of M, q^*, and $\bar{v}$.

Equations (1), (2), (3), (4), (5), and (6) give us six equations for the determination of the six quantities

$$\nu_L, V_L, Q_L, Q_c, \nu_c, V_c. \tag{16}$$

Thus, M and q_0 determine not only the general shape of the animal but also its internal structure.

Strictly speaking, relations (2) and (5) will involve m_L and m_c, the masses of the lungs and of the heart respectively. These may be left as undetermined parameters. Then, according to the principle of maximum simplicity, we shall take for m_L and m_c the smallest values that permit real positive solutions (15) and (16) of our equations. That such minimum values of m_L and m_c, different from zero, must exist is physically obvious.

The establishment of the form of f_L (eq. [2]), F_L (eq. [3]), f_c (eq. [5]), F_e (eq. [6]), etc., form the main part of our problem. This is to be done through a theory of lung and heart activity.

We may introduce equations for other organs. Thus the mass m_k of the kidney will be determined by the maximum metabolism $\sum_\kappa Q_k$, which determines the necessary excretion. The mass of the liver will be at least partially determined by the amount of glycogen stored, which may be mobilized during the running, to supply the necessary q^*.

Notice that $\sum_k Q_k'$ represents fundamentally the basal metabolism. It may be possible that, expressed as a function of M, $\sum_k Q_k'$ will vary approximately as $M^{2/3}$, in spite of the fact that $Q_0 \propto M$. If this were so, we should have Rubner's law derived from the above equations.

In the above considerations we have entirely disregarded the skeleton as an internal structure. We may introduce it in the following manner.

Instead of (12) we shall have, denoting by L_s and s_s the length and thickness of the spine,

$$L_s = F_2(M, s_s)\,; \tag{17}$$

this may be subject to the condition that the ratio

$$R = \frac{L_s\, s_s^2}{M} \tag{18}$$

would have a minimum. Expressing L_s in terms of M and s_s from (17), we find

$$R = R(M, s_s),$$

and we determine s_s from

$$\frac{\partial R}{\partial s_s} = 0. \tag{19}$$

This would be in line with the principle of maximum simplicity, for it will give us the minimum weight ($\propto$ volume) of the skeleton.

Relation (13) should, strictly speaking, determine the cross-section of the bones of the extremity. The muscular cross-section may be argued to be proportional to the latter, because the stronger the bones of the legs, the stronger the muscular forces and torques which they may support without breaking.

If we add

$$M = \sum M_L + M_c + M_i + M_s\,,$$

we may perhaps eliminate one of the three determining parameters.

As a matter of illustration only, without any claim to any correspondence to the real situation, we shall briefly outline a possible theory of the lungs and heart.

Let us consider the plausible case, that Q_L, Q_c, and Q_i are negligible compared to $Mq^* + Q_0$, and let the latter roughly follow Rubner's law, being proportional to the surface of the animal, or, for similar animals, to $M^{2/3}$. Then

$$V_L \nu_L \propto M^{2/3}. \tag{20}$$

Let us also assume that the volume V_L is proportional to the mass M_L of the lungs. The linear dimensions are then proportional to $M_L^{1/3}$, and the acceleration in the periodic breathing movements is proportional to $M_L^{1/3}\nu_L^2$. Hence the inertial forces are proportional to $M_L^{4/3}\nu_L^2$. Since the muscular forces of the lungs vary approximately as the cross-section of the muscles, they will be roughly proportional for similarly built lungs to $M_L^{2/3}$. As the lung pumps air back and forth, it has to overcome the resistance of the air flow through all the parts of the lung. That force of resistance may be taken as roughly proportional to the total pressure, which is proportional to the volume velocity, $V_L\nu_L \propto M_L\nu_L$. The force of resistance will also be proportional to the total area S in which that pres-

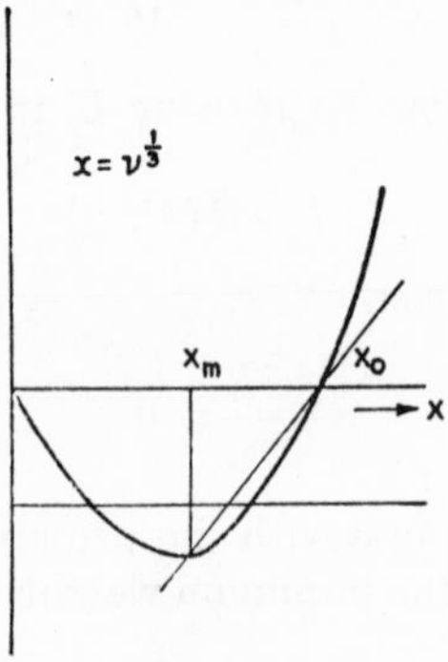

FIG. 1

sure is exerted. If the size and number of alveoles per cubic centimeter is roughly constant, then $S \propto V_L \propto M_L$, and the resistance force is proportional to $M_L^2\nu_L$. Since the muscular force must be equal to the sum of the inertial forces and of the forces of air resistance, we have, denoting by a and b two coefficients,

$$M_L^{4/3}\nu_L^2 + aM_L^2\nu_L - bM_L^{2/3} = 0\,. \tag{21}$$

From (20) and (21) we have, remembering that $V_L \propto M_L$,

$$M^{4/9}\nu_L^{5/3} + aM^{8/9} - b\nu_L^{1/3} = 0\,. \tag{22}$$

The graph of equation (22) is represented in Figure 1. From it we see that (22) has two positive roots, one increasing with M, the other decreasing. It follows from (20) that the smaller root, which increases with M, gives a larger value of M_L. By the principle of maximum simplicity of structure, we must therefore choose the larger root, which gives a smaller size of lung.

A very rough solution of equation (22) may be obtained in the following way:

Put

$$\nu_L{}^{1/3} = x; \quad M^{4/9} = A. \tag{23}$$

Equation (22) now becomes

$$Ax^5 - bx = -aA^2. \tag{24}$$

The abscissa of the minimum of the left side is

$$x_m = \alpha \left(\frac{b}{A} \right)^{1/4}, \tag{25}$$

where α is a numerical coefficient. The ordinate of that minimum is

$$y_m = (\alpha^5 - \alpha) b \left(\frac{b}{A} \right)^{1/4}. \tag{26}$$

The point x_0 of intersection of the left side with the axis of abscissa is

$$x_0 = \left(\frac{b}{A} \right)^{1/4}. \tag{27}$$

Very roughly we may approximate the portion $y_m x_0$ of the curve (Fig. 1) by a straight line passing through those points. The equation of this straight line is

$$Bx - B\left(\frac{b}{A} \right)^{1/4} = y; \quad B = \frac{b(\alpha^5 - \alpha)}{1 - \alpha}.$$

Substituting that for the left side of (24), we find

$$x = -\frac{a_1}{B} A^2 + \left(\frac{b}{A} \right)^{1/4}. \tag{28}$$

For not too large masses, the second term of the right-hand side of (28) prevails, and, because of (23), we find

$$\nu_L \propto M^{-1/3}. \tag{29}$$

From (29) and (20) we find

$$M_L \propto M. \tag{30}$$

Relations (29) and (30) are fairly well satisfied by actual data, as seen from Figures 2 and 3.

An interesting problem is presented in this connection by the lungs of birds. Their relative size is rather small, compared to those of mammals. But their structure and their mechanism of action are apparently more complicated.[3] The lung seems to be bathed by a

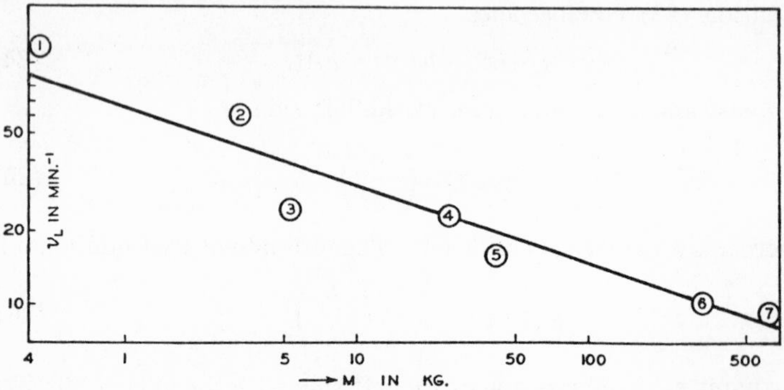

FIG. 2.—Frequency ν_L of breathing plotted against mass M of the animal on logarithmic scale. The straight line has the theoretically required slope of — 1/3. *1*, rat; *2*, rabbit; *3*, cat; *4*, dog; *5*, sheep; *6*, bear; *7*, horse. Data from Crile[1] and Oppenheimer and Pincussen.[2]

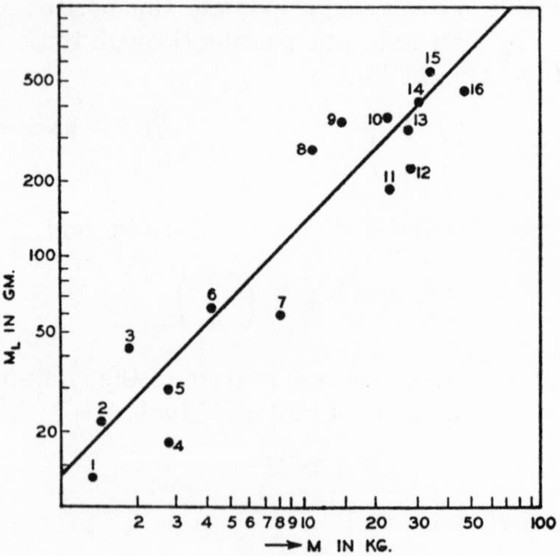

FIG. 3.—Mass M_L of lungs plotted against mass M of animal on logarithmic scale. The straight line has the theoretically required slope of 1. *1*, cat; *2*, cat; *3*, hare arctic; *4*, hare African; *5*, jackal; *6*, beaver; *7*, coyote; *8*, dog; *9*, dog; *10*, greyhound; *11*, police collie; *12*, capibra; *13*, mountain lion; *14*, huskies; *15*, jaguar; *16*, leopard. Data from Crile.[1]

continuous stream of air, owing to a peculiar mechanism. From considerations of diffusion it can be readily seen that the ventilating efficiency of a bird's lung is several times higher than that of a mammal. This permits a smaller volume, which is essential in a bird, in order to reduce weight and give room for the muscles operating the wings. It may perhaps be possible in the future to show mathematically, by developing a more exact theory of the lungs, that a lung of the mammal's type would be incompatible with flying and other functions of the birds and that the structure of the bird's lung is the simplest that satisfies the necessary requirements.

Somewhat similar considerations may be made about the heart.

Consider a capillary of length l and radius r. Let that capillary supply with oxygen a region of radius R and length l. Denoting by $\bar{c}$ the average oxygen concentration in the capillary, assuming no radial gradients, and denoting by c^* the concentration of oxygen in the tissue, by h the permeability, and by αq the rate of oxygen consumption per cubic centimeter per second proportional to the rate of energy metabolism q, we have

$$2\pi rlh(\bar{c} - c^*) = \pi(R^2 - r^2)l\alpha q\,, \tag{31}$$

or

$$R^2 = r^2 + \frac{2rh}{\alpha q}(\bar{c} - c^*)\,. \tag{32}$$

If $\bar{c}$ and c^* are considered as approximately constant, then, for a given r, equation (32) gives R. The higher the q, the smaller the R, hence the larger the number of capillaries per cross-section of tissue. Since q increases with decreasing mass, according to Rubner's law, smaller animals should have a larger number of capillaries per unit cross-section of tissue. This seems to be the case.[4]

If v denotes the velocity of blood flow, then $\pi r^2 v\bar{c}$ is the amount of oxygen entering the capillary at the arterial end per second. Considering, for simplicity, that at the venous end the concentration of oxygen is zero (the general case is treated similarly), we have

$$\pi r^2 v\bar{c} = 2\pi rlh(\bar{c} - c^*)\,; \tag{33}$$

or, putting

$$\bar{c} - c^* = c\,, \tag{34}$$

$$vr\bar{c} = 2lhc \tag{35}$$

or

$$v = \frac{2lhc}{r\bar{c}}. \tag{36}$$

From Poiseuille's law we have, for the pressure difference along the whole capillary,

$$\Delta p = a\frac{lv}{r^2}; \quad a = 8\mu; \quad \mu = \text{viscosity}. \tag{37}$$

Equations (36) and (37) give

$$\Delta p = b\frac{l^2}{r^3}, \tag{38}$$

where

$$b = \frac{2hac}{\bar{c}}. \tag{39}$$

Most of the blood pressure is across the capillaries. If we schematize the circulatory circuit, as shown in Figure 4, we see

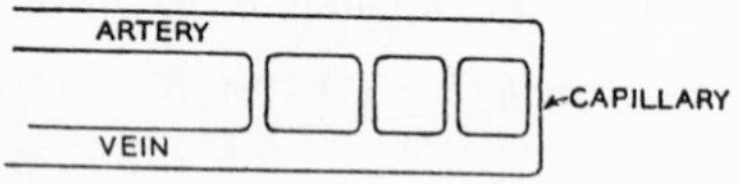

FIG. 4

that (38) gives approximately the average blood pressure. Approximately, in similarly built animals, the length l of the capillaries varies as the linear dimensions of the animal or as $M^{1/3}$. If r is the same for all animals, then $\Delta p \propto M^{2/3}$. Actually, Δp varies little with M, within a rather wide range of M's.[4] Hence, if Δp is approximately constant, we must have

$$r^3 \propto l^2. \tag{40}$$

There may be different reasons for such a relation. They may be purely mechanical. A larger capillary may have to be thicker in order not to break because of natural stresses, to which it is subjected by the tissues.

One might think that an upper limit for r is set by the requirement that the radial gradients should be very small. If c_1 and c_2 are the concentrations on the axis and at the periphery of the capillary, so that

$$\bar{c} = \frac{c_1 + c_2}{2}, \tag{41}$$

then we have, denoting by D the diffusion coefficient,

$$\pi r l \frac{2D(c_1 - c_2)}{r} = 2\pi r l h (c_2 - c^*) , \tag{42}$$

or

$$\frac{c_1 - c_2}{c_2 - c^*} = \frac{rh}{D}. \tag{43}$$

If

$$\frac{c_1 - c_2}{c_2 - c^*}$$

should be below a small quantity ε, we have

$$r \lesseqgtr \frac{D\varepsilon}{h}.$$

This does not connect r with l in any way.

To derive equations for the size and frequency of the heart, we may argue as follows:

Assuming the beat volume of the heart to be roughly proportional to the actual maximum volume V_c and denoting by ν_c the frequency, we have

$$V_c \nu_c \propto Mq \propto M^{2/3} , \tag{44}$$

according to Rubner's law.

The mass of the heart is proportional to V_c, its linear dimensions to $V_c^{1/3}$. Hence the acceleration is proportional to $V_c^{1/3}\nu_c^2$, and the inertial force to $V_c^{4/3}\nu^2$. The total force necessary to overcome the blood pressure p is proportional to $pV_c^{2/3}$. The mechanical force of the heart muscle is proportional to $V_c^{2/3}$, their cross-section. Hence denoting by a, b, and c coefficients of proportionality, we have

$$aV_c^{4/3}\nu_c^2 + bpV_c^{2/3} = cV_c^{2/3} , \tag{45}$$

or

$$V_c^{2/3}\nu_c^2 = A ; \qquad A = \frac{c - bp}{a}. \tag{46}$$

Equation (44), solved for V_c and introduced into (46), gives

$$\nu_c = \frac{A^{3/4}}{M^{1/3}} \tag{47}$$

and

$$M_c = \frac{M}{A^{3/4}}. \tag{48}$$

To what extent relations (47) and (48) are actually satisfied in nature is shown in Figures 5 and 6.

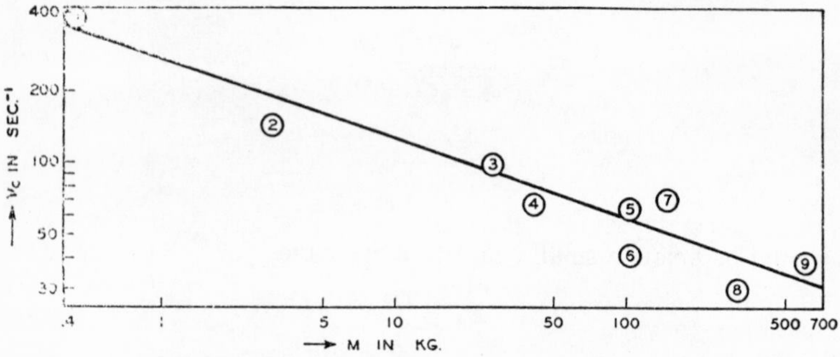

FIG. 5.—Heart frequency ν_c plotted against mass M of the animal on logarithmic scale. The straight line has the theoretically required slope — 1/3. *1*, rat; *2*, rabbit; *3*, dog; *4*, sheep; *5*, tiger; *6*, lion; *7*, pig; *8*, camel; *9*, horse. Data from Crile[1] and Oppenheimer and Pincussen.[4]

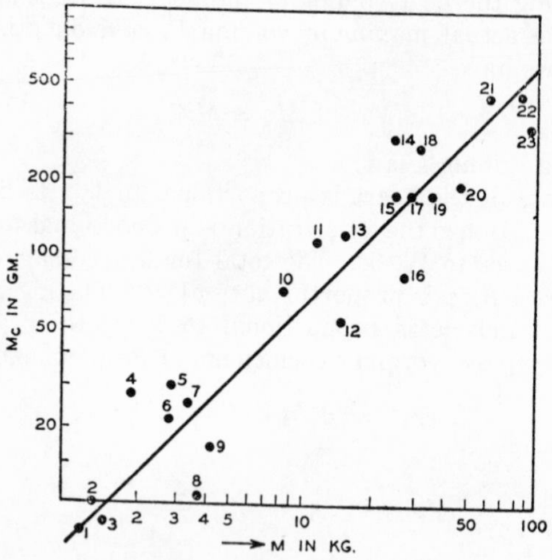

FIG. 6.—Mass M_c of heart plotted against the mass M of the animal on logarithmic scale. The straight line has the theoretically required slope 1. *1*, cat; *2*, agouti; *3*, cat; *4*, hare Arctic; *5*, hare African; *6*, jackal; *7*, fox; *8*, rabbit; *9*, beaver; *10*, coyote; *11*, dog; *12*, capibra; *13*, dog; *14*, greyhound; *15*, police collie; *16*, capibra; *17*, mountain lion; *18*, huskies; *19*, jaguar; *20*, leopard; *21*, hyena; *22*, lion; *23*, lion. Data from Crile.[1]

If the principle of determination of structure by function is to hold generally, it should apply also to single cells. Physicochemical functions are more likely to be of importance here than locomotion is. The determining variables may be different chemical parameters. The rates of reactions are dependent on the concentrations of metabolites, and the average concentrations of those are determined by the solutions of the diffusion equations, which involve the geometrical shape and structure of the system. The solution of the fundamental problem of the nucleus and cytoplasm may be sought in that direction. If a cell of given mass is to be the seat of certain reactions, which are quantitatively specified as to their rates, and if that cell is characterized by the presence of catalysts, which control those reactions, then it may well happen that the necessary results may be obtained *only* if some catalysts and some reactions are spatially segregated in a region which we call "nucleus." A number of new problems in cellular biophysics are suggested by such considerations.

Some of the relations obtained in this chapter have been derived by B. Günther and E. Guerra[5] from dimensional considerations based on a *principle of biological similarity.*

REFERENCES

1. G. W. Crile, *Intelligence, Power, and Personality* (New York: McGraw-Hill Book Co., 1941).

2. C. Oppenheimer and L. Pincussen, *Tabulae biologicae,* Vol. 3 (Berlin: W. Junk, 1926).

3. A. Bethe, *Handb. d. norm. u. path. Physiol., herausgegeben von A. Bethe et al.,* Vol. 2 (Berlin: J. Springer, 1925).

4. C. Oppenheimer and L. Pincussen, *Tabulae biologicae,* Vol. 1 (Berlin: W. Junk, 1925).

5. B. Günther and E. Guerra, *Acta Physiol. latinoamer.,* 5, 169, 1955; E. Guerra and B. Günther, *Bol. Soc. Biol.,* Concepcion (Chile), 29, 87, 1956; *Acta. Physiol. latinoamer.,* 7, 1, 1957.

CHAPTER XXVII

ANOTHER APPLICATION TO THE INTERNAL STRUCTURE OF ANIMALS

An interesting application of the general line of thought outlined in the preceding chapter has been made by David L. Cohn[1, 2].

Unfortunately Cohn's papers suffer from several inaccuracies. The following presentation is based on the general ideas of Cohn but is in many essential aspects different from it.

Instead of speaking of the "principle of maximum simplicity," we may perhaps better speak of the "principle of optimal design." Though Cohn makes nowhere any explicit definition of such a principle, his approach definitely suggests the following formulation:

For a set of prescribed biological functions an organism has the optimal possible design with respect to economy of material used, and energy expenditure, needed for the performance of the prescribed functions.

The above formulation has the advantage over the formulation given in chapter xxi (p. 248) that it avoids the somewhat indefinite term "simplicity." A certain amount of indefiniteness may, however, be still inherent in the term "optimal design." Just like in the case of simplicity, we must consider here the possibility of existence of several designs, which are equivalent in their economy of material and energy expenditure for a given set of biological functions to be performed. Moreover, it is quite possible that a design which is optimal with respect to economy of material is not optimal with respect to energy expenditure needed for the performance of the prescribed functions. Thus one design may be more economical as regards the saving in building material, another may be more economical from the energetic point of view. In such a case, in order to obtain a unique solution, we may have to minimize not the amount of material and the energy requirements separately, but some linear combination, or more generally some other combination of the two. This will introduce the problem of determining the proper combination.

Inasmuch as we are only beginning to look for some general mathematical principles in biology, we can hardly expect to find at once the correct and precise formulation. We must resign ourselves to inevitable revisions and improvements, and see what we can do even with the tentative formulations which we are able to make now. It is interesting and possibly important that even with those inadequate formulations we are already in a position to draw significant conclusions.

Situations like this have arisen many times in the physical sciences. The Periodic Table of chemical elements as originally formulated by Mendeleyeff in terms of atomic weights looks different from the present one, formulated in terms of atomic numbers. Yet the *basic* idea remains the same. Again, the formulations of the postulates involved in Bohr's model of the atom, 1913, looks certainly very inadequate compared with the present day formulation of the principles of quantum mechanics. Yet again, the latter would have been impossible without the former.

We shall apply the principle of optimal design to the problem of the structure of the arterial system.

The first question which we ask is what determines the size of the aorta. From the point of view of economy of material the smaller the radius of the aorta, the better. However, the aorta must be large enough in order not to offer too much resistance to the blood flow and not to require therefore extra energy expenditure on the part of the heart for overcoming the pressure drop along the aorta. The pressure drop in the aorta of animals is, however, known to be negligible as compared with the pressure necessary to force the blood through the rest of the vascular system, especially through the capillaries. Hence it would seem that a further reduction of the size of the aorta would improve the design, since considerable saving of "building material" would be effected without appreciable increase in necessary energy expenditure. Why then is the aorta not much smaller?

D. Cohn suggests that its size is limited by the requirements of what is known as laminar flow, that is by absence of turbulences. Whenever turbulences in flowing fluid are present, they are connected with loss through dissipation of energy and thus increase the energy requirements necessary to maintain the flow. It is known from hydrodynamics[3], that the flow of a fluid becomes turbulent when a certain quantity R, known as the Reynolds number, exceeds a critical value. The Reynolds number itself depends on the velocity of flow, on the density and viscosity of the fluid, and on the size of the system through which the fluid flows. For a flow of a fluid of specific gravity σ and viscosity η through a cylindrical tube of radius r with a velocity v, the Reynolds number is given[3] by:

$$R = \frac{\sigma v r}{\eta}. \tag{1}$$

The critical value of R above which turbulent flow sets in, varies from fluid to fluid. Equation (1) gives us R for a fluid with a given σ and η, and for a given v and r, but it does not tell what the critical value of R is. This critical value must be determined experimentally for each fluid. It is found to be about 1100 for blood[4].

Denote by C the total volume of blood flowing through the aorta, in $\text{cm}^3\ \text{sec}^{-1}$. This is the cardiac output. If r is the radius of the aorta then the average velocity $\bar{v}$ of blood flow is equal to

$$\bar{v} = \frac{C}{\pi r_a^2} \text{ cm sec}^{-1}. \tag{2}$$

If we substitute in (1) r_a for r, and $\bar{v}$ for v, and introduce (2) into (1), we obtain the average value of Reynolds number for the aorta:

$$R = \frac{\sigma C}{\pi r_a \eta}. \tag{3}$$

We notice that the Reynolds number R for the aorta increases with decreasing size of the latter. Hence, if the flow through the aorta is to remain non-turbulent, r_a cannot decrease below a certain size. The requirement of non-turbulence is $R \leqq 1100$, or from (3):

$$\frac{\sigma C}{\pi \eta r_a} \leqslant 1100, \tag{4}$$

which gives

$$r_a \geqslant \frac{\sigma C}{1100 \pi \eta}. \tag{5}$$

According to the principle of optimal design, r_a will be as small as compatible with non-turbulence. Since turbulence sets in as soon as R exceeds the critical value, we should expect r_a to be determined by the equality sign in (5). Thus

$$r_a \cong \frac{\sigma C}{1100 \pi \eta}. \tag{6}$$

This result, as well as others to be discussed below may be compared with a set of systematic data published by H. G. Green[5] for the vascular system of a dog which weighed 13 kg. The cardiac output is given as $C = 2400$ ml $\text{min}^{-1} = 40\ \text{cm}^3\ \text{sec}^{-1}$. The ratio η/σ for aortic blood is given as $0.027\ \text{cm}^2\ \text{sec}^{-1}$. Introducing these values into (6) we find:

$$r_a \cong 0.43 \text{ cm} \tag{7}$$

The value found by Green for the dog in question is 0.5 cm., which is a very fair agreement.

No comparison will be made of equation (6) with well known data on average values of r_a and C for human beings, as it is preferable to use for comparison data obtained on the same animal. It is, however, readily seen that the order of magnitude of the human aorta is such as would be expected from Cohn's considerations.

We now pass to the basic problem of how the arterial system could be branched and how the branches should be arranged in space in order to insure an adequate supply of blood to every element of the tissues.

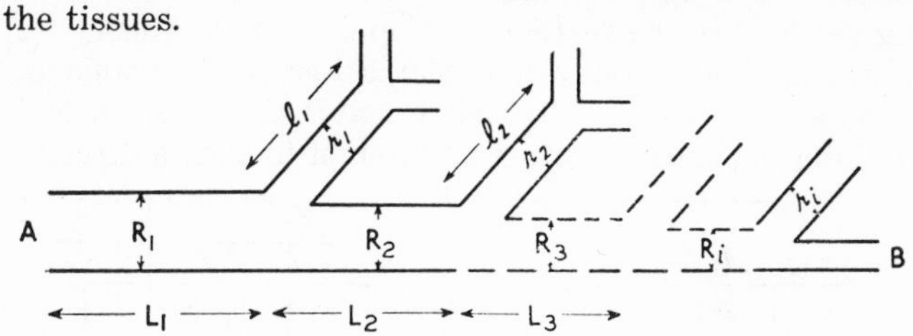

FIG. 1

The irregularity of the shapes of animals makes this problem particularly difficult. One of the simplest conceivable structures of the arterial system would be obtained if the aorta would bifurcate, each branch would bifurcate again, and so forth. Actually this is not the case. From Table 1 on p. 231 of the above mentioned paper by H. D. Green[5], we see for example that in the dog the aorta gives rise to 40 large arteries, which in turn give rise to 600 main branches. The new branches do not originate by bifurcation, but actually are branched off the larger artery along its course, as shown schematically in Figure 1. However, in the column before last of his Table Green gives the "equivalent bifurcations." Those are the number of bifurcations which would have led to approximately the observed number of arteries of a given type.

This suggests a purely theoretical, abstract study of a system of arteries that would be obtained by pure bifurcations. Such systems do not actually occur in animals. It is, however, interesting that some quantitative conclusions drawn from the study of such "equivalent bifurcation systems" agree fairly well with actual data. This may seem strange at first glance, in view of the gross dissimilarity between such an abstract system and the actual ones. Yet it is no more strange than the agreement with experimental data of results of the kinetic theory of gases, in which the molecules are considered as elastic spheres. Certainly the difference between our conceptual "equivalent bifurcation system" and the actual arterial system is not greater than the difference between an elastic sphere and what we now believe to be the structure of actual atoms.

Just as we idealize the laws which govern the branchings of the arterial system, so we shall idealize the shape of the tissue which is to be supplied by blood through this system. We shall investigate the following theoretical question: How can a cube be supplied in a simple manner with an adequate system of bifurcating vessels? In the further development of the theory we will have to consider other more irregular shapes and arrangements, some of which are likely to resemble better the actual arterial system. D. Cohn[2] has already made an attempt in such a direction.

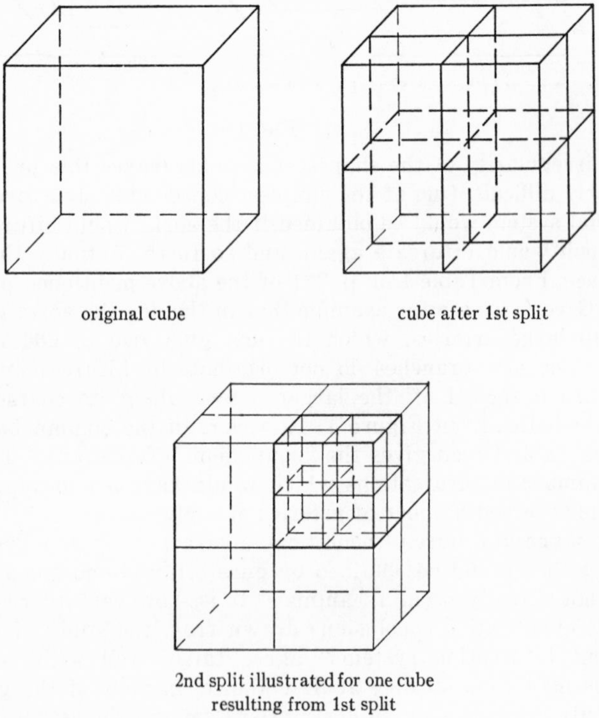

original cube

cube after 1st split

2nd split illustrated for one cube
resulting from 1st split

FIG. 2

Consider a cube with edges of length L. (Figure 2a). By means of three mutually perpendicular planes we may subdivide the cube into eight smaller cubes, with edges $L/2$ each (Figure 2b). We shall call this the first subdividision of the cube. Repeating the process for each of the eight partial cubes *simultaneously,* we subdivide the original cube into 64 smaller cubes each with edges of length $L/4$. We may repeat the process indefinitely. Thus the first subdivision divides the original cube into 8 cubes; the second subdivision results in 64 cubes, etc. If m is the number of subdivisions, then the number of small cubes resulting from those subdivisions is 2^{3m}.

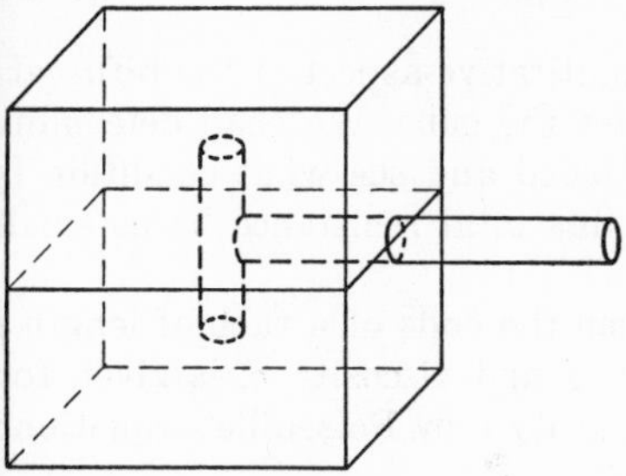

FIG. 3A

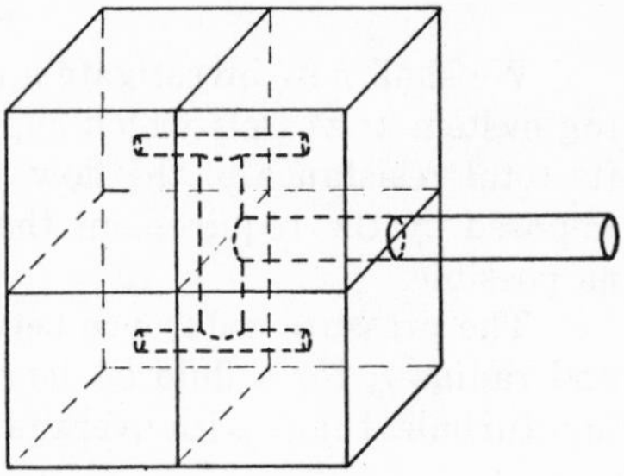

FIG. 3B

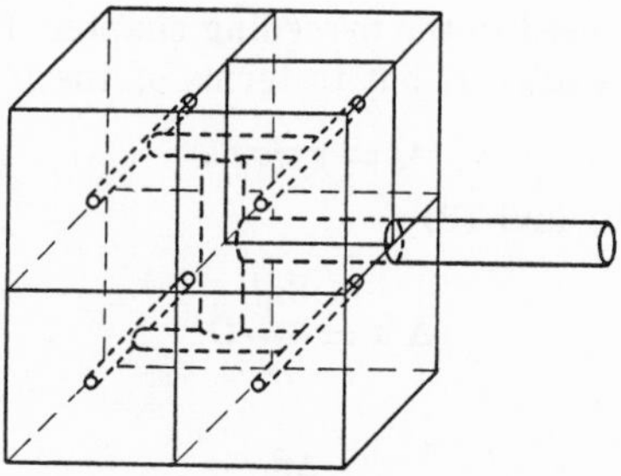

FIG. 3C

To supply each of the 2^m small cubes with a branch of a vessel we proceed as shown in Figure 3. The main branch enters at the center of one surface and extends to the center of the cube. There it splits as indicated in Figure 3A. Each primary branch extends to a length of $L/4$ and then splits as shown in Figure 3B. The next branching of the system of vessels is shown in Figure 3C. We notice that by effecting 3 branchings of the system of vessel we supplied a small vessel to each cube of the *first* subdivision. Proceeding further in the same manner we find that the nth branching of the arterial system provides a blood vessel to the cube which corresponds to the $(n/3)$th subdivision. Thus

$$m = \frac{n}{3}. \tag{8}$$

The volume of the small cube which is supplied by a vessel of the nth generation is given by

$$V_n = \frac{L^3}{2^n} = \frac{L^3}{2^{3m}}. \tag{9}$$

We shall now investigate a quantitative aspect of the bifurcating system of vessels which supplies the cube. We shall determine its total resistance to the flow of blood and see what condition is imposed by the requirement that this total resistance be as small as possible.

The pressure difference between the ends of a tube of length l and radius r, for a fluid of density σ and viscosity η, is given for non-turbulent flow with average velocity v by Poiseuille's equation:

$$\Delta p = \frac{8\eta l v}{r^2}, \tag{10}$$

which we already used in the preceding chapter. Expressing Δp not in terms of the velocity v, but in terms of the total flow

$$Q = \pi r^2 \sigma v\,, \tag{11}$$

we find, from (10) and (9):

$$\Delta p = \frac{8\eta l}{r^4} Q\,. \tag{12}$$

The ratio

$$\Omega = \frac{\Delta p \cdot \sigma}{Q} \tag{13}$$

of the pressure to volume flow may be taken as measure of the total resistance to the flow of the tube of length l and radius r. Hence from (13) and (12) we obtain:

$$\Omega = \frac{8\eta l}{\pi r^4}. \tag{14}$$

If we have m identical tubes in parallel, their total resistance to the flow is $1/m$ of the resistance of each tube. Hence if $\Omega_a, \Omega_1, \ldots, \Omega_n$ denote correspondingly the resistances of the aorta of each first, of each second, and each nth branch of the system, then the total resistance of the system is equal to

$$\Omega_T = \Omega_a + \tfrac{1}{2}\,\Omega_1 + \tfrac{1}{4}\,\Omega_2 + \ldots + \frac{1}{2^n}\,\Omega_n\,. \tag{15}$$

We shall consider the oversimplified case in which the lengths of all branches of the same "generation" are the same. Let l_i be the length of each branch of the ith generation. Then, denoting by Ω_i the resistance of each such branch, we have

$$\Omega_i = \frac{8\eta l_i}{\pi r_i^4}\,. \tag{16}$$

From (15) and (16) we find

$$\Omega_T = \frac{8\eta}{\pi}\frac{l_o}{r_o^4} + \frac{8\eta}{\pi}\sum_{i=1}^{n}\frac{1}{2^i}\frac{l_i}{r_i^4}\,. \tag{17}$$

If Δ is the thickness of the wall of a blood vessel, then the mass of each branch, assuming its density to be 1, is $2\pi r\Delta l$. We shall assume that Δ is proportional to r, that is that the larger vessels are thicker. If α denotes a constant of proportionality, we have

$$\Delta = \alpha r \tag{18}$$

and therefore the mass M_i of each branch is

$$M_i = 2\pi\alpha r_i^2 l_i\,. \tag{19}$$

Hence the total mass of the arterial system is, remembering that there are 2^i branches in the ith "generation,"

$$M = \sum_{i=0}^{n} M_i = 2\pi\alpha r_0^2 l_0 + 2\pi\alpha\sum_{i=1}^{n} 2^i r_i^2 l_i\,. \tag{20}$$

From (20) we obtain

$$r_o^2 = \frac{1}{l_0}\left(\frac{M}{2\pi\alpha} - \sum_{i=1}^{n} 2^i r_i^2 l_i\right). \tag{21}$$

Introducing (21) into (17) we find:

$$\Omega_T = \frac{8\eta}{\pi}\,\frac{l_0^3}{\left(\dfrac{M}{2\pi\alpha} - \displaystyle\sum_{i=1}^{n} 2^i r_i^2 l_i\right)^2} + \frac{8\eta}{\pi}\sum_{i=1}^{n}\frac{1}{2^i}\frac{l_i}{r_i^4}\,. \tag{22}$$

We shall now determine the optimum radii r_i of the different branches for a prescribed total mass M of the arterial system and for prescribed values of l_i. These optimal values will be the ones that minimize the total resistance Ω_T. To this end we form the partial derivatives $\partial\Omega_T/\partial r_i$. We find, remembering (21)

$$\frac{\partial\Omega_T}{\partial r_i} = \frac{8\eta}{\pi}\left(4\frac{2^i r_i l_i}{r_0^6} - 4\frac{l_i}{2^i r_i^5}\right). \tag{23}$$

By putting

$$\frac{\partial\Omega_T}{\partial r_i} = 0\,, \tag{24}$$

we obtain an expression for the r_i's which maximize or minimize Ω_T.

Introducing (23) into (24) we find:

$$r_i = 2^{-i/3} r_0\,. \tag{25}$$

Introducing (25) into (21) we find relation between r_0, M, and the l_i's, thus

$$r_o = f(M, l_1, l_2, \ldots, l_n)\,. \tag{26}$$

We shall see later that the values l_i are determined from different considerations. Since r_o is given by (6), therefore this approach implies that M is also determined from considerations of optimal design.

By taking the second derivative of Ω_T with respect to the r_i's, we verify after some elaborate calculations that the extremum given by (24) is a minimum.

From (25) we obtain:

$$\frac{r_{i+1}}{r_i} = \frac{2^{-(i+1)/3} r_0}{2^{-i/3} r_0} = 2^{-1/3} = 0.794\,. \tag{27}$$

Thus at each branching the ratio of the radius of the branch to the radius of the preceding artery should be 0.794.

If n is the *last* generation of the blood vessels, that is if it corresponds to capillaries, then the volume V_n must be the largest possible volume of the tissue which still can be adequately supplied with oxygen and food by one capillary. Of all the metabolites oxygen is required at the highest rate. If a capillary supplies an adequate amount of oxygen to a given volume it is safe enough to assume that it will supply an adequate amount of other metabolites.

If s is the distance from the capillary to which the necessary metabolites still penetrate from the capillary by diffusion in sufficient amounts, and if l_n is the length of a capillary, then

$$V_n = \pi s^2 l_n . \tag{28}$$

Let c_0 be the concentration of a metabolite in a capillary, the radius of which is small compared to the distance s. Let D be the average diffusion coefficient of the metabolite in the surrounding tissue, to which we count also the capillary wall. Let q be the constant rate of consumption of the metabolite in the tissue, expressed in gm cm^{-3} sec^{-1}. We approximate the radial gradient of concentration of the metabolite in the tissue by a linear one. The concentration is thus c_0 in the capillary, and equals to zero at some distance. Since we are calculating the distance s over which an adequate supply of metabolites takes place, therefore s cannot be the distance at which the concentration becomes zero, because at distances near the limit the concentration of the metabolite will be already very low and its supply inadequate. Arbitrarily we may put the distance at which the concentration becomes zero as equal to $2s$.

If r_n is the radius of the capillary, then the concentration gradient is

$$\frac{c_0}{2s - r_n} . \tag{29}$$

If we consider the case that $r_n << s$, an assumption which will be justified presently, when we consider the numerical results, then the gradient may be written

$$\frac{c_0}{2s} . \tag{30}$$

The outward flow per unit length of the capillary is equal to

$$\frac{2\pi r_n D c_0}{2s} \tag{31}$$

and this in turn is equal to the total rate of consumption in the volume πs^2 which corresponds to the unit length of the capillary. This total rate of consumption is

$$\pi s^2 q. \tag{32}$$

Equating (31) and (32) and solving for s we find:

$$s = \left(\frac{r_n D c_0}{q} \right)^{1/3} . \tag{33}$$

We now compute s for oxygen. For the radius r_n of the capillary we have $r_n = 5 \times 10^{-4}$ cm. The concentration c_0 of oxygen in the capillary corresponds to a partial pressure of about 0.1 atm. Since at atmospheric pressure there is 1.5×10^{-3} gm cm^{-3} of oxygen, therefore $c_0 \sim 1.5 \times 10^{-4}$ gm cm^{-3}. Considering again the dog described by H. D. Green[5], we find for its total oxygen consumption at rest the value 155 ml min^{-1} or, approximately 2.5 cm^3 sec^{-1}. Since the oxygen supply by capillaries must remain adequate during exercise, when the resting consumption may increase as much as 12 times, we obtain the value of q by multiplying 2.5 cm^3 sec^{-1} by 12, dividing by 13000, the total weight of tissue volume of the animal, and converting into grams by multiplying by 1.5×10^{-3}. We thus find: $q = 3.5 \times 10^{-6}$ gm cm^{-3} sec^{-1}. For the coefficient of diffusion we take $D = 10^{-6}$ cm^2 sec^{-1}. Equation (33) now gives

$$s \cong 28 \times 10^{-4} \text{ cm}. \tag{34}$$

This justifies the approximation $r_n << s$.

There are altogether 2^n capillaries. The total cardiac output C eventually divides into individual flows through each capillary, so that the flow per capillary is

$$f_c = \frac{C}{2^n}. \tag{35}$$

If we denote by v_n the velocity of flow through the capillary, then the total flow is given by

$$f_n = \pi r_n^2 v_n. \tag{36}$$

From (25) it follows that

$$r_n = 2^{-n/3} r_0. \tag{37}$$

Equating (35) and (36), solving for v_n and remembering (37), we find:

$$v_n = \frac{C}{\pi r_0^2 2^{n/3}}. \tag{38}$$

If l_n is the length of the capillary, then a given volume of blood stays in the capillary roughly for time $\tau = l_n / v_n$. From (37) we find

$$\tau = \frac{\pi l_n r_0^2 2^{n/3}}{C}. \tag{39}$$

Imagine for a moment that instead of flowing continuously, the blood containing a metabolite would fill the capillary and remain stationary until the metabolite has sufficiently diffused. The concentration of the metabolite in the blood must at first be in excess of that in the surrounding tissue, and then gradually reach a value which corresponds to a stationary state.

From equation (37) of chapter i of Volume I we see that the time which it takes for a metabolite to reach a stationary state of diffusion is of the order of magnitude of the quantity Λ. When $t > \Lambda$, the time dependent term in equation (37) of chapter i of Vol. I already becomes much smaller than its initial value. For a diffusion with a cylindrical symmetry we find an expression for Λ by putting in equation (35) of chapter i of Vol. I, $r_1 = \infty$; $r_2 = r_n$; $\delta = r_n$.

We are now interested in the time which it takes a slowly diffusing metabolite to leave the capillary. We therefore consider principally the diffusion *in* the capillary itself and put accordingly $D_e = h = \infty$.

We then find

$$\Lambda = \frac{r_n^2}{6D_i}. \tag{40}$$

The blood actually flows continuously but if the time τ which it stays in the capillary is much less than Λ, then by the time the blood leaves the capillary the concentration of the metabolite in the blood will be still in excess of that in the tissue. Thus optimal conditions require that $\tau \simeq \Lambda$.

The smaller the coefficient of diffusion D_i of the metabolite through blood, the longer time blood must stay in the capillary in order to achieve an efficient exchange, and the longer therefore must be the capillary. Equating approximately the right side of (39) and (40) and solving for l_n, we find, remembering (37):

$$l_n = \frac{C}{6\pi D_i 2^n}. \tag{41}$$

Introducing now (41) into (28) and the latter into (9) we find that 2^n cancels out and obtain

$$s^2 = \frac{6L^3 D_i}{C}. \tag{42}$$

It must be kept in mind that D_i here is not the same as D in equation (33). The latter denotes the coefficient for diffusion of oxygen through the tissue, while D_i is the coefficient of diffusion of the *slowest* diffusing metabolite through blood in the capillary. Thus in general we would expect $D_i << D$.

Introducing (37) into (33) we obtain

$$s = \left(\frac{2^{-n/3} D r_0 c_0}{q} \right)^{1/3}. \tag{43}$$

We now introduce expression (43) into (42) and obtain

$$\left(\frac{2^{-n/3} r_0 D c_0}{q} \right)^{2/3} = \frac{6L^3 D_i}{C}. \tag{44}$$

From equation (44) we find

$$2^{2n/9} = \frac{C}{6L^3 D_i} \left(\frac{D r_0 c_0}{q} \right)^{2/3} \tag{45}$$

or

$$n = \frac{9}{2 \log 2} \log \frac{C}{6L^3 D_i} \left(\frac{D r_0 c_0}{q} \right)^{2/3} \tag{46}$$

Putting $D_i \sim 10^{-9}$ cm^2 sec^{-1}, and using the previous values of the other constants, we find $n \approx 39$. Then equation (37) gives us

$$r_n \approx 0.6 \times 10^{-4}\ cm. \tag{47}$$

as compared with the actual size of 5×10^{-4} cm. Finally equation (41) gives $l_n = 0.004$ cm, as compared to the actual length of 0.07 cm.

The total number of capillaries should be $2^{39} \approx 5 \times 10^{11}$. Table 1 of H. D. Green's paper[5] puts this number at 1.2×10^9. The agreement here is definitely not good. However, we must remember, that the constants in equation (46) were chosen rather arbitrarily. With a slightly different choice of constants, n may be easily reduced to about 33-34. This will bring the calculated number of capillaries into better agreement with the observed one, and will not change the order of magnitude of the other calculated constants. We must in particular remember that the body of an animal is not a cube filled with tissues. Following D. Cohn, we may arbitrarily take for a 13 kg dog the value of L to be slightly larger than 25 cm, in other words take L^3 larger than 13 000 cm^3. Considering the crudeness of the approximation used, the overall agreement is not bad.

From considerations of optimal design we thus can express the structural constants of the arterial system, such as radius of aorta, radius and length of capillaries, and number of capillaries, in terms of such constants as cardiac output, mass of animal, and different parameters characteristic of the tissue, such as coefficients of diffusion, rate of metabolism, concentration of oxygen, etc. The agreement with observation will naturally be crude at this stage, in view of the crudeness of the theory and of not too exact observations. The usefulness in principle of the approach is, however, well illustrated.

REFERENCES

1. D. L. Cohn, *Bull. Math. Biophysics*, **16**, 59, 1954.
2. D. L. Cohn, *Bull. Math. Biophysics*, **17**, 219, 1955.
3. L. Hopf, "Zähe Flüssigkeiten". *Handb. d. Physik*, **7**, 91, Berlin: J. Springer, 1927.
4. N. A. Coulter and J. R. Pappenheimer, *Am. J. Physiol.*, **159**, 401, 1949.
5. H. D. Green, in *Medical Physics*, Vol. II, p. 228, (Chicago: The Year Book Publishers, Inc., 1950).

CHAPTER XXVIII

RELATIONS WITHIN AND BETWEEN ORGANISMS

MAPPINGS IN BIOLOGY AND MATHEMATICS

Some readers who have read the first volume of this work and the present volume up to this point may perhaps feel impressed by the vast array of biological phenomena which have been made amenable to mathematical treatment and which range from cell division to some complex phenomena of behavior such as learning or abstract thinking.

Against this array of successes must be weighed the following shortcomings. First, there are still a large number of biological phenomena to which the attention of the mathematical biologist has not been turned. While serious, this is the least important shortcoming — time may easily remedy it. A very serious shortcoming is this: All the theories mentioned above deal with separate biological phenomena. There is no successful mathematical theory which would treat the *integrated* activities of the organism as a whole. It is important to know how pressure waves are reflected in blood vessels. It is important to know that diffusion drag forces may produce cell division. It is important to have a mathematical theory of complicated neural networks. But nothing so far in those theories indicates that the proper functioning of arteries and veins is essential for the normal course of the intracellular processes; nor does anything in those theories indicate that a complex phenomenon in the central nervous system, by eventually resulting, for example, in the location of food, becomes very indirectly, yet intimately, tied up with some metabolic process of other cells of the organism. Nothing in those theories gives any inkling of a possible connection between a faulty response of a neural net, which leads to the accidental cutting of a finger, and the cell divisions which thus result from a stimulation of the process of healing. And yet this integrated activity of the organism is probably the most essential manifestation of life.

So far as the theories mentioned above are concerned, we may just as well treat, in fact *do* treat, the effects of diffusion drag forces as a peculiar diffusion problem in a rather specialized physical system, and we do treat the problems of circulation as special hydrodynamical problems. The fundamental manifestation of life mentioned above drop out from all our theories in mathematical biology.

Against this criticism, one may object that this is also a matter of time. When the physicochemical dynamics of a cell are worked out, the dynamics of interaction of cells, and thus the dynamics of cellular aggregates, will become possible. This will eventually lead to the theory of the organism. Attempts in this direction have been made in chapter xxvi and xxvii of the first volume of this work. Of all branches of mathematical biophysics described in this work they are, however, the least successful. These failures do not mean, of course, that a successful attempt may not actually be made. Let us, however, appraise the problem realistically. In celestial mechanics, where we deal with forces varying as simply as the inverse square of the distance and acting on rigid masses, the three-body problem, let alone the n-body problem, still defies in its generality the ingenuity of mathematicians. The forces between cells are much more complex; they are non-conservative, and the cells themselves are not merely displaced but also changed externally and internally by these forces. What are the chances within a foreseeable number of generations to even approximately master the problem of an organism as an aggregate of cells, considering that this organism consists of some 10^{14} cells, hundreds of different tissues, and thousands of complex interrelated structures. Pessimism is not a healthy thing in science, but neither is unrealistic optimism.

But if we abandon the hope of developing a mathematical theory of the organism starting at the cellular level, does it mean abandoning the hope of developing a physicomathematical theory of the organism and, therefore, of life at all? We shall see later that this is not necessarily the case.

We may look at the whole situation from a different angle. If we may for a moment indulge in comparisons (which, in general, is a risky procedure), we must say that in spite of the sometimes rather elaborate nature of some of the theories, mathematical biology is now in a pre-Newtonian stage of development. In pre-Newtonian physics there existed, since the days of Archimedes, mathematical treatments of some separate physical phenomena. But it was Newton, who, in his laws of motion, introduced the first general principles which rapidly were applied to practically all domains of physics. In present day mathematical biology we use a great number of more or less ingenious mathematical models, based on sound physical principles. The use of models is well known to the theoretical physicist. But in physics these models are based on the *fundamental principles.* Newton's laws were used in 19th century models, like that of the billiard ball molecule of the kinetic theory of gases. Einstein's principles are used in contemporary models. A mathematical model is of a transient nature, while a general principle, once found, enjoys greater permanency. The supplanting of the Newtonian mechanics by general relativity in no way discards the former. Newton's laws of motion are found to be approximations, frequently very close approximations to the relativistic laws of motion.

As we have seen, a direct application of the physical principles, used in the mathematical models of biological phenomena, for the purpose of building a theory of life as an aggregate of individual cells is not likely to be fruitful. We must look for a principle which connects the different physical phenomena involved and expresses the biological unity of the organism and of the organic world as a whole.

In chapters xxi to xxvii of this volume we introduced as a possible general principle in biology the principle of maximum simplicity or of optimal design. The studies carried out so far in that direction are definitely promising. The precise formulation of this principle will undoubtedly be eventually changed, (c.f. chapter xxvii, p. 292), but in one form or another it is likely to remain. But even if it should prove useful in the future, this principle cannot claim the necessary generality which we seek. It leaves the problem of integration practically untouched. It is likely to lead to the understanding of the mechanical integration of an organism as a locomotor unit, or to the physical integration as a unit in which distribution of food and oxygen are concerned, but the problem of the general integration of entirely diverse functions seems to be beyond its scope.

There is still a third angle from which we may view our problem and which will indicate to us the way to its solution. Thus far mathematical biology has emphasized almost exclusively the *metric* aspects of biological phenomena. In the study of physical, as well as of biological, phenomena the quantitative aspects are all-important. Every physicist and mathematical biologist knows that a qualitative statement or prediction is usually of very limited value and frequently is meaningless. Without finding a quantitative expression for the forces which may produce cell division and without comparing them quantitatively with forces that are necessary to divide a cell, no meaningful prediction can be made. When we observe the phenomena of biological integration we notice, however, not quantities, varying continuously or discontinuously, but certain rather complex *relations*. In some of its branches, for example in topology, mathematics has excellent tools to deal with such relations. Kurt Lewin[1] advocated long ago the application of topology to psychology without, however, using any of the actual mathematical apparatus of topology. Implicitly topological relations are contained in even older considerations of D'Arcy W. Thompson[2]. Thompson's observations that skulls or other skeletal parts of different animals can be "transformed" into each other by simple continuous univalent transformations amount, in essence, to the statement that the different shapes of skulls are not only homeomorph but even homotop.

These are, however, relatively superficial relations. Topological analogies go much deeper in the realm of the living when we observe not merely structural but functional (in a biological sense) relations. The unity of the organism and the unity of all life is expressed by just that kind of relations. A paramecium performs some relatively simple movements which either bring it in contact with food or with another paramecium, with which it conjugates. These relatively simple movements are produced as responses to simple chemical stimuli. After coming in contact with food, the paramecium ingests and then digests it, excreting undigestible waste. It reacts to light and avoids harmful stimuli. The relatively simple responses to simple stimuli result in movements which serve either the preservation of the individual or that of the species.

A bird flying after food or after its mate performs much more complex movements, which are responses to much more complex sets of stimuli. It also performs very complex movements with its larynx which result in the production of sounds. The latter have a definite survival value both for the individual and the species. Thus again we have a set of movements as a response to a set of stimuli, which result in either obtaining food, a mate, or avoiding harmful situations. When food is obtained, it is ingested and digested by a series of much more complex mechanisms than those in a paramecium. But the general pattern is the same.

A human being performs still more complex movements, serving either the survival of the individual or of the species. Considering the existing evidence[3] that thought is but a covert speech we notice that the thinking of a scientist or inventor is another very complex form of minute muscular movements which much more indirectly than in the case of a bird or paramecium contribute to the survival of the individual or of the species. And the composition of a love sonnet by a poet and its writing down are again another highly complex set of covert and overt motions which may result in the finding of a mate and which correspond to the much simpler movements of a paramecium that produce the same result. The purely vegetative functions of ingestion and digestion of food, and other connected phenomena, are very much more complicated in the human being, but again follow the same general pattern as that in a protozoan.

When we consider the sessile plants, we still find fundamentally the same pattern of relations, which are more complex than in a unicellular organism but much less complex than in man. Although it is customary to say that autotrophic plants manufacture their own food, it is perfectly logical to consider the solar energy and carbon dioxide as the primitive food, taken from outside. Phenomena of phototropism involve entirely different mechanisms form those found in the movements of a paramecium or higher animals, but these movements again occur in response to a stimulus and result in a better "contact" with food — the radiant energy of the sun.

These relations go even further, and many features of animal and, especially, human societies show similar relations. This has led to frequent considerations of society as a kind of organism. Just as numerous biological functions of a simple cell eventually specialize and are divided between many cells of a metazoan, so are different functions of a human being specialized and divided between many individuals in a society.

What we described in the preceding paragraphs is generally known, in fact it is so well known as to be apt to be overlooked. Yet it is this correspondence that is the essential feature of the organic world and that constitutes the unity of everything living.

To a simple physiological function of a protozoan corresponds a large set of similar physiological functions in a higher animal. The various complex biophysical and biochemical phenomena involved in the act of vision of man correspond to a simple light sensitivity of the protoplasm of a protozoan. Similarly, the very large number of complex muscular movements in human locomotion corresponds to a relatively simple movement of the protozoan. But the relation between the simple light sensitivity process in a protozoan and its avoiding motion[4] and the relation between the sight of a tiger and the running motion of the man is basically the same.

What we described above, especially what we said in the preceding paragraph may also be stated in the following manner: All organisms can be *mapped* on each other in such a manner that certain basic relations are preserved in this mapping. Several detailed properties of a higher organism are in general mapped on a lesser number or on only one property of the lower organism.

If we wish to describe and investigate this and similar situations mathematically, we must turn our attention to those branches of mathematics which deal with mappings and relations. There are several such branches, for example theory of sets, theory of relations, topology, and theory of groups. Those disciplines are the representatives of a large division of mathematics which may be called qualitative or relational mathematics. Recently it has been occasionally used in psychology and in social sciences. With one notable exception, however, it has hardly been used at all in general biology. The notable exception is the work of J. H. Woodger[5], who made an attempt at a systematic application of the theory of relations to biology. His approach does not emphasize, however, the above mentioned general fact of mapping. We shall therefore seek a different approach.

Every organism is characterized by a collection of certain biological properties, which make us recognize an organism as such. Thus from the above examples we see that organisms are endowed with the property of being sensitive to certain stimuli. We shall call this property S. In many organisms, as our examples also illustrate, a stimulus evokes certain movements. The property to move we shall designate by M. Movements may result in ingestion of food. All organisms ingest food, and the property of ingesting food we shall designate by I. Again the ingested food is digested, in very different ways by different organisms. The property of an organism to digest we shall denote by D. We do not need to enumerate all possible biological properties of organisms. But even without enumerating them we may say that an organism is, at least partly, characterized by a collection of various biological properties, such as those mentioned above.

In mathematics a collection of any kind of "things" is called a set. The things themselves may be quite real, or they may be conceptual abstractions. Thus we may speak of the set of biological properties of an organism. Or we may speak of the set of chairs in a room, or of the set of readers of this book. Then again we may speak of the set of integers from 1 to 10, or of the set of all integers. We may just as well speak of the set of points on an infinite line, or on a stretch of line. Again we may speak of the set of all points in a plane, or within a circle of radius r. We also can consider a set of five-dimensional non-Euclidian spaces.

The things, or objects, the collection of which constitutes a set, are called the elements of the set. Thus a chair may be an element of the set of chairs in my dining room. Some sets are made of a finite number of elements, like the set of chairs in my dining room, or the set of integers 1, 2, 3, 4, 5, 6. Such sets are called finite. Other sets are made of an infinite number of elements, like the set of all integers 1, 2, 3, . . . or the set of all real numbers between 0 and 1;

in other words the set of such real numbers x, for which we have $0 < x < 1$. Such sets are called infinite.

Consider the set of integers $\{1, 2, 3, 4\}$, and denote it by S_1. We shall express the above sentence symbolically by writing

$$S_1 = \{1, 2, 3, 4\}. \tag{1}$$

Similarly consider another set $\{3, 4, 5, 6, 7, 8\}$, and denote it by S_2, so that:

$$S_2 = \{3, 4, 5, 6, 7, 8\}. \tag{2}$$

The elements 3 and 4 belong to both sets S_1 and S_2. They themselves form a set $\{3, 4\}$. This set, which consists of all elements that are contained in both S_1 and S_2 is called the intersection of the sets S_1 and S_2 and is denoted by $S_1 \cap S_2$. Thus

$$S_1 \cap S_2 = \{3, 4\}. \tag{3}$$

On the other hand consider the set $\{1, 2, 3, 4, 5, 6, 7, 8\}$. It consists of elements such that each belongs either to set S_1 (elements 1, 2, 3, and 4), or to S_2 (elements 3, 4, 5, 6, 7, and 8), or to both (elements 3 and 4). The set $\{1, 2, 3, 4, 5, 6, 7, 8\}$ is called the union of S_1 and S_2 and is denoted by $S_1 \cup S_2$. Thus

$$S_1 \cup S_2 = \{1, 2, 3, 4, 5, 6, 7, 8\}. \tag{4}$$

Let S_3 denote the set of all real numbers x, such that $0 \leqslant x \leqslant 1$. In other words the numbers 0 and 1 are included in the set. Let S_4 denote the set of all real numbers x, such that $1/2 \leqslant x \leqslant 3/2$. Then the intersection $S_3 \cap S_4$ is equal to the set of all real numbers x, such that $1/2 \leqslant x \leqslant 1$, because all such numbers belong both to S_3 and S_4. The union $S_3 \cup S_4$ is equal to the set of all real numbers x, such that $0 \leqslant x \leqslant 3/2$.

The fact that 3 is an element of the set $S_1 = \{1, 2, 3, 4\}$ is expressed by $3 \in S_1$. Consider the set $S_5 = \{2, 4\}$. Every element of S_5 is also an element of S_1. In such a case we say that S_5 is included in S_1, and express it symbolically thus:

$$S_5 \subset S_1. \tag{5}$$

The set S_5 is also called a *subset* of S_1.

In particular every set is included in itself; in other words every set is a subset of itself. However, if a subset of the set S_1 is not identical with S_1, then that subset is called a *proper subset* of S_1. Thus the set $\{1, 3\}$ is a proper subset of $\{1, 2, 3, 4\}$.

A set which contains no elements is called empty and is denoted by $\emptyset$. It may seem simpler to say that this is no set at all, but the concept of an empty set proves to be very useful in mathematics.

Consider the set S_1, given by (1), and the set $S_6 = \{5, 6, 7\}$. The two sets have no elements in common; hence their intersection is the empty set. We write

$$S_1 \cap S_6 = \emptyset. \tag{6}$$

Sets, the intersection of which is the empty set, are called disjoined. The sets of all real numbers x such that $0 \leqslant x \leqslant 1$, and the set of all real numbers such that $2 \leqslant x \leqslant 3$, are disjoined.

When we look at a set of points which constitute an infinite or a finite line and which represent either all the real numbers, or the real numbers within a given finite interval, we are apt to think of such a set as of one-dimensional space. This, however, is not correct. A collection of points which are in no way related to each other, is merely a set, but not a space. This holds equally for the collection of points represented by the line of Figure 1a, as for the collection of points represented in Figure 1b. If, however, there exist certain relations between the points of a set then the set is called a space. We shall now consider some possible relations between the points of a set. We shall begin with one that is probably the most important in topology, but also possibly the least obvious. We shall introduce the notion of neighborhood.

In common parlance neighborhood is a somewhat indefinite word. We may speak of our neighbors across the landing in an apartment house, or of our neighbors next door on the street, or across the street, or even in the next block. If we arbitrarily consider as our neighbors only the people across the landing, then by definition our neighborhood is confined to the particular floor on which we live. If we consider next block neighbors, then our neighborhood is extended to several blocks. In a city rarely would anyone consider people living two miles away as neighbors. Yet English and pre-revolutionary Russian country squires would consider as neighbors such individuals, whose estates may be 10 miles away. Christ taught us to consider everybody as our neighbors. This extends the notion of neighborhood to the whole world.

A snobbish person may consider as his neighbors the wealthy individuals who live in the same building, but he may not consider as a neighbor the janitor who may live in the basement of the same building. Another person in the same building will consider everybody in the building, including the janitor, as his neighbor. Thus distance alone is not always sufficient to define neighborhood in ordinary life. And while A may consider B as his neighbor, and vice versa, C may be considered as a neighbor by A, but not by B.

When we pass to an abstract definition of neighborhood in a set of points, we meet with a somewhat similar indefiniteness and arbitrariness. For a given set of points we can define the neighborhoods as we please, and there are almost no restrictions imposed on our definition. Thus in the set of points which represent all real numbers we may define the neighborhood of a point x in the following manner:

a) Choose an arbitrary positive number ρ, and consider that the neighborhood of every point x consists of all points for which $|x - y| < \rho$. As there is an infinite number of possible values of ρ, we have for each point x an infinite number of neighborhoods, depending on the chosen value of ρ. The neighborhoods in this case are defined in the same manner for all points x.

We may, however, define in the same set of points the neighborhoods in a less "democratic" manner[6].

b) Define for every point $x \lesseqgtr 0$ the neighborhood in the above manner. For the point $x = 0$ define it, however, in the following way: Let n be a positive integer. Define the neighborhood of $x = 0$ as consisting of all points y such that $|y| < \rho$, except the points which correspond to the numbers $1/n$, where n can take *any* integral value. The points $1/n$ are not to be considered as belonging to the neighborhood of $x = 0$. The point $x = 0$ corresponds to the snobbish individual in our previous example.

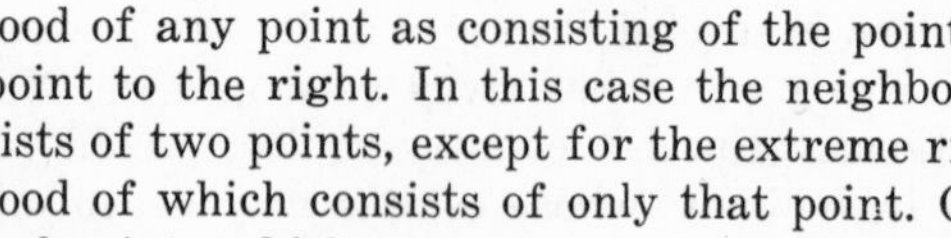

FIG. 1

In the set of points shown in Figure 1b we may define the neighborhood of any point as consisting of the point itself and of the next point to the right. In this case the neighborhood of each point consists of two points, except for the extreme right point, the neighborhood of which consists of only that point. Or, in analogy to the set of points which represents real numbers, we may introduce an arbitrary integer n, and define the neighborhood of a point in Figure 1b as consisting of the point itself and of all points that are less than n points removed from it. If $n = 10$, then the neighborhood of every point in Figure 1b consists of all the ten points which constitute the set. If for example $n = 3$, then the neighborhood of the two extreme points consists each of only 3 points while the neighborhood for example of 4th or 5th point from the left contains 5 points.

As a rule, certain restrictions are imposed in topology on the definitions of neighborhoods. This is done in order to study special cases, imposed by those restrictions. Basically, however, we can define the neighborhoods as we please. In particular, the definition of neighborhood given at the beginning of the preceding paragraph is essentially the same as used in an example by R. L. Wilder (reference 6, p. 170).

We shall denote a neighborhood of a point a by $U(a)$.

Once the neighborhoods have been defined in a set of points, this set is considered, *by definition,* as a space. In other words a space is a set of points in which neighborhoods have been in some manner assigned to each point. If for the set of points which represent all real numbers we assign the neighborhoods in the first manner mentioned above, that is if the neighborhood of x consists of all points y such that $|x - y| < \rho$, we obtain a one dimensional space. Similarly the set of ten points shown in Figure 1b becomes a space, in the general sense of this word, when we assign neighborhoods to each of its points. The notion of a "space" consisting of a finite number of discrete points appears at first somewhat unusual. However, the generalization of the word "space," which includes even such unusual spaces, proves to be useful not only in pure mathematics but also in biology.

Making a set into a space by assigning neighborhoods does not make it cease to be a set. Thus not every set of points is a space, but every space is a specialized set of points[6].

Thus far we have said nothing about *distances* in our spaces. Spaces exist, in which distances are not defined at all. Those spaces are said not to be metrized. There are spaces which are even not metrizable[6, 7, 8]. It is true that the difference $|x - y|$, which we introduced in our definition of neighborhoods, looks very much like a distance between the points x and y. But this is actually not so. If we define as $|x - y|$, the distance between x and y along the line of points which represent the real numbers, then we obtain the usual Euclidean one-dimensional space. But distances may be defined even in such a manner, that the distance from x to y is not equal to the distance from y to x. For example, if $y < x$, let us define the distance from y to x by $|x - y|$, while the distance from x to y is defined as $(x - y)^2$. A physical example of such "peculiar" definitions of distance is given by P. Alexandroff and H. Hopf on p. 29 of their book[8]. The distance between two points along a river may be defined in terms of the time it takes to row a boat from one point to another. Rowing down-stream takes less time than rowing upstream. Thus the distance from a point up stream to a point down-stream is less than the distance between the same two points in the opposite direction. If for the set of points which represent the real numbers we define as neighborhood of every point x all points such that $|x - y| < \rho$, and if at the same time we *define* the distance between x and y by $|x - y|$, then we may restate the definition of the neighborhood by saying that the neighborhood of every point x consists of all points y, the distances of which from x are less than ρ. This is called a spherical neighborhood of radius ρ, or simply a ρ-neighborhood. We shall denote it by $U(x, \rho)$, thus indicating that U is the neighborhood of the point x and has the radius ρ.

The usefulness of the concept of neighborhood can be seen when we examine the mappings of different spaces on each other. It was the consideration of mappings of different organisms on each other that led us to the discussion of the purely mathematical problems.

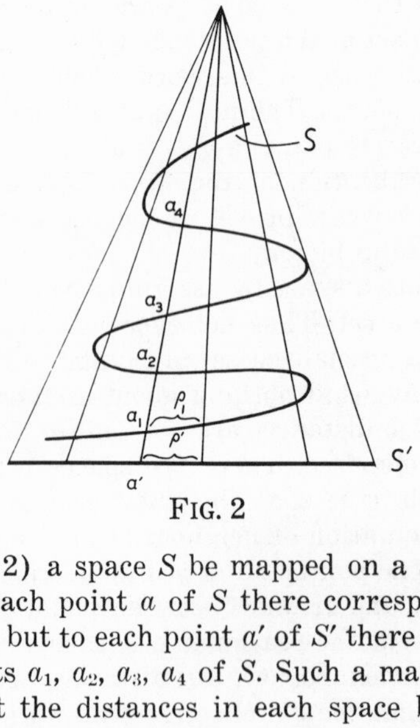

FIG. 2

Let (Figure 2) a space S be mapped on a space S', in such a manner that to each point a of S there corresponds one and only one point a' of S', but to each point a' of S' there correspond in general several points a_1, a_2, a_3, a_4 of S. Such a mapping is said to be many to one. Let the distances in each space be defined as on a Euclidian line and the neighborhoods defined as spherical neighborhoods. The mapping in Figure 2 is obtained by means of a bundle of straight half-lines which originate at the point O. The point a' is called the image of a_1, or of a_2, etc.

Consider a neighborhood of the point a' in S' with the radius ρ' (Figure 2). To this neighborhood there corresponds a neighborhood of the point a_1 in S, with the radius ρ_1. It is readily seen that in case of the mapping shown in Figure 2, all the points which lie within the neighborhood ρ_1 of a_1 in S_1 map on points which lie within the neighborhood ρ' of a' in S'. In other words all images of the points of the neighborhood of a_1 are included in the neighborhood of a'. This holds for *every* neighborhood of *any* point in S', regardless of the chosen value of ρ'. The same situation holds for the points a_2, a_3, and a_4 of which a' is the image.

Under these conditions the mapping of S on S' is said to be *continuous*. The situation may be summed up briefly in the following definition:

c) A mapping of a space S on a space S' is said to be continuous if for *every* point a' in S' and for *every* neighborhood $U'(a')$ of a' there exists a neighborhood $U(a)$ of the corresponding point in S such that the image points of all points of $U(a)$ are included in $U'(a')$.

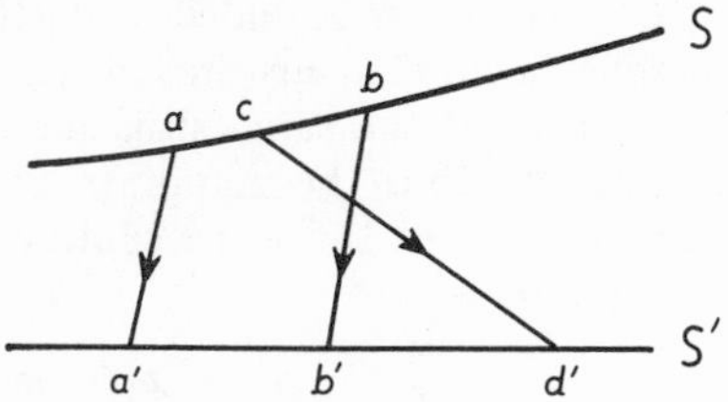

FIG. 3

This definition sounds quite natural to everyone familiar with continuous functions. It prevents the possibility of the situation shown in Figure 3. Here a maps on a', b maps on b', but c which is between a and b maps on d'. There exists now a neighborhood $U'(a')$, defined by the distance ρ' such that not all the points of the corresponding neighborhood of a map *inside* that neighborhood $U'(a')$. Such a mapping would be also intuitively felt as discontinuous.

The above definition of continuity permits us to apply the notion of continuous mapping to spaces which consist of discrete points, as shown in Figure 1b. Let us again define the neighborhood of each point as consisting of the point itself and of the next point to the right. Consider a mapping of one such space S on another, as shown in Figure 4. Here a space consisting of six points is mapped in a many to one way on a space consisting of three points. According to our definition c) this mapping is continuous. We notice that while in the preceding case each point has a neighborhood for every value of ρ, now each point has only one neighborhood. The words *every neighborhood* in definition c) does now mean *the* neighborhood. An inspection of Figure 4 shows that to the neighborhood of a', which consists of a' and b', there is a corresponding neighborhood of a, which consists of a and a_1. *All* points of that neighborhood map on a'. In other words the image points of the points of the neighborhood of a are included in the neighborhood of a'. The point a' is also the image point of a_1. The neighborhood of a_1 con-

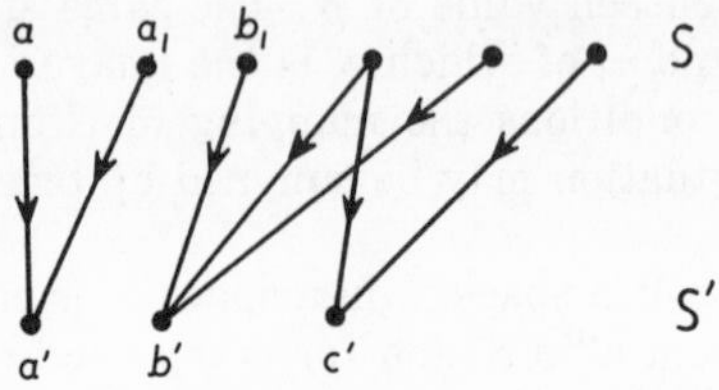

FIG. 4

sists of the set $\{a_1, b_1\}$. But a_1 is mapped on a' and b_1 on b'. As we remarked on p. 312 every set is included in itself. Hence the image points of the neighborhood of a_1 are included in the neighborhood of a'. We easily verify that the same situation holds for all other points and their images. Thus the mapping shown in Figure 4 is continuous, though the use of the word continuous in case of discrete points may sound odd.

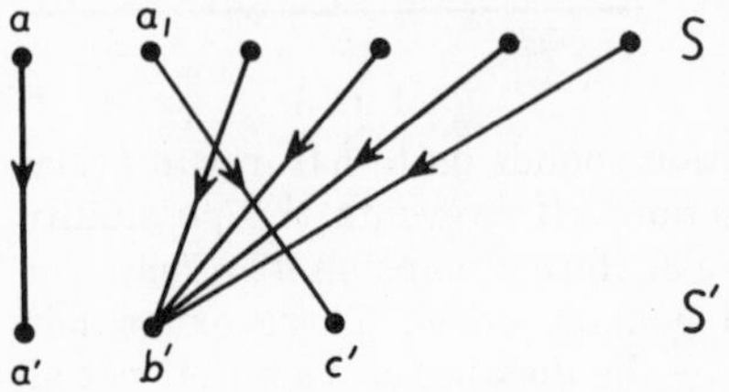

FIG. 5

The mapping shown in Figure 5, where the same two spaces are involved, is not continuous. It does not fulfill the conditions of definition c). The point a' in S' has the only neighborhood $\{a', b'\}$. There is no corresponding neighborhood of a in S, such that all its image points would fall within $\{a', b'\}$. In fact a has only one neighborhood $\{a, a_1\}$, but the point a_1, which belongs to the neighborhood of a, maps on c' which is *not* included in the neighborhood of a'.

As we already remarked, in this case each point has only one neighborhood. Therefore, in this particular instance we state the definition of a continuous mapping in a somewhat less rigorous but shorter form, namely: A mapping is continuous, if neighborhoods map on neighborhoods.

When we define a neighborhood, in other words, when we introduce certain criteria by means of which we can decide whether a given point y belongs to the neighborhood of x, we define in effect a certain *relation* between x and y. Continuous mapping preserves the basic relation of neighborhood.

As we have remarked, an organism is characterized by a set of biological properties. Those properties are not unrelated. The detailed relations between them are not all known. Yet some basic relations are manifest. Thus a stimulation causes excitation, and the latter results in contraction of some motile organ. This contraction, however, requires also a metabolic energy supply of some kind. Metabolic energy in its turn on one hand is necessary to produce contraction, on the other hand it is a necessary antecedent of some synthetic process. Thus we may establish a set of relations of "immediate precedence," or perhaps "immediate causation" between the different properties of an organism. If we represent the set of properties which characterize an organism, by a set of points, we may define neighborhoods in such a set in a rather natural manner by the following procedure: We define the neighborhood of a point which represents a property as consisting of the point itself and of all points which represent other properties which are immediately preceded, or caused by the given property. In this manner we make our set of properties into a space. The requirement, which we know empirically to be true, that in the mapping one organism on another the basic biological relations are preserved, then translates into the requirement that the abstract spaces which represent any two organisms should be mapped on each other continuously.

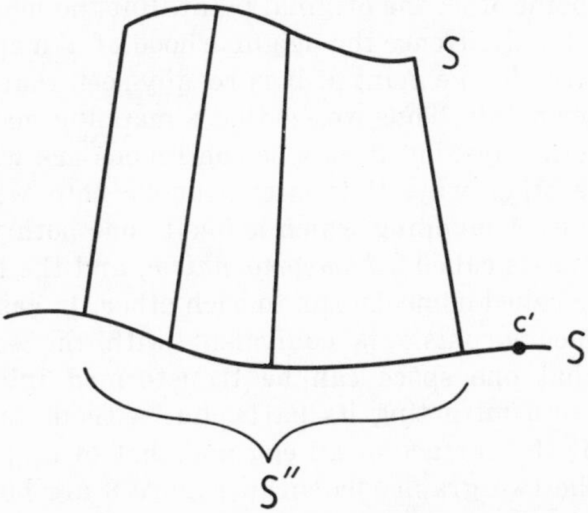

FIG. 6

In Figure 6 the linear space S is mapped only on a subspace S'' of the space S'. In such a case to each point of S there corresponds a point of S', but the reverse does not hold: There are some points of S' to which no points of S correspond, for example, the point c'. In such cases we say that S is mapped *into* S'. The mapping may, however, be a one-to-one mapping, as in Figure 6. An inspection of Figure 2 and 6 shows that in both cases not only is S mapped continuously onto or into S', but in Figure 2 the space S' is also mapped continuously onto S, and in Figure 6 the subspace S'' is mapped continuously onto S. Consider, however, the mapping shown in Figure 7. Let again in both S and S' the neighborhood of each point consist of the point itself and of the next point to the right. The mapping shown in Figure 7 is one-to-one. The mapping of S on S'

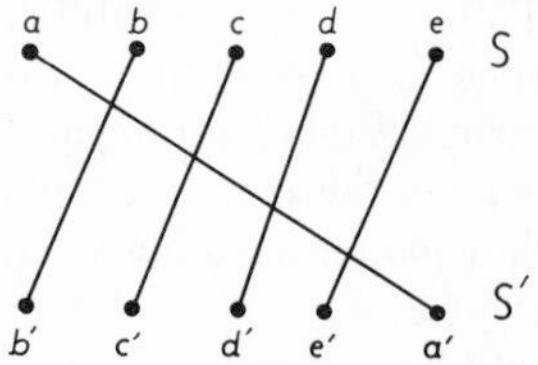

FIG. 7

is, however, not continuous, because the neighborhood of the image point a' consists of a' only, while the neighborhood of the point a consists of a and b. Since b maps on b', which does not belong to the neighborhood of a', therefore the neighborhood of a does not map on the neighborhood a', although a maps on a'. Consider, however, the inverse mapping of S' onto S. It is continuous, because a is now the image point of a', the original point. But the neighborhood of a' consists of a' only. Hence the neighborhood of a' maps on the neighborhood of the image point a. It is readily seen that the same holds for the other points. Thus we see that a mapping may be one to one, and onto both ways, but it may be continuous one way and not continuous the other way. If it is continuous both ways, it is called bi-continuous. A mapping which is one-to-one both ways, onto, and bi-continuous, is called a *homeomorphism*, and the two spaces thus mapped are called homeomorph to each other. In case of continuous spaces homeomorphism is equivalent with the easily visualized property that one space can be transformed into the other by stretching or contracting its parts, but without tearing anything apart. Thus the surface of an egg and that of a sphere are homeomorph. The two graphs shown in Figure 8 are homeomorph.

Two continuous lines AB and $A'B'$ of finite length L_1 and L_2, respectively, are homeomorph. The one-to-one bi-continuous mapping in this case may be expressed rather simply analytically. Consider on AB the coordinate of a point x as being the distance of x

from A taken along the line; similarly consider the coordinate of a point x' of $A'B'$ as the distance s' of that point from A', taken along the line. Let now to each point s of AB correspond the point $s' = s\ L_2/L_1$. The point A which corresponds to $s = 0$ maps on A'; the point B for which $s = L_1$, maps on B', for which $s' = L_2$. The mapping is also everywhere continuous.

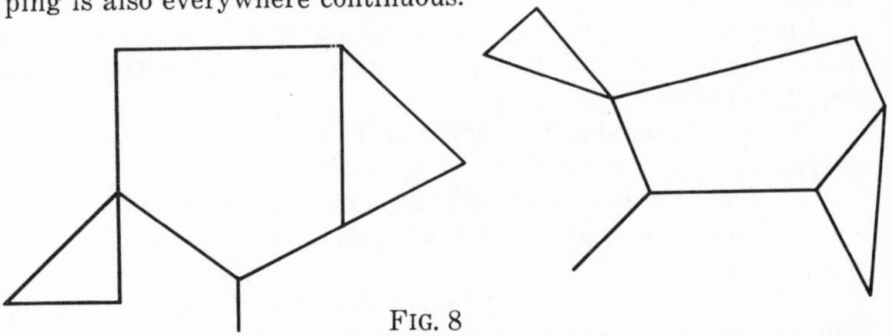

FIG. 8

Consider the set of points which represent the real numbers. Define the distance between two points x and y by $\rho = |x - y|$ and introduce ρ — neighborhoods for every point x, thus making it into a space R_1. If from *any* neighborhood of a given point x we remove the point x itself, the remaining set of points, in other words the set $\{U(x, \rho) - x\}$, for any value of ρ, no matter how small, will still contain a number of points of the space R_1. We describe this by saying that x is a *limit point* of the space R_1. A limit point of a set does not need to belong to the set itself, as is seen from the following examples. Consider the set S, defined by $0 < x < 1$. The points 0 and 1 do not belong to this set. Yet, if we introduce again ρ — neighborhoods, we see that both 0 and 1 are limit points of the set, because *any* neighborhood of 0, or of 1 contains an infinite number of points of the set. The point 0 is also a limit point of the subset A of S, which consists of all points $1/n$, where n is an integer, because by taking n sufficiently large we see that in any ρ — neighborhood of 0 there are points different from 0 but belonging to $1/n$. If, however, we assign in S or in the set of all real numbers, the neighborhoods as we did in the definition b) on p. 314, then we see that the point 0 is not a limit point, of the subset A either in R_1, or in S, because the points $1/n$ were by definition excluded from the neighborhood of the point 0. Thus, whether a point x is or is not a limit point of a space depends on the definition of neighborhood.

As we have said on p. 319, a continuous mapping preserves the basic relations of neighborhood. From what has been said about limit points it follows that a continuous mapping also preserves limit points. In other words if S is mapped continuously on S' then the image of a limit point of S is a limit point of S'.

The union of a set A with *all* its limit points is called the closure of A and is denoted by $\bar{A}$. Consider the set A_1 defined by $0 \leqslant x \leqslant 2$. All the limit points of this set are included in it. Therefore the set A_1 is identical with its closure. We have $A_1 = \bar{A}_1$. But consider the set A_2 of all points such that $0 < x < 2$. Here the points 0 and 2, which are limit points, are not included in the set A_2. Therefore, according to the definition of a union of sets, the closure $\bar{A}_2$ of A_2 consists of A_2 and of the points 0 and 2. Thus in this case $\bar{A}_2$ is different from A_2.

We now generalize the definition of a limit point to any kind of spaces:

d) Just as above we say that a point x is a limit point of a set S if for any neighborhood of x the set $U(x) - x$ includes some points of S.

We have made the set of points in Figure 1b into a space by defining the neighborhood of each point as consisting of the point itself and of the next point to the right. With this definition all points in the space thus obtained are limit points, with the exception of the extreme point to the right. The neighborhood of the extreme point to the right consists only of that point. If we remove that point from its neighborhood, what is left is an empty set, which does not contain any points of the space considered. But for any other point the removal of it from its neighborhood still leaves in that neighborhood one point that belongs to the space. In our definition d) of limit points we speak of *any* neighborhood $U(x)$. We must, however, again remember that with the definition of neighborhoods used here for the set in Figure 1b, *any* neighborhood of x reduces to the only neighborhood of x.

Consider again the space R: $0 \leqq x \leqq 1$. Remove any point $0 < x < 1$, say $x_0 = 1/4$ from it. The space R now consists of two spaces A and B, such that A consists of all points $0 \leqq x < 1/4$, while B consists of all points $1/4 < x \leqq 1$. Intuitively these two spaces are seen to be separated by the removal of the point $x_0 = 1/4$. We must, however, introduce the concept of separateness or non-connectedness in such a manner as to make it applicable to spaces which consist of discrete points. We notice that the point $x_0 = 1/4$ is a limit point of both A and B, but does not belong to either A or B, since it has been removed from the original space R. From what we have discussed above, the closure $\bar{A}$ of A consists of A and of the point x_0. But since x_0 is not included in B, therefore according to the definition of the intersection on p. , we have $\bar{A} \cap B = \emptyset$. Similarly $A \cap \bar{B} = \emptyset$. Thus in this case

$$\bar{A} \cap B = A \cap \bar{B} = \emptyset. \tag{7}$$

Condition (7) may be used as a definition of what is meant by a non-connected space. If (7) is not satisfied, no matter how we choose the two subspaces A and B, then $R = A \cup B$ is said to be connected.

With this definition the space obtained from the set of points in Figure 1b by defining the neighborhood of each point as consisting of the point itself and the next point to the right, is connected. Consider, for example, the subspace A which consists of the first 4 points, and the subset B which consists of the last 6 points. The fourth point, which belongs to A, is as we have seen a limit point of B, though it does not belong to B. Thus $\bar{B}$ consists of the last seven points, and has a point in common with A. Thus

$$A \cap \bar{B} \neq \emptyset. \tag{8}$$

and therefore the space is connected.

FIG. 9

If in the set of points which represent the properties of an organism, we define neighborhoods through biological relations between the properties, as we did before, then we can show that the space which represents any organism must be connected. To prove this we remark that if a space is not connected, there exists, by definition, two such subspaces, A and B, that A does not contain any limit points of B and vice versa. Otherwise $\bar{A} \cap B$ or $A \cap \bar{B}$ would not be empty and the space would be connected. This implies that no point of A belongs to a neighborhood of B and *vice versa.* For if a point of A belongs to a neighborhood of B, then that point of B would be a limit point of A. But if neighborhoods are defined through the biological relations between the properties of an organism, then the above statement that no point of A should belong to a neighborhood of B and *vice versa* means that no property in the subset A is in any way related to any property in the subset B and *vice versa.* But then we would have not one but two separate *unrelated* organisms.

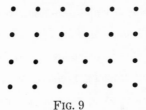

We conclude this chapter by the following remark: If in the set of points shown in Figure 9 we define the neighborhood of each point as consisting of the point itself and of the next point to the right we obtain a non-connected space, which consists of four disconnected components, each being a connected space. If, however, we define the neighborhood of a point x as consisting of the point x itself, the next point to the right of x, and the next point above x, then the whole space is connected.

REFERENCES

1. Kurt Lewin, *Principles of Topological Psychology* (New York, McGraw-Hill, 1936).

2. D'Arcy W. Thompson, *On Growth and Form,* Cambridge: At the University Press, 1917).

3. E. Jacobson, *Am. Journ. of Physiol.*, **95**, 694, 1930; **95**, 703, 1930; 97, 200, 1931.

4. R. Buchsbaum, *Animals Without Backbones* (Chicago: The University of Chicago Press, 1938).

5. J. H. Woodger, *Axiomatic Method in Biology* (Cambridge: Cambridge University Press, 1937).

6. R. Wilder, *Topology of Manifolds* (New York: American Mathematical Society, 1949).

7. H. Seifert and W. Threlfall, *Lehrbuch der Topologie* (Leipzig and Berlin: B. G. Teubner, 1934).

8. P. Alexandroff, and H. Hopf, *Topologie* (Berlin: Springer, 1935).

CHAPTER XXIX

A GENERAL PRINCIPLE AND ITS APPLICATIONS

At the beginning of the preceding chapter we emphasized the well known general fact that different organisms can be mapped on each other, preserving certain basic biological relations. From the subsequent discussion of that chapter it follows that one of the most natural ways of expressing and studying this fact mathematically is to represent the properties of an organism and the relations between those properties by an appropriate abstract connected space and to study the continuous mapping of such spaces on each other. This is by no means the only way of approaching the problem, but it seems to be so natural as to be worth investigating. Perhaps it may be possible to represent an organism in a more abstract form, namely by a class of relations. Then we could study mappings of such classes of relations. This possibility must be kept in view for the future. A more general mathematical representation of the relational aspects of organisms and of their mappings will be discussed in chapter xxxiii. In the meantime we shall investigate the approach suggested in the preceding chapter.

Any mapping of spaces is basically a *transformation* of one space into another. This transformation need not necessarily be given by an analytical expression. It may be expressed by a set of purely geometric rules. We have so far discussed the many-to-one mapping of a more complicated organism on simpler ones. Consider the inverse mappings, which are also given by some transformation. All organisms originated from some simpler organism, or possibly from a few different such organisms. This initial organism, or those few initial organisms, may, or more likely, may not even exist any more. But to the extent that they represent, or represented, the smallest sets of biological properties which we still would recognize as organism, all subsequently appearing organisms, whether higher multicellular ones, or complicated unicellular, still would map in the above described manner on this "primordial" organism. The inverse mapping in a way represents the manner in which the more complicated organisms arose from the simpler ones, in particular from the primordial. If we seek for any regularities in the mapping observed in the living, regularities which have predictive value, we are of necessity led to the following principle:

The topological spaces or complexes by which different organisms are represented are all obtained from one or at most from a few primordial spaces or complexes *by the same transformation,* which contains one or more parameters, to different values of which correspond different organisms.

It must be emphasized that there is nothing hypothetical about this principle, which, for brevity, we may call the principle of biotopological mapping. If we do not accept it, we admit the absence of any regularity in the different mappings which we know to exist. But then the scientist has nothing to do. The principle states a known fact coupled with our basic belief in the uniformity of nature, without which no *science can exist.*

Within this principle a theory of organisms can be developed by studying different topologically interesting transformations and their properties and seeing which of them leads to the best agreement with observation. Such was fundamentally the procedure used in the development of Newtonian mechanics. Such is also fundamentally the procedure used in Einstein's general relativity theory. Newton's basic principle, his laws of motion, are too general to say anything in a specific situation, until the forces are specified as functions of the coordinates, and until all forces acting on a given body are specified. A failure of agreement between observation and theory, as in the case of the residual motion of Uranus, is not laid down to the failure of the basic principle,

$$m\frac{d^2x}{dt^2} = F\,,$$

but to the inadequate assumption about F. An additional force, due to an unknown planet, was to blame for the discrepancy.

The basic concept of the general relativity theory, namely, that our four-dimensional space-time is non-Euclidian, that its geometry is determined by the distribution of masses, and that the world-lines of particles are geodesics in this non-Euclidian hyper-space, cannot lead, important as they are, to any prediction or description of physical facts, until equations are established which determine the metric tensor as a function of mass distribution. In establishing these equations, a hypothetical element enters. The equations originally proposed by Einstein in 1916 were soon modified by him so as to include the cosmological term. Since H. Weyl's attempt to generalize the space-time metric so as to incorporate electromagnetic phenomena, numerous modifications have been proposed. The question is still unsettled, though the latest generalization proposed by Einstein himself carries great promise.

Our problem is thus to find, amongst infinite number of possible transformations the one that corresponds to actual organisms. To do this it will most likely be necessary to study in abstracto many different types of conceivable transformations, in order to eventually find the appropriate one. As always in such cases, we may be guided by certain principles of simplicity.

We shall denote certain properties by the letter P provided with a capital Latin subscript to designate the specific property. Thus P_S stands for sensitivity to external stimuli; P_C — for property to conduct excitation; P_M — for orderly movement (as contrasted with thermal agitation); P_A — for absorption, etc. Lower case Latin letters will be used for running subscripts. Thus we shall write P_i $(i = S, C, M, \ldots)$.

In a unicellular organism the one cell which constitutes it, possesses all the basic properties P_i. Those properties are related in a manner to be discussed below. One of the characteristics of multicellular organisms is that in the latter different cells specialize in different properties. Some cells retain some properties and lose others. The relation between two different properties P_i and P_k, whether they belong to the same cell of a multicellular organism or to different cells, remains the same as in a unicellular organism. E.g. one type of cells may be sensitive to external stimuli, but not be motile; another cell may not be sensitive but possess motility. Yet just as in a unicellular organism a stimulus produces under certain conditions a movement, so will a stimulus applied to the sensory cell result in a movement of the motile cell.

Another characteristic of more complex multicellular organisms is the much larger number of different properties as compared with the simpler or unicellular ones. Thus a sensory cell in a lower organism may be sensitive to chemical stimuli in general. In a higher organism, different sensory cells may be sensitive to different chemical stimuli. For example, different taste cells of the human tongue are sensitive to salty, sour, sweet, and bitter. We shall refer to those as "subproperties." The sensitivity to bitterness, which we shall denote by P_{S_1}, and the sensitivity to sour P_{S_2} are included in the sensitivity P_S. Thus P_S is a set of subproperties $P_{S\alpha}$ $(\alpha = 1, 2, \ldots)$. The $P_{S\alpha}$'s are subsets of P_S. The same holds for any other property P_i. Denoting a "subproperty" by $P_{i\alpha}$ $(i = S, C, M, \ldots)$ $(\alpha = 1, 2, 3, \ldots)$ (in other words numbering the subproperties in an arbitrary manner) we have

$$P_{i\alpha} \subset P_i \,. \tag{1}$$

When we examine the mapping of different organisms on each

other, we see that the set $S_1(P_{ia})$ of the subproperties of P_i in one organism maps on the set $S_2(P_{i\beta})$ of another organism; and both map on the set P_i of the primordial. The set P_i is thus the largest or the most inclusive of all subsets P_{ia}.

The family of subsets P_{ia} of P_i may be conceivably infinite. Thus P_S contains amongst its elements the sensitivity $P_{S\lambda}$ to radiation of wave length λ. Thus the family of subsets of P_S has, at least theoretically, the power of the continuum. Actually, however, in any given concrete organism, the family of subsets of P_i are all finite, though some of them may have very large cardinal numbers. An arbitrary ordering of the subsets P_{ia}, as done above, does not present therefore any practical difficulty.

It must be also noted that two subsets P_{ia} and $P_{i\beta}$ of P_i are not necessarily disjoined, so that we may have

$$P_{ia} \cap P_{i\beta} = \emptyset \cdot \wedge \cdot P_{ia} \cap P_{i\beta} \neq \emptyset \,, \tag{2}$$

where $\wedge$ denotes the exclusive "or." As an example we have the secretion of proteins and the secretion of regulatory substances. Both are included in "secretion" in general. *Some* secreted proteins are regulatory substances, and *some* regulatory substances are proteins.

Let us examine more closely some of the sets P_i.

We have already discussed some of the subsets P_{Sa} of P_S. Special considerations should be given to the sensitivity to pain. As an example let us consider that a painful stimulus may be a stimulus of any modality with an intensity above a certain injurious limit. Let P_{Sa_i} denote the sensitivity to a stimulus of modality α_i, while $P_{Sa_i|(\beta)}$ denotes the sensitivity to the stimulus of modality α_i and intensity β. Then we have

$$P_{Sa_i(\beta)} \subset P_{Sa_i} \tag{3}$$

and the sensitivity to pain by stimuli of modality α_i is represented by

$$P_{Sa_i(\pi)} = \bigcup_{\beta \geq \beta_0} P_{Sa_i(\beta)} \tag{4}$$

where β_0 is the threshold of pain. The sensitivity to painful stimuli of any modality is then represented by the subset of P_S:

$$P_{S\pi} = \bigcup_{P_{Sa_i} \subset P_{S_i}} P_{Sa_i(\pi)} \,. \tag{5}$$

The set which represents the property of conduction, P_C, consists of subsets P_{Ca}, which are conductions at different rates. Other subsets are conductions mediated chemically and conductions mediated electrophysiologically.

Of special interest is the set P_M of all orderly movements. In this set are included such movements as those of cilia and flagella, as well as the movement involved in the protrusion of a pseudopod. The fact that different pseudopoda may succeed each other in a random fashion does not make the movements in each pseudopod disorderly or random. On the other hand movements of transport due either to diffusion or to active transport, secretion or absorption, are also subsets of P_M. Thus one important subset of P_M is the set P_{M_1} of all movements which may be called movements on the physically molar level. An other important set is the set of orderly movements P_{M_2} on the molecular level.

The set P_A of properties of absorption includes as subsets P_{A_1} absorption of building substances for the organism, and P_{A_2} of energy-yielding substances. The absorption P_{A_3} of energy is a subset of P_A. That absorption may either proceed through absorption P_{A_4} of radiant energy directly, as in autotrophic plants, or by absorption of energy-yielding substances, P_{A_2}. We have

$$P_{A_3} \subset P_{A_2}; \text{ and } P_{A_3} \subset P_{A_4}. \tag{6}$$

Hence

$$P_{A_2} \cap P_{A_4} \neq \emptyset. \tag{7}$$

This gives us another example of (2).

The set P_{Me} of the properties of metabolism includes as subsets the anabolism or synthesis, P_{Me_1}, catabolism P_{Me_2}, and storage P_{Me_3}. Those contain other subsets. Thus, e.g. synthesis of proteins is included in P_{Me_1}; storage of fats and storage of sugars are both included in P_{Me_3}, etc.

How are the different sets, P_S, P_M, etc. related in the primordial organism? We do not know the full answer to that question, but certain partial relations may be inferred from the logical analysis of what is usually meant by the concept of organism. An organism is a set S_0 of sets P_i in which certain relations of "immediate succession" is established.

As we have seen in the preceding chapter we may consider one biological property P_i as immediately succeeding another, P_k, if the manifestation of P_i causes the manifestation of P_k without involving the manifestation of any third property P_l ($l \neq i; l \neq k$). As examples we may give excitation and conduction. However, to the extent that both P_i and P_k contain subsets $P_{i\alpha}$ and $P_{k\beta}$, a sequence of manifestations of *different* subsets may be involved in the sequence $P_i \rightarrow P_k$. Thus, for example, the excitation of a nerve is immediately followed by conduction of an impulse. But in different types of nerves both the excitation and the conduction may represent a sequence of somewhat different physico-chemical processes.

It is convenient to designate the relation of immediate precedence or immediate succession by an arrow. If P_i immediately precedes P_k, we shall write $P_i \rightarrow P_k$.

There will be a general agreement at least on the relations between some properties of the primordial organism. Thus we have in general $P_S \rightarrow P_C$, and $P_C \rightarrow P_M$. In some organisms we have only P_{M_2}, while in others both P_{M_1} and P_{M_2} are present, but at least one of the two sets of properties is exhibited by *all* organisms. As a result of P_{M_1} as well as of P_{M_2} we have in general ingestion, P_E, or excretion of substances. Thus $P_M \rightarrow P_F$. The process of digestion, which corresponds to a set P_D of properties, occurs either as a result of P_{M_1} or of P_{M_2} or both. Hence we also have $P_M \rightarrow P_D$. Then again $P_A \rightarrow P_{Me}$. Metabolic processes being essential to the proper performance of sensitivity, conduction, and motion, we have also $P_{Me} \rightarrow P_S$; $P_{Me} \rightarrow P_C$; $P_{Me} \rightarrow P_M$. The metabolic processes are also essential for the reproduction P_R of the organism. Hence $P_{Me} \rightarrow P_R$, and by the same token, $P_M \rightarrow P_R$.

There is even in the primordial organism also a set P_H of properties of homeostasis. The connection between P_H and the other P_i is not directly evident from *a priori* considerations. However, undoubtedly there is a connection $P_{Me} \rightarrow P_H$, as well as a connection of P_M to nearly all other P_i's.

We have already noticed the important fact that in a multicellular organism the different $P_{i\alpha}$ ($\alpha = 1, 2, 3, \ldots$) map on the P_i of the primordial. Let S_0' be the set of sets P_i which represents a multicellular organism, and S_P' — the set of sets P_i which represets the primordial organism.

Those sets are not yet spaces, since no neighborhoods have been introduced into them. By connecting the different points P_i of S_P, or P_i of S_0 by appropriate arrows which indicate the relations of immediate succession, we can obtain a one-dimensional continuous space, if we consider the arrows as continuous lines. Such a one-dimensional space is called a graph. We have already met graphs in chapter xxviii of volume I. But actually those arrows merely indicate the relation of immediate succession. As lines they have no *physical* meaning. It is therefore much more logical to construct spaces S_O and S_P by introducing into the sets S_O' and S_P' a topology by an appropriate definition of neighborhoods. Considering the P_{ia} and P_i as points in the spaces S_O and S_P, respectively, this can be done in the simplest manner by defining in S_O and S_P the neighborhoods in the following way.

The neighborhood of a point in S_O (or S_P) consists of the point itself and of all those points which it immediately precedes.

Since the relation of immediate succession can be represented by an arrow of a graph, we see that to each S_O, and to S_P there is a corresponding graph. Instead of saying that a point a immediately precedes b, we may say that "a is connected to b by an arrow." Then the above definition of neighborhoods can be stated thus: The neighborhood of a point in S_O (or S_P) consists of the point itself and of all points to which arrows originate from it. We have seen that the mapping of S_O onto S_P must be continuous. If now the space of the primordial organism is given, the possible spaces S_O are obtained in the following manner:

As we have remarked on page 327, the more complex an organism, the "narrower" the specialization of its cells. In other words, the smaller a subset P_i each cell type represents and therefore the larger the number n of subsets. Denote by $P_{ia}^{(n)}$ any set of n subsets of P_i. Denote by $P_{ia_r}^{(n)}$ $(r = 1, 2, 3, \ldots, n)$ the n subsets of $P_{ia}^{(n)}$. For example, if $i = S$, and $n = 2$, and if P_S had only three possible subsets, P_{S1}, P_{S2}, P_{S3}, which denote respectively the sensitivities to light, sound, and touch, then $P_S^{(2)}$ would be either (P_{S1}, P_{S2}), or (P_{S1}, P_{S3}), or (P_{S2}, P_{S3}). Actually, of course, each P_i includes much more than two subsets. We now proceed as follows:

(A). For each set P_i in S_P, which is represented by a point on the corresponding graph, we choose n_i subsets $P_{ia}^{(n_i)}$. These subsets, for all possible values of i, will be the points of the space S_O. If in S_P the point P_i immediately precedes the point P_k, in other words, if the point P_i is connected by an arrow to the point P_k, then in S_O *at least one* point $P_{ia}^{(n_i)}$ immediately precedes *at least one* point $P_{k\beta}^{(n_k)}$, in other words in S_O at least one point $P_{ia}^{(n_i)}$ is connected by an arrow to *at least one* $P_{k\beta}^{(n_k)}$, the directions of the arrows being properly preserved. If in S_O, P_i is not connected by an arrow to P_k, then no P_{ia} is connected to any $P_{k\beta}$.

In this manner neighborhoods of S_0 are mapped on neighborhoods of S_P. The mapping is continuous.

Although for our purposes the rule(A)is quite sufficient and we shall use it throughout this chapter, yet it may be considerably generalized, without affecting any of the following conclusions. We may establish in any arbitrary manner relations of immediate precedence and immediate succession between all the points of the subset $P_{i\alpha}$, in other words between points belonging to the same i but to different α's. In terms of the associated graph, we may connect all points $P_{i\alpha}$, (i = const), by arrows in any manner. As long as all such points map on P_i, the mapping will still be continuous.

The above procedure of constructing S_0 from S_P does not prevent the possibility that more than one $P_{i\alpha}^{(n_i)}$ will have an arrow pointing to a $P_{k\beta}^{(n_k)}$, or that one $P_{i\alpha}^{(n_i)}$ has arrows pointing to several $P_{k\beta}^{(n_k)}$. The total number of possibilities for prescribed values of n_i ($i = S, C, M$, etc.) is very large. To each possible set of arrows permitted by (A) there corresponds a different multicellular organism. Moreover, it must be remembered that the set P_i can be divided in many different ways into $P_{i\alpha}^{(n_i)}$ subsets. Thus we may have two sets S_0 which are homeomorph, but in which two topologically identical points $P_{i\alpha_r}^{(n_i)}$ represent different subsets of P_i. Such two sets represent again different multicellular organisms.

It is an interesting combinatorial problem to determine the total number N of possible different sets S_0 which correspond to a given S_P. This number will give us the total number of possible organisms. If any of the P_i's are infinite sets, then of course N will be infinite. As we remarked, actually for any given organism, n_i are always finite. But inasmuch as theoretically some if not all, of the P_i's may be infinite and even not enumerably infinite, we have here a possibly interesting problem in set theory. Namely, for given cardinal numbers of the P_i's what is the cardinal number of the set of possible sets S_0?

The organism may be considered as the more complex, the more arrows there are in S_0 between the different $P_{i\alpha}^{(n_i)}$ and $P_{k\beta}^{(n_k)}$. The maximum degree of complexity is obtained when each point $P_i^{(n_i)}$ has an arrow pointing to each $P_k^{(n_k)}$. We shall call such a S_0 the *maximal* S_0.

The rule (A) for constructing S_0 from S_P is very general and contains only the restriction of continuity. We must, however, add to it another restriction. A space S_0 constructed according to (A) is not necessarily connected. To see this we may consider the particular case when all n_i's are equal ($n_i = n$). Each point $P_{i\alpha}^{(n)}$ of

S_0 would then have an arrow in the direction of just one corresponding point $P_{k\beta}^{(n)}$ in such a manner that we have n disjoined graphs, each of which is homeomorph with S_P. This corresponds exactly to the example mentioned at the end of the preceding chapter. It is to be noted that with the above definition of neighborhoods in S_0 a connected graph implies a connected space S_0, in the more general topological meaning of the word "connection."

Hence we require:

(B). S_0 *is connected.*

If we speak in terms of graphs which correspond to our spaces, then requirement (B) implies some geometrical and combinatorial relations in S_0, relations which are in general by no means simple, but which may have definite biological predictive value. We shall not discuss here this question in detail, but merely illustrate its nature on an example.

Let again $n_i = n$, and consider the graph of S_0. In the absence of requirement (B) this graph may consist, as we have seen, of n disjoined identical graphs.

Because of $n_i = n$, we can conveniently number all the $P_{ia_q}^{(n)}$ and $P_{ka_r}^{(n)}$ in such a manner, that $q = r$, in other words, so that the point $P_{ia_q}^{(n)} \rightarrow P_{ka_r}^{(n)}$.

To make the whole space, and therefore also the graph, connected we must have at least $n - 1$ lines joining *different* non-corresponding points of the n identical graphs. Let such arrows be made between the points $P_{ia_r}^{(n)}$ and $P_{ka_{r+1}}^{(n)}$. Since we already have $P_{ia_{r+1}}^{(n)} \rightarrow P_{ka_{r+1}}^{(n)}$ therefore the point $P_{ka_{r+1}}^{(n)}$ will have two predecessors, namely $P_{ia_r}^{(n)}$ and $P_{ia_{r+1}}^{(n)}$. Each of the last two points will have at least one immediate predecessor.

We call a point a a predecessor of b, if a precedes b. However, a may precede b either immediately, or not immediately by having intermediate points between a and b. Accordingly we shall speak of immediate and non-immediate predecessors. Hence, requirement (B) assures us that of the n points which correspond to P_i, $n - 1$ points will have more predecessors in S_0 than P_i has in S_P. In other words, while a certain point P_k in S_P may be reached from only one point P_i, in S_0 we shall have at least $n - 1$ points corresponding to P_k, each of which will have at least two immediate or non-immediate predecessors. The maximal S_0 is of course always connected.

If P_i is a predecessor of P_k, then anything that affects P_i is going to affect P_k. Hence the biological meaning of the above is that in a multicellular organism, due to requirement (B) the number of biological properties which affect a given property is greater than in a unicellular organism.

At this point we shall introduce some terminology from the theory of graphs, which will be also used in subsequent chapters.

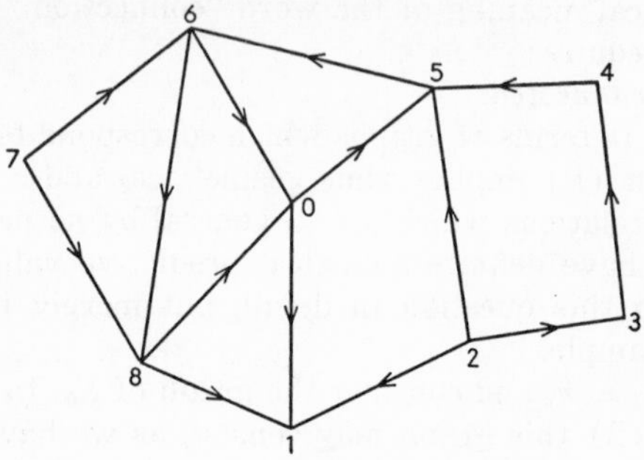

FIG. 1

We define a *path* as a sequence of adjacent lines of a graph, regardless of whether the two adjacent lines have the same direction or not. A point following a path will follow, in general, some of its lines in the direction of that line, some in the opposite direction. Thus in Figure 1 the sequence 01234 is a path; also the sequence 25067.

A path in which all lines are directed in the same manner is called a *way*. Thus in Figure 1 the sequence of lines 345681 is a way leading from the point 3 to the point 1.

Theorem I: If in the graph of S_P there is way from P_i to P_k, which goes through one or more intermediate points P_e, then in the maximal S_0 the number of disjoined ways from any point $P_{ia_q}{}^{(n_i)}$ to any $P_{ka_k}{}^{(n_r)}$ is equal to n_{min}, where n_{min} is the smallest of all n_e's, which belong to any of the intermediate points P_e.

Proof. If n_{min} is the smallest of all n_e's, then we can pick out n_{min} points amongst every of the n_e's, and construct n_{min} disjoined ways from $P_{ia_q}{}^{(n_i)}$ to $P_{ka_r}{}^{(n_k)}$. More than n_{min} disjoined ways are impossible, because some of them would have common points amongst the n_{min} points of $P_m{}^{(n_m)}$.

How about unicellular organisms? They exhibit a great variety of properties P_i, and they also map on each other and on the primordial. Some microorganisms, as we remarked on page 330 do not have any P_{M_1} (non-motile microorganisms), but all of them have

P_{M_2}. Similarly different microorganisms have different P_S, but at least some elements of P_S occur in all of them. Generalizing by induction, it is natural to postulate:

(C). The spaces S_{ou} which represent all possible unicellular organisms are obtained from S_P by assigning to one cell any possible space S_o, with the exception of such elements $P_i^{(n_i)}$ of combinations thereof, as would be incompatible with the size of a cell or with physical laws.

The last restriction is essential for example in the following case: Consider the property P_H of homeostasis. Amongst its elements the set P_H contains the subset P_{H_t} of temperature regulation, While some microorganisms show other homeostatic properties P_H, for example, osmoregulation[1], no unicellular organism can have temperature regulation, because, as simple calculations show, the maintenance of any appreciable difference in temperature between a single cell and its environment would require such rates of heat producing reactions as are incompatible with known physicochemical laws, because of the tremendous specific surface of a single cell.

In addition to (C), we postulate:

(D). All possible multicellular organisms are represented by S_o, and conversely, any organism which corresponds to an S_o is possible.

A number of interesting conclusions follow almost immediately from (A) — (D), without a more detailed specification of the structure of the primordial space S_P.

From (A) it follows, that if we have an S_o, in which $P_{i\alpha} \to P_{k\beta}$ then in the primordial we have $P_i \to P_k$. Hence, from (D) it follows that there exist organisms, in which $P_{i\mu} \to P_{k\nu}$, where μ and ν are in general different from α and β. From (C) it follows that there exist unicellular organisms, in which $P_{i\mu} \to P_{k\nu}$ unless the existence of either $P_{i\mu}$ or $P_{k\nu}$, or both, is incompatible with the size of a single cell.

Thus from observations of some relations within an organism, we may infer the existence of other organisms, in which different, but corresponding relations exist.

Let us consider the sequence $P_S \to P_C \to P_M$. As we have seen, an important subset of P_M is P_{M_1}, the subset of molar orderly movements. In a unicellular organism this may be represented by amoeboid movements, or ciliary or flagellary movements, which we shall denote correspondingly by P_{M_a}, P_{M_c}, P_{M_f}. We have

$$P_{M_a} \subset P_{M_1}; P_{M_c} \subset P_{M_1}; P_{M_f} \subset P_{M_1}. \tag{8}$$

In a higher animal different cells specialize in the three different subsets: the leucocytes, for example, in P_{M_a}; cells of respiratory epithelium in P_{M_e}; spermatozoids — in P_{M_f}.

A subset of P_{M_1} is represented by contractile muscular tissues. A movement of a unicellular organism, for example, an amoeboid movement, plays several roles in the life of the organism.

(a). It propels the organism as a whole in space, towards food, or away from the enemy.

(b). It orients the organism differently with respect to different stimuli, thus

(c) changing possibly the effectiveness of the stimulus;

(d) it helps ingestion of food into the digestive vacuole, and

(e). It may cause an eventual movement of food to the latter. It also

(f) in general affects the transport of substances inside the cell.

The sets of movements which produce correspondingly the effects (a), (b), (c), (d), (e), and (f) are included in $P_{M'_1}$. In line with (A), (B), and (D), different cell types specialize in some higher organisms in each of those subsets of movements, which we shall denote correspondingly by $P_{M(a)}$; $P_{M(b)}$; $P_{M(c)}$; etc. We have

$$P_{M(a)} \subset P_M \tag{9}$$

similarly for $P_{M(b)}$ and the others.

The skeletal muscles are general representatives of $P_{M(a)}$; they also represent the subset $P_{M(b)}$. The ciliary muscle of the eye, or the muscles of the tympanic membrane have properties which belong to $P_{M(c)}$.

Instead of the general sensitivity P_S we also have in a higher animal several subsets of P_S, some of which we discussed above. The same holds for P_C.

Let P_{Sv} denote the set of visual sensitivities of all kind. We have

$$P_{Sv} \subset P_S \,. \tag{10}$$

In a primordial we have $P_S \to P_C \to P_M$. Hence it follows from (A) that in *some* higher organism we must have:

$$P_{Sv} \to P_C \to P_{M(d)} \,. \tag{11}$$

In other words: There exists higher organisms, in which gastrointestinal movements are affected by visual stimuli. A well known example is the vomiting at the sight of some unpleasant things. By the same argument, we have more generally:

$$P_{Sa} \rightarrow P_C \rightarrow P_{M(d)}\,, \tag{12}$$

which states that in some animals different sensory stimuli affect the gastrointestinal motility.

As we have seen, the more complex an animal, the more subsets $P_{i\alpha}$ are connected to a given subset $P_{k\beta}$, if $P_i \rightarrow P_k$. Hence, the higher the animal, the greater the variety of sensory stimuli, which affect the gastrointestinal motility. Man is the highest of the presently existing animals, though there is no reason to assume that it is represented by a maximal S_0. We should, however, expect the human gastro-intestinal tract to be more sensitive to a great variety of sensory stimuli, than in any of the other animals.

To the extent that our psychological experiences are manifestations of a complex interplay of sensory activities, we may state that it follows from (A), (B), and (D) that in man, as well as in some animals, psychic disturbances produce gastrointestinal troubles. This is a well known fact. It does not follow and cannot follow from any metric biophysical theory, unless specifically assumed. It does follow, however, from the general principle of biotopological mapping, as formulated here.

This result cannot be deduced from considerations of natural selection, since its adaptive value is, if anything, negative, at least for man's usual occupations.

By the same argument we see that there exist animals, in which sensory stimuli and specifically in man, psychic disturbances, affect the cardio-vascular phenomena. We merely substitute in (12) P_{Mf} for $P_{M(d)}$. In this connection it is interesting to note that "stimulation of almost any afferent nerve of the body can affect the heart rate" (Reference 2, p. 161).

From $P_S \rightarrow P_C \rightarrow P_M$ it follows, according to (A), that

$$P_{Sa} \rightarrow P_{C\beta} \rightarrow P_{M\gamma} \tag{13}$$

where $P_{M\gamma}$ is any subset included in P_M.

Hence we may substitute for $P_{M\gamma}$ any subset contained in P_{M_2}. But P_{M_2} represents the different molecular orderly movements, such as, for example, secretion. In particular the set $P_{M\epsilon}$ of "secretions of different digestive enzymes" is included in P_{M_2} and hence in P_M. Therefore we have

$$P_{Sa} \rightarrow P_{C\beta} \rightarrow P_{M\epsilon}\,. \tag{14}$$

In words: In some animals sensory stimuli affect the secretion of digestive enzymes. In man we should expect psychological states to affect such a secretion.

A biological property of an organism is affected whenever any predecessor is affected. If a given P_{ia} has, say, n predecessors, and if we assume equal probability for any of them being disturbed, then the probability that an observed disturbance of the property P_{ia} is actually due to a disturbance of a predecessor, and not of P_{ia} itself, is $(n-1)/n$. To know the total number of predecessors for a given P_{ia} we must know the structure of S_P, which we do not know. But even from a simple general consideration as that made on p. 330 we see that for P_M, and therefore for any $P_{M(d)}$ of P_M, $n = 4$, at the very least. Hence the probability of a given gastro-intestinal disturbance being due to disturbances of other parts of the organism is greater than 0.75. To the extent that the psychological disturbances involve P_S's and P_C's, we can infer that the number of observed gastro-intestinal disturbances due to psychic disturbances is greater than 75%. It is said to be actually over 80%. Consider now in S_P the relation of P_M to some following P_i's. Molar movements are followed by feeding reactions P_F. So are the molecular orderly movements, because diffusion gradients and active transport bring food from the surrounding towards the cell in non-motile cells. Hence

$$P_M \to P_F \tag{15}$$

in the primordial. Denote by $P_{M(sec)}$ the subset of P_M which contains all the secretory properties. Since $P_{M(sec)} \subset P_M$, therefore from (15) and from (A) and (B) it follows:

$$E(S_o) : P_{M(sec)} \subset S_o \cdot P_{Fa} \subset S_o \cdot P_{M(sec)} \to P_{Fa} \, . \tag{16}$$

In words: There are organisms in which secretory phenomena produce feeding reactions. An example of this is offered by *Urechis* (reference 1, p. 145), which secretes mucous bags, which filter out food particles and are eventually swallowed. Another example is the secreted spider-web which catches the prey.

In some unicellulars the movements P_{M_1} affect the transport of substances both within the cell (by stirring "the protoplasm") and outside of it. (Ingestive movements of cilia). Denoting phenomena of transport in general by P_T, we thus have:

$$E(S_{ou}) : P_{M_1} \subset S_{ou} \cdot P_T \subset S_{ou} \cdot P_{M_1} \to P_T \, . \tag{17}$$

Hence, using the sign of implication $\supset$, it follows from (A) and (C):

$$P_M \subset S_P \cdot P_T \subset S_P \supset P_M \to P_T \, , \tag{18}$$

that is, in the primordial we have $P_M \rightarrow P_T$. But then it follows from (A):

$$E(S_o) : P_{M_1 a} \subset S_o \cdot P_{T\beta} \subset S_o \cdot P_{M_1 a} \rightarrow P_{T\beta} . \qquad (19)$$

Put for $P_{M_1 a}$ the movements of skeletal muscles, which are propelling the organism in space. Put for $P_{T\beta}$ the set of circulatory phenomena. Then (19) states that in some higher organisms such movements of skeletal muscles affect the circulation. Example: The venous circulation in man is largely due to the "kneading" action of skeletal muscles. Effects of body musculature on circulation are also known in a number of lower animals.[1]

The general principles (A)—(D) apply to both animals and plants. The latters are perhaps characterized by the fact that $P_{M_a} = \emptyset$; the subset of all amoeboid movements of the cell is empty. We have $P_{M_a} \subset P_{M_1}$. But $P_{M_1} \neq \emptyset$, since we have the flow of water in plants. The set of flagellate movements is not empty in lower unicellular plants. Similarly the subset of P_C which contains the conduction due to electrochemical phenomena (nerve conduction) is empty in plants. However, from $P_S \rightarrow P_C \rightarrow P_M$ in the primordial it follows:

$$E(S_o) : P_{Sa} \subset S_o \cdot P_{C\beta} \subset S_o \cdot P_{M\gamma} \subset S_o \cdot P_S \rightarrow P_C \rightarrow P_{M\gamma} . \qquad (20)$$

This applies to plants as well as to animals. If P_{Sa} denotes any sensitivity to external stimuli, $P_{C\beta}$ — chemical mediation, and $P_{M\gamma}$ denotes either the movement of water through tracheae, or the movement of food-containing solvents through sieve cells, then (20) states that adequate stimulation of plants, say by light, affects both the flow of sap and the translocation of metabolites.

The subset of all secretions, which is included in P_{M2}, includes such subsets as secretion of wastes, secretion of poisons, secretion of substances useful to other organisms, and secretion of substances lethal or otherwise harmful to other organisms. From (C) it follows that there must exist microorganisms, which secrete substances that are lethal or otherwise harmful to some other organisms. The toxins of some pathogenic bacteria is one example. The set of substances harmful to some other organisms includes the subset of substances harmful to some microorganisms. The antibiotics, like penicillin, are an example.

By the same token there must exist microorganisms, which produce substances that are useful to other organisms, which is a well known fact.

The finding of different possible subsets of a set P_i may be a matter of logic. A set P_i consists of all conceivable subsets included in it, as long as the existence of such subsets is compatible with physical laws. Sometimes the possibility of a subset P_i is shown by experiment.

In many relatively higher animals there are cells which upon stimulation with appropriate substances, the antigens, produce special proteins, the antibodies. The production of antibodies is thus the subset of the set P_{Me} of metabolic phenomena. The sensitivity to antigen is a subset of the set P_S. We shall designate the former by $P_{Me(a)}$, the other by $P_{S(a)}$. From (C) it follows that there must exist unicellular organisms which produce antibodies when stimulated by an appropriate antigen. So far no such microorganism has been definitely found, though there is a report of antibody production by yeast[3, 4].

This is an example of prediction made from the general principles proposed here.

Another conclusion seems to be actually verified. We have $P_{S(a)} \subset P_S$ and $P_{Me(a)} \subset P_{Me}$. We also have in higher organisms:

$$P_{S(a)} \rightarrow P_{ia} \rightarrow \ldots P_{m\gamma} \rightarrow P_{Me(a)} , \tag{21}$$

where $P_{ia} \rightarrow \ldots P_{m\gamma}$ denotes the possible intermediate sequence of points of S_o, which as yet are unknown. From (A) and (21) it follows that in a primordial

$$P_S \rightarrow P_i \rightarrow \ldots P_m \rightarrow P_{Me} . \tag{22}$$

and then again from (A) that there exist multicellular organisms, in which

$$P_{S\mu} \rightarrow P_{iv} \rightarrow \ldots P_{m\omega} \rightarrow P_{Me(a)} . \tag{23}$$

Here $P_{S\mu}$ stands for sensitivity to any stimulus, such as light, heat, etc. Expression (23) states that *in some cases* antibodies may be formed in multicellular organisms by "physical stimuli." This reminds us of the "physical allergy" phenomena[5], which seems, at least in some cases, to be connected with actual formation of "something" that can be transferred passively by the serum[6]. Alternative explanations of the observed phenomena seem, however, possible[5]. Thus the above conclusion cannot be regarded as verified. Neither does it seem to be yet disproved.

By the same line of reasoning we should expect that some plants produce antibodies. Indications of the existence of such a phenomenon have been found[7]. Again, however, a different interpretation of the observations has been suggested[8]. The evidence against production of antibodies by plants is considered to be conclusive[4]. However, in view of the fact that as yet very few plants have been investigated, the search would be worth while to be continued. Should, however, such a search fail definitely, this would lead to definite conclusions, which are again verifiable by experiments. As has been remarked, in plants the set P_{M_a} of amoeboid movements is empty. There are other subsets P_i which are empty in plants. Plants are characterized by the sets P_o of subsets P_i which are empty in them. If plants do not produce antibodies, then $P_{Me(a)}$ is empty in plants. Either then $P_{Me(a)}$ is an element of P_o, and in a sense enters into the definition of plants, or there must be some physicochemical relation between some of the P_i' and $P_{Me(a)}$, such that the absence of P_i' implies the absence of $P_{Me(a)}$. The first possibility does not seem very likely. The second possibility suggests immediately a possible physicochemical connection between P_{M_a} and $P_{Me(a)}$. There may be a common biophysical or biochemical factor involved in certain type of movements of the cell and production of antibodies. It may, perhaps, be significant that antibodies are apparently produced by reticuloendothelial cells, which resemble more than others some amoeboid forms. If there is a relation between P_{M_a} and $P_{Me(a)}$, then, however, we should look for antibodies production by unicellulars not to yeasts, but rather to amoebae.

The above is meant to illustrate that even in its immediate and simplest consequences, the postulates (A)—(D) do have a predictive and heuristic value. More of this should be found by further elaborating the set-theoretical properties of S_o and S_P.

We have considered two subsets of P_C, the subset of what may be called nervous conduction, and the subset of humoral chemical conduction. We shall denote the former by P_{C1}. The set P_{C1} includes two important subsets, P_{C1_0} and P_{C1_h}, such that

$$P_{C1_0} \subset P_{C1}; \text{ and } P_{C1_h} \subset P_{C1}. \tag{24}$$

The first one, P_{C1_0}, we shall call, for lack of better term, nonhysteresis conduction, the second, P_{C1_h}, hysteresis conduction. The first is characterized by independence of a given conduction phenomenon on the past history. The other is characterized by the fact that the character of the conduction depends on past conductions. No more detailed specifications are necessary here. In its simplest form a hysteresis conduction may manifest itself merely by the fact that a given response to a given stimulus is facilitated by repetition. In its most complex manifestations hysteresis conduction may result in most complicated phenomena of learning in higher animals. Whatever physiological or biological theory of learning we accept, whether we consider it based on the existence of self-circuited neurons, as in chapter ix and xiv, or on synaptic changes of a physical or chemical nature[9], or any other different conceivable mechanism, in all of them we deal with hysteresis conduction in the central nervous system. Conduction here is understood not only along a nerve-fiber, but including synaptic transmission as well.

From (C) it follows that there must exist unicellular organisms which exhibit some form of hysteresis conduction. The turning around of a paramecium in a capillary tube with fewer turns after several trials is an example of this (Reference 1, p. 842). Whether we call such phenomenon elementary acts of learning or not, is immaterial. Relationally they are isomorphic to the more complex phenomena of learning in higher animals.

So far as relations between the different P_i's and P_k's are concerned, we have considered only the relation of immediate precedence R, and immediate succession $\breve{R}$, its converse. If we represent S_o and S_P by directed graphs, then we have here a graphical representation of the class of relations R. We can apply to this some standard expressions of the theory of relations, but we so obtain only relatively trivial results[10].

A systematic application of theory of relations to biology and an attempt to build an axiomatic biology on this basis, has been made in the noteworthy researches of J. H. Woodger[11]. Though Woodger's approach differs seemingly very radically from ours, the possibility cannot be denied that the further development of both approaches may establish a number of points of contact between them. In any case, to Woodger belongs the credit of having clearly emphasized the importance of relational aspects in biology and to have made the first systematic mathematical study of these relational aspects.

The principal difficulty found in the present approach is that the graphs of S_P or S_o do not represent merely such simple relations as immediate succession. Two biological properties of which one immediately succeeds the other are usually characterized by other relations, which are more inclusive than the relation R of immediate succession. In chapter xxxiii we shall discuss one possible way out of the difficulty.

No elaborate scientific system can be developed on the basis of one or two general principles only. Other principles or postulates will have to be added in the future to those presented here. Some of them are likely to be of a restricting nature, reducing somewhat the generality of (A) or (C), just as (B) does restrict (A). The principle of maximum simplicity or optimal design, discussed in preceding chapters, may be used as another general mathematical principle, together with the principle of biotopological mapping. The principle of optimal design may possibly eliminate some of the possibilities presented by (A).

It may be asked as to whether we should not expect on the basis of the foregoing to have organisms which are sensitive to X-rays or γ-rays or which can perform other tasks than those so far observed. The answer is in the affirmative, since e.g. sensitivity to γ-rays is included in sensitivity to radiation. Does it then follow that we must predict organisms to develop in the future which will have such properties? Not necessarily.

Through science and technological invention man has found means to detect γ-rays and to perform numerous tasks which no organism can do directly. All such performances we do not consider as part of the biological properties of the human organism. But all such performances are definitely the result of biological manifestations of the human organisms, in particular of the brain. And *relationally* it is quite consistent to extend the notion of organism to include the results of the direct biological properties. Relationally there is no difference between the *Urechis* secreting a mucous bag, which catches food, and then swallowing it, or the spider secreting its web, and a human being manufacturing as a result of his brain-work a machine which processes food and makes it possible for it to be swallowed.

Such an extension of the relational principles will necessitate a more detailed study of relations between organism and surroundings, which thus far have been considered only sketchily. The principle of optimal design may then lead to the conclusion that organisms which perceive X-rays or γ-rays directly, may not develop because it is simpler to develop an appropriate brain, which can invent technological devices for the performance of such tasks, than to develop an organism which performs them directly.

An extension of the relational principles, such as mentioned above, will also include many aspects of social relations, both in man and animals.

Can the principle of bio-topological mapping be incorporated into the scheme of physical laws which govern the organic world? The way to do this would seem to be as follows:

The physicist must derive the possibility of a living molecule or simple small aggregate of molecules, proving its stability as a dynamic system and hence its ability of continued existence. Then it would be necessary to prove a general theorem to the effect that any physical system, derived from such a "primordial" by a transformation rule (A) or another related rule, has the same stability properties. This would reduce the principle of bio-topological mapping to already established physical principles.

REFERENCES

1. C. L. Prosser, *Comparative Animal Physiology.* (Philadelphia, W. B. Saunders Co. 1950).

2. A. J. Carlson and V. Johnson, *The Machinery of the Body.* 4th Ed. (Chicago: The University of Chicago Press, 1953).

3. S. W. Fox and E. Plaisted, "The Precipitability of Two Modified Proteins". *Proc. Soc. Expl. Biol. Med.*, 84, 392, 1953.

4. J. E. Cushing and D. M. Campbell, *Principles of Immunology.* (New York: McGraw-Hill, 1957).

5. W. C. Boyd, *Fundamentals of Immunology.* 3rd Ed. (New York: Interscience Publishers, 1956).

6. W. B. Sherman and P. M. Seebahn, J. Allergy, 21, 414, 1950.

7. J. M. Wallace, "Immunological Properties of Plant Viruses". in *Viruses* (M. Delbrück, Ed.) California Institute of Technology, 1950.

8. S. E. Luria, "Comment of the Paper by J. M. Wallace". *Viruses*, pp. 98-99, 1950, (Ed. by M. Delbrück). (Passadena: California Institute of Technology).

9. A. Shimbel, *Bull. Math. Biophysics,* 12, 241-275, 1950.

10. N. Rashevsky, *Bull. Math. Biophysics,* **20**, 71, 1958.

11. J. H. Woodger, *Axiomatic Method in Biology.* (Cambridge: Cambridge University Press, 1937).

CHAPTER XXX

ORGANISMS AND GRAPHS

We have seen in the preceding chapter, that with the topological space which represents an organism can be associated a graph. In the discussions of chapter xxix this graph played a rather subordinate role. We could completely dispense of it.

In his first attempt to introduce topological considerations into biology, N. Rashevsky[1] began with considerations of graphs, rather than with the set-theoretical approach, as we do here. This graph-theoretical, or so called, combinatorial approach did not lead to the rather large number of verifiable conclusions and to the predictions, which were discussed in chapter xxix. However that approach leads to some other conclusions which at first glance do not seem to follow from the set-theoretical approach. In a new field of science we should not be biased by one particular promising approach, but should try as many different approaches as possible. We shall present in this and the next chapter the combinatorial approach, and show in chapter xxxii how the set-theoretical and the combinatorial approaches are related.

The word "organism" itself provides us with a clue. It derives from the same root as "organization." For organizations in human societies there is a standard, well adapted method of geometric representation: the organization diagram or chart. Topologically it is a one-dimensional complex or graph. Moreover it is a *directed* or oriented graph[2] (c.f. chapter xxviii of vol. I). The relations between the different properties of an organism can also be represented by a graph, and such graphs are not infrequently used in physiology.

Unfortunately, we do not know enough even about the simplest protozoa to describe their graphs in any detail. From the knowledge we have we can, however, make some plausible surmises. Let us see what the graph of a relatively simple organism may look like.

It should first be very strongly emphasized that neither the proposed graph shown in Figure 1 nor the transformation to be discussed presently is to be considered as hypotheses proposed for a development of a theory. As such hypotheses they are definitely not good. They are introduced here only as illustrations of the basic idea. Even when later on in this chapter we discuss some biological implications of the suggested transformation, we do so only to show what kind of biological implications may follow from a future properly selected transformation. It is more than likely that an abstract study of different types of transformations hitherto not studied in topology will have to precede any further development of a biologically applicable theory.

The feeding mechanism begins with the contact of the organism with food, which we represent by the point C in Figure 1. This is followed by the ingestion of food, usually into the food vacuole,

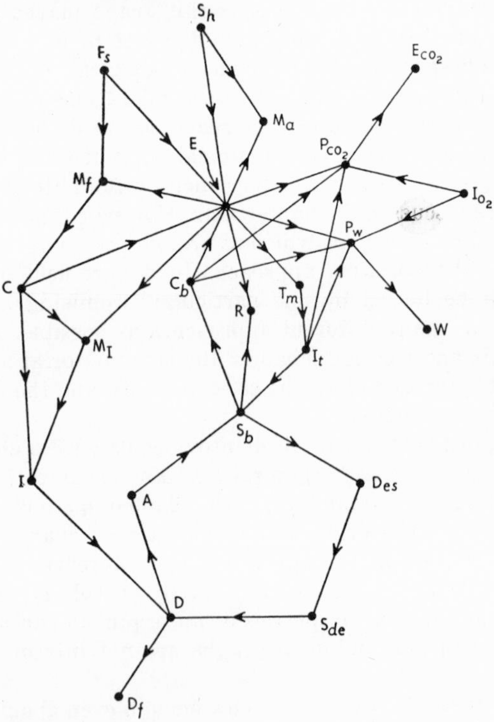

FIG. 1

which process is represented by the point I, the arrow $C \rightarrow I$ indicating that I follows C. The ingested food is digested, digestion D following I. This is followed by the absorption A of the digested food into the protoplasm of the cell, as well as by the rejection of indigestible waste, or excretion D_f. The absorbed food is transported to various parts of the cell where a synthesis S_b of the body of the cell follows. These general synthetic processes result among other things in the synthesis D_{es} of digestive enzymes. This is followed by the secretion S_{de} of the digestive enzymes into the digestive vacuole, where they come into contact with the ingested food, and digestion D results. The directed path $IDAS_bD_{es}S_{de}D$, which contains the cycle $DAS_bD_{es}S_{de}D$, expresses a very fundamental property of every organism: in order that food may be assimilated and the body of the organism synthetized, the organism must be already present. The convergence of the arrows $I \rightarrow D$ and $S_{de} \rightarrow D$ upon the point D expresses that digestion cannot take place without previous ingestion of food, nor can it take place without digestive enzymes, which presuppose the existence of the organism producing them. Similarly, the synthesis S_b needs both a previous absorption A, and a transport of the absorbed substance through the protoplasm of the cell. This inner transport I_t in a protozoan usually takes place by diffusion. However, protoplasmic streamings or other mechanisms may conceivably be possible. The above is expressed by the convergence on S_b of the arrows $I_t \rightarrow S_b$ and $A \rightarrow S_b$. The process S_b is also followed by catabolic processes C_b. At this stage the intake I_{O_2} of oxygen (for aerobic organisms) combines with C_b to produce on one hand a release of energy E, on the other production P_{CO_2} of carbon dioxide, which is followed by the elimination E_{CO_2} of carbon dioxide, as well as the production P_W and the elimination W of other catabolic waste products. Some of the released energy is necessary to maintain the inner transport I_t. If the latter involves any special movements like protoplasmic streamings, then E affects first that movement T_m, and the latter results in I_t, as indicated by the arrows. In the light of present biochemical knowledge[3] we should not regard the liberation of energy as directly connected with oxygen consumption, and, therefore, we do not connect I_{O_2} with E on the graph. This in some cases may be a debatable question, which is, however, not essential for our purposes. The graph on Figure I is rather tentative anyway, and used largely as an illustration.

A stimulus of some kind coming from the food results in the process of stimulation, F_s. How this process acts in a protozoan is little known. In some ways it affects the energy liberation E, and through this it produces certain movements M_f (cilia, flagella, protrusion of pseudopods), which bring the organism in contact C with food. This contact with food again acts as a stimulus, which in a similar way produces some movements M_I which result in food ingestion. A harmful stimulus S_h results in a similar manner in a motion M_a, the avoiding movement. It is very likely that M_f and M_a are in some way connected through a mechanism which produces a reciprocal inhibition of the two functions. We shall not, however, go into this in detail.

Last but not least the body synthesis S_b, as well as the release E of energy, result eventually in the more or less complicated processes R of reproduction.

Thus constructed, the graph of Figure 1 strikes us with its complexity. Yet the true graph of a protozoan is undoubtedly more complex. We have not one digestive enzyme but many, produced through different processes which would be represented by separate points. There is a sensitivity for stimuli of different modalities which again complicates the graph. The synthesis S_b is not a single process, but a series of separate processes.

The determination of the graph of a unicellular organism is ultimately a matter of experimental study. There is, however, a large proportion of aprioriness in our construction, which is due to the generally accepted definition of an organism. For some non-motile bacteria, for example, we may perhaps omit the points F_s, M_f, and M_l. But the chemotropic accumulation of some bacteria in regions of higher oxygen concentration is of the nature of a stimulus-and-response phenomenon. We hardly would speak of something as a living organism if it did not show something essentially similar to the cycle $DAS_bD_{es}S_{de}D$.

If we wish to consider, as some do, that the viruses are living unimolecular parasitic organisms, we can do so mainly because we find for them a fundamentally similar graph. The attachment of the virus to the host cell[4, 5] is due to electrostatic forces. The electrostatic attraction plays the role of the stimulus F_s and results in a movement M_f of the virus toward the host, establishing the contact C. From here on little is known as to what happens in detail. But the lysis of the host is undoubtedly due either to enzymes liberated by the virus molecule, that is, by parts of molecules that are split off from the virus, or else to the virus itself. Certain parts of its surface probably act as lytic enzymes. In either case the enzymatic action is due to previous synthetic activity S_b which produced the virus molecule in question. This synthetic activity must involve intramolecular displacements and deformations, in which the digested food (results of lysis) which must "enter" (point A) the molecule, participates. Thus we have fundamentally the sequence $CDAS_bD_{es}D$ which is obtained from the graph of Figure 1 merely by omitting the points I and S_{de}. But if a penetration of a constitutent part into the virus molecule occurs, then the point I may also be incorporated. Whether through oxidation or otherwise there must be energy liberation by the virus molecule in the course of its life cycle and this implies catabolic processes. This leads to a part of the graph involving the points C_b, E, W, and possibly others. J. von Neumann[6] in his discussion of self-reproducing molecules points out that such a molecule must send out information-carrying units into the surrounding medium to pick out of a mixture of potential building units the proper ones. Add to this that the building units must be first obtained by breaking down *in a proper way* larger units, which are actually given as "food," and we formally come again to a cycle similar to $DAS_bD_{es}S_{de}D$.

We may now restate the principle of biotopological mapping in the following manner: There exists one, or very few, primordial organisms, characterized by their graphs; the graphs of *all* other organisms are obtained from this primordial graph or graphs by a transformation, which contains one or more parameters. Different organisms correspond to the different values of those parameters.

Our problem is to establish within the principle of biotopological mapping proper hypotheses as to the structure of the primordial graph and as to the transformation law. In regard to the first we have already suggested in Figure 1 a possibility which is at present as good as any. In regard to the second part of the problem, observation provides us with a clue. We shall specify our transformation as a set of rules which permits the construction in a unique way of more complicated graphs from the primordial graph.

Consider a colony of n identical cells, thus all having the same graph. The graph of the colony is simply the sum of n identical but distinct graphs, and symbolically we may represent, without loss of generality, the graph of the colony by a single graph of any one cell.

The growth of organisms in complexity proceeds through differentiation of tissues and through their *specialization*. A biological property, f_i, which originally is possessed by all cells, is lost by some of them and retained by others. These other cells are said to have specialized in the property f_i. At the same time as a rule, those cells which lost the biological property f_i specialize in another biological property f_k, which in its turn becomes lost in those cells which specialize in f_i. A "division of biological properties" is thus established, and instead of n identical cells, represented by the original graph, we now have two classes of cells, the cells of one differing from those of the other. The problem is to derive the graph of this organism from the graph of the original homogeneous colony.

We construct first two identical distinct original graphs, i and k (Figure 2a). Since we are dealing now with the transformation

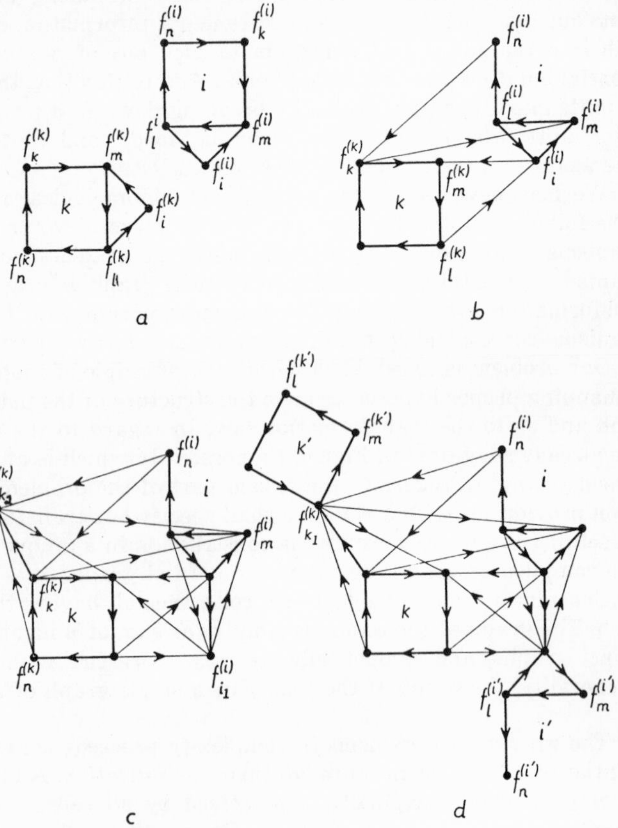

FIG. 2

which should be applicable to *any* primordial graph, the graphs i and k in Figure 2 are drawn without any reference to the hypothetical graph of Figure 1. They are just any arbitrary graphs. Let the parts of the original homogeneous colony which correspond to graph i specialize in f_i, those of the graph k in f_k. In line with the biological fact of specialization, we remove the point f_k from graph i and f_i from graph k (Figure 2b). We shall denote the point f_k belonging to graph i by $f_k^{(i)}$, that belonging to graph k by $f_k^{(k)}$, with similar notations for other points. Since k lost the biological property $f_i^{(k)}$, therefore, this property must be taken over by the property $f_i^{(i)}$ of i. In addition to the connection of $f_i^{(i)}$ in i to the point $f_l^{(i)}$ and $f_m^{(i)}$ we connect $f_i^{(i)}$ to the points $f_l^{(k)}$ and $f_m^{(k)}$ *in the same manner*, that is, since the arrow in i is in the direction $f_l^{(i)} \rightarrow f_i^{(i)}$, the arrow of the new connection is $f_l^{(k)} \rightarrow f_i^{(i)}$. Similarly we have $f_i^{(i)} \rightarrow f_m^{(k)}$. In the same manner $f_k^{(k)}$ is connected to $f_n^{(i)}$ and $f_m^{(i)}$, and we obtain the graph shown in Figure 2b.

This, however, does not describe the biological facts in all their generality. When a group of cells of an organism specializes with respect to a given biological property, the performance of this biological property usually becomes more complicated. The biological property breaks up in several *subsidiary* ones. Thus the specialized eye of a higher animal is much more complicated than the sensitive spot of the protoplasm of an amoeba on which it may be mapped. The number of separate biological properties involved in the process of vision of a higher animal is greater than that involved in the process of light sensitivity of an amoeba.

The simplest assumption which we can make about this increase in number of subsidiary biological properties is that to each lost biological property the cell or tissue acquires one property subsidiary to that in which it specializes. Actually the situation may be more complicated, and to each lost biological property there may be p subsidiary specialized properties added. Or to q lost biological properties a number $w(q)$ subsidiary specialized may be added where $w(q)$ is a mathematical function of q. Since present day knowledge does not give us any reasons to choose between these and other possible assumptions, we shall make here the simplest one. In some cases it is likely to be a sufficiently good approximation to actual facts.

On the basis of this assumption, in the case of Figure 2, the complex i receives an additional subsidiary point $f_{i_1}^{(i)}$, while k receives a point $f_{k_2}^{(k)}$. These we connect to the other points of the graph in the same manner as $f_i^{(i)}$ and $f_k^{(k)}$ respectively. Moreover, we assume that $f_{i_1}^{(i)}$ connects with $f_i^{(i)}$ through $f_i^{(i)} \rightarrow f_{i_1}^{(i)}$, and $f_k^{(k)}$ connects with $f_{k_2}^{(k)}$ through $f_k^{(k)} \rightarrow f_{k_2}^{(k)}$. This latter assumption is again one of the simplest ones, which we adopt provisionally. It may perhaps be more likely to assume two-way connections, such

as

which forms a diangle. But restricting ourselves to the simplest assumption we find the graph of Figure 2c.

The latter graph corresponds to an organism in which two biological properties are specialized and enhanced. The biological property $f_i^{(i)}$ and $f_{i_1}^{(i)}$ are seen to "belong" to the original graph i, those $f_k^{(k)}$ and $f_{k_1}^{(k)}$ to the graph k. Actually, specialization involves not two biological properties but very nearly all of them. Some biological properties, however, notably those connected with synthesis of cell proteins and with energy yielding oxidative processes are not specialized. Thus those tissues which lost the ability to digest food receive digested products from the specialized tissues. But we do not know of a tissue which would have lost the ability for its own synthesis, and would receive ready synthesized product from another tissue. Nor do we know of a tissue which would have lost the ability of performing energy yielding oxidative processes, and would receive the energy needed for the maintenance of its life from other tissues. Thus in the primordial graph there are certain points, which correspond to the biological properties that are never specialized and which, therefore, do not undergo the transformation shown in Figure 2. We shall call those points, which remain unspecialized in a given transformation, *residual points,* and the partial graph composed of them and their connecting arrows the *residual graph.* We shall also speak of *residual biological properties.*

Mathematically a residual graph may not be a connected one, or it may even degenerate into a set of disconnected points. This will happen, for example, if in a square we specialize the two diagonally opposite points. Biologically this would be meaningless. Therefore in what follows we assume that the residual graph is connected.

The subsidiary specialized biological properties are each performed by special cells or tissues, which retain their own residual biological properties. Therefore, in the case of Figure 2, the points $f_{i_1}^{(i)}$ and $f_{k_1}^{(k)}$ must be each connected to a residual graph, which in this case is composed of f_l, f_m, and f_n. Thus finally we obtain the graph of Figure 2d, in which the residual graphs are designated by i' and k'.

From the very simple graph of Figure 2a we arrived by a transformation, which in essence describes the process of cell and tissue specialization, to the very complicated graph 2d. True enough, we made a number of assumptions, but they were the simplest compatible with observations and were largely generalizations drawn from those observations. The results become even more complicated when we generalize the transformation so as to describe the specialization of m biological properties by m cell-types. The situation is further complicated by the fact that we must consider the specialization of a class of cells not in one property, but in a group of biological properties. Thus in the simplest metazoa we notice the specialization of the ectoderm and entomesoderm in the whole group of animal, respectively vegetative functions. Following the same argument as before, the transformation rules can be stated thus:

Let n biological properties f, all arbitrarily numbered from 1 to n, become specialized in m groups of $n_1, n_2, \ldots, n_m$ points each. We have $\Sigma\, n_r = n$. Let group i specialize in n_i biological properties f_l, where l designates one of the n_i points, and lose $n - n_i$ biological properties f_k, where k designates one of the $n - n_i$ points. The $n - n_i$ biological properties f_k are divided into $m - 1$ groups, each consisting of $n_1, n_2, \ldots n_{i-1}, n_{i+1}, \ldots n_m$ points respectively. We now formulate the following transformation rules $T^{(1)}$:

$T_1^{(1)}$. Draw m distinct primordial graphs. The number m is a parameter of the transformation.

$T_2^{(1)}$. Remove from a graph i $(i = 1, 2, \ldots m)$ those $n - n_i$ points which correspond to its lost biological properties.

$T_3^{(1)}$. Connect each specialized point $f_l^{(i)}$ of a graph i to those remaining points $f_p^{(k)}$ of each graph k $(k = 1, 2, \ldots i - 1, i + 1, \ldots m)$ which correspond to those points $f_p^{(i)}$ of graph i to which $f_l^{(i)}$ is connected, preserving the directions of connections.

$T_4^{(1)}$. Choose a distribution of $n - n_i$ elements into n_i sets, so that the lth set has a number $\nu_l^{(i)}$ of elements with

$$\sum_{l=1}^{n_i} \nu_l^{(i)} = n - n_i\,. \qquad (1)$$

Some of the $\nu_l^{(i)}$'s may be zeroes. This will always happen when $n_i > n - n_i$. This arbitrary chosen distribution plays the role of another parameter of the transformation. A third parameter is the choice of the n_r's.

$T_5^{(1)}$. In a graph i add $n - n_i$ subsidiary points, and divide them into n_i sets containing each $\nu_l^{(i)}$ points. Connect each of the $\nu_l^{(i)}$ points of a set to all the other points in the same way as the specialized point $f_l^{(i)}$ is connected to them, preserving the directions of connections and also make the connections

$$f_l^{(i)} \to f_{l,1}^{(i)} \to \ldots f_{l^{(i)}\nu_l^{(i)}} \,. \tag{2}$$

$T_6^{(1)}$. Connect each point $f_{l,r}^{(i)}$ $(r = 1, 2, \ldots \nu_l^{(i)})$ to a residual graph in the same manner as $f_l^{(i)}$ is connected to its own residual graph.

The complexity of the graph thus obtained seems to defy any visualization. But so does the complexity of a higher living organism. In fact, the circumstance that a set of rather simple transformation rules applied to a relatively simple original graph leads to such a complicated result possibly indicates that we are on the right track.

We shall denote the primordial graph by P, the transformed one by $T^{(1)}(P)$. When reference is made to one of the m primordial graphs of which $T^{(1)}(P)$ is composed according to $T_1^{(1)}$, we shall speak of the *component primordial graph,* to distinguish it from the primordial P.

Let us now see how *a graph thus obtained can be mapped on the original graph.*

The transformed graph contains the m original residual graphs, according to $T_1^{(1)}$. In addition, each of the specialized points gives rise to ν_l subsidiary points. Each of the m primordial graphs receives $n - n_i$ subsidiary points, according to $T_5^{(1)}$. The total number of subsidiary points is, therefore,

$$\sum_{i=1}^{i=m} (n - n_i) = n(m-1). \tag{3}$$

Each of those, according to $T_6^{(1)}$ is connected to its own residual graph. Thus there are altogether $m + n(m-1)$ residual graphs. Since they are all identical and each is a partial graph of the primordial, therefore, all corresponding points and lines may be mapped on the corresponding points and lines of the partial graph of the primordial, in an $m + n(m-1)$ to one mapping.

Of the non-residual points, each $f_l^{(i)}$ has given rise to $\nu_l + 1$ points $f_l^{(i)}, f_{l,1}^{(i)}, \ldots, f_{l,\nu_l^{(i)}}$. Each of these can be mapped on the tion $f_{i,r}^{(i)} \to f_q^{(k)}$ can be mapped on the connection $f_i \to f_q$ of the primordial graph. The connections (2) are all mapped on the zero connection of a point to itself. In other words, all lines (2) are mapped onto one point.

In the present discussion we consider a graph as a one-dimensional "multiply connected" space, and ascribe geometrical reality to all its lines. As we have seen in chapter xxviii, any two continuous lines can be mapped continuously on each other. If we take care in the above mapping to map all lines of $T^{(1)}$ continuously on the corresponding lines of the primordial graph, then the whole mapping is a continuous one.

We now shall prove

Theorem 1. The transformation rules $T^{(1)}$, when applied to two different primordial graphs, result, for the same choice of the parameters, in different graphs.

We define two graphs as different if either one of them contains at least one connection which is not contained in the other. Connections $a \rightarrow b$ and $b \rightarrow a$ are considered as different.

Consider two different primordial graphs, *I* and *II*. Let f_1f_2 be a connection of *I*, not contained in *II*. Suppose f_1f_2 belongs to the residual partial graph. Since the transformed graph contains $m + n(m - 1)$ residual graphs, therefore, there will be $m + n(m - 1)$ connections in the transformed graph *I* which are not contained in the transformed graph *II*. The two will be different. Let now f_1f_2 connect in *I* either two specialized points or a specialized point with a point of the residual graph. In the transformed graph of *I* there will be a connection between the points that are mapped on f_1 and f_2 correspondingly, according to $T_5^{(1)}$. But in the transformed graph *II* there will be no such connections. Hence the two graphs are different.

Theorem 1 is important because it demonstrates the verifiability and predictive value of the theory. From that theorem there follows as a corollary that it is possible to determine in principle the original primordial graph, if a given transformed graph and the transformation rules are known. This possibility in principle is, however, of no practical value, because of the tremendous complexity of the graphs of the higher organisms. The following theorem 2 is of more practical value.

Theorem 2. The transformation rules T transform any partial graph of the primordial in such a way that points of the transformed graph which correspond to the points of the original are connected in the same manner as those of the original.

The theorem is again a consequence of $T_5^{(1)}$.

Because of that theorem, we may choose an experimentally

convenient small number of biological properties in an organism, and compare the partial graph to the corresponding partial of the primordial.

As remarked above, a directed cycle, as one in Figure 3a, implies fundamentally the self-perpetuation of a set of properties, and the impossibility of perpetuation when any member of the set is missing. In the circuit of Figure 3b the convergence of arrows on f_1 may mean either that the biological property f_1 can be manifested only if f_2 or f_3 are both manifested, or if either of them is.

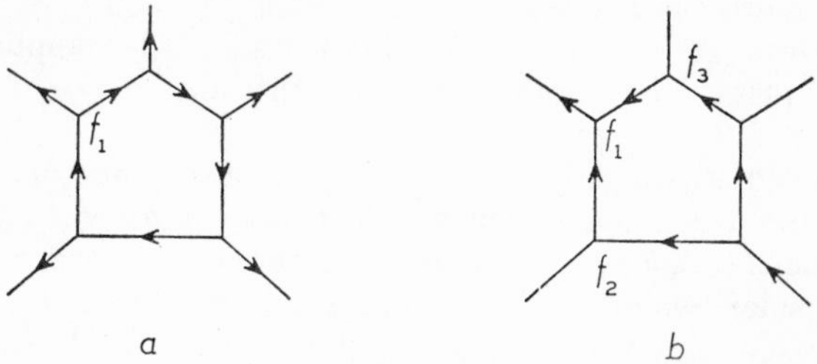

FIG. 3

In the second instance the circuit implies an extra stability, a coefficient of safety. One of the next steps in the development of the theory of biotopologic mappings is to study how the transformation $T^{(1)}$ affects circuits of different types.

It must be kept in mind that the transformation $T^{(1)}$ does not determine the physicochemical nature of the subsidiary points. Thus the secretion of an inactive substance may give rise in the process of the specialization to the secretion of venom by a snake, or to the secretion of odorous substances, as in the case of a skunk. The specialization of some metabolic processes may lead to a subsidiary point which represents a chemoluminescent reaction in some animals, though in others the subsidiary point may represent a non-luminous reaction. The biologist determines the biological homology of some apparently diverse functions from comparative anatomical and physiological studies. The studies of the organism's graph together with the knowledge of the proper transformation may be of great help in those problems.

The transformation $T^{(1)}$ does not, of course, tell the whole story. It may be applied in steps. First one or a few biological properties become specialized, then others. Some general rule must now be looked for, which determines the sequence of different steps. Again we have some clues in observation. The earliest specialization seems to be in the separation of the two groups of biological properties, the animal and vegetative. This separation is closely related with the formation of the two embryonic layers — the ectoderm and the entomesoderm, which are the only two layers in *Coelenterata*. A differentiation of the mesoderm begins with *Platyhelminthes* and marks the next step.

To illustrate what we mean by such a rule which determines the sequence of steps, let us give here a hypothetical example, which, most likely, has no meaning in reality. It is conceivable that at first a given group of biological properties in the "animal" partial graph begins to specialize, and that the specialization of other properties comes the later, the greater their distance, measured in terms of minimum number of intermediate points, is from a given point.

One interesting consequence of the proposed $T^{(1)}$ must be noted. While the number of possible transformed graphs is very large (we shall discuss it in the next chapter), it is nevertheless finite. When, with the exception of the residual biological properties, all others are completely specialized, so that every tissue corresponds to only one specialized biological property, the process stops.

The question is whether the application of $T^{(1)}$ does stop here, or whether it can now be applied to this higher unit, perhaps with a different choice of parameters. In other words, we can now consider the final transformed graph as a primordial or as a starting point of the transformation $T^{(1)}$. Now the specializable biological properties may be different, but the transformation rule remains the same. If this is so, we obtain in this way a set of graphs, which connect higher organisms in their interreaction, much in the same way as the cells are connected in an organism. In other words we construct graphs of social relations. In human society the division of labor and social differentiation are not connected with physiological and anatomical differentiation. This is rather the exception than the rule. In insect societies social and biological differentiations are sometimes observed together.

These considerations bring out, however, another aspect of the problem. We see that some primordial cell may be considered as a unit of first order, while a metazoan plays the role of a unit of second order, being in the same relation to a social aggregate as a cell is to the organism. We also noticed the high complexity of the graph of even a simple protozoan. Is it not possible that the graph of a cell is already a transform of a graph of a living unit of smaller order, say, a living molecule? Evidence for or against such a possibility may be obtained by an experimental study of some partial graphs of a cell with the application of theorem 2. We have already remarked that certain points, for example, S_b, D_{es}, C_b in Figure 1 actually stand for several points each. If those several points are subsidiary points then by theorem 2 each subsidiary point belonging to, say, S_b should be connected with each other point of the graph in the same way. Whether this is so can in principle be verified by physiological and biochemical experiments. If the experiments confirm the above, then on the basis of the principle of biotopological mapping we will have to conclude that there exists a lower primordial graph, perhaps that of a living "undifferentiated" molecule. Such a living molecule would perform the essential living functions (cf. p. 347). Then it may gradually differentiate and form a complicated aggregate of molecules, which all perform different functions.

In connection with this possibility, one would naturally think of viruses. All evidence, however, indicates that viruses are derived from cells, rather than vice versa[4, 5]. Also the parasitic nature of viruses precludes them from being considered as the primordial organisms. The idea of "naked genes," as primordial organisms has, however, been suggested. The big problem is why, if such primordial organisms exist, we do not find them now. In this connection we may point out that should a living virus-like molecule exist which "feeds" on dead organic matter or even on inorganic matter like an autotrophic plant, it may easily escape detection. Viruses were discovered by their effects. If putrefaction, for example, is affected by some submicroscopic organism, but if it is also usually produced by bacteria, due to their universal presence, then, unless very precise quantitative measurements of all metabolic rates involved are made nothing will suggest the presence of the unknown organisms. In any case the study of partial graphs of some cells will contribute to this important question.

If we choose a different primordial graph, or a different transformation, or both, we shall in general be led to different conclusions. Each choice gives us an abstract system of biology, within the framework of the general principle of biotopological mapping. Our goal is to find a system which is isomorphic, or as nearly isomorphic as possible, with the actual biological world. In order to eventually reach this goal, it may well be necessary to develop first a general theory of such abstract systems of biology. The system based on the primordial which may be given by the graph of Figure 1 and on the transformation $T^{(1)}$ is just one of the infinite number of possible ones, just as Euclidean geometry is only one of an infinite number of possible geometries. An abstract study of the systems of geometry of necessity preceded their application to the physical universe. A study of the abstract systems of biology will possibly have to precede any fruitful application of topology to biology.

In line with this idea we shall now study some different transformations, as well as a slightly different manner of representation of an organism by a graph.

Leaving the discussion of the primordial graph still on a purely abstract theoretical level, let us nevertheless discuss some possible modifications and improvements over the graph proposed above.

There is one process in even the simplest organism which occupies a somewhat special position both biologically and topologically. Even a simple cell is not homogeneous, and the different biological and biochemical reactions take place in different parts of the cell. A connection between such processes is made possible only by transport phenomena. The principal mediator of transport is diffusion, though sometimes convection may play a part.

To indicate that a reaction f_k cannot take place without the reaction f_i previously taking place, but that f_k also needs a transport f_T of reaction products from the site of f_i to that of f_k, we symbolically made converge on the representative point of f_k two

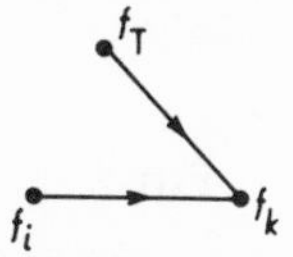

FIG. 4

arrows: one connecting f_i and f_k, the other connecting the representative point f_T of the transport to f_k, as illustrated on Figure 4. With this method of representation the assumption is made that in the primordial graph a biological property is manifested only if *all* the immediately preceding biological properties are manifested.

The method of representation illustrated in Figure 4 has obvious disadvantages. The direct connection $f_i \rightarrow f_k$ does not mean the same thing as the direct connection $f_l \rightarrow f_m$ between representative points of two reactions of which one follows the other without transport. Yet topologically the two connections are of the same kind. If transport takes place by convection, then the same convection current designated by a representative point f_T (Figure 5) may carry the end products of reaction f_i to the site of f_k, as well as the end product of reaction f_r to the site of f_s, resulting in a diagram shown in Figure 5. That graph does not indicate clearly that f_T stands for the transport of two different substances by the same means.

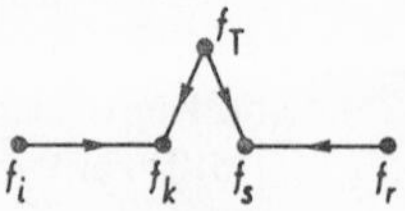

FIG. 5

We shall, therefore, introduce a different possible method of representation which obviates those shortcomings. The proposed new representation will have particular advantages when we discuss the transport in a differentiated organism represented by a transformed graph.

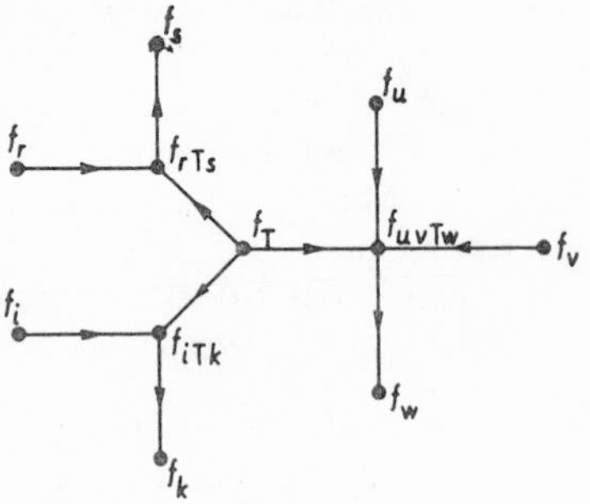

FIG. 6

We represent the general notion of transport by a representative point f_T (Figure 6). This transport may carry different substances from different sites and involving different reactions f_i. If the end products of the reaction f_i are transported to the site of f_k, we represent the transport of that particular product by a point f_{iTk}. Since that particular phase of the transport cannot take place without the existence of the general transport mechanism f_T, we therefore make the connection $f_T \rightarrow f_{iTk}$ as in Figure 6. Then we make the connection $f_{iTk} \rightarrow f_k$. If there is a transport between two other reactions represented by the points f_r and f_s, we represent it by the point f_{rTs} and again make the connections $f_T \rightarrow f_{rTs}$ and $f_r \rightarrow f_{rTs} \rightarrow f_s$.

A situation may arise where a reaction represented by f_w will take place only if end products of *two* other reactions f_u and f_v are transported to the site of f_w. The transport of the two kinds of end products is represented by the point f_{uvTw} (Figure 6), with the connections: $f_T \rightarrow f_{uvTw}$; $f_u \rightarrow f_{uvTw}$; $f_v \rightarrow f_{uvTw}$; and $f_{uvTw} \rightarrow f_w$.

In line with this method of representing transport phenomena, let us consider as an illustration only the following possible primordial graph. For convenience we use new numbers for the subscripts of the points f_i. The biological property represented by each point is explained in the text.

Ingestion f_1 (Figure 7) is followed by digestion f_2 which leads on one hand to excretion f_3 and on the other to absorption f_4. The absorbed materials are transported via f_{4T5} to the sites of synthetic processes f_5. Then the synthesis of digestive enzymes, represented by f_6, follows via transport f_{5T6}. Those enzymes are transported via f_{6T7} to the site of secretion, represented by f_7, and digestion f_2 again follows.

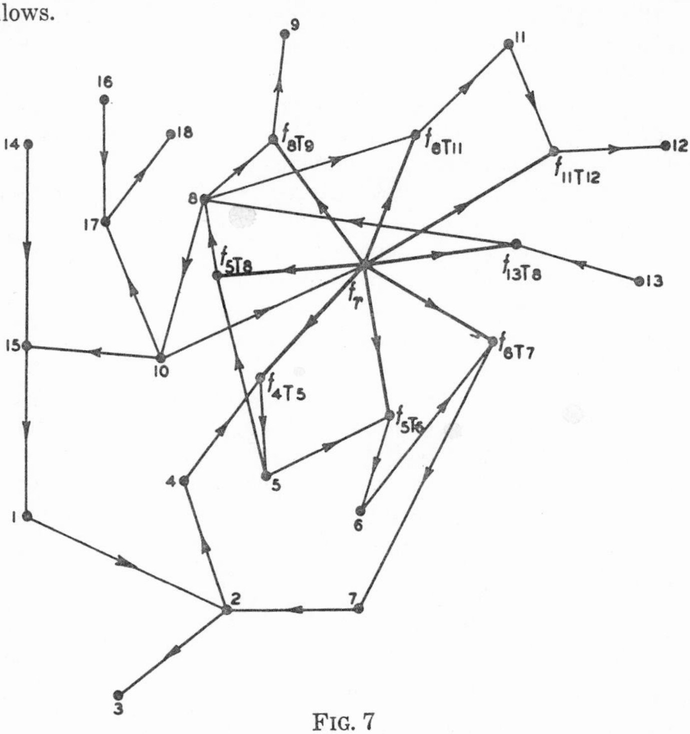

FIG. 7

On the other hand, some of the synthetized products are transported via f_{5T8} to the site of the catabolic processes, which are represented by f_8. Products of catabolism are transported via f_{8T9} to the site of elimination of waste products, and there elimination, represented by f_9, takes place. Catabolic processes result in the liberation of energy, represented by f_{10}, which in turn provides the possibility of transport f_T. On the other hand, after a transport f_{8T11} the catabolic reactions give rise to the production f_{11} of CO_2. the latter is transported within the cell via f_{11T12}, and this eventually results in the elimination of CO_2, this process being represented by f_{12}.

The intake of O_2 from the outside, represented by f_{13}, results in a transport of O_2 to the sites of different reactions involved in catabolic processes[3]. Liberation of energy combined with anabolic processes as well as with other biological properties results in the process of multiplication, which is not indicated in Figure 6 to simplify the latter.

All the above discussed biological properties belong to the class of vegetative functions. A partial graph of the animal functions may be represented as follows:

A stimulus f_{14} combined with energy release f_{10} results in some kind of protoplasmic motility f_{15} which leads to the ingestion f_1. A different kind of stimulus f_{16}, combined with energy release f_{10}, results in a different set of motility processes f_{17} which produce an avoidance reaction f_{18}.

The primordial graph suggested here is different from the one discussed as a possibility and possibly somewhat more realistic. It is, however, still as schematized as the other. We still omit a tremendous number of biochemical reactions of an enzyme nature which are connected to the different biological properties shown in Figure 7. The omission of a number of points, while making the graph much simpler, is not necessarily objectionable in principle. What is left after such an omission is a partial graph, and if we use the transformation $T^{(1)}$, we can apply theorem 2 and thus derive some properties of the corresponding partial graph of higher organisms.

A more serious objection is the already mentioned circumstance, that some points of the suggested primordial stand actually for possibly a very large number of points that are interconnected in an intricate manner. Thus point f_5 represents actually a very complex set of reactions in which very large numbers of different organic substances are synthetized. If those different points are specialized in different tissues, then the permissibility of such a "lumping" of whole partial graphs into one point may be seriously questioned. This problem will be discussed below after a study of different transformations.

In discussing the transformations of the primordial graph, we considered that all points of the primordial are divided in two classes: specializable and residual points. We considered the situation in which a biological property when specialized by one cell type is lost in all other cell types. While this is true with respect to some biological properties, it is definitely not true for all of them. Such biological properties as transport, intake of oxygen, elimination of CO_2, and elimination of other waste products are retained by all cells, although in higher organisms specialized organs possess those biological properties for the organism as a whole. Such biological properties we shall call *specialized residual*. A closer examination reveals that they are not as numerous as the above list suggests.

While it is true that every cell of a higher organism takes in oxygen, this intake is different from that of a protozoan because the latter receives the oxygen from the inorganic environment directly, whereas each cell of a higher organism takes in oxygen from blood which, while being exterior to the cell, is nevertheless an integral part of the organism. The specialized organs, such as gills or lungs, retain the property of taking up oxygen directly from the extraorganismic inorganic environment. The same holds about elimination of carbon dioxide and of other waste products. A somewhat different position is occupied by digestive processes. In the highest animals all digestion occurs extracellularly in a specialized organ (the intestinal tract) so that practically all other cells have lost the ability of intracellular digestion. In lower forms, such as *Platyhelminthes, Nemertea,* and others, which do possess a more or less differentiated and specialized gastrointestinal tract, digestion takes place partly intracellularly, partly extracellularly. Thus in spite of specialization not all cells lose the intracellular digestive functions.

We must, however, keep in mind that even intracellular digestion is extra-protoplasmic, occuring in the digestive vacuole. Technically the digestive vacuole is inside the cell. Yet it is not part of the living protoplasm. In bacteria digestion takes place partly extracellularly. Thus we may say that what is actually specialized in a higher organism is the secretion of digestive enzymes, represented by f_7 in Figure 7. The process of digestion is basically an external process. All other cells of the organism lose the ability of secreting digestive enzymes though some specialize in their production. Thus f_7 is a specializable point, and it may be said that f_2 and f_7 always specialize in the same organ.

What actually happens in the case of oxygen intake or carbon dioxide elimination is that those two biological properties are specialized by an organ consisting of several tissues and that first oxygen is carried by the intracellular transport of those tissues then taken over by the specialized general transport, if it exists, then taken over again by the intracellular transport of each cell and carried there to the site of f_8 (Figure 7) or any other appropriate site. It is, therefore, more appropriate and rigorous to designate f_{13} as the point representing intake of oxygen from inorganic environment, f_{12} as representing elimination of carbon dioxide into inorganic extraorganismic environment, and so forth.

The organ *par excellence* of the specialized transport in animals is the circulatory system proper. However, the lymphatic system as well as the interstitial fluids may, in general, be considered as part of the specialized transport. There remains the important question as to whether the properties of the vascular system, the lymphatic system, and the interstitial fluids are to be considered as specializations of three distinct transport properties present in the primordial graph, or whether they are biological properties which correspond to different subsidiary points in the specialization of a single biological property, that of general transport. The latter view appears to be more attractive. However, only further detailed studies of different possible transformations will enable us to decide the above question. Whenever we shall speak of specialized transport in this chapter, we shall explicitely understand the cardiovascular transport. But we do not commit ourselves here as to whether to consider the lymphatic system as being represented by subsidiary points or not.

Thus, the only specializable residual points of the graph of Figure 7 are the transport points f_T and the f_{iTk}'s. Their specialization may be described in the same manner as that of other points. In other words, if for example the sth component primordial graph specializes in all or some of the transport points, it loses some of the other specializable points, and a corresponding number of subsidiary points is added to the specialized residual points which represent the transport. Although biologically apparently either all or no transport properties specialize, yet mathematically we may consider the case in which only some of the points f_T, f_{iTk} specialize.

In the ith component primordial graph which specializes in some non-transport points only, we now connect each specialized point $f_l^{(i)}$ not necessarily directly with those remaining points $f_p^{(k)}$ of each graph k $(k = 1, 2, \ldots i - 1, i + 1, \ldots, m)$ which correspond to those points $f_p^{(i)}$ of graph i to which $f_l^{(i)}$ is connected. We do this only if $f_p^{(k)}$ is *not* a transport point. If it is, in other words, if $f_p^{(k)} = f^{(k)}{}_{lT\ldots}$ or $f_p^{(k)} = f^{(k)}{}_{\ldots Tl}$, where the dots stand for some other letters, and if no transport points are specialized, then, in line with what was said above, we connect $f_{lT}^{(i)}\ldots$ to all $f_{lT}^{(k)}\ldots$'s, in such a manner that

$$f_l^{(i)} \rightarrow f^{(i)}{}_{lT}\ldots \rightarrow f^{(k)}{}_{lT}\ldots \tag{4}$$

would be a directed way from $f_l^{(i)}$ to $f^{(k)}{}_{lT}\ldots$. Or if $f_p^{(k)} = f^{(k)}\ldots{}_{Tl}$, then we connect $f^{(i)}\ldots{}_{Tl}$ to all $f^{(k)}\ldots{}_{Tl}$ in such a manner as to have a directed way

$$f^{(k)}\ldots{}_{Tl} \rightarrow f^{(i)}\ldots{}_{Tl} \rightarrow f_l^{(i)}. \tag{5}$$

If, however, the transport point $f_{lT}\ldots$ or $f\ldots{}_{Tl}$ is specialized, say in the sth component primordial, then we connect $f^{(i)}{}_{lT}\ldots$ (resp. $f^{(i)}\ldots{}_{Tl}$) first to $f^{(s)}{}_{lT}\ldots$ (resp. $f^{(s)}\ldots{}_{Tl}$) and to all its subsidiary points $f^{(s)}{}_{lT\ldots,\alpha}$ (resp. $f^{(s)}\ldots{}_{Tl,\alpha}$); $[\alpha = 1, 2, \ldots, \nu^{(s)}{}_{lT}\ldots$; or $\alpha = 1, 2, \ldots, \nu^{(s)}\ldots{}_{Tl}]$ and then connect $f^{(s)}{}_{lT}\ldots$ (resp. $f^{(s)}\ldots{}_{Tl}$) and all the subsidiary points to each $f^{(k)}{}_{lT}\ldots$ (resp. $f^{(k)}\ldots{}_{lT}$) in such a manner that a set of directed ways

$$f^{(i)}{}_{lT}\ldots \rightarrow f^{(s)}{}_{lT}\ldots \rightarrow f^{(k)}{}_{lT}\ldots \text{ and } f^{(i)}{}_{lT}\ldots \rightarrow$$

$$f^{(s)}{}_{lT\ldots,\alpha} \rightarrow f^{(k)}{}_{lT\ldots,\alpha} \tag{6}$$

respectively

$$f^{(i)}\ldots{}_{Tl} \leftarrow f^{(s)}\ldots{}_{Tl} \leftarrow f^{(k)}\ldots{}_{Tl} \text{ and}$$

$$f^{(i)}\ldots{}_{Tl,\alpha} \leftarrow f^{(s)}\ldots{}_{Tl,\alpha} \leftarrow f^{(k)}\ldots{}_{Tl,\alpha} \tag{7}$$

would be formed. Thus each specialized biological property which is preceded or followed by transport is connected to others via transport in its own cell type, systemic transport, and transport in each of the kth cell types.

We now shall formulate a number of transformation rules, which are different from the rules $T_i^{(1)}$ given on p. 353.

Instead of connecting the subsidiary points in this manner

$$f_l^{(i)} \rightarrow f^{(i)}{}_{l,1} \rightarrow \ldots f^{(i)}{}_{l,\nu_l^{(i)}} \tag{8}$$

we may connect them thus:

$$f_l^{(i)} \leftarrow f^{(i)}{}_{l,1} \leftarrow \ldots f^{(i)}{}_{l,\nu_l^{(i)}} \tag{9}$$

Or we may connect them thus:

$$f_l^{(i)} \rightleftarrows f^{(i)}{}_{l,1} \rightleftarrows \ldots f^{(i)}{}_{l,\nu_l^{(i)}} \tag{10}$$

Finally we may not connect the subsidiary points to each other at all, connecting them only to those points to which $f_l^{(i)}$ is connected. We shall symbolically denote this by

$$f_l^{(i)} \ldots f^{(i)}{}_{l,\,1} \ldots f^{(i)}{}_{l,\,\nu_l^{(i)}} \tag{11}$$

Instead of connecting a specialized point with its subsidiary points "in series" as indicated by (8), (9), or (10), we may connect them "in parallel," and this in three different ways. Either we make the connection

$$f_l^{(i)} \rightarrow f^{(i)}{}_{l,\,1};\, f_l^{(i)} \rightarrow f^{(i)}{}_{l,\,2};\, \ldots f_l^{(i)} \rightarrow f^{(i)}{}_{l,\,\nu_l^{(i)}} \tag{12}$$

or the connections

$$f_l^{(i)} \leftarrow f^{(i)}{}_{l,\,1};\, f_l^{(i)} \leftarrow f^{(i)}{}_{l,\,2};\, f_l^{(i)} \leftarrow f^{(i)}{}_{l,\,\nu_l^{(i)}} \tag{13}$$

or, finally

$$f_l^{(i)} \leftrightarrows f^{(i)}{}_{l,\,1};\, \ldots f_l^{(i)} \rightleftarrows f^{(i)}{}_{l,\,\nu_l^{(i)}} \tag{14}$$

We now define the following transformations:

$T^{(2)}$ is identical with $T^{(1)}$, except that (9) is substituted for (8).
$T^{(3)}$ is identical with $T^{(1)}$, except that (10) is substituted for (8).
$T^{(4)}$ is identical with $T^{(1)}$, except that (11) is substituted for (8).
$T^{(5)}$ is identical with $T^{(1)}$, except that (12) is substituted for (8).
$T^{(6)}$ is identical with $T^{(1)}$, except that (13) is substituted for (8).
$T^{(7)}$ is identical with $T^{(1)}$, except that (14) is substituted for (8).

Now we define a transformation $T^{(8)}$ in line with the discussion preceding the definitions of $T^{(2)} \ldots T^{(7)}$.

Let n biological properties f, all arbitrarily numbered from 1 to n, become specialized in m groups of $n_1, n_2, \ldots, m_m$ points each. We have as before

$$\Sigma\, n_r = n;\, n_r > 0. \tag{15}$$

Let group i specialize in n_i biological properties f_l, where l designates one of the n_i points. Since, in general, n may include some of the transport properties which are both specializable and residual, therefore, now the number of points lost in group i is not necessarily $n - n_i$. We shall denote it by $\bar{n}_i$. We have

$$\bar{n}_i \leqslant n - n_i, \tag{16}$$

because transport points are included in the n points, but they are never lost.

Let f_k designate one of the $\bar{n}_i$ lost biological properties.

The transformation rules for $T^{(8)}$ are:

$T_1^{(8)}$. Draw m distinct primordial graphs. The number m is a parameter of the transformation.

$T_2^{(8)}$. Remove from graph i ($i = 1, 2, \ldots, m$) those $\bar{n}_i$ points which correspond to its lost biological properties.

$T_3^{(8)}$. (1). If $f_p^{(k)}$ is a remaining point of one of the $m - 1$ graphs k ($k = 1, 2, \ldots, n_{i-1}, n_{i+1}, \ldots, m$), which corresponds to a point $f_p^{(i)}$ to which $f_l^{(i)}$ is connected, and if $f_p^{(i)}$ is not a transport point, then connect $f_l^{(i)}$ to each such $f_p^{(k)}$, preserving the directions of connections between $f_l^{(i)}$ and $f_p^{(i)}$.
(2). If an $f_p^{(i)}$ is a transport point $f^{(i)}{}_{lT\ldots}$ or $f^{(i)}{}_{\ldots Tl}$ and if no transport points are specialized, then connect $f^{(i)}{}_{lT\ldots}$ (resp. $f^{(i)}{}_{\ldots Tl}$) to all points $f^{(k)}{}_{lT\ldots}$ (resp. $f^{(k)}{}_{\ldots Tl}$), preserving the directions of connections, in other words so that expression (1), respectively (2) would hold.
(3). If an $f_p^{(i)}$ is a transport point $f^{(i)}{}_{lT\ldots}$ (resp. $f^{(i)}{}_{\ldots Tl}$) and if that point is specialized in the sth graph, then connect $f^{(i)}{}_{lT\ldots}$ (resp. $f^{(i)}{}_{\ldots Tl}$) to $f^{(s)}{}_{lT\ldots}$ (resp. $f^{(s)}{}_{\ldots Tl}$) and the latter to each $f^{(k)}{}_{lT\ldots}$ (resp. $f^{(k)}{}_{\ldots Tl}$) ($k = 1, 2, \ldots, n_{i-1}, n_{i+1}, \ldots, m$) so as to have a directed way from $f^{(i)}{}_{lT\ldots}$ to $f^{(k)}{}_{lT\ldots}$ (resp. from $f^{(i)}{}_{\ldots Tl}$ to $f^{(k)}{}_{\ldots Tl}$).

$T_4^{(8)}$. Choose a distribution of n_i elements into n_i sets, so that the lth set has a number $\nu_l^{(i)}$ of elements with

$$\sum_{l=1}^{n_i} \nu_l^{(i)} = \bar{n}_i\,. \tag{17}$$

Some of the $\nu_l^{(i)}$ may be zero. This will always happen when $n_i > \bar{n}_i$. This arbitrarily chosen distribution plays a role of another parameter of the transformation. A third parameter is the choice of the n_r's.

$T_5^{(8)}$. In graph i add $\bar{n}_i$ subsidiary points and divide them into n_i sets containing each $\nu_l^{(i)}$ points. Connect each of the $\nu_l^{(i)}$ points of a set to all other points to which the specialized point $f_l^{(i)}$ is connected, in the same way as $f_l^{(i)}$ is connected to them, preserving the directions of connections, and also make the connections

$$f_l^{(i)} \rightarrow f^{(i)}{}_{l,\,1} \rightarrow \ldots f^{(i)}{}_{l,\,\nu_l^{(i)}}\,. \tag{18}$$

$T_6^{(8)}$. Connect each point $f^{(i)}{}_{l,r}$ ($r = 1, 2, \ldots, \nu_l^{(i)}$) to a residual graph in the same manner as $f_l^{(i)}$ is connected to its own residual graph.

Application of $T_5^{(8)}$ to the component primordial graph in which transport points are specialized insures connections (6) and (7) automatically.

In a similar manner as we obtained transformations $T^{(2)} \ldots T^{(7)}$ from $T^{(1)}$, we can obtain six other transformations $T^{(9)} \ldots T^{(14)}$ from $T^{(8)}$. We list them here:

$T^{(9)}$ is obtained from $T^{(8)}$ by substituting (9) for (18) in $T_5^{(8)}$.
$T^{(10)}$ is obtained from $T^{(8)}$ by substituting (10) for (18) in $T_5^{(8)}$.
$T^{(11)}$ is obtained from $T^{(8)}$ by substituting (11) for (18) in $T_5^{(8)}$.
$T^{(12)}$ is obtained from $T^{(8)}$ by substituting (12) for (18) in $T_5^{(8)}$.
$T^{(13)}$ is obtained from $T^{(8)}$ by substituting (13) for (18) in $T_5^{(8)}$.
$T^{(14)}$ is obtained from $T^{(8)}$ by substituting (14) for (18) in $T_5^{(8)}$.

It is clear that from a biological point of view $T^{(8)} \ldots T^{(14)}$ are much more realistic than $T^{(1)} \ldots T^{(7)}$.

Let us see now how $T^{(8)}$ (P) maps onto the primordial graph P. The transformed graph contains m component primordials. In addition each specialized point gives rise to ν_l subsidiary points. Each of the m primordial graphs receives $\bar{n}_i$ subsidiary points according to $T_5^{(8)}$. The total number of subsidiary points is, therefore,

$$\sum_{i=1}^{i=m} \bar{n}_i. \tag{19}$$

Let n_T denote the total number of transport points in the primordial graph. In Figure 7, for example, $n_T = 9$. Let n_{Ti} denote the number of specialized transport points in the ith component primordial. Then

$$\sum_{i=1}^{i=m} n_{Ti} = n_T. \tag{20}$$

We now have

$$\bar{n}_i = n - n_i - (n_T - n_{Ti}). \tag{21}$$

Because of (21), (20), and (15) expression (19) becomes

$$\sum_{i=1}^{i=m} \bar{n}_i = (n - n_T)(m - 1). \tag{22}$$

Each of the $(n - n_T)(m - 1)$ subsidiary points is connected according to $T_6^{(8)}$ to its own residual graph. Thus there are altogether $m + (n - n_T)(m - 1)$ residual graphs. All their corresponding points and lines map on the corresponding points and lines of P in an $m + (n - n_T)(m - 1)$ to one mapping.

All the subsidiary points belonging to a given specialized point map on the corresponding point of P. Every direct connection

${f^{(i)}}_{l,r} \to {f_p}^{(k)}$ maps upon the line $f_l \to f_p$ of P, while all the connections (18) map on the zero connection of a point to itself, in other words, on the point f_l of P. The connections ${f^{(i)}}_{lT\ldots} \to {f^{(k)}}_{lT\ldots}$ (resp. ${f^{(i)}}_{\ldots Tl} \leftarrow {f^{(k)}}_{\ldots Tl}$) which appear in ${T_3}^{(8)}$ (2), as well as the connections ${f^{(i)}}_{lT\ldots} \to {f^{(s)}}_{lT\ldots} \to {f^{(k)}}_{lT\ldots}$ (resp. ${f^{(i)}}_{\ldots Tl} \leftarrow {f^{(s)}}_{\ldots Tl} \leftarrow {f^{(k)}}_{\ldots Tl}$) and the corresponding connections of the subsidiary points map on the point $f_{lT\ldots}$ (resp. $f_{\ldots Tl}$) of P.

Just as before we prove the two theorems given on p. 355 .

Of greater practical importance is a theorem which justifies the "lumping" of several points of the primordial graph into one.

Such a lumping may be considered as a special case of a many-to-one self-mapping of the primordial in which a partial graph P_A of P is mapped on the point A of P; another partial graph P_B of P is mapped on the point B of P, and all connections between any point of P_A and any point of P_B are mapped on the connection $A \to B$. This can be done only if every line connecting a point of P_A with a point of P_B is directed from a point of P_A to a point of P_B. If there were some lines directed from a point of P_B to a point of P_A, then those lines could not be mapped on $A \to B$. Such a self-mapping, of which there may be very many different ones, results in a simplification of the actual primordial graph, reducing the number of its lines and points. A graph obtained by such a self-mapping will be called a *simplified primordial* graph P_S. The graphs shown in Figure 1 and in Figure 7 may be perhaps simplified primordials.

If we apply any transformation $T^{(1)} \ldots T^{(14)}$ to P, then the different points of P_A, unless they are all residual points, will in general be specialized in different component primordials of $T(P)$. The same is true about the points of P_B. Each of those specialized points will, in general, give rise to several subsidiary points. Because of ${T_3}^{(u)}$ ($u = 1, \ldots, 14$) and ${T_5}^{(u)}$ some of those points, which we shall call Q-points and which arise as a result of specialization of points of P_A, will be connected to some points, R-points, which arise as a result of specialization of points of P_B. However, because of ${T_3}^{(u)}$ and ${T_5}^{(u)}$, every point Q of $T^{(u)}(P)$ is connected directly or indirectly with a point R of $T^{(u)}(P)$ in such a manner that the arrow leads from Q to R: $Q \to R$.

Denote by $T^{(u)}(a)$ the set of points of $T^{(u)}(P)$ which arises as a result of specialization of the point a of P under the transformation $T^{(u)}$. Then $T^{(u)}(A)$ is a subset of the set of the Q-points, and $T^{(u)}(B)$ is a subset of the set of the R-points. We can now map in several different ways the set Q on $T^{(u)}(A)$ and the set R on

$T^{(u)}(B)$, mapping each point of $T^{(u)}(A)$ and of $T^{(u)}(B)$ onto itself. The residual graph belonging to the Q-points and to the R-points are correspondingly mapped on the residual graphs of the point of $T^{(u)}(A)$ and $T^{(u)}(B)$. As a result of such a mapping we obtain a simplified transformed graph which is the transformed graph of the simplified primordial P_S. Thus we have

Theorem 3. There exists a $[T^{(u)}(P)]_S$ which is identical with $T^{(u)}(P_S)$.

All empirically determined physiological graphs are simplified graphs. Theorem 3 enables us to operate with simplified graphs and to obtain conclusions which can be verified experimentally. Thus in a simplified primordial graph absorption f_4 is connected via f_{4T5} to synthesis f_5, which is a simplification. In a transformed graph, for a given choice of parameters, there will be considerably more complex connections between groups of absorption phenomena and groups of synthetic processes, each of which represents a "lumping" of a still greater number of such processes. The simplified transformed graph may be still amenable to experimental study, whereas the actual complete transformed graph may be too complicated for it. It may be possible by considering primordial graphs of a different degree of simplification to work a method of successive approximations for the study of the transformed graphs.

REFERENCES

1. N. Rashevsky, *Bull. Math. Biophysics*, **16**, 317, 1954; **17**, 111, 1955; **17**, 207, 1955; **18**, 113, 1956; **18**, 173, 1956.

2. Denes Konig, *Theorie der endlichen und unendlichen Graphen*, (Leipzig: Akademische Verlagsbuchhandlung, 1936).

3. B. T. Sheer, *Comparative Physiology* (New York: John Wiley and Sons, 1948).

4. S. E. Luria, *General Virology* (New York: John Wiley and Sons, 1953).

5. E. Pollard, *The Physics of Viruses* (New York: Academic Press, 1953).

6. J. von Neumann, "The General and Logical Theory of Automata", *Cerebral Mechanisms in Behavior* (New York: John Wiley and Sons, 1951).

CHAPTER XXXI

SOME CONSEQUENCES OF THE FOREGOING

We have already remarked on p. 357 , that the total number of possible transformed graphs $T^{(1)}$ is finite, though it may be very large. An actual estimation of this number is very difficult. The great variety of possible transformed graphs is due to the many possibilities of choosing the number m in $T_1^{(1)}$, the ν's in $T_4^{(1)}$, and the n_r's for a fixed m. The number of possibilities depends on the number of specializable points in the primordial graph, and increases very rapidly with that number of points. Very rough estimates made by N. Rashevsky[1] gave a value of about 10^8. An exact treatment of the problem has been given by E. Trucco[2].

The meaning of the above is that only a finite number of different organisms is possible. The actual number of known species is of the order of 10^6. The plant kingdom would be represented by such choice of parameters, which corresponds to the specialization of vegetative functions only.

The total number of theoretical possibilities is thus well in excess of the known number of living species. This excess is further accentuated if we admit the possibility that species, or at least subspecies, differ not in their graphs, but in metric relations which give the intensities of the different biological properties. If this is so, then the total number of possibilities should give us the total number of genera, rather than of species. The number of species per genus varies very much. For example, there are 70 genera of *Brachiopoda,* with 225 species[3], or about 3 species per genus. There are 6 genera and 30 species of *Chaetognata.* On the other hand, in the plant kingdom there are, for example, about 150 genera of *Cyanophyta,* containing 1400 species, or about 9 species per genus, and about 300 genera of *Chrisophyta* containing about 5,700 species, or 17 species per genus[4]. Taking as a plausible average 10 species per genus, the total number of genera is of the order of 10^5.

However, the assumption that species within the same genus differ only metrically may not be true. Moreover, not only have there been a large number of extinct organisms, but there is no reason whatsoever to assume that all possible organisms have by now developed. In fact, new species do appear. Thus even 10^7 possibilities may not be too large.

On the other hand, it is possible that the transformation $T^{(1)}$ is too general, and that a restricting condition may have to be added, which will reduce the number of possibilities. The restriction may be of purely biological nature, requiring, for example, that only biological functions "adjacent" on the graph can be specialized together in the same tissue. Possibly, however, the restriction may be of purely topological character. For example, of all the transforms only those may be admissible whose fundamental group is homomorph to that of the primordial graph. Whether or not this is a restriction cannot be said without further study.

By assuming that the specialization of different points proceeds not independently, the total number of theoretically possible organisms is considerably reduced, as has been pointed out by N. Rashevsky[5].

Basically similar considerations hold for all the other transformations studied in the preceding chapter. It may be very difficult indeed to ever prove or disprove by observation whether the total number of possible organisms is finite. The implication, however, is a very interesting one. In a very remote way it may be of a somewhat similar nature to the conclusion of the finite size of the universe. Direct measurements may be impossible. Indirect evidence may be suggested by further development of the theory.

We have remarked in the preceding chapter (p. 358) that some properties of a system of abstract biology are determined only by the choice of the transformation, regardless of the choice of the primordial graph. Others are determined by both. Systems which depend only on the choice of the primordial graph are of little interest since they deal only with the properties of the primordial organism. We have studied altogether 14 different transformations $T^{(u)}$ $(u = 1, \ldots, 14)$. Two different conceivable primordial graphs, one represented in Figure 1, the other on Figure 7 of chapter xxx, have been hitherto considered. We shall denote them respectively by P_1 and P_2. We shall denote a system determined by a given transformation $T^{(i)}$ and a given primordial P_k by $(T^{(i)}P_k)$, indicating, if necessary, in additional parentheses the range of variation of the indices i and k. Thus we may have $(T^{(i)}P_k)$ $(i = 1, \ldots, 8; k = 1, 2)$. The class of systems which is determined by a given $T^{(i)}$ and any P_k shall be denoted by $(T^{(i)}X)$. Thus if a theorem holds for $(T^{(i)}X)$, it means that it holds for all systems based on $T^{(i)}$ regardless of the choice of P_k.

In any given system $(T^{(u)}X)$ $(u = 1, \ldots, 14)$ the number n of specializable points is fixed. Moreover, for any m all n points are specialized in one of the component primordials, according to $T_2^{(u)}$. We may now restrict the transformations $T^{(u)}$ $(u = 1, \ldots 14)$ by assuming that of the n specializable points only $m \leqq n$ are actually specialized for a given m. This means that for any given choice of m as parameter of the transformation some m of n specializable points are actually specialized, that is, each component primordial loses $m - 1$ points, specializing only in one rather than in n_i biological properties. The remaining $n - m$ specializable points remain non-specialized, that is, they are not lost by any of the m component primordials. Each component primordial receives now only one specialized point, losing $m - 1$ others. The step $T_4^{(u)}$ $(u = 1, \ldots, 14)$ is now eliminated while the step $T_5^{(u)}$ becomes much simpler. Thus the one specialized point receives now $m - 1$ subsidiary points.

The maximum amount of specialization is obtained when $m = n$, when all n specializable points become actually specialized. The residual graphs, attached to the subsidiary points should not contain any specializable points. To each transformation $T^{(u)}$ $(u = 1, \ldots, 14)$ we now obtain a corresponding simplified transformation $T^{(u)\prime}$.

We now shall prove two theorems for $T^{(1)}X)$, which have interesting biological interpretations. First we make the following

Definition. If in a directed graph we have a cycle such that all arrows are in the same direction, in other words, a cycle which is a closed directed way, such a cycle is called a *uniformly directed cycle.* Examples of uniformly directed cycles are the cycles $AS_bD_{es}S_{de}DA$ and $S_bC_bEM_IIDAS_b$ in Figure 1 of chapter xxx. In the same Figure the cycle $F_sEM_fF_s$ is *not* a uniformly directed cycle. We now state

Theorem 1. If r specializable points $f_1, f_2, \ldots, f_r$ of the primordial graph P all belong to a uniformly directed cycle, and if no two of them are adjacent, then in the transformed graph $T^{(1)}(P)$ those points each belong to at least m different uniformly directed cycles that have no common sides, where m is the parameter in $T_1^{(1)}$. The m cycles have the r points $f_1, f_2, \ldots f_r$ in common. If some of the points are adjacent, then in the transformed graph $T(P)$ each of the points $f_1, f_2, \ldots f_r$ again belongs to at least m uniformly directed cycles, but those m uniformly directed cycles have as many sides in common as there are pairs of adjacent points in the set $f_1, f_2, \ldots f_r$.

Proof. When a point f_u is specialized to graph i, it is removed from each of the $m - 1$ primordial graphs, except the ith, and $f_u^{(i)}$ is connected to each of the $m - 1$ graphs according to $T_3^{(1)}$. This is the same as fusing all points $f_u^{(l)}$ $(l = 1, 2, \ldots m)$ into one.

Hence the operations $T_2^{(1)}$ and $T_3^{(1)}$ result in the fusion of all corresponding specialized points of the m primordials. Therefore each point f_i ($i = 1, 2, \ldots, r$) in $T^{(1)}(P)$ belongs simultaneously to m uniformly directed cycles. If a pair of points f_i, f_k are adjacent, then operations $T_2^{(1)}$ and $T_3^{(1)}$ also result in the fusion into one line of all the m lines $f_i \rightarrow f_k$. Hence $f_i \rightarrow f_k$ is a common side of m cycles.

Corollary. If in the primordial graph P a uniformly directed cycle contains only the specializable points $f_1, f_2, \ldots f_r$, then those points belong in $T^{(1)}(P)$ to only one uniformly directed cycle.

Proof. The m cycles each consist of r sides. Since there are r adjacent pairs of points, therefore the m cycles have r sides in common; in other words, they fuse into one cycle.

The theorem and corollary hold, as is readily seen, for non-uniformly directed as well as non-directed cycles also. The reason for our emphasizing the uniformly directed cycles is as follows.

We have seen (chapter xxx, p. 347) that if in a uniformly directed cycle one biological property is destroyed, the remaining biological properties represented by the points of the cycle also are destroyed, since each following biological property depends on the preceding. If in the primordial organism the r specializable points $f_1, \ldots, f_r$ all belong to only one uniformly directed cycle, then the destruction of a biological property represented by any residual point of the cycle destroys all other biological properties in that cycle, in particular, the specializable biological properties $f_1, f_2 \ldots, f_r$. In $T^{(1)}(P)$, however, except for the very special case of the corollary, destruction of one point in one of the m cycles breaks only the chain of biological properties, in this particular cycle. There still remain $m - 1$ intact cycles, to each of which the set of biological properties, represented by the points, $f_1, f_2, \ldots f_r$ belongs. Thus in this case those biological properties are not affected by the injury. Two adjacent points f_k and f_{k+1} are joined by only one line. But, in general, two points are joined by m lines. We may remove *at least* $m - 1$ residual points between any two specialized non-adjacent points f_k and f_{k+1}, still leaving one way $f_k \rightarrow f_{k+1}$ intact. (We can remove more than $m - 1$ such points if there is more than one residual point between f_k and f_{k+1} in P.) Hence if v denotes the number of pairs of adjacent points in $f_1, f_2, \ldots, f_r$, then we can remove at least as many as $(r - v)(m - 1)$ residual points and still leave at least one uniformly directed cycle intact.

Translating this topological result into biological language, we may say that the greater m, that is, the more developed and differentiated an organism, the greater are its possibilities of withstanding the loss of some residual biological properties or functions, the role of which is taken over by other corresponding residual biological functions.

In the same manner as theorem 1, we can prove generally the following

Theorem 2. If in the primordial graph P there are p directed ways that lead from a specializable point f_i to another specializable point f_k, through some residual points, then in $T^{(1)}(P)$ there are at least mp directed ways leading from f_i to f_k.

The biological implication of theorem 2 is the same: a larger number of directed ways between f_i and f_k provides a greater safety factor against results of destruction of some of the biological properties which are "between" the biological properties represented by f_i and f_k.

A similar situation holds for the destruction of a specialized biological property represented by one of the points of the set $f_1, f_2, \ldots, f_r$. In the primordial graph P let the point f_k be preceded by the point f_k' and followed by f_k''. These two points may either be residual points or they may be elements of the set $f_1, f_2, \ldots f_r$. In this case $f_k' = f_{k-1}$; $f_k'' = f_{k+1}$. According to $T_5^{(1)}$ in $T^{(1)}(P)$ the point f_k has in general a subsidary point, f_{k_ν}, which is connected to f_k' and f_k'' in the same way as f_k is connected to them. Hence the removal of f_k from the uniformly directed cycle still leaves the other points $f_1, f_2, \ldots, f_{k-1}, f_{k+1}, \ldots, f_r$ belonging to a uniformly directed cycle, the point f_k being "by-passed," and the directed way $f_k' \rightarrow f_k \rightarrow f_k''$ being substituted by $f_k' \rightarrow f_{k_\nu} \rightarrow f_k''$. Thus, a higher organism has a greater ability to adapt itself to such a loss of biological function by substitution of other biological functions. This is a well-known fact of biology.

We may go even further. In chapter xxx (p. 357) we suggested that when the differentiation is completed, that is, when $m = n$ (where n is the total number of specializable points), we may apply the transformation $T^{(1)}$ to this "completed" graph $T^{(1)}(P)$ as we applied it to the primordial graph P. In this way we describe specializations between various individuals and obtain a topological representation of social relations. We may, however, apply the transformation $T^{(1)}$ to any $T^{(1)}(P)$, not necessarily to the completely differentiated one. This corresponds to actual facts, since social differentiation is found among some relatively lower animals. The specialization may be either a social one, a biological one, or both, different individuals of the species being biologically different for the performance of different biological functions. The most common example is the sexual differentiation, which in human society is both biological and social. Sociology may justly be considered as the ecology of human society.

Purely biological specializations occur at rather low levels of development. Thus plants specialize in producing organic material from water, carbon dioxide, and inorganic salts. Some animals use this organic material by feeding on plants. An organism is never completely isolated. A large part of its environment is formed by other organisms with which it interacts biologically. Therefore, the representation of an organism by a graph that describes the interactions within the organism is an unrealistic abstraction. We should consider the graph of an organism as a partial graph of a more general one, which includes other species with which the organism interacts. Since the number of species interacting with a given one is finite, though sometimes very large, we still are dealing with finite graphs.

We may now apply the transformation $T^{(1)}$ to this general graph as we applied it to the primordial. Since theorems 1 and 2 are independent of the choice of the graph to which we apply $T^{(1)}$, we therefore arrive at the same results, only with a much broader biological scope. The removal of some specialized points now may mean the destruction of some of the organisms on which the given organism feeds, or of some particular food component. Interpreted biologically, theorems 1 and 2 again mean that the higher an organism, the more adaptable it is to changes in biological environment.

Thus regardless of the choice of the primordial graph, the transformation $T^{(1)}$ leads us to the well-known biological law: that of increased adaptibility with increasing development. We may, however, pose the interesting question: What conditions must the transformation satisfy in order to lead to given known biological laws? The answer to that question will narrow the possible choices of a proper transformation.

Within this given system of abstract biology we may, however, find other general laws by further study of the general properties of different $(T^{(i)}P_k)$.

Different types of general laws will be obtained by studying such topological properties as are invariant with respect to $T^{(u)}$. The law derived above deals with *differences* between organisms of different degrees of development. The laws obtained from the study of invariance will emphasize the *similarities* between different organisms.

The following example illustrates a still different kind of biological relation which may be derived in this system of abstract biology.

It is natural to interpret m as the number of organs of an organism because each of the m component primordial graphs contains some specialized points as well as their subsidiary points and forms a natural unit of the graph $T^{(1)}(P)$. Each of the $n - n_i$ subsidiary points is attached to a residual graph. In the interpretation which we have given in chapter xxx those residual graphs correspond to different cell types of the organ. Therefore the total number τ of different cell types in the organism is equal to the total number of residual graphs in $T^{(1)}(P)$. But that latter is equal to $m + n(m - 1)$. Hence we have the relation

$$\tau = m + n(m - 1), \tag{1}$$

which connects the total number of different cell types with the number m of organs and the number n of specializable biological properties.

Equation (1) above is verifiable empirically. It may even seem to be easily verifiable because τ and m could be directly counted. For a given organism, we then could determine n. With this value we should obtain for all other organisms which are derived from the same primordial a relation between τ and m, free of arbitrary parameters. Since the number of primordials is either one or is very small, the verification of (1) would seem to present no particular difficulties.

Actually the situation is not quite so simple, because neither τ nor m has ever been systematically counted for different organisms.

Therefore there are no data now available in the literature which would enable us to verify (1) over a wide range of organisms. The method outlined above is, however, valid, and whether equation (1) proves to be correct or not, it definitely suggests a new avenue of experimental research. It is again a problem that seems quite foreign to the metric approach.

In $(T^{(u)\prime}X)$ $(u = 1, \ldots, 7)$ (page 373) equation (1) is simplified by making $n = m$, to

$$\tau = m^2, \tag{2}$$

that is, the number of cell types of an organism is equal to the square of the number of organs. Since neither $(T^{(u)}X)$ nor $(T^{(u)\prime}X)$ are likely to correspond to biological reality, we should not expect either (1) or (2) to hold actually.

From equation (22) of chapter xxx, it follows that in $(T^{(u)}X)$ $(u = 8, \ldots, 14)$ we have instead of (1)

$$\tau = m + (n - n_T)(m - 1). \tag{3}$$

In the corresponding $(T^{(u)\prime}X)$ $(u = 8, \ldots, 14)$, we have instead of (2)

$$\tau = m^2 - n_T m + n_T. \tag{4}$$

A systematic observational search for a relation between τ and m would be well worth while and would throw light on the biotopological relations in the organic world.

In $(T^{(u)\prime}X)$ $(u = 1, \ldots, 7)$ there is only one specialized point per component primordial, and it has $m - 1$ subsidiary points to each of which is attached a residual graph. Hence all organs are monofunctional and have the same number of residual graphs for each component primordial. In biological terms we have the following:

Theorem 3. In $(T^{(u)\prime}X)$ $(u = 1, \ldots, 7)$ the number of cell types in all organs is the same and is a function of the number of organs only.

It does not seem likely that such a relation actually holds in nature, but it is certainly an empirically verifiable relation.

The situation is different for $(T^{(u)}X)$ $(u = 1, \ldots, 7)$. Here if a component primordial contains n_i specialized points, it contains a total of $n - n_i$ subsidiary residual graphs, or, together with the given component primordial, a total of $n - n_i + 1$ partial graphs. Hence all component primordials, which contain the same number n_i of specialized points, though the actual points may differ from one component primordial to another, give rise to the same number of partial primordial graphs. In biological language we have

Theorem 4. In $(T^{(u)}X)$ $(u = 1, \ldots, 7)$ all polyfunctional organs of an organism, which perform the same number of different biological functions, consist of the same number of different cell types.

Theorem 2 states that in $(T^{(1)}X)$ if two nonadjacent specializable points of the primordial are connected by a way, then the same two specialized points are connected in the transformed graph by at least m ways. One biological consequence drawn from this theorem was that the more complex organisms are more adaptable to possible losses of some biological functions. There is, however, another important consequence of that theorem. Let m ways lead from a specialized point f_i to a specialized point f_k. If the biological function represented by f_i is in some manner impaired, this impairment will affect all biological functions to representative points of which there is a way from the point f_i. But that means that more biological functions will be affected in a complex organism than in a simpler one, due to impairment of the same specialized biological function f_i. Any affected biological function manifests itself either as an objective *sign*[6] or, in humans, as a subjective *symptom.* Thus many signs or symptoms will be produced by the impairment of a biological function. A complex of symptoms constitutes a *syndrome*[6]. We shall use here the word syndrome somewhat loosely as referring both to signs and symptoms. Therefore, from theorem 2 there follows

Theorem 5. In $(T^{(1)}X)$ the complexity of a syndrome due to the impairment of a specialized biological function increases with increasing complexity of the organism.

We now shall prove a theorem which at the present stage of development is probably biologically irrelevant, but which illustrates another interesting possible application of topological considerations.

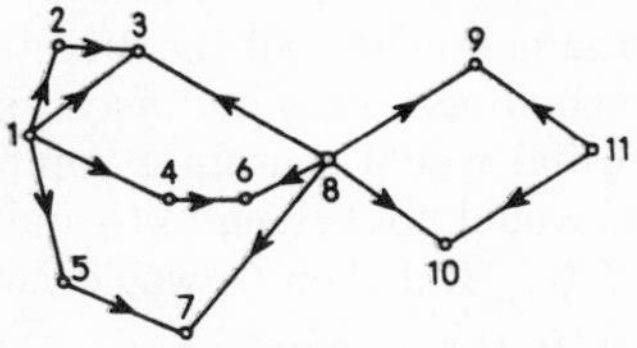

FIG. 1

Let us consider the so-called fundamental sets[7] (Grundmenge of König[7]). A fundamental set is defined in the following way. Denote by Π_a the set of points which can be reached by a directed way from the point a. If Π_a is not a proper subset of any other Π_b, where b is not included in Π_a, then Π_a is called a fundamental set G_a, with the point a as its source. If directed cycles are present, then a fundamental set may have more than one source. In general, different fundamental sets of a graph have a non-empty intersection. Some of them may, however, be disjoined. For example in the graph of Figure 1, G_1 consists of the points 1, 2, 3, 4, 5, 6, 7; G_8 consists of 8, 3, 6, 7, 9, 10; G_{11} — of 11, 9, 10, G_1 and G_{11} are disjoined. G_1 and G_8 have a non-empty intersection consisting of points 9, 10.

If the sets G_i and G_l are disjoined, then no point of G_i can be reached by a way from any point of G_l $(l \neq i)$, and *vice versa.*

Our theorem is stated as follows:

The number of mutually disjoined fundamental sets, each having a specialized point as its only source, is an invariant of the transformation $T^{(1)}$.

Proof. Let the primordial graph contain k mutually disjoined fundamental sets G_i $(i = 1, 2, \ldots, k)$ with corresponding sources S_i $(i = 1, 2, \ldots, k)$. The transformed graph $T^{(1)}$ consists of m component primordials, which all have the points S_i in common, and of a number $n(m - 1)$ of subsidiary residual graphs.

In the primordial graph P let the fundamental set G_i consist of r_i points $a_{i_1}, a_{i_2}, \ldots, a_{i_{r_i}}$. Denote the points which correspond to a_i in any of the m component primordial graphs by $a_i^{(q)}$ $(q = 1, 2, \ldots, m)$. Then in $T^{(1)}$ there are mr_i points $a_{i_1}^{(q)}, a_{i_2}^{(q)}, \ldots, a_{i_{r_i}}^{(q)}$ $(q = 1, 2, \ldots, m)$, which can be reached by a directed way from S_i. In addition some points in the subsidiary residual graphs which belong to S_i according to $T_5^{(1)}$ and $T_6^{(1)}$ may be reached from S_i.

a) We shall now prove that all those points together with the point S_i itself form a fundamental set $G_i^{(T)}$ of $T^{(1)}$. Suppose this were not the case. Then there would exist at least one point A of T not belonging to $G_i^{(T)}$ such that $G_i^{(T)}$ would be a proper subset of $\Pi_A^{(T)}$. But since all the points and all the directed ways of $T^{(1)}$ can be mapped on corresponding points and ways of the primordial P, therefore, the primordial would contain a point A_0, on which A is mapped, such that A_0 would not belong to G_i and such that G_i would be a proper subset of Π_{A_0}. But then G_i would not be a fundamental set, which is contrary to the assumption.

Thus the mapping of a set $\Pi_i^{(T)}$, which is not a fundamental set in $T^{(1)}$ onto P gives also a non-fundamental set in P. By a similar argument we prove that the mapping of any fundamental set of $T^{(1)}$ onto P gives a fundamental set in P.

b) Next we shall prove that all fundamental sets $G_i^{(T)}$ are mutually disjoined. If $G_i^{(T)}$ and $G_l^{(T)}$ $(i \neq l)$ were not disjoined then there would be at least one way in $T^{(1)}$ which would lead from a point $a_{i_p}^{(q)}$ of $G_i^{(T)}$ to some point $a_{l_v}^{(u)}$ of $G_l^{(T)}$. But this way would map on a way from a_{i_p} of G_i to a_{l_v} of G_l. On the primordial P this would mean that G_i and G_l are not disjoined, which is contrary to the assumption.

From a and b it follows that to each G_i $(i = 1, 2, \ldots, k)$ of P there corresponds a $G_i^{(T)}$ of $T^{(1)}$ with the same source S_i. Hence there are at least k fundamental sets $G_i^{(T)}$ in $T^{(1)}$ with corresponding sources S_i $(i = 1, 2, \ldots, k)$.

c) Now we must complete our proof by showing that there are not more than k disjoined fundamental sets $G_i^{(T)}$ such that each has a specialized point as its only source. Suppose there were a $(k+1)$st fundamental set $G_{k+1}^{(T)}$ with a specialized point S_{k+1} as source, and that $G_{k+1}^{(T)}$ were disjoined with all other fundamental sets $G_i^{(T)}$. All the points and ways of $G_{k+1}^{(T)}$ will map on corresponding points and ways of P. Hence, contrary to the assumption, P would contain a $(k+1)$st fundamental set, disjoined from all other G_i's.

Thus our theorem is demonstrated.

Let us now translate it into biological language. As remarked above, if the biological property represented by the point S_i is disturbed, this will result in a disturbance of all biological properties which are represented by the other points of G_i. All these disturbances form a syndrome. We shall call two syndromes disjoined if they do not have any symptoms in common. Our theorem then means biologically that the number of disjoined syndromes, due to disturbances of some specialized biological property, is the same for all organisms. Inasmuch as the theorem has been proved as valid only for the transformation $T^{(1)}$, which is a biologically implausible one, therefore no direct applications of the above are to be expected. Moreover, practically no one has ever bothered to study syndromes of any kind in lower animals. However, when it comes to the all important problem of extrapolating results of medical experimentation on higher animals to human beings, the study of relations of such type as the above may prove to be of great practical value.

An important class of specializable biological properties is formed by internal secretions which play a coordinating role in the over-all functioning of the organism. More and more hormones are being discovered, and a few dozens are known now in humans. How many hormones are there altogether in a given organism? This is a question which hardly has a place in metric mathematical biology, but to which topological biology may perhaps give an answer some day. To suggest a physico-chemical scheme for the chemo-regulatory processes which regulate all the hundreds of separate physiological functions of a complex organism is a hopeless task. To suggest a similar scheme for a relatively simple primordial organism may be quite feasible. We may, for example, assume that each of the specializable biological properties of a primordial organism is regulated by a special hormone or that one hormone coordinates the biological activities in a "block" of such properties which specialize in a correlated manner. Relatively simple interactions between the hormones of the primordial may be postulated. Once this is done a proper transformation $T^{(u)}$ will give us the number of subsidiary biological properties to a given specializable internal secretion, and those subsidiaries may be interpreted also as additional internal secretions. Moreover $T^{(u)}$ also gives us all the connections between the points which represent the different additional internal secretions. As we have seen a very simple partial of the primordial is, in general, transformed into a very complicated partial of the resulting graph. A guess at a correct partial graph for the internal secretions of a complex organism is a hopeless task. But such a correct complex graph may well be *derived* from a much simpler primordial which is much easier to postulate.

Adding even only a few internal secretions to the primordial will increase its complexity and therefore increase the number N of possible organisms. With specialization in "blocks" we obtain, however, for $(T^{(u)\prime}P_1)$ $(u = 1, \ldots, 7)$ a value $N = 10^3$ which is much too small. Hence there may well be room for the addition of more points to the primordial.

If, out of n specializable points of the primordial, n_1 stand for internal secretion, then in a completely differentiated graph, in which $m = n$, the total number of points will be n^2, since each of the n points receives n subsidiaries, whereas the number of points which represent the internal secretions in the completely differentiated graph is equal to nn_1. Hence the ratio of the number of internal secretions to the total number of specialized organs is the same in the completely specialized graph as in the primordial. Inasmuch as we remarked above that even in humans there are polyfunctional organs, whereas a completely differentiated organism could have only monofunctional organs, we see that no completely differentiated organism has yet been evolved. But in intermediate steps the ratio of the number of internal secretions to the total number of organs is not equal to n_1/n. In fact, for the same value of m it may vary depending on the distribution of the specializable points between the m component primordials (Step $T_2^{(u)}$). A simple expression for all the possibilities can be derived in $(T^{(u)\prime}X)$ $(u = 1, \ldots, 7)$.

In $T^{(u)\prime}$ only $m < n$ of the specializable points actually specialize. The total number of possible choices of those m points out of n is $\binom{n}{m}$, when all points specialize independently. Amongst the n points there are n_1 which represent the internal secretions. In how many ways, K, can we choose m points out of n in such a way that $k < m$ of those points will be from the group of the n_1 points, which represent the internal secretions? There are $\binom{n_1}{k}$ ways of choosing k points out of n_1. For each choice there remains $n - n_1$ points, not belonging to n_1, from which we can choose $m - k$ points to be added to k making a total of m. But there are $\binom{n - n_1}{m - k}$ ways of making that latter choice. Hence the answer to our question is

$$K = \binom{n - n_1}{m - k} \binom{n_1}{k}. \tag{9}$$

For each possibility in which k of the n_1 points are specialized, each of the k points gives rise to $m - 1$ subsidiaries or to a total of m points each. The total number of points generated by the k points is mk. Hence the total number of possibilities of generating mk points is given by (9).

We now can compute the average number $\bar{n}_h$ of points which correspond to internal secretions for all organisms with a given m, assuming equal probability of all combinations. To this end we multiply (9) by mk and sum for all values of k, that is, from $k = 1$ to $k = m$, if $m < n_1$; and from $k = 1$ to $k = n$, if $m > n_1$. Then we divide the result by the total number $\binom{n}{m}$ of possible combinations of n points by m. We thus find

$$\bar{n}_h = \frac{\sum_{k=1}^{m} \binom{n - n_1}{m - k} \binom{n_1}{k} mk}{\binom{n}{m}}, \text{ for } m < n_1 \tag{10}$$

and

$$\bar{n}_h = \frac{\sum_{k=1}^{n_1} \binom{n - n_1}{m - k} \binom{n_1}{k} mk}{\binom{n}{m}}, \text{ for } m > n_1 \tag{11}$$

The value of $\bar{n}_h$ is a function of m, n, and n_1. Thus (10) and (11) give us the average number of internal secretions in the class of organisms characterized by a given number m of different organs, for a system $(T^{(u)\prime}P_r)$ $(u = 1, \ldots, 7)$ in which P_r is arbitrary except for containing n specializable points, of which $n_1 < n$ represent hormonal secretions. Here again we have a prediction of a type of relation which has never been looked for in biology.

Corresponding relations for $(T^{(u)}P_r)$ $(u = 1, \ldots, 14)$ are much more complicated.

N. Rashevsky[8] investigated the behavior of the so-called "point bases"[7] of the primordial graph under the transformation $T^{(1)}$. He suggested a biological interpretation of his results, which may throw light on the decrease of regenerating ability of lost parts with growing complexity of the organism. E. Trucco[9] corrected and generalized Rashevsky's theorem about point bases.

REFERENCES

1. N. Rashevsky, *Bull. Math. Biophysics*, **16**, 317, 1954.
2. E. Trucco, *Bull. Math. Biophysics*, **19**, 309, 1957.
3. T. I. Storer, *General Zoology*, (New York: McGraw-Hill, 1951).
4. H. J. Fuller and O. Tippo, *College Botany*, (New York: Henry Holt), 1953.
5. N. Rashevsky, *Bull. Math. Biophysics*, **18**, 173, 1956.
6. Stedman, *Practical Medical Dictionary*, (Baltimore: Williams and Wilkins, 1946).
7. Denes Konig, *Theorie der Endlichen und Unendlichen Graphen.* (Leipzig: Akademische Verlagsgesellschaft), 1936.
8. N. Rashevsky, *Bull. Math. Biophysics*, **17**, 111, 1955.
9. E. Trucco, *Bull. Math. Biophysics*, **18**, 65, 1956.

CHAPTER XXXII

COMPARISON OF THE SET — THEORETICAL AND COMBINATORIAL APPROACHES. POSSIBLE OUTLOOKS.

In chapter xxix we outlined a set-theoretical approach to topological biology. We reached a number of conclusions which are in agreement with well known facts and therefore throw light on the understanding of those facts. Other conclusions predict the existence of definite experimentally verifiable relations.

In chapter xxx and xxxi we outlined a combinatorial topological approach. Although we pointed out in chapter xxix that with the topological spaces used there are associated certain graphs, yet the two approaches seem to be different in many respects. The combinatorial approach leads also to the prediction of various relations within organisms which are outside of the scope of metric mathematical biology. Yet those relations such as for example the relation between the number of cell-types and the number of organs [Equation (1) of chapter xxxi] are less specific. They depend on additional hypotheses. The set-theoretical approach leads us directly, for example, to such conclusions as that emotional disturbances should result in gastro-intestinal or cardio-vascular disturbances. The combinatorial approach does not lead us to any of those conclusions. On the other hand, the set-theoretical approach does not seem to have any room for considerations of relations between number of organs and number of cell types, as well as for other relations discussed in the preceding chapter.

An examination of the two approaches shows that this apparent deficiency of the otherwise more general and apparently more powerful set-theoretical approach lies in the circumstance, that in our combinatorial approach the *combinatoric* proper and the *topology* are essentially independent of each other. Thus equation (1) of chapter xxxi holds not only for $T^{(1)}$, but for any $(T^{(i)}X)$, $(i = 1, 2, \ldots, 14)$. Yet certain topological aspects of these different $(T^{(i)}X)$ are different.

This remark makes it possible to incorporate some of the aspects of the graph-theoretical approach into the set-theoretical one. Such an incorporation means a restriction on some of the possibilities offered by the set-theoretical approach. But this perhaps is just what we need. As pointed out in chapter xxix, p. 343, the spaces

S_o discussed there may be too general and a restrictive additional assumption may be needed. As long as this additional assumption does not invalidate the useful conclusions drawn from the set-theoretical approach, it may prove to be itself useful.

The argument which leads to equation (1) of chapter xxxi namely

$$\tau = m + n(m-1), \tag{1}$$

can be used almost without change in the set-theoretical approach. Instead of assigning to each property P_i in S_P any arbitrary set of subproperties $P_{i\alpha}$ in S_o, we now proceed as follows.

Consider an aggregate of identical cells, each possessing all the basic properties P_i. Let n be the number of the basic properties P_i. Divide the aggregate into m aggregates. Let the cells of the rth aggregate specialize in n_r properties of the n basic properties and loose the $n - n_r$ remaining ones. We again have as on p. 366

$$\sum_{r=1}^{n} n_r = n. \tag{2}$$

We now can make one of the following assumptions:

a) When an aggregate loses $n - n_r$ basic biological properties P_i, then $n - n_r$ new aggregates are formed, each of which has acquired some sub-property $P_{i\alpha}$ of one of the non-lost basic properties P_i. We shall call those additional aggregates "subsidiary aggregates." The $n - n_r$ subproperties $P_{i\alpha}$ are all different. In other words we have altogether $n - n_r$ subproperties $P_{i\alpha}$, $\alpha = 1, 2, \ldots, n - n_r$.

b) When an aggregate loses $n - n_r$ basic biological properties P_i, then $n - n_r$ new subsidiary aggregates are formed, each of which acquires a subproperty $P_{i\alpha}$ of *any* of the basic properties P_i, whether lost or retained by the rth aggregate. The $n - n_r$ subproperties $P_{i\alpha}$ are all different.

The number of subproperties which thus appear as a result of the assumed specialization for any of the m sub-aggregates is $n - n_r$. Therefore the total number of sub-properties is equal because of (2), to:

$$\sum_{r=1}^{m} (n - n_r) = n(m-1). \tag{3}$$

This is also the number of subsidiary aggregates. If we add to them the original m aggregates, we obtain for the total number of different aggregates or cell-types the expression (1). If now we identify

m with the number of organs, we can interpret (1) in the same manner as we did in the preceding chapter.

The different subproperties P_{ia} are related to other subproperties P_{ik} in the space S_o, according to rule A of chapter xxix, p. 331. We thus obtain a subset of the set of all spaces S_o. While, as we have seen, the set of all spaces S_o may be infinite, yet, by the same argument as used on page 357, we see that the subset of this set of all possible spaces S_o is finite. In other words, with either assumption a) or assumption b), the total number of possible organisms is finite. This total number depends on n, the number of basic specializable properties in S_P. Yet for a given S_P this number is in general not equal to the number of possible organisms in $(T^{(i)}P)$, $(i = 1, \ldots, 14)$, where P is the primordial graph which is associated with S_P. The reason for this is that we have not considered here the possible distributions of the subproperties P_{ia} among the different P_i. Thus the counterparts of operations $T_4^{(i)}$ and $T_5^{(i)}$ $(i = 1, 2, \ldots, 14)$, are missing in the assumptions a) and b). An introduction of corresponding additional assumption will mean a further restriction on S_o.

Since the set $\mathfrak{S}$ of all possible spaces thus obtained is a subset of the set $\mathfrak{S}_0$ of all possible spaces S_o discussed in chapter xxix, therefore all conclusions drawn there remain valid.

Assumption b) is biologically much more realistic than assumption a). According to the latter, an organ would consist only of cell-types which specialize in one or a few basic properties P_i and in the subproperties P_{ia} of *those* properties. Actually this is not so. The eye, organ of vision, consists not only of cells which specialize in photosensitivity to light of different wave-lengths. It consists also of different types of muscles, secretory cells, etc. The same holds for other organs. Assumption b) added to the postulates of chapter xxix divides all the subproperties P_{ik} of the organism or all of the points P_{ik} of S_o into groups of subproperties which "belong together" by virtue of their construction through assumption b). They may be considered as belonging together also by virtue of performing a common complicated biological function. Thus if the rth aggregate of cells specializes in the property P_S of sensitivity to external stimuli, then the subsidiary aggregate with the subproperties P_{Ma} of different orderly movements may represent muscles which serve in the process of vision, e.g. eye muscles, ciliary muscles, etc. We may introduce the following explicit assumption:

c) The cell types which are characterized by the subproperties P_{ia} and which correspond to a given rth aggregate of the original m aggregates, are all segregated spatially in an organism and constitute an organ.

From a postulational point of view the above may be regarded not as an assumption but as a definition of an organ.

The above considerations suggest another interesting possibility.

As already remarked every organ has subproperties of most of the basic biological properties. A gland does not have any muscles elements. But it certainly exhibits some subproperties of the molecular orderly movements, P_{M_2} (chapter xxix). While a gland does not possess sensitivity to direct external stimuli it can be stimulated endogenically. All organs receive food from the blood, which is part of the circulatory system of the organism as a whole. Blood is the "milieu interieur" of the organism. It is, however, an external medium for the cells which constitute the different organs. Tentatively we may consider the following postulate which may be incorporated into the system of postulates given in chapter xxix.

Postulate. Each individual organ can be mapped continuously on S_P and the organism as a whole can be mapped continuously on each of its organs.

Certain interesting conclusions follow almost immediately from this postulate. In S_0 an external stimulus results in molar or molecular orderly movements, which in their turn result in an uptake of food from the environment. In a gland the orderly movements are of the molecular type, and represent either secretion, or uptake of substances from the blood which plays now the role of the external environment. Hence, proper stimulation of a gland should result directly in a higher uptake of food substances from the blood. Stimulation of the eye by light should also result directly in a higher absorption of food from the blood. The mechanism of this may be manifold: a vaso-dilation which results in an increased blood flow through the organ, an increase of permeability of some cells, etc. Similar conclusions follow about any other organ. Those conclusions may sound trivial, but they are by no means self-evident truths.

Another interesting conclusion is the following. The organism as a whole picks up food from the environment. In the digestive mechanism that food is split into parts that are useful to the organism and are absorbed by it, and into other parts that are rejected, being of no use to the organism. According to our postulate a situation relationally isomorphic to this should be found in individual organs. The food, which a cell of an organ takes from the blood is very different from the "raw" food which the organism takes from its environment. It is already digested and no intracellular digestion takes place in organs of the higher organisms. Yet a relational isomorphism with the phenomenon of digestion must be present if the organism can be mapped on the organ. The basic relational feature of digestion, quite regardless of any particular biochemical mechanism involved, consists of a substance A being taken up, split into two or more substances, $A_1, A_2, \ldots A_k$, of which some are retained, some excreted back. We should therefore expect that in any organ reactions of that type will occur even with the substances which are already digested in the ordinary sense, and are present in the blood. That every cell of an organ takes in different substances from the blood and returns other substances to the blood is, of course, a generally known phenomenon. But our postulate requires that among the excreted substances there must be *some,* which are direct fragments of the substances that have been taken in. This in principle is an experimentally verifiable statement.

The above discussed postulate is independent on the principle of biotopological mapping. It may, if necessary, be added to it. There is, however, one conclusion which does follow from the general principle.

Consider any biochemical chain of reactions, for example, the reaction of sugar metabolism. Such a reaction may be schematically represented by a directed graph. Or, if we prefer, the reaction chain may be represented by a topological space, in which neighborhoods are defined as on p. 331. This set of reactions, like any other biochemical reactions is a part of the organism. The individual reactions of the set are particular properties or subproperties of the organism. Therefore, according to the principle of biotopological mapping, we should expect that the graphs of the corresponding sets of reactions in different organisms should map continuously onto each other. The graphs of the reactions of the higher organisms will be in general more complicated. To each reaction of a set in a simpler organism there will correspond several reactions in a higher organism. But a mapping of one set onto another should be possible with the preservation of the basic biochemical relations.

CHAPTER XXXIII

THE ORGANISM AS A SET OF MAPPINGS CATEGORIES AND EQUIVALENCES

In representing an organism by either an abstract topological space or by a graph, we made the points of the space or the vertices of the graph correspond to different biological properties of the organism. We now shall discuss a different approach following Robert Rosen[1]. To the points of the abstract space or of the graph we shall make correspond actual *parts* of an organism. Those parts may be of very diverse nature. They may be organs, like the eye, the stomach, the kidney. They may be parts of organs, like the crystalline lens, the digestive glands of the stomach, the tubules of the kidney. Or they may be groups of physiologically identical cells, like the erythrocytes, or the insulin secreting cells of the Langerhans islets. Finally these parts may be simple cells or even parts of cells, like nuclei, or chromosomes. All such parts of the organism we shall designate by the common name of *component*.

Consider as an example of a component the digestive system of an animal. It receives from outside a number of substances. After digesting them, it returns to the outside certain indigestible residues, and supplies the products of digestion to the remaining of the organism. Quite generally any component which participates in the metabolic activities of the organism, receives either from the environment of the organism or from other components certain substances, and gives off either to the environment or to other components other substances. The substances which enter a component shall be denoted as the *inputs* of that component. The substances which leave a component shall be called its *outputs*. In general inputs and outputs do not necessarily need to be substances. Thus the retinal cells of the eye receive radiations of different wavelengths as some of their inputs. In addition they have as inputs also various metabolites from the blood stream. The output of the retinal cells consists of various metabolites, the production of which in general depends both on the input of light and on the input of other metabolites. The electrical action potentials of the retinal cells which are produced as a result of the input of light plus input of metabolites are part of the cells' output.

Returning again to the example of the digestive system, we notice that not all substances are used or accepted as inputs. Certain solids, like stones, are not even taken in by the animal. No animals will also drink kerosene or mineral oil. The digestive organ of some animals will not digest certain types of fats or of carbohydrates. The human digestive tract, for example, does not digest cellulose. Similarly the eye is sensitive to only a relatively small spectral range of light, and the ear — to a limited range of audio frequencies.

Thus the input into the digestive system consists of classes or sets of admissible substances. There is a class of admissible fats, each individual type of admissible fat being an element of that class or set. Similarly there is a set of admissible proteins, and a set of admissible carbohydrates, etc. As a result of digestion a given admissible protein yields a definite set of aminoacids as output. From other admissible proteins other sets of aminoacids are obtained as output. Similarly a given acceptable fat will yield as output a definite set of fatty acids. Thus the outputs are also sets of various "objects" such as aminoacids, fatty acids, monosacharides, etc. The different sets of output objects correspond to different sets of input objects. The correspondence is in general not a one-to-one correspondence. To a given aminoacid in the output there may correspond several different proteins in the input, all those proteins in fact which contain the given aminoacid. Similarly to a given protein in the input there correspond in general several different aminoacids in the output. This correspondence constitutes a mapping of a more general nature than the ones which we discussed hitherto. We do not visualize this type of mapping geometrically. We merely say that a mapping between an input set and an output set exists, if for a given input set there exists a definite output set. This is actually the case. For if, for example, we specify all the proteins in the input, then we can specify all aminoacids in the output.

In the mappings which we discussed in the preceding chapters, the rules of mapping were prescribed either as analytic expressions (p. 321) or as certain geometrical rules. But a mapping may be described by rules of a very different nature. In the present example the structural characteristics of the protein determine what set of aminoacids will be given as output if a given set of proteins is given as input. Similarly the chemical knowledge of the properties of the enzymes and of the particular linkages which it breaks up in a given protein enables us to determine what type of polypeptides will appear as output, when a given class of proteins is introduced as input.

All admissible inputs consist of sets of proteins, fats, and other substances. All possible outputs consist of sets of aminoacids, fatty acids, etc. The chemical rules provide us with a criterion as to which input set is mapped on which output set. Thus we have not only a number of input and output objects, but also a collection of different mappings. In chapter xxviii we defined a set as a collection of any objects, real or conceptual. A mapping is also such a conceptual object, and therefore we see that each component of an organism is associated with a set of input objects, a set of output objects, and a set of mappings. If a given set A of input substances does not correspond to a given set A' of output substances, we may consider this statement as a generalized case of mapping.

Let us now consider smaller components of the digestive system. For example consider as component that part of the digestive enzyme system which breaks up first the proteins into polypeptides. Another component breaks the polypeptides into aminoacids. The inputs of the first component are the proteins, its outputs are the resulting polypeptides, and again there is a mapping of the set of proteins on the set of polypeptides. The polypeptides which are the output of the first component form the input of the second component, the output of which is formed by aminoacids. There is again a mapping of the input sets on the output sets.

If we know the rules which enable us to find from a given set of input proteins the corresponding set of output polypeptides in the first component, and if we know the rules which enable us to find for the second component the output aminoacids from the known input polypeptides, then we also know the rules by means of which we can find for the whole digestive system the output aminoacids from the known input proteins. Designate the first set of rules, or the first mapping (proteins — polypeptides) by the letter f. Designate the second mapping (polypeptides — aminoacids) by g. Finally designate the mapping of proteins on aminoacids by h. The application of the mapping f followed by a subsequent application of g is denoted by gf. Then the above statement may be made in the form: If f and g are given, then we also know the mapping $h = gf$.

A given set A of input objects can of course be always mapped on itself. Such a mapping leaves the set unchanged. We shall denote such a mapping by i_A. It is possible that certain substances which enter a component as inputs remain unchanged and leave the components also as outputs. In that case the set of inputs is mapped on the corresponding set of outputs by the mapping i. It is called the identity mapping.

Similar considerations apply to components the inputs or outputs of which are not substances, but some physicochemical factors, such as light, sound, electrical potentials, etc.

In particular in a system of neurons certain adequate stimuli of the afferents form the inputs, while the response of the efferents form the outputs. Again we have a mapping between input and output.

Summing up we see that an organism may be considered as a set of objects between which certain mappings are defined.

In the examples considered there is only one possible mapping. In general two sets may be mapped in many different ways. Thus the set of numbers 1, 2, 3, 4 and the set 7, 8, 9 may be mapped in the following manners:

```
1, 2, 3, 4          1, 2, 3, 4              1, 2, 3, 4
|  |  |      ;      |     |  |  , or        |  |     |
7, 8, 9             7,    8, 9              7, 8,    9
```

In all those mappings, the relation $\leqq$ (less than or equal to) is preserved. We may say that to each pair of sets (A, A') in the biological example given above there corresponds a set of mappings, which either consists of only one element ,or is empty. The latter happens when A does not correspond to A'. For example, A may be a set of fats, A' a set of monosacharides. If in line with the principle of biotopological mapping, we wish to map different organisms on each other, preserving the basic relations, we are confronted with the problem of mapping of one set of mappings on another. The objects of one organism will be mapped on corresponding objects of another organism. In other words, to each object in one organism there corresponds an object in another organism. Moreover the rule must be given such that to a mapping in the first organism there corresponds a mapping in the second, and that the relations between the corresponding mappings are preserved. This means that if in one organism we have the mappings f', g', and h', and if $fg = h$, then $f'g' = h'$.

The situation which we just discussed is a very special concrete case of a general abstract theory developed in 1945 by S. Eilenberg and S. MacLane[2]. Robert Rosen[3] recently recognized the possible importance of this "Theory of Natural Equivalences" to biological problems. For a detailed presentation of the mathematical theory we refer the reader to the paper by Eilenberg and MacLane[2]. For a discussion of the possible biological applications the reader is referred to the paper by Rosen[3]. Here we shall merely give now the definition of the mathematical concepts involved. The reader will readily see in those abstract definitions a close analogy to the very concrete biological situations which we discussed above.

The following is called a *category*:

1. A collection of objects, designated by A, A', A'', etc.
2. A function, or a rule, which assigns to each pair (A, A') of objects a set $H(A, A')$ of mappings of A on A'.
3. A function, called composition, which assigns to certain pairs (f, g) of mappings, such that $f \in H(A, A')$, $g \in H(A', A'')$ a mapping $h = fg$ such that $h \in H(A', A'')$.

If $\mathfrak{A}$ and $\mathfrak{B}$ are two categories, then we say that a *covariant* functor T consists of a pair of mappings or transformations. One mapping of the pair maps every object A in $\mathfrak{A}$ on a corresponding object, denoted by $T(A)$ in $\mathfrak{B}$. The second mapping or rule assigns to each mapping $f \in H(A, A')$ in $\mathfrak{A}$ a corresponding mapping $T(f) \in H[T(A), T(A')]$ in $\mathfrak{B}$, such that

1. $T(gf) = T(g)T(f)$ whenever gf is defined,
2. $T(i_A) = i_{T(A)}$ for each A

We notice that this abstract formulation covers a much greater variety of cases than the biological examples discussed above. The "objects" do not need to be input and output substances of a component of an organism. The mappings need not be chemical rules. The objects may, for example, be topological spaces, and the mappings f, g, etc. — continuous mappings. Or the objects may be groups and the mappings f, g, etc. — homomorphisms. To the extent that the theory of natural equivalences considers correspondence between different categories, and to the extent that the "objects" which are associated with the components of an organism are categories, the study of different aspects of the theory of categories may well lead us to the discovery of new aspects of biology.

Thus far a direct application of this theory of categories has been made only to some aspects of the central nervous system, in which the different neurons follow the McCulloch-Pitts rules of Boolean algebra[3].

REFERENCES

1. R. Rosen, *Bull. Math. Biophysics*, **20**, 245, 1958.
2. S. Eilenberg and S. MacLane. *Trans. Am. Math. Soc.*, **58**, 231, 1945.
3. R. Rosen, *Bull. Math. Biophysics*, **20**, 317, 1958.

CHAPTER XXXIV

AN INTERESTING CASE OF BIOTOPOLOGICAL TREATMENT OF THE ORGANISM

As we have seen in the preceding chapter, any component of an organism receives in general some outputs from the environment, some — from other components. If an output of the component M_i serves as input of the component M_k, we may indicate this by connecting M_i to M_k by an arrow directed from M_i to M_k. Each output or input is to be represented by a different arrow. If M_i receives an input from the environment, we shall represent this by drawing an arrow marked with an E, and *ending* on M_i. If M_i gives off an output into the environment, we shall represent this by an arrow marked with an E and originating at the point M_i. We thus obtain a graph, such as is, for example, represented in Figure 1. We shall not, however, ascribe to the points of such a graph, which represents components of an organism, any particular biological properties as we did in the graphs shown in Figure 2 and 7 of chapter xxx. Nor shall we ascribe any particular biological meaning to the corresponding inputs or outputs. We just shall consider a system of components, inputs, and outputs of any kind. This is a kind of abstract picture of an organism. Such an abstract system introduced first by Robert Rosen[1], we shall call a biological system. An actual organism is a particular, concretized case of a biological system. Rosen[1] has shown that the study of such abstract biological systems may lead to interesting biological conclusions. One of them we shall discuss in this chapter.

A component of a biological system $\mathfrak{M}$ which accepts an environmental input shall be called an *origin* of $\mathfrak{M}$. A component which produces an environmental output shall be called a *terminus* or *terminal component* of $\mathfrak{M}$. A component can be both an origin and a terminus as is the component M_5 in Figure 1.

We shall call a subsystem $\mathfrak{M}'$ of $\mathfrak{M}$ a subset of the set of components of $\mathfrak{M}$, if the elements of this subset are connected by arrows in the same manner as in $\mathfrak{M}$, if the environmental outputs of $\mathfrak{M}'$ contain a subset of the environmental outputs of $\mathfrak{M}$, and if no input to $\mathfrak{M}'$ is an output of a component of $\mathfrak{M}$.

In Figure 1 the sets of points $\{M_1, M_4, M_5\}$ with their connections constitute a subsystem. Also the sets $\{M_1, M_2, M_4, M_5\}$ and $\{M_1, M_2, M_3, M_4\}$, with their connecting arrows are subsystems. But $\{M_1, M_2, M_3\}$ is not a subsystem, because in this set M_2 receives an input which is an output of the component M_4 of $\mathfrak{M}$ which does not belong to $\mathfrak{M}'$.

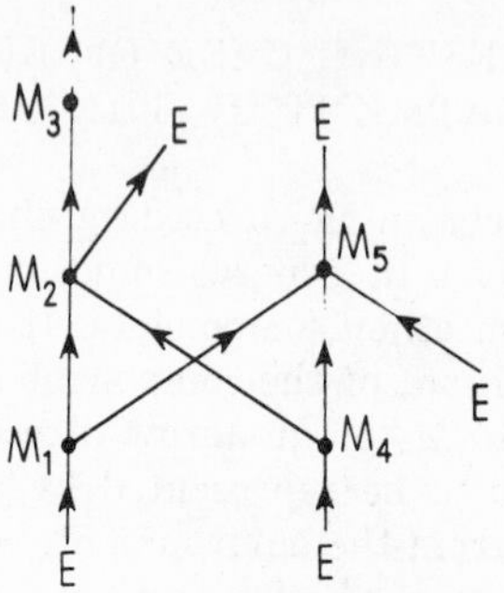

FIG. 1

Since each component affects directly or indirectly other components therefore a removal, destruction or inhibition of a component M_i of a biological system will in general result in an impairment of some other components of that system. In particular the removal of M_i may result in the cessation of some environmental outputs of $\mathfrak{M}$. Denote by θ the set of all environmental outputs of $\mathfrak{M}$ and by S_i the set of all environmental outputs of $\mathfrak{M}$ which are stopped by the removal of the component M_i. The set S_i is a subset of θ. Thus $S_i \subset \theta$. The set S_i is not necessarily a proper subset of θ, because the removal of M_i may stop all environmental outputs of $\mathfrak{M}$. The set S_i shall be called the *dependent set* of the component M_i.

We may take it as a general fact that catabolic processes result in a constant destruction of every part of the organism. This destruction is compensated by a continuous building up of those parts by anabolic processes. If the anabolic processes would stop any part of an organism would exist only for a finite time. In addition to anabolic processes ordinary tear and wear also gradually destroy all parts of the organism. But in the specially organized anabolic processes every part of the organism possesses an appropriate repair mechanism which renovates the part and counteracts the effects of catabolism and of natural tear and wear.

It is therefore natural to consider such abstract biological systems in which every component M_i has an appropriate repair mechanism R_i. This repair mechanism R_i is itself a component of a more general system, which consists of the components M_i and of the corresponding components R_i. With Robert Rosen[1] we shall call such a generalized system an $(\mathfrak{M}, \mathfrak{R})$ — system. We shall consider the special case where each R_i receives as inputs *some* of the environmental outputs of $\mathfrak{M}$. Thus the set θ_i of inputs into R_i is a subset of θ. We shall consider that the only output of R_i is the process of replication or rebuilding of M_i. We shall, moreover, make the assumption that R_i requires all the elements of θ_i for its proper functioning. The missing of a single input of the set θ_i will make R_i inoperative. This assumption is somewhat restrictive but not implausible. We also assume that the operation of each M_i requires *all* its inputs.

Just as in the case of a system $\mathfrak{M}$, the destruction of a component M_i of an $(\mathfrak{M}, \mathfrak{R})$ — system will in general result in a cessation of the biological functions of some parts of the $(\mathfrak{M}, \mathfrak{R})$ — system. If the destruction or removal of M_i results in a complete cessation of the functions of the whole $(\mathfrak{M}, \mathfrak{R})$ — system, then the component M_i is called a *central component* of the $(\mathfrak{M}, \mathfrak{R})$ — system. If a component M_i is not central, then there exists a subsystem $\mathfrak{M}_i'$ of the system $\mathfrak{M}$ which forms a part of the $(\mathfrak{M}, \mathfrak{R})$ — system such that it is not affected by the destruction of M_i. This subsystem $\mathfrak{M}_i'$ is called the *related subsystem* of the component M_i.

The set of all environmental outputs *not* produced by $\mathfrak{M}_i'$ in $\mathfrak{M}$ will be called the *augmented dependent set* of M_i, and will be denoted by $\bar{S}_i$. In general some of the environmental outputs of the set $\bar{S}_i$ will not necessarily be abolished by the removal or destruction of M_i. But on the other hand any element of the dependent set S_i of the environmental outputs which are abolished by the destruction of M_i are certainly *not* produced by $\mathfrak{M}_i'$, for otherwise they would not be abolished. Hence $S_i \subseteq \bar{S}_i$.

Having thus defined the abstract biological $\mathfrak{M}$ — system and the $(\mathfrak{M}, \mathfrak{R})$ — system, we may now study systematically their properties. For the details of such a study we refer the reader to the original paper by R. Rosen[1]. Here we shall prove only one interesting theorem, to illustrate the type of conclusions that are reached in such a study.

We inquire into the conditions under which a destroyed component M_i of an $(\mathfrak{M}, \mathfrak{R})$ — system will be re-established or repaired. This will be possible only if the destruction of M_i does not abolish any of the environmental outputs of the set θ_i. The abolishing of M_i leaves now $\mathfrak{M}_i'$ as a functioning biological system. In order that M_i be re-established, R_i must operate, and therefore all the environmental outputs of the set θ_i must be present. But this means that no element of θ_i shall be an element of the set $\bar{S}_i$ of the environmental outputs of $\mathfrak{M}_i'$. In other words, in order that M_i be re-establishable, we must have $\theta_i \cap \bar{S}_i = \emptyset$.

We now prove the following theorem due to Rosen.

Theorem. If in an $(\mathfrak{M}, \mathfrak{R})$ — system the corresponding system $\mathfrak{M}$ is represented by a connected graph, then it is impossible for *every* component M_i to be re-establishable.

Proof. Suppose the theorem is false. Then there exists an $(\mathfrak{M}, \mathfrak{R})$ — system Λ in which every component is re-establishable. Let M be a terminus of the system $\mathfrak{M}$ in Λ. Then M is re-establishable. If M is the only terminus of $\mathfrak{M}$, then only its own outputs are available as inputs to the corresponding R_M. But then M cannot be re-establishable, because its destruction would abolish all inputs into R_M. Hence the outputs of M must serve as inputs to some R_i, by definition of the $(\mathfrak{M}, \mathfrak{R})$ — system. The re-establishability of M_i implies that those outputs cannot serve as inputs to such an R_i which corresponds to such an M_i that M can be reached by a directed way from it. Because in such a case the destruction of M_i would result in an abolishment of M, which would make the inputs into R_i unavailable, and would make M_i not re-establishable. Hence there must exist another terminus N which can be reached along a way from the component M_i, such that $\theta_i \cap \bar{S}_M$ is not empty. By hypothesis N is also re-establishable. Hence no output of N can serve as input to an R_j which corresponds to such an M_j that N can be reached from M_j by a directed way. If M and N were the only termini of $\mathfrak{M}$, then the connectedness of $\mathfrak{M}$ implies that there exists a component M_k from which both M and N can be reached along a directed way. But then M_k would not be re-establishable, because its destruction would abolish the outputs of M and N, which are the only ones available as inputs to R_k. Hence there must be a third terminus. The argument may again be repeated, and we find again that there either must be another terminus or there exists a non re-establishable component. Since the number of termini is finite, we eventually arrive at the conclusion that a Λ system does not exist. This proves the theorem.

The biological implications of the above theorem are evident. A number of other theorems of similar purport have been proven and discussed by Rosen[1].

One decidedly weak point of the above outlined theory is the question as to what happens when an R_i component is destroyed. Does it become re-established and if so, how? Or are the R_i components not re-establishable? In the latter case we have a biologically somewhat unlikely situation. Catabolic processes must take place also in the R_i components. Therefore after a while those components will cease to exist and the M_i components will become not re-establishable. On the other hand, if for some reason or other the life span of the R_i components is much greater than that of the M_i components, in other words if they decay much more slowly, then the above situation may not appear to be quite so unlikely. We may perhaps associate some phenomena of ageing with the decay of the R_i components, inasmuch as it is known that with age the self-repairing ability of an organism in general decreases.

However, it would seem decidedly desirable to investigate different possibilities, namely such where a re-establishment of the R_i components takes place. The most interesting of such possibilities is to consider that some M_k system or several of them may play the role of R-systems with respect to some R_i-systems. This will impose certain conditions on the whole $(\mathfrak{M}, \mathfrak{R})$-system, and the study of the resulting possibilities is likely to offer a fertile field for biotopological investigations.

Another possibility, which is probably the simplest possible one, is to assume that an R_i component, if destroyed, becomes re-established automatically as long as the corresponding set θ_i of environmental outputs of $\mathfrak{M}$ remains intact.

Regardless of the above, a very interesting aspect of Rosen's $(\mathfrak{M}, \mathfrak{R})$-systems is that they may offer a clue to a possible biotopological treatment of the problem of reproduction.[2] Hitherto, both in chapter xxix and in chapter xxx we considered reproduction just as another basic biological property, on par with any other property P_i. Yet somehow this seems to be inadequate, because reproduction seems to occupy a central position among the other properties. Reproduction causes the spread of life on earth and all other biological activities of the organism seem to converge towards that result.

The theory of the $(\mathfrak{M}, \mathfrak{R})$-systems has no connection with the principle of biotopological mapping. It is basically a topological model of the organism. Inasmuch as our aim, as stated in chapters xxviii and xxix, is to discover fundamental general principles in biology, we should attempt to reduce any models, topological or otherwise, to the general principles. We shall now *very tentatively* suggest a possibility of deriving the $(\mathfrak{M}, \mathfrak{R})$-systems from the principle of biotopological mapping combined with a proper *definition* of the primordial.

At the beginning of chapter xxix we already hinted that the primordial organism may not be an actually existing one. We may go now a step further and say that the primordial need not be even an organism that ever existed. For our purposes it may perfectly well be an abstraction, defined as the smallest set of basic properties which still would be considered as an organism. According to chapter xxix, a basic property P_i is the logically most inclusive set of all subsets P_{ia}. If we apply this point of view, then we can considerably reduce the cardinal number of the set of basic properties of a primordial. Essentially, as we already remarked elsewhere[3, 4] and as we shall discuss in the next chapter, the many properties of an organism are logically different aspects of *selection.* An organism, through its sense organs, selects the proper location and proper character of its food. Through either molar or molecular movements P_M it continues the selection of the proper food. The digestive enzymes act *selectively* on certain substances and break them down in a selective manner. Thus the idea is naturally suggested to consider all the above mentioned basic properties as subproperties of the more inclusive property P_{sel} of selection. Some of the subproperties and therefore P_{sel} itself would be inputs into the primordial, some — outputs. The next set of properties all deal with metabolic activities and may perhaps be all considered as subproperties of another basic property P_T, which can be denoted as *transformation.* This transformation includes both production of enzymes and of waste products, and the proper arrangement of the selected molecules, obtained as a result of the operation of property P_{sel}, into a new organisms. In line with Robert Rosen's views outlined in the preceding chapter, we shall consider the property P_T neither as input nor as output, but as a mapping of outputs on inputs, or as relations between inputs and outputs.

In line with this view the simplest organism recognizable as such would consist of two components. One, M, will have as outputs certain enzymes, or enzymatic properties connected with the organism directly (if the organism consists of only one molecule). The effect of this output would be to produce, by selection, from the fragments of food, of a set of molecules which can be used as building stones for the organism. The second component, R, would take those in as inputs and produce as output through synthetic processes, a new organism.

The graph, representing such an organism would be a simple open circuit with an additional environmental input into M and an output from M, as shown in Figure 2.

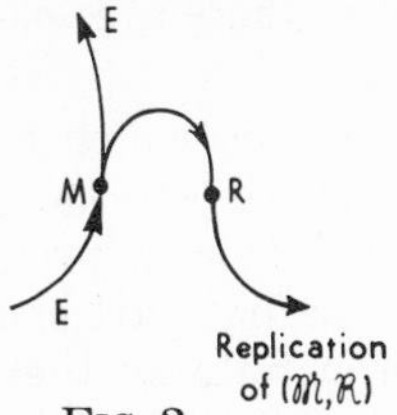

FIG. 2

We may remark that a virus molecule is not too dissimilar from the above scheme. The virus must either act directly as lytic agent on the cytoplasm of the host, or send off small catalytic particles to do that. Its selectivity is well known. Once the building stones are obtained by lysis, the replication mechanism, presumably DNA, produces other virus molecules.

If now we apply either transformation rule(A)of chapter xxix in its generalized form, or the rules $T^{(u)}$ $(u = 1, \ldots, 14)$ of chapter xxx to the primordial which we just suggested, we can obtain very complex structures. Formally the above transformation rules can be applied to an $(\mathfrak{M}, \mathfrak{R})$-system, for it does not make any difference topologically whether the points represent biological properties or components. Instead of one output of M in the primordial, there will be now a number of "suboutputs," in which different components M_i will be specialized. The same holds about R. In effect we obtain an $(\mathfrak{M}, \mathfrak{R})$-system.

Such an $(\mathfrak{M}, \mathfrak{R})$-system differs, however, from the one introduced by Rosen, and discussed above in one very essential feature: the components M_i are not merely repaired, but they multiply. There is, however, a close relation between repair of parts of an organism and the multiplication of its constituent cells. Multiplication does not occur, however, unless repair is needed. An explanation of this situation may lie in an assumption which we already made in chapter xxix of Volume I of this work, and which is almost inescapable, if we are to account for the cessation of growth of the whole organism after a certain time, and yet understand the potentially unlimited cell multiplication which will go on in an excised piece of tissue of such an organism, if the tissue is placed in a proper medium. We must assume that the different cells of an organism exert some kind of mutual inhibition on each other, and that when number of cells in the organ reaches a certain limit, the inhibition becomes complete. The situation is *formally* not unlike that studied in chapter iii of this volume for the case of mutually inhibiting neurones. When there are too many of them, the inhibition is complete.

With such an assumption, which may possibly eventually become a general principle, the $(\mathfrak{M}, \mathfrak{R})$-system, obtained by a biotopological transformation from a proper primordial will behave just as we discussed in the first part of this chapter.

We now run, however, into another difficulty. The primordial reproduces itself, but the $(\mathfrak{M}, \mathfrak{R})$-system obtained from it by a biotopological transformation, only repairs its parts.

The solution of this difficulty is likely to lie in an extension or sharpening of the principle of biotopological mapping, to which we alluded already in chapter xxx (page 357). A complex higher organism is not obtained from a simpler one by a single transformation but through a series of steps. The rule(A)of chapter xxix and the rules $T^{(u)}$ $(u = 1, \ldots, 14)$ of chapter xxx, give us the end result of the transformation. They do not tell anything about the steps in which it proceeds and which correspond to the steps of both phylogenetic and ontogenetic development. In *ontogenesis* an organism does not develop from a primordial but from an already rather complex, though unicellular organism, the ovum. This does not contradict the principle of biotopological mapping, because if a simpler and a more complex organism both map continuously onto a primordial, then the more complex will map onto the simpler one. Hence we can introduce into the topological space or graph of an organism a subspace or partial graph, O, which represents the ovum, and from which the whole organism develops in successive steps. In terms of the $(\mathfrak{M}, \mathfrak{R})$-system, O would be a subsystem. If we now assume that the subsystem O is the only one that is not inhibited, then all other components and subsystems will merely be re-established, while O will from time to time multiply and reproduce the whole organism.

As to the steps of the transformation from the representative space S_P of a primordial to the representative space S_o of a complex organism, the most natural and simple thing to consider is that at first the more inclusive subproperties P_{ia} develop, and later the less inclusive ones. Thus if $P_{ia}' \subset P_{ia}$, then P_{ia} will develop first. Since, according to chapter xxix any choice of P_{ia}'s is permissible, *several* different situations are possible. We may have a series of organisms of increasing complexity, such that the set $\mathfrak{S}_{i+k}$ of all subproperties of the more complex one includes the set $\mathfrak{S}_i$ of the less complex one, thus $\mathfrak{S}_i \subset \mathfrak{S}_{i+k}$. Such a linear arrangement will, however, be a rather special one. More generally we shall find that for two organisms, i and k, of either the same or of different complexities

$$\mathfrak{S}_i \cap \mathfrak{S}_k \neq \emptyset; \; \mathfrak{S}_i \cup \mathfrak{S}_k \neq \mathfrak{S}_i; \; \mathfrak{S}_i \cup \mathfrak{S}_k \neq \mathfrak{S}_k, \tag{1}$$

which means that $\mathfrak{S}_i$ and $\mathfrak{S}_k$ have elements in common, but neither is included in the other. The point at which the above relation holds may be reached at a certain degree of complexity prior to which the consecutive $\mathfrak{S}_i$'s are included in each subsequent one. With increasing complexity, the cardinal number of the intersection $\mathfrak{S}_i \cap \mathfrak{S}_k$ may become smaller, and finally $\mathfrak{S}_i$ and $\mathfrak{S}_k$ may even become disjoined. They will both contain subproperties of the same basic properties P_i, but different subproperties.

A development of this type is not representable by a linear series or by a line. It corresponds to a branched tree, just as is the case in actual evolution.

REFERENCES

1. R. Rosen, *Bull. Math. Biophysics*, 20, 245, 1958.
2. N. Rashevsky, *Bull. Math. Biophysics*, 20, 275, 1958.
3. N. Rashevsky, *Bull. Math. Biophysics*, 17, 207, 1955.
4. N. Rashevsky, *Bull. Math. Biophysics*, 18, 31, 1956.

CHAPTER XXXV

THE GEOMETRIZATION OF BIOLOGY

In 1909 Hermann Minkowski, inspired by the profound discovery by Einstein in 1905 of the relativity of space and time, indicated a way of reducing physical phenomena to something which is outside of physics, even outside of any other natural science, namely, pure geometry. Minkowski showed that the basic concept of mechanics, and possibly of all physics, the concept of motion, may be interpreted as an orthogonal transformation of a system of coordinates in a four-dimensional hyperspace with one imaginary coordinate. Inspired by Einstein, this discovery in its turn eventually led Einstein to the creation of the General Theory of Relativity, in which not only the concept of motion, but also concepts of acceleration, mass, and force, and especially the notion of gravitation received a geometrical interpretation in a four-dimensional non-Euclidean hyperspace.

True enough, a *complete* geometrization of physics is still a relatively distant goal. One of the stumbling stones are Maxwell's equations. Beginning with the ingenious — though unsuccessful attempt by Herman Weyl[1] — attempts at a reduction of electromagnetic phenomena to geometric concepts have continued, and Einstein's own later contribution[2] seems to carry a great deal of promise.

But even to the limited extent that geometrization of physics has been achieved, it proved to be important. Not only has it shown an unusual predictive value both in physics and astronomy, but it is different from the old attempts to reduce physics to one of its branches in that the reduction of actual natural phenomena is made to purely mathematical concepts. Those concepts are creations of the human mind, and basically are therefore much more intuitive than the physical ones, even though a visualization of multidimensional spaces may be barred to us. Basically, what modern physics does, is to map the observable physical phenomena isomorphically onto an abstract geometric structure. Certain concepts of physics, like motion, acceleration, etc., map on purely geometrical concepts of coordinates, curvature, etc. The theorems of geometry, which establish metric relations between different geometrical concepts, then lead directly to laws of physics by the use of a sort of glossary or dictionary which shows the name of the physical concept that is to be substituted for the name of a geometric concept. A "translation" of physical laws into geometric theorems and *vice versa* is thus possible.

Compared with physics in age, biology is almost a newborn baby. Whenever we experience outside of ourselves any manifestations of life we do it only through its physical manifestations. Certain introspective psychological experiences, as well as the more immediate contact with life than with the nonliving, may have led some biologists to assume that phenomena of biology are basically different from those of the nonliving physical world. An utterly useless and time-wasting argument ensued between the vitalists and the mechanists, which are now better called physicalists, as to whether phenomena of life are something *sui generis,* nonphysical in nature, or are basically reducible to the laws of physics. As remarked above, the only objectively scientific study of life can be made through the study of its physical manifestations. This holds also for the so-called mental phenomena. We can know what another person thinks only by his telling us, or writing it, which are both physical acts, or we may infer about his thoughts from some other of his overt behavior, which again must be physically manifested if we wish to observe it. Therefore the scientific study of biology has become a study of different very special physicochemical situations, with the applications of the methods of both experimental and theoretical physics. This approach has proved to be of tremendous success. As to whether all phenomena of biology can be explained in terms of contemporary (1958) physics is a question which cannot be answered by any general speculation. All we can say that attempts at such explanation, when made competently, have been hitherto crowned with success. It is, however, impossible to deny that a biological phenomenon may be discovered which cannot be explained in terms of physical laws known at present. But far from proving anything "unphysical" about life, such a discovery will merely mean the need of an extension of physics[3, 4], just as the impossibility of explaining some spectroscopic phenomena in terms of classical physics has led to its extension by introducing quantum mechanics. No one will ever call quantum mechanics "unphysical."

If physics, in its present or in its extended form, is to be reduced to geometry, then it follows from all the above that eventually a geometrization will be also the fate of biology. When we come to consider this possibility more closely, we notice one very essential difference between some laws of biology and the laws of physics. All phenomena of physics are quantitative in nature. They not only *can* be measured, but even more, unless they are measured, very little if anything significant can be said about them. Many biological phenomena are also quantitative in nature, and the biologist is now becoming used to both measurement and mathematical analysis. But, as we have seen, very many biological phenomena, and perhaps the most basic of them, are not quantitative but *relational*. Yet very definite statements can be made about them, and their importance is unquestionable.

If we wish to describe mathematically this situation, we need a different mathematical apparatus from the one used hitherto in physics or in mathematical biology. Such an apparatus is provided by topology, which is a geometry of relations rather than of quantities. The topological approach described in the preceeding chapters is to some extent a move in the direction of a geometrization of biology. However, the geometrization of biology, as attempted by topological biology, is still something very different from the geometrization of physics. In the former we do not interpret in geometrical terms any of the biological functions, such as digestion, assimilation, etc. We may perhaps say that we eliminate from biology the elusive concept of "organization," and substitute for it the geometrical notion of the topological properties of the graph or of a topological space of an organism. But except for that, we still manipulate with such concepts as digestion, assimilation, locomotion, stimulation, etc. We consider those concepts as given, and all we do is to study topological relations between those concepts, in an abstract space.

The geometrization of physics goes much further. It interprets the basic concepts of physics in geometrical terms. It eliminates, in a sense, those concepts from physics. It does not merely seek formal geometric relations between different masses, velocities and acclerations. This has been done long ago by classical kinematics and does not constitute a mapping of physics onto geometry.

If we wish to achieve the same thing for biology, we must go much further than topological biology has done so far.

The whole universe, physical and biological, is a set of "elements," the word element not being used in the chemical sense. In order to avoid confusion with the chemical connotation of the word element, we shall use it in quotation marks when set theoretical connotation is implied, and without quotation marks when the chemical connotation is used. Perhaps the most basic way of looking at it is to consider the universe as a set of world lines. We may, however, consider as "elements" of the sets, groups of the world lines, or their points of intersections, or other configurations. Different chemical reactions may be considered as the "elements" of the set. In any case, however we define the "elements" of this set, the biological phenomena are a subset of it.

What are the characteristic properties which make us recognize an organism as such? Perhaps the most basic thing about an organism is that it selects certain "elements" from the inorganic environment even if those elements form parts of other subsets (page 309). Once a selection is made, those selected "elements" are organized in a definite pattern eventually becoming themselves "elements" of the organism, and leading to a duplication of the latter. In this case the "elements" are the different chemical molecules, radicals or complexes.

This process of selection is accompanied by a loss of some "elements" of the organism. This loss may be a complete breakdown into waste products, or it may be constituted by the secretion of a molecule of a digestive enzyme which "attacks" a food particle and selectively breaks from it the desired molecular configuration. Usually the secretion of a digestive enzyme is not considered on the same level as a catabolic breakdown. But *logically* they both resemble each other, and they both may be necessary for the process of selection. For while in some microorganims, like nonmotile bacteria, the selection goes on at a purely chemical level; in higher organisms it is more complicated. The sight of possible food; the locomotion towards it; the breaking up of food either by teeth, or by hands, or by hand-made machinery; the picking up and consumption of the proper parts of the food — all this constitutes a process of selection, and for many such processes in higher organisms the energy released by catabolic processes is needed. Thus everywhere in the process of selection some loss of its constituents by the organisms seems essential.

Any selection process implies rejection of the unwanted material. Digestion, followed on one hand by absorption, on the other by excretion are only the logical aspects of the selection process. Thus these three very basic biological functions may be described in terms of selection. And as we have just said, a number of other biological functions, which acquired typically biological names, are also basically logical aspects of the process of selection.

If we could interpret selection geometrically — or more specifically topologically — we would thus reduce some biological concepts to geometric ones.

Let us make the next logical step. Selection implies the division of the "elements" of some subset in two classes: those selected and those rejected. Division in two classes is not at all uncommon in topology. Thus a point of the one dimensional space of real numbers induces a Dedekind cut, and, therefore, a division of all other points in two classes. A closed Jordan curve in E^2, the Euclidean plane, divides all points of E^2 in two classes: the inner and the outer ones. Both cases are examples of a subset M of a space S dividing $S - M$ in two classes. But those simple cases do not help us any. As we have seen, the division by the organisms of the set of "elements" which constitute the environment of an organism in two classes is contingent on the organism, considered as a set, losing some of its own "elements." Moreover, if one or more of the selected "elements" are added to the subset M which is the organism, the relation between that subset and the complement $S - M$ remains the same: the organism continues to select. That second property is exhibited in the following example. Let M be a subset of S not closed in S. Then M divides all the points of $S - M$ in two classes: those that are the limit points of M, and those that are not. Except for the very special case in which the first class is a degenerate subset, when some of the limit points of M are added to M the resulting subset M' still divides the points of $S - M'$ in two classes: those that are limit points of M', and those that are not.

A particular case of the above offers some remote analogy to the first necessary property, that of a loss by breakdown. Let S be the space of real numbers and let M be the subspace obtained from S by omitting all rational points in the closed interval $(0, 1)$. All rational points of S within that interval are limit points of M; those outside are not. The subspace M is not connected, however, and this loss of connectivity may be regarded as a remote analogy of a breakdown process. In this example there is no division by M of $S - M$ in two classes, that is, no selection, without loss of connectivity of M.

The above examples have, of course, no scientific value whatsoever. They are used only to illustrate a point which, if given an abstract formulation, may be difficult to make clear. Namely, if we can find a topological space, such that its different topological properties stand in the same logical relation to each other as do different basic biological concepts, then by substituting the names of those biological concepts for the names of the corresponding topological properties, we could, using again a glossary, translate every theorem about such a space into a corresponding biological law, just as it is done in the geometrization of physics. The purely mathematical study of the properties of such a properly chosen space would yield us all the laws of biology, both already known and those not yet discovered. If this ever becomes possible, it would indeed be a triumph of geometry, more generally, of pure mathematics.

This idea, suggested by the twentieth century physics, may appeal to some and not appeal to others. But even to those to whom it may appeal, it still is of no use. We cannot do much with a bare idea unless we at least show how, in principle, the idea *might* be realized. Here we must consider two logical possibilities.

Topology is still a young science; yet, it has already ramified in many directions, and a very great variety of its aspects have been studied. It is not precluded that the necessary types of spaces or other topological structures have already been studied and only need to be taken over, but that thus far we have failed to perceive the proper possibility. After all, the basic apparatus of non-Euclidean geometry has existed for a fairly long time; yet, it took Einstein to see that phenomena of physics are isomorphic to some of those already well known geometric properties. The rational problem-solving and the reduction of new situations to already known ones has psychologically and biophysically some similarity with the discovery of a "hidden picture" as has been shown in chapter xv. Thus, we may hope that an inspiration by a mathematician or a mathematical biologist may indicate the solution, which will apepar rather obvious after it is discovered.

But we cannot discount the other possibility, namely, that appropriate topological spaces have not yet been studied and that the needs of biology may provide a stimulus to the topologist to make new discoveries in his field, just as the needs of physics have provided in the past the stimulus for new mathematical discoveries. Gauss has actually credited physics with many of his purely mathematical inspirations.

But here again we must be somewhat more definite and therefore, even without hoping to formulate at present the necessary purely mathematical problem and to describe the necessary type of topological space, give at least a few examples of the kind of thinking that may be required. Those examples we shall give again *as an illustration only*. Their actual biological and mathematical values are nil. But they may serve, as the French say, "pour fixer les idées."

Let us return again to the basic logical property of the organism. Certain "elements" of the environment are selected, that is, begin to belong to one of two classes if some "elements" of the organism itself are detached from the latter. Considering again the organism as a subspace M in the space S and considering the "elements" as points in these spaces, we may translate the above logical property into topological language. In order that M should induce a division of the points of $S - M$ in two classes, it is necessary that some points of $S - M$ would possess some property P with respect to M, which others do not possess. In order that the division of the points of $S - M$ in two classes becomes possible only after M loses some "elements," some points of $S - M$ must acquire the property P with respect to M only after certain points of M are removed. The simplest example of such a situation is offered by a closed Jordan curve, from which one point, α (Figure 1), is removed. Let such a Jordan curve with a point removed be the subspace M in the space $S = E^2$. It is actually a Jordan arc, the ends of which are separated by the point α only. Thus M is a single connected subspace of E^2. The point α does not belong to M, but belongs to $S - M$. Let property P consist of making M connected. Since M is already connected, therefore α does not possess property P. But if we remove from M any other point, say β (Figure 1), then M becomes non-connected, and α acquires the property P.

Instead of a closed Jordan curve with one point removed, consider the structure shown in Figure 2, in which the points α_1, α_2, and α_3 are removed. As a subspace M of $S = E^2$, it is connected. If, however, we remove the point β from M, it breaks up into four components, and the *set of points* $(\alpha_1, \alpha_2, \alpha_3)$ acquires the property P. Thus the removal of one point, β, makes M divide the different subsets of $S - M$ in two classes: one class, consisting only of one element — the subset $(\alpha_1, \alpha_2, \alpha_3)$ — has the property P; the other does not. The subsets of the two different "classes" are not all disjoined. Thus the subset $(\alpha_1, \alpha_2, \alpha_4)$ does not have property P, but $(\alpha_1, \alpha_2, \alpha_4) \cap (\alpha_1, \alpha_2, \alpha_3) \neq 0$.

In a similar space like the one shown in Figure 2, but having instead of 4 lines $n + 1$ lines connected by the point β, the removal of the point β will make a set of n points of $S - M$ acquire the property P, where n is an arbitrary positive integer.

We shall call such subspaces of E^2, as those shown in Figure 2, λ_n-spaces. Now connect an infinite number of λ-spaces in a manner shown in Figure 3, in which all $\lambda_n = \lambda_2$. Considered as subspace M of $E^2 = S$ the space thus obtained is connected, non-compact, dense in itself and nowhere dense in S, and not closed in E^2, since all the α points are its limit points. It satisfies the four Hausdorf axioms. It has the property that the removal of any β_i makes a set of points $(\alpha_i^1, \alpha_i^2, \ldots \alpha_i^n)$ acquire the property P. Any subspace of S that has this property we shall call a λ-space.

We can make the λ-space shown in Figure 3 bounded in $S = E^2$ and derive a more complicated λ-space. To achieve this, take the spiral with the equation in polar coordinates ρ, θ:

$$\rho = \frac{\theta - 1}{\theta} \, ; \theta \geqslant 1 \, . \tag{1}$$

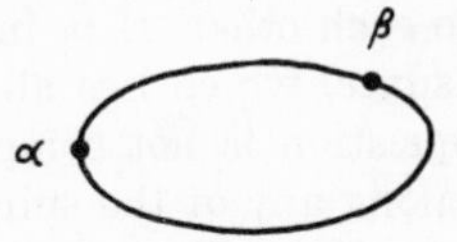

FIG. 1

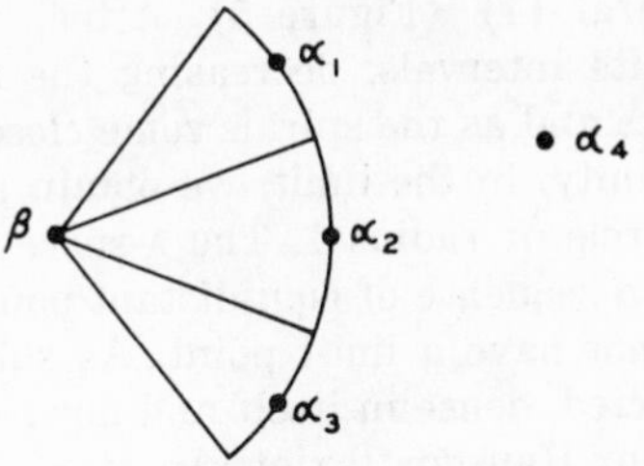

FIG. 2

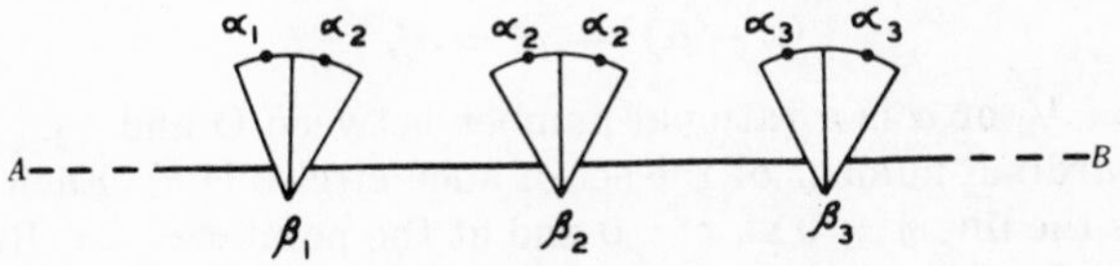

FIG. 3

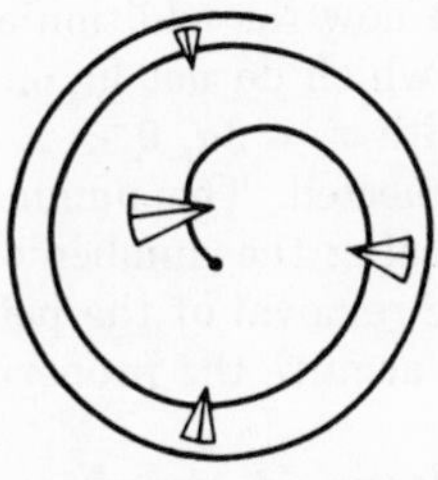

FIG. 4

FIG. 5

At equal, or unequal intervals, along the line (1), which begins at $\rho = 0$ and approaches asymptotically the circle $\rho = 1$, attach to it λ_n-spaces, as they are attached in Figure 3 to the line AB, (Figure 4), making the size of each λ_n-space smaller, as the windings of the spiral become closer, so that no λ_n-space would be intersected by the line (1). Then take spirals given by:

$$\rho = \frac{\theta - \left(1 + \dfrac{\pi}{m}\right)}{\theta} \, ; \theta \geqslant 1 + \frac{\pi}{m} \, , \qquad (2)$$

where m is an arbitrary integer different from zero. The spirals (2), obtained for different values of m, lie all between the windings of spiral (1) (Figure 5). Attach to each spiral (2) a λ_n-space, at finite intervals, decreasing the size of λ_n-spaces as the m increases and as the spirals come closer to each other. If m increases to infinity, in the limit, we obtain a λ-space, which lies all within the circle of radius 1. The λ-space in question is not compact because a sequence of equi-distant points along any of the spiral lines does not have a limit point. As subspace M of E^2, the λ-space is connected, dense in itself and nowhere dense in $E^2 = S$. It satisfies the four Hausdorf axioms[5].

We now shall construct a different space M, in which the removal of one point makes an infinite set of points of $S - M$ acquire property P. Consider the family of circles in E^2:

$$(x - \alpha)^2 + y^2 = \alpha^2, \tag{3}$$

where $\alpha = 1/2$ or α is a rational number between O and $1/2$.

The cardinal number of the set of such circles is $\aleph_0$. Each circle intersects the line $y = 0$ at $x = 0$ and at the point $x = 2\alpha$. Remove in each circle the point $x = 2\alpha$. The space M obtained by this removal from the family of circles (3), considered as a subspace of $S = E^2$, is connected. Removal from M of the point 0 which we shall designate by β, makes it not connected. But now the addition of all points of the segment (0, 1) of the x-axis which do not lie on any circle of the family, that is, of all points with $x \neq 2\alpha$, $0 < x < 1$, $y = 0$; will make the resulting space connected. The number of points to be thus added is non-countable, being the number of all *irrational* points between 0 and 1. Thus the removal of the point β makes all points $x \neq 2\alpha$, $0 < x < 1$, $y = 0$ acquire the property P. We shall call such a space a λ'-space.

Now consider a space which is made up if λ'-spaces such that each λ'-space is in a plane which passes through the x-axis, in a sequence of planes with each two adjacent planes forming an angle π/n, where n may be as large as we wish, then the point $\beta = (0, 0, 0)$ will be a disconnecting point, and the set of irrational points of the x-axis $(0 < x < 1)$ will acquire property P. This space we may call λ''-space.

The following theorem can be readily proved about the λ-, λ'- and λ''-spaces.

The analytical intersection of two λ-, (λ'-, λ''-) spaces is not a λ-, λ'- or λ''-space, and is always not connected.

As we have emphasized already, the above examples of "fancy" topological spaces are of no value either biologically or topologically and are used only to illustrate a point. We shall now use them for such an illustration.

An organism, as we have seen, selects from the environment some "elements" which have some special properties with respect to that organism. The selection of a set of "elements" becomes possible only after the organism loses some other set of its own "elements," and, in general, a specific set must be lost in order to make the selection of a given set possible. The selection, as we also have seen, is logically equivalent to inducing the division of all the "elements" of the environment in two classes: those that possess certain properties, and those that do not.

The λ-, λ'-, and λ''-spaces are, from a logical point of view, selecting the specific sets from the environment $S - M$ upon losing other specific sets. We have here a description of a biological phenomenon in topological terms. Or we may put it this way. If we make the "elements" of an organism, which must be lost in order to make a selection from the environment, correspond to the β-points of the λ-, λ'-, or λ''-space and the selected "elements" to the α-points, then the logical relation between the loss of "elements" by an organism and its selection activities are mapped isomorphically on the topological relations between the α- and β-points.

In an organism the loss of an "element" is compensated by the addition of the properly selected "elements" of the environment. If, after we remove a β-point, we add the corresponding α-points, we compensate by this addition for the loss of the β-point and restore the original connectedness of the λ-, λ'-, or λ''-space.

Now, to continue the illustration, let us just for a moment imagine that the λ-, λ'-, and λ''-spaces would be used not only for illustration, but so to say, taken seriously.

The selection of "elements" of the environment through loss of some of its own "elements" is a basic property of the organism. We have seen that an intersection of two λ-, λ'-, or λ''-spaces is not a connected space, and it does not possess the property of selection which the λ-, λ'-, and λ''-spaces possess. Let us translate the theorem into biological language. It reads thus: the common part of two organisms is not an organism and does not itself select the proper "elements" from the surroundings. Since a cell is an organism, we may restate the above as follows: The common part of two cells does not possess the ability of selecting proper elements from the environment by losing some of its own elements.

But the only possible common part of two cells could be the cell membrance which separates two adjoining cells. Hence from topological considerations, we reach the biological conclusion that the cell membrane in such cases does not make a selection of proper material from the environment in a manner which the cell as a whole, and possibly some of its parts, do. Whether this is true or not, it is certainly an experimentally verifiable conclusion.

The above example illustrates how the approach suggested in this paper, if properly made, can lead to verifiable predictions.

Very many objections can be raised against the λ, λ', and λ'' — spaces. Inasmuch as they are used only for illustration, we do not need to worry about the numerous possible objections. One point, however, may be mentioned perhaps as possible suggestion for the directions future research may take.

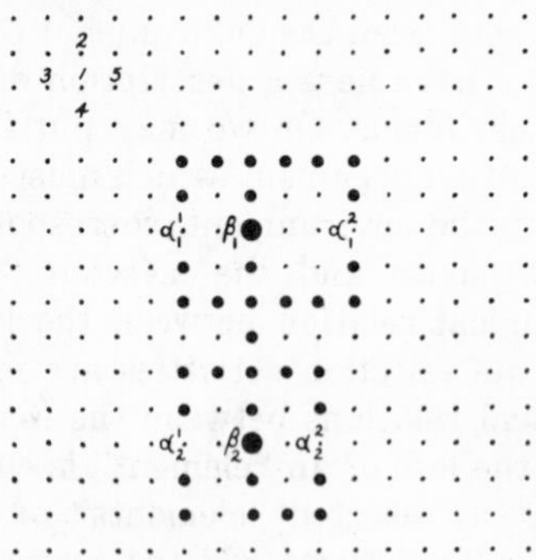

FIG. 6

The number of "elements" of which an organism is composed is very large but finite, whereas the number of points in the λ-, λ'-, and λ''-spaces is infinite. Moreover in the λ-space the cardinal number of all points is $\aleph$, while the cardinal number of β- and α-points is $\aleph_0$. We may say that only an infinitesimal fraction of the total number of points of the λ-space take part in the "selection" process. This is certainly not so in a biological system.

It seems to be desirable to study spaces with a finite number of points. As an example used again for illustration purposes only, let S be the space formed by the points in a plane arranged in an infinite square lattice (Figure 6) and in which the neighborhoods are defined as follows: the neighborhood of a point consists of that point and of the four adjacent points which lie on the lines of the lattice. Thus the neighborhood of point 1 in Figure 6 is constituted by the points 1, 2, 3, 4, 5. With neighborhoods so defined, S is connected because there exists no partition $S = A|B$ such that $A \cap \bar{B} = \bar{A} \cap B = \emptyset$. The subspace M, which consists of the points marked by heavy dots, is also connected and has a finite number of points. The removal of point β_1 from M makes the points α_1 and α_2

of $S - M$ acquire the property P; while the removal of the point β_2 makes the points α_2^1 and α_2^2 of $S - M$ acquire the property P. More complicated spaces of that kind can be readily constructed.

The following last example shows the possibility of having spaces which, as a result of a selection followed by addition of the selected "elements" (assimilation in biology), may *duplicate themselves.* The biological interest of such spaces is quite obvious.

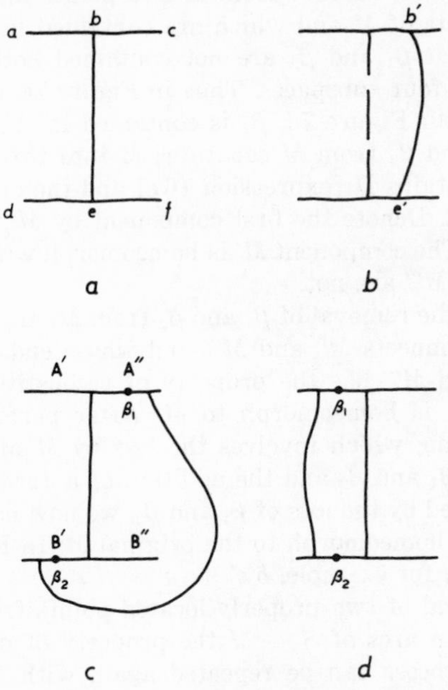

FIG. 7

Consider in $S = E^2$ the space M shown in Figure 7a. From the point of view of combinatorial topology, M is a tree with the bicenters b and e. We shall consider it, however, from a set topological point of view as a subspace of $S = E^2$. M is irreducibly connected about its subspace

$$C = A \cup B\,, \tag{4}$$

where A and B denote respectively the segments ac and df:

$$A = ac\,; \quad B = df\,. \tag{5}$$

Hence the segment be, which we shall denote by D, may be defined as

$$D = M - C\,. \tag{6}$$

The end points of D are cut points of A and B respectively. They divide A and B each in two components: A', A'', and B', B''. If we remove from M either a point or a nondegenerate subset of D which does not contain the cut points of A and B, then M loses its connectedness, and any Jordan arc in $S = E^2$ which joins the sets A and B has the property P. In Figure 7b, line $b'e'$ has, for example, the property P.

Let us, however, remove from M two points β_1 and β_2, which are not end points of M and which are contained in A', A'', B', or B'', and such that β_1 and β_2 are not contained both in the same one of the above four subspaces. Thus in Figure 7c, β_1 is contained in A'', β_2 in B'; in Figure 7d, β_1 is contained in A', β_2 in B'. The removal of β_1 and β_2 from M separates M into three components, one of which contains D [expression (6)] and the other two which do not contain it. Denote the first component by M', the other two by M'' and M'''. The component M' is homeomorph with M; the components M'' and M''' are not.

Now, after the removal of β_1 and β_2 from M, any Jordan arc in $S = E^2$ which connects M'' and M''' and whose end points are cut points of M'' and M''' has the property of reconstituting a second space M_1, which is homeomorph to M. After performing thus a specified operation, which involves the loss by M of two properly specified points β_1 and β_2 and the addition of a Jordan arc from a set of arcs selected by the loss of β_1 and β_2, we now have two spaces M' and M_1, each homeomorph to the original M. In Figures 7c and 7d such arcs are, for example, $b'e'$.

Thus, removal of two properly located points from M imposes on certain Jordan arcs of $S - M$ the property of duplicating the space M. The process can be repeated again with M' and M_1 indefinitely. It is true that the sizes of the subspaces which correspond to A', A'', B', and B'' decrease with each "reproduction." However, we are interested here not in the metric, but only in the topological properties. And topologically all the "daughter spaces" are homeomorph to the original space.

By study of appropriate topological spaces, it thus may be possible to map the properties of the simplest conceivable organism onto a proper topological space. Using then the principle of biotopological mapping, it may be possible to construct, by proper transformations, more complicated spaces, which map continuously in a many-to-one manner on the simpler space, and the study of the topological properties of those spaces may lead us to the discovery of new biological properties of multicellular organisms.

Continuing our fantastic excursion into the possible future of topological biology, we shall now take a look at another branch of topology which, perhaps, may also be destined to contribute its share to mathematical biology.

With the present-day reduction of physics to geometry, the physical events are represented geometrically by the intersections of the world lines of different particles. The metric characteristics of those intersections, or as the physicists call them, space-time coincidences, describe also the metric characteristics of the physical events. Inasmuch as an organism is composed of physical particles and obeys the laws of physics, the living phenomena are also representable by the intersections of world lines of the particles of which the organism is built. However, the characteristic and basic properties of life being of a relational character rather than of a metric one, it is the topological relations between the intersections of world lines that are important now. The branch of topology which comes close to the study of such types of relations is the theory of knots[6] and especially its subdivision, E. Artin's theory of braids[7].

Artin studies braids in a three-dimensional space, but an extension to four dimensions seems to be natural and worth trying. Since again we shall use here some elementary notions of the theory of braids only for purposes of illustration, we shall confine ourselves to the three-dimensional case, studied by Artin. In fact, we shall consider even for simplicity only a degenerate two-dimensional case.

A braid is basically a set of lines interwoven in a regular manner. Consider the three lines of Figure 8. Let them first run parallel and then, at a certain point, begin an orderly interweaving. Such an interweaving constitutes, as Artin has shown, a group. The elements of that group are defined in the following manner.

Let us number at any place of the braid the lines from left to right, 1, 2, ... If the first line crosses the second *over* it, as in the upper crossing of the Figure 8a, we denote this process by σ_1. If the first line crosses the second *underneath*, as in the second crossing in Figure 8a, we denote this process by σ_1^{-1}. Clearly σ_1^{-1} is the inverse of σ_1, for, as seen from Figure 8a, a successive application of the two, $\sigma_1\sigma_1^{-1}$, results in the reestablishment of a situation which is homotop to the initial situation. It is seen from Figure 8a that a mere homotopic deformation reduces 8a to just a set of parallel lines which do not cross at all. In a similar manner the relation between the second and the third line are denoted by σ_2

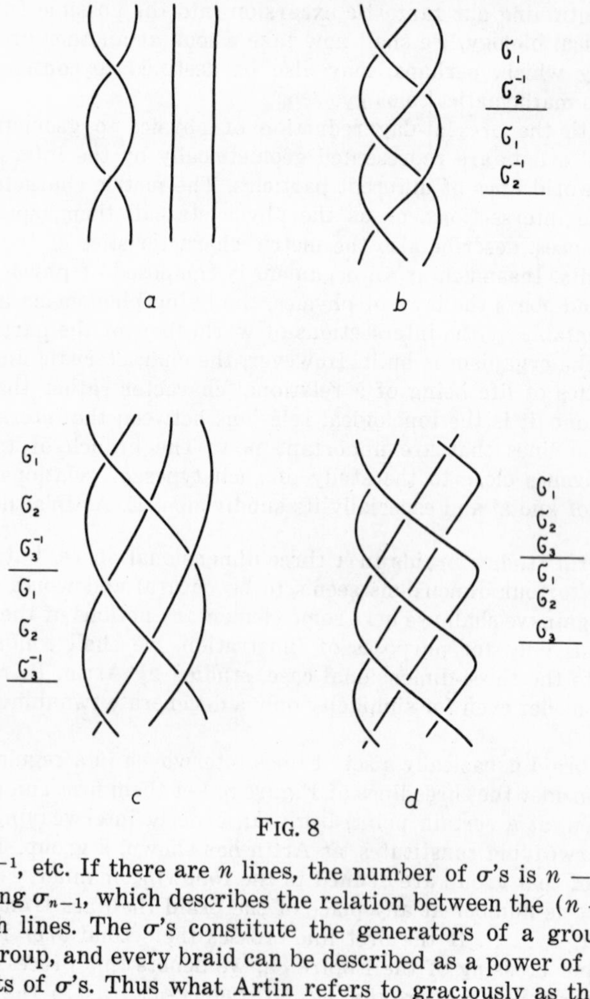

FIG. 8

and σ_2^{-1}, etc. If there are n lines, the number of σ's is $n - 1$, the last being σ_{n-1}, which describes the relation between the $(n - 1)$st and nth lines. The σ's constitute the generators of a group, the braid group, and every braid can be described as a power of proper products of σ's. Thus what Artin refers to graciously as the ordinary ladies' braid is given by

$$(\sigma_1\sigma_2^{-1})^m. \tag{7}$$

That this is so is intuitively clear from Figure 8b.

Figure 8c represents a braid; the group-theoretical expression for which is

$$(\sigma_1\sigma_2\sigma_3^{-1})^m, \tag{8}$$

while Figure 8d represents a braid

$$(\sigma_1\sigma_2\sigma_3)^m. \tag{9}$$

The two examples show that the braid group is noncommutative. It is readily seen that braids of any complexity can thus be represented.

We shall considerably simplify the examples to follow by considering a special case, discussed by Artin, namely, when it does not matter whether one line is above or below the other. Then the σ_k^{-i}'s are the same as σ_k^{i}'s. The braid of Figure 8b now becomes

$$(\sigma_1\sigma_2)^m \tag{10}$$

and is represented in Figure 9.

Artin considers all the lines of a braid as indistinguishable, which is the case when they are just abstract lines. If, however, each line represents the world line of a particle, then if the particles are distinguishable physically, the lines must be distinguishable also. In a drawing we may represent them in different colors, or by full, broken, and dotted lines, etc.

A braid may be deformed homotopically and the metric relations in it, such as the actual distance along a line between points of intersection, will change. But the topological properties expressed by (7) — (10) remain invariant. It is, therefore, rather natural to consider the relational properties of the organism as corresponding to the topological properties of the four-dimensional braid of world lines of the particles, of which the organism is composed. A braid being a special kind of a knot, it may well turn out to be literally true that life is a knotty problem!

It is, however, readily seen that the concept of an organism as a simple braid of world lines is utterly inadequate. An organism undergoes continuous catabolism and anabolism. While the chemical constitution of an organism may remain relatively constant, no constituent atom or molecule remains in the organism for any length of time. Some molecules are continuously lost and are just as continuously replaced by other similar molecules. In terms of a braid, we have a braid which is constantly unwoven and rewoven from other threads, something like a "Belgian lace." This, at first glance, seems to complicate the topological problem tremendously. Actually it does not.

At any point of a braid we may "pull out" a thread or line homotopically[8] without disturbing the topological properties of the braid. Thus the braids of Figures 8b and 10a are topologically the same, being homeomorph. We may make the loop larger and larger, and in the limit move the point a (Figure 10a) into infinity, still preserving the topological properties. In the limit we obtain the situation shown in Figure 10b, where the braid loses a line (l_1) and gains one (l_2). This can be done to any line of the braid at any point, except a point of intersection. In a finite four-dimensional world even the removal of the point a to infinity is not necessary. A mere removal to a sufficient distance is enough.

Thus in our following discussion we may disregard the constant unweaving and reweaving of the braid and consider the classical form of Artin.

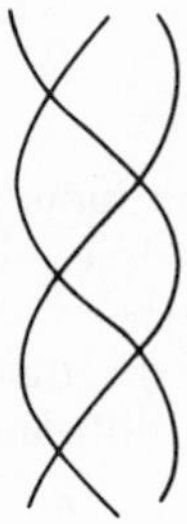

FIG. 9

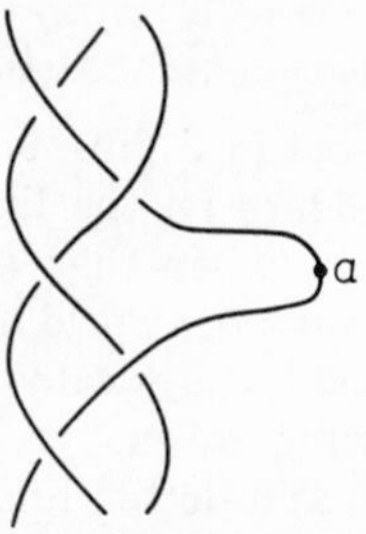

FIG. 10 a.

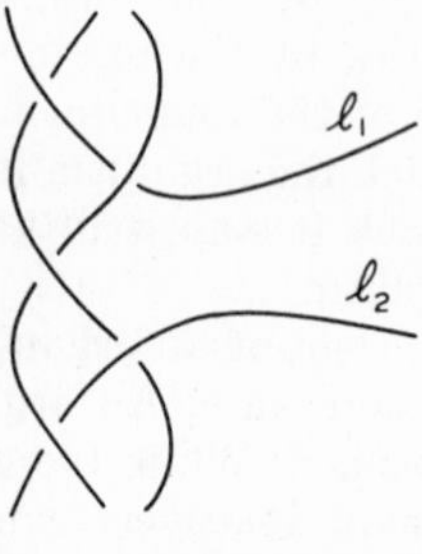

FIG. 10 b.

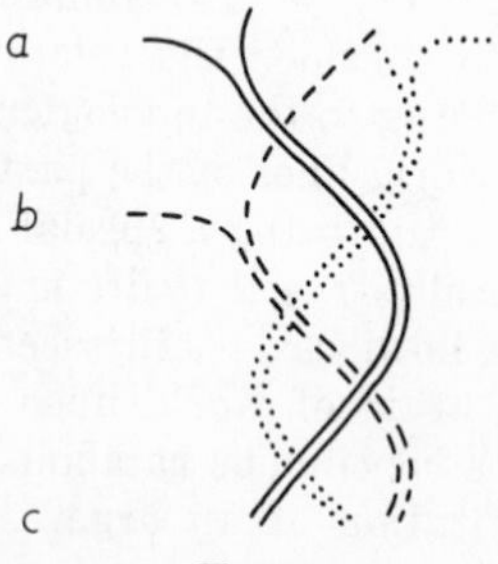

FIG. 11

An organism usually grows when it assimilates more molecules than it loses to the environment. In terms of a braid this means that more lines are woven in than are unwoven. In the situation shown in Figure 10, for each line lost there is one gained. We need, therefore, consider only the weaving in of the excess lines. This can be done in many different ways. Since, as we said above, the lines now are all physically distinguishable, we may, for example, postulate that every line which is at any given position on the outside of the braid "catches" a similar line unless there are already two lines of that kind in the braid. Such a "caught" line then remains adjacent to the other, making a "double thread" of identical lines until all lines are duplicated. The process is illustrated for three lines in Figure 11. At *a* the full and the dotted lines each "catch" a similar one; at *b* the broken line which here becomes an outside line, "catches" a similar line. After those two steps, all lines are duplicated. If there are more than three lines, there will be more than two steps, and the number of steps, in general, depends on the structure of the braid, that is, on the structure of its group. Each time a new line is woven in, in this way, a new generating element σ is introduced into the braid group. When each line is duplicated, we must make some further assumption as to what happens. For example, we may assume that, from that moment on, the braid is determined by the group of all 6! permutations of the six threads of which it now consists, the permutations being obtained by a prescribed sequence of transpositions. After a definite number of steps the situation will be reached in which we shall have the sequence: full, broken, dotted; full, broken, dotted. In other words, the original braid is now duplicated in two similar ones. From this moment the interweaving may continue only amongst the first three and the second three lines, and thus the process begins all over again with two identical braids instead of one. We have here a topological model of the duplication and continued multiplication of an organism through assimilation.

Instead of the above assumptions about the method of "catching" and weaving in of new lines, we could have made an infinite number of different ones which lead to an eventual duplication of the braid. The important part is that each set of assumptions leads, if translated into biological terms, to different verifiable conclusions. The number of steps between the beginning of the process and the duplication of every line depends, as we have said, on the assumption made. So does the number of steps between stage *c* of Figure 11, and the stage at which the actual multiplication begins. But each step would correspond to some biological process, since each step represents an intersection of two world lines, a space time coincidence, that is a physically observable phenomenon. Thus the number of physically observable processes between the different stages of the life cycle of an organism are predicted by the topological assumptions made.

Instead of assuming that the interweaving in separate groups of three begins only when the situation

full, broken, dotted; full, broken, dotted **(11)**

is reached, we may consider the case in which it begins at the stage

full, full, dotted; broken, broken, dotted. **(12)**

This stage will also eventually be reached after a definite number of steps. We have now a case which biologically corresponds to an unequal division with differentiation. One of the new braids has now an excess of full lines, the other an excess of broken lines. We may now consider braids of second order, in which the role of lines is played by the braids of the first order. We may, in particular, consider the case in which a braid with an excess of full lines interweaves with one that has an excess of broken lines, in the same way as the full line interweaves with the broken line in a first order braid. In the second-order braid, which may represent a multicellular organism, some of the individual first-order braids will stand to each other in the same relation as their corresponding components (lines) stand to each other in the first-order braid. But this is just the kind of relation which is found in biology

In a braid of the second order there may also be a sort of division of functions. In two dimensions only two first-order braids will be "on the outside." Only those two can "catch" new lines from outside, and, as in the case of Figure 11, those new lines may "move inward" by a process of interweaving. When such a line has moved completely inward so as to become adjacent to an inward second-order braid, only then can the line be woven into that inner second-order braid.

Thus the outer second-order braids may be said, to use biological terminology, to specialize in ingesting outside lines and to pass them along to the inner braids.

Again we repeat that all the above examples are not to be taken seriously in any way. They are used only to illustrate a point which is undoubtedly very suggestive for different possible directions of future research both in mathematical biology and in pure mathematics. The λ-spaces seem to be new in topology; the theory of braids is an established branch of the latter. As remarked on p. 409, we cannot be sure that some already well developed branch of topology does not carry in it the solution of the problem of geometrization of biology.

Should such a geometrization, as anticipated in this chapter, ever become a reality, it will be the greatest triumph of geometry and of pure mathematics in general. The doors to every science can then carry the inscription which appeared over Plato's Academy:

Μηδειζ αγεωμετρινοζ εισιτω.

REFERENCES

1. Hermann Weyl: *Raum, Zeit, Materie.* (Berlin: Julius Springer, 1921).
2. A. Einstein: *The Meaning of Relativity.* (Princeton: Princeton University Press, 1953).
3. N. Rashevsky: *Phil. of Sc.*, 1, 176, 1934; *Bull. Math. Biophysics*, **16**, 317, 1954; *ibid.*, 17, 45, 1955.
4. N. Rahhevsky: *Bull. Atom. Scientists*, 11, 193, 1955; *Bull. Math. Biophysics*, 17, 111, 1955; *ibid.*, 17, 207, 1955; *ibid.*, 17, 229, 1955.
5. R. L. Wilder: Topology of Manifolds. (New York: American Mathematical Society, 1949).
6. K. Reidemeister: *Knotentheorie.* (Berlin: Julius Springer, 1932).
7. E. Artin: *Abh. Math. Semin. Hamburg Univ.*, 4, 17, 1925.
8. H. Seifert and W. Threlfall. *Lehrbuch der Topologie.* (Leipzig and Berlin: G. B. Teubner, 1934).

CHAPTER XXXVI

THE ORGANIC WORLD AS A WHOLE

The relation between different characteristics of an organism is in many cases due to the biophysical constants of the organism itself. If two different characteristics, x and y, are determined by the same physicochemical factors, there will be a definite quantitative relation between those two characteristics. If, however, the two characteristics are determined, in general, by two different groups of factors, with only a few factors being common to the two groups, we shall find, instead of a definite mathematical relation between x and y, only a certain correlation, which will be the closer to unity, the more common factors the two groups possess. The future development of the mathematical biophysics of the organisms as a whole should thus eventually lead us to the theoretical prediction of the correlation coefficients between different pairs of characteristics of an organism. Such a theory would be of particular value because it would render useful a wealth of empirical data accumulated in this field by biometrists.

It must be pointed out, however, that there is another possible cause for the appearance of correlation between different characteristics of an organism. This cause lies in the effects which these given characteristics may have upon the interaction of different organisms and thus, indirectly, upon the preservation of the species. Certain values of the two characteristics may be more favorable to the preservation of the species. Organisms characterized by such values will have a better chance for survival, and such values will therefore occur more frequently than one would expect on the basis of a random distribution.

Let us first consider the case in which two characteristics x and y vary discontinuously and may have only discrete values, x_1, x_2, x_3, $\cdots$, x_n; y_1, y_2, y_3, $\cdots$, y_n. Let the number of organisms, characterized by the values x_i, y_k, be equal to N_{ik}. We shall refer to an organism, characterized by x_i, y_k, as organism (ik). The values x_i and y_k determine, among other things, the interaction of the particular organism with its inorganic surroundings; and through that interaction they determine the rate of net increase, $a_{ik}N_{ik}$, with respect to time of the total number of organisms of that kind. But that rate of increase also depends on the interaction of the organism (ik) with other organisms (ik) as well as organisms (mn), where m and n are different from i and k. We may set that part of the rate of increase as being of the form

$$N_{ik} \sum_{n} \sum_{m} b_{ik}^{mn} N_{mn}. \tag{1}$$

We thus have for the total rate of increase of all organisms,

$$N = \sum_{i} \sum_{k} N_{ik}, \tag{2}$$

the expression

$$\frac{dN}{dt} = \sum_{i} \sum_{k} a_{ik} N_{ik} + \sum_{i} \sum_{k} N_{ik} \sum_{m} \sum_{n} b_{ik}^{mn} N_{mn}. \tag{3}$$

Natural selection acts so as to maximize expression (3), and the conditions of the maximum of (3) give us the values of N_{ik}'s. These values are determined by the requirement:

$$\frac{\partial}{\partial N_{ik}} \left(\sum_{i} \sum_{k} a_{ik} N_{ik} + \sum_{i} \sum_{k} N_{ik} \sum_{m} \sum_{n} b_{ik}^{mn} N_{mn} \right) = 0, \tag{4}$$

which leads to a system of equations,

$$a_{ik} + \sum_{m} \sum_{n} b_{ik}^{mn} N_{mn} = 0. \tag{5}$$

By a procedure familiar in the theory of integral equations, we may pass to the case of continuously varying x's and y's. In this case the a_{ik}'s and the N_{mn}'s become functions $a(x, y)$ and $N(\xi, \zeta)$ of x and y, and ξ and ζ. The coefficients b_{ik}^{mn} become functions $b(x, y, \xi, \zeta)$ of four variables. The system of linear equations (5) reduces to the integral equation:

$$a(x, y) + \int\int b(x, y, \xi, \zeta) N(\xi, \zeta) \, d\xi d\zeta = 0. \tag{6}$$

where $a(x, y)$ and $b(x, y, \xi, \zeta)$ are known. The solution of (6) gives us the distribution function $N(x, y)$ for both characteristics. This function $N(x, y)$ determines the average values $\bar{x}$ and $\bar{y}$ of the characteristics. The correlation coefficient between x and y is then given by

$$r = \frac{\overline{(x-\bar{x})(y-\bar{y})}}{\sqrt{\overline{(x-\bar{x})^2}\,\overline{(y-\bar{y})^2}}}. \tag{7}$$

and is completely determined by $N(x, y)$.

The solution of the integral equation (6) represents the *mathematical* problem involved in the development of the suggested theory. The *biophysical* problem lies in the determination of $a(x, y)$ and of $b(x, y, \xi, \zeta)$ and represents a different problem for every different meaning of x and y. For instance, x may stand for the weight of the animal, and y for its speed of locomotion. In determining $b(x, y, \xi, \zeta)$, we shall have to consider that a large x is beneficial for the preservation of the species by offering a protection against smaller enemies. A large y is also beneficial, by enabling avoidance of enemies, on the one hand, and catching prey, on the other. But the effect of ξ and ζ is opposite. In general, in this case $b(x, y, \xi, \zeta)$ will increase with x and y and decrease with ξ and ζ.

We may set, approximately, $b(x, y, \xi, \zeta)$ and $a(x, y)$ as linear functions of x, y, ξ and ζ, with indeterminate coefficients and then determine these coefficients from the observed correlations.

The salient feature of the situation is that the characteristics of an organism depend on the structure of the whole organic world. A particular distribution function, $N(x, y)$, is determined by its contribution to the maximizing of the rate of reproduction of the organic world as a whole and not of a particular species. We thus may find that certain characteristics of an organism exist that are of no apparent use to *that* organism, such as, for example, the appendix and the caecum.

Instead of considering the maximum rate of reproduction as the determining factor, we may consider other biological or biophysical functions. The environment of each organism being principally composed of other organisms, the organic world as a whole is characterized by an incessant interaction between different organisms. Some of them provide food for the others. Some are detrimental to others either by feeding on them or by inhibiting the activities of these others by metabolic by-products. Thus the whole organic world is a system in which continuous exchanges of matter and energy take place, a system of complex flows of matter and energy.

A. J. Lotka[1] suggested as a possible general biological principle that the processes of life run in such a way as to maximize the total flow of energy in the organic world. We shall attempt to develop this suggestion further and to formulate it in mathematical form.

Let any organism be completely determined by n determining parameters

$$x_1, x_2, x_3, \cdots, x_n \,. \tag{8}$$

Consider, first, the case that those parameters have only a finite set of discrete values:

$$\begin{array}{c} x_1^{(1)}, \; x_2^{(1)}, \; x_3^{(1)}, \; \cdots, \; x_n^{(1)} \\ x_1^{(2)}, \; x_2^{(2)}, \; x_3^{(2)}, \; \cdots, \; x_n^{(2)} \\ \cdot \quad \cdot \quad \cdot \quad \cdot \quad \cdot \quad \cdot \quad \cdot \\ x_1^{(m)}, \; x_2^{(m)}, \; x_3^{(m)}, \; \cdots, \; x_n^{(m)} \,, \end{array} \tag{9}$$

where, in general, $m > n$ and m is in no way related to n. Subsequently, we shall pass to the continuous case, letting all x_i's vary continuously.

Consider an organism that is characterized by the following set of determining parameters:

$$x_1^{k_1}, x_2^{k_2}, x_3^{k_3}, \cdots, x_n^{k_n}, \tag{10}$$

and let the total number of such organisms in the organic world be

$$N_{k_1, k_2, \ldots, k_n}. \tag{11}$$

Let another organism be characterized by a set of values

$$x_1^{l_1}, x_2^{l_2}, x_3^{l_3}, \cdots, x_n^{l_n}, \tag{12}$$

and the total number of organisms of that type be

$$N_{l_1, l_2, \ldots, l_n}. \tag{13}$$

We may assume that the energy exchange due to the interaction of the first kind of organisms with the second kind is of the form

$$a_{k_1, k_2, \ldots, k_n; l_1, l_2, \ldots, l_n} N_{k_1, \ldots, k_n} N_{l_1, \ldots, l_n}. \tag{14}$$

The coefficient $a_{k_1, \ldots, k_n; l_1, \ldots, l_n}$ is to be considered as positive if the interaction is such that it increases the energy content of the first type of organisms and negative if it decreases the energy content.

The total energy of interaction or total exchange in the whole organic world is then given by the sum

$$I_0 = \sum_{k_i} \cdots \sum_{l_i} a_{k_1, \ldots, k_n; l_1, \ldots, l_n} N_{k_1, \ldots, k_n} N_{l_1, \ldots, l_n}. \tag{15}$$

We may also consider the interaction of each type of organism with the inorganic world; this will be of the form

$$I_i = \sum_{k_i} b_{k_1, \ldots, k_n} N_{k_1, \ldots, k_n}. \tag{16}$$

It may be remarked that we do not need necessarily to have $a_{ik} = - a_{ki}$, as one might be inclined to assume at first. The antisymmetry would be required only if the organisms interacted in isolated pairs. In general, when there is simultaneous exchange of energy between many organisms, $a_{ik} \gtrless - a_{ki}$.

We may now consider different types of postulates that lead us to interesting equations governing the development and behavior of the organic world.

First, we may postulate that the configuration of the whole organic world tends to such a configuration as will maximize the value $I_0 + I_i$. When such a configuration is reached, no further changes occur, and, if $F(N_{k_1, \ldots, k_n})$ is any function of $N_{k_1, \ldots, k_n}$,

$$\frac{dF(N_{k_1, \ldots, k_n})}{dt} = F'(N_{k_1, \ldots, k_n}) \frac{dN_{k_1, \ldots, k_n}}{dt} = 0, \tag{17}$$

where F' denotes the derivative.

At the same time, when $I_0 + I_i$ has a maximum,

$$\frac{\partial(I_0 + I_i)}{\partial N_{k_1, \ldots, k_n}} = 0. \tag{18}$$

Hence, denoting by F a function to be determined later by biological considerations, it is natural to put

$$\frac{dF(N_{k_1, \ldots, k_n})}{dt} = \frac{\partial(I_0 + I_i)}{\partial N_{k_1, \ldots, k_n}}, \tag{19}$$

because then F, and hence $N_{k_1, \ldots, k_n}$ tend to such values, for which $I_0 + I_i$ has a maximum. Introducing equations (15) and (16) into (19), we find

$$\frac{dF(N_{k_1, \ldots, k_n})}{dt} = \sum_{l_i} a_{k_1, \ldots, k_n; } N_{l_1, \ldots, l_n} + b_{k_1, \ldots, k_n}. \tag{20}$$

If we now let the values of $x_i^{(m)}$ vary continuously, the coefficients $a_{k_1, \ldots, k_n; l_1, \ldots, l_n}$ become functions of the values $x_1, x_2, \cdots, x_n$ of the first organism and of the values $x_1', x_2', \cdots, x_n'$ of the second. The coefficients $b_{k_1, \ldots, k_n}$ become functions of $x_1, x_2, \cdots, x_n$; $N_{k_1, \ldots, k_n}$ becomes a function $N(x_1, \cdots, x_n)$ of $x_1, x_2, \cdots, x_n$; $N_{l_1, \ldots, l_n}$ becomes a function $N(x_1', \cdots, x_n')$ of the x_i''s; and the system of linear differential equations (20) becomes an integro-differential equation of the form

$$\left.\begin{aligned} F'\{N(x_1, \cdots, x_n, t)\} \frac{\partial N(x_1, \cdots, x_n, t)}{\partial t} \\ = \int\int \cdots \int K(x_1, \cdots, x_n; x_1', \cdots, x_n') \\ N(x_1', \cdots, x_n') dx_1' \cdots dx_n' \\ + f(x_1, x_2, \cdots, x_n), \end{aligned}\right\} \tag{21}$$

the integration being extended over the whole range of variation of the x_i''s.

If the kernel $K(x_1, x_2, \cdots, x_n; x_1', \cdots, x_n')$ and the function $f(x_1, x_2, \cdots, x_n)$ are known, the integrodifferential equation (21) determines for given initial conditions,

$$N(x_1, \cdots, x_n, t) = N_0(x_1, \cdots, x_n)$$

for $t = 0$, the function $N(x_1, \cdots, x_n, t)$ for any time $t > 0$. Since the values of $x_1, x_2, \cdots, x_n$ determine the shapes and sizes and, in general, the anatomic structure of the organism, the knowledge of $N(x_1, x_2, \cdots, x_n, t)$ gives us thus the distribution of different types of organisms in the organic world at any time $t > 0$. For certain values of the x_i''s the function $N(x_1, \cdots, x_n, t)$ may be zero. Organisms with anatomic structure corresponding to such values of the determining parameters will not exist. As we have seen, the knowledge of the distribution function $N(x_1, \cdots, x_n, t)$ gives us also the correlation coefficient between the different determining parameters, if $n = 2$. For practical purposes, whatever we may wish to obtain from (21), it will be rather difficult to do for such a large number of determining parameters as is likely actually to occur. We may, however, fix our attention on any pair x_r, x_s, of the n determining parameters and attempt to find the correlation between them, when the remaining $n - 2$ determining parameters vary at random. To this end, we may integrate the function $N(x_1, x_2, \cdots, x_n)$ with respect to all the variables except x_2 and x_3, the integration to be extended over the whole range of variation of those n—2 variables. Thus we obtain

$$\left.\begin{aligned} \bar{N}(x_r, x_s, t) = \int \cdots \int N(x_1, \cdots, x_n, t)\, dx_1 dx_2 \\ \cdots dx_{r-1} dx_{r+1} \cdots dx_{s-1} dx_{s+1} \cdots dx_n \,. \end{aligned}\right\} \tag{22}$$

Since, denoting by $N(t)$ the total number of organisms in the world at the time t, we have

$$\int \cdots \int N(x_1, \cdots, x_n)\, dx_1 \cdots dx_n = N(t)\,; \tag{23}$$

therefore

$$\int\int \bar{N}(x_r, x_s, t)\, dx_r dx_s = N(t). \tag{24}$$

Hence $\bar{N}(x_r, x_s, t)$ may be considered as a distribution function for x_r and x_s for random values of the other determining parameters.

By introducing, similarly, a function

$$\bar{K}(x_r, x_s; x_r', x_s') = \int \cdots \int K(x_1, \cdots, x_n; x_1', \cdots, x_n')\, dx_1 \cdots dx_{r-1} dx_{r+1} \cdots dx_{s-1} dx_{s+1} \cdots dx_n \cdots dx_1' \cdots dx'_{r-1} dx'_{r+1} \cdots dx'_{s-1} dx'_{s+1} \cdots dx'_n$$

and by applying the same reasoning to $\bar{N}(x_r, x_s)$ in regard to mutual interaction, we find

$$\left. \begin{aligned} &F'\{N(x_r, x_s, t)\} \frac{\partial \bar{N}(x_r, x_s, t)}{\partial t} \\ &\quad = \int\int \bar{K}(x_r, x_s)\, \bar{N}(x_r', x_s')\, dx_r'\, dx_s' = \bar{f}(x_r, x_s), \end{aligned} \right\} \qquad (25)$$

where

$$\bar{f}(x_r, x_s) = \int \cdots \int f(x_1, \cdots, x_n)\, dx_1 \cdots dx_{r-1} dx_{r+1} \cdots dx_{s-1} dx_{s+1} \cdots dx_n .$$

Equation (25) may be used for the determination of the coefficient of correlation between x_r and x_s; and, to the extent that those may determine certain features of the anatomic structure, it may be used for a theoretical prediction of the correlation between some anatomic structures.

Equation (21) describes the gradual development of the whole organic world. The change of $N(x_1, \cdots, x_n, t)$ in time gives us the change of the general structure of the organic world with changes from one type of organism to another, as is found in paleontology. One of the problems of the theory is to determine $K(x_1, \cdots, x_n; x_1', \cdots, x_n')$ and $f(x_1, \cdots, x_n)$ from theoretical considerations and to see whether this will give us such an $N(x_1, \cdots, x_n, t)$ as would roughly describe paleontological facts.

If $f(x_1, \cdots, x_n) > 0$ for any values of $x_1, \cdots, x_n$, equation (21) implies that, even when $N(x_1, \cdots, x_n) = 0$, still for every set of values of $x_1, \cdots, x_n$, $\partial N(x_1, \cdots, x_n)/\partial t > 0$. This would mean that organisms of any type could be spontaneously generated from nonliving material. Since this is not the case, $f(x_1, \cdots, x_n)$ cannot be positive everywhere. Neither can it be negative or zero everywhere, since, then, the organic world could never have started, because if $f(x_1, \cdots, x_n) \leqq 0$, then for $N(x_1, \cdots, x_n) = 0$, $\partial N(x_1, \cdots, x_n)/\partial t \leqq 0$. At some geological epoch life must have started out of the nonliving. And it did start with the simplest organisms for which most of the x_i's are zero, and the others, perhaps only M and q, rather small. To obtain this result, let us consider, as an illustration only, that $f(x_1, \cdots, x_n)$ is of the following form:

Let

$$x_1 = M, \qquad x_2 = q,$$

and let Δ, ε_1, and ε_2 be small positive quantities. Then let

$$\left.\begin{aligned} f(x_1, x_2, \cdots, x_n) = \Delta \quad &\text{for} \quad 0 < x_1 < \varepsilon_1, \\ 0 < x_2 < \varepsilon_2, x_3 = x_4 = &\cdots = x_n = 0, \\ f(x_1, x_2, \cdots, x_n) = 0 \quad &\text{for any } x_i > 0, \quad i > 2. \end{aligned}\right\} \tag{26}$$

With such a form of f, we shall find that even when

$$N(x_1, \cdots, x_n) = 0, \qquad \partial N(x_1, \cdots, x_n)/\partial t > 0$$

for such organisms, which correspond to $0 < x_1 < \varepsilon_1$; $0 < x_2 < \varepsilon_2$. But $\partial N(x_1, \cdots, x_n)/\partial t = 0$ for all higher organisms, which have any of the x_i $(i > 2)$ greater than zero.

Such a situation would still imply that, even at the present time, the spontaneous generation of some lowest forms of organisms takes place. Though there is no direct evidence against that, if such evidence were forthcoming, it could be met in two different ways.

A. The first and simplest way is to make f depend on one or more parameters $\eta(t)$, which vary with time. Those parameters may characterize the physicochemical properties of the environment, such as temperature, pressure, humidity, etc., at different times. We may now make a different requirement, instead of (26), namely:

Requirement (26) holds only for $\eta < \eta_0$; for $\eta > \eta_0$ we have $f(x_1, x_2, \cdots, x_n) = 0$ for any values of x. If, now, η increases with time, being originally less than η_0, then, after a while, spontaneous generation will become impossible for any kind of organisms, no matter how simple.

B. The second way is to make f not a function of the x_i's, but a functional of $N(x_1, \cdots, x_n)$; in Volterra's notations $f|[N(x_1, \cdots, x_n)]|$, such that

$$f|[N(x_1, \cdots, x_n)]| > 0$$

when $N(x_1, \cdots, x_n)$ is different from zero only for $0 < x_1 < \varepsilon_1$; $0 < x_2 < \varepsilon_2$, $x_3 = x_4 \cdots = x_n = 0$ and

$$f|[N(x_1, \cdots, x_n)]| = 0$$

for any other forms of $N(x_1, \cdots, x_n)$. In that case, f will become zero as soon as the organic world develops sufficiently to have even a few organisms with $x_i > 0$ $(i > 2)$.

The equation

$$K(x_1, \cdots, x_n; x_1', \cdots, x_n') = 0 \tag{27}$$

defines for a given set of values $x_1, \cdots, x_n$, considering x_i''s as variables, an n-dimensional hypersurface, which divides the whole space of the variables x_i' into two regions, one for which $K > 0$ and another for which $K < 0$. The hypersurface (27) may be multiply connected. Let us denote by V_+ the region in the hyperspace for which $K > 0$, and by V_- the region for which $K < 0$. Remembering that $N(x_1, \cdots, x_n, t) \geqq 0$, and thus denoting by vertical lines absolute values, we may write (21) in the following form:

$$\left.\begin{aligned} &F'\{N(x_1, \cdots, x_n)\} \frac{\partial N(x_1, \cdots, x_n, t)}{\partial t} \\ &= \int_{V_+} \cdots \int |K(x_1, \cdots, x_n; x_1', \cdots, x_n')| N(x_1', \\ &\cdots, x_n') \, dx_1' \cdots dx_n' - \int_{V_-} \cdots \int |K(x_1, \cdots, x_n; x_1', \\ &\cdots, x_n')| N(x_1', \cdots, x_n') \, dx_1' \cdots dx_n' + f , \end{aligned}\right\} \tag{28}$$

both integrals being positive.

Considering $x_1, x_2, \cdots x_n$ as fixed, we may interpret the first integral of (28) as the increase of organisms of type $(x_1, x_2, \cdots, x_n)$ by birth, while the second integral may be interpreted as the decrease of the number due to death. Both birth and death rates thus appear as depending on the presence of other organisms. For values of the x_i's, for which $f > 0$, the function f adds to the birth rate, while for values for which $f < 0$, it adds to the death rate. To bring equation (28) into the usual form, when the birth and death rates are proportional to the population, we must put

$$F\{N(x_1, \cdots, x_n)\} = \log N(x_1, \cdots, x_n). \tag{29}$$

Equation (28) then becomes

$$\left.\begin{aligned}
&\frac{\partial N(x_1, \cdots, x_n, t)}{\partial t} \\
&= N(x_1, \cdots, x_n, t) \int_{V_+} \cdots \int |K(x_1, \cdots, x_n; x_1', \cdots, x_n')| \\
&\qquad N(x_1', \cdots, x_n') \, dx_1' \cdots dx_n' \\
&- N(x_1, \cdots, x_n, t) \int_{V_-} \cdots \int |K(x_1, \cdots, x_n; x_1', \cdots, x_n')| . \\
&\qquad N(x_1', \cdots, x_n') \, dx_1' dx_n' + Nf .
\end{aligned}\right\} \quad (30)$$

This may be considered as a more general form of the usual growth equation:

$$\frac{dn}{dt} = an - bn^2 ,$$

which may be written in the form

$$\frac{dn}{dt} = a'n - (b' + c'n)n$$

with

$$a = a' - b' ; \qquad b = c' .$$

Thus, if the kernel, K, is known, we may determine by means of equation (27) the birth and death rates for any species characterized by a given set of values $x_1, \cdots, x_n$ of the determining parameters.

It may appear strange that both birth and death rates depend on the presence of other organisms. Concerning the birth rate this is, however, quite natural. For the multiplication of organisms goes on only under proper conditions of nutrition, which involves the destruction of other organisms. Even as regards some simplest microörganisms, which feed on nonliving media, they do not multiply in a culture where only a few organisms are present.

In regard to the death rate, the conclusion is no less natural. Equation (30) gives the actual death rate, which is due to all possible causes. And, with rare exceptions, death occurs because of interaction with organisms. Death of pure old age is exceedingly rare, even among humans. If $f > 0$, then in terms of our equations (30) we may express that death rate by taking the integral

$$\int \cdots \int K(x_1, \cdots, x_n; x_1', \cdots, x_n') \, dx_1' \cdots dx_n' \qquad (31)$$

over a very narrow strip of values in the immediate neighborhood of the hypersurface (27). If η_1 is a small quantity, we may integrate over the range

$$x_i^0 - \eta_1, \qquad x_i^0 + \eta_1, \tag{32}$$

x_i^0 being a coordinate of a point of the hypersurface (27) and η_1 being considered as the range of biological variations of the characteristics of the species. Expression (31), integrated over the range (32), may be divided again into a positive and a negative part, the latter giving us the death rate from purely old age. Owing to the smallness of η_1, it will be very small.

The problem of handling equation (30) resolves itself into two parts: first, the problem of determining from physicochemical and biological considerations the form of $K(x_1, \cdots, x_n; x_1', \cdots, x_n')$; and second, the solution of the nonlinear integrodifferential equation (30). The similarity of (30) to some nonlinear systems of differential equations with many variables, studied by V. Volterra,[2] suggests the approach to the second problem by a transition to the continuous case from Volterra's equations. The first problem opens a very wide field for further theoretical studies.

It is important to remark that the limits of integration in equations (21) and (30) are not all constant. As we have seen in chapter xxi, if M and q are prescribed, the velocity v may have, in general, an upper limit, which will be a function of M and q. Thus, if we deal, for instance, with only three determining parameters, $x_1 = M$, $x_2 = q$, and $x_3 = v$, we may integrate with respect to x_1 and x_2 from 0 to ∞, but with respect to x_3 only from 0 to a value $v(M, q)$. In other words, the total space is limited by the planes $q = 0$, $M = 0$, $v = 0$, and the surface $v = v(M, q)$.

Limiting ourselves, for simplicity, to only two determining parameters, M and n (cf. chap. xxi), we may, for instance, determine the form of K by the following considerations: For any small value of n the interaction between the two organisms M and M' will be such that the greater the ratio M/M', the greater the interaction. By definition (p. 427) the interaction of M and M' is positive when it favors M. This will hold, however, only within a certain range of ratios M/M'. A too large ratio M/M' may be unfavorable to the first organism.

Thus, while an elephant may readily have the better of a tiger, yet it may be quite helpless against some pathogenic bacteria with which its interaction will be negative. Hence K must, for a fixed n, vary in such a way as to have a positive maximum for a certain M/M', then drop again and become negative.

But, as n increases, the advantage of a larger mass becomes less and less important. A smaller animal with greater nervous coordination may have the better of a larger one with a less developed nervous system.

Without solving equation (30), we may surmise what the consequences of such a choice of K will be. Given an initial condition, when only small values of M and n are present, we shall find that the larger the value of M, the larger the birth rate and the smaller the death rate. Hence $\partial N(M, n, t)/\partial t$ will be the largest for large values of M, and the value of $N(M, n, t)$ will become large for large M's. As, however, the value of $N(M, n, t)$ increases for all values and therefore the number $N(M, n, t)$ of organisms with large n also increases, the birth rate will become largest for organisms with a large n. Such organisms begin to prevail, and those with large M but small n actually die out. Such considerations may give a clue to the understanding of the preponderance of large reptiles in the Jurassic era and their recession.

As a final generalization of our approach, we may suggest that, instead of postulating the maximizing of the expression $I_0 + I_1$, as given by expressions (15) and (16), we may introduce a Hamiltonian principle and postulate that[3]

$$\int_{t_1}^{t} (\delta F + \Sigma Q_{k_1, \ldots, k_n} \delta N_{k_1, \ldots, k_n}) = 0. \tag{33}$$

With

$$F = I_0 + I_i ; \qquad Q_{k_1, \ldots, k_n} = -\frac{1}{N_{k_1, \ldots, k_n}} \frac{dN_{k_1, \ldots, k_n}}{dt}, \tag{34}$$

requirement (33) leads us to a system of nonlinear equations, which, in passing to the continuous case, lead again to equation (30).

Equation (30), or the more general equation (21), represents a theory of the development of the whole organic world. Known facts of paleontology should be deducible from those equations in principle, provided that we can overcome the mathematical difficulties of solving them.

We may apply the same principle which leads to equation (21) or (30) to a number of more restricted, though no less important, problems by generalizing it somewhat. We may assume that the principle (33), or the requirement of the maximum of $I + I_0$, holds not only for the organic world as a whole but for any part of it. We may apply it, then, either to limited organic groups or even to individual organisms or cells.

An example of such a limited group is human society. While the gross physiological properties of man may be considered as rather uniform constants, different psychological traits vary considerably from person to person. The social interactions of two individuals are determined by the values of the parameters which measure those psychological traits. By exactly the same argument as before we shall arrive at an integrodifferential equation of the form (30) for the determination of the distribution function of different traits. Not only does this equation give the distribution function, but it also gives its variation with time. As has been shown elsewhere,[4] such a distribution function determines the social structure of society and its variation with time. Thus mathematical sociology actually becomes a branch of mathematical biology, and history may in a sense be considered as a small branch of paleontology.

The distribution of different psychological types may also be studied in this way. The methods of theoretically predicting the correlation between any pair of determining parameters suggests a possible approach to a theory of the experimentally found correlations between Thurstone's primary factors.

The same procedure should lead to a theory of distribution of different pathological variations, giving us the incidence of certain organic diseases.

All human activities may be considered as biological manifestations and the principle of maximum energy flow may be applied to all of them. If so, then even such problems as the distribution of wealth may be treated in a similar way. Wealth is an important factor producing energy flow, and the Pareto distribution may perhaps be derived from considerations of maximizing that flow.

It has been suggested by N. Rashevsky[6] that Lotka's principle of maximum energy flux may apply not only to the organic world as a whole, but to individual organisms and even cells as well. It was suggested[7] that the Hamiltonian principle in physics be generalized in such a way that the Hamiltonian function contains a term which depends not only on the energy of the system but also on the energy flows within the system. Such a generalized Hamiltonian principle has been applied by N. Rashevsky[8] to the dynamics of cell division. Henry E. Stanton[9] showed that the equations thus obtained are empirically equivalent to those derived by H. D. Landahl and discussed in chapter xiv of Vol. I. The problem of biological organization has also been discussed by N. Rashevsky[10] from the point of view of a maximum principle.

REFERENCES

1. A. J. Lotka, *Proc. Nat. Acad.*, 8, 146, 151, 1922.

2. V. Volterra, *Leçons sur la théorie mathématique de la lutte pour la vie* (Paris: Gauthiers-Villars, 1931).

3. E. T. Whittaker, *A Treatise on the Analytical Dynamics of Particles and Rigid Bodies* (Cambridge: At the University Press, 1927).

4. N. Rashevsky, *Psychometrika*, 7, 117, 1942.

5. L. L. Thurstone, *Multiple-Factor Analysis* (Chicago: University of Chicago Press, 1947).

6. N. Rashevsky, *Bull. Math. Biophysics*, 5, 49, 1943.

7. N. Rashevsky, *ibid.*, 4, 65, 1942.

8. N. Rashevsky, *ibid.*, 5, 99, 1943.

9. H. Stanton, *Bull. Math. Biophysics*, 6, 71, 1944.

10. N. Rashevsky, *Bull. Math. Biophysics*, 5, 165, 1943; *Acta biotheoretica*, 8, 60, 1946.

INDEX

Abscissae, 47, 65, 239
Absence of locomotion, 251
Absence of turbulences, 293
Absolute inhibition, 208, 212
Absolute intensity of stimulus, 94
Absolute value, 59, 62, 155
Absolute values of excitation intensities, 107
Absorption, 327, 329, 345, 346, 347, 361, 370
Abstract biological system, 395, 396 f.
Abstract relation, 95
Abstraction, mathematical biophysics of, 175 ff.
Accommodation, muscular movements of, 108
Ackerman, W., and Hilbert, D., 229
Acoustic, Gestalt, 109
Acoustic nerve, fibers of, 11
Acoustic perceptions, 113
Activated circuit, 137
Activity, 50
Adaptation, 69
Adjacent points, 374
Adjustment, speed of, 72
Adrian, E. D., 6, 7, 17, 36
Aerodynamic profile, 270, 271, 273, 275
Aerodynamics, 3, 270
Aesthetic perception, 2 f.
Aesthetic sensation, theoretical values of, 162
Aesthetic value, 35, 161, 163, 172, 173
Aesthetics
  experimental, 245
  visual, 154 ff.
Afferent end, 37
Afferent level, 175
Afferent nerve, 91, 337
Afferent neuroelements, 35, 125
  cross-inhibitory, 199
Afferent pathways, 32, 94, 175, 185, 202
Afferent side, 87
Aggregate of cells, 246
  dynamics of, 307
Aggregate of molecules, 344
Aggregate, social, 357
Aggregates, subsidiary, 386
Air resistance, forces of, 284
Alexandroff, P., and Hopf, H., 315, 324
Algebra, Boolean, 3, 6, 207 ff., 394
All-or-none law, 7
All-or-none phenomena, transmission of excitation, 13
Allergy, physical, 340
Alley, 134
  blind end of, 135
  entries into, 135
  length of, 135
  running into, 134
  sight of, 135
Altitude, maintenance of, 271
Alveoles, 284
Amelotti, E., and Householder, A. S., 132, 133, 135, 184
Amoeboid movements, 335, 336, 339, 341
Amytal, sodium, effect of on memory, 188
Anabolic processes, 362, 396
Angle, 157, 160, 163
Animals, 95, 134, 135, 304, 339
  internal structure of, 280 ff.
  irregularity of shapes of, 295
  mass of, 305
  problem of form, 246
  skeletal parts and skulls of, 309
  speed of, 135
Antibiotics, 339
Antibodies, 340, 341
Anticipation
  of future events, 196 f.
  intensity of, 201
Antigens, 340
Anxiety neuroses, 204
Aorta
  of dog, 295
  resistance of to blood flow, 298
  size of, 293, 294, 295, 305
Appendix, 426
Arbitrary functional, 111
Aristotelian logic, 219
Aristotelian mode, 222
Arrangement of neuroelements, 103
Arterial system
  branches of, 300
  mass of, 299
  structural constants of, 305
  structure of, 293, 295, 296, 297
Arteries, of dog, 295
Arteries and veins, proper functioning of, 306
Arthropods, 269
Artin, E., 417, 418, 419, 420, 423
Association, strength of, 201
Associative connection, 202
Asymptotic state, 94
Asymptotic values, 19, 24, 86, 127, 133, 154
Atom, Bohr's model of, 293
Atoms, 296
Attention, 31
Auditory data, 40, 44, 55, 67
Auditory stimuli, 54, 55
Autonomous nervous system, 78
Autotrophic plants, 310, 358
Avoidance reaction, 362
Axiomatic biology, 342

Axis, 65
Axons, 3, 9, 10, 231, 232, 233, 235, 236, 237, 238, 241
  and neurons, structures of, 230

Background, 31, 98
Bacteria
  digestion in, 363
  pathogenic, 339, 434
  and putrefaction, 358
Ball on a curved surface, 69
"Bases, point," 384
Behavior, psychoneurotic, abolition of, 200
Berger, G. O., 39
Bertalanffy, L. v., 4
Bethe, A., 250, 425
Betz, A., 279
Bi-continuous mapping, 320
Bifurcating system of blood vessels, 298
Bifurcations
  of aorta, 295
  equivalent, 295
Biological functions, 292
Biological homology, 356
Biological integration, 308
Biological organization, 436
Biological similarity, principle of, 291
Biological system, 35
  abstract, 395 f., 396 f.
Biological unity of organism and of organic world, 306, 308
Biology, 311, 359, 405, 409
  axiomatic, 342
  geometrization of, 406, 422
  mathematical, 1, 231, 307, 406, 422
    general principles in, 292
  metric mathematical, 381, 385
  topological, 381, 406
    set-theoretical approach to, 385
Biophysical theory, metric, 337
Biophysics
  of abstraction, mathematical, 175 ff.
  mathematical, 307, 308
    of central nervous system, 6, 218, 246, 247
    of color vision, 116
Biotopological mapping, 326, 337, 343, 344, 349, 356, 358, 389, 393, 399, 402
Biotopological transformation, 402
Bird
  flight and form, 270 ff.
  limit of mass, 273
  mass of, 270, 273
  responses of, 309
  velocity of locomotion of, 271, 277 f.
Birkhoff, G., 161, 162, 163, 174
  theory of, 171
Birth rate, 432, 433, 434
Blind end of an alley, 135
Blood circulation, 280, 298
Blood flow
  in arterial system, 295, 298
  in capillary, 303
  critical value of R for, 294
  total, 302
  velocity of, 287, 293, 302
Blood pressure, 288, 289
Blood vessels, 296, 297, 298, 299, 300, 389
  reflection of pressure waves in, 306
  size and structure of, 281
Body surface and metabolism, 264
Bohr's model of atom, 293
Bonin, G. von, 45
Boolean algebra, 3, 6, 394
  of neural nets, 207 ff.
Bothe, W., 68
Boyd, W. C., 344
Brachiopoda, 371
Braids, theory of, 417-22
Brain, 3, 5, 31, 35, 48, 59, 99, 112, 135, 155, 230, 343
  complexity of, 1
  function of the, 5
  lesions of, 230 f.
  number of neurons in, 222, 223, 231
  physiology of, 98
  resemblance to, of physicomathematical systems, 1 f.
Brain center, 91, 95, 96, 98, 101, 102, 103, 104, 105, 106, 107, 108, 131, 132, 134, 155, 156, 159
  spontaneous activities of, 78
Brain tracts, 99
  myelinated, 99
Branch of a nerve fiber, 8, 9,
Branching-point, 8
Breathing movements, 284, 286
Brightness, 98, 108
  discrimination of, 98
Brodhun, E., and König, A., 53, 54
Bronk, D. W., 18
Brown, V., 17, 165
Buchsbaum, R., 324
Buddenbrock, W. van, 274, 279
Bulb, terminal, 12, 15, 207
Bundle of nerve fibers, 46
Busch, A. K., Hofstatter, L., and Smolik, A., 206
Bush, R. R., and Mosteller, F., 142, 143

Caecum, 426
Calculus, logical, 3
Campbell, D. M., and Cushing, J. E., 344
"Canonic" form, 114
Capillaries
  calculated number of, 304, 305
  radius and length of, 301, 302, 305
Capillary, 287, 288, 300, 301, 302
  metabolic diffusion in, 303, 304
Capillary pressure, 288
Capillary wall, 301
Carbon dioxide, 310, 363, 364
Cardiac output, 294, 302, 305

Cardio-vascular disturbances, 385
Cardio-vascular phenomena, 337
Cardio-vascular transport, 364
Carlson, A. J., and Johnson, V., 344
Cartesian coordinates, 76
Catabolic processes, 347, 349, 361, 362, 396, 398
Categories, theory of, 394
Cattell, J., McK., 39
  and Hoagland, H., 17
Celestial mechanics, 307
Cell aggregates, 246
Cell division, 246, 306, 436
Cell respiration, 245
Cells, 69, 335
  dynamics of interaction of, 307
  essential features of, 182
  living, 73
  metabolism in, 182
  motile, 327
  nonmobile, 280
  non-motile, 338
  not homogeneous, 359
  photosensitive, 116
  physicochemical dynamics of, 307
  primordial, 357
  reticuloendothelial, 341
  retinal, 212
  secretory, 387
  sensory, 327
  sieve, 339
  sizes of, 107
  specialization, 327, 331, 336, 349, 351, 352, 353, 363
  synthesis of body of, 346
Cellular aggregates, dynamics of, 307
Center, 162
  for discrimination of sizes, 108
  sensory, 156, 157
Central end of neuroelement, 21
Central excitation, 6 ff., 11 ff., 35, 36, 71, 129, 130, 159, 165, 166, 173, 202, 203
Central inhibition, 6 ff., 11 ff., 138
Central nervous system, 5, 6, 11, 59, 69, 108, 123, 306, 342
  inhibition of function of, 197, 198
  mathematical biology of, 1, 231
  mathematical biophysics of, 6, 218, 246, 247
  systematic neurobiophysical theory of, 142
Central neuroelements, 155
  cross-inhibition of, 198
Central retina, 98-102, 108, 109, 114, 117 f.
Chaetognata, 371
Chain
  of neuroelements, 39, 178, 188
  of neurons, 13, 14, 32, 173
  of pathways, 177, 187, 188
Change of size of a visual object, 106
Character of synaptic transmission, 6, 12, 207
Chemical mediation, 339
Chemoluminescent reaction, 356
Chemo-regulatory processes, 381
Chrisophyta, 371
Cilia, 329, 335, 338
Ciliary muscle of eye, 336, 387
Circuits
  activated, 137
  circulatory, 281-88
  conditioning, 128, 129
  excited, 15 ff., 136, 137
  neuronic, 11 ff., 16, 17, 231
  of one neuron, 214
  reverberating, 215, 221, 224
Circulation, problems of, 306
Circulation, venous, 339
Circulatory circuit, 281-88
Circulatory phenomena, 339
Circulatory system, 364, 388
Classes of relations, mapping of, 325
Closed circles of neurons, 219 f.
Closed circuit, 74, 214, 216, 231, 232, 233, 235
Coefficient
  of correlation, 424, 425, 430
  of diffusion, 289, 301, 302, 305
    of oxygen, 303 f.
    of metabolite, 303, 304
  of inhibition, 168
  of proportionality, 157, 166
  of static friction, 256
Coelenterata, 357
Coghill, G. E., 45
Cohn, David L., vii, 292, 293, 295, 296, 304, 305
Cold receptor, cutaneous, 208
Cold, sensation of, 208
Cold, stimulus, 208, 210
Collateral, 47, 159, 160
Collateral fiber, 9
Collateral pathway, 80, 91, 94, 99, 101
Color discrimination, 98, 230
Color triangle, 116, 122, 123
Color vision
  mathematical biophysics of, 116
  mechanism of, 116, 117
Colors, 98, 122, 123
  primary, 116 f., 124, 125
Combination of stimuli, 88
Combinatorial topological approach, 345, 385
Common response path, 179
Complete transformed graph, 370
Complex stimulus pattern, 200 f.
Complex structure, 5
Complexity of brain, 1
Complexity and order, 163
Component
  in abstract biological system, 395, 396 f.
  as part of organism, 390, 393, 394
  terminal, 395, 398 f.
Component primordial, 354, 378, 380, 382
Component primordial graphs, 376

Component stimulus, 180, 181, 182, 183
accidental, 182
essential, 182
frequency of occurrence of, 180, 181
Components, organism of two, 400 f.
Computers, electronic, 1
Concentrated solution, 74
Concentration
of delayed reflexes, 129, 135
gradient, 301
metabolic, 291, 301, 303
of oxygen, 287, 302, 305
ratio of, 70
Concept of ordinal numbers, 226
Conditioned circuits, 198
Conditioned connection, 202
Conditioned reflex, 80 ff., 90, 134, 198
delayed, 127 ff., 134
extinction of, 198
intensity of, 90, 135
internal inhibition of, 91 f.
reinforcement of, 90, 91
Conditioned response, 91, 127, 131, 133, 135
intensity of, 129
Conditioned stimulus, 83, 90, 127, 130, 131, 135
Conditioning, 83, 86, 87, 90, 95, 129, 131, 133, 134, 135, 160
process of, 134
Conditioning circuit, 128, 129
Conditioning connections, 87, 202
"Conditioning" pathways, 197
Conditioning system, 91
Conduction, 329, 330, 342
humoral chemical, 341
hysteresis, 341, 342
nerve, 339
nervous, 341
non-hysteresis, 341
time, 42, 207
Configuration
of equilibrium, 69, 70, 71, 72
of a system, 70
Connected graph, 333
Connected space, 322, 323, 324
Connection, 10, 11, 19, 22, 25, 27, 28, 30, 31, 33, 34, 35, 36, 37, 38, 39, 40, 41, 42, 44, 47, 48, 49, 50, 58, 59, 80, 81, 82, 87, 88, 89, 91, 94, 99, 100, 101, 102, 103, 104, 128, 154, 156, 175, 176, 177, 185, 187, 188, 202, 231
associative, 202
conditioning, 87, 202
contour, 101
definition of, 13
delay, 10, 17, 187
inhibition of, 185, 187, 188
inhibitory factor at, 190
multiple, 127
retardation of, 23
transmission of, 44
Connective delay, 21, 38, 40, 82
Consciousness, nature of, 185
Conservative synapsings, 237
Constancy of size of an object, 108
Constant, 38, 40, 44, 58, 59, 62, 64, 155, 160, 162
of proportionality, 50
Constant current, 7
Constant intensity of stimulation, 19, 37, 61
Constant ratio of excitation, 107
Constant stimulus, 11, 47, 154
suddenly established, 127
Constant velocity, 157
Constants, 304
external, 69
of neuroelements, 197
of pathways, 175, 176, 194, 198
structural, of arterial system, 305
Consumption of metabolite, rate of, 301
Continuity
definition of, 317
perception of, 155
restriction of, 332
Continuous differential equations, 4
Continuous excitation, 7, 25
Continuous mapping, 317, 318, 319, 320, 321, 325, 331
Continuous stimulation, 7, 11, 12, 30, 36, 82, 91, 99, 125, 217
Contour, 100, 101, 102, 103, 104, 105, 106, 107, 156
Contour connection, 101
Contour effect, 113, 114
Contour pathways, 102
Contour perception, 98
Contractile muscular tissue, 336
Contrast, sharp, 98
Convection, 359
Coordinates
Cartesian, 76
of the extremum, 120
functions of, 326
polar, 103
rectangular, 118
variable, 109, 110
Coordination
and movement, 249
nervous, 247, 248, 249, 250, 435
Correct judgment, 57, 62
Correct response, 59, 60, 67, 137, 139
Correct stimulus, 138, 139
Correlation coefficient, 424, 425, 430
Cortex, 78, 185, 193, 202
sensory projection area in, 226
Cortical excitation, 202
in manic-depressive psychoses, 195
periodic fluctuations of, 194, 195
Cortical inhibition, 199
periodic fluctuations of, 194
Cortical level, 185
Coulter N. A., and Pappenheimer, J. R., 305
Covert speech, thought as, 309
Crawling, 249

Crile, G., 264, 268, 269, 286, 290, 291
Critical value of R for blood, 294
Culbertson, J. T., vii, 113 f., 115
Current, constant, 7
Curve, fourth degree, 178
Cushing, J. E., and Campbell, D. M., 344
Cutaneous cold receptor, 208
Cutaneous heat receptor, 208
Cyanophyta, 371
Cycle of neurons, 232 f., 234, 235
  directed, 356
  non-directed, 374
  non-uniformly directed, 374
  uniformly directed, 373, 374, 375
Cycle saturation, 233

Danziger, L., and Landahl, H. D., 205, 206
Data
  auditory, 40, 44, 55, 67
  experimental, 62, 63, 64, 65, 67, 162, 163
  gustatory, 40, 41
  visual, 40, 44, 67
Davis, H., 79
  and Galambos, R., 17
Davis, R. C., 161, 162, 163, 174
Death rate, 432, 433, 434
Decay, 66, 67
  rate of, 15, 17
Dedekind cut, 407
Definite integral, 111
Definition of primordial, 399 f.
Delay
  at connection, 10, 17, 187
  connective, 21, 38, 40, 42
Delay, synaptic, 12, 14, 16, 207, 208, 211 f., 219, 221, 227
  as unit of time, 207
Delayed conditioned reflex, 127 ff., 134
Delayed reflexes, 127 ff.
  concentration of, 129, 135
Dendrites, number necessary to each neuron, 114
Density
  of pathways, 118, 119, 124
  of excitation, 119, 120, 123
  distribution of neuroelements, 123
Dependence of final state of a system on rate of variation of external parameters, 72
Depression, 200
Depth perception, monocular, 56
Desire for attention and physiological disturbance, 200
Difference, perception of, 176, 177
Difference mechanism, 177
Difference reaction, 177
Difference response, 178-79
Differences, just noticeable, 3
Different modalities, stimuli of, 109
Differential equation, 2, 3,
  continuous, 4
Differentiated organism, 382
Differentiation, social, 375
Diffusion coefficient, 289, 301, 302, 303, 305
  of oxygen, 303 f.
Diffusion equation, 291
Diffusion drag forces and cell division, 306
Diffusion gradients, 338
Diffusion of metabolite, coefficient for, 303, 304
Diffusion and transport, 359
Digestion, 309, 311, 330, 346, 347, 361, 363, 389
  intracellular, 363, 388
Digestive enzymes, 337 f., 347, 361, 400
Digestive mechanism, 388
Digestive system, as a component, 390 f., 392
Digestive vacuole, 347, 363
Dilation of pattern, 114
Directed cycles
  non-uniformly, 374
  uniformly, 373, 374, 375
Directed graph, 345, 356, 373, 382, 389
Discharge
  frequency of, 4, 11, 12
    in peripheral fiber, 6
  periodic, of fiber, 211
Discontinuous interaction between neurons, 3
Discontinuous molecular impacts, 3
Discrimination, 57
  of absolute intensities, 92
  of brightness, 98
  of color, 98, 230
  psychophysical, 67, 177
  of relations, 94 ff.
  of sizes, center for, 108
  between stimuli, 138, 139
  of stimulus patterns, 92
  theory of, 50, 172
  threshold of, 96
  of weights, 62, 65
Disinhibition, 91, 95, 96, 188, 189
Disjoined fundamental sets, 380, 381
Disjoined graph, 333
Disjoined sets, 313
Disjoined syndromes, 381
Disjunction, logical, 207
Displacement, 110, 113
Dissimilarity judgment, 178, 180
Distances, 56
Distribution
  of excitation, 104, 110
  randomness of, 230
  transformation of, 111
Distribution density of neuroelements, 123
Distribution function, 47, 61, 63-66, 87, 88, 105, 110, 127, 162
  normal, 61, 62, 65
  normal error, 119
Disturbance, 69, 70
  external, 77
Division, dynamics of cell, 246

Dodd, Stuart C., 241
Dog
 aorta of, 295
 oxygen consumption of, 302
 vascular system of, 294
Dunker, K., 36
Duration
 of excitation, 156
 of stimuli, 64
Dynamic processes, 5
Dynamical laws of interaction, 5
Dynamics
 of cell division, 246
 of cellular aggregates, 307
 of interaction of cells, 307
 of locomotion, 269
 physicochemical, of a cell, 307

Economy of neurons, 112, 114
Ectoderm, 353, 357
Edge, 98
Efferent neuroelements, 89, 185, 186, 187, 188
Efferent paths, 108, 198
Efferent pathways, 181
Efferent side, 42, 49, 87, 91
Eilenberg, S., and MacLane, S., 393, 394
Einstein, A., 404, 409, 423
Einstein's principles, 307, 326
Elastic sphere, 295, 296
Elasticity, modulus of, 252
Electrochemical phenomena, 339
Electromagnetic phenomena, 326
Electronegativity, 69
Electronic computers, 1
Electrostatic forces, 348
Element, 161
 exciting, 6
Elements of the set, 311
"Elements" as theoretical set, 406 f., 408, 409 f., 413, 414, 415
Elimination
 of waste products, 281, 346, 361, 363, 364
 of a wrong alley, 135
Empty sets, 313, 322
End of alley, 135
End-feet on neuron, 4
End-organs, 40, 41
Endocrine activities, role in mental phenomena, 204
Endogenically stimulated, 388
Energy
 free, 69, 70
 potential, 70
 release, 361, 362
Engram, 186, 189, 190, 191, 192, 193
 intensities of, 193
Engramic neuroelement, 189
Enteroceptive stimuli, 59
Entomesoderm, 353, 357
Entries into an alley, 135
Entropy, 69, 70
 maxima of, 69
Environment, 73
 inorganic, 363, 364
 inorganic, extraorganismic, 364
 and organism, 246
 as part of organism, 395
Environmental input, 395, 396, 397 f.
Environmental output, 395, 396, 397 f., 399
Environmental properties, 431
Enzymes
 digestive, 337 f., 347, 361, 363, 400
 lytic, 348, 400
 as outputs, 400
Epidemics, spread of, 240 f.
Epithelium, respiratory, cells of, 336
Epstein, H., and Rapoport, A., 210
Equations
 continuous differential, 4
 differential, 3
 finite difference, 32
 functional, 131
 integral, 34, 35
 integrodifferential, 36
 linear differential, 2
 of motion, 248, 267
 Poiseuille's, 298
 transcendental, 239
Equilibrium, 71, 72, 73, 77
 stable, 70, 71, 77
 unstable, 77
Equilibrium configuration, 69, 70, 71, 72
Equivalence of geometrical figures, 172
"Equivalences, Theory of Natural," 393
Equivalent bifurcations, 295
Erect posture, maintenance of, 249, 250
Error
 distribution function, normal, 119
 elimination of, 127 ff.
 as function of number of trials, 141
Esser, M. H. M., 254, 255
Euclidean
 geometry, 358
 line, 316
 plane, 407 f.
 space, 315, 326
Event
 anticipated, 196 f.
 directly perceived, 197
 remembered, 197
Evolution, 72
Excitability, increase in, 62
Excitation, 7, 9, 10, 11, 20, 21, 22, 25, 31, 36, 39, 41, 42, 44, 59, 80, 85, 94, 95, 98, 99, 101, 102, 112, 123, 128, 154, 155, 162, 330
 of angle center 165, 166
 brief, 154
 of a center, 35
 central, 6 ff., 11 ff., 35, 36, 129, 130, 159, 165, 166, 173, 202, 203
 character of, 156

Excitation—*Continued*
of closed circuit, 216
constant ratio of, 107
continuous, 7, 25
and contraction, 319
cortical, 202
density of, 119, 120, 123
distribution of, 104, 110
duration of, 156
external, 80
fluctuations of, 176, 177, 227
gradual extinction of, 189
intensity of, 7, 9, 10, 11, 15, 16, 19, 20, 32, 33, 37, 38, 39, 47, 48, 61, 74, 75, 89, 90, 97, 102, 108, 110, 119, 127, 128, 131, 154, 155, 156, 160, 161, 163, 167, 173, 185, 188, 192, 201, 202, 217 f.
level of, 203
as measure of pleasantness, 186
as measure of unpleasantness, 186
mechanism of, 112, 207
net, 119
of neuroelement, 122, 124, 185, 186, 187, 188, 197, 202
of neuron, 4, 219, 224, 227
of pathways, 217, 227
peripheral, 6, 202
of peripheral nerve, 12
of peripheral pathways, 159
property to conduct, 327
proprioceptive, 160
random, 59
reversible, 188
spontaneous fluctuations of, 59
spread of, 231
state of, 75
of terminal bulbs, 212
total, 154, 164, 171, 172
velocity of propagation, 75
wave of, 130, 131
Excitation intensities, absolute values of, 107
Excitation pattern, 35, 98, 112, 123
Excitation threshold, 185, 188, 189
Excitatory action, 32
Excitatory factors, 9, 41, 58, 75, 125
Excitatory fiber, 9, 10, 15, 21, 221, 225
Excitatory level, 204, 205
Excitatory neuroelements, 32
Excitatory neuron, 13, 217
Excitatory pathway, 19, 21, 22, 27, 28, 31, 33, 47, 58, 99, 136, 162, 175, 185, 186, 187, 194
chain of, 58
Excitatory process, 27, 171
Excitatory stimulus, 10
Excitatory type, 58
Excited circuit, 15 ff., 136, 137
Excited interval, 51
Excited pathway, 128, 129
Excited region, 125
Excited state, 80, 81, 83
Exciting element, 6
Excretion, 330, 346, 361, 389
Existential operator, 213, 214, 215
Experimental aesthetics, 245
Experimental data, 62, 63, 64, 65, 67, 162, 163
External conditions, 69, 70
External constants, 69
External disturbance, 77
External excitation, 80
External inhibition, 91
External stimuli, sensitivity to, 311, 327, 330, 339, 387, 388
External stimulus, 7, 74, 75, 77, 78, 81, 155, 183
Exteroceptive stimuli, 59
Extremities
folding and unfolding of, 267
length of, 265, 268
number of, 249, 250
optimum number of joints of, 268
repelling action of, 265, 266
second-order, 250
thickness of, 265, 266, 268
of unequal length, 268
volume of, 266
Extremum, 73, 121
coordinate of, 120
Eye, 108, 155, 161, 351, 387, 388
ciliary muscle of, 336
Eye movement, 158, 159
path of, 155
Eye muscles, 155, 156, 157
Eye, stimulation of, 388

Factor, excitatory, 9, 41, 58, 75, 125
Factors, inhibitory, 58, 125
Fechner, T., 125
Fechner's law, 49
Feeding mechanism, 338, 345, 346 f.
Fibers, 7, 8, 9, 10, 89
of acoustic nerve, 11
conveying touch, 11
excitatory, 9, 10, 15, 21, 221, 225
inhibitory, 9, 12, 16, 21, 33, 167, 225, 226
of muscle end organs, 11
optical, 211, 212
perfectly adapted, 12
periodic discharge of, 212
peripheral, 6, 7
polymerized, 175
rapidly adapting, 11, 213
sensory, 7, 226
slowly adapting, 11, 13, 212
Final common path, 80
Finite difference equation, 32
Finite graphs, 376
Finite group of transformations, 110 f.
Finite size of neuroelements, 107
Fischer, M. H., 279
Fischer, O., 250
Fisher, R. A., 67
Flagella, movement of, 329, 335, 339
Flicker fusion, 126
Flight and form
of birds, 270 ff.
in insects, 270 ff.

Flight velocity and insect size, 275
Flow
  of metabolites, 251, 253
  laminar, 293
Fluctuation, 65
  of excitation, 176, 177, 227
  in the organism, physicochemical, 183
  spontaneous, 59
  of the thresholds, in nerve fibers, 14, 15
Fluids, interstitial, 364
Food
  absorption and plant form, 251
  digestion of, 309, 311, 336
  ingestion of, 309, 310, 311, 336
  stimulus from, 347
Force of heart muscle, 289
Forces
  of air resistance, 284
  inertial, 270, 274, 284, 289
Form
  of animals, problem of, 246
  of plants, 251 ff.
  of quadrupeds, 262 ff.
  of snakes, 256 ff.
Form, "canonic," 114
Fourier, theory of heat conduction, 247
Fox, S. W., and Plaisted, E., 344
Free energy, 69, 70
  minima of, 69
Frequency, 7
  of discharge, 4, 11
    in peripheral fiber, 6
  of heart beat, 281
  of respiration, 280
  of sound, 11
  of wing movement, 272, 274, 278
Friction, static, 257
Fright reaction, 198
Frog, neurons of the, 5
Frontal lobes, 198, 200
Fuller, H. J., and Tippo, O., 384
Fulton, J. F., 17
Function, 111
  of arteries and veins, 306
  of the brain, 5
  of coordinates, 326
  distribution, 47, 61, 63-66, 87, 88, 105, 110, 127, 162
  linear, 47, 50, 52
  linearly increasing, 154
  of neuronic circuit, 11
  normal error distribution, 119
  symmetric, 65
  two-parametric, 66
Functional, 111, 112, 113, 114
  arbitrary, 111
Functional equations, 131
Functional relation, 57
Functions, 48, 49, 50, 59, 61, 62, 64, 65
  biological, 292
  monotonically increasing, 58, 127, 128
"Functor," 209
Fundamental sets, 379
  of a graph, 379
  mutually disjoined, 380, 381
Fusion, flicker, 126
Fusion, of points in graphs, 374

Galambos, R., and Davis, H., 17
Ganglia, sympathetic, 12
Gas, van der Waalsian, 74
Gases, kinetic theory of, 295, 307
Gasser, H. S., 18
Gastro-intestinal disturbances, 337, 338, 385
Gastro-intestinal movements, 336, 363
Gauss, C. F., 409
Geckeler, J. W., 255, 269
Geiger, H., and Scheel, H., 68
Gelb, A., and Goldstein, K., 115
General graph, 376
General relativity, 308
  theory of, 404
"Genes, naked," 358
Geodesics, 326
Geological changes, 73
Geometric arrangement, 5
Geometric progression, 85
Geometrical figure, 123
  equivalence of, 172
  invariance of, 102
Geometrical pattern, 2 f., 107, 110, 156
Geometrical shape, 105
Geometrization
  of biology, 406, 422
  of physics, 404, 406, 408, 417
Geometry, non-Euclidean, 409
Gestalt, vii, 98 ff., 113 f.
  acoustics, 109
  invariance, 109, 113 f.
  optical, 109, 110
  perception, 109, 230
  psychology, 35
  transposition, 98, 106, 109
Gills, 363
Gland, 388
Glycogen, 282
Goldstein, K., and Gelb, A., 115
Graded response, 7
Graded stimulus, 7
Gradient
  of concentration, 301
  diffusion, 338
  radial, 287, 288, 301
Graham, C. H., and Hartline, H. K., 17, 116, 126
Granit, R., 116, 117, 126
Graphs
  component primordial, 367
  connected, 333, 398
  differentiated, 382
  directed, 345, 373, 389
  disjoined, 333
  finite, 376
  fundamental sets of, 379
  general, 376

Graphs—*Continued*
one-dimensional space, 330 f., 332, 355
partial, 355, 356, 357, 358, 362, 369, 376, 378, 382, 402
partial primordial, 356, 378
physiological, 370
primordial, in abstract biology, 350, 351, 352, 353, 354, 355, 357, 358, 359, 361, 362, 364, 366, 368, 369, 370, 371, 372, 373, 374, 375, 376, 377, 380, 384, 387, 400, 402
representation of an organism by, 345, 348, 349, 354, 359, 376, 390, 395
residual, 352, 354, 355, 367, 368, 370, 373, 377, 378, 380
simplified primordial, 369, 370
simplified transformed, 370
of social relations, 357
specialized, 382
theoretical approach to, 345, 385
theory of, 334
transformed, 345, 346, 349, 350, 352, 353, 354, 355, 357, 360, 370, 371, 372, 373, 375, 376, 378, 380, 381, 382, 384
Green, H. D., 294, 295, 302, 304, 305
Groups of neurons, as units, 17
Groups, theory of, 311
Guerra, E., and Günther, B., 4, 291
Guilford, J. P., 64, 65, 66, 68
Gulliksen, G. H., 139, 142, 143
Günther, B., and Guerra, E., 4, 291
Gustatory data, 40, 41

Hamiltonian function, 436
Hamiltonian principle, 435, 436
Hartline, H. K., and Graham, C. H., 17, 116, 126
Hausdorf axioms, 412
Heart, 282, 283, 287, 289, 290
effective volume of, 281
muscle, force of, 289
rate, 337
Heart-beat, frequency of, 281
Heat conduction, theory of, 247
Heat receptor, cutaneous, 208
Heat, sensation of, 208, 210
Helmholtz, H., 116
Hilbert, D., and Ackerman, W., 229
Hilgard, E. R., 142, 143
Hill, A. V., 261, 266, 269
History, 69
as branch of paleontology, 436
Hoagland, H., and Cattell, J. McK., 17
Hofstatter, L., Smolik, A., and Busch, A. K., 206
Homeomorph sets, 332
Homeomorph, shapes of skulls, 309
Homeomorphism, 320
Homeostasis, 330, 335
Homology, biological, 356
Homotop, shapes of skulls, 309
Hopf, H., and Alexandroff, P., 315, 324
Hopf, L., 305
Horizontal stimulus, 165, 166
Hormonal secretions, 383
Hormones, 381, 382
Householder, A. S., 2, 19, 33, 36, 45, 50, 52, 54, 55, 56, 78, 79, 174, 213, 229
and Amelotti, E., 132, 133, 135, 184
and Landahl, H. D., 6, 17, 19, 36, 45, 67, 78, 79, 117, 126, 139 143, 206, 229
Humidity, 431
Humoral chemical conduction, 341
Hydrodynamics, 293, 306
Hydrogen ion concentration, per terminal bulb, 15
Hypersurface, 70, 71
Hypothesis, 155
"Hypothetical" neurons, 2, 3
Hysteresis, 69 ff., 72, 74
conduction, 341
threshold, 80
Hysteria, 200
Hysterical behavior, abolition of, 200

Illumination
inside, 102
intensity of, 102
outside, 102
Image
displacement of, 110
of a limit point, 321
points, 317, 318
Impulse
conduction of, 330
inhibitory, 225
nervous, 7, 12, 37, 253, 254, 255
postsynaptic, 12
presynaptic, 12
proprioceptive, 108, 156, 157, 158
sequence of, 14, 16
synchronous, 14
Incorrect response
average effect of, 139
self-inhibiting, 137
Independent variables, 111
Individual, preservation of, 309
Inertial forces, 270, 274, 284, 289
Inflection point, 71
Ingestion, 309, 310, 311, 330, 336, 338, 346, 347, 361, 362
Inhibiting effect, as function of distance between neuroelements, 134
Inhibiting elements, 6
Inhibiting pathway, 218
Inhibiting synapse, 208, 212
Inhibition
absolute, 208, 212
central, 6 ff., 11 ff., 138
of connections, 185, 187, 188
as correlate of unpleasantness, 186
cortical, 194, 199
differential, 24, 30, 34, 92, 94, 95, 129, 132, 134, 136
external, 91

Inhibition—*Continued*
internal, 91 f.
interneuronic, 6
lasting, 154
mechanism of, 9
mutual, 58, 202
of neuroelement, 186, 187
of unpleasant stimulus, 185
Inhibitory coefficient, 168
Inhibitory constant, 202
Inhibitory effect, 32
Inhibitory factor, 58, 125, 190
Inhibitory fiber, 9, 12, 16, 21, 33, 167, 225 f.
Inhibitory impulse, 226
Inhibitory mechanism, 90
Inhibitory neurolement, 21
of intermediate type, 92
Inhibitory neuron, 208
Inhibitory neuronic chains, 102
Inhibitory pathway, 19, 21, 26, 27, 28, 30, 31, 33, 47, 48, 50, 51, 58, 91, 95, 96, 99, 100, 101, 128, 131, 139, 162, 171, 173, 175, 181, 187, 189, 190, 191, 194, 197, 199, 218
stimulation of, 21
threshold of, 173, 192
Inhibitory state, 127
Inhibitory stimulus, 31
Inhibitory type, 58
Initial conditions, 94
Innervation, reciprocal, 58
Inorganic environment, 363, 364
Inorganic extraorganismic environment, 364
Inputs, into a component, 390, 391 f., 392 f., 395 f.
Inputs, environmental, 395 f., 397 f.
Inputs, into a primordial, 400
Insect
flight and form of, 270 ff.
locomotion of jumping, 269
size and flight velocity of, 275
societies, 357
Inside illumination, 102
Integral, definite, 111
Integral equation, 34, 35
Integration, 51, 61
in organism, 21, 308
Integrodifferential equations, 36
Intensities of stimuli, 82
Intensity, 11, 46, 49, 53, 57, 58, 108, 156, 158, 162
of anticipation, 201
change of, 155
of conditioned reflex, 90, 135
of conditioned response, 129
constant, stimulus of, 19, 37, 61
of excitation, 7, 9, 10, 11, 15, 16, 19, 20, 32, 33, 37, 38, 39, 47, 48, 61, 74, 75, 89, 90, 97, 102, 108, 110, 119, 127, 128, 131, 154, 155, 156, 160, 161, 163, 167, 173, 185, 188, 192, 201, 202, 218
of illumination, 102
of optical stimulus, 117
peripheral, 166
of peripheral stimulus, 23, 202
of reflex, 90
of stimulation, 7, 27, 31, 74, 131
of the stimulus, 6, 11, 12, 13, 40, 41, 45, 46, 49, 51, 52, 154, 212, 213, 217
continuous, 11
discharge frequency and, 6
and number of impulses, 13
Intensity-time curve, 44
Interaction
of cells, dynamics of, 307
dynamical laws of, 5
of large number of individuals, 229
of neurons, 2, 3, 6, 11
of organism, 424, 426, 427, 433, 434
Interaction, discontinuous, of neurons, 3
Interaction, quasi-continuous, 4
Intermission, length of period of, 125
Intermittently applied stimulus, 125, 126
Internal inhibition, 91 f.
of a conditioned reflex, 91
Internal secretions, 381, 382, 383
Interneurons, 21, 66, 226
Internuncial, 16, 17, 40, 212, 219, 223, 226
Intersection of the sets, 312, 322
Interstitial fluids, 364
Interval, 49, 50, 162
excited, 51
preparatory, 43
between stimulations, 86
Intestinal tract, 363
volume of, 281
Intracellular digestion, 363, 388
Intracellular processes, 306, 364
Invariance, 113
Invariance of a geometrical figure, 102
Invariance, Gestalt, 109, 113 f.
Invariant response, 107
Irreversible process, 71
Irritable elements, 6
Isomorphism, 342, 348 f.
Isotropic structure, 103

Jacobson, E., 324
Johnson, V., and Carlson, A. J., 344
Jordan arc, 410, 416
Jordan curve, 407 f., 410
Judgment
correct, 57, 62
of dissimilarity, 178, 180
psychophysical, 3
of similarity, 177, 178, 180
two-category, 64
wrong, 62
Jurassic era, 434
Just noticeable differences, 3

Kidney, 282

Kinematic degrees of freedom, 248
Kinematics of vertebrate movements, 248
Kinetic theory of gases, 295, 307
Klüver, H., 172, 174
Knots, theory of, 417
Köhler, W., 5, 17, 108, 115
König, A., and Brodhun, E., 53, 54
König, Denes, 370, 384, 415

Laminar flow and size of aorta, 293
Landahl, H. D., ix, 2, 4, 18, 33, 36, 39, 40, 41, 43, 45, 62, 63, 64, 66, 67, 117, 124, 125, 126, 135, 136, 139, 141, 142, 143, 176, 177, 184, 210, 213, 227, 229, 436
  and Danziger, L., 205, 206
  and Householder, A. S., 6, 17, 19, 36, 45, 67, 78, 79, 117, 126, 139, 143, 206, 229
  and McCulloch, W. S., and Pitts, W., 6, 17
Landau, H. G., and Rapoport, A., 240
Lashley's jumping apparatus, 138
"Latent addition," period of, 12, 217, 220, 227
Law
  Fechner's, 49
  Poiseuille's, 288
  Rubner's, 264, 283, 287, 289
Learning, 69, 342
  of alley, 135
  of extremities, and mass of animal, 265, 268
  theory of, 142
Length of capillaries, 302, 305
Lesions of brain, 230 f.
Lethal substances, 339
Lettvin, J., and Pitts, W., 205, 206
Leucocytes, 336
Level, afferent, 175
Lever-propelled system, 248, 249
Lever structure of organism, 248
Lewin, K., 308, 324
Life, origin of, 73
Light, 7
Light sensitivity and vision, 310
Limit points, 321, 322, 323
Limited existential operator, 213, 215
Limiting value, 47, 81
Limits, of possible variations, 51
Linear arrangement of nerve centers, 130
Linear differential equations, 2
Linear function, 47, 50, 52
Linearly increasing function, 154
Lines, 162
  segments of, 157
  straight, 158, 160
Linksz, A., 126
Liver, 282
Living cell, 73
Living organisms, 72, 354
Lloyd, D., 16, 18
Lobes
  frontal, 198, 200
  occipital, 98, 99, 210
Lobotomized patients, 198
Lobotomy
  "partial," 200
  prefrontal, 198, 200
Locomotion
  absence of, 251
  average velocity of, 247
  crawling, 249
  dynamics of, 269
  of jumping insects, 269
  of organism, 247, 248
  and plant form, 251
  in quadrupeds, 262 ff.
  of snakes, 256 ff.
  speed of, 134, 249, 261, 267, 426
  use of extremities in, 249
  velocity of, in air, 271, 278
Logarithms, natural, 239
Logic
  Aristotelian, 219
  symbolic, 207
Logical calculus, 3
Logical disjunction, 207
Lorente de Nó, R., 16, 18
Lotka, A. J., 426, 437
Lotka, principle of maximum energy flow, 436
Lowest threshold, 12
Lung, 47, 282, 283, 284, 285, 286, 363
  mammalian, 286, 287
  movement of, 280
  ventilation of, 287
  volume of, 280
Luria, S. E., 344, 370
Lymphatic system, 364
Lysis, 348, 400

McCulloch, W. S., vii, 211, 214, 219, 229
  and Landahl, H. D., and Pitts, W., 6, 17, 207, 208, 211, 214, 219, 229
  and Pitts, W., 3, 4, 6, 16, 17, 109, 110, 111, 112, 113, 114, 115, 210, 214, 219, 229, 394
Macdonald, P. A., and Robertson, D. M., 56
MacLane, S., and Eilenberg, S., 393, 394
"Macro-circuit," 227
"Macroscopic" theory, 3, 213
Magnitude, orders of, 44, 107
Maintenance
  of altitude, 271
  of erect posture, 249, 250
Mammal, lung of, 286, 287
Man
  physiological properties of, 436
  psychological traits of, 436
  social interactions of, 436
Mapping
  bi-continuous, 320
  biotopological, 326, 337, 343, 344, 349, 356, 358, 389, 393, 399, 402, 417

Mapping—*Continued*
of classes of relations, 325
continuous, 317, 318, 319, 320, 321, 331
graph on graph, 354, 355, 369
identity, 392 f.
of neighborhoods, 331
one-to-one, 320
of organ, 388
of organisms, 310, 311, 325, 327 f., 334, 388
of outputs and inputs, 391
self-, 369, 370
of a set, 380, 391, 392
of spaces, 325
of transformations, 368, 416
Mappings and relations, 310 f., 316
Marey, E. J., 270, 271, 278
Mass
of bird, 270, 273
of quadruped, 263, 264, 265, 268
Mass distribution, 326
Mathematical biology, 306, 307, 308, 406, 422
of central nervous system, 1, 231
metric, 381, 385
Mathematical biophysics, 307
of abstraction, 175 ff.
of central nervous system, 6, 246, 247
of color vision, 116
Mathematical models, 142, 143, 307, 308
Mathematical modes, 142
Mathematical sociology, 436
Mathematical theory of neural networks, 306
Mathematical theory of the organism, 306, 307
Mathematics, 422
qualitative or relational, 311
Matrix, 70, 73
Matthews, B. H. C., 17
Maxima, 50, 51, 52
of entropy, 69
Maximum, 35
Maximum central excitation, 35, 36
Maximum energy flow, principle of, 436
Maximum simplicity, principle of, 292, 308, 343
Maze, 134
Measure of pleasantness, 162
Mechanical function and organism shape, 249
Mechanical system, 69, 70
Mechanism, 155
of color vision, 116
digestive, 388
for dilation of pattern, 114
of discrimination, 56
of excitation, 112, 207
of Gestalt perception, 109
of inhibition, 9
neural, 109, 112, 113
neurological, 47, 142, 157
neuron-saving scanning, 113
for rotation of pattern, 114
Mechanists, 405
Membrane, tympanic, 336
Mediation, chemical, 339
Memory
complexity of situation, 189
conscious, 189, 193
nature of, 185
subconscious level of, 188
subconscious, limits of, 193
weakening of, 189, 191
Mendeleyeff, 293
Mental phenomena, mathematical biophysics of, 185 ff.
Mesoderm, 357
Metabolic activity, 59
Metabolic concentration, 291
Metabolic energy and snake velocity, 261
Metabolic energy supply, 319
Metabolic forces, 246, 247
Metabolic phenomena, 340
Metabolic processes, 330, 356, 400
as transformation, 400
Metabolic rates, 358
Metabolism, 276, 282, 329
and body surface, 264
cellular, 182
rate of, 305
role of, in mental phenomena, 204
sugar, 389
Metabolite
coefficient for diffusion of, 303, 304
concentration of, 301, 303
translocation of, 339
Metabolites
flow of, 251, 253, 300, 301
rate of consumption of, 301
Metabolizing systems, 247, 248
Metazoan, 310, 353, 357
Metazoan plant, 247
Metric aspects of biological phenomena, 308, 326
Metric biophysical theory, 337
Metric mathematical biology, 381, 385
Metric, space-time, 326
Metrized spaces, 315
Microorganisms, 334 f., 339, 340
non-motile, 334 f.
Microscopic properties, 3
Minima, of free energy, 69
Minimum difference, 49
Minimum perceptible angle, 160
Minkowski, H., 404
Modalities, 175
different, stimuli of, 109
of pathways, 176
Mode, Aristotelian, 222
Models, vii
mathematical, 142, 143, 307, 308
neurobiophysical, 142
Modulus of elasticity, 252

Molar movement, 335, 338, 388, 400
Molecular movement, 329, 337, 338, 388, 400
Molecule, living, 344, 357, 358
Molecules, as elastic spheres, 295
Monkeys, 108
Monocular depth perception, 56
Monofunctional organs, 378, 382
Monotonically increasing function, 58, 127, 128
Morphological structures, 32
Mosauer, W., 256, 261
Mosteller, F., and Bush, R. R., 142, 143
Motile cell, 327
Motility
  of organism, 247
  protoplasmic, 362
Motion, 330
  equations of, 248, 267
  of wings, 270, 271, 276
Motor reactions, 47
Movement
  amoeboid, 335, 336, 339, 341
  of eye, 158, 159
  flagellate, 329, 335, 339
  kinematics of, 248
  of lung, 280
  molar, 335, 338, 388
  molecular, 338, 388
  of muscle, 161, 250
  orderly, 327, 329, 337
  of organism, 250, 311
  peristaltic, 280
  snake, action of head, 257 f.
Movements
  and coordination, 249
  superimposed, 156
Multicellular organism, 327, 330, 332, 334, 335, 340, 422
Multiple connection, 127
Multiple response, 46
Multiplication, 362
Muscles
  ciliary, 387
  of eye, 155, 156, 157, 336, 387
  skeletal, 336, 339
Muscular apparatus and snake velocity, 258
Muscular contraction, 157
  wave of, 257, 258
Muscular force, in flight, 272, 274
Muscular movement, 161, 250
  of accommodation, 108
Muscular tissues, contractile, 336
Mutual inhibition, 58, 202
Muybridge, E., 267, 269, 270, 278
Myelinated brain tracts, 99

N-body problem, 307
"Natural Equivalences, Theory of," 393
Natural logarithms, 239
Natural selection, 337, 425
Neighborhood, definition of, 331
Neighborhood, mapping of, 332
Neighborhood of a point, 331
Neighborhoods, 313, 314, 315, 316, 317, 318, 319, 320, 321, 322, 323, 324, 331, 333
Nemertea, 363
Nerve, 46
  acoustic fibers of, 11
  afferent, 91
  optic, 108
Nerve activity, spontaneous, 78
Nerve centers, 6, 32, 35, 49, 94
  linear arrangement of, 130
Nerve conduction, 339
Nerve excitation, 12, 330
Nerve fiber, 7, 8, 342
  branch of a, 8, 9
  bundles of, 46
  definition of, 13
  threshold of, 10
Nerve impulse, 7
  velocity of propagation of, 10, 39
  volley of, 7, 8
Nerve trunk, 46
Nervous activity, theory of, 6
Nervous conduction, 341
Nervous coordination, 247 f., 249, 250, 435
  in standing, 249, 250
Nervous impulse, 7, 12, 37, 253, 254, 255
Nervous system, 10
  autonomous, 78
  central, 1, 5, 6, 11, 59, 69, 108, 123, 142, 231, 306, 342
  visceral, 11
Net excitation, 119
Net, neuronic, 241
"Nets with bias," 231
Neumann, J. von, 349, 370
Neural elements, 98
Neural mechanisms, 109, 112, 113
Neural net, 111, 114, 207, 208, 209, 231, 306
Neural networks, 306
Neural pathways, 118, 123
Neural structures, 207, 230
Neurobiophysical mechanisms, 185
Neurobiophysical models, 142
Neurobiophysical parameters, 173, 174
Neurobiophysical theory of central nervous system, 142
Neuroelement, 163, 202
Neuroelements, 5, 6, 27, 29, 33, 38, 40, 42, 44, 45, 46, 47, 48, 49, 50, 74, 86, 87, 90, 91, 92, 94, 95, 99, 100, 101, 108, 117, 119, 120, 122, 127, 131, 134, 154, 158, 162, 230
  afferent, 35, 125
  arrangement, 103
  central, 155
  central end of, 21
  chain of, 39, 178, 188
  constants of, 197
  cross-inhibition of, 198
  definitions of, 17

Neuroelements—*Continued*
distribution of, 123, 230
efferent, 89, 185, 186, 187, 188
engramic, 189
excitation of, 122, 124, 185, 186, 187, 188, 197, 202
excitatory, 32
finite size of, 107
geometrical arrangement of, 37
group of, 159, 160
of higher order, 159
inhibition of, 186, 187
inhibitory, 21
location of, 198
and pathways, structures of, 230
peripheral, 118
self-circuited, 185, 214
self-circulated, 188
stability of, 189
time constant of, 194
Neurological diagrams, 37
Neurological mechanisms, 47, 142, 157
Neurological observations, 74
Neurological structure, 57
Neuron, 9, 10, 88, 89, 110, 114, 209, 216, 221 ff., 225 f., 231, 232, 233, 234, 235, 236, 237, 238, 239, 241
circuit of one, 214
closed circles, 219 f.
excitation, 219, 223 f., 226-28
excitatory, 13, 216 f.
of frog, 5
higher-order, 12, 208
"hypothetical," 2, 3
inhibitory, 208, 401 f.
initial, 14
intensities of excitation among, 110
interaction, 6, 11, 50
internuncial, 17
of man, 5
path between, 235
in physicomathematical systems, 2
physiological properties of, 5
receptor, 208
refractory phase of, 12
second-order, 213
Neuronic chain, 32
excitatory, 173
inhibiting, 173
inhibitory, 102
Neuronic circuit, 11 ff., 16, 17, 231
"average" life-span of, 16, 17
finite life-span of, 16
function of, 11
"natural" life-span of, 16, 17
Neuronic group, as unit, 17
Neuronic nets, 241
Neuronic structure, 40
Neuron-saving scanning mechanism, 113
Neurons, 112, 114, 230
and axons, structures of, 239
chain of, 13, 14
cycle of, 232 f., 234, 235
economy of, 112, 114
interaction of, 2, 3, 4, 6, 11
number in brain, 222, 223, 231
in retina, 117
self-circuited, 214, 342
threshold of, 220, 221, 224
Neuropathways, 123
Neurophysical assumptions, 155
Neurophysiological interpretation, 21
Neurophysiological picture, 157
Neurophysiological processes, 59
Neuroses, anxiety, 204
Neutral stimuli, 91
Newton, I., 307, 308, 326
No-difference response, 178, 179
Non-adjacent points, 374
Non-connected space, 322, 323, 324
Non-directed cycles, 374
Non-Euclidean geometry, 409
Non-Euclidean hyper-space, 326
Nonexcitation, 74
Nonexcited state, 129
Non-fundamental set, 380
Non-hysteresis conduction, 341
Non-luminous reaction, 356
Non-motile cells, 338
Non-motile microorganisms, 334 f.
Non-specializable points, in graphs, 373
Non-uniformly directed cycles, 374
Normal distribution function, 61, 62, 65
Normal error distribution function, 119
Number of errors and number of trials, 141
Number of extremities
of arthropods, 269
determination of, 250
and organism size, 250
and stabilization, 250
Number of impulses
as function of stimulus intensity, 13
per unit time, 13

Occipital lobes, 98, 99, 123, 210
Odorous substances, 356
One-to-one correspondence, 105
One-to-one mapping, 320
Ontogenetic development, 402
Opatowski, I., 254, 255
Oppenheimer, C., and Pincussen, L., 264, 269, 286, 290, 291
Optic nerve, 108
Optic perceptions, 113
Optical fibers, 211 f.
Optical Gestalts, 109, 110
Optical patterns, 114
Optical stimulus, intensity of, 117
Optimal design, principle of, vii, 292, 293, 294, 300, 305, 308, 342
Optimism, 204
Optimum radii of branches of arterial system, 300
Optimum stimulus pattern, 35

Order
  and complexity, 163
  of magnitude, 44, 107
Ordinal numbers, concept of, 226
Organ, definition of, 388
Organ, mapping of, 388
Organic molecules, 73
Organic world, 73
  as a whole, 245 ff., 308, 424 ff.
Organisms, 329, 330, 335, 336, 338, 343, 345, 351, 352, 355, 356
  anatomic structure of, 429, 430
  biological properties of, 311, 319, 356
    set of points representing, 319, 323
  biological unity of, 308
  differences between, 376
  differentiated, 382
  energy content of, 427
  and environment, 246
  and feeding mechanism, 347
  finite number of, 371
  function and shape of, 249, 292
  integrated activities of, 306
  integration in, 21, 308
  interaction of, 357, 424, 426, 427, 433, 434
  lever structure of, 248
  living, 72, 354
  locomotion of, 247, 248
  mapping of, 310, 316, 325, 327 f., 359, 388
  mathematical theory of, 306, 307
  motility of, 247
  movement of, on rough terrain, 250
  multicellular, 327, 332, 334, 335, 340, 422
  multiplication of, 401, 433
  nervous coordination in, 247 f., 249, 250, 435
  nonmobile cells of, 280
  physicomathematical theory of, 307
  primordial, 329, 330, 331, 349, 381
  primordial, in abstract biology, 358, 372, 400
  primordial, mapping of, 325
  properties of, 400
  propulsion of, 247, 248, 249, 336, 339
  rate of increase in, 424, 425, 426
  repair of, 401
  reproduction of, 330
  response to stimuli of, 311
  shape of, 248, 249, 252, 269
  similarities between, 376
  society as a kind of, 310
  spontaneous generation of, 431
  and surroundings, relation between, 343
  theory of, 307, 326
  transport in, 360
  two-component, 400 f.
  unicellular, 327, 334, 335, 336, 338, 340, 348
  unity of, 309
  useless characteristics of, 426
  as a whole, 245 ff.
Organs
  end-, 40, 41
  internal, size and shape of, 280
  monofunctional, 378, 382
  polyfunctional, 382
  specialized, 363
Organization, biological, 436
Origin of life, 73
Osmoregulation, 335
Outputs
  from a component, 390, 391, 392 f., 395 f.
  environmental, 395 f., 397 f., 399
  as enzymes, 400
  into a primordial, 400, 401
Outside illumination, 102
Ovum, 402 f.
Owen, R., 264, 269
Oxygen
  coefficient for diffusion of, 303 f.
  concentration of, 287, 302, 305
  consumption of, 287, 302
  energy equivalent of, 280
  intake of, 363 f.
  supply, 280, 281, 300, 302

Pain, 328
Pain-center, 199
Pain stimulus, 31, 95
Pair of stimuli, 95, 175
Pappenheimer, J. R., and Coulter, N. A., 305
Parabola, inverted, 52
Paramecium, 309, 342
Parameters, 11, 41, 50, 53, 59, 61, 66, 70, 71, 72, 141, 142, 183, 184, 231, 273, 282, 283, 291, 305, 349, 355, 357, 370, 426, 427, 429, 431, 433, 434, 436
  neurobiophysical, 173, 174
  of pathways, 123
  of the transformation, 366, 367
Paranoia, 204, 205
  surgical treatment of, 199
Partial graph, 355, 356, 357, 358, 362, 369, 376, 378, 382
"Partial" lobotomy, 200
Partial primordial graphs, 356, 378
Path of a graph, 334
Pathogenic bacteria, 339, 434
Pathological variations, 436
Paths between neurons, 235
Pathways, 38, 40, 46, 59, 61, 75, 81, 90, 97, 103, 104, 105, 117, 119, 127, 154, 155, 156, 161, 165, 172
  afferent, 32, 94, 175, 185, 202
  branching of the, 37
  chain of, 177, 187, 188
  of class I, 27, 28
  of class II, 27, 29, 30
  collateral, 80, 91, 94, 99, 101
  conditioning, 197
  constant, 175, 176, 194, 198
  contour of, 102
  cross-inhibitory, 163, 185, 187, 190, 199

Pathways—*Continued*
  definition of, 13
  density of, 118, 119, 124
  distribution of, 230
  efferent conditioned, 181
  excitation of peripheral, 159
  excitatory, 19, 21, 22, 27, 28, 31, 33, 47, 58, 99, 136, 162, 175, 185, 186, 187, 194
  excited, 128, 129, 216 f., 227
  inhibitory, 19, 21, 26, 27, 28, 30, 31, 33, 47, 48, 50, 51, 58, 91, 95, 96, 99, 100, 101, 128, 131, 139, 162, 171, 173, 175, 181, 187, 189, 190, 191, 194, 197, 199, 217 f.
  of intermediate type, 94
  modalities of, 176
  neural, 118, 123
  and neuroelements, structure of, 230
  parameters of, 123
  peripheral, 31, 37, 47, 91
  proprioceptive, 156, 157, 160
  randomly distributed, 99
Patterns, 91, 115
  dilation of, 114
  excitation, 112, 123
  geometrical, 2 f., 107, 110, 156
  optical, 114
  rotation of, 114
  stimulus, 35, 36, 49, 91, 109, 111, 175, 178, 179 ff., 186, 187, 218 f.
  transformation of, 110
Pavlov, I. P., 81, 90, 91, 93, 135
Pecher, C., 18
Penicillin, 339
Perception,
  acoustic, 113
  aesthetic, 2 f.
  of angles, 160
  of continuity, 155
  of contour, 98
  of depth, 56
  of difference, 176, 177
  Gestalt, 109
  optic, 113
  of similarity, 176, 177
  visual, 108, 155
Performance, 67
Period of intermission, length of, 125
Period of latent addition, 12, 217, 220, 227
Period of stimulation, length of, 125
Periodic discharge of fiber, 211 f.
Periodic Table, 293
Peripheral afferents, 197
Peripheral excitation, 202
  two-factor theory of, 6
Peripheral fiber, frequency of discharge in, 6, 7
Peripheral intensity, 166
Peripheral neuroelement, 118
Peripheral nerve excitation, 12
Peripheral pathway, 31, 37, 47, 91
  excitation of, 159
Peripheral photosensitive processes, 212
Peripheral sensory fibers, 7
Peripheral stimulus, 10, 35, 38, 39, 49, 86, 127, 130, 154, 155, 163
  intensity of, 23, 202
Peripheral vision, 113
Periphery, 27, 29
Peristaltic movement, 280
Permanently excited state, 14
Persons, contact of, analogy to synapse, 240
Pessimism, 204
pH, 15
Pharynx, 47
Phase, refractory, 12
Photochemical reaction, 212
Photoreceptors, 116 f., 124
Photosensitive cells, 116, 387
Photosensitive process, peripheral, 212
Phototropism, 310
Phylogenetic development, 402
Physical characteristics, 160
Physicalists, 405
Physically molar level of movements, 329
Physicochemical dynamics of a cell, 307
Physicochemical processes, 330
Physicochemical relation, 341
Physicochemical system, 69, 72, 74
Physicomathematical systems, resemblance to brain, 1 f.
Physicomathematical theory of the organism, 307
Physicomathematical theory of visual perception, 155
Physics, geometrization of, 404, 405, 406, 409, 417
Physiological conditions, 46
Physiological disturbance and desire for attention, 200
Physiological function, correspondence of in lower and higher animals, 310
Physiological function and organism shape, 249
Physiological graphs, 370
Physiological properties of the neuron, 5
Physiological stimulus, 7
Piéron, H., 40, 41
Pincussen L., and Oppenheimer, C., 264, 269, 286, 290, 291
Pitch, 47
Pitch scale, 112
Pitts, W., vii, 19, 36
  Landahl, H. D., and McCulloch, W. S., 6, 17
  and Lettvin, J., 205, 206
  and McCulloch, W. S., 3, 4, 6, 16, 17, 109, 110, 111, 112, 113, 114, 115, 207, 208, 210, 214, 219, 229, 394
Plaisted, E., and Fox, S. W., 344

Plane, 157
Plant form and food absorption, 251
Plants, 371
  autotrophic, 310, 358
  branched character of, 251
  flow of metabolites in, 251, 253
  form of, 251 ff.
  production of antibodies by, 340 f.
  sessile, 310
  stimulation of, 339
  unicellular, 339
Plato's Academy, 422
Platyhelminthes, 357, 363
Pleasantness, measure of, 162
Pleasurable sensation, 36
Pleasure, 36
"Point bases," 384
Point-to-point correspondence, 98, 99
Points
  adjacent, in graphs, 373, 374
  image, 317, 318
  interconnected, 362
  non-adjacent, 374
  non-transport, 364
  residual, 362 f., 369, 374, 375
  of a set, 313, 379
  specializable, 362 f., 364, 372, 373, 374, 375, 377, 378, 382, 383
  specialized, 355, 366, 367, 368, 369, 371, 372, 373, 374, 377, 378, 380
  subsidiary, 356, 358, 365, 366, 367, 368, 369, 375, 377, 378
  topologically identical, 332
  transport, 367, 368
Poiseuille's equation, 298
Poiseuille's law, 288
Poisons, secretions of, 339
Polar coordinates, 103
Pollard, E., 370
Polyfunctional organs, 382
Polygon, 161, 162, 163
  axes of, 167
  central symmetry of, 170
  permutation of sides of, 166, 167
  symmetry of, 167, 168, 170
  variable angles of, 167, 168
Polygonal contour, 161, 162
Polymerized fibers, 175
Position, 108
Postsynaptic impulse, 12
Posture, erect, 249, 250
Potential energy, 70
Prediction, 340, 343
Prefrontal lobotomy, 198, 200
  beneficial effects of, 200
Preparatory interval, 43
Preparatory stimulus, 42
Preservation of species, 309, 424, 426
Pressure, 7, 431
  blood, 288, 289
Pressure waves, reflected in blood vessels, 306
Presynaptic discharge, frequency of, 12
Presynaptic impulse, 12
Primary colors, 116 f., 123, 124, 125
Primordial, 328, 330, 334, 336, 338, 339, 340, 344, 365, 382
Primordial cell, 357
Primordial component, 378, 380, 382
Primordial, definition of, 399 f.
Primordial graph, 350, 351, 352, 353, 354, 355, 356, 357, 358, 359, 361, 362, 364, 366, 368, 369, 370, 371, 372, 373, 375, 377, 380, 384, 387
  component, 367
  partial, 378
  simplified, 369, 370
Primordial, inputs and outputs of, 400 f.
Primordial organism, 329, 330, 331, 349, 358, 381, 400 f.
  in graphs, 325, 372, 373, 377
Primordial space, 335
Primordial, suboutputs of, 401
Principle of biological similarity, 291
Principle of biotopological mapping, 326
Principle of maximum energy flow, 436
Principle of maximum simplicity, vii, 292, 308, 342
Principle of optimal design, vii, 292, 293, 294, 298, 308, 342
Principles of quantum mechanics, 293
Probability, 60, 61, 63, 67, 338
  of correct response, corrected for chance, 139
  for correct statement, 57
  of formation of closed circuit, 231
  of synapses, 235, 236, 237, 241
Probability integral, 61
Problem of animal form, 246
Process
  conditioning, 134
  photosensitive, 212
  of selection, 407
    interpreted topologically, 407 f.
Processes
  anabolic, 396
  catabolic, 361, 362, 396, 399
  chemo-regulatory, 381
Production
  of excitatory factor, 58
  of inhibitory factors, 58
Progression, geometrical, 85
Projection area, sensory, 226
Propagation, velocity of, 39
Proper subset, explanation of, 312
Properties, environmental, 431
Properties, set of, 319, 356
Proportionality
  coefficient of, 157, 166
  constant, 50
Proprioceptive excitation, 160
Proprioceptive impulses, 108, 156, 157, 158
Proprioceptive pathways, 156, 157, 160
Proprioceptive stimulus, 59
Propulsion, 247, 248, 249, 336, 339

Prosser, C. L., 344
Protein, 340, 352
  secretion of, 328
Protoplasmic motility, 362
Protoplasmic streamings, 347
Protozoa, 310, 345, 347, 348, 357, 363
Pseudopod, movement of, 329
Psychic disturbances, 337, 338
Psychology, 308, 311
Psychological disturbances, 338
Psychological experiences, 31, 337
Psychoneurosis, 205
Psychoneurotic behavior, abolition of, 200
Psychophysical constitution, 36
Psychophysical discrimination, 67, 177
Psychophysical judgment, 3
Psychosis, 205
Putrefaction, 358

Quadrupeds, form of, 262 ff.
  locomotion, of, 262 ff.
  mass of, 263, 264, 265, 268
  size of legs of, 263, 264
  trunk of, 262
Qualitative mathematics, 311
Quantum mechanics, principles of, 293
Quasi-continuous types of interaction, 4
Quasi-homogeneous structure, 5

Radial gradient, 287, 288, 301
Radius of aorta, 293, 294, 295, 305
Radius and length of capillaries, 301, 302, 305
Radius vector, 103
"Random nets," 3
Randomness of distribution, 230
Rank-order method, 163
Rapidly adapting fibers, 11, 213
Rapoport, A., ix, 3, 142, 143, 232, 233, 240, 241
  and Epstein, H., 210
  and Landau, H. G., 240, 241
  and Shimbel, A., 231, 241
  and Solomonoff, R., 241
  and Rebhun, L., 241
Rashevsky, N., 4, 6, 17, 18, 45, 73, 74, 79, 109, 113, 114, 115, 132, 135, 163, 172, 174, 177, 178, 184, 205, 206, 218, 229, 254, 255, 265, 269, 344, 345, 370, 371, 372, 384, 403, 422, 423, 436, 437
  and Brown, V., 165, 174
Rate
  of consumption of metabolites, 301
  of decay, 15, 17
  of metabolism, 305, 358
  of reaction, 291
  of reproduction, 424, 425, 426
  of variation of external parameters, dependence of final state of system on, 72
Ratio of length to width, 42
Reaction, 42, 43, 44, 46, 49, 58, 59, 80, 128, 144, 145, 359, 360
  feeding, 338
  photochemical, 212
  rate of, 291
  of a system, 69
Reaction times, 3, 37 ff.
Reaction velocities, 73
Reactions
  avoidance, 362
  catabolic, 362
  chemoluminescent, 356
  non-luminous, 356
  wrong, 60
Reasoning, speed of, 228 f.
Rebhun, L., and Rapoport, A., 241
Rebound phenomenon, 27, 97
Receptor neuron, 208
Receptors, 124
  cold, 208
  heat, 208
  tactile, 12
Reciprocal innervation, 58
Rectangular coordinates, 118
Recti inferiors, 157
Recti superiors, 157
Rectus lateralis, externus, right, 157
Rectus lateralis, internus, left, 157
Reflex, 80, 81, 87, 131
  conditioned, 80 ff., 90, 134, 198
    intensity of, 90
  delayed, 127 ff., 134
Reflex arcs, 40
Refractory phase, 12, 214
Refractory time, 7
Regulatory substances, secretion of, 328
Reidemeister, K., 423
Reinforcement of conditioned reflex, 90, 91
Relational mathematics, 311
Relations
  discrimination of, 94 ff.
  mapping of classes of, 325
  social, topological representation of, 375
  theory of, viii, 311
Relative intensity, 49
Relativity
  general, 308, 326
  general theory of, 404
Relaxation, 158, 160
Release of energy, 361, 362
Removal of waste products, 281
Repeated stimulus, 214-17, 228 f.
Repelling action of extremities, 265
Repetitions, 129
  necessary to produce an elimination of a wrong alley, 135
  number of, in conditioning, 134
  and response, 341
Representation, topological, of social relations, 375
Reproduction, 330, 348, 399
Reproduction rate, 424, 425, 426

Residual graphs, 352, 354, 355, 367, 368, 370, 372, 376, 378, 380
Residual points, 362 f., 369, 374, 375
Residual, specialized, 363
Residual transport properties, 366
Resistance of tissue to flow of blood, 298, 300
Respiration
  cellular, 245
  frequency, 280
Respiratory epithelium, cells of, 336
Response, 91, 94, 95, 131, 132, 134, 136 ff., 160
  of bird, 309
  complete invariance of, 107
  conditioned, 83, 91, 121, 131, 133, 135
    intensity of, 129
  correct, 59, 60, 67, 137, 139
  difference, 178-79
  equality, 60
  incorrect, 137, 139
  invariant, 107
  multiple, 46
  of neuron, 4
  no-difference, 178, 179
  of paramecium, 309
  probable speed of, 228
  of protozoan, 310
  and repetition, 341
  self-inhibiting, 138
  self-reinforcing, 138
  similarity, 179
  unconditioned, 134
  wrong, 59, 60, 137, 139, 140, 142
Response path, common, 179
Restriction of continuity, 332
Retardation, connection, 23
Reticuloendothelial cells, 341
Retina, 98, 107, 110, 117, 123, 210
  central, 114, 117 f.
  displacements on, 113
  neurons in, 117
  optical Gestalts on, 109 f.
  photosensitive cells in, 116
  visual sensations of, 175
Retinal cells, 212
Retinal elements, 98
Retinal image, 108
Retinal size of object, 108
Retracing of steps, 134
Reverberating circuit, 215, 221, 224
Reversible variations, 71
Reversibly interacting substances, 70
Reynolds number, 293
Riesz, R. R., 55
Robertson, D. M., and Macdonald, P. A., 56
Rosen, Robert, viii, ix, 390, 393, 394, 395, 397, 398, 399, 400, 401, 403
Rotation of pattern, 114
Rubner's law, 264, 283, 287, 289
Rules, transformation, 365, 366
Rumor spreads, 241
Running into alley, 134
Sacher, G., 78, 79
Saddle point, 71
Saturation, cycle, 233
Scanning, 158, 159, 160
Scheel, H., and Geiger, H., 68
"Second-order" extremities, 250
Second-order neuron, 213
Secretion of digestive enzymes, 347
Secretion, internal, 381, 382, 383
Secretions, 328, 329, 337 f., 339, 356, 361, 363, 388
  hormonal, 383
Secretory cells of the eye, 387
Secretory properties, 338
Seebahn, P. M., and Sherman. W. B., 344
Segments, 158, 159
  parallel, 160
Seifert, H., and Threlfall, W., 324, 423
Selection, interpreted topologically, 407 f., 414
Selection, process of, 407
Self-circuited neuroelement, 185, 214
Self-circuited neuron, 214, 342
Self-mapping, 369, 370
Sensation
  of cold, 208
  of heat, 208, 210
  of pleasure, 36, 162
  of touch, 11, 175
  visual, 175
Sensitivity, 336, 340
  to external stimuli, 311, 327, 330, 339, 387, 388
  pain, 328
  visual, 336
  to X-rays and radiation, 343
Sensory cell, 327
Sensory center, 156, 157
Sensory fibers
  peripheral, 7
  reaching cortex, 226
Sensory projection area, 226
Sequence of impulses, regular, 14, 16
Sequences of stimuli, temporal, 218 f.
Sessile plants, 310
Set, selection of, 413
Set of points, 313, 315, 316, 321, 322, 323, 324, 379
  considered as space, 313, 315
  disjoined fundamental, 379, 380
  fundamental, 379, 380
  mapping of, 380, 391
  neighborhood in, 314
  non-fundamental, 380
  representing properties of organism, 319
Set-theoretical approach to topological biology, 345, 385, 386
Sets
  definition of, 311
  elements of, 311
  examples of, 312, 313
  inputs as, 391
  intersection of, 312

Sets—*Continued*
outputs as, 391
theory of, 311, 406 f.
Shape, 108
of animals, irregularity of, 295
of the contour, 156, 157
of the curve, 44
of a figure, 155
geometrical, 105
of organism, 248, 249, 252, 269
Sharp contrast, 98
Sheer, B. T., 370
Sherman, W. B., and Seebahn, P. M., 344
Sherrington, C., 27
Shimbel, A., 143, 344
and Rapoport, A., 231
Shock therapy, 205
Sides, 161
Sieve cells, 339
Sight of alley, 135
Similarity
biological principle of, 291
perception of, 176, 177
reaction, 177
response, probability of, 179
Similarity judgment, 177, 178, 180
Simplicity, principle of maximum, vii, 292, 308, 342
Simplified primordial graph, 369, 370
Simplified transformed graph, 370
Simultaneous presentation, 58
Size, 104, 107, 108, 109
of animal, 266
of aorta, 293
of cell, 107
change of, 106
discrimination of, 108
variation of, 108
Skeletal muscles, 336, 339
Skeletal parts of animals, 309
Skeletons, minimal weight of, 283
Skin and sensation of touch, 175
Skulls, shapes of, 309
Skunks, 356
Slowly adapting fibers, 11, 13, 212
Smith, Mrs. Elaine, ix
Smolik, A., Busch, A. K., and Hofstatter, L., 206
Snakes
form of, 256 ff.
gliding velocity of, 257, 258
locomotion of, 256 ff.
maximum speed of, 261
and metabolic energy, 261
movement of, 257 f.
and muscular apparatus, 258
venom of, 356
Social aggregate, 357
Social relations
differentiations of, 375
graphs of, 357
topological representation, 375
Social sciences, 311
Social structure, 436
Societies, insect, 357
Society as a kind of organism, 310
Sociology, 376
Solar energy, 310
Solomonoff, R., and Rapoport, A., 241
Solution, concentrated, 74
Sound frequency, as parameter, 11
Space
connected, 322, 323
topological, 345, 389, 390, 408, 409, 412, 416
Space time coincidence, 421
Spaces
distances in, 315
mapping of, 325
metrized, 315
non-connected, 322, 323
in set of points, 313, 315, 323
Specializable points in graphs, 362 f., 371, 372, 373, 374, 375, 377, 378, 382
Specializable residual points, 364
Specialization of cells, 327, 331, 336, 349, 351, 352, 353, 363
Specialization, process of, 356, 357
Specialized graph, 382
Specialized organs, 363
Specialized points, 355, 364, 365, 366, 367, 368, 369, 372 f., 373, 374, 377, 378, 380
Specialized residual, 363
Specialized transport, 364, 365, 366
Species preservation, 309, 424, 426
Spectrum, 117
Speech, thought as covert, 309
Speed
of adjustment, 72
of animal, 135
of locomotion, 134, 249, 261, 267, 426
of reasoning, 228, 229
of response, 228
Spermatozoids, 336
Spherical neighborhood, 316
Spider-web, secreted, 338, 343
Spontaneous activities of brain centers, 78
Spontaneous generation, 431
Spontaneous nerve activity, 78
Spontaneously and constantly excited center, 95
Spread of epidemics, 240 f.
Spread of rumors, 241
Square, 98
Stability
of neuroelement, 189
properties, 344, 356
Stabilization, and number of extremities, 250
Stable equilibrium, 70, 71, 77
Standard weight, 62, 65
Standing
and muscular movement, 250
and nervous coordination, 249, 250
as unstable process, 249

Stanton, H. E., 56, 436, 437
State of excitation, 75
Static friction, 257
  co-efficient of, 256
Stationary state, 28, 47, 66, 125
  of metabolic diffusion, 303
Stedman's Practical Medical Dictionary, 384
Stimulated endogenically, 388
Stimulation, 30, 86, 87, 319
  chemical, 327
  continuous, 7, 11, 12, 30, 36, 82, 91, 99, 125, 217
  of eye, 389
  from food, 347
  of inhibitory pathway, 21
  intensity of, 7, 27, 31, 74, 131
    constant, 19, 37, 61
  length of period of, 125
  of plants, 339
Stimuli, 37, 41, 45, 57, 58, 60, 65
  comparison of, 67
  difference of, 57
  of different intensities, 175, 176
  of different modalities, 109, 175
  discrimination between, 138, 139
  duration of, 64
  enteroceptive, 59
  equal, 57
  of equal intensity, 31
  exteroceptive, 59
  greater (stronger), 57
  neutral, 91
  pair of, 95, 175
  peripheral, 202
  physical, 340
  proprioceptive, 59
  of same modality, 175
  sensitivity to, 311, 327, 330, 337, 339, 340, 387
  sensory, 337 f.
  temporal, 213, 218 f.
  variety of, 337
  varying with respect to time, 36
Stimulus, 7, 11, 41, 42, 43, 46, 47, 50, 52, 53, 62, 80, 81, 88, 89, 91, 94, 95, 96, 128, 134, 362
  absolute intensity of, 94
  "accidental" component, 182
  afferent centers of, 181
  cold, 208, 210
  component, 180, 181, 182, 183
  conditioned, 83, 90, 127, 130, 131, 139
  constant, 11, 47, 94, 154
    intensity of, 19, 37, 61
    suddenly established, 127
  continuous, 11, 12, 217 f.
  correct, 138, 139
  "essential" component of, 182
  excitatory, 10
  external, 7, 74, 75, 77, 78, 81, 155, 183
    sensitivity to, 311, 327, 330, 337, 339, 340, 387
  frequency of occurrence of, 180, 181
  horizontal, 165, 166
  inhibitory, 31
  intensity of, 6, 11, 12, 13, 40, 41, 45, 46, 49, 51, 52, 154, 212, 213, 217 f.
    optical, 117
  intermittently applied, 125, 126
  pain, 31, 95, 328
  peripheral, 10, 35, 38, 39, 49, 86, 127, 130, 154, 155, 163
  physiological, 7
  pleasant, 138, 185, 187
  preparatory, 42
  proprioceptive, 12
  repeated, 215 f., 217 f., 228 f.
  and response, 136 ff., 309, 310
  unconditioned, 83, 90, 91, 92, 95, 131, 134, 135
  unpleasant, 138, 185, 186, 187
  visual, 11, 164 ff., 336
  warning, 42, 43
Stimulus combination, 88
Stimulus pattern, 35, 36, 49, 91, 109, 111, 175, 178, 179 ff., 185, 186, 187, 218 f.
  complex, 201
  components of, 180
  conditioning to, 180
  discrimination of, 92
  multimodal, 178
  optimum, 35
  response to, 180 ff., 336
  transformation of, 110
Stirling's formula, 234
Storer, T. I., 384
Straight line, 158, 160
  segment of, 155, 157, 159, 160, 161
Strength of association, 201
Structure
  complex, 5
  isotropic, 103
  lever, 248
  morphological, 32
  neural, 207, 230
  of neuroelements and pathways, 230
  neuronic, 40
  social, 436
Subject, 95
Subset, 312, 321, 379, 402, 408, 410
Subsidiary aggregates, 386
Subsidiary point, in graphs, 356, 358, 365, 366, 367, 368, 369, 375, 377, 378
Substitution of integrals for sums, 33
Sugar metabolism, 389
Superliminal, 29
Superthreshold of excitation, 14, 15
Symbolic logic, 207
Symmetric functions, 65
Symmetric scheme, 58
Symmetry
  effect of, on aesthetic value, 172
Sympathetic ganglia, 12

Synapse, 6, 12, 14, 16, 207, 208, 214, 231, 232, 233, 235, 236, 237, 238, 240
analogy to personal contact, 240
definition of, 13
failure of, 15, 16, 17
inhibiting, 208
Synapses, probability of, 235, 236, 237, 241
Synapsings, conservative, 237
Synaptic changes, 342
Synaptic delay, 12, 14, 16, 207, 208, 211 f., 219, 221, 227
Synaptic transmission, 6, 12, 207, 342
Synchronous impulse, 14
Syndrome, 379, 381
disjoined, 381
Synthesis, 346 f., 352, 362, 370
of digestive enzymes, 361
System, 69, 70, 71, 75, 77, 78, 83
abstract biological, 395 f., 396 f.
arterial, structure of, 293, 295, 296, 297, 305
mass of, 298
biological, 35
circulatory, 364, 388
conditioning, 91
lever-propelled, 248, 249
lymphatic, 364
metabolizing, 247, 248
physicochemical, 69, 72, 74
vascular, 364
Systematic neurobiophysical theory of central nervous system, 143
Systematic transport, 365

Tachermak, A., 174
Tactile data, 56
Tactile receptors, 12
Tactile stimuli, 56
Tarski, Alfred, viii
Taste, 36, 327
Temperature, 70, 431
Temperature regulation, 335
Temporal lobe, 112
Temporal sequences of stimuli, 218 f.
Temporally separated stimuli, 213 f.
Terminal bulbs, 12, 15, 207, 212, 220, 227
excitation of, 212
failure of, to function, 15
Terminal component, 395, 398 f.
Terminology, 59
Thalamus, flow of impulses to, 193, 194
Theoretical values, 63, 65, 67, 162
Theory
of braids, 417-22
of discrimination, 50, 172
of heat conduction, 247
of knots, 417
of learning, 142
"macroscopic," 213
of natural equivalences, 393
of nervous activity, 6
of relativity, general, 404
of visual perception, physicomathematical, 155
Thermodynamic systems, 74
Thermodynamics, 70
Thompson, D'A. W., 309, 324
Thought, as covert speech, 309
Three-body problem, 307
Threlfall, W., and Seifert, H., 324, 423
Threshold, 7, 19, 38, 44, 46, 47, 48, 50, 58, 59, 61, 62, 74, 80, 83, 87, 95, 103, 104, 112, 127, 128, 129, 167, 173, 207, 213, 215
of discrimination, 96
excitation, 185, 188, 189
of inhibitory neuroelement, 33
of inhibitory pathway, 173, 192
lowest, 12
of nerve fiber, 10
of neuron, 220, 221, 224
permanent excitation, 185, 188, 189
of response for neuron, 4
value, 176
variation in, 15
Thickness of extremities, and mass of animal, 265, 268
Thurstone, L. L., 436, 437
Time, 42, 61, 67
conduction, 42, 207
conduction along fibers, 207
constant, 45
factor, 45
reaction, 3, 40, 41, 42, 43
refractory, 7
of transmission, 40
variation with, 37
Time-interval, 128
Tippo, O., and Fuller, H. J., 384
Tissues, 352
to be supplied with blood, 296, 303
contractile muscular, 336
resistance of, to flow of blood, 298
specialization of, 352, 353, 357, 363 f.
Tongue, 47
Tonic contraction, 160
Topological application, 379
Topological approach, combinatorial, 385
Topological biology, 381, 406, 417
set-theoretical approach to, 385
Topological interpretation of selection, 407 f., 413 f.
Topological mapping, 326, 416
Topological properties
of a braid, 419 f., 421
laws from, 376
Topological representation of social relations, 375
Topological results into biology, 374
Topological space, 345, 389, 390, 402, 408, 409, 412, 416
Topologically identical points, 332
Topology, 308, 309, 311, 313, 315, 331, 345, 359, 406, 409, 415, 417, 422

Total central excitation, 164
Total excitation, 154, 171, 172
Total inhibition, 168, 171
Touch, sensation of, 11, 175
Toxins, 339
Tracheae, 339
Tract, 103
Transcendental equation, 239
Transformation
  biotopological, 402
  of a distribution, 111
  in graphs, 345, 346, 350, 352, 353, 354, 355, 356, 357, 358, 359, 360, 362, 368, 369, 372, 373, 375, 376, 378, 380, 381, 382, 384
  as metabolic activity, 400 f.
  of one space into another, 325
  parameter of the, 366, 367
  rules, 344, 365, 366
  of stimulus-pattern, 110, 111
Transformations, 52, 326, 327, 352, 364
  continuous univalent, 309
  finite group of, 110 f.
  mapping of, 368
Transformed graph, 357, 370, 371, 373, 378, 380
  simplified, 370
Transforms, 114
Translation, 114
  of patterns, 110
Translocation of metabolites, 339
Transmission
  connection, 44
  direction of, 37
  of excitation, 12, 13, 17
    all-or-none phenomenon in, 13
    mechanism of, 9
  synaptic, 6, 12
    character of, 207
  time of, 40
Transport, 338, 359, 360, 361, 362, 363 f., 365, 366, 367
  points, 367, 368
  properties, 366
Transposition, Gestalt, 98, 106, 109
Trees, form and mechanical properties of, 254
Triangle, color, 116, 122, 123
Trucco, Ernesto, ix, 371, 384
Trunk of quadrupeds, mechanical strength of, 262
Turbulences, absence of, 293
Two-factors, 38
Two-parametric curve, 44
Tympanic membrance, 336

Unconditioned reflex, 131
Unconditioned response, 134
Unconditioned stimulus, 83, 90, 91, 95, 131, 134, 135
"Undifferentiated" molecule, 358
Unexcited state, 80
Unicellular organism, 327, 334, 335, 336, 338, 341, 348
Unicellular plants, 339
Uniformity of nature, 326
Uniformly directed cycle, 373, 374, 375
Units, 50
Univalent transformation, continuous, 309
Unlimited existential operator, 213 f., 215
Unstable equilibrium, 77
Uranus, 326
Urban, F. M., 65, 66, 68
Urechis, 338, 343
Uspensky, J. V., 241

Vacuole, digestive, 347, 363
Variable coordinates, 109, 110
Variables, 52
  independent, 111
Variation
  of size of visual object, 108
  in wing area, 274
  in wing mass, 274
  in wing velocity, 274
Variations
  pathological, 436
  reversible, 71
  with time, 37
Vascular system, 294, 364
Vegetative functions, 353, 362, 371
Veins and arteries, proper functioning of, 306
Velocity
  of blood flow, 287, 293, 298, 302
  constant, 157
  of contraction, 158, 160
  of locomotion, 247, 271, 278
  of propagation of nerve impulse, 10, 39
  reaction, 73
  and size of animal, 266
  wing, 271, 276, 277, 278
Venom, snake, 356
Venous circulation, 339
Vertebrate movement, kinematics of, 248
Vertebrates, sensitivity to colors, 117
Vertical stimulus, 165, 166
  effect of variation in, 165 ff.
Vessels, blood, 296, 297, 298, 299, 300
Virus molecule, 401
Viruses, 348, 349, 358
Visceral nervous system, 11
Vision, color
  mathematical biophysics of, 116
  mechanism of, 116, 117, 387
Vision and light sensitivity, 310, 351
Vision, peripheral, 113
Visual aesthetics, 154 ff.
Visual data, 40, 44, 67
Visual lengths, 56
Visual pattern, elements of, 172
Visual perception, 108
  physicomathematical theory of, 155
Visual sensation, 177
Visual sensitivities, 336

Visual stimulus, 11, 164 ff.
aesthetic value of, 164, 173
elements of pattern, 172
equivalence of geometrical figures as, 172
polygons, 164, 174
symmetry and aesthetic value in, 172
Vitalists, 405
Volley of nerve impulses, 7-8
Volterra, V., 431, 434, 437
Volume
of extremities, 266
of intestinal tract, 281
of lung, 280
Vomiting, 336

Wallace, J. M., 344
Warning stimulus, 42, 43
Washington Public Opinion Laboratory, 241
Waste products, removal of, 281, 346, 361, 363
Wastes, secretion of, 339
Wave-front, 130, 131
Wave lengths, 117
Way of a graph, 334
Weight
discrimination of, 62, 65
standard, 62, 65
Weights, 56
Weyl, H., 326, 423
Whittaker, E. T., 437
Wilder, R. L., 315, 324, 423
Wing
as aerodynamic profile, 270, 271, 273
frequency of movement of, 272, 274, 278
limit of size of, 273
movement of, 272, 274, 278
as propeller blade, 271
velocity of, 271, 276, 277, 278
Woodger, J. H., viii, ix, 311, 324, 342, 344
Woodrow, H., 43
Wrong alley, 135
number of repetitions necessary to produce elimination of, 135
Wrong judgment, 62
Wrong response, 59, 60, 137, 139, 140, 142
average effect of, 139
probability of, 137, 139

X-rays, sensitivity to, 343

Yeast, antibody production by, 340, 341
Young, G., 159
Young, Thomas, 116